Gouverneur Morris

ALSO BY JAMES J. KIRSCHKE

Henry James and Impressionism

Willa Cather and Six Writers from the Great War

Not Going Home Alone: A Marine's Story

Author, Statesman, and
Man of the World

Gouverneur Morris

JAMES J. KIRSCHKE

THOMAS DUNNE BOOKS

ST. MARTIN'S PRESS

NEW YORK

THOMAS DUNNE BOOKS.
An imprint of St. Martin's Press.

www.stmartins.com

Book design by Susan Walsh

Library of Congress Cataloging-in-Publication Data

Kirschke, James J.
    Gouverneur Morris : author, statesman, and man of the world / James J. Kirschke.—1st ed.
      p. cm.
    Includes bibliographical references (pp. 277–352) and index.
    ISBN 0-312-24195-X
    EAN 978-0-312-24195-7
    1. Morris, Gouverneur, 1752–1816. 2. Statesman—United States—Biography. 3. United States. Constitution—signers—Biography. 4. United States—History—Revolution, 1775–1783—Biography. 5. New York (State)—History—Revolution, 1775–1783—Biography. 6. United States—Politics and government—1775–1783. 7. United States—Politics and government—1783–1789. I. Title.

E302.6.M7K57 2005
973.4'092—dc22
[B]

                                        2005051942

First Edition: December 2005

10 9 8 7 6 5 4 3 2 1

To Nancy Kirschke
with love and thanks

CONTENTS

PERSONAL CHRONOLOGY: THE LIFE OF GOUVERNEUR MORRIS

1752 Gouverneur Morris is born on January 31 at Morrisania, his family's estate in what is now the South Bronx.

1761 Morris goes to study at the Academy of Philadelphia, a school founded by Benjamin Franklin. In Philadelphia, Morris stays with his half-sister, Mary Ann (Morris) Lawrence, and her husband, Thomas L. Lawrence, Jr. Like his father, Lawrence serves as mayor of Philadelphia.

1764 Morris enrolls in King's College (later Columbia) in New York City. He is the youngest student.

1766 Morris is badly scalded, losing much of the flesh on his right arm.

1768 Morris receives a bachelor of arts degree from King's College and is elected by the college literary society to present the oration at commencement.

1768–71 Morris reads law and clerks in law office.

1771 Morris receives master of arts degree from King's College; three months after receiving the degree, at just under 20 years of age, Morris is licensed as attorney-at-law.

1772–74 Morris practices law, mainly in New York State; he begins to speculate in land.

1775 Despite his severe physical handicap Morris is chosen as lieutenant colonel of the New York State Militia, one of the state's four highest-ranking militia officers. He becomes one of the few elected representatives to New York's First Provincial Congress; Morris is the only such elected official to serve simultaneously two separate districts: Westchester and Albany.

Morris drafts and presents orally an important currency report to the Congress. He serves on the Provincial Congress's Committee of Safety, as Chair of the Committee of Correspondence, and as member of the Committee of Budget and Finance.

1776   Morris makes an important speech on May 24, advocating independence at the Fourth Provincial Congress in the Exchange Building in New York. The Provincial Congress changes its title to the Convention of the Representatives of the State of New York two months later.

1777–78 Morris works with John Jay and Robert Livingston to draft the first New York State Constitution. A New York delegate to the Continental Congress, he signs the Articles of Confederation and serves on numerous committees in Congress.

1779–80 Morris publishes *Observations on the American Revolution.* He loses his left leg as a result of a runaway carriage accident on Dock Street, Philadelphia. He conducts commercial business in Philadelphia.

1781–84 Morris serves as first and only American Assistant Superintendent of Finance, working closely with the Finance Office Superintendent, Robert Morris (no relation).

1785–86 Morris conducts commercial ventures, maintains extensive correspondence.

1787   Morris elected as one of the seven-member delegation from Pennsylvania to the U.S. Constitutional Convention, where he does important work.

1788–91 Morris serves in Europe first as a private commercial agent, then at Washington's request as the new nation's first official secret agent overseas.

1792–94 Morris serves as first official U.S. minister plenipotentiary to France.

1795–98 Morris travels in Europe, providing steady advice to British Foreign Secretary William Grenville. Commercial land ventures, in the United States mainly, continue.

1799   Morris returns to Morrisania, repairing the family estate and restoring the grounds; he resumes his legal practice and continues financial dealings.

1800–03 Morris is elected to serve an unexpired term in the U.S. Senate.

1804   Morris helps found the New-York Historical Society. Business ventures resume; extensive correspondence.

1809   Morris marries Anne Cary Randolph, his head housekeeper.

1811   Morris is elected as one of nine commissioners of the Erie Canal Commission (construction of the canal begins in 1817).

1813   Gouverneur Morris, Jr., only child of Anne and Gouverneur Morris, is born.

1816   Gouverneur Morris dies on November 6 in the upstairs front room at Morrisania, where he first drew breath.

HISTORICAL TIME LINE: THE WORLD OF GOUVERNEUR MORRIS

1752 Gouverneur Morris born.
       Benjamin Franklin conducts experiments with kite and lightning.
1753 British and French quarrel over Ohio River basin.
1754 Louis XVI born.
       French military forces defeat Virginia militia under George Washington at Fort Necessity.
1755 French forces defeat the British, led by General Edward Braddock, at Fort Duquesne; French and Indian War (1755–1763).
1756 Britain declares war on France; Seven Years' War (1756–1763).
1757 Britain gains ascendancy in India.
1759 British capture Quebec City. Montcalm and Wolfe die in the battle.
1760 British capture Montreal; end of New France.
       Accession of Britain's George III.
       Benjamin Franklin invents bifocal lens.
1761 Collapse of French power in India.
1762 Rousseau publishes *The Social Contract.*
1763 Treaty of Paris ends the Seven Years' War.
       France cedes Canada and India to Britain, Louisiana to Spain, but regains Martinique and Guadeloupe.
       Charles Mason and Jeremiah Dixon begin survey of Pennsylvania-Maryland boundary.
1764 Burdened by heavy postwar debt, Britain seeks revenue from the American colonies under the Sugar Act and the Currency Act (the latter mainly targets Virginia).
       Voltaire publishes the *Philosophical Dictionary.*

John Adams marries Abigail Smith.

John Jay graduates from King's College, New York.

1765 Quartering Act requires American civil authorities to provide barracks and supplies for British troops.

Stamp Act is the first direct tax levied by British Parliament upon America.

1766 A second Quartering Act extends first enactment and mandates quartering and billeting in inns, alehouses, and unoccupied dwellings in the colonies.

Declaratory Act asserts wide-ranging Parliamentary authority over America.

British trade laws with North American colonies modified; Stamp Act repealed.

1767 Townshend Acts: British Parliament mandates import duties on five commercial products (glass, lead, paints, paper, and tea) being shipped to America.

North American colonists agree to reinstate their 1744 boycott of English luxury goods.

John Quincy Adams and Andrew Jackson born.

1768 Massachusetts Circular Letter, by Samuel Adams, connects the thirteen colonies in communication against British Crown.

British customs officials seize John Hancock's sloop, *Liberty;* violent demonstrations follow.

1770 Lord North becomes British Prime Minister, a post he retains until 1782.

First performance of Handel's *Messiah* in New York.

Townshend Act duties limited to tea.

In court, John Adams successfully defends British troops involved in Boston Massacre.

Marie-Antoinette marries the French dauphin, who will reign as Louis XVI in 1774.

Sons of Liberty clash violently with British forces at Golden Hill, New York.

First Quartering Act allowed to lapse.

G.W.F. Hegel born.

1771 James Madison receives degree from College of New Jersey.

Louis XV dissolves courts *(Parlements)*.

1772 Rhode Islanders burn British revenue cutter *Gaspée*.

1773 American colonists expand Committees of Correspondence. Tea Acts, followed by Boston Tea Party.

1774 Riots over the tax on tea continue; tea is dumped in New York harbor.
First "Intolerable Acts," or "Coercive Acts," including the Boston Port Bill and the Quebec Act, serve to unify the colonies further.
Quartering Act extends to occupied buildings.
First Continental Congress convenes in Philadelphia.

1775 In Massachusetts first shots fired in the Revolutionary War.
Edmund Burke delivers his speech "On Conciliation with America" in House of Commons.

1776 British forced to evacuate troops from Boston.
British forces drive American army from Canada and occupy much of New York State.
Congress approves the Declaration of Independence.
Thomas Paine publishes *Common Sense.*

1777 Lafayette arrives in America and serves as volunteer on Washington's staff.
Howe defeats George Washington and occupies Philadelphia.
Liberty Bell moved to Allentown, Pennsylvania.
Gates defeats Burgoyne near Saratoga.
Articles of Confederation drafted (but not ratified until 1781, when Maryland signs).

1778 France signs Treaties of Amity and Commerce with the Americans.

1779 Spain declares war on Britain.

1780 Virginia state government moves from Williamsburg to Richmond.
British capture Charleston, South Carolina.

1781 Battle of Yorktown, Virginia.

1783 Britain and the United States sign the Treaty of Paris, recognizing the colonies' independence and settling boundaries.
Washington Irving born.

1784 Congress ratifies peace treaty with Britain on January 14.

1787 Constitutional Convention convenes in Philadelphia, with George Washington presiding. Northwest Ordinance passes, establishing the first territory of the U.S., prohibiting slavery in what was to become the present states of Ohio, Indiana, Illinois, Michigan, Wisconsin, and part of Minnesota (officially known as the Territory Northwest of the River Ohio).

1788 Ratification of the U.S. Constitution by ninth state, New Hampshire, means Constitution legally adopted.

1789 Constitution declared officially in effect.
George Washington elected President of the United States (he receives 69 electoral college votes).

Bill of Rights submitted to states.

James Fenimore Cooper born.

The Bastille in France stormed.

1790 Benjamin Franklin dies.

Burke publishes *Reflections on the Revolution in France.*

1791 Bill of Rights goes into effect.

Vermont becomes fourteenth state.

1792 George Washington reelected President (receives 132 electoral votes).

1793 Louis XVI and Marie-Antoinette executed.

France declares war on Britain, Holland, and Spain.

1794 Dolley Payne Todd and James Madison marry.

1796 Washington refuses third term; his Farewell Address published.

John Adams elected President (receives 71 electoral votes).

1799 George Washington dies.

Pennsylvania state capital moves from Philadelphia to Lancaster.

Patrick Henry dies.

Napoleon's 18 Brumaire coup d'état ends French Republic.

USS *Constellation* captures French frigate *L'Insurgente.*

By order of Napoleon, French raids on U.S. shipping stop.

Britain forms Second Coalition (with Russia, Austria, Turkey, Portugal, and Naples) against France.

1800 Thomas Jefferson elected President (73 electoral votes) only after the House of Representatives breaks tie vote of the presidential electors.

U.S. capital moves from Philadelphia to Washington, D.C.

1803 Louisiana Purchase nearly doubles the size of the United States.

Ralph Waldo Emerson born.

1804 Jefferson reelected (162 electoral votes).

Lewis and Clark expedition begins.

Burr-Hamilton duel.

Amendment XII, designed to avoid a repeat of the 1800 election fiasco by separating the votes for president and vice president, is ratified.

1808 James Madison elected President (122 electoral votes).

1809 Thomas Paine dies.

Robert Fulton patents commercial steamboat.

Washington Irving publishes *A History of New-York by Diedrich Knickerbocker.*

Franz Joseph Haydn dies.

Abraham Lincoln born.

1811 Harriet Beecher Stowe born.

1812 Madison reelected (128 electoral votes) on war platform.

War of 1812 begins.

1814 Treaty of Ghent ends War of 1812.

1815 Americans, commanded by Andrew Jackson, defeat British at Battle of New Orleans, neither side knowing that a peace treaty had been signed.

Battle of Waterloo.

United States signs important commercial convention with Britain.

1816 James Monroe elected President (183 electoral votes).

Second Bank of United States founded.

Indiana becomes 19th state.

DeWitt Clinton obtains state funding to begin construction of Erie Canal, New York.

Gouverneur Morris dies.

PREFACE

THE AMERICAN PEOPLE are singular among the peoples of the earth in governing themselves on the basis of a charter written more than two centuries ago and only sparsely and infrequently amended since. The author of the final draft of this remarkable document, as well as of its lucid, economical, and inspiring Preamble, is the subject of this biography. Gouverneur Morris (1752–1816) was, moreover, one of only six individuals to sign both the Articles of Confederation (1777) and the Constitution of the United States (1787). As an elected delegate to the Constitutional Convention in Philadelphia, he served on the important Committee of Electoral Representation. Morris spoke more often than anyone else at the Convention, and sometimes his speeches had great effect. In recognition of his abilities, Morris was named to chair the Convention's Committee of Style. In this position he quickly wrote the final draft of our valuable and enduring document.

Often during his public life, Morris read the future correctly; and during these years some of his utterances and writings influenced America's political destiny for the better. During the Constitutional Convention's debates in Philadelphia, Morris proposed a presidential Cabinet, to consist of those positions that eventually proved the offices most important to the new nation. He believed that the people, not the Congress, should elect the president and vice president. He argued, too, for the abolition of slavery.

The United States Constitution, like most such documents, has its origins in a variety of sources. By sifting the records of the proceedings at the Constitutional Convention, and by examining the extant state documents, foreign constitutions, and other political writings, I have attempted to chart the major lines of influence on the Preamble and the Constitution of the United States.

Great men and women tend to make bold use of their opportunities, and this characteristic was true of Gouverneur Morris. In 1775 he sat, as the representative from Westchester County, in the fourth and last New York Provincial Congress, which established the governmental apparatus that served the colony when it became a state. Morris not only worked on the plan for a state government but also served on the committee concerned with citizens' civil rights. In this capacity he championed a bill of rights that would strengthen civil liberties. His eloquent speeches argued trenchantly for the abolition of slavery and the equal treatment of all male citizens, irrespective of race or religion. In the New York Congress, too, Morris urged the wisdom of separation from England and proved a bold and effective advocate for American independence. As his actions and the testimony of his contemporaries reveal, he seldom did things by halves.

In the New York legislature, Morris collaborated with John Jay and Robert Livingston on the Constitutional Committee, which in 1777 drafted the first New York State constitution. This document not only served as the framework for the state's government for nearly half a century; many of its provisions subsequently found their way into the Constitution of the United States.

On October 3, 1777, Gouverneur Morris was elected to serve as a delegate from New York at the Second Continental Congress (1778–1779). Here he chaired some crucial committees, gained the enduring admiration of George Washington, and accepted the directive from Congress to write some of the most critical official documents originating from these proceedings. His pamphlet *Observations on the American Revolution* (1780) lucidly states the Americans' grievances and minces no words in rejecting Lord North's offer of a peace marked by neither the surrender of the British forces nor their withdrawal from the colonies.[1] Morris also wrote the report of the Continental Congress's Committee on Finance, which manifests sound comprehension of the issue of paper money in the colonies.

After Congress dissolved, Morris went into commercial business, mainly land purchases and tobacco, in Philadelphia. There he published a series of articles on finance. These so impressed Robert Morris (no relation), the newly created U.S. Superintendent of Finance, that he promptly asked the younger man to become his principal assistant and deputy. Gouverneur Morris held this position from 1781 to 1785, during which time he developed the basic plan for the U.S. decimal coinage system that, with modification, remains in use today.

Many of the political questions of the Revolutionary era and the Confederation period involved problems of public finance. That these were adequately resolved is owed in large part to Robert Morris and Gouverneur Morris. The two men were instrumental in the planning and establishment of the Bank of North America, the first central bank on this continent. Morris's reasoning about fiscal policy developed, through various permutations, in the essays he first published in Pennsylvania magazines and then presented to Robert Morris and to Congress.

The art of speaking and the art of writing are essentially different. Orations and addresses, however much they delight their original listeners, when read in later years, often hang limp like flags on a still day. Gouverneur Morris's speeches are mostly exceptions to this rule, as the moving oration he delivered at Hamilton's funeral testifies. The speeches Morris gave as U.S. senator from New York (1800–1803) are works of impressive rhetorical artistry.

Scholars have wondered at Morris's failure to seek a commission in the Continental Army and serve on the battlefield during the war. Even Morris's great-grandniece, Beatrix Cary Davenport, in her introduction to Morris's *Diary of the French Revolution,* comments, "Why a young stalwart should have served [during the American Revolution] with tongue and pen instead of sword in hand remains unexplained."[2]

Perhaps surprisingly, historians have overlooked the biographical evidence. From adolescence onward, Morris suffered from severe physical disabilities: much of the flesh had been scalded off his right arm in an accident during his years at King's College (later Columbia). Nonetheless, he entered the New York militia, and in early 1776 his fellow militiamen elected him to serve as lieutenant colonel, a field position in the 4th Regiment.[3] To that date, only four men in the colony had been selected for a higher rank.[4]

It is true that Morris's state and national service were primarily civilian. His militia unit was not activated until the autumn of 1776, and by the summer of that year Morris was serving in the fourth New York Provincial Congress, deeply involved in drawing up a new constitution for the state. Almost immediately he also joined the New York Council of Safety, whose few members could not be spared for military service. He was also exempted from militia service as a delegate to the Continental Congress from his election in October 1777 through 1779 and then again as assistant finance minister from 1781 to 1785. In any case, the last exemption was moot: Morris's left leg had been amputated below the knee in May 1780, after he "broke his leg by jumping out of his phaeton, as the horses were running away."[5]

Not long after the Constitutional Convention, Gouverneur Morris sailed to England as a private commercial agent. Here, at George Washington's request, he soon became the new United States' first governmental private agent.[6] In this capacity, he attempted to conduct negotiations and to make inquiries concerning the seeming indisposition of the British to accept fully the terms of the Treaty of Paris. Recent scholarship, however, shows why Morris's dealings with the British were sabotaged from the outset.

In 1792, while Morris was still abroad, Washington appointed him U.S. minister to France, succeeding Thomas Jefferson and William Short. The 1790s, of course, were the years of the French Revolution. As the only foreign envoy to remain in France throughout the Terror, Morris proved, as glimpsed in his voluminous letters and fascinating diary of the period, a perceptive and courageous American diplomat-author, one of a distinguished line that includes Benjamin Franklin, Jefferson and Short, James Monroe, Washington Irving, John L. Motley, James Lowell, Brand Whitlock, Lewis Einstein, and William C. Bullitt. Gouverneur Morris may be the most reliable of all witnesses to the French Revolution; France's great nineteenth-century historian Hippolyte Taine seemed to think so and drew heavily on the American's writings for his volumes dealing with the Revolutionary period.[7]

Like many other great men and women, Gouverneur Morris evidently attracted love and hatred of a force from which meaner natures generally are exempt. His character was not admirable in all respects, but the vitality and intelligence that survive in Morris's writing suggest the potent effect of the man himself. Moreover, among the architects and builders of the government of the United States, Morris possessed one of the most robust senses of humor.

That many women could not resist his charm quickly becomes apparent to anyone studying the period. By all reports, as well as by the evidence provided in the surviving portraits, Morris was a big man, with a heavy, sensual face, a large nose, a broad forehead, and a worldly manner. As regards female charms, he seems to have felt that the only way to get rid of temptation was to yield to it.

His choice of a wife was characteristically unusual and independent, for he married late, in 1809, after his term in the Senate, and he chose a woman he had at first brought into his household as the head housekeeper. His wife, Anne Cary Randolph, had had a life of extreme difficulty in her earlier years, but their marriage was a happy one. And when Morris was sixty-one, their son was born. During his last years he proved instrumental, along with Robert Fulton, in gaining approval for construction of the Erie Canal, and then became the first chairman of the canal commission. Facing death with some of the same spirit with which he had lived, Gouverneur

Morris died, at age sixty-four, in the same room at Morrisania where he had first seen light.

Considering Morris's importance to history and the interest of his character, the bibliography on him is not large, though it is fairly impressive. Jared Sparks's early, three-volume *Life* is that writer's weakest work.[8] By Sparks's own admission, the *Life* was done in haste, in the roughly nine months before he undertook his biography of Washington.[9] Nearly two-thirds of Sparks's *Life* is devoted to the expurgated publication of Morris's writings; and the scholar was probably too close to the Founding period to have presented his subject in an optimally clear light. Sparks's annotations and chronological arrangements are sometimes in need of correction; he omits without indication parts of many of the letters; and he silently changes spelling, punctuation, and capitalization.

The work nevertheless deserves the same respectful consideration due all such pioneer biographical efforts. Sparks obtained considerable information regarding the life of Gouverneur Morris from men who had known Morris, including General Morgan Lewis and Jacques-Donatien Leray de Chaumont. The biographer consulted the archives of the State of New York that were destroyed by the fire in 1911. And the *Life* profits from an extensive correspondence with Madison and Lafayette, among others.

Theodore Roosevelt's *Gouverneur Morris* was completed in 1887 for the American Statesmen series and published in 1888.[10] Written in haste, it shows a lack of care in the planning, research, composition, and execution. Roosevelt tends to judge Morris too simplistically, and the volume manifests a deficiency of attention to proportion. Roosevelt's *Morris* is a weak book: the ability to fight political battles and administer affairs of state do not especially fit a man or woman for literary endeavor.

The next life of Morris is Howard Swiggett's *The Extraordinary Mr. Morris*.[11] Although admirable in attempting to present as faithfully as possible Morris's many-sided character, Swiggett's book is "popular" in the less complimentary sense. Mary-Jo Kline's brief *Gouverneur Morris and the New Nation, 1775–1788* is a published version of her doctoral dissertation.[12] As its title implies, Kline's book examines Morris mainly during the Revolutionary and early Federal periods. Nonetheless, Kline does thorough work on the period she covers. This is an admirable book.

Until recently the only excellent biographical scholarship on Gouverneur Morris had been done by Max M. Mintz, whose work provides the fullest and best-balanced account of Morris's life and career, but Mintz's fundamental work was completed more than forty-five years ago. His doctoral dissertation, "Gouverneur Morris, 1752–1779: The Emergence of a Nationalist," is unpublished and difficult to obtain, and his book, *Gouverneur Morris and the American Revolution,* published in 1970, adds little, if anything, to the dissertation.[13] Since then new scholarship has offered fascinating insights on the subject that were not available before.

Richard Brookhiser's *Gentleman Revolutionary: Gouverneur Morris— The Rake Who Wrote the Constitution* appeared when my biography was in the advanced stages of production,[14] and thus I have not been able to profit from his insights and analyses. Clearly, however, Brookhiser's biography is a lively and engaging narrative of Morris's life and achievement.

William Howard Adams's *Gouverneur Morris: An Independent Life,* like all of this scholar's books, is intelligently conceived, thoughtfully researched, and urbanely written.[15] But Adams's biography also appeared too late for me to have had time to properly absorb and fully incorporate his elegant insights.

My biography uses contemporary perspectives, broad access to primary documents from the eighteenth century, and recent scholarship to shed new light on this remarkable man. In working from these sources, I have attempted to place Morris's achievements more fully in the context of his times than any other biography heretofore. For the man, I try to indicate how his independent spirit triumphed over accidents and reversals that might have crushed a lesser soul. For his major writings and speeches, I have sought to provide accurate descriptions of the texts while relating them to the world in which they were first presented.

The U.S. Constitution, in particular, has its origins in various sources from ancient Greece and republican Rome to the French philosophers, British political traditions, and colonial charters. My work involved sifting the records of the proceedings of the Constitutional Convention, examining the extant state documents, foreign constitutions, and other political writings, and threading the influence of these ideas through the many articles that the Convention, after votes of approval, passed to Morris for the Committee of Style. By these means, I have tried to chart the major lines of influence that led Morris to give the Preamble and the Constitution of the United States the shape and content that govern and inspire us today.

Gouverneur Morris

{ 1 }

FAMILY ROOTS AND EDUCATION

Every so often a man or woman happens to be given a name that fits so well it might have been chosen by a poet or a novelist. Such an individual came into this world in the large, upstairs front bedroom of Morrisania Manor, in the early morning of the last day of January 1752. Gouverneur Morris's name unites the last names of his mother, Sarah Gouverneur (1714–1786), and his father, Lewis Morris, Jr. (1698–1762). *Gouverneur* is, of course, French for "governor." It is closely related to the nautical terms *gouverner,* which means "to steer," and *gouvernail,* "the helm." And a "morris" is a sprightly dance, performed in eighteenth-century America and in Britain, where morris dance troupes still exist. By 1725 the term "morris" had come to be used as an intransitive verb meaning "dance." As this biography intends to reveal, Gouverneur Morris's full name proved fitting in both regards.

The Morrisania estate of Gouverneur's father occupied 1,920 acres of hilly, scenic, and valuable real estate in the southernmost part of the Bronx. It was across the Harlem River from Manhattan Island, ten miles north of the city, and was bordered on the south by the East River. In the eighteenth century these rivers were scenic, busy with commercial shipping, and almost pollution-free. Today this tract of land covers roughly the area of the Bronx south of U.S. 98, and southeast of the Deegan Expressway.

The family history of a great man or woman often forms an important part of his or her biography, and this is evidently so of Gouverneur Morris.[1] His mother was grateful for the arrival of Gouverneur, her only son after four daughters. That she had given birth to a child so late—Sarah was thirty-eight years old—added even more to her feeling of satisfaction.

Sarah had been married to Gouverneur Morris's father, Lewis, on

November 3, 1746, by the minister of the Westchester, New York, parish. She was his second wife. Her family, originally French Huguenots, had immigrated to America in 1663 from Holland, where they had fled from Normandy at least as early as 1594. Their departure from Normandy resulted from their desire to escape the Catholic-inspired persecution that forced a massive emigration of French Protestants, which continued until the 1598 promulgation of the Edict of Nantes. Sarah's first traceable ancestor, Guillaume Gouverneur, was one of many Huguenots who fled abroad to escape the religious wars that had raged in France for three decades. His decision to make a new life in Holland shows not only that he held firmly to his religious beliefs but that his character was prudent, practical, and determined.

Guillaume's direct descendant, the merchant Nicholas Gouverneur, married a Dutch woman, Machtelt De Riener, in Amsterdam in 1670. This couple had two sons, Abraham and Isaac. The latter married Sarah Staats, whose family was rich and well-known. Isaac and Sarah produced three sons, all of whom became wealthy merchants. They also had a daughter, Sarah, born in New York on October 14, 1714, who became Gouverneur's mother.[2]

Men and women tend to acquire certain traits in youth or never. The French term *comme il faut,* describing a well-bred correctness of social behavior, almost always characterized Gouverneur Morris, and he learned his manners primarily from his parents. The mother of four daughters and stepmother to three grown men, Sarah became especially close to Gouverneur, her only son.

From the paternal side, too, Gouverneur had advantages. His great-grandfather Richard Morris, having fought in Cromwell's armies, immigrated to America via Barbados on the restoration of Charles II in 1660 and founded the manor of Morrisania, in what was then New Netherland. Gouverneur's paternal grandfather, Lewis Morris (1671–1746), inherited this manor and also a large estate from his uncle in East Jersey (now in Monmouth County).

In the early 1690s, New Jersey comprised two political entities, East and West Jersey. In East Jersey a pair of legally unique groups, known as the English and Scottish Proprietors, governed the region. West Jersey was governed by the West Jersey Society. The East Jersey proprietors and the West Jersey Society claimed they had received their rights of governance by reason of grants from the original proprietor of New Jersey, the Duke of York. As scholars have often noted, however, under British law only the king could rightfully delegate sovereignty to his subjects. Thus, sovereignty in the Jerseys at this time was legally uncertain. During his months abroad in

London in the early 1700s, Lewis Morris was an influential advocate for the unification of what eventually again became known as New Jersey. This unification process allowed Morris and the other landed families to retain predominance in the reunited colony.[3]

A member of the New Jersey Council in 1703, Lewis Morris was suspended by the governor, Lord Cornbury, in mid-1704 for having failed to attend to the governor's summons to discuss a criminal assault case involving an Indian man and an English woman, but was elected a member of the Assembly in 1707. He then led that body in opposition to Cornbury. Lewis was reelected in 1709 and was made president of the council in 1710 under Governor Robert Hunter, whose administration (1710–1720) he staunchly supported in 1711. Morris became a justice of the Supreme Court of New Jersey. From 1715 until 1733 he served as chief justice of the court, where he and the other justices handled appellate jurisdiction in all criminal cases and in civil cases involving property worth more than twenty pounds.[4] Late in 1731, Lewis Morris was sent to England by the popular party to present their grievances to the king. He served as governor of New Jersey from 1735, when he was sixty-four, until his death on May 21, 1746, at age seventy-four.

In the early 1700s Lewis was appointed the first American member of the Society for the Propagation of the Gospel, a newly created Anglican missionary organization. He also proved one of the major early financial contributors to Trinity Church in New York City.[5]

Eugene Sheridan's *Lewis Morris, 1671–1746* and Stanley N. Katz's *Newcastle's New York* both reveal the "fiercely independent" nature, in Katz's words, of Gouverneur's paternal grandfather. Sheridan and Katz also provide interesting examples of Lewis Senior's sometimes reckless behavior and remarkable changes of political direction—bewildering traits that also surfaced occasionally in Gouverneur's life. In *Newcastle's New York,* for instance, Katz observes that "despite the strength" of his pre-1700 views against the Crown's appointment of a governor for New Jersey, Lewis greeted with approval the reappointment, in 1699, of Andrew Hamilton, a more sympathetic governor than the anti-proprietary Jeremiah Basse, and readily resumed the undergovernor's office, which he had previously denounced as unconstitutional.[6] From his paternal grandfather, then, Gouverneur Morris inherited a tradition of public service, combined with a sense of political independence.

In *The Origins of American Politics,* Bernard Bailyn adjudges Lewis Morris "the least egalitarian of men." Abundant records cited in Sheridan's *Lewis Morris* and in his three-volume edition of *The Papers of Lewis Morris* indicate that Bailyn's assessment is largely accurate. This elitism was inherited by Gouverneur Morris.[7]

When this Lewis Morris—Gouverneur Morris's paternal grandfather—died, he left all that part of the manor west of the Mill Brook, called Old Morrisania, to his wife, Isabella. He left the remainder of the estate, east of the Mill Brook, to his son, Lewis Junior. Upon the death of his mother, Lewis Junior became the owner of the entire manor. He had served for decades as a judge of the vice-admiralty court of New York. His first wife was Elizabeth Staats. By her he had three sons. The first, who was the third Lewis (1726–1798), was a signer of the Declaration of Independence. Staats Long Morris (1728–1800) became a general in the British army, and married Catherine, Dowager Duchess of Gordon. Staats's stepson instigated the anti-Catholic "Gordon riots" in London in 1780. Richard Morris (1730–1810) married into the wealthy Ludlow family, and was admitted to the bar in New York in 1752, the same year his half-brother, Gouverneur, was born. A judge of the Court of Admiralty at the outbreak of the Revolutionary War, Richard was a reluctant patriot.

Morrisania, although not so large as the estates owned by the Livingstons, the Schuylers, and other socially elite New York families, was nevertheless one of the largest manors in the region at the time. "A landed estate is an engrossing business," Eustace Percy has aptly observed, "even when it is small enough to be a hobby."[8] Gouverneur's father needed considerable skill to manage Morrisania, even if that skill was narrow in its range.

The example of his father's insouciant but capable management of the Morrisania estate may have provided a model for Morris's own confidence in handling important public business. Gouverneur also seems to have experienced little of the unhealthy opposition from close relatives that often saps the energy of natively talented individuals.

The Morrisania house was a large, three-story dwelling, which commanded a splendid view of the East River to the south and overlooked Bronx Kills and Randall's Island. Jared Sparks reports that sources who knew Gouverneur as a boy characterized him as an athletic lad, who "made excellent use of" the estate hills, meadows, woods, and streams.[9]

Among apparent Morris legacies from the paternal side, perhaps not least important was Gouverneur's intelligently cultivated social sense. Lewis held many a social evening at Morrisania, where he often strolled around wearing a hat of loon's skin with full feathers. The Morrises frequently had guests, whom they received in the Wilton-carpeted, black-walnut parlor, with its mahogany furniture, its silk-bottomed chairs, its card table, its teaboard and its large settee.[10] From early adolescence through his last years, the Morrises' son knew how to entertain people of all ages, and when he died, he left one of the country's largest and best-stocked wine collections.

Under the tutelage of a Swiss émigré named John Peter Têtard, Morris studied in New Rochelle, New York, from age six through eight. Here the boy began to learn that habit of high-toned courtesy which, in some fields of endeavor, sometimes presages greatness. Dominie Têtard, a graduate of the University of Lausanne, had preached to Huguenot congregations in South Carolina from 1752 to 1758. From him the boy imbibed the essentials of the Christian faith, which helped sustain him throughout his life.[11] He also began to learn French—then the tongue of the European political and cultural elites—although he did not become fluent until he lived abroad, in the 1790s. Nonetheless, in the service of his country, Morris's grasp of French, which he began to develop as a pupil of Têtard, proved important. The French that Gouverneur learned in New Rochelle and at Morrisania also helped prepare Morris in his legal studies. The French element in legal vocabulary is large: *proposal, effect, society, assurance, insure, schedule, duly, signed, agreeing, policy, subject, rules, forms, terms, conditions, date, entrance, contract and accepted,* for example, are all from French.

In late summer of 1761, when he was nine, his parents sent him to study in Philadelphia. He lived with his half-sister, Mary Ann Lawrence, and her spouse, Thomas L. Lawrence, Jr., who, like his father, was the city's mayor.

The school in which Gouverneur enrolled was Benjamin Franklin's Academy of Philadelphia, located on the square formed by Arch, Fifth, Market, and Fourth Streets. He attended the Latin (that is, precollege) School, where the curriculum included Greek and Latin grammar and classical writers: Virgil, Caesar, Sallust, Xenophon, Livy, Lucian, Ovid, Homer, Terence. The boys also studied the Greek Testament, mathematics (at which Gouverneur always proved quite adept), geography, history, and literary composition.[12] The pupils read and wrote steadily, and one day a week they learned the fundamentals of oratory by reciting poetry and prose. Among the roughly sixty pupils were several from eminent families: Samuel Schuyler, of New York, and, from Philadelphia, Thomas Morris, brother of the already famous Robert Morris, and Gouverneur's nephew John Lawrence. The boys amused themselves with footraces around Academy Square (circumference roughly eight hundred yards), as well as by swimming in and skating on the Delaware and Schuykill Rivers.

Gouverneur's half-brothers had begun their university studies at Yale, but in 1746, six years before Gouverneur was born, their father had withdrawn them from the college after a dispute of some sort. Whatever it was, it had left Lewis permanently hostile toward Connecticut men. Although

his will, dated November 19, 1760, stated his "desire that [his] son, Gouverneur Morris, have the best education that is to be had in Europe or
America," it also directed that the boy "never be sent to the Colony of
Connecticut, lest he should imbibe in his youth that low craft and cunning,
so incident to the people of that Colony, . . . though many of them, under
the sanctified garb of Religion, have endeavored to impose themselves on
the World for honest men."[13] Lewis Junior's will, however, shows evidence
of an endearing humility. Gouverneur also manifests this trait, especially in
his diary, a small indication that even very self-confident-seeming people
often feel inadequate. Lewis Junior, for example, begins his will: "My actions have been so inconsiderable in the world that the most durable mon-
ument would but perpetuate my folly while it lasts. My desire is that
nothing be mentioned about me, not so much as a line in a News Paper to
tell the World I am dead. That I have lived to very little purpose, my children will remember with concern when they see the small pittance I have
left them. . . ."

Lewis died in 1762. Details regarding the family's grieving are not known.
In 1764, Sarah Gouverneur Morris enrolled her son in New York City's
King's College (later known as Columbia). At twelve, he was the college's
youngest student, roughly three years younger than the average first-year
student.[14]

In the words of the historian James K. Martin, "the rarest sort of individual
in prerevolutionary America was the college-educated man," but "woman"
would have been rarer yet. Not surprisingly Morris and his fellow King's
men, most of whom came from the New York social elite, provided a high
percentage of the colonial and Revolutionary leadership, and this despite the
Loyalist cast of the King's administration and faculty.[15]

Among Gouverneur's fellow students were Peter Van Schaack, who left
college in his fourth year, but returned and graduated with Morris's class of
1768; Robert R. Livingston, B.A. 1765, M.A. 1768; John Jay, who earned his
bachelor of arts in 1764 and his master's in 1767; and John Stevens, class of
1768 (Stevens became a famous engineer, inventor, and pioneer in the field
of mechanical transportation). Like many people, Morris often found his
college acquaintances helpful in professional advancement.

King's College then occupied a single three-story stone building, set on
an eminence roughly three hundred and fifty yards from the Hudson. This
building contained the library, lecture rooms, a scientific laboratory, a dining room, and roughly two dozen student apartments. Morris lived in one of
these apartments throughout his time at King's. Room and board cost, on
average, less than six pounds a year. The students attended chapel daily, ate

three meals a day together, and from Monday through Friday morning during term attended classes together. Afternoons were devoted to study. In the evenings the students either studied or enjoyed such amusements as the austere statutes of the college allowed. The cook's kitchen was in the basement. And the library was on the second floor, probably for the sake of the natural light and the relative freedom from damp.[16]

During Morris's years as a student at King's, 1764 through 1771, the newly matriculated students were ranked by their academic distinction when they were accepted. Morris ranked sixth in his class of nine. Attrition was surprisingly high. Two of Morris's cohort dropped out, one "at the end of his third year" and the other "in his second year having behaved very indifferently." Cornelius Jauncey of the class admitted in 1765 "left College in his second year after having behaved very indifferently." Daniel Kemper "left College in his second year, having not behaved so well as he ought to." Viner Van Lant "left College in his third year and was not much regretted." The record reveals that the graduate students could be as ill regarded as the undergraduates. At the bottom of his 1765 M.A. class foundered Richard Clark, who "had a Bachelor's Degree in this College but was not educated in it."

Egbert Benson, a New York State legislator who met Morris in college, told Jared Sparks that, although not a brilliant student, Morris absorbed information quickly and easily. In mathematics and science, he distinguished himself by being able to solve complicated problems without writing down his calculations. These talents would prove useful; the flair for mathematical problems is much in evidence, for instance, in Morris's proposals for a system of coinage and for a pension plan for Revolutionary officers.[17]

Morris also had a strong literary sense. His attentive reading of Shakespeare's plays and sonnets contributed much to his dramatic abilities—subtle talents, which steadily favored his later successes in private commerce and public finance, as well as his successes, such as they were, in statesmanship and diplomacy.[18]

During the Georgian age letters and politics were not separate. Early in his career in the Continental Congress, Morris was appointed to draft a high percentage of official responses and directives: a report on the conditions of the troops at Valley Forge; a wide-ranging, monograph-length response to the British offer of "peace" in 1778; instructions to the American negotiating team working to bring the French into the war on our side.

The literary schooling at King's prepared Morris well for these duties. The "Plan of Education" adopted by the college authorities in the fall of 1763 made first-year students responsible for reading, in the originals, Sallust's histories; Caesar's *Commentaries;* Ovid's *Metamorphoses* and other poetry; Virgil's *Eclogues;* Aesop's *Fables;* Lucian's *Dialogues;* and Grotius's *De veritate.* Also required were translations from Latin and Greek, as well as frequent themes in Latin and in English emphasizing subjects suggested by the readings. During 1764, following the passing of Grenville's Revenue Act—the so-called Sugar Act—and the Currency Act prohibiting the colonies from issuing paper money, James Otis (1725–1783) published his forceful tract *The Rights of the British Colonies Asserted and Proved.*

The fall of Morris's second college year, 1765, followed the British enactment of the Quartering Act; on November 1, Parliament passed the Stamp Act. The readings for this year included at least the following: Terence's comedies; Ovid's *Epistulae heroidum;* Virgil's *Aeneid* and *Georgics;* Flavius Arrian's *Enchiridion;* large chunks of Xenophon and Quintilian; Sanderson's *Composition;* and *Elementa Philosophica* and *Noetica,* by the Samuel Johnson who had been the first president of King's College. There were frequent "repetitions to learn the Art of speaking." The students composed weekly themes "set" after their reading.

The third-year program was similar; readings included Cicero's orations and *De Oratore;* selections from Quintilian; the *Epistles* of Pliny the Younger; large sections of Catullus, Propertius, and Horace; Aristotle's *Nicomachean Ethics* and *Poetics;* Plato's dialogues; Xenophon's *Anabasis;* and a compendium of readings in ethics. There were formal "Syllogistic Disputations" (formalized debates); more Latin themes and English essays, as well as, for the first time, the writing of Latin and English verse; and more "repetitions." This academic year followed the March 1766 repeal of the Stamp Act, but coincided with the passage of the Declaratory Act, asserting Parliament's right to make laws binding the colonies.

The fourth-year curriculum included Cicero's *Tusculan Disputations;* the histories of Livy and of Tacitus; Lucan's *Pharsalia;* the satires of Juvenal and of Persius; the comedies of Plautus; Thucydides' *History; On the Sublime,* which in that day was thought to be by Longinus; Demosthenes' orations; and Dionysius of Halicarnassus and Isocrates *in extenso.* The collegians studied Hebrew grammar and read large selections from the Old Testament, selections from either Grotius or Pufendorf, Hutcheson's *System of Moral Philosophy,* additional selections from other moral philosophers previously studied, and some English verse. They wrote Latin themes and declamations, philosophical essays in English and in Latin, and their own English-language verse. The faculty organized debates and the presentation of famous orations in the College Hall.[19] This academic year followed the May 1767 enactment of the Townshend Acts.

For Gouverneur, every day began with an obligatory two hours of prayer: between five A.M. and seven A.M. in fall and winter, and six and eight in spring and summer. Students attended the church of their choice; Morris chose the college chapel, where Myles Cooper conducted Anglican services. There were two months and two days of vacation—one month beginning at the end of May, two weeks at Michaelmas (September 29), two weeks at Christmas, and two days at Whitsuntide (the seventh Sunday after Easter).

Candidates for the bachelor's degree were examined "publicly . . . in the college hall, about six weeks before commencement, by the president, fellows, professors and tutors, and such of the governors as please to attend, and such of the said candidates as appear to be duly qualified (having fulfilled the conditions prescribed)." Morris received his degree in late spring of 1768, having placed second among the seven graduates. The one student to outrank him was the future Loyalist Peter Van Schaack (1747–1832); he was more than five years Gouverneur's senior. Morris remained at King's and obtained a master's degree in 1771.[20]

What generalizations can be made about the King's curriculum? It should be noted in the first place that each year brought stiffly sharper requirements. Graduates received more than adequate training in speaking at great length on a subject.

What is the genesis of existing things? How do we learn of that which is behind nature, as it were, and makes it possible? Is the whole world of one substance or more? These important questions seem to have been first pursued in a systematic way by the ancient Greeks. And these searches, properly conducted, take us into the fascinating world of metaphysics. The King's College curriculum emphasized heavily the Hebrew Testament, and stressed the major metaphysical questions.

The advance of knowledge often depends upon the ability to attend to what is unusual, and to observe its connections with what is already familiar. For reasons that should be obvious, the steady production of literary themes, based on topics drawn from the great classical authors, enhanced these abilities.

Through their reading, the King's undergraduates became thoroughly familiar with literary figures and tropes. Moreover, four years of close study of several foreign languages seems to have led Morris to see qualities of expression in his own language, such as suppleness of diction and syntax, which he would not otherwise have known.

Morris's speeches from his mature years have a well-balanced cadence, developed through extensive readings in Cicero, Demosthenes, and Horace.

His style generally manifests harmony and elegance of design in adapting the parts of the composition to the whole and to each other.[21]

Morris learned a valuable stylistic directness from such masters of brevity as Tacitus, Aristotle (in the *Physics* and *Poetics* especially), Quintilian, and Euclid. It shows to good effect in his funeral orations on the deaths of Alexander Hamilton and George Washington, as well as in many of his addresses to the Constitutional Convention, to Congress, and to learned societies. Few speeches read as well as these do.

The King's curriculum is noticeably light in scientific studies and is perhaps unduly conservative. The only roughly contemporary writers included are comparative philosophical and literary moderates: Francis Hutcheson (1694–1746) and the American philosopher Samuel Johnson (1696–1772). The formal program omits such "long eighteenth century" statesmen and philosophers as Shaftesbury (1671–1713), Berkeley (1685–1753), Hume (1711–1776), and Anthony Collins (1676–1729). The social theorists— Bernard Mandeville (1670–1733) and Adam Smith (1723–1790), for example—are also missing. And none of the major European Enlightenment thinkers made the reading list.

The Morris family's Bronx estate included a library of roughly four thousand volumes, to which Gouverneur of course had access. Unfortunately, he routinely neglected to record what he read, no inventory of the books exists, and during their occupation of New York, the British burned, stole or otherwise dispersed virtually every library they could lay hands on, the Morrises' included.[22] This was the condition of Manhattan in 1783, when the defeated British finally left:

> All the churches except St. Paul's Chapel had been demolished or desecrated. There were no charitable institutions at all, no banks or insurance companies. Trade was at a standstill, education had been suppressed. . . . The residence section stopped short of Murray Street, with quantities of vacant lots besides the burned-out areas still littered with ashes. The whole population at the time of evacuation comprised scarce 20,000 souls.[23]

Though the details are lost, we can be fairly sure that Gouverneur Morris had access to the same contemporary writers and works as had an Oxford or Cambridge undergraduate of the 1760s.[24] The smallest range of Morris's possible readings among his now classic contemporaries is suggested by the many books available to the delegates of the Constitutional Convention.[25]

In their influence on Morris and their pertinence to his time and his thinking, some of the writers in the King's curriculum stand out. One such is Isocrates, who was studied only at King's and at Harvard. This Athenian orator (436–338 B.C.) flourished during an especially tumultuous period, during which the Greek city-states waged one internecine war after another. His works include abundant political speeches and pamphlets on nationalist sentiment, on the perils of internal political strife, and on the adverse effects of being a colony.[26]

In his *Aeropagiticus,* for instance, Isocrates advocates the restoration of a strong supervisory function to the Council of the Aeropagus, the Athenian body of former high officeholders, largely aristocratic at first, whose functions were variously advisory and judicial. Its power had increased as that of the Athenian monarchy waned, but as democratic institutions advanced the council weakened. By Isocrates' time it had lost political influence entirely. In Isocrates' address are the seeds of a number of the Federalist-style arguments presented by Morris and such close Federalist contemporaries as Alexander Hamilton, Henry Knox, Rufus King, and John Dickinson. In the *Philippus,* written before Isocrates learned that Philip had moved to seize central Greece, the author called on Philip to lead Greece against Persia.

Morris was also influenced by Isocrates' "To Nicocles"; the burden of this argumentative discourse is the superiority of monarchy to either oligarchy or democracy. "To Nicocles" seems to have helped make Morris more resistant to the earliest Revolutionary American arguments, more inclined to think aristocratically, and more disposed to favor the monarchy during his ministership to France.

King's was the only well-established colonial American college to require students to read the Roman historian Sallust (86–35 B.C.). In contrast to Isocrates, who never actually entered politics, Sallust became a tribune and a senator. After not altogether successful military expeditions in Africa, he returned to Rome, where he faced charges of political corruption. Although he was eventually exonerated on charges of extortion, he probably did misbehave in office. This incident, along with Caesar's assassination, led Sallust to retire from politics. In a series of monographs on such subjects as the conspiracy of Catiline, he traces the essential qualities—honor and virtue—that he believes led to the rise of ancient Rome, then adumbrates what he sees as the main cause of Roman decline—namely, extreme wealth, with its tendencies to induce sloth and weakness. In Sallust's *History of the War with Jugurtha,* he examines with especial care the effects in turn of virtue and of vice on the human system.[27]

King's College was also alone in the colonies in placing Tacitus's *Histo-ries* and Herodotus on the curriculum. With Caesar, Tacitus is one of the best classical Latin authors from whom to learn the terseness that can lead to elegance. (Only Harvard, which produced the orators and pamphlet-eers James Otis (1725–1783) and Winthrop Sargent (1753–1820), and King's required intensive study of Caesar's *Commentaries,* a masterpiece of stylistic and historical concision.) Herodotus (484–424 B.C.) is the first historian to draw an engaging and relatively polished narrative out of the welter of plots and anecdotes that before him passed for historical writing. Herodotus had an eye, too, for the unusual example and the striking, if slightly bizarre, detail. His influence on Morris's writings and thinking is manifest in Gouverneur's letters, reports, and diaries.

Thucydides (fl. second half of fifth century B.C.) was read only at King's and the upstart College of Philadelphia. From his *Peloponnesian War* Morris learned ways to compose a moving funeral speech (see, for instance, the ora-tion by Pericles, II, 34–46), techniques of intelligent debate (see the debate on Mitylene, III, 36–50), and how to write effectively on war, military con-ditions, and military encampments (see the narratives of the revolution at Corcyra, III, 82 ff., of the battle in the Great Harbor at Syracuse, and on the destruction of the Athenians, VII, 51–87).

Perhaps more than any of his famous contemporaries, Morris was in sev-eral key ways an elitist. His extensive reading in the history of the Roman Re-public would have made it seem appropriate that, in a crisis, a country would turn for political leadership to its best-educated citizens. As Charles Nicolet and Matthias Gelzer have both demonstrated, a "very small collection of people . . . constituted the Roman political [leadership] class" during the Re-public.[28] Morris believed that, at first, the United States would need to rely on its most educated citizens primarily in its governmental offices.

Morris's education was both rigorous and relevant. But, as anyone knows who has taught in a university, the disparity between students' intelligence and their maturity sometimes proves astonishing. In the second half of his sophomore year, Morris and two classmates, Richard Dolier and John Troup, circulated what the college authorities termed a "Scandalous report . . . vir-ulently attacking the Moral Character of Professor Harpur." John Vardill drew a cartoon that portrayed Harpur's alleged onanist activities and put it up on a hallboard. The college trustees conducted hearings, obtained con-fessions from some unnamed students, and concluded that the charges of scandalizing Harpur, as presented, were unfounded. To keep his degree, nonetheless, Vardill, who later became a leading Loyalist, had to publicly admit guilt and make a retraction before the board, the professors, and the tutors; Dolier and Morris were admonished by the college president. However, the following year, on February 6, 1767, the trustees accepted Harpur's resignation.[29]

In August 1766, Gouverneur sustained severe burns when he overturned a kettle of boiling water in the family kitchen. A contemporary wrote that he had been seized by "a Fit"—no doubt an outburst of exuberance often characteristic of healthy adolescents.[30]

Morgan Lewis, a young friend, was visiting, and the accident resulted from their antics. Gouverneur was so seriously burned that Dr. Clossy set aside his duties at King's to come treat him. Lewis said that Gouverneur dealt with the pain "with a fortitude that would have done honor to an Indian Brave."[31] The injury left Morris's right arm almost fleshless, and his right side extensively scarred. Nonetheless, significantly Morris made no explicit mention of this experience in his writings.

Commencement took place on Tuesday, May 15, 1768, at St. Paul's Chapel in New York City. First in the class of seven was future Loyalist Van Schaack. John Stevens and Benjamin Moore also received the B.A.; Robert Livingston, the future statesman, and the future jurist Egbert Benson took their master's. According to the local papers, all of which printed the same account, "Exercises . . . were highly applauded by a numerous and polite Audience."[32]

As mentioned earlier, the College Literary Society had chosen Morris to give the commencement address. The manuscript of "On Wit and Beauty" is the earliest known essay by Morris to survive. A reading makes clear that the sixteen-year-old Gouverneur ("in the early spring of life," as he wrote) was father to the man. Morris's wit stamped the adult Gouverneur as did his continued interest in female charms, in particular. He observes that the   human is dominated by extreme passions, tempered only by the instinct for beauty:

> Philosophers who find themselves already living in society say that Mankind first entered into it from a Sense of their mutual Wants. But the Passions of Barbarians must have had too great an Influence upon their Understandings to commence this arduous task. Those who were in the prime of Life would never have been persuaded to labor for *their* Support who were

or had not arrived at that State. And even if they *consented* to do it yet the Love of Liberty so natural to all must have prevented both old & young from giving up the right of acting as they pleased & from suffering themselves to be controlled by the Will of another. Besides Reason unassisted by Beauty would never have smoothed away that Savage Ferocity which must have been an inseparable Bar to their Union.[33]

Morris's diverse illustrations of his twin subject draw cleverly on the character of the youthful Philip of Macedon. (Morris does not name him, but the references are clear.) That mighty and highly successful military conqueror also became an ardent devotee of worldly beauty.

More significant, perhaps, is that although King's was by far the most Loyalist of American colleges, Morris sounded surprisingly patriotic; he referred to himself and his audience, for instance, as "we who can boast of the glorious title of free-born Americans." This was, at the time, very bold. As Morris knew, in the audience were New York's royal governor, the Earl of Dunmore; the senior British military officer in New York, General Thomas Gage; and the members of the New York Provincial Council.

After three additional years of uninstructed, unsupervised, virtually unguided reading (not altogether unlike a present-day Rhodes scholarship at Oxford), at a fee of £150 per annum, Gouverneur, along with five fellow students, received a master's degree. Morris addressed this commencement, too, this time offering a smooth essay on love, "the bright and steady lodestar of the Moral World."[34] Hegel contended that we can understand men and women by understanding whom they worship. To take a single angle of investigation seldom proves optimally revelatory, and good sense suggests that no one can ever be completely understood. Still, the topics Gouverneur chose to examine in his commencement orations provide some early insights into his nature and character: wit, beauty, and love are topics in which Morris remained interested lifelong.

Gouverneur Morris was the youngest son of a father who had already had a large brood. Lewis's will promised him a legacy of two thousand pounds, but this money was to be paid at some vague time in the future. Moreover, his mother's inheritance was (perhaps revealingly) smaller than that of the children from Lewis's first marriage. The wealth of his father and grandfather had allowed Gouverneur access to an excellent education. But, with his bachelor's completed, Gouverneur had immediately to find a way to manage on his own, since he did not have ready, direct access to the family money.

Given his education, talents, presence, family connections, and well-connected friends, law seemed a natural professional choice; so, as he studied for his M.A., Morris also began, semiofficially, to prepare for the New York bar. Probably he joined the New York City Debating Society, which was formed by a group of King's students and alumni shortly after he received his B.A. As a member, he would have attended the meetings and contributed to the debates on legal and political topics.[35]

At some time during this period—I have been unable to learn precisely when—he also began an apprenticeship as a law clerk in the offices of a longtime family friend, William Smith, Jr.

Until the early twentieth century, this was the usual practice; most American law students "read law" in the office of a practicing lawyer, and learned mainly by observing and doing.[36] In New York (also in North Carolina and New Jersey), all attorneys were technically appointed to the bar by the royal governor, but in practice the appointments were usually made on the recommendation of either a judge or a court.[37]

In the 1760s, New York students had to serve a three-year apprenticeship at a fee of £120 to qualify for membership in the bar, although Morris's apprenticeship was briefer than this. Practicing lawyers were permitted to accept only two clerks at a time. By 1767 Gouverneur's proctor, William Smith, Jr., had already become a well-regarded lawyer and had been appointed to a seat in the provincial council by New York's royal governor. Nonetheless, Smith strongly opposed many British policies in New York. He was the author of a well-written history of the colony of New York, and had completed extensive studies in Greek philosophy and ancient Hebrew texts. A devout Presbyterian, Smith also exerted substantial political influence in the colony.

He supplied his law clerks with a study outline, done by his father, William Smith, Sr., in 1747. Smith senior wrote that "the sciences necessary for a lawyer are 1. The English, Latin and French tongues, 2. Writing, Arithmetic, Geometry, Surveying, Merchant's Accounts or Bookkeeping, 3. Geography, Chronology, History, 4. Logick and Rhetorick, 5. Divinity, 6. Law of Nature and Nature and Nations, 7. Law of England."

Smith's priorities are especially interesting when viewed from the perspective of twenty-first-century legal schooling. The eighteenth-century student was first required to understand the legal philosophy of the period, next to master the leading texts, and only then to concentrate on legal techniques. At the time of Morris's apprenticeship, Henry de Bracton (d. 1268) and Edward Coke (1552–1634) were the law's mostly highly regarded authorities; after 1770 and throughout Morris's life, William Blackstone

(1723–1780) assumed steadily more importance. New York lawyers also virtually all owned and used the legal calendar *Year Books,* which were speedily going out of fashion in Britain. Legal documents in New York Province often cite works such as Hugo Grotius's *De jure belli ac pacis* (1625) and Samuel von Pufendorf's *De jure naturae et gentium* (1672) with a tone of reverence.

Smith had his clerks begin with Jacques Bossuet's *Discourse on Universal History.* Bossuet argued that civil government is a salutary and necessary brake on humankind's evil passions, and that the best form of government is monarchy, presided over by a reasonable and just sovereign. After Bossuet, Smith wrote, apprentices should read histories, such as Herodotus and Tacitus.

The readings in law began with Thomas Wood's *The New Institute of the Imperial or Civil Law,* the edition of 1721. In this textbook, Wood (1661–1722) examines in some detail the work of Gaius (c. A.D. 110–180), an early compiler of Roman law. Wood's legal writings anticipated Blackstone, although they lacked Blackstone's stylistic polish. Next came Pufendorf's *De jure naturae,* followed by works of British common law and constitutional theory.[38]

The legal historian Peter Stein has argued compellingly that an exposition of legal institutions and doctrines must consider the social context in which they have developed.[39] Fortunately for Morris and his fellow law students in provincial New York, context-illuminating documents were available. The New-York Historical Society Manuscript Collections include a 150-page manuscript, "Treatise on the Nature and Law of Evidence" (circa 1770), which Morris had read. This treatise discusses such matters as how to manage legal procedure in presiding over civil cases before the Supreme Court of New York in the late eighteenth century. The writer offers a useful discussion of the value of different kinds of testimony, a long and informative essay on "the Evidence that ought to be offered to a Jury and [by what] . . . Rules of Probability it ought to be weighed and considered," and an analysis of "the Degrees of Assent from full Assurance and Confidence quite Down to Conjecture Doubt distrust and disbelief."[40] Morris's study of such essential matters as jurisprudential technique, sound rules for gathering and presenting evidence, and ways to elicit optimal kinds of testimony benefited him in his extensive committee service and report writing in Revolutionary New York and Pennsylvania, not to mention in the preparation of his letters from Britain and Europe during the Washington administration.

Gouverneur furthermore profited from membership in the Moot Club, a New York lawyers' debate society founded in November 1770. The club met until April 7, 1775; thereafter in the words of one member, it had to be disbanded on account of the events at Lexington, "which [were] the precursor in this city as elsewhere of the dissolution of many social ties." At the first meeting, November 12, 1770, Morris, although not yet an elected member, was one of the eight men present, along with William Smith, William Livingston (who would later represent New Jersey at the First Continental Congress), John Jay, Egbert Benson, and the Tory lawyer Samuel Jones. Joining soon after were James Duane, the future New York attorney general John Tabor Kempe, Peter Van Schaack, Benjamin Kissam, John Morin Scott, and Stephen De Lancey—all to be important figures in late colonial and revolutionary America. During this period, the club met on the first Friday of every month, alternately at Barden's King's Arms Tavern and at the Queen's Head. The club consistently assembled the greatest governmental, judicial and literary talents of any such group in pre-Revolutionary America.[41] It rapidly became the most prestigious debating club in New York, and its discussions influenced a number of New York Provincial Supreme Court decisions.

In what ways and to what extent did Gouverneur's training in the law influence his subsequent career? The New York bar had sixty-two members in 1775, of whom exactly half sided with the Loyalists and half with the forces of independence. Had Morris not been a trained lawyer by the mid-1770s, for instance, he probably could not have served New York nearly so effectively as a legislator. He would not have performed such sterling service at the Constitutional Convention. Nor is it likely that Washington would have appointed him to negotiate for the new United States in Europe, an appointment that profoundly affected his life from 1789 onwards.

Morris's legal education proved nearly indispensable to his service in the independence movement; imperial constitutional law and the Crown's prerogatives in its North American colonies were key issues in the Revolution. In shaping revolutionary and constitutional rhetoric, lawyers proved essential. Moreover, many of the predominant issues were ultimately questions of law—for instance, the patriots attacked the Stamp Act as not a simple revenue measure but rather a form of taxation unconstitutional by British standards.[42] In important respects, therefore, the American Revolution could be characterized as a lawyers' revolution, since legal issues, and the ways they were interpreted by American lawyers, provided much of the fuel that steadily fed the hostilities.

Gouverneur's apprenticeship was comparatively brief. On October 26, 1771, Governor Tryon issued him a license to practice law. On the same day,

Gouverneur—three months shy of twenty years old—took the attorney's oath before the New York Province Supreme Court of Judicature. After that, a large party went to the house of Samuel Fraunces, where Morris and two other newcomers were sworn in and then the tavern keeper supplied proper libations.[43]

Morris's legal training was particularly helpful to him as a writer, a businessman, and a statesman. An important requisite for the study and practice of the law is what Felix Frankfurter called "the capacity for discriminating reading."[44] Virtually every aspect of Morris's schooling furthered his development of this valuable quality. Lawyers also know better than most people that it is impossible to alter form without in some way changing content. In Morris's drafting of the final version of the U.S. Constitution, this understanding is manifest, dramatically so.

Gouverneur's legal training, along with his earlier schooling, taught him to absorb the gist of an argument with extraordinary speed. His legal studies also helped develop in him what many contemporaries saw as a dreadful honesty. Moreover, as his response to the Carlisle Commission's offer of "peace" reveals, Morris's study of law had perfected his formidable ability to digest readily other men's stated opinions, and to respond to them with appropriate strength.

Gouverneur joined the New York bar at a propitious time: the profession was about to rise rapidly in public esteem. He and his King's College contemporaries, of course, were among the prime reasons for that rise.[45]

{ 2 }

EARLY LEGAL PRACTICE AND
NEW YORK POLITICS

ONE OF MORRIS'S several major advantages in life was that his family background and education put him socially in the upper tier of his period in New York. Benjamin Moore, John Stevens, James Duane, John Jay, Robert R. Livingston, Egbert Benson, Peter Van Schaack, John Vardill, Rufus King, George Clinton, and Alexander Hamilton—all would have been important in any civilized nation at any time, and all either were, or soon would be, on excellent terms with the tall, handsome young attorney Gouverneur Morris. Not long afterward, Benjamin Franklin, George Washington, Thomas Jefferson, James Madison, and Robert Morris came to know him well. His good looks were another asset. More than six feet tall and powerfully built, Morris had blue eyes and light brown hair.

To know exactly what one wants is never common, perhaps especially uncommon for young men and women. Though he had so many talented and interesting companions in the colonies, the new lawyer had "thoughts of sailing in the *Miller*" to have a year in England. On February 20, 1772, he wrote William Smith:

> I hope to form some acquaintances, that may hereafter be of service to me, to model myself after some persons, who cut a figure in the profession of the law, to form my manners and address by the example of the truly polite, to rub off in the gay circle a few of those many barbarisms, which characterize a provincial education, and to curb that vain self sufficiency, which arises from comparing ourselves with companions who are inferior to us.

Gouverneur concedes he may be excessively inclined to enjoy worldly pleasures; he assures Smith, however, that the overseas venture would not lead to profligacy: "if it be allowed that I have a *taste* for pleasure, it may naturally follow that I shall avoid those low pleasures which abound in as great an exuberance on this as on the other side of the Atlantic." He goes on to write, significantly, that "I have somehow or other been so hurried through the different scenes of childhood and youth, that I have still some time left to pause before I tread the great stage of life."[1]

Eighteenth-century London may have been less civilized than young Gouverneur thought: bare-knuckle fighting, bull- and badger-baiting, and cockfighting all had avid followings. Press-gangs roamed the streets seeking "conscripts"; and, with very few exceptions, felonies—including theft of an astonishingly small sum, generally forty pence—were punished by death. Until 1777 Jacobites' heads remained spiked on Temple Bar. Few Londoners of any class bathed much. And drinking among the privileged classes was routinely excessive: the phrase "drunk as a lord" was coined in this era.

Morris always seemed to know how to relax. Had he gone to London then, he would have spent a great deal of money and would likely have missed opportunities to make money. More important, if he had overstayed (as he seems to have done when he finally did visit the Continent), he might have missed his chance to make history.

Knowing Morris as well as he no doubt did, therefore, William Smith did well when he advised him against sailing overseas. "Remember your uncle Robin [Robert Hunter Morris]," he warned.

He saw England thrice. No man had better advantages, either from nature or education. He began to figure with 30,000 [pounds]. He did not leave 5,000. I know others that never saw the east side of the great lake [the Atlantic], who had no other friends than their own heads and their hands, to whom your uncle was in bonds. What! *Virtus post nummos?* [Virtue comes after ready cash?] Curse on inglorious wealth. Spare your indignation. I too detest the ignorant miser. But both virtue and ambition abhor poverty, or they are mad. Rather imitate your grandfather [Lewis Morris], than your uncle. The first sought preferment *here,* and built upon his American stock. The other *there,* and died the moment before shipwreck. . . .

Upon the whole, I must refer you to your mother. She must spare a great deal before you can resolve with prudence. And when the guineas lay at your feet, think! think! think! I love you with great sincerity, or I should not be so much puzzled.

Dutch influence remained surprisingly strong in New York City long after the British conquest.[2] Yet the city was a cosmopolitan place even in the mid-eighteenth century, with immigrants not only from England but also from Holland, France, Scotland, Ireland, and the German Palatinate. By 1772 New York was a major port, attracting more foreign shipping than any other in North America.

In 1772, roughly 28.2 percent of the white males and nearly 26.1 percent of the white females were older than sixteen. Among African Americans in New York City, roughly 31.3 percent of the males and 26.1 percent of the females were older than sixteen.[3]

As late as 1770, the Province of New York consisted of a fringe of settlements on the Hudson River; Manhattan; and Long Island. New York City was a burgeoning mercantile town that contained most of the province's population; a census made in 1771 had counted 18,726 whites and 3,137 African Americans.[4] With so few people, with the roadways not very well developed, and with transportation rather unreliable, the pace of life was fairly slow despite the port's importance and success.

But for a young man with Gouverneur's background, the city offered a larger variety of social activity than almost anywhere else in America. The social historian Karin Calvert has written that in eighteenth-century America "to dance was crucial, and to dance badly was perhaps worse than not dancing at all." Of music, too, there was a surprising abundance. The symphony had not yet been developed, but the sonata had; and Handel, the eldest Bach, Haydn, the two Scarlattis, Geminiani, and Corelli were among the composers well known in New York. Every well-off household had its spinet, harpsichord, or clavichord; and Bach's *Well-Tempered Clavier* and Handel's English Suites and French Suites were especially popular. Singing groups and musical associations existed by the dozens.

Organ recitals were frequent in several of the city's churches, while "secular" concerts often took place in the New Exchange or Assembly Room. In general, admission cost six shillings; concerts began at six in the evening and usually ended with dancing—to minuets, gigues, gavottes, rigadoons, sarabandes, allemandes, courantes, passepieds, bourrées, and chaconnes.[5]

Although all this had a sophisticated air, the world of musical and dramatic theater had rougher edges. A great deal of theft took place at theater performances. In 1764, a mob wrecked the theater that David Douglass had built in Chapel Street. As Charles Hamm has noted, in his *Music in the New World,* "theatrical companies in eighteenth-century America played in an atmosphere not too far removed from that of Elizabethan England," full of rowdiness, drunkenness, gambling, and prostitution. In May 1762, Douglass, who was manager of the American Company, placed a notice in the New York newspapers offering rewards to whoever could identify the person or persons "so rude as to throw Eggs from the Gallery upon the Stage . . . by which the Cloaths of some Ladies and Gentlemen were spoiled and the performance in some measure interrupted." Performances were often disrupted by more friendly members of the audience, climbing onstage to see the actresses close up. Boston and Philadelphia audiences could be similarly troublesome; the *Pennsylvania Gazette* of November 10, 1773, stated flatly "that the Playhouse in this city [Philadelphia] is a common nuisance."[6] In October 1774, the newly formed Continental Congress found it advisable to pass a resolution to eliminate "every species of extravagance and dissipation, especially horseracing, and all kinds of gaming, cock-fighting, exhibition of shows, plays, and other expensive diversions and entertainments." (It was enforced, and for a decade there were no stage performances in America.)

Mostly because of the variety of immigrants to New York, several Christian denominations flourished there during Morris's life: the Dutch Reformed, the Lutherans, the Presbyterians, the Anglicans, and eventually (in no small measure thanks to Gouverneur's efforts on the first New York State Constitution) even the Catholics. (During Morris's youth, the latter were subject to a 1701 statute disenfranchising any who refused to take a special oath.)

Although New Amsterdam had been the first colony in North America to have a Jewish community, as late as 1773 New York still had just thirty Jewish families. Perhaps this was because in 1737 the Assembly had deprived Jews of the franchise.[7]

Most of New York's private houses stood in what is now lower Manhattan. They were generally of brick, and some as tall as three stories, with the gable end facing the street, and with roofs of tile. Some of the houses were in a simple colonial style, using mortise-and-tenon frame construction, and virtually all had at least a small garden in the rear.

From 1762, when Gouverneur was ten years old, Manhattan's streets had been lighted, at public expense, with lamps on posts. The introduction of the efficient and inexpensive Franklin stove in the early 1740s had revolutionized heating for the very wealthiest, while, from about 1750 onward, several kinds of functional lamps had been introduced. To have reasonably well-lit and well-heated rooms must have added greatly to the number of winter hours Morris and his contemporaries could spend reading.[8]

In an October 20, 1778, letter to his cousin Robert Morris (not the future finance minister), Gouverneur Morris comments, "I speak too often and too long. . . . To my sorrow I am by no Means improved in my public Speaking."[9] On the few occasions when he wrote self-reflectively, Gouverneur

Morris seems unduly hard on himself, though Morris scholars have often characterized him as arrogant. But a contemporary—Thomas Jones, a future Loyalist judge from New York—remarked that Morris was "witty, genteel, polite, sensible, and a judicious young fellow," who possessed "more knowledge than all his three older brothers put together."[10]

Many others, less difficult to impress, agreed with Jones, but of course Morris's family and social connections abetted his success in law and in business. As Max Mintz points out, Morris represented his widowed mother in lawsuits for which he received impressive fees. His oldest brother, who was directly responsible for Gouverneur's start in the political arena, also made rain for his law practice.[11]

Morris's legal cases often brought fees as high as three hundred pounds.[12] Among the talented opposing counsels were several very distinguished lawyers, such as John Jay and Alexander Hamilton. The distinguished lawyers were canny, too. Jay represented the defendant in an action begun in early summer 1772. As Morris noted in his register, "This Cause put off at circuit for small Mistake in Notice, one word being used for another [of] which Mr. Jay took ungenerous Advantage." As often happens, the litigation went on for more than a year and, on September 6, 1774, the "Case went off for Want of Jury."[13]

In *King v. Benjamin Ferris* (1773), Gouverneur Morris was one of the defendant's three lawyers, with Richard Morris and Benjamin Kissam. Ferris was accused of bringing a gang of thugs to a dwelling and forcibly evicting the lawful residents.[14]

John Tabor Kempe's notes on the trial indicate that the defense, led by Gouverneur Morris, took the clever line that no evidence had been produced to show that the landlord actually lived on the premises, that therefore only the tenant had been dispossessed, and that in any event actual dispossession had not been demonstrated. On October 25, 1773, judgment was then ordered "for the defendant nisi"—in other words, the defense had prevailed because the charges were not proven.

Morris represented clients in a wide variety of matters. Gillard Honeywell and Isaac Leggett were parties to disputed election cases in 1773–74. In both instances John Jay was the opposing counsel, and in both cases Morris's clients won: in July 1774, Honeywell was admitted to the office of Westchester borough alderman, and Isaac Leggett was installed in the Westchester borough office of common councilman.[15] On his mother's behalf, Gouverneur made an estate-related business trip to New England in fall 1772. And in 1773, he served as agent in the sale of New York houses that had been owned by his uncle Nicholas Gouverneur.[16]

In fall of 1773 Morris speculated in land for the first time. Like Robert Morris on a much larger scale later, he failed. At an auction in New York, he purchased a tract in what is now Saratoga County, bidding more than £777. In payment, he presented a bond of £475 backed by his mother. Morris never paid the seller and on June 17, 1784, a court ordered the bond forfeit and charged Sarah Morris the difference, in addition to nearly £50 in interest. Mrs. Morris evidently absorbed the cost as a sort of maternal gift.[17]

Between 1762 and 1776, three of Gouverneur's four sisters married. In 1762 the eldest, Isabella, married an Anglican minister, King's class of 1760. The next youngest sister, Catherine, married a paternal cousin, a New York merchant, Vincent P. Ashfield, in 1770. Euphemia (born 1754), the youngest sister, to whom Morris was closest, married in 1775. The fourth sister, Sarah, remained single (she died in 1781).

Gouverneur himself would not marry until more than three decades later, but he flirted extensively, notably with the socially popular Kitty Livingston. This dalliance cooled amicably. "I am (as you know), constitutionally one of the happiest Men," Gouverneur wrote in early August 1772, in a note acknowledging Kitty's having gently turned him aside. Fifteen years later she married Matthew Ridley, a British-born merchant from Baltimore who was a longstanding friend of Morris's.[18]

In mid-December 1773, Morris went down to Philadelphia, where he was "up all night making merry," mostly in celebration of the dumping of the large quantities of tea into Boston Harbor. And in late winter of 1774 the young attorney was elected to the Moot Club, which, at that time, dined during the cold months at the same Fraunces Tavern where he and his friends had drunk after being admitted to the New York bar.[19] A club like the Moot allowed ample access to rewarding social exchanges, valuable conversations, and long, leisurely meals. In April, Gouverneur attended John Jay's wedding to Sally Livingston in the great parlor at Liberty Hall, William Livingston's extravagant New Jersey estate. Among the guests were not only many Livingstons and Jays but also a younger figure: Alexander Hamilton. Hamilton later married Elizabeth Schuyler, daughter of the wealthy general Philip Schuyler.

On May 10, 1774, the Bostonians learned that, in response to the Tea Party, the port would soon be forcibly closed; on May 17, the British general Thomas Gage landed in the city. Gage was to replace Thomas Hutchinson as governor, with a view to punishing those responsible for the Tea Party and enforcing the port closure until Boston had reimbursed the East India Company for its jettisoned tea.

As a result of the Tea Act of 1773, import duties on tea to the ports of

Boston, Charleston, New York, and Philadelphia had been so reduced as to allow the East India Company to sell tea in America at a price even below smugglers' prices. Merchants in the other cities refused to accept this monopoly arranged by Parliament to shore up the financially weakened British-owned East India Company's position in India. But in Boston the selected consignees, several of whom were relatives of the royal governor, Thomas Hutchinson, wished to sustain the reduced price tea imports. After the governor and the consignees clearly indicated their refusal to send the tea to England, Samuel Adams led a small band of the Sons of Liberty, disguised as Native Americans, to board the three ships with the tea cargo and "deep-sixed" all of it. Soon all thirteen colonies, including (with less enthusiasm than the others) heavily Loyalist New York, responded to the call from Massachusetts in the form of a circular letter asking for patriot support.

As late as the beginning of that year, Gouverneur seemed oblivious or indifferent. He wrote a joint letter to his friends Mr. and Mrs. John Penn, in Philadelphia. To John Penn:

> Politics I dislike, and only look on with pity, while the madness of so many is made the gain of so few, exclaiming with poor Hamlet, "What's Hecuba to him, or he to Hecuba?" Religion—the very word demands respect, and as B [possibly their mutual friend Elias Boudinot] says of his wife, "I speak of her with reverence." Love—as dull as a tale twice told.

He was not much occupied with love, either, he went on; the problem, he said, was his need to devote himself to his rapidly growing legal practice: "Business . . . Has so transformed, and transmigrated and almost transubstantiated me, as hardly to leave the memory of what I was." To Mrs. Penn, he wrote:

> What a terrible life do I lead. Worse than at Philadelphia. There I was all night up it is true, but it was [with] a company, marking merry. Here up all night writing, and like his grace the Duke of C [Cornwall?] nobody with me but myself! Pity it is you are not here—balls, concerts, assemblies—all of us mad in the pursuit of pleasure.[20]

In response to the news from Boston, on May 19 the American patriot leaders in New York Province convened an outdoor meeting to elect a Committee of Correspondence, which would direct the revolutionary efforts in New York. And at this gathering assembled two parties: the Sons of Liberty, with twenty-five candidates' names offered, and the party of the merchants, who were led by the Delanceys and had a final list of fifty. In the election that day, all free males present voted, and the merchants won. Francis Lewis, a Son of Liberty, was promptly added to the committee to make it bipartisan.

Morris did not think much of the relatively proletarian Sons of Liberty. To John Penn, he wrote that it was a party of all

> [t]he tradesmen, *etc*. Who tho't it worth their while to leave daily labor for the good of the country. The mob begin to think and reason. The gentry begin to fear this. Their committee will be appointed [to take unified action against Great Britain], they will deceive the people [about the real nature of their activities], and again forfeit a share of their confidence. . . . I see, and I see it with fear and trembling, that if the disputes with Britain continue, we shall be under the domination of a riotous mob.

Morris has often been criticized by historians for referring, in this private letter to close friends, to the May 19 election crowd as "Poor Reptiles." The critics, however, unjustly fail to examine this matter in the larger pattern of Morris's life and times. First of all, Morris's observations on the political crisis were mostly correct. He found the closing of the port of Boston intolerable, but—what may have been nearly true—believed that "the interest of all [American] men at the time is for reunion with the parent state." Nevertheless, he argued, "we ourselves are competent to regulate our internal peace, and to refuse taxes, laid on us for government or defense. . . . She [England] cannot destroy our trade and still derive a profit from it." Moreover, he maintained, "men are by nature as free as air [and] have an antecedent right to the utmost liberty, which can be enjoyed consistent with the general safety." Morris predicted, accurately, that the aristocrats would use the committee for their own advantage, and that the power of the classes whose members made up the Sons of Liberty would grow as the power of the aristocrats waned: The gentry's "committee will be appointed, they will deceive the people and again forfeit a share of their confidence, and if the instances . . . of perfidy shall continue to increase—farewell aristocracy."[21]

In the eighteenth century generally—as perhaps largely even in the twenty-first—important cultural standards tended to form at the top and flow downwards, as Jonathan Powis has noted.[22] In an ideal democracy, however, the *polis* should probably seek not equality of type but equality of opportunity. But such an ideal can only be approached, as many wise people have noted, through sound education. And what sort of education was available to ordinary people in prerevolutionary America? For far more than 99 percent of Americans education was limited to the basics of arithmetic, writing (mostly penmanship), and rudimentary reading. Even this was often available only to boys, and only for several years, while teachers had to be paid by private funds. The academies that existed offered a fine education, but they were few. The same goes for the colleges. To the latter, of course, only males were admitted. So societal advancement through education alone would indeed have proven a hard task.

"Above all things I hope the education of the common people will be attended to; convinced that on their good sense we may rely with the most security for the preservation of a due degree of liberty": these words are Thomas Jefferson's.[23] Surely the subject of education undergirds Jefferson's correspondence with John Adams, where the two discuss the desirability of an aristocracy in America, and where Jefferson emphasizes the need for natural aristocrats, whose foundation consists of "virtue and talents."[24]

Morris had access to an excellent education, and he used that access superbly. He was also rich in what the philosopher Santayana would call personal capital. Armed with these gifts, he indeed "made his own way" to a great extent.

At the same time, it was his family's financial status and social connections that gave him access to the splendid education: he emerged from his law training with sixteen years of possibly the finest schooling then available in North America; and he acquired that education without incurring the burden of a single loan. Nor did he need to work for money while studying for his bachelor's degree at King's.

As for the M.A. degree at King's, it was noted earlier that the annual fee for the three years of unsupervised study was £150. The fee for Morris's law apprenticeship was £120 per annum. And this at a time when the average adult white man's *total* wealth, excluding slaves and indentured servants, was £47.5. The three years of Gouverneur's postgraduate schooling therefore cost more than seventeen times as much as the average free white wealthholder could have mustered in pounds sterling.

Gouverneur also enjoyed some additional advantages of the kind Jefferson called artificial. His grandfather Lewis had served as New York's chief justice from 1715 to 1733. Although he was not a formally trained lawyer, many contemporaries considered him unrivaled in the knowledge and understanding of the law. Moreover, Lewis evidently learned most about the law by reading in his large personal library—to virtually all of which Gouverneur had easy access.[25]

It is difficult to know how much Morris's family connections helped him in his legal practice; certainly he earned his large fees honestly in the cold arena of litigation. Still, he was fortunate (and must have been relieved) that his mother was sufficiently well off to be able to forgive outright an early loan (for his first, failed land speculation) that with interest totaled well over seven times the value of the average free white male American's complete financial assets; that is, wealth plus human capital (slaves); and roughly eleven times the entire financial assets of the free white male non-slaveholders.

In light of all this, Morris's misgivings about the almost entirely unlettered citizenry may appear in a special light. "Young, ignorant, destitute and single"—thus does the British historian Nicholas Canny characterize the majority of the early English settlers in America. Until the Revolution and well beyond, they had little or no chance of advancement through education. By the beginning of the Revolution, true, as many circulation libraries existed as there were colonies, but most of them charged a membership fee that very few who were not merchants or professionals could have afforded. Moreover, during their occupation of New York, the British troops did their mean-spirited best to destroy any American vehicles for the development of valuable learning, such as libraries, schools, and printing presses.[26]

No one has ever accused Gouverneur Morris of being a Pecksniff (unctuously hypocritical). His views, like those of most people, deserve to be seen in the pattern of his times. No one so vividly aware of the horrors executed in the Gordon Riots and in the French Terror could too simple-mindedly idealize "the common man." On this complex subject perhaps many of us would do well to concur with the poet Robert Frost: "The People—yes and no." The Framers of the United States Constitution in many respects did.

All that having been said, it is also true that as a member of major legislative and deliberative bodies, Gouverneur Morris worked to try to eliminate the inequalities of sumptuary and inheritance provisions in American wills, spoke very boldly against slavery, and consistently argued for the broadest possible religious freedoms.

In his seminal discussion of New York politics of the period, Carl L. Becker observes correctly that before roughly 1765 the most important political struggle in what became the state of New York was contention between the governors and the Assembly. But Becker exaggerates slightly when he states that "technically the assembly did not represent the people."[27] The essential point he evidently intended to convey was that the Assembly more often than not represented its own elite members' interests rather than those of rank-and-file New Yorkers. Westchester County (which then included the Bronx)—which is as important politically now as it was then—offers a dramatic example. The county then included six manors, which together made up more than half its area. Although Morrisania,

Fordham and Pelham in the south were comparatively small, together with Scarsdale (owned by Caleb Heathcote), Cortland Manor, and Phillipsburgh, they covered many square miles of the choicest New York land. One of the most important privileges given by the Crown's charters to the lords of these New York manors was the right to administer justice within the boundaries of their manors. Given this reality, combined with all the strength that such enormous landholdings bestow on their owners, it is not surprising that the already large number of smaller landholders often received short shrift from their elected representatives in the Assembly. This was so especially when the small landholders were in conflict with the prerevolutionary governors, as the Assembly often was.[28]

Certainly this political-economic tension was made more extreme by reason of prerevolutionary New York's status as a royal province. From the beginning of the eighteenth century until the War for Independence, the royal province was the prevailing form of colonial government. It differed from the proprietary province in that the king was the proprietor, with a royal executive and judicial system. The relation between the Crown and its legislature and officials was immediate, so the royal provinces cannot be understood apart from the concept of direct imperial control. Small wonder that revolutionary-minded New Yorkers felt the need to supplant the Assembly with the Provincial Congress.[29]

The Convention for the First Provincial Congress of New York met in the city on April 20, 1775, and continued until Saturday, April 22. One year earlier, the Sons of Liberty dumped eighteen cases of tea from the ship *London* into New York Harbor. Hardly had the tea episode concluded when the Coercive Acts opened the way for the city's conservative bloc to try to gain ascendancy. Probably on May 13 they posted a notice at the Coffee House, inviting the merchants to meet at the home of Samuel Fraunces on Monday, May 16. At about the same time, the radicals held a meeting attended by several merchants and the majority of the mechanics. This group named a committee of twenty-five, which included the leading members of the former committee of the Sons of Liberty, as well as a number of conservatives. Clearly the radicals wished to checkmate the conservative move by presenting this committee at the meeting on Monday. The widespread outrage in New York aroused by the Boston port act no doubt led the radicals to suppose there would be no firm opposition to the appointment of such a committee or to a return to the key radical policy: absolute nonimportation.

Hearing of the rebels' victory at Lexington, a number of the most ardent of the Sons of Liberty, led by John Lamb (1735–1800), looted the arsenal in the city, where firearms were distributed to roughly six hundred actively determined citizens who announced plans to take over the city government. This group seized the public supply depots and promptly closed the Customs House. The British soldiers remained in barracks.[30]

Membership in the First Provincial Congress's Convention was determined by each county's delegation. By means of arrangements not altogether clear, however, Gouverneur Morris, from Westchester, was appointed the sole representative from both Westchester and Albany; thus, with an unorthodoxy typical of Gouverneur's entire career, his first public office was this position on the important Committee of Safety of the First New York Provincial Congress, a committee on which he controlled two of the twelve votes. No other delegate was elected to represent two counties. Almost immediately this committee became extremely busy, and from the outset, Morris was a central figure, and not just because of his extra vote.

This committee's work was extremely important at this crucial juncture in New York history. The first Committee of Safety received appointment on July 8, 1775. Membership in the committee was apparently determined by each county's delegation. To the first Committee of Safety was entrusted almost the entire power of Congress. As early as September, the committee had recommended the disarming of all prospective Loyalists. But in October, the second New York Congress voted down this recommendation, although the Continental Congress had already authorized the measure.

In the third New York Congress, however, a committee on "intestine enemies" was appointed. This second committee was appointed sometime after May 24 (no record of appointment found). This committee, on which Morris served as one of seven members, had very extensive responsibilities. In effect these duties included the following: summoning, arresting, and bringing before the committee numerous New Yorkers from a list initially supplied by the third New York Congress. The list contained New Yorkers believed to be corresponding with the British army and navy and prepared to join the British forces when they arrived. The committee's wide-ranging duties likewise included inquiring of persons brought before it if they had provided aid to the British fleet, dissuaded any colonists from associating for defense, decried the value of Continental money, or retarded in any way the congressional measures for the safety of the colony. If innocent, the New Yorkers interviewed were discharged with certificates. If guilty, however, the suspects were to be confined or dismissed on parole to their homes or to some prescribed district in a neighboring colony.

This committee on which Morris served was furthermore authorized to investigate and try other suspected New Yorkers in the same manner as the persons on the list supplied by the congress. Lastly, the committee on "intestine enemies" was charged with arresting certain persons, either royal officials or notoriously disaffected citizens. In this group, those found innocent were to be discharged with certificates. If guilty these individuals were to be paroled in neighboring colonies, or, on refusal, to be confined. The committee's decisions were to be based on the evidence of paid witnesses, sworn to tell the truth.

All persons in New York in arms against America at this time were to be arrested and tried by the Provincial Congress. These traitors' property was seized after they were disarmed, forcibly if necessary. Some Loyalists were paroled, many were exiled to Connecticut, and the jails in New York soon became full. The list of persons investigated thus by Morris and his colleagues was very long. Not many twenty-four-year-olds have shouldered as much responsibility as Morris did during his months of service in this committee.[31]

One year after Morris's May 1774 letter to the Penns in Philadelphia, he had moved from being a neutrally disposed conservative to becoming one of the leaders in the revolutionary movement in the colonies. A committee of fifty-one delegates from New York was elected on May 16 to try to determine what shape the resistance to the British would take. Delegates were elected by the votes of similar groups of free white males throughout the Province. New York then formed an association of representatives from these delegations. This association traveled to the First Continental Congress in Philadelphia in September 1774. Congress there adopted the Continental Association. This group promised to hold its thirteen member colonies to stern measures on nonimportation, nonexportation, and nonconsumption of British commercial goods and food stuffs.

After the fighting at Lexington, Concord, and Bunker Hill, in the spring of 1775, most patriotic Americans knew that for their political and economic situations to improve, the rebellion had to succeed. Like many members of the other educational, social, political, and economic elites throughout the colonies, Morris still hoped for a rapid and peaceful compromise. At the same time, when forced to choose, he chose the patriot side. His family roots cherished independence and American self-government. As early as 1768, his commencement address at King's expressed pride in claiming "the glorious title of free born American[s]."

In typical Morris fashion, once he decided to side with the rebellion, he went into the conflict wholeheartedly. On May 8, 1775, when a group of freeholders at White Plains elected representatives from Westchester to a

Provincial Congress that had been proposed for New York, Morris was chosen as a delegate. Thus, when the Provincial Congress met at the Exchange on May 23, he was not only present but played a leading role.[32]

Following Morris's brilliant May 30 speech on "the expediency of emitting a Continental Paper Currency," the Provincial Congress appointed a committee to formulate a scheme of reconciliation with Britain. On June 2, this committee formed and Morris became one of its members. Gouverneur then presented a lengthy report he had drafted to attempt a prompt and practicable compromise, "to which," John Jay wrote, "they could make no objections excepting that none of them could understand it."[33]

Morris next presented a briefer plan. This epitome of his first effort recommended that the colonists insist upon the right of self-taxation and allow parliamentary regulation of the trade of the empire with just payment of all duties to the colonial treasuries, along with entirely voluntary colonial contributions to the empire's defense. The New York committee accepted this plan, but added a pair of issues to which Gouverneur much objected. These were a repeal of all subsequent Parliamentary strictures on colonial trade and fisheries and a denunciation of "popery." These new issues amounted to an objection to the 1774 Quebec Act, which, among other details, extended the Quebec province south to the Ohio River. Morris naturally believed that the first demand was so radical as to guarantee a blunt British rejection. And he reasoned that the statement concerning Catholicism was "most arrant Nonsense." He opposed it vigorously; nonetheless, the committee approved the amended plan in a close vote.

As late as mid-June 1775, for mostly mercantile reasons, sentiment remained strong within New York for reconciliation with Britain. Majority opinion notwithstanding, the members of the committee agreed, apparently unanimously, to associate the Provincial Congress with the Continental Congress. Among the foremost subjects deliberated by the New York Provincial Congress was the matter of how to raise enough money to pay for military preparations and other arrangements for a government and defense independent of Britain. As a member of the committee addressing these matters, Morris wrote a cogent and detailed plan.

The report he wrote assumes at the outset that the war-induced crisis will immediately demand a very large sum of money, and more than can be raised by taxation. Paper currency, therefore, would be indispensable, and the difficulty to be settled was how best to arrange its issuance. After a review of the pecuniary resources of the colony and the overall operations of a paper medium, the Morris report suggests three possibilities. One, each colony might print the sum apportioned for it by the Continental Congress.

Two, the Congress could print all the money deemed necessary, and then each colony should pledge to contribute its proportionate share. Three, the Congress should print the whole amount and apportion a share to each of the colonies. In characteristic Gouverneur Morris fashion, the report analyzes the situation as a whole and demonstrates how each method would accrue advantages not only to New York but also to the other twelve American colonies. In the event, the New York committee voted for the third alternative, because it backed the currency with specified credit, secured a broader circulation for the paper money, and strengthened the bond among the colonies by establishing a common interest in the circulating paper and in its eventual redemption.

Egbert Benson (1746–1833) wrote a sketch of Gouverneur in which he discussed Morris's presentation of the paper currency issue. Benson remarked that this subject "more than any other" occupied the Provincial Congress in 1775, "as being our only *money sinew* of war. Mr. Morris appeared to have comprehended it throughout, and as [if] it were by intuition. He advanced and sustained opinions new to all. There was none who did not ultimately perceive and acknowledge them to be just."[34]

When Morris spoke out firmly to expunge religiously bigoted language, as in his private letter to John Jay, dated June 30, 1775, he knew Jay would share the letter with the rest of the New York delegation. Morris struck another blow for liberty that same year in his defense of the British-born newspaperman James Rivington (1724–1802).

In 1773 Rivington had started a newspaper, *Rivington's New-York Gazetteer.* During the following two years New York had become divided politically along Whig (Patriot) and Tory (British) lines. *Rivington's* published criticism of New York's Sons of Liberty, and the paper's Tory editorial policy provoked anger against him not only throughout the city but also in the Middle Atlantic colonies and New England. With resentment simmering among the patriots, the Provincial Congress committee, which was led by the Sons of Liberty, sent John Jay and Philip Livingston on March 8, 1775, to confront Rivington about the factual basis for some of his statements. Soon afterward, this committee referred the matter to the Continental Congress.

The Congress had made no decision when, two months later, an angry patriot mob confronted Rivington. Morris thereupon pleaded with such influential friends as Richard Henry Lee, Virginia's mercurial delegate to the Continental Congress, and Charles Lee (1732–82), a British-born soldier of fortune, who in 1775 was appointed by Congress a major general in the Continental Army (at the time, only Washington outranked Lee), to urge restraint of such "Excess . . . zeal." Morris pointed out that, hardly a month before Rivington had been threatened by his fellow New Yorkers, most of the city's residents had been either Tories or sympathizers.

In cold fact, the young lawyer was correct. He did not carry his objections to the charges against Rivington because procedural matters made it impossible to thwart the prosecution.[35] But his admirable letters defending Rivington's right to freedom of the press, quickly understood and hailed by Richard Henry Lee, are another example of Morris's courage in expressing and defending unpopular ideas. Already Morris seems to have been what today would be termed a First Amendment absolutist. But his concern for freedom of the press was genuine and may in the long run have proved salutary for the new nation. In addition, like almost all of the major American Founders, Morris was the kind of conservative who abhorred mob violence. This action, he sensed correctly, would soon be visited upon Rivington.

After Rivington's shop was wrecked, the printer published a brief retraction and signed a loyalty pledge put before him by the Provincial Congress. He then sailed for England, but returned in 1777 with a royal commission as the King's Printer in New York (the British occupied the city throughout most of the war). He established an arrangement with other New York newspaper publishers that resulted in the first daily newspaper in America, *The Royal Gazette*. This Rivington-owned publication reported American military losses in great detail and ignored American victories. As regards his anti-Americanism, however, there was more than met the eye of his contemporaries: by war's end Rivington had become an important spy for the Americans, of which more will be said when we reach the Yorktown section of our story.

Morris always disapproved of "legislation" by mob action, as he demonstrated—along with a large amount of physical courage—on June 6, 1775, when he attempted to prevent the seizure of five carts filled with "spare arms" that the British had been in process of evacuating. After unsuccessfully confronting a large mob of patriots on this question in the Broadway, he wrote to the Provincial Congress on June 10, 1775, arguing for the restoration of the carts of weapons and ammunition. The proposal carried nineteen votes to four.

This incident too, though, is typical of Morris in another way. His confrontation with the leader of the raiding party, Marinus Willet (1740–1830), was brave, and we may applaud his instinct to be fair to the mob-besieged British forces. Under terms of an agreement with the Provincial Congress, promulgated June 3, the British troops that had not been withdrawn, under threat, from New York City were to be allowed to leave peacefully. The precise date of the withdrawal the British kept secret. On June 6, however, as the last British subunit, the "Royal Irish" regiment, began marching to the docks, a crowd of New Yorkers surrounded the British troops, commanded by Major Isaac Hamilton. The self-appointed "citizens' army" insisted that the British depart without any spare arms, as this they claimed would be in keeping with the formal agreement regarding the British evacuation. Indeed, the duly approved regulations for the British retirement did include an explicit committee statement that in their withdrawal from New York the King's troops were not to remove "spare arms," which the five carts of arms surely represented. As often in Gouverneur's life, he acted valiantly and promptly, and his opinion carried the day. On reflection, however, we can see that, from the standpoint of the duty a public official owes his constituency, in this instance, as in some others, Morris probably did not do altogether right.[36]

From mid-July 1775 onward it became increasingly difficult to secure a quorum of either the particular delegations on which he served or of the Congress. (In nearly twenty-four months Morris was absent only seven times—less than the average.) Nevertheless, from the first meeting in late spring through the autumn, Morris and his New York congressional colleagues worked with remarkable diligence. Gouverneur's duties were exceptionally demanding: he was a member of the Committee of Safety and also chairman of the Committee of Correspondence. In the latter capacity, he was responsible for drafting numerous letters and resolutions to the Continental Congress and to the associated revolutionary colonies. On the Committee of Safety, of which he was one of six supervisory members, his duties included often urgent deliberations involving the carrying out of the orders issued by the Continental Congress, the superintendence of the military affairs of New York, compliance with requisitions made by the generals of the Continental Army, the appropriation of money for the necessary public services, and setting the time and place at which the Provincial Congress would convene. The Committee of Safety alone proved the equivalent of a very demanding full-time job, in particular because John Jay, also a supervisory member, often had to be away on other official business. In consequence, Morris was elected one of the supervisory delegates. Since one, however, the great legal mind John Jay, was perforce so often absent, the other six members of this Committee for Safety became so deluged with pressing concerns that they had to meet almost daily for weeks at a time. "We grow weary," writes Morris, "of being called together to deal with Tories. That has been our whole business ever since we have been formed into a committee."[37]

As early as September 1775, the Committee of Safety of the First New York Provincial Congress had recommended the disarming of all so-called non-associators. In October, however, the same Congress, to Gouverneur's understandable chagrin, had voted down the recommendation, even though the Continental Congress had already authorized such action. (In fact, neither the First nor the Second Provincial Congress took the systematic measures that could have smothered the innumerable Tory fires in New York; and thus the bonfires became steady conflagrations.)[38]

The most frequent Tory subversions took the following forms: production of counterfeit money; correspondence with the British, including the divulgence of patriot secrets, military dispositions, and information on fortifications; affording aid to the King's fleet; sowing sedition by encouraging Loyalist enlistments; strong disparagement of the worth of the Continental currency; and making preliminary but detailed plans for espionage. Since each of the dozens of such cases would ideally have called for, in effect, a major criminal espionage investigation, the reader can perhaps imagine how exhausting it was to serve conscientiously on the Committee of Safety. It is true that the weakness of the Continental Congress, as well as of the First and Second Provincial Congresses, on the executive and judicial sides provided a strong stimulus for the development of a new government on both levels. But those deficiencies made Morris's New York service much more difficult.[39]

The committee asked for (and got) the raising of a strong militia to overawe the Loyalists of Dutchess County; a similar but more permanent show of strength was, at roughly the same time, needed in Queens. How loyal to the Revolution was the militia in far Ulster County? This question required investigation. In late June, the committee aided in uncovering a large conspiracy to capture George Washington, which had originated in Tryon and involved both the mayor of New York, David Matthews, and one of Washington's bodyguards, Thomas Hickey. Matthews was arrested for his malversation, and on June 28 Hickey was hanged.[40] To the great credit of the patriots, few if any American Loyalists lost their lives merely for holding certain beliefs and expressing them, a revolutionary record that may be unequaled.

In New York, the Tory problem was exceptionally difficult because the province was almost certainly the most Loyalist of the mainland colonies (Canada excepted), and it was also huge. Also, though New York ranked only seventh of the colonies in population, that still gave it (1775) nearly 203,000 people, including roughly 4,000 indentured servants and almost 18,150 slaves. The sheer size of the population made checking out people's loyalties in New York very difficult.[41]

As head of the Committee of Correspondence, Morris was chosen to draft a letter from the New York Congress to the Canadians, assuring them that no military action against them would come from New York. The letter was sent in late summer of 1775. The Continental Congress made a similar declaration. And yet, within ten weeks a seemingly formidable expedition was ordered assembled and marched into Quebec, under the command first of General Philip Schuyler and then, when Schuyler became ill, of General Richard Montgomery. This force—raised almost wholly in New York, by the way—captured Montreal from the British. But in the battle of Quebec, on New Year's Eve, a clever British counteroffensive defeated the Americans. Montgomery was killed in the battle and Canada was lost to the future United States.[42]

Thus ended the first foreign offensive launched by the American Continental forces. The Continental Congress did not authorize privateers to strike outside American waters until March 23, 1776. This was nearly six months after the British had seized and burned Falmouth (Portland), and nearly three months after British forces had cannonaded and then burned Norfolk, Virginia, on New Year's Day, 1776. It was also the day when Washington first raised the Continental flag, with thirteen stripes, before his headquarters in Cambridge, Massachusetts.

Not until April 13, 1776, did Washington arrive in New York from Cambridge with the main part of his army. With the siege of Boston over, General Washington feared that the British General Howe was preparing his forces in Halifax, Nova Scotia, for a military confrontation in New York that would isolate the northern colonies from the southern colonies. On April 4, therefore, Washington took the major portion of his army south to New York, where they arrived on April 13. Only the day before had the Provincial Congress of North Carolina instructed its delegation to the Continental Congress to stand for independence. They were the first.

Washington left General Israel Putnam in charge of the troops and rode to Philadelphia to confer with the Continental Congress. Putnam then effected the defenses outlined by Major General Charles Lee before the latter had moved south in February. An additional concern for the American patriots was the rumor that the British had hired mercenaries from Germany and were preparing to expand the war to include the entire eastern seaboard.

On May 10, 1776, the Continental Congress finally adopted a measure urging each colony without a clear governmental apparatus to develop one promptly. To this time, only New Hampshire (on January 5, 1776) and South Carolina (on March 26, 1776) had developed, written, and ratified constitutions.

On May 24, New York acted. At nine o'clock sharp, on a clear, sunny morning, twenty-four-year-old Gouverneur Morris took the floor of the Exchange to address what had by now become the Fourth Provincial Congress of New York. He spoke for three hours, relying on notes and an outline. The speech survives only as a sixteen-page manuscript entitled "Oration on Necessity for Declaring Independence from Britain," which Morris drafted after the fact—but even these fragments show that its eloquence must have been luminous. Its burden is to urge the necessity of independence, and to assert that no reason exists to delay the establishment of a new, ratified state government, since the Continental Congress has already become a sovereign law-making body.[43]

A few words about the context of this oration are in order. In making such a consequential speech there and then, in comparatively Loyalist-leaning New York, the last colony to ratify the Declaration of Independence, Gouverneur Morris crossed an emotional-political Rubicon. In his family of over a dozen adults (counting in-laws), the only declared supporters of independence were his sister Euphemia's husband, Samuel Ogden (1746–1810); Gouverneur's brother Lewis (1726–1798); and Isaac Gouverneur, a maternal cousin who lived in the Dutch West Indies. Gouverneur's duller older brother Richard (1730–1810) temporized for a long time before he declared for the American side. And as for Gouverneur's mother, Sarah Morris herself was an early and outspoken Tory.[44]

Yet, on Friday, May 24, 1776, Gouverneur spoke for independence strongly. This should come as no surprise. Despite the severe burns he had sustained as an adolescent, Morris had volunteered for the New York militia. (To his patriotic brother Lewis, he wrote on February 26, 1775, "You well know that the Offers of my Service were merely for the Benefit of the general Cause[,] conscious that my little abilities were more adapted to the Deliberations of the Cabinet than the glorious Labours of the Field.")[45]

According to the manuscript, Morris began his speech by outlining the origins of the political crisis. The governmental arrangements between home country and colonies, he said, had been dissolved and were not to be revived. Now, he said, the occasion presented itself for America to assume the mantle of self-confident sovereignty. Reconciliation was a chimera:

> Undoubtedly you will find some state carpenter, ready to frame this disjoined government, and warrant his work. And if there should be some flaws, considering the *protection* you receive from Britain, you ought to put up with them. I know he will tell you so. *Protection,* Sir, is a very good thing, yet a man may pay too much for diamonds. There is a common story

of a certain juggler, who would undertake to cut off a man's head, and clap it on again so neatly, as to cure him without a scar. Much such a sort of juggling business is this protection we are about to receive. Great Britain will not fail to bring us into a war with some of her neighbors, and then protect us as a lawyer defends a suit; the client paying for it.

This is quite in form, but a wise man would rather, I think, get rid of the suit and the lawyer together. Again, how are we to be protected? If a descent is made upon our coasts, and the British navy and army are three thousand miles off, we cannot receive very great benefit from them on that occasion. If, to obviate this inconvenience, we have an army and navy constantly among us, who can say that we shall not need a little protection against them? We may indeed put a clause in the agreement, that Britain shall not use them to enslave us; and then all will be safe, for we cannot suppose they will *break their promise.*

Thus I find, Sir, that with the help of a little paper and ink, we may draw out a long treaty, filled with cautious items, and wise *et ceteras.* Then the whole affair is settled. America is quite independent of Great Britain, *except* that they have the same King; for although the British Parliament is allowed to possess, under the name of supremacy, an immense train of legislative powers, there are contained in the agreement strict inhibitions from using any one of them. Thus it is settled, I say, for seven years. Not a day further. The very next parliament, not being bound by the acts of the former, the whole is in law as to them a nullity. Our acknowledgment of supremacy binds us as subjects, and our most exquisite restrictions, being contrary to the very nature of civil society, are merely void. Remember, too, that no faith is to be kept with rebels.

In this case, or in any other case, if we fancy ourselves hardly dealt with, I maintain there is no redress but by arms. For it never yet was known, that, when men assume power, they will part with it again unless by compulsion. Now the bond of continental union once broken, a vast load of debt accumulated, many lives lost, and nothing got, I wonder whether the people of this country would again choose to put themselves into the hands of a Congress, even if a general attack were made upon their liberties. But undoubtedly the whole continent would not run to arms immediately, upon an attempt against one of the colonies, and thus, one after another, we should infallibly be subjugated to that power, which we know would destroy even the shadow of liberty among us.

Continued union with Britain, then, was impossible. What of independence? First, Morris defined it, and next he explained the extent to which it already existed, even in New York. Then he dropped the other shoe: "[T]o make a solid and lasting peace, with liberty and security, is utterly impracticable. My argument, therefore, stands thus. As a connexion with Great Britain cannot again exist, without enslaving America, *an independence is absolutely necessary*. I cannot balance between the two. We run a hazard in one path, I confess, but then we are infallibly ruined if we pursue the other." He urged his fellow congressmen to "candidly examine" what independence would mean, and he described its "grand lineaments and characteristics": for the society itself, "legislation and distributive justice"; as the society interacts with others, "the coining of money, raising armies, regulating commerce, peace, war, and treaties."

With respect to legislation, he concludes, "we do not find, that there was any immediate and personal act of the overseas prince necessary for the exercise of the law unless perhaps the affixing a piece of wax now and then to a piece of paper or parchment. And I believe we may find men in this country, quite as well skilled in that manufacture, as any English workmen. . . . We have lawyers among us, to tell what the law books say." Morris follows the above statements with an analysis of the degree of justice, which he believes Congress wields better than Parliament for the colonies.

Of his fellow American legislators he remarks, "coining money, raising armies, regulating commerce, peace, war, all these things you are not only adept in, but masters of. Treaties alone remain, and even those you have dabbled at." He then presents the example of Georgia, once recalcitrant but now "received . . . upon repentance." By the summer of 1775 Georgia had only had twenty years of self-government. In addition, she was probably the poorest colony. Furthermore, her numerous Native American neighbors remained loyal to British Indian superintendent John Stuart. Her undefended coastline and the British garrison at St. Augustine would make her a ready target for the British military were a rupture to come. Moreover, in British governor Wright the Georgians had a very important and influential royal official. Although Georgia had at first scorned membership with the American colonies to her north, she soon reversed her position and joined the patriots. All these factors being known by most if not all of the members of the audience that May 24 at the Exchange, Morris's mention of even Georgia's movement to solidity with the twelve other colonies was a cogent argument.[46]

Morris also cited the Congress's current dealings with Canada. And "France and Spain," he presciently remarks, "you ought to treat with." Morris goes on:

I believe, Sir, the Romans were as much governed, or rather oppressed, by their emperors, as ever any people were by their king. But *emperor* was more agreeable to their ears, than *king*. Some, nay many persons in America, dislike the word *independence*. For my own part, I see no reason why *Congress* is not full as good a word as *States-General,* or *Parliament,* and it is a mighty easy matter to please people, when a single sound will effect it.

What would be the benefits of a separation from Britain? Morris examines these, under the separate headings of peace, liberty, and security. Peace: "[E]xperience, Sir, has taught those [European] powers, and will teach them more clearly every day, that an American war is tedious, expensive, uncertain, and ruinous"—owing to geography ("that great gulph which rols [*sic*] its waves between Europe and America") and the fighting qualities of the Americans. Liberty: Morris believed it impossible that the Continental Congress would turn oppressive, whereas how can "we pretend to say—that we have political liberty, while subject to the legislative control of Great Britain?

"The last consideration, Sir, is *security,* and so long as the system of laws by which we are now governed shall prevail, it is amply provided for in every separate colony." For the moment, this was mostly wishful thinking. To come were six more years of continuous fighting, not to mention the depredations by British raiders during the so-called War of 1812.

Independence had yet more advantages: a healthy commerce; development of wealth; increase of population; and diffusion of knowledge. That last would induce "all nations to resort hither as an asylum from oppression."

Nothing more remains but to say a word on the *inconveniences,* to which an independent form of government would subject us. And what are they? A war with Great Britain. And in that very war we are already engaged. *Perhaps some gentlemen may be apprehensive of losing a little consequence, and importance, by living in a country where all are on an equal footing. Virtue in such a country will always be esteemed, and that alone would be respected in any country.* If these gentlemen would reflect, that free republican states are always most thickly inhabited, perhaps they may be of opinion with me, that [if] the indulgence of a few in luxurious ease, to the prejudice of their fellow creatures, is at best not to encourage a general profligacy of manners, it is then criminal in the highest degree [emphasis added].

As this passage should suggest, those who characterize Morris as no more than a snobbish aristocrat have failed to measure the man altogether accurately.

Concerning New York's formal declaration of separation from Britain, Morris's peroration is as follows:

> Now let me earnestly ask, why should we hesitate? Have you the least hope in treaty? Will you even think of it, before certain acts of Parliament are repealed? Have you heard of any such repeal? Will you trust these commissioners? Is there any act of parliament passed to ratify what they shall do? No, they come from the King. We did not quarrel with the King. He has officiously made himself a party in the dispute against us. And now he pretends to be the umpire. Trust Crocodiles, trust the hungry wolf in your flock, or a rattlesnake nigh your bosom, you may yet be something wise. But trust the King, his Ministers, his commissioners, it is madness in the extreme! Remember, I conjure you to remember! You have no legal check upon that legislature. They are not bound in interest, duty, or affection to watch over your preservation, as over that of their constituents; and those constituents are daily betrayed. What can you expect? You are not quite mad. Why will you trust them? Why force yourselves to make a daily resort to arms? Shall we never again see peace! Is this miserable country to be plunged in an endless war? Must each revolving year come heavy laden with those dismal scenes, which we have already witnessed? If so, farewell liberty, farewell virtue, farewell happiness!

Examination of the manuscript offers rewarding insight into the twenty-four-year-old Morris's compositional style and intellectual development. First of all, the sixteen pages have remarkably few alterations; on some pages even a high-powered magnifying glass fails to reveal a canceled word or phrase. Unnecessary words, such as the occasional "which" or "that," Gouverneur invariably strikes. He makes careful stylistic changes, such as substituting "yet" for "and" where his argument hesitates rather than pushes ahead. Every change he makes adds clarity or force. For example, one sentence in the draft began "To affirm then, that distributive . . ." Gouverneur amends this to read: "To affirm that the Distribution of Justice is not in the Hands of this House, argues great want of attention, and ignorance of our public Proceedings." The change from "distributive justice" to "the Distribution of Justice" sharpens his emphasis and highlights the concept he presents. (It should be remembered, too, that the eighteenth-century practice was to capitalize for emphasis.)

The speech is marked by Gouverneur's characteristically interesting use of metaphors, like that comparing England to a decapitating juggler, or, in his peroration, the remarkable "Trust Crocodiles"—a device to make even a Cicero smile.

It may be remembered that during his King's College years, Morris had studied Isocrates *in extenso,* as well as the Scottish philosopher Francis Hutcheson. Isocrates' works abound with passages expressing nationalist sentiment, examining the hazards of internal political feuding, and expostulating in detail on the disadvantages of being a colony. With these matters Isocrates was very familiar, since his Athens had lived through all of them. As for Hutcheson, he emphasized steadily the citizens' moral right to revolt against tyrannical oppression, a right that in his view applied clearly to colonies' relationships with the mother country.[47]

Morris's oration also shows the technical influences of Demosthenes. As Demosthenes does, most notably in the *First Philippic,* Gouverneur takes his time itemizing the facts of the political situation, and builds his details in a cumulative manner before he explicitly advocates a policy direction. In *On the Symmories,* Demosthenes does not make known the main theme of his speech until very late, when he reveals his answer to the twenty symmories' important financial problems, and recommends temporary military inaction.[48] Gouverneur's circuitous method in the May 24, 1776, speech evidently draws in important ways on Demosthenes. Also, like the Demosthenes of the *First Philippic,* Morris presents a speech virtually absent an ego. And like the perorations in the *Philippics* and *Olynthiacs,* Morris's peroration relies strongly, if unconventionally, on narration, which seems characteristic of Morris. In a very high percentage of his diary entries, letters, speeches, and reports he seems to be telling stories perhaps as much as describing, explaining, or persuading. Of course, Morris's narrative almost always intends exposition or argumentation, yet the narrative aspect of Morris's discourse tends to make his verbal and literary productions interesting well beyond the ordinary.

Morris followed his speech with a motion for the popular election of a new body to frame a government for New York. On May 31, after about a week of debate, the Provincial Congress agreed.[49]

Although New York was almost certainly the most Loyalist of the thirteen colonies, its political leadership steered it briskly toward the independence movement. On May 15, 1776, Virginia directed its delegates to vote for independence at the Continental Congress; subsequently Richard Henry Lee moved that the Congress pass a resolution for independence. But New York was not so far behind. As early as May 13, 1776 (this date precedes by two days Richard Henry Lee's promulgation of the Virginia resolves, generally assumed to be the first official movement to independence), the Provincial Congress had formed the small "Secret Committee," whose brief was to confer regularly with George Washington and pass on to him all strategically and tactically significant information. Morris, who had been named to the Secret Committee on June 21, promptly became the key New York liaison with Washington, and just as promptly the two men developed a warm relationship that lasted until the older man's death. (Not surprisingly Martha Washington asked Gouverneur to present a eulogy at her husband's funeral.)

"The secret of the world," writes Emerson, "is the tie between person and event. Person makes event, and event person." The same concept illuminates the relationship between Morris and Washington. They enjoyed two dozen years of friendship, one that seems to have generally enriched the governmental contributions of both men. Morris and Washington first met on June 25, 1775. Shortly after nine o'clock that morning the New York Provincial Congress ordered Morris, along with three other members of the congress, to meet Washington at Newark, New Jersey, and escort him to New York. To avoid the British warship *Asia,* with its sixty-four guns, the party crossed into New York via the upper ferry from Hoboken to Colonel Lispenard's country estate, two miles north of the city. By the time Washington and his escorts arrived, greeted on the beach by nine companies of militiamen and numerous patriot leaders, Washington and Morris had already been in each other's company for seven hours. On the morning of June 26 the New York Provincial Congress approved an address by Washington, and appointed Morris and Isaac Low to inquire of Washington when the members should assemble to hear Washington's speech, which he delivered at five in the evening.

Almost one year later (on June 21, 1776), Morris was appointed as one of the three members—Philip Livingston and John Jay were the other two—to the Secret Committee to confer with Washington regarding security arrangements in New York.

During Morris's 1778–79 service on the Continental Congress, he did more committee service than any other member. Many of these committees dealt with war issues and required Morris to work with Washington. None more so than the Committee of Conference, which worked closely with Washington to improve the conditions, morale, and efficiency of the Continental Army. From Congress, Morris wrote to Washington on such subjects as naval prisoners of war, flag shipments, conditions in Congress, and U.S. prisoner of war accounts.

At the Constitutional Convention in Philadelphia, over which Washington presided, Morris and Washington had steady personal and professional contact for more than three months. As Assistant U.S. Finance Minister, also, Morris attended regular weekly meetings with George Washington in Philadelphia. After the Philadelphia Convention, when Washington hesitated to have his name put forward in nomination for the presidency, Morris's letter to Washington at Mount Vernon ("The Exercise of Authority depends on personal character" and "you are the *indispensablest* man") evidently helped induce Washington to assent to become the first President of the United States.

When Morris first went to Europe on private business, Washington provided the younger man with valuable letters of introduction. On November 12, 1788, Morris wrote Washington:

> I am about shortly to take my Departure from Philadelphia for the Kingdom of France and expect to visit both Holland and England. When I desire to be favored with your Commands it is not the mere ceremonious Form of Words which you every Day meet from every Man you meet and which you know better than any Man to estimate at its true Value. Whether I can be useful to you in any Way I know not but this I know that you may command my best Endeavors.

For Morris, Washington wrote letters of introduction to Chastellux, to Jefferson, to Lafayette, to Rochambeau, and to Arthur Young, among other influential people in Europe. Washington's letter of November 27, 1788, to Chastellux is interesting for the general's compliments regarding Gouverneur: "As for Mr. Morris, only let him be once fairly presented to your French Ladies, and I answer for it, he will not leave the worst impression in the world of the American character. . . . I rely upon it he will make his way good."[50]

In Europe, under Washington's new presidency, Morris received an assignment as the first U.S. private agent (or presidential envoy, as we would now describe him), inquiring mainly regarding Britain's disposition to act on the terms of the Treaty of Paris.[51]

As first official U.S. Minister to France after the Constitution had taken effect, Morris steadily wrote informative letters to Washington on such issues as the French revolutionaries and the British alliance, the French tobacco trade, and the French debt.

Washington's esteem remained constant, even after Morris had returned from his decade in Europe. Within a year of his death, the former President wrote comments at the foot of the pages of James Monroe's introduction to a pamphlet entitled *A View of the Conduct of the Executive of the United States.* In these comments the physically ailing Washington vigorously defended

Morris, "a man of first-rate abilities," with "integrity and honor [that] had never been impeached" against Monroe's criticisms of Morris's service in France (January 1792–94) as U.S. Minister during the French Revolution.

The Morris-Washington friendship and close working relationship might seem at first puzzling. The general was nearly twenty years Morris's senior. At the same time Morris generally got along well with older and younger associates when he wished to: Robert Morris, John Penn, James Duane, Benjamin Franklin, William Short and Elias Boudinot, for instance. Both men also, interestingly, had lost their fathers when still prepubescent; Washington's father died when he was eleven years old.

As our story below indicates, Morris and Washington were two of the most powerfully built American leaders of the period. Morris's physique was so similar to Washington's that he was asked by the sculptor Houdon, with Washington's consent, to pose his body as Washington's when Morris was in Europe and Washington in the United States. (Houdon had already made a cast for Washington's head.)

The Virginian had less formal education than any other U.S. President, except for Andrew Jackson and Abraham Lincoln. At the same time, Washington always admired the signs of a good formal education in others. Unlike Morris, Washington was anything but flamboyant. But like Morris, he knew and understood people—men and women—well. Like Morris, too, from his teen years onward Washington wrote voluminously—letters and a journal, mainly.

The American Revolution, like most others, was largely stimulated by an influential minority. In large measure, it was planters, merchants, and lawyers who led the mass of the people into the movement. The constitutional and legal reasoning on which the Revolution built, and the application of the doctrine of the rights of man, were necessarily the work of highly educated people—James Otis, Stephen Hopkins (1707–1785), John Adams (1735–1826), Samuel Adams (1722–1803), James Warren (1726–1808), Alexander Hamilton (1755–1804), Thomas Jefferson (1743–1826), and John Dickinson (1732–1808).[52] But, subsequently, the Revolution was carried out mainly by carpenters, mechanics, shopkeepers, farmers, and other men of limited formal education, social status, and financial stability.

The American Revolutionary War began, of course, with the fighting at Lexington and Concord on April 19, 1775, and continued soon afterward with the battle of Bunker Hill. The emotional and intellectual lead-up to the war, however, probably first dramatically occurred with James Otis's representation of Boston merchants versus the Writs of Assistance as early as 1761. Carl Jung is no doubt generally correct in observing that "most crises or dangerous situations have a long incubation, only the conscious mind is not aware of it."[53]

On September 28, 1774, Joseph Galloway, a Pennsylvania delegate to the First Continental Congress, proposed a constitution that would keep the colonies an internally self-governing part of the British empire while providing them with elected representatives to a Grand Council, whose consent to imperial regulations would be required. The plan was at first tabled and then rejected. At this point, the outbreak of fighting, which led directly to the formal July 2, 1776, declaration of war, can be seen as inevitable. But to many contemporary observers it did not seem so. Such eventual American patriots as Benjamin Franklin, John Dickinson, and Gouverneur Morris were still speaking cautiously quite late in the day. The British visitor Nicholas Cresswell recorded, as late as October 30, 1775, that "the people here [in New England] are ripe for a revolt"[54]—as if it had not already begun.

Morris's historical importance stems in large part from his activities in the independence movement, so a few words concerning the most important of the reasons for the revolt are in order. Certainly the British military was a proximate cause. From the outset, the colonists had fought off so-called Indian attacks. Since the French and Indian War, in particular, the British army and navy had become increasingly visible; and from roughly the 1760s on, the colonists gradually came to perceive the British military more as occupiers than as protectors. The sentiments stimulated by the Quartering Acts may have much aggravated the colonists and done much to change their perceptions. These new perceptions no doubt led directly to the Boston Massacre (March 1770), not to mention producing in the Rhode Islanders a penchant for attacking British ships. (By 1776, at least four such attacks had occurred: in 1764, 1765, 1770 [the *Gaspée*], and 1775.) Indeed, the well-respected historian George L. Beer argues in *British Colonial Policy* that "the controversies that led ultimately to the American Revolution . . . grew out of this military question."[55]

I have already alluded to a second cause—namely, the issues stimulated by questions of constitutional law. In *The American Revolution,* C. H. McIlwain shows how the Americans went back to precedents dating from before the Revolution of 1688 to distinguish between the Crown, whose sovereignty they accepted within limits, and Parliament, which they considered a local British legislative assembly only.[56] Indeed, at the outset the Americans objected not so much to royal claims as to the claims of subjects in one part of the King's dominions to be sovereigns over their fellow subjects in another part of his dominions. "The sovereignty of Britain I do not understand. . . . We have the same King, but not the same legislature."[57] Needless to say, this reasoning did not impress the British authorities.

Still another cause of the Revolution may have been the most basic of all: the geographic separation between Britain and America. Three thousand miles of ocean constituted a formidable barrier (as Morris's separation speech of May 24, 1776, emphasizes), which often took three months to cross. One of the first after-the-fact commentators on the Revolution, David Ramsay, emphasized "the distance of America from Great Britain," which fostered a spirit of independence in the colonies.[58] By 1770, these territories included virtually everything east of Lake Superior and south from contemporary Duluth through New Orleans, on none of which had either the King or his most relevant cabinet secretaries ever set foot. The insularity of the British may have contributed as much to the development of the American Revolution as any cause besides geography. No eighteenth-century British monarch had ever visited even Wales, Scotland, or Ireland; that remote America remained "undiscovered" is therefore no surprise.

At Dettingen, in 1743, during the War of the Austrian Succession, George II (George III's grandfather) became the last reigning British monarch to lead his subjects in battle. George III ascended to the throne in 1760, when he was twenty-two, and reigned for sixty years. When he died, at eighty-one, in 1820, he had fathered fifteen children. He was a man of strong mind, diligence, and business ability, but he had little of the imagination a statesman needs, and what little he had largely failed him when it came to the American question. One of George III's characteristically boneheaded moves was his crucial letter, castigating "every branch of [British] Government" for remaining silent on Charles Townshend's proposal concerning "the American tax" in late March 1763. The tax referred to was the revision of the Molasses Act of 1733, which imposed a duty of sixpence a gallon on molasses imported from the French West Indian Islands into the North American colonies. On March 19, when Charles Townshend introduced before the Parliamentary Committee of Ways and Means an alteration of a continuance of the original Molasses Act "with amendments," his evident intent was to shift this act into a revenue duty, aimed at obtaining taxes from the colonies for already restricted imports.

This episode served as "a dress rehearsal," as Romney Sedgwick phrases it, for Townshend's behavior in 1767. In this year, without consulting any of his colleagues, Townshend committed the British government to the taxes that led to the war with America. But the middle step had been taken for Townshend by George Grenville. In the session following the one in which

Townshend's 1763 proposal was left to wither, Grenville introduced "a comprehensive measure to raise a colonial revenue and to reform the old colonial system both in its administrative and its economic features." This measure passed and became known as the Sugar Act. This act effectually adopted Townshend's principle by converting a prohibitive tax into a revenue duty. The point bearing on the King's responsibility, however, is that George III evidently strongly urged both of Townshend's endeavors, as well as Grenville's intermediary step. From 1770 to 1782 George had, as prime minister, Lord North, a man who was so manifestly unequal to handling the difficulties of the American crisis that, in letter after letter, he begged the King to let him resign.[59]

Demographics no doubt also loomed large among the Revolution's causes. As James Henretta has noted, as late as 1700 there were twenty English men and women for every American-born colonist, whereas by 1775 the ratio of English citizens to Americans had fallen to three to one. And as Henretta observes, the generally acute shortage of labor, in a land of so much fertile acreage, encouraged American population growth throughout the eighteenth century.[60]

Another annoyance to the colonists was what we may call the religion problem: although more and more Americans had their origins in countries other than England, the British government continued to attempt to impose Anglicanism as an official religion. This policy was certain to alienate a population of diverse creeds.

The colonists had economic grievances, too. The *Proceedings and Debates of the British Parliament* during the period leading up to the violence presents a picture of an empire interested above all in exploiting the wealth of its North American colonies.[61] Owing to the Acts of Trade and a government policy to discourage all manufacturing in the colonies, the balance of trade worked permanently in favor of the mother country; by the time of James Otis's 1761 speech on the Writs of Assistance, the balance of trade on Britain's side exceeded £2 million. Sales of such export-oriented British items as woolens and metalware grew more than ninefold during the first seven decades of the eighteenth century in America. As a result, by the 1770s the colonies had been drained of specie, which flowed all too heavily to Britain, while population growth, the necessary expansion of trade, and the inconvenience of barter all increased the demand for currency.[62]

One of the most radical American leaders, Samuel Adams, asserted even before the 1770s that "things will never be properly settled in America until the Parliament has repealed all the Acts affecting the American Trade": the Navigation Laws, the Enumerating Laws, and the Stamp Act. The colonists also, of course, vocally resented "taxation without representation." By this, most colonists meant that taxes should be imposed by a body such as a colonial assembly, in which they believed themselves more directly represented, not by Parliament. Englishmen who thought about this problem, however, generally remarked that almost every adult male in Britain paid some taxes, but only about 10 percent had the vote. The rest were hardly better represented in Parliament than the colonists were.[63] At the same time, the distance from Britain, combined with the complete absence of voting representation in Parliament, led the colonists to feel particularly aggrieved.

An additional cause of the Revolution was the longstanding system of transporting convicts from British jails to British colonies. This must be called an extension of the empire's commercial policy. Upon conviction, the felon's personal estate was forfeit to the King. During the eighteenth century alone, Britain transported to the colonies more than 50,000 convicts, including over two-thirds of all felons convicted at the Old Bailey, London's chief criminal court. This system of course served the British by steeply reducing their jail population. At the same time, the payments made in pounds sterling to the all-British transporters by the American merchant convict supervisors further enriched Britain commercially. This is not to say that the American merchants who promptly hired the released felons did not also have a lucrative arrangement. Such a policy, nonetheless, is not likely to endear any mother country to its colonies. Well before the outbreak of armed hostilities, we find Benjamin Franklin, with something of Swift's sharp-edged irony, urging Americans to send the British rattlesnakes in exchange for the felons.

(Colonial newspapers were quick to take note of any of the felons' crimes in the New World [where they were free to move about]. The records reveal that in fact the transportees committed surprisingly few offenses. But transportation was a cynical policy; that it seems to have done the colonists little harm did not lessen their outrage.)[64]

So the colonists had substantial economic reasons to revolt, the more so since England's mercantilist tendencies had probably never been stronger than during the two decades preceding 1775. The revolutionists' political motivation was likewise great, for reasons touched upon in Morris's May 1776 speech. With few exceptions, every official in a royal colony exercised his authority by virtue of a grant from the King—either directly, through one of the executive departments in England, or indirectly, through the royal governor or secretary in the province. This created in the colonies a group of officeholders who held their offices at the King's pleasure and considered themselves responsible to the King alone. Important posts, such as those of governor, lieutenant governor, secretary, attorney general, deputy auditor, provost marshal, sheriff, and collector of customs, as well as officerships in the navy, were held as properties from which a profit might often be made. In a system in which virtually all these offices represented the Crown, the colonists must have come to feel very keenly what Evarts B. Greene calls "the sense of divergent interests."[65]

Some problems with King George III's imperial administration were common to several colonies, some unique to one. In Gouverneur Morris's New York, as in prewar Massachusetts and North Carolina, the legislative assemblies' independence was somewhat curtailed by the governor's intimidating practice of sitting and voting with them. In New York, judges served at the King's pleasure; but New Yorkers (like Jamaicans, New Jerseyans, and North Carolinians) came increasingly to believe that their judges should hold office during good behavior or for life, and that the New Yorkers themselves should be the ones to assess the former. In New York, the legislative representatives gained a measure of control over the personnel of the courts by appropriating salaries for individuals, rather than by position. Nevertheless, the New York Assembly never sustained a permanently successful challenge of the right of the King's agents to fill all judicial offices.[66]

The last of the obvious causes of the Revolution might be most accurately termed moral, and stems from the colonists' perception that they must be free from British restraint. And when the relationship between the mother country and the American colonies was nearly at its most strained, England made the gross error of applying pressure, rather than giving slack.

Once the conflict began, the British lost mainly because they lacked effective strategic leadership—not surprisingly, given the geographical distances and the astonishing insularity of the government's upper reaches—and because their naval forces were overcommitted, and consequently outnumbered at the most crucial times.

Nevertheless, as the sagest analyst of the war, Piers Mackesy, compellingly argues, the war's outcome was not inevitable. With the vital help of the French, with assistance from some Prussian mercenaries, with some valuable Spanish aid, the Americans attained victory. A Captain Levi Preston, of Danvers, Massachusetts, was asked, years after the war, "What did you mean in going into the fight?" The veteran infantry officer supposedly replied, "Young man, what we meant in going for those redcoats, was this: we always had governed ourselves and we always meant to. They didn't mean we should."[67]

That has the ring of essential truth. With the exception of New York, which in 1664 the British seized by force (as they did also Jamaica and Nova Scotia), all of the thirteen colonies were founded by private individuals or groups of private individuals for specific purposes of their own. Consequently they had, in essence, thirteen separate governments. This situation fostered a spirit of separation and at times reduced the combined military strength of the colonies almost to a nullity; nonetheless, it increased the flexibility of colonial institutions, allowed for more political experimentation, and helped the colonists clarify their ideas concerning appropriate governmental administration.[68]

On Morris's motion, the Provincial Congress voted 18–4 in late May to hold popular elections by all white adult male freeholders to a New York legislative body. The election was held in June and the so-called Convention first met on July 8, 1776, in White Plains. (The British army threatened New York.) The following day the duly sworn-in body ratified the Declaration of Independence, which had recently arrived with a cover letter from John Hancock.[69] The colonies were unanimous.

John Hancock's letter accompanying the Declaration concluded: "the important consequences to the American States of this Declaration of Independence, considered as the ground and foundation of a future government, will naturally suggest the propriety of having it proclaimed in such a manner, as that the people may be universally informed of it." To Morris was entrusted the honor of drafting the congratulatory and affirming reply to the delegates from New York in the Continental Congress, which he did on July 11.

The drafting of the Declaration of Independence and its prompt ratification deserve as much attention as they have received, since they represent a strong expression of the patriots' unified thought and emotion. Nine colonies favored the resolution by Richard Henry Lee on July 1 and only two, South Carolina and Pennsylvania, opposed. Delaware's vote was divided until their third delegate, Caesar Rodney, arrived during the final vote on July 2 and swung them in favor. The two states in opposition changed their votes, the New York delegation abstained, and the resolution for independence passed 12–0. But all too many Americans seem to believe the Declaration and the celebratory ringing of bells marked the start of independence; in fact, independence was won by means of a long war. And in some ways the Declaration was even redundant, because fighting had begun more than a year earlier. It went on for nearly seven more years, with at least 1,331 engagements, the last of which took place on April 17–24, 1783, at Fort Carlos III (now in Arkansas). Here a British trader, James Colbert, led a small force of Choctaws and other partisans in an attack on the Spanish outpost, the only Revolutionary War battle west of the Mississippi River. According to Howard H. Peckham, the Americans who were killed in action or died in service totaled at least 24,324—a little less than 1 percent of the American population of 2,781,000 in 1780. (Deaths in service include the high toll of death from disease, illness, and infections. Many thousands of our soldiers and sailors perished in captivity.) Peckham cites the number of American wounded as at least 8,445. Needless to say, these figures do not take account of the casualties sustained by our allies— chiefly French line forces, naval and ground, and Prussian mercenaries, primarily artillery and infantry.[70]

In New York City, on the evening of July 11, General Washington had his troops drawn up and the Declaration of Independence read at the head of each brigade. The officers and men then sang a part of the Eighteenth Psalm ("The Lord is my rock, and my fortress . . ."), and gave three cheers. Meanwhile a crowd pulled down and beheaded the bronze equestrian statue of George III, so that the royal troops might have "melted majesty fired at them."

Of the reality of the bloody toll of independence, the New York Convention had already become aware. The Americans had so strengthened their position in Boston that the British forces must have felt much relieved when they evacuated the city on March 17, 1776, and moved to Halifax, Nova Scotia, accompanied by nine hundred civilian Loyalists. Having obtained reinforcements in Halifax, General Howe took possession of Staten Island in July 1776. In anticipation of Howe's plans, Washington shifted his army from Boston and occupied Brooklyn Heights, which commanded the town of New York, then confined to the southern tip of Manhattan Island. But Howe quickly crossed to Long Island (of which Brooklyn is a part), defeated the American divisions in front of Brooklyn Heights, and compelled Washington to take refuge on Manhattan Island, north of Harlem. In mid-September, once he finally decided to launch his offensive, Howe briskly occupied the town of New York.[71]

This series of British victories caused a scene of confusion in New York that deranged the proceedings of the Convention. It sat first at White Plains, as was mentioned earlier, then successively at four different locations (King's Bridge, Philipse Manor, Poughkeepsie, and Kingston), before settling temporarily in Fishkill, a small trading village about fifty miles north of Manhattan, on the east bank of the Hudson. Fishkill was, at least temporarily, beyond British reach. Owing to this series of hasty retreats, meetings were, for a while, sparsely attended. Most of the executive work during this period was performed by the Committee of Safety, the Committee of Correspondence, and the Monetary Committee to establish a state fund. Morris sat on each of these small but vital committees and chaired the last. Under Morris's chairmanship, it borrowed large sums of money, issued bills of credit, and pledged the faith of the new state for higher payment.

The tactical emergency in mid-1776 in New York forced the Convention to suspend further consideration of a new form of government. However, on August 1 a committee of thirteen members was appointed, with instructions to draft and report a plan for the governance of the State of New York. Gouverneur Morris, Robert R. Livingston, and John Jay, who had by now returned from his delegation to the Congress in Philadelphia to rejoin the New York Convention, were elected to this committee.

By the time Jay returned, the Convention had moved from New York City to White Plains. In letters to friends and associates he expressed contempt for the move and displeasure with Morris for having suggested it. To Robert R. Livingston, he wrote, on July 1: "[T]o my great mortification our Convention, influenced by one of G. Morris['s] vagrant plans, have adjourned to the White Plains. . . . This precipitate ill-advised retreat I fear will not be a little injurious to the public. . . . This stroke of Morrisania Politics quite confounds me."[72] But Morris's suggestion may well have averted disaster. Had the convention not moved to White Plains, its members would have had to be tremendously clever and lucky to avoid capture. Even if they then had not been killed, they would have been sent to the British prison ships and hastily established jails, where so many captured American soldiers perished.

From the summer of 1776 throughout 1777, certainly, the task of governing was seriously complicated by New York's status as the principal battleground of the Revolution. Finally having fetched up from the White Plains to Kingston, the convention drafted the first New York constitution (March 12, 1777), extensively debated it, and ratified it.[73]

On August 1, 1776, Morris was appointed one of the thirteen members of the committee to file a report on this first constitution and bill of rights. At least in part because of the threatening military situation, the committee took more than seven months to present the drafts to the convention. (From August 1776 on, British troops occupied five entire New York counties and large parts of two others; moreover, the military pressures throughout 1777 came from virtually all sides toward the interior, where the Convention's committees were at work.) But another reason for the delay was surely Morris's months-long absence from the Convention. For reasons not clear, he had stayed with Washington's army on the retreat across the Jerseys. In November he wrote from Boonton to the convention at Fishkill the kind of insouciant letter that tended to do his reputation harm:

The truth is, a series of accidents, too trifling for recital, have prevented me the pleasure of attending the convention for upwards of a month past. Among the last, let me mention the loss of all my horses. As soon as I can find any of them, or purchase another, I shall hasten to Fishkills.

Apparently Gouverneur had felt an obligation to remain with the army as long as he could. The loss of his horses during the retreat must have kept him longer than expected. As for why he was with Washington's army in the first place, a letter to him from Robert R. Livingston (October 8, 1776) suggests that he was actually under arms.[74]

On December 9 Morris returned to the convention, which these days was meeting at the still-standing Dutch Reformed church in Fishkill. No sooner had he arrived than new, steady rounds of committee assignments resumed (service with Washington's army might have seemed restful by contrast). The Committee of Budget and Finance and the Committee of Safety immediately occupied much of Gouverneur's time. Meanwhile, on the military front, matters were about to go somewhat better.

Sometimes daring is prudence: on Christmas night, 1776, Washington crossed the Delaware to smash the British forces at Trenton—taking prisoner more than a thousand Hessians (December 26) and giving the Americans encouragement they sorely needed. After defeating the British at Princeton (January 3, 1777), Washington retreated to winter quarters on the easily defensible high ground at Morristown, New Jersey, while General Howe's cautious retirement to Burlington left most of New Jersey free from British control.

Morris had received a personal blow that must have tempered his patriotic exultation: in December 1776, his sister Euphemia had died. On December 19, Gouverneur wrote his mother a letter of condolence. It reads in part as follows:

There is one comforter, who weighs our minutes, and numbers out our days. It is He who has inflicted upon us the weight of public and private calamities, and He best knows when to remove the burthen. I am sorry it is not in my power to see you at present. I know it is your wish, that I were removed from public affairs; indeed, as far as relates to my own ease and enjoyments, I wish so too. But I know it is the duty of every good citizen or man to preserve that post, in which by a superior order he is placed. *Where the happiness of a considerable part of our fellow creatures is deeply concerned, we soon feel the insignificancy of an individual.* . . .

What may be the event of the present war, it is not in man to determine. Great revolutions of empire are seldom achieved without much human calamity; but the worst, which can happen, is to fall on the last bleak mountain of America, and he who dies there, in defense of the injured rights of mankind, is happier than his conqueror, more beloved by mankind, more applauded in his own heart.

The death of my sister has incapacitated me for mirth; my letter, therefore, is of an improper complexion to one already afflicted. My love to my sister, to Wilkins, whose integrity I love and respect . . .

Pray believe me most sincerely your affectionate son.

Gouverneur Morris[75]

This rare letter from Gouverneur, still only twenty-four, provides a glimpse of a young man with a maturity and sense of patriotic purpose decades beyond his years. Indeed, he seems here more like a boorish older brother or a self-important uncle to his mother than a son. Because of the exigencies of the war, Gouverneur's mother never saw him after 1776, and they were able to send only one poignant letter apiece through the British lines. Sarah Gouverneur Morris died after the Revolution; Gouverneur neither saw nor spoke to her from the time he was twenty-four. Such all but complete isolation from his family constituted one more considerable sacrifice for American independence.

On March 7, 1777, five days before the submission of the first draft of the New York Constitution, Morris presented to the New York Convention the Safety Committee's recommendations concerning Loyalists. With respect to former inhabitants who had "gone, [been] sent out of the state, or confined as disaffected persons," Morris's report, as adopted by the Convention, prescribed an oath for them to take. Those who took it would be pardoned; those who refused would be sent behind British lines. That such a capacious forgiveness was granted on the basis of an oath alone suggests Morris and his fellow delegates had more faith in a citizen's word than we do nowadays.

The offer of pardon did not extend to those "charged with taking up arms against the United States, with enlisting men for the service of the enemy, accepting a warrant or commission for that purpose, supplying them with provisions, or conveying intelligence to them." Those people were to undergo a criminal trial. Two months later Morris and John Jay were named to a new committee, charged with preparing "an act of grace for such of the inhabitants of this state as have been guilty of treasonable practices against the State." Their report, presented by Jay and adopted on May 10, offered pardon to those who took an oath of allegiance.[76]

The first draft of the New York State Constitution was submitted on March 12, 1777; the Convention discussed this draft almost daily for about a month, and revised the text extensively. On April 20 the revised text was accepted, with only one opposing vote. Like the other state constitutions enacted up to that time, New York's went into effect without the approval of the voters.

Massachusetts, the first of the future states to frame a government independent of the King, deviated as little as possible from its previous charter. Assuming the governorship vacant as of July 19, 1775, the colony recognized a provincial congress (a completely extralegal body of recently elected delegates) as the legal successor to its executive power. The Massachusetts constitution was not ratified until 1780.[77]

On January 5, 1776, New Hampshire chartered its government much as Massachusetts had. In late March, South Carolina shaped a provisional constitution, but only two years later was a permanent constitution introduced, by an act of the legislature. Rhode Island's charter was already so thoroughly republican that the rejection of monarchy, in May 1776, required very little change. Much the same applies to Connecticut.

Virginia was first to adopt a completely new government, in July 1776. Soon her legislative system was formulated, and then adopted also by New Jersey, Delaware, Maryland, North Carolina, and Georgia. The Pennsylvania convention adopted its constitution on September 28, 1776, but Pennsylvania delayed its thorough organization and enactment for five months.

New York's constitution was thus rather a latecomer. Yet in many ways it surpassed the other states' in humane liberality.

Since the other twelve governmental charters had already been drafted and communications were reasonably good, it may be presumed that the statesmen of New York were familiar with the prior constitutions when they set out to develop their own. The extent to which they were influenced by the other states' work we do not know, but the subject at least deserves to be borne in mind as we consider the process of drafting, and the document produced: the constitution adopted in April 1777 provided the framework by which New York was governed for half a century, and it influenced the development of the U.S. Constitution as well.

To backtrack a little: on August 1, 1776, then, Morris moved the appointment of a committee to prepare a plan for a new state government. As was mentioned earlier, the Convention set up a committee of thirteen; but, as often happens, a much smaller group—comprising John Jay (age thirty-two), Morris (age twenty-four), and Robert R. Livingston (age thirty)—did the lion's share of the work. Although authorship of the state constitution cannot be ascribed conclusively to one individual, most historians accord John Jay the central role.[78]

The constitution begins with a long and otiose preamble listing the colonial grievances against Britain; to this is appended the Declaration of Independence. The state constitution proper comprises forty-two articles on a wide range of subjects. The complete 1777 document has the following major features. The governor was to be elected by eligible £100 freeholders—that is, free white men without debts who had not been convicted of a felony and who also had £100 or more of tangible wealth. This high freehold was a unique characteristic of the New York constitution. The governor served for three years, and was eligible for immediate re-election. This was an unusually long term, and a fairly permissive re-election policy. Only Delaware and Pennsylvania also gave the governor a three-year term; most of the new states allowed just a year. And only six other states—Delaware, New Hampshire, Massachusetts, Connecticut, Rhode Island, and New Jersey—permitted *immediate* reelection. In Pennsylvania and South Carolina, a governor who wanted to serve again had to wait four years for another chance.

In New York, appointment power in the executive branch was assigned to a body called the Council of Revision, a part of the judiciary branch that included the governor, the chancellor, and the Supreme Court judges. Appointments were confirmed by a Council of Appointments. No other new state government required the agreement of the governor *and* some other body for a veto. Only Massachusetts also limited the governor's veto power. As regards the executive's veto power, we find that, aside from the prospective restraints implied by New York's stipulation that required additional authorization by the Council of Revision, only Massachusetts allowed for a qualified veto by its governor. As has already been remarked, however, the Massachusetts state constitution was not effectively written and enacted until 1780, three years after New York's.

Historians and political scientists have generally held that the first New York state government provided for a weak executive; and it is true that only New York obliged its governor to share his appointive power. Yet these historians may have overlooked that the governor had some veto power, the length of his term, and the liberal rules for reelection. Furthermore, the governor commanded the state's armed forces and could prorogue the legislature.

New Hampshire, Massachusetts, Connecticut, and Rhode Island as well as New York provided for direct election of the governor by voters. In the other eight—New Jersey, Pennsylvania, Delaware, Maryland, Virginia, North Carolina, South Carolina, and Georgia—he was elected by an intermediary body: the legislature, the "General Assembly" (Delaware), or a council elected by the voters. The five direct-election states came closest to the U.S. constitutional system of presidential election. Of those states New York was least close, but its three-year gubernatorial term with eligibility for immediate reelection resembled federal constitutional provisions more than any other state's did. The shared appointive power (Council of Revision plus Council of Appointments) resembles the U.S. constitutional system, in which the Senate is the sole legislative body with power to confirm appointments. Last and not least, the New York provision for a veto power residing in the governor and the Council of Revision is the only state provision to resemble in any way the U.S. presidential veto power.[79]

The New York constitution, moreover, had a lieutenant governor who presided *ex officio* over the state senate. He was elected by the popular vote of male, £100 freeholders, just as the governor was. The framers of the U.S. Constitution made the President's powers and duties devolve upon the Vice President in the event of the President's removal, death, resignation, or inability. New York State's provisions for the governor and lieutenant governor were remarkably similar, except that where the U.S. Constitution cites "inability" the state constitution cited "absence from the state." The powers and duties of the New York State lieutenant governor were unique; it seems, then, that the state constitution, in which Gouverneur Morris's ideas had such importance, greatly influenced the shape of the U.S. presidency and vice presidency.

The composition of New York's legislative branch has its interesting aspects, too, though these are less striking. All the first state constitutions but Pennsylvania's divided the legislature (generally called the Assembly) into two houses; the lower house was always the larger. Except in Georgia, the members of both were to be elected by popular vote. Voters generally had to be freeholders, a requirement that almost entirely restricted the franchise to men (New Jersey stipulated "inhabitants of a 50 pound estate," which made legally adult women eligible).[80] Georgia and South Carolina explicitly limited the vote to "free, white males." New York was unique in that to vote for a senator required a freehold of £100, to vote for a representative, a freehold of £20 or rent of forty shillings. Thus, as late as 1790 in New York only one adult male in ten could vote for either the governor or a senator.

New York's legislature was assigned uniquely important and wide-ranging functions. New York State's elected delegates were elected to serve, overall, almost the longest continuous terms—four years for the Senate (only Maryland senators served longer terms; namely, five years). Only New Hampshire and New York specified no qualifications for legislators.

Readers may need reminding that in the 1789 version of the U.S. Constitution, the members of the House were popularly elected, but the Senate was elected by state legislators. And both U.S. senators and representatives, then as now, had to meet requirements of both age and duration of citizenship.

New York was alone among the states in setting a retirement age (sixty) for judges. All the states gave their judges tenure of office as long as they demonstrated "good behavior," but New York was one of only four states to omit from its first constitution any explicit mention of impeachment. In this respect, the four (Connecticut, Rhode Island, and Delaware were the other three) differed substantially from the U.S. Constitution. However, in providing that state judges be appointed by the chief executive "and the Council," New York's constitution to some extent prefigured the U.S. constitutional procedure by which federal judicial appointments are made by the President and approved by the Senate.[81]

The New York State constitution of 1777 also presages the tripartite division of power established by the federal Constitution: in New York, the powers delegated to the governor and council were, at least in form, executive, legislative, and judicial. (Of course, the three divisions are also discernible in both British and colonial precedents.) There is strong evidence that Jay, Livingston, and Morris were unwilling to entrust either the legislature or the executive with untrammeled power in its arena. In the words of Charles Z. Lincoln, "the [New York] constitution shows a manifest intention to reserve to and invest in each department some authority over the others."[82]

Owing to the property qualifications for voting, the New York Senate was certain to be dominated by a narrow base of wealthy men. Only by a two-thirds vote of both houses could a veto be overridden.

As we learned earlier, the drafting of the New York Constitution was delayed by Morris's long absence with Washington's forces. Further delays resulted because Jay had departed from mid-March through April to plan the obstruction of the Hudson against the invasion under way by the British. At least partly in consequence, the first draft was a terse instrument, engaging few subjects. Some important provisions, such as the matter of the Council of Revision and the Council of Appointments, were added while the convention was in session. John Jay's correspondence makes clear he intended to suggest, on the floor, other additions, but he then had to leave because his mother had died. While he was gone, the constitution was adopted—in his view, which he stated to Morris and Livingston among others, somewhat hastily.

The first draft was discussed for a month before being presented to the Convention on March 12, 1777. In the Convention, Morris had worked hard to simplify the motion on the powers of the Assembly, and with Livingston had moved to limit the qualifications of voters to owners or leasees of real property. Morris successfully attempted to have state senators elected by viva voce vote rather than by ballot. John Jay unsuccessfully argued (and I believe most would agree) that balloting would lead to much less intimidation by the wealthier segment of the voters. And Morris succeeded in tightening eligibility to vote for the Assembly; the draft had required only a freehold, while, as the reader will remember, the final document required voters to have property worth at least £20, or rent of forty shillings.[83] Morris also proposed liberalization of the nominating process in case a legislative seat became vacant on the member's election to Congress or resignation for other reasons. This provision became Article 30 of the constitution.

John Jay proposed harshly worded anti-Catholic amendments, and Livingston one that was milder but more broadly antireligious. Jay wished to see erected "a wall of brass around the country for the exclusion of Catholics." His earlier motions having been defeated, Jay proposed a statement to the effect that "the liberty hereby granted shall not be construed to encourage licentiousness or be used to disturb or endanger the safety of the state." Gouverneur promptly followed with an emendation comparatively liberal and inoffensive, altering Jay's motion to read "the liberty of conscience hereby granted shall not be so construed as to excuse acts of licentiousness." The convention adopted Morris's change unanimously. The New York Constitution of April 20, 1777, declared freedom from "spiritual oppression and intolerance wherewith the bigotry and ambition of weak and wicked priests and princes have scourged mankind" and proceeded to "ordain, determine, and declare, that the free exercise and enjoyment of religious profession and worship, without discrimination or preference, shall forever hereafter be allowed, within this State, to all mankind."[84]

At the convention Morris advocated an even stronger executive than he got.[85] He moved to make naturalization—then still a state matter—as simple as possible, but in this matter Jay prevailed, and for the next decade New York required an oath abjuring certain specified loyalties.[86] Sarah Morris had inherited slaves, and Gouverneur inherited one slave from his father, but he freed this slave, as throughout his life he abhorred "the peculiar institution." He moved that the following be added to the constitution's preamble:

And whereas a regard to the rights of human nature and the principles of our holy religion, loudly call upon us to dispense the blessings of freedom to all mankind; and in as much as it would at present be productive of great dangers to liberate the slaves within this state; it is, therefore, most earnestly recommended to the future legislature of the state of New York to take the most effectual measures consistent with the public safety, and the private property of individuals, for abolishing domestic slavery within the same, so that in future ages every human being who breathes the air of this state shall enjoy the privileges of a freeman.

Morris opposed slavery and would argue against it again during the U.S. Constitutional Convention. Here he seems to have bowed to pressure from the many slaveholding New Yorkers and succumbed to fears concerning immediate emancipation; yet he sought to include in his state's constitution at least a pledge of future liberation for the slaves. His colleagues, even more nervous about emancipation than he, and much more worried about touching the wallets of wealthy slaveholders, induced him to give way. The next day, he proposed instead: "Inasmuch as it would be highly inexpedient to proceed to the liberating of slaves within this state, in the present situation there of . . ." This amendment was then adopted by a vote of 24 to 12.[87]

We could rightly call Sunday, April 20, 1777, when the Convention adopted the new constitution, the birthday of the State of New York. Like virtually every such document, the new constitution was the result of numerous compromises, a fact Morris certainly recognized.[88] Yet, although he was one of about a hundred representatives to the Convention—one of four from Westchester County alone—his influence on the completed document had been substantial.

After the constitution was ratified but before elections could be held (the enabling law was passed on May 8, 1777), the Convention named a fifteen-member Council of Safety "with full powers to provide for the safety and preservation of the State until a meeting of the legislature"—that is, to act as a government pro tem. On May 7, as a member of this committee, Morris put forth a bill to remit "all quit rents due" and to abolish quitrent in the state. Morris's surprising measure would have abolished not only the quitrents, specifically appropriated by the fledgling state, which had been owed to Great Britain but also the quitrents due American landowners. Quitrents originated in New York as prescribed payments to the British King, his heirs and successors, and were to be made on a regular basis by New Yorkers living on much of the Province's lands. A list had been kept for decades of all owners of lands, with situation and number of acres. This list, known as the rent-roll, had been maintained since the 1660s by a Receiver General. This specially appointed officer of the Proprietary interests visited all the New York counties at prearranged times and extracted the quitrents. These payments were made either in farm products or else in colonial currency. The quitrents, needless to say, profited the King and the British treasury at first and toward the mid-1750s through the Revolutionary era profited the largest American landholders in New York. Of course, the debate was lengthy. Such a proposal from virtually anyone else would likely have died instantly, but because it came from Morris, it was discussed in a committee that included Morris, John Jay and John Morin Scott; only then did it go under.

So leveling a notion as abolishing quitrent may seem uncharacteristic, but Morris was seldom mundanely predictable and ever, as James Madison much later noted, willing to put forward ideas few other people would have touched. And, as Max Mintz has observed, Morris always insisted on the unrestricted right of free property.[89]

On May 13, 1777, the New York Convention elected a fresh slate of delegates to the Continental Congress: Philip Schuyler, Philip Livingston, James Duane, William Duer, and Morris. (So loose were administrative arrangements, though, that Morris served on the New York Convention for over five more months.)[90]

Morris became involved with the Continental Army when he was appointed an inspector after the American rout at Fort Ticonderoga. As the summer of 1777 began, Major General Philip Schuyler was in command of the American troops at Fort Ticonderoga and General John Burgoyne was heading south from Canada in a British attempt to cut New England apart from the other colonies. This plan had been approved by Lord Germain in London, where he presided over the American Department. He viewed New England as the heart of the rebellion and hoped to isolate this region and split the colonies by moving British forces north from Manhattan and south from Lake Champlain to dominate the Hudson River. Once the crossing points of the Hudson were seized, the plan called for the invasion of New England on a broad front, from the landward side, in conjunction with a narrower thrust from Rhode Island.

Burgoyne had a comparatively fresh army of roughly 4,000 British regulars, 3,000 German mercenaries, 650 Canadians and Loyalists, and 500 Native Americans. Schuyler had only 3,000 American troops. British reconnaissance revealed that Schuyler had foolishly neglected to position a unit on the hill

overlooking Fort Ticonderoga. Burgoyne promptly laid in a battery of artillery there and briskly bombarded the fort. The American troops soon
abandoned Ticonderoga and fled. The retreat became a stampede when
Schuyler's men, under the immediate command of Major General Arthur
St. Clair (1736–1818), of Pennsylvania, took off in disarray after they
had sustained only a few casualties. On receiving the news, Washington
wrote to Schuyler reassuringly, and in the event presciently, that the confidence Burgoyne "derived from success may hurry him into measures which
will in their consequences be favorable to us."

Understandably alarmed by the fall of Ticonderoga, the New York legislature appointed Robert R. Livingston and Abraham Yates, Jr. (1724–1796),
to visit General Schuyler at his headquarters, in order to investigate the details surrounding the debacle at Ticonderoga. On July 10, Morris replaced
Livingston, whose father had just died. Yates and Morris traveled separately,
no doubt for security reasons: better that only one should be captured.
Morris set out from Kingston first, reaching Albany by July 14, where he
was delayed by heavy rains, but on July 16 he arrived at Fort Edward. At the
time Schuyler's army consisted of about 2,600 Continental troops and 2,000
militia, plus an outpost of some 500 men stationed to the west. "Excepting
the General [Schuyler] and General Sinclair," Morris wrote about the
American troops in Fort Edward at the time, "you have not a general officer
here worth a crown"; his assessment seems correct.[91] The next day Morris
and Schuyler made a reconnaissance to Saratoga to get a sense of possible
British attack routes. Morris wrote the president of the Council of Safety
"that if we lay it down as a maxim, never to contend for ground but in the
last necessity, and to leave nothing but a wilderness to the enemy, their
progress must be impeded by obstacles, which it is not in human nature
to surmount."[92] He advised Schuyler accordingly.

On July 30, Burgoyne and his forces reached Fort Edward, now abandoned by the Americans, and the broad valley of the navigable Hudson
stretched before them. However, Burgoyne felt he could not advance further until he had amassed thirty days' supplies. Indeed, he paused long
enough—until September 12—to bring up a train of fifty-two cannon and
the necessary accouterments. As one contemporary observer trenchantly
noted, "All [Burgoyne's] wants were owing to his having too great an abundance."[93] Meanwhile, General Schuyler had been withdrawing his forces,
this time in a much more orderly manner. By August 3, Schuyler was at
Stillwater, some miles south of Fort Edward and only thirty miles north of
Albany.

On August 4, John Hancock wrote, on behalf of the Continental Congress, a letter ordering Schuyler's relief by General Horatio Gates. On August 27, Morris wrote Schuyler from Kingston, offering advice that might have enabled him to hand over a tactically victorious army, if he had followed it. Morris sympathized with Schuyler: "[W]e did not arrive at [headquarters] Philadelphia, until the day it had been determined to send Gates to take the command of the northern department [in relief of Schuyler]. You will readily believe, that we were not pleased with this resolution, and I assure you for my own part, I felt exceedingly distressed at your removal, just when changing fortune began to declare in our favor. . . . In misfortunes, great minds rise superior to adversity, and this too, whether they are of a public or private nature." Morris went on:

> [W]ith that incautiousness natural to me, and of which I scorn to divest myself among my friends, let me say, that I think you will find it for your honor to resign, but in this, *festina lente* [make haste slowly], the hour is not yet come. . . . It seems to me we should contrive to possess the height to the northward of Fort Edward, if it be practicable to maintain it, and then, by keeping parties around Burgoyne's army, intercept his supplies, and force him to quit his post at Batten Kill. This is a reverie, but clearly something capital may be done; perhaps he may be attacked with success in his lines. I am inclined to believe, that the unexpected sight of our troops, advancing with fixed bayonets without firing a shot, would so intimidate his soldiers, that they would not stand. . . . I could wish that having digested your plan, you would send it to Gates, as the continuation of what you intended . . . Introduce it to him under the idea, that you think it your duty to contribute to the success of the American arms . . . And send a copy of the whole to Congress, in which you may also, with great propriety, mention as a reason why you have not obeyed their order, that General Gates was so long on his journey.[94]

Morris's plan would likely have succeeded, but as he acknowledges, would have laid General Schuyler open to charges of disobeying orders, since Schuyler knew he was to stay where he was.

On September 18, Morris, ever the faithful friend, wrote a consolatory letter to Schuyler, remarking of General Gates that "Fortune may make him a great man, in the estimation of the vulgar, who will fix their estimation at their own price, let the intrinsic value be what it will, but it is not in the power of fortune to bestow those talents, which are necessary to render a person superior to her malice. This being the case, it is but equal, that, between competitors, she should take the weaker side to preserve the natural equality of mankind."

Morris went on to underestimate Gates's abilities, stating his belief that his army lacked the "skill to manage" a battle with Burgoyne. But as Piers Mackesy has aptly remarked, Burgoyne's "long pause [for supplies] at Fort Edward had enabled the Americans to collect their strength."[95] And a failure in communication had also damaged the British strategy: Lord Germain had sent Burgoyne to march down the Hudson from Canada without positively ensuring that General Howe was on the way up the Hudson to meet him. As a result, Howe lingered in Philadelphia, while General Benedict Arnold's forces aggressively moved on Burgoyne's inner lines. Burgoyne's army had dwindled from some 8,000 troops to roughly 3,500 effective fighting men. Even these were outnumbered by the Americans five to one since his forces had become reduced by desertions, disease, and casualties. In the event, though General Horatio Gates was the officer in command, it was Arnold's intrepid leadership that led to the British defeat at Bemis Heights. Gates defeated the British at Saratoga on October 17, 1777, with the help of 2,000 "Hampshire Grants" (Vermont) militiamen posted on the heights north of Fort Edward.[96] Burgoyne's surrender meant the end of the attempt to split the colonies. It also meant the entrance of France into the war.

In the September 18 letter to Schuyler that Morris wrote from Kingston, Morris sounded weary and impatient with the state government he has already elected to leave:

> The Chief Justice [Jay] is gone to fetch his wife. The Chancelor [Livingston] is solacing himself with his wife, his farm, and his imagination. Our Senate is doing, I know not what. In Assembly we wrangle long to little purpose. You will think so, when I tell you, that from nine in the morning till dusk in the evening, we were employed in appointing [four members] to be the council of appointment. I tremble for the consequences, but I smile, and shall continue to do so, if possible. We have not appointed delegates, nor do I know when or whom we shall appoint.

These are the words of a professional for whom it is time for a new prospect, and Morris soon had one. On October 3, 1777, when the legislature convened, another slate of delegates to the Continental Congress was appointed; as has been mentioned, Morris was again elected, although he does not appear to have taken his seat until January 20, 1778.

He had spent three years in amassing a small fortune as a lawyer, then roughly three years in a busy public life. Extremes of talent are often drawn forth by exigencies, and this was so during the Revolution. At age twenty-six, Gouverneur Morris entered the Continental Congress with a reputation for intelligence, zeal, and a special kind of integrity.

{ 3 }

MORRIS AND THE CONTINENTAL CONGRESS

W HEN GOUVERNEUR MORRIS reported for service in January 1778, the Continental Congress was still sitting in York (then known as Yorktown), Pennsylvania, where it had fled in September 1777, when British forces under the command of General Howe seized Philadelphia. The delegates assembled, under the presidency of John Hancock, in the small courthouse in the town square. The day of his arrival, Morris was given the honor of an appointment to the five-man Committee on the Encampment at Valley Forge. This committee was of vital importance in determining whether the colonies would become a nation. The army under Washington at Valley Forge was discouraged and demoralized by cold and scarcity of food, clothing, firewood, and munitions. In concert with the general-in-chief, the encampment committee formed a plan to reorganize the army, clothe and feed the men, and regulate the military medical department.[1]

From 1778 through most of 1779, Morris devoted his attention to the diplomatic and financial matters that came before the Congress as well as to its military concerns. He served on about a third of the congressional committees, chairing several important ones, and drafted many significant foreign policy documents. In addition to the encampment committee, Morris served on the Financial Committee, the Committee on Public Safety, the Committee on Marine Activities, the Committee on the Treasury Administration Reorganization, the Committee on the Treatment of Prisoners and on Foreign Officers and Soldiers, the Medical Committee, the Committee to Provide Instruction to Our Foreign Commissioners, the Committee on Ratification of the Treaty with France, the Committees for Military Recruitment and Commissions, the Committee on Mississippi River Navigation, and several others. He was also chosen to draft many important papers: the response to the 1778

British offer of "peace," the instructions for negotiating with the Six Nations of the Iroquois, and missives on numerous other matters large and small.

Morris had first been elected to the Continental Congress shortly after the New York State constitution was adopted. In July the Committee of Safety sent him to Fort Edward to report on conditions there and the advance of Burgoyne's troops southward. And with war raging across the state, travel from New York to Pennsylvania was impossible. A second election, held in assembly and council on October 3, 1777, repeated the results of the first, naming Morris, Philip Livingston, James Duane, Francis Lewis, and William Duer as delegates. The New Yorkers' credentials were delivered to Congress in York, Pennsylvania, nearly six weeks later, on Friday, November 14. Morris finally reported to York on January 20, 1778, roughly nine weeks after that. As usual, his papers provide no explanation; he seems, however, to have been visiting the Ogdens, his sister and brother-in-law, in New Jersey.[2] Such behavior might suggest an unprofessional and possibly, under the circumstances, an unpatriotic attitude.

At the time Morris and his fellow committee members arrived at Valley Forge, the Continental Army was still busily chopping down every tree large enough to be called such, in order to construct huts, assemble chevaux-de-frise, brace the earthen entrenchments, and furnish fuel for campfires. Even in verdant Valley Forge, therefore, large acreages of mostly hardwoods, such as oak, walnut and hickory, were soon denuded. The oaks and walnut trees mostly went into the construction of the living huts and the defense works, whereas hickory wood was especially treasured as the raw material for charcoal. As anyone who has done even a little such logging will attest, it is exhausting. And the men had to drill besides.[3]

Washington had carefully considered the choice of a winter encampment site before deciding on Valley Forge, as an aide-memoire of December 17, 1777, shows:

> The General ardently wishes it were now in his power to conduct the troops into the best winter quarters; but where are they to be found? Should we retire to the interior of the State, we would find it crowded with virtuous citizens, who, sacrificing their all, have left Philadelphia and fled hither for protection; to their distress humanity forbids us to add. This is not all. We should leave a vast extent of country to be despoiled and ravaged by the enemy, from which they would draw vast supplies, and where many of our firm friends would be exposed to all the miseries of an insulting and

wanton depredation. A train of evils might be enumerated, but these will suffice. These considerations make it indispensably necessary for the army to take such a position as will enable it most effectually to prevent distress, and give the most extensive security; and in that position we must make ourselves the best shelter in our power.

Once settled at Valley Forge, Washington wrote to the Continental Congress five times between December 22, 1777, and January 28, 1778, appealing for help. In his first letter, the general wrote that, unless the commissary department, then under Quartermaster General Thomas Mifflin, was reorganized "suddenly," then the Continental Army "must inevitably . . . starve, dissolve or disperse." Of the 11,000-odd soldiers who marched to Valley Forge, more than a quarter did not survive the winter. Inadequate provisions caused most of the deaths. While the American army went hungry through much of the war, the British army appears to have been adequately victualed. The British government provided each man serving in America with a third of a ton of food a year, every year of the war.[4]

In his fifth appeal, Washington proposed that the congressional committee then visiting the Valley Forge camp effect this reorganization. The encampment committee, known also as the Committee of Conference, officially consisted of Morris, Francis Dana, Joseph Reed, Nathaniel Folsom, John Harvie, and perhaps Charles Carroll.[5]

As usual, Morris had involved himself in controversy even before he reached Valley Forge. On their way to join the committee, Morris and the Virginian, Harvie, passed through Lancaster, Pennsylvania; there they encountered some British officers, with an American escort and under a flag of truce, on their way to provide clothing and medicine to British prisoners in American hands. This party stopped to eat at the same tavern where Morris and Harvie were spending the night after having crossed the Susquehanna. The British paid for their meal in gold and silver coin. They had agreed with the tavern owner on an amount, but one of the American officers accompanying them took issue. He held that the bill should be settled at the exchange rate fixed by the Pennsylvania Council, which set a higher value on American currency. The British officers argued that the truce agreement with Washington obliged them only to pay "reasonable rates," and they appealed to Morris and Harvie, as members of the Continental Congress, for support.

Morris, seeing a threat to national prestige, agreed with them. He promptly declared that the case "was alone to be determined by the Law of Nations," for the British "were not subject to the municipal Laws of the separate States so long as they demeaned themselves [that is, conducted themselves] consistently with the terms they had either tacitly or expressly agreed to." Then and there he wrote a letter protesting the American officers' conduct to Thomas Wharton, Jr. (1735–1778), the president of the Pennsylvania Council of Safety, who was then at the height of his political influence.

When Morris arrived at Valley Forge, on January 24, his committee colleague Joseph Reed told him he had been imprudent: Morris should have spoken to Wharton in person on this matter, he said, rather than writing him.[6] Morris responded that he was not personally acquainted with Wharton. Reed ended his lengthy remonstrance with a statement that Morris had acted in haste and "would not do it if it was to do again."

This altercation did not end matters, however, for Wharton sent a strong complaint to the Continental Congress, which agreed with him. Washington, on the other hand, had already written to the Board of War, criticizing the American officers involved for picking a fight with the British and then detaining them. What might have come of all this brouhaha is a subject for speculation. The Pennsylvania Council and the Continental Congress each wanted Morris and Harvie to appear and "defend themselves," but as both men had more important obligations, the matter was allowed to fizzle out.[7]

Surprisingly, the president of Congress, Henry Laurens, a man of good sense, was not disposed to pour water on the dispute. Laurens's opinion of Morris was decidedly mixed; in an early 1778 letter to Lafayette, he expressed regret that the Marquis had allowed Morris to read some of his— Lafayette's—correspondence, and called Morris "a Gentleman who though very sensible appears to me, and has given some proof, to be often guardless and incautious."[8]

Morris and Harvie managed to join their committee colleagues without further incident. The delegation mainly billeted at the Moore (sometimes spelled Moor) house, several miles from Washington's encampment. Francis Dana of Massachusetts, a lawyer, jurist, and diplomat with a Harvard degree, was elected chair. He and Morris seem to have done the most important work on the committee, but Morris's influence grew steadily.

Morris was astonished by his early tours of the camp: "An army of skeletons appears before our eyes, naked, starved, sick, discouraged," he wrote John Jay on January 31.

Thomas Mifflin (1744–1800) had resigned as quartermaster general in July 1777, thus aborting an investigation of his mismanagement. Since then no new supplies had been provided through this office, for Joseph Trumbull, who had been elected to replace Mifflin, was too infirm to fill his post, and for some reason no replacement had been sought. "In truth not a little Regulation, hath become necessary," Morris understatedly wrote Jay on February 1.[9]

Almost at once the committee wrote Congress to recommend that Philip Schuyler replace Trumbull and that Jeremiah Wadsworth (1743–1804), formerly a Connecticut merchant, be named commissary general. Wadsworth's appointment was approved swiftly but Schuyler was in bad odor owing to the Fort Ticonderoga disaster and the committee's suggestion was rejected. The post went to "the fighting Quaker," Nathanael Greene (1742–1786). Born in Rhode Island and self-educated, Greene was elected to the General Assembly of Rhode Island in 1770. In 1775 he was appointed brigadier general of the Rhode Island regiments sent to join the Continental Army besieging the British in Boston. Greene earned Washington's esteem for his military service in the New York City area, won promotion to major general, and fought in the battles of Princeton, the Brandywine, and Germantown. Greene held the quartermaster generalship from 1778 to 1780.[10]

The committee soon found it necessary to restructure the Continental Army's procurement system, a task largely handled by Morris. They dictated efficient accountancy methods to all the army departments, and prompt reports were required on all available personnel, stocks, and stores. Through roughly March 20, the committee also dealt with officers' complaints regarding supply, distribution, and promotion and handled the administrative details of recommending promotions and appointments to the Congress. Meanwhile, the committee also managed to formulate its army reorganization proposal, which it presented in a letter to Congress dated February 5, 1778, less than two weeks after its arrival in Valley Forge. The proposal called for reduction of the number of battalions, and recommended that the number of enlisted men and noncommissioned officers in each infantry battalion be reduced from 692 to 553; each battalion would have twenty-nine commissioned officers. The new battalions were to have nine companies, one of which would be a light infantry unit. The "surplus" soldiers could be used to reinforce the Continental Army's skimpy cavalry and artillery, of which there would be four battalions each. The reconfigured army would include nearly 54,000 noncommissioned officers and men. This new army would cost substantially less in monthly salaries and rations. In rations needed for the troops there would be a reduction of nearly 5,000 units a month.

The final draft of the committee's report to Congress was written by Joseph Reed and signed by Francis Dana, but the first draft was by Gouverneur Morris. Both versions show his stamp: like Washington, for example,

Morris believed in supplying line units with plenty of first-quality officers, a policy emphasized in his initial draft of the report and retained in subsequent versions. Morris also clearly recognized the need for swift movement in combat against the enemy infantry. Having trained primarily for war in mainland Europe, where set-piece battles were the rule, the British forces were less mobile than they needed to be in this American war. The suggestion to streamline the infantry battalions is also Morris's. (Incidentally, Washington agreed with him.)

For reasons not clear from the records, Congress delayed action on the original reorganization plan. On March 3, the committee wrote President Laurens a letter proposing the establishment of an "Army Corps of Engineers." This would comprise a pair of battalions, each with eight companies of one hundred enlisted men and a heavy complement of officers with a large repertoire of relevant skills, especially in civic and mechanical field engineering. (The committee remarked that its members believed strongly in the importance of such an engineer wing but had not included the proposal in the earlier report because they had not yet been unanimous on the point.) The March 3 letter is signed by Dana but is in the handscript of Gouverneur Morris.

The committee plan as spelled out in both letters was presented to Congress by Henry Laurens on May 18, debated for several days, and approved with no significant alterations on May 27. But, for complicated administrative reasons with which Morris had nothing to do, the army was not reorganized until late November 1778.[11]

Although the substitution of Nathanael Greene for Thomas Mifflin as quartermaster general, and Greene's prompt personnel changes, produced immediate improvements in the situation at Valley Forge, by the spring of 1778 the lack of provisions had led to three near mutinies.[12]

Some of the material deficiencies not rectified by the army's reorganization had nothing to do with food. Although clothing was plentiful in the colonies throughout the eighteenth century, "patriotic" civilians failed utterly to manufacture and deliver enough clothing for the American army; by early summer 1779, Congress had to call for the importation of a comprehensive list of clothing items for our troops from France. Even such readily available articles as hats, collars, shirt buttons, garters, needles and thread, hooks and eyes, and shoes and stockings, as well as shoemaking tools of all kinds, had, as of 1779, to be imported from our new ally.[13]

At least partly because of the shortages, by April 1778 American officers were asking Washington for permission to resign at the rate of two or three a day; already, enlistments had been dropping steadily since 1776.[14] On

January 28, 1778, George Washington urged Congress to provide his officers half-pay for life and pensions, to encourage them to stay. (He had made the same proposal earlier, but it had been rejected on January 13. The general pressed his case for many more months.)[15]

Gouverneur Morris eagerly supported Washington on this matter as on so many others. In a letter to the general, he described himself as "an Advocate for the Army. I loved them from Acquaintance with some Individuals and for the Sufferings which as a Body they had bravely and patiently endured."[16] From the spring of 1778 through the spring of 1779, he sponsored (unsuccessfully) half-pay and pension laws, drafted and sent more than a dozen letters to influential members of Congress, and corresponded steadily with Washington. He must also have conducted numerous face-to-face negotiations.

Finally, after several tries and defeats, in August 1779 and 1780 Congress passed bills providing officers half-pay for seven years past the end of the war and giving a similar allowance to the widows of officers killed on active duty. The latter was the first national pension law for the benefit of widows and orphans. By the time it passed, Morris was no longer a member of Congress, but his labors had contributed much to its success.

The Committee of Conference returned to its congressional duties on April 15, having left Valley Forge five days earlier. Their work had had direct military benefits. Even during the darkest days at Valley Forge, the American army conducted offensive training. In addition, they built effective obstacles against Howe's forces, billeted less than twenty-five miles away,[17] and they performed valuable bayonet, musketry, and gun drills, as well as rehearsing maneuvers.[18]

On Wednesday, April 15, 1778, when Morris returned to the Congress in York, he was immediately chosen to serve on three committees. Along with Francis Dana, again, and Samuel Chase, he was elected to prepare a report on the terms offered by the British and Loyalist turncoats; and, with Dana and William Duer, was elected to prepare a draft of strategic military instructions to Major General Gates. In addition, he was added to the Committee of Representation for the General Assembly of New Jersey.

Three days later Morris was chosen for the Clothier General's Committee, the Medical Committee, and a new Committee for Settling Cartel Problems. On Saturday, April 25, he and two others were named to another new committee, to deal with miscellaneous questions of resupply, morale, and training that George Washington had written to the Congress about two days earlier. And on May 1 Morris was selected to report proper instructions to the commissioners at foreign courts. (The other members chosen for this strategically important committee were Richard Henry Lee and Roger Sherman.)

So in the fifteen days since his return to York, Gouverneur Morris had been selected to serve on eight congressional committees, six of which were newly constituted. Each of these disparate committees required steady rounds of conferences and correspondence. (And newly formed committees generally require much more work than established ones.)

On April 20, 1778, the Congress elected Morris to chair a committee to respond to the Carlisle Commission and its peace offer.[19] The peace efforts of the Carlisle Commission are best considered in the context of the American strategic situation at the time.[20] On October 17, 1777, after suffering heavy losses, the British general Burgoyne had capitulated at Saratoga, New York. The American victory had emboldened the French. At this point, it occurred to the British that conciliation might be in order. In February of 1778, Lord North had introduced the Conciliatory Propositions to the House of Commons. Though they caused an uproar because of perceived British concessions to the colonies, the propositions were passed. A peace commission was chosen, led by the Earl of Carlisle, and embarked for the colonies to negotiate the proposals, which had been received by the Americans in advance. The commission's brief was to make peace with the rebels without surrendering militarily and without conceding the colonies' independence. By this time—with the French alliance signed—there was no chance for the commission to succeed.

For several reasons, the victory at Saratoga was not, as the historian Cecil Headlam suggests, "a negative success" which might have been retrieved, but rather a timely victory for the Americans—it served as the direct stimulus for the French entry into the war—and a crucial defeat for the British.[21] In the words of Piers Mackesy, "the disaster at Saratoga . . . altered the framework of the American War entirely." With the aid of the French army and the first-class French navy, the American rebels were able to conduct the military campaigns and naval maneuvers—in the West Indies, the English Channel, and the Mediterranean, as well as on the American coast and in mainland North America—that won the war.[22]

The alliance with France was crucial in terms of morale and money as well. In 1777 war fever on the British side was at its height, and the Whig opposition, in which Charles James Fox (1749–1806) was rapidly taking the lead, was becoming despondent. On the other side of the Atlantic, by 1778, support for the war was declining: many American civilians, at least, had begun to believe the Revolution doomed. The paper money—that clear measure of public faith—issued by the Congress and by the states was almost worthless. French loans, which by 1784 amounted to $6,352,000, contributed materially to the Revolution's success.

The year after France allied itself with America, Spain decided to join it in military operations against Britain, in the English Channel and especially in the Mediterranean. In 1780, the Dutch too went to war against Britain. They had been negotiating with America since August 1778, when the first Dutch-American treaty was negotiated at Aix-la-Chapelle. When the British captured Henry Laurens en route to Holland, they discovered the text of this treaty and demanded that the Dutch government punish the official who had signed the draft of the treaty. The Dutch refused, and Britain, after declaring war on December 20, 1780, captured the Dutch West Indian port of St. Eustatius.[23]

France and Spain were the only European enemies of Britain whose money contributed substantially to American success in the Revolution. Spain advanced $174,000 in 1780–1782, but it had already provided a generous sum in munitions for the American forces. Dutch bankers did venture loans totaling $1,304,000, but not until 1782–1783, when the Americans had already won. Later, Gouverneur Morris would have much to do with these international dealings, especially those with France and the Netherlands.

On January 8, 1778, two of the three American negotiators in Paris met with Count Gérard, the first secretary of the French Foreign Ministry; the next day, Gérard told the American commissioners Benjamin Franklin and Silas Deane that his government had become convinced that the Americans intended to maintain (he might more justly have said "attain") their independence, and had decided to help. Negotiations began at once, and on February 6 the plenipotentiaries of the United States and France signed two treaties. The first was commerical—it granted America most-favored-nation trading privileges—and the other declared the nations' military alliance. This latter hinged on a war between France and Britain, but that war was on its way and the signatories knew it. The British possessions on the continent of North America were reserved for conquest by the United States, and France was given a free hand to dispose of the British island colonies, the Bermudas excepted.

Vergennes, the French foreign minister, had the ambassador to London deliver the treaties to the British government in early March. By the middle of the month, relations had been severed. In late spring 1778, Lord North expelled the French ambassador from London, but even then he did not declare war. The first fighting came in June, with a naval skirmish near the island of Ishant, off Brittany. On July 10 Britain declared war; by then, a French expeditionary force commanded by Admiral Comte Charles Henri d'Estaing (1729–1794) had already sailed for America.

In the year after Saratoga, Britain had to redeploy her military forces for a greatly widened war. In midsummer of 1778, Philadelphia had to be evacuated in order to reinforce the West Indies and Florida. France had attacked the former, beginning to hamper British communications with and resupply to the American mainland. And the French alliance further emboldened American privateers, led by John Paul Jones (1747–1792), to harass British shipping in the Atlantic and in British territorial waters. He even raided in the British Isles proper; for the first time during the war, the British had to deploy naval and land forces at home. Even before the alliance went into effect, evidence presented to the British House of Lords in February 1778 indicates that at least 173 American privateer vessels had already captured or destroyed at least 559 British ships. Once the French alliance was concluded the number of prizes taken and ships sunk by American privateers increased greatly.[24]

America did not win its independence alone, but with the moral, financial, and military support of France, without which the colonial rebellion would likely have failed; with mainly indirect aid from the Spanish and the Dutch, because fighting them made it impossible for Britain to concentrate on America; and with some help from German individuals and mercenary units.

The English had had some notice that trouble was on its way. In fall 1777 rumors spread through official circles in London that the French court had declared in favor of open recognition of America and of making a treaty with the nascent nation. And although, as has already been noted, France did not immediately send the British government a copy of the alliance treaty, London very promptly received copies of both treaties. They were delivered by Commissioner Deane's private secretary, Dr. Edward Bancroft (1744–1821), an American who spied for Britain throughout the Revolutionary War. Bancroft was very well placed: not only did he act as Deane's secretary from the time of the latter's arrival in Europe on his "secret" mission to establish contact with the French through the completion of the two treaties, but he also served as secretary to the joint commission to establish a Franco-American alliance, later to Benjamin Franklin as minister to France, and finally as secretary to the American peace commission of 1781–1783. In all this time, the only American to suspect him was the third commissioner,

Arthur Lee. In very large part because Lee had voiced these suspicions, Deane and Franklin seem to have conducted as much official business as possible in Lee's absence. Although Bancroft's perfidy was not known for certain until more than a century had passed, aspects of his conduct should have raised the red flag that Lee, seemingly alone, noticed. Ironically, Franklin, writing from Philadelphia in 1776, had recommended to Congress's Secret Committee of Correspondence with France that Silas Deane first contact Bancroft as a reliable source of information on British war plans; this was why Deane arranged to meet "the even-tempered patriotic Doctor" (Deane's words) at Calais in July 1776. At this time, Bancroft agreed to become Deane's private secretary while Deane was in Paris making "secret arrangements" for the French to supply the Americans and beginning to lay the foundations for the 1778 treaties.[25]

The British had an almost ludicrous number of well-placed spies operating for them and against the Franco-American alliance. In addition to Bancroft, they included Paul Wentworth, Joseph Hynson, John Vardill, and Hugh Elliot. Furthermore, George Lupton and a Mr. Thornton, in particular, proved ready to step in when needed as special kinds of supernumeraries. Paul Wentworth came from New Hampshire but earned his fortune in London, where he offered to serve as a spy when the conflict broke out. His network included Edward Bancroft, his former accountant. As secretary for Silas Deane, Bancroft had access to transcripts from Deane's secret meetings with the French and transmitted them to Wentworth, who passed them on to the head of the British secret service, William Eden. Captain Joseph Hynson also worked for Silas Deane in mercantile affairs, his apparent patriotic zeal obscuring his dealings with the British, until the fall of 1777. George Lupton, an Englishman, stayed in France and communicated his observations of American activity directly to Eden. John Vardill taught at King's College in New York while spying for the British.

In *L'Europe et la révolution française,* Albert Sorel memorably depicts the cutthroat nature of European politics in the latter half of the eighteenth century. The performance of the American commissioners, diplomats, and ministers abroad will hardly surprise any reader who bears Sorel in mind and remembers that America's representatives overseas sprang from a young and naïve nation.[26]

The background of the French commitment is enlightening in its own right and, besides, affected events important in Gouverneur Morris's service. The Duc de Choiseul, Louis XV's long-serving minister of foreign affairs, as early as the mid-1760s perceived in Britain's increasingly agitated American colonies a likely arena for France to try again to embarrass Britain.

In 1770, however, Choiseul left office. The Comte de Vergennes, who was well schooled in the savage European diplomacy of the period, took over the Ministry of Foreign Affairs in 1774, with the accession of Louis XVI. He revived Choiseul's ideas concerning the American question, and presented them in numerous dispatches and *aides-mémoires*. "You will show them [the Americans] that it is only because of them that we are in it [the armed conflict with Britain], that thus the engagements we have undertaken with them are absolute and permanent, that our causes are common causes that can now never be separated"—thus he instructed Gérard when the latter was setting out for America in the summer of 1778.[27]

As early as December 1774, however, British supporters of America had indirectly approached Vergennes and suggested secret French assistance. Vergennes then resisted, but only because he feared the British government would give in to the American colonists; the result might be a hydra-headed problem for the French. A year later, though—five months after Lexington—the foreign minister was convinced that both the British government and the American leadership were firm in their resolve. He secretly sent Julien Achard de Bonvouloir (1749–1783) to America, to encourage the colonists, to intimate that France did not desire the return of Canada, and to convey that France did not disapprove of independence for the colonies. Furthermore, America would be free and welcome to trade with the French.[28]

By April 1776, too, we now know, the dramatist and secret agent Pierre-Augustin Caron de Beaumarchais (1732–1799) had written proposals to Vergennes, which the latter had stitched into his own memoranda presented before the king and council, advocating French intervention, on all relevant fronts, against the British. Devoted to the American cause, Beaumarchais also saw the colonies' break with Britain as a means for France to avenge the disadvantageous 1762 treaty that ended the Seven Years' War. He proposed a French loan to America that would enable them to purchase gunpowder. In a May 1776 letter he wrote, "The Americans are in as good a situation as they can be. Army, fleet, food supplies, courage—everything is excellent. But without gunpowder and without engineers, how can they be victorious or even defend themselves? Are we going to let them perish rather than lend them one or two millions?"[29] The cumulative effect of the Beaumarchais memos, as filtered through Vergennes, strongly predisposed France to ally with America. The only major voice in dissent seems to have been Anne Robert Jacques Turgot (1727–1781), Louis XVI's minister of finance, who feared that the cost of helping the revolutionists might bankrupt France. Vergennes argued that after the war, France would become America's chief trading partner. This would effectively exclude Britain from North America and, following Choiseul's 1770 proposals, perhaps France would even sup-plant Britain in American waters. Vergennes's arguments prevailed, and what was essentially his policy was decreed from Versailles on May 2, 1776. After a period of reflection, Turgot resigned on May 12. But time proved him largely correct: the commitment to America did much to drain the French treasury, and soon after losing the colonies, Britain again became America's chief trading partner.

Louis XVI promptly ordered that one million livres' worth of munitions be sent to the colonists from French arsenals. These arrangements were ef-fected through Roderigue Hortalez et Cie, a front for the French govern-ment, operated by Beaumarchais. Through the same "Company" Louis influenced his cousin, Charles III of Spain, to contribute an equivalent amount. Thus, roughly two months before the Declaration of Indepen-dence, and long before any agent of the American colonies had come to France to try to establish an alliance, the French government, largely in or-der to undermine the power of Britain and thus aggrandize its own, poured no small amount of oil on the nascent flames of American rebellion.[30]

The Carlisle Commission was about to leave on its mission of reconcilia-tion. As Lord North proposed to Parliament on February 19, 1778, the commission was established to negotiate peace with Congress and was au-thorized to suspend or abolish taxation, and to "treat, discuss, and conclude upon every point whatsoever." (The commissioners were to take full advan-tage of the scope Parliament granted them.)[31]

The commissioners were Lord Carlisle, William Eden, and George John-stone, who had been named to replace Richard Jackson (1722–1787). (Lord Howe, who of course was already in the colonies, had also been named at first but soon resigned.)[32] Probably few people so ill qualified had ever headed such an important mission. Frederick Howard, the fifth Earl of Carlisle (1748–1825), a friend of the opposition leader, Charles James Fox, was young and inexperienced, with few substantial credentials. The com-mission was his first work of public service. Morris, though several years younger, had far more relevant experience and was on his home turf. The second member, William Eden (1744–1814), a lawyer working for the British secret service, had developed under the mentorship of Lord Suffolk, and for this reason alone he held an important though uncertain place in British public life. Eden had already served as secretary for Ireland and am-bassador to France. His older brother, Robert, had been governor of Mary-land, and his father-in-law, Sir Gilbert Elliott, had many powerful friends. Thanks to family connections, Eden had also become friends with Germain. In terms of relevant experience and political strength, then, he was the sheet-anchor of the commission. George Johnstone (1730–1787) had served as governor of Florida and had been detailed to keep up with the "secret" Franco-American negotiations in Paris. The commission's secretary was Adam Ferguson (1723–1816), a scholar who became best known for his 1783 *History of the Progress and Termination of the Roman Republic.* [33]

On March 13, the commissioners, along with Germain; the British solicitor general, Edward Thurlow (1731–1806); and Alexander Wedderburn (1733–1805), the attorney general, met at Lord North's to discuss the mission. Carlisle commented afterward that "little passed of any real importance; and I confess I came away shocked at the slovenly manner with which an affair so serious in its nature had been dismissed."[34]

Why so "slovenly"? Through Bancroft's traitorous offices, Johnstone at least knew the French-American alliance was imminent. Yet despite that knowledge and the clear early warning of the Saratoga defeat, Lord North failed to allow Germain to schedule the first planning session for the commission until mid-March 1778. So perhaps the commissioners were inattentive at that meeting because they were aware, at some level not altogether conscious, that their efforts would come too late.[35] Yet somehow, the British government hoped, the commission might both forestall further French military action and persuade Congress not to ratify the treaties. Had the British declared war on France, France would have been able to invoke her defensive alliances with Austria and Spain.

The French treaties and the Carlisle Commission in effect raced across the Atlantic; the treaties arrived first, reaching York on May 4, 1778. (Congress had been driven out of Philadelphia on the second of the month.) Both treaties were immediately ratified. In July a French battle fleet arrived, bringing the first diplomatic representative accredited to the United States, Conrad Alexandre Gérard, Minister Plenipotentiary of Louis XVI. In a hearty end of the summer reception ceremony, planned in part by Gouverneur Morris, Gérard, his staff, and his hosts, the members of Congress, lavishly supped (twenty-one toasts!) on fine clams, terrapin, and wine, which the Carlisle Commission had sent ahead as a goodwill offering.[36]

After the first communication arrived from the Carlisle Commission, in late spring 1778, a committee of Dana and South Carolina's William Henry Drayton, chaired by Morris, reported to Congress its opinion that "the United States cannot hold a conference or treaty with any commission on the part of Great Britain unless they first withdraw their fleets and armies and acknowledge the independence of the United States." After a debate, Congress approved this position unanimously. So, thanks in great part to the timely arrival of the news from France, the American war, much as France desired, seemed bound to continue for some years more.[37]

Congress did not learn that the twin compacts with France had been made until April 27. On February 5, however, the day before the endorsements in Paris, George Johnstone, privy to Lord North's plans, had informed Robert Morris that the Carlisle Commission would soon sail for America.[38] When the news finally reached Philadelphia in late April, Gouverneur Morris quickly (and in some ways correctly) interpreted the signal. The next day he wrote John Jay, then in Peekskill, "Great Britain seriously means to treat. . . . If the minister from France were present as well as him from England, I am a blind politician if the thirteen States (with their extended territory) would not be in peaceable possession of their independence three months from this day. . . . Probably a treaty is signed with the house of Bourbon [France] ere this; if so, a spark hath fallen upon the train which is to fire the world."[39]

Here is an irony that no loyal American official could have appreciated at this time—and no doubt many never did connect the dots. The Continental Congress first learned that the treaties were about to be signed from a letter drafted the day before the event by a member of the Carlisle Commission, which was sent to short-circuit congressional ratification of those very treaties.[40]

On June 13, 1778, a large package from the Carlisle Commission in British-held New York reached Congress in York, Pennsylvania. It contained the commissioners' address to Congress, a copy of their commission to treat, and three relevant acts of Parliament. Henry Laurens began to read the address, but Gouverneur Morris stopped him on the ground that an official reading in Congress would offend the king of France. Principally, however, he said, "I oppose going on with it [the reading of the address], and thereby we will strike conviction to the souls even of Tories that Great Britain is reduced to imploring a peace from America." Morris's motion was defeated three days later, on June 16. The Continental Congress no doubt felt that it would be wise to enter the formal British terms into the official record. On the same day that his motion went under, the British began their secretly planned evacuation of Philadelphia. This movement was an early harbinger of their defeat.

After the reading, a committee of five distinguished congressmen— Richard H. Lee, Samuel Adams, William Henry Drayton (1742–1779), John Witherspoon (1723–1794), and Morris—was selected to consider the documents.[41] Lee and Witherspoon drafted responses that very day; on the next,

Congress approved for transmittal a letter, written by Morris, who drew upon the drafts of Lee and Witherspoon. It said, essentially, that unless Britain both recognized American independence and withdrew her entire military force from American territory, no peace negotiations could take place. Drayton and Morris also wrote long letters—essays, really—which appeared pseudonymously in the June 20 *Pennsylvania Gazette,* having been presented to Congress on June 17 (Drayton) and June 20 (Morris). It is fair to highlight Morris's response, since he had already written the resolves of April 22 answering Lord North's peace proposals. (Those resolves were read before Parliament, which praised them.)[42]

The Carlisle Commission offered to guarantee that British military forces would be garrisoned in America only "with consent" (whose consent is not specified), a very equivocal reference, and to allow the American colonies representation in Parliament, another opaque "concession." The British government might adopt policies to raise the value of colonial paper money and to attempt to discharge the American public debt. All four points were vague to begin with, and the commission presented them in suitably obfuscatory terms. In the first response, drafted by Morris, Henry Laurens rejected the commission's offer as an insult to the king of France and an affront to "the people of America," whom the proposals assumed to "be still subject to the Crown of Great Britain."[43]

Morris wrote and published three additional responses over the next few months. The one dated July 21, 1778, is in some ways the most interesting of the four. In its opening paragraph, a kind of preamble, Morris remarks upon the commissioners' presentation of "one more fruitless negociatory essay," and regrets that Lord Carlisle, in particular, since thus involved, "should be raised up as the topstone on a pyramid of blunders." Morris subsequently remarks that "Great Britain must acknowledge" America's independence: "How idle of you to talk of insuring or enlarging what is out of your power and cannot be enlarged." He next dismantles the two reasons the commission asserts for the presence of British military forces in American territory.[44] The first of these reasons was that the British forces were a precautionary measure against Britain's "ancient enemies." But Morris points out that it is difficult to understand how the British army in America is a protection against France, unless Britain is using the opportunity to divert French attention before invading France itself. In which case, offers Morris sarcastically, "Your armies are doubtless assembled in readiness for the descent, which, considering the unprovided state of that country, cannot but prove successful; and therefore I congratulate your lordship on the fair prospect you enjoy of seeing your Sovereign make his triumphant entry through the gates of

Paris." The commission also claimed the necessity of British military protection for the Tories. "Let them take care of themselves," responds Morris. "I offer you this consolation, my lord, because we both know that you cannot protect the Tories, and because there is every reason to believe that you cannot protect yourselves."

In private letters to close friends, such as John Jay, Morris expressed satisfaction with the series of responses to the Carlisle Commission. The congressional leadership, too—speaking chiefly through Laurens—also made its pleasure known. Morris's prose in the responses is precise, elegant, lively, and as befits a revolutionary, rather cheeky. In the September 19 letter, for example, he promises "to undeceive you in some matters you seem to have mistaken, and to state the true ground on which you stand with respect to America," then concludes:

> My Lord, you are come hither for the very modest purpose of persuading a free and independent nation to surrender their rights and privileges. You are confessedly incompetent to subduing them and are therefore to proceed by what you call reasoning. . . . I wish your King would mind his own affairs, and not trouble other people. But if he will send armies to fight, we must e'en [continue to] fight. And so I wish your Lordship a good morning. I am my Lord, with the most profound veneration, Your Lords most obedient, and most humble servant. AN AMERICAN.

On March 4, 1779, he wrote a letter from Philadelphia, addressed to George Johnstone; this followed the printing of Johnstone's November 27, 1778, address to Parliament, explaining the failure of the Carlisle Commission. Morris's letter concludes:

> But I beg pardon, Sir, for political disquisitions to so refined a politician, and for mentioning the means of peace to one enamoured of war. To the force of necessity; to the embarrassment of your finances; to that wheel of fortune which you wish not to be thrown out of, and whose revolutions will place your country as low in this as she was high in the last war; to these I leave you. When all other views are precluded, then you will see your true interests, and then you will join in a prayer for peace with Your most obedient and humble servant, AN AMERICAN.[45]

The device here is anaphora, in which a word or phrase is repeated in several successive clauses, uniting them. Morris's fine sense of balance and rhythm are also on display. Small wonder he was chosen to do so much of Congress's writing.

Although they may not constitute, as Jared Sparks asserts, Morris's "most essential service . . . during his career in Congress," his responses to the Carlisle Commission give him a claim to some historical honor. They were, after all, official responses to Britain on behalf of the Continental Congress. True, the commissioners were not altogether formidable intellectual opponents. But the essays were published in periodicals and, in 1779, in book form. The book was published in Britain at almost the same time, as an issue of John Almon's *Remembrancer*, a monthly anthology of materials related to the revolution in the colonies. The American volume alone promptly sold thirteen hundred copies. This timely, broad public exposure is important. Through 1779, most of the British public and their officials seem to have backed the war, while from 1777 through 1779 American morale had been steadily sagging. Morris's rather brassy writings likely encouraged the Americans and had the opposite effect, to some extent, on the British. In this ocean-spanning effect, then, Morris may rival the impact of Paine's *Common Sense,* which seems to have appealed far more to an American than to a British audience.[46]

During the late spring and early summer of 1778, Morris drafted for the committee of Richard Henry Lee, Chase, and himself an eloquent "Address to the Inhabitants of North America." To reach as many people as possible, the piece was written to be read from every church pulpit in America, a largely Christian country at the time. Its burden is a commentary on the significance of the alliance with France and a plea for sustained American patriotism. With no end in sight for the war and morale beginning to flag, Morris chose to write this inspiriting essay.

Not long after, Morris and the two Lees then in Congress put together the manifesto to the Nova Scotians on the matter of fishing rights. With Duer and Drayton, Morris was also soon assigned to the committee for recruitment of Continental battalions for the remainder of the war. Despite all this work, Morris found time in the summer of 1778 to write letters to many of his friends and (probably in late July) to draft a lengthy memorandum on American fiscal and administrative reform. He had been reflecting on the latter throughout June and most of July 1778, so when he wrote he wrote fluently.[47]

The memorandum, entitled *Proposals on Fiscal and Administrative Reform,* begins with the incorrect prediction "that America must be victorious if she can prosecute the war since it is impracticable for Great Britain to pursue it much longer." (Actually, the peace treaty was five years away, and the fighting in America alone continued through 1782.)[48] Morris continues: "Now America can prosecute the war so long as she can keep an Army in the Field, but to keep an Army it is necessary to have Men to clothe, arm, Feed and pay them. To all these Purposes Money is the great Thing needful." But the "Paper Circulation" was depreciating seriously—a problem to which, as Morris points out, the "Want of Men" was closely related. He goes on to describe the eight leading causes he sees for the depreciation.

To "restore the Value of [its] Money," Morris writes, America should "lessen the Quantity & Kinds to provide Ways and Means to procure Funds for carrying on the War." His first idea made excellent economic sense: "every State should instantly by Law cry down their own Emissions and redeem them with Continental Loan Office Certificates." The replacement of state money with federal money would enable the next critical steps, procuring credit and obtaining loans in Europe and establishing taxes on such transported commodities as flour, salt, rum, and beef. He also proposes a Treasury Board, to consist of a treasurer, an auditor, and a comptroller.

His other suggested administrative reforms include the establishment of a "Navy Board or Board of Admiralty," a "Commercial Board, and a coordinated Board of War." The Navy Board was to consist of "five Intelligent Sea Officers well acquainted with maritime Affairs and otherwise qualified as Men of Business." The Commercial Board would require "the five most intelligent Merchants to be met with"; the Board of War, on the other hand, would require "Men of Experience." Morris did not, however, offer any candidates for these positions, seeing himself as primarily engaged in formulating the "System."

Morris also proposes the formation of a committee of three, or else a single officer, as "Chief of the States Who should superintend the Executive Business." That is, roughly nine years before the formulation of the U.S. Constitution, Morris had outlined the leading elements of an executive branch. His is the first detailed, written exposition of the idea that has been recorded.

In mid-June 1778, the British evacuated Philadelphia and Congress returned. Soon the city was again the cultural and financial capital of the colonies as well as the seat of government. (It retained its preeminence through 1789, at least.) But Philadelphia had been ravaged. Before the British entry into the city, there had been about 33,000 inhabitants; roughly a third of them had fled, and those who remained were subject to substantial depredations.

Even by the accounts of some decided Loyalists, the British troops burned numerous houses and "plunder'd and ill-used" many Philadelphians.[49] Morris and his colleagues no doubt enjoyed the spaciousness of their Philadelphia quarters after their sojourn in the town of York, but the British occupancy had left its marks. The State House, which the British had used as a hospital, was not immediately fit for use, and a stench, emanating from a nearby pit filled with garbage and the bodies of men and horses, permeated the air. Many deserted houses in the city had been ransacked, including the library in Franklin's residence; later estimates put the losses for city residents at just under £200,000.

In June, Morris served on committees to address matters as diverse as orders concerning army provisioning, questions of property ownership, and a Beaumarchais proposal about cargo.[50] The fleet of ships organized by the Frenchman delivered guns and ammunition to America, and Congress promised to compensate him with produce, including tobacco, a debt that remained unpaid forty years later. Morris also conducted some of Congress's official correspondence with, for example, Robert Morris and George Clinton. Robert Morris wrote Gouverneur from Valley Forge on June 16, in a tone that suggests his attitude had warmed considerably in the past six months: "My time for joining you is near at hand and I had rather it shou'd be in Philad[elphi]a than York Town. I long to take you and Duer by the hand as also some other Worthies your associates and with sincere regard remain Dear Sir, Your most obedient, humble servant, Robt Morris." The standard of the day was a courtly one, but even so this is uncommonly friendly.

But Morris continued to have detractors in Congress. Josiah Bartlett (1729–1795), for example, wrote to the New Hampshire merchant and legislator William Whipple (1730–1785) that the delegate from New York, Gouverneur Morris, was "an eternal speaker," and others may have agreed.[51] Nevertheless, Rousseau's observation, that fluency of speech is often inability to hold the tongue, is not always correct.

Morris's foundational work on the committee setting up the Quartermaster's Department has not been recorded directly but can be judged by his correspondence with General Nathanael Greene, who seems often to have taken his advice.[52] During that same summer of 1778, Morris's warm friendship with Washington grew deeper. On August 2, he wrote the general from Philadelphia: "I was in your Debt. It is my Fate always to be so with my Friends. But believe me my Heart owes Nothing. Let me add that you can do me no Favor so great as to comply with your Wishes except an Opportunity to serve the Public which indeed is your highest Wish." Morris agreed with Washington in wishing to prevent seemingly undue promotions for foreign officers, such as Von Steuben: "The Baron has a claim . . . but . . ." He concluded this letter by observing: "You have Enemies on our side. It is happy for you that you have. A Man of Sentiment has not so much Honor as the Vulgar suppose in risquing Life and Fortune for the Service of his Country. He does not Value them as highly as the Vulgar do. Would he give the highest evidence let him sacrifice his Feelings. In the History of last Winter posterity will do you Justice."

Whatever Washington's enemies were saying, Morris had praise for him: "Let me however congratulate you on the Affair at Monmouth. On the *whole* Affair. It might have been better it is said. I think not for you have even from your Enemies the Honor of that Day."[53]

Around mid-June the main British forces in Philadelphia decided to return to New York by way of New Jersey. Within hours of the British army's departure from Philadelphia, American cavalry arrived in the city. Of course, units of the American army also followed the British force, led by General Sir Henry Clinton.

On June 26, the British reached Freehold, New Jersey, followed closely by Washington and a large cohort of American soldiers. On June 28, at Monmouth, Washington ordered Charles Lee to attack Clinton's rear, which guarded a seven-mile-long baggage train in a sunken road, in broiling heat. The attack seemed a good idea at the time, since the rear guard seemed near heat exhaustion. Moreover, the most aggressive British units were at the head of Clinton's column. In addition, with the baggage train in a sunken road, it and its security force were more vulnerable than usual.

Lee attacked but, after a little skirmishing, ordered a general retreat. When Washington arrived, he stemmed what had quickly become a rout, halted the advance of the British troops, and thereby prevented what could have become a large-scale slaughter of hundreds of Lee's troops. Because of his conduct during this battle, Morris's former ally, Charles Lee, was relieved of his command. He was subsequently court-martialed and suspended from command for one year. After he refused to accept his one-year suspension, he wrote an insolent letter to the Continental Congress, and he was removed from the army.

At first Clinton believed this could become the decisive battle his instructions from London (sent March 8) had called for, and were it not for Washington it might have become so. Colonel John Laurens wrote to his father, Henry, on June 30, describing "All [the] . . . disgraceful retreating, passed without the firing of a musket, over ground which might have been disputed inch by inch. . . . Fortunately for the honour of the army, and the welfare of America, Gen'l Washington met the troops retreating in disorder, and without any plan to make an opposition." By force of will he pushed them to make of a nearly full-scale rout an admirable defense—a major feat of leadership. In this "brillant though capricious and indecisive conflict on the plains of Monmouth," as William Gilmore Simms calls the encounter, Clinton suffered by far the worse casualties: 327 killed, 500 wounded, and 95 captured. The American forces lost 63 killed and 210 wounded. The supply train, however, continued unmolested.[54]

On several occasions during 1778, Gouverneur Morris's friends felt the need to warn him of whispering enemies. On July 4, 1778, John Jay evidently wrote him (the letter is lost) that according to rumor Morris had a hand in the till. (Indeed, many of his colleagues during the Revolutionary and early Federal periods were stealing; no evidence exists concerning Morris.) With fitting terseness, Gouverneur responded, "I have no apprehension that these Money Matters can affect *me*. I have not taken nor would I on any Consideration have taken the Agency of the Business." And he continues, "Your Caution however is useful and proper and I thank you for it. On no Occasion do I wish to give Room for the Exercise of Slanderous Tongues much less where money Matters are in Question for they are indeed delicate, very delicate."

Jay seems also to have told Morris he had a number of all-around enemies. The still only twenty-six-year-old Morris somewhat petulantly responds: "As to the Malevolence of Individuals It is what I have to Expect. It is by no means a Matter of Surprize that I should be hated by some Men but I will have my Revenge. By laboring in the public Service so as to gain the Applause of those whose Applause is worth gaining I will punish them severely."

A few months later, on October 21, Jay told Morris he was politically suspect, too: "Your enemies talk much of your Tory connections at Philadelphia. Take care. Some people of importance in your city apprehend ill consequences to yourself as well as the State from it, and wish you to be more circumspect." (Morris was always gracious in dealing with rumors and perceived slights. One unnamed Philadelphia eminence was peeved at being left off the committee arranging the banquet for the French emissary Gérard. Morris wrote to Jay: "he inquired of me in a Stile which really put it out of my Power to give him satisfactory Answers. It is a pity for his own Sake that he appeared to feel the Omission. . . .")[55]

Whether or not Morris was making financial use of his position, he may well have needed the money. In August 1778 he confided to Robert Livingston, "I think I cannot [afford to] much longer attend [Congress].

The depreciation here rapidly increasing hath arrived at such a pitch that I am confident my expenses are between fifteen and twenty dollars per day."[56] By point of comparison, a soldier named Charles Powell, in the First Artillery, made nine dollars a month in the summer of 1778. After a promotion to sergeant later that year, he pulled in ten dollars a month, with the pay coming as a mix of New York currency and English pounds. Late that same summer, Morris corresponded with George Washington about the chronic difficulty of recruiting soldiers, writing of the proposal in Congress to offer "ten Dollars in Specie and ten Square Dollars to Recruits."[57] Morris did not clearly register his reasons for opposition, but the shortage of funds must have been foremost in his mind: "I fear to inflame the Rapacity of Soldiers with the Love by the Possession of a Metal of which we have such a plentiful Lack."

At the same time, he was assigned to "prepare a Manifesto on the Cruelties of the British [to American prisoners]." The summer of 1778 in Philadelphia was steambath hot and humid, and one can imagine the stuffy indoor working conditions. Morris remarked in letters at the time to John Jay and Robert Livingston that his duties were so demanding that his only daily exercise was the fifty-yard walk each way from his apartment to the congressional meeting hall.

As summer turned to fall, Morris also began preparing the monograph based on his responses to the Carlisle Commission: "Observations on the American Revolution." Although commentators on the "Observations" have frequently implied that it simply reprints those responses as they had appeared in the *Pennsylvania Gazette,* this is not so.

After a brief preamble—"Great Britain claimed revenue and dominion. We refused the one, and disputed the other"[58]—comes an overview of recent colonial history and of the colonists' grievances against "the authors of this arbitrary [current governmental] arrangement," meaning, of course, England. The essential correspondence between the Carlisle Commission and the Congress appears along with a clever running commentary.

Morris's prose in the "Observations" is rather heated, even feverish:

> At length that God of battles in whom was our trust, hath conducted us through the paths of danger and distress to the threshold of security. It hath now become morally certain that, if we have courage to persevere, we shall establish our liberties and independence.— The haughty prince, who spurned us from his feet with contumely disdain,—and the parliament which proscribed us, now descend to offer terms of accommodation. Whilst in the full cares of victory, they pulled off the mask, and vowed their

intended despotism: But, having lavished in vain the blood and treasure of their subjects in pursuit of this execrable purpose, they now endeavor to ensnare us with the invidious offers of peace. They would seduce you into a dependence, which necessarily, inevitably leads to the most humiliating slavery.

Having elaborated on Britain's failures thus far, he exhorts his American readers: "Arise then! To your tents! And gird you for the battle! It is time to turn the headlong current of vengeance upon the head of the destroyer." Throughout, "Observations" is marked by what used to be called the *argumentum ad baculum*: the threat of force, used as a tool of debate. The sentences and paragraphs finish, whereas most writers' simply end.[59] His language "invests the subject with grandeur," as Longinus puts it.[60]

The portion of the "Manifesto" section that refutes British claims builds in intensity, as the orations of Socrates and Demosthenes sometimes do. Some of Morris's sentiments prefigure those given voice by Emma Lazarus. Victory, he says first, is in reach:

By such [military and economic] steps we shall frustrate the designs of our enemies, and hasten that moment when the United States of North America, rising from distress to glory, shall dispense to their citizens the blessings of that peace, liberty and safety for which we have virtuously and vigorously contended.

Then he goes on to articulate ideals that still endure:

The portals of the Temple we have raised to Freedom, shall then be thrown wide, as an Asylum to mankind. America shall receive to her bosom and comfort and cheer the oppressed, the miserable and the poor of every nation and of every clime. The enterprize of extending commerce shall wave her friendly flag over the billows of the remotest regions [of the world]. . . . We shall learn to consider all men as our brethren, being equally children of the Universal Parent—that God of the heavens and of the earth, whose infinite Majesty, for providential favour during the late revolution, almighty power in our preservation from impending ruin, and gracious mercy in our redemption from the iron shackles of despotism, we cannot cease with gratitude and with deep humility to praise, to reverence and adore.[61]

To skip ahead a bit, to 1780, the reprinting of "Observations" in London that year may have had some effect on British public opinion. Britain's campaign in America had not proven really successful so far. In the south-east, Cornwallis had achieved some tactical victories, but by the end of the year his forces had entrenched in a precarious position, their supply and communications routes threatened everywhere. Still, in many ways the American situation must have seemed even more dismal. Though it was only a year away from its final success, the Continental Army had not won a clear victory since Saratoga. The British held Georgia and the Carolinas, as well as much of Virginia. American currency, even with French and Spanish aid, continued to decline in value, and Congress proved unable to secure suffi-cient revenue from the states. Moreover, one of the Americans' four best generals, Benedict Arnold, had deserted to the British. With the Americans' prospects seemingly at their bleakest, the republication of Morris's "Obser-vations" in *The Remembrancer* may have come at a propitious time. Its pub-lisher, John Almon (1737–1805), was a Liverpudlian by birth. Because he had many friends in Parliament, as early as 1771 he was able to publish a brief report of each day's debates in his *London Evening Post*. In 1774 he began producing the first monthly record of the proceedings, *The Parliamentary Register*. Subsequently he burnished both his reputation and his finances with a still valuable account of the parliamentary debates from 1742 on.

Almon sympathized greatly with the American colonies—indeed, had aided them enough to have been penalized by British law. In the 1770s he was tried for libel more than once for selling a reprint of a "Junius" letter, one of a series of public letters containing personal and political invective written by a Whig known only by his pseudonym. A shrewd and successful businessman with a keen eye for the market of influential readers, Almon began publishing *The Remembrancer* in 1775, and by 1780 it had the kind of steady devoted readership that *The New York Times* has today. It is quite possible that reading "Observations" again in 1780 prompted many of those readers to support the American cause.[62] In the 1780s Almon was ac-cused of libeling King George and is thought to have fled to France, but eventually he surrendered to the British authorities and was imprisoned for two years.

September 1778 was another typical month for Morris in the Congress. On September 9 he was chosen as one of four members of a committee on the treasury. Five days later he and four other members were chosen "to pre-pare a letter of credence to his most Christian majesty, notifying [him of] the appointment of Dr. [Benjamin] Franklin as minister plenipotentiary of these States at the court of France." On September 17, he, Robert Morris, John Witherspoon, Samuel Chase, and Richard Henry Lee were asked to make a preliminary criminal investigation and prepare a report for the Board of War concerning $1 million that had been advanced to General Mifflin, the quartermaster general. And on September 26, Gouverneur Morris and two other members were assigned to come up with seals for the treasury and the navy.[63] His service on the Medical Committee involved, for example, drafting orders to the Continental Army doctor Jonathan Potts to move certain "medicines and stores" from the Middle Department to the Eastern Department, as well as writing, on Congress's behalf, to numerous correspondents, among them George Clinton and Robert Livingston. Morris wrote to Clinton about some cannon that had arrived in North Carolina from Spain. Congress needed to decide whether to move them to protect Philadelphia or to sell them to a southern state; these cannon were eventually sold to Virginia and North Carolina. Morris also rallied Clinton's support for the Congress's solution to the "rapid Depreciation of the Continental money." "Taxation," he wrote, "is the only Remedy." Morris's communication with Livingston was of a more personal nature; he reported to Chancellor Livingston on the social standing and nature of a Dr. Thomas Tillotson, who was to marry Livingston's sister the next year.[64] Just as they do today, members of Congress had constituent requests to deal with, as well. For instance, a New Yorker named Abby Hamilton asked Morris to help her two elderly parents.[65]

Morris was just twenty-six in 1778, but his letters evince a maturity well beyond his years. In September he wrote to a former King's College classmate, Peter Van Schaack, "that matters of conscience and faith, whether political or religious . . . are beyond the ken of human legislatures. In the question of punishment for acts, it hath been my constant axiom, that the object is [to provide an] example." Van Schaack (1747–1832), a lawyer from New York, had landed in political trouble over a matter of conscience. He had been exiled to England for seven years after refusing on conscientious principles to swear allegiance to the New York State government. Morris recognized that, as he had written to Clinton, "it is not good Policy to banish useful Citizens," and vowed to Van Schaack to "continue in public life till the establishment of the liberties of America."[66]

As mentioned above, in May, Morris was chosen, along with Richard Henry Lee and Roger Sherman, to help draft Congress's instructions to the American peace commissioners. In mid-September he chaired a committee to prepare a draft of instructions to Benjamin Franklin, then America's minister plenipotentiary at Versailles. The draft Morris produced was mostly approved by Congress on October 22. (Only his proposed last article was rejected.)

On October 26 the "Draught of Instructions" was mailed under Henry Laurens's signature, along with a plan, also drafted by Morris, for a joint attack on Quebec and an important essay, this too by Morris, "Observations on the Finances of America" (of the latter, more later). The instructions and the attack plan proved controversial.[67]

In performing his public duties, Morris generally manifested the quality Henry James called artistic "insistence"; that is, "the act of throwing the whole weight of the mind, and of gathering it at the particular point . . . in order to do so."[68] On his own initiative, for instance, Morris arranged to consult with the newly arrived French minister before he drafted the documents by which the Congress addressed France.

A draft dated October 21, 1778, of Franklin's letter of credence exists in Morris's hand. It is much in his style of long sentences and elevated diction; the tone is perhaps best characterized as lofty: "Great faithful and well beloved Friend and Ally," it calls Louis, and, after a statement concerning the "Principles of Equality and Reciprocity on which you have entered into Treaties with us," it states, "We have nominated Benjamin Franklin esqr [Esquire] to reside at your Court in Quality of our Minister Plenipotentiary that he may give you more particular Assurances which you have excited in us and in each of the united States."

Like many of the products of Gouverneur's pen, the instructions to Franklin include an inspiring preamble and an earnestly devout closing salutation. The preamble begins, "We the Congress of the United States of North America, having thought it proper to appoint you their Minister . . . , you shall in all things according to the best of your knowledge and Abilities promote the Interest and honor of the said States at the Court." Even here Morris's intensive study of the classics is evident. For example, his Virgilian version combines an elevation of tone with Tacitean economy.

The first article emphasizes the need for Franklin to express appropriate gratitude for his "most Christian Majesty['s] . . . Exertions in . . . [our] favor." The "speedy Aid" provided by the French is "a Testimony of . . . fidelity" and "an earnest of that Protection." (Congress had rejected "further assistance," perhaps Morris's phrase, in favor of "Protection.")

The second and third items press Franklin promptly to assure the king and his cabinet "that neither the Congress nor any of the States they represent have . . . swerved from their Determination to be Independent," a sage inclusion, which is a kind of preemptive reassurance of the colonies' determination. Item four urges the expungement of Articles 11 and 12 of the treaty of commerce, a stroke soon made also by France.[69]

The fifth item, drafted by William Duer, concerns the exchange of prisoners held aboard ships of the major combatants. Congress first approved this proposal, then rejected it, and then reapproved it, although Duer drafted the article so badly as to confuse any otherwise uninstructed minister.[70] Article 6, by Morris again, attempts to drive home the advantages to the French of the prisoner exchange. The seventh article urges Franklin "to suggest the fatal consequences which would follow to the Commerce of the Common Enemy" if the French fleet were to attack English shipping in a concentrated way. Next the instructions emphasize the stated importance of "reducing Halifax and Quebec." Article 9 is rather desperate: "you are to lay before the Court, the deranged state of our finances and show the necessity of placing them on a more respectable footing." Ten, Franklin is to do everything possible "to promote a perfect harmony" with the French; eleven, he is "not to make any Engagements or stipulations on the part of America" without the consent of Congress. This last constitutes a serious stricture, since communications then took on average eight weeks to cross the Atlantic, when they arrived at all. While his negotiating powers were somewhat limited, Franklin received the news of his appointment as minister plenipotentiary with some relief, dismissing his colleagues Arthur Lee and John Adams, who considered Franklin corrupt and untidy, respectively. As sole American representative, Franklin met with various French ministers, attended court, oversaw purchases and shipping, and carried out endless other mundane duties, having no one to assign duties to.

The congressional packet also included the elaborate "Plan of Attack" on Canada, outlining five major steps, four advantages to France, and six advantages to America, among them the devastation of Britain's Newfoundland fisheries and the "accession of two states to the union." Franklin was instructed to expound on the beneficial consequences "if, by confining the war to the European and Asiatic seas, the coasts of America could be so freed from the British fleet as to furnish a safe asylum to the frigates and privateers of the allied nations and their prizes." The editors of the Franklin Papers have seen in this plan similarities to a strategic proposal outlined by the Marquis de Lafayette (1757–1834) for all of North America. Lafayette may have had some influence in the general conception, since at this time he and Morris were still on mutually respectful terms. But it greatly resembles, in style and conception, the plan Morris suggested to George Clinton for recapturing New York; its military overambitiousness and its elegant literary style, too, are pure Morris. The plan detailed that men were to be stationed along the Mohawk River, where they would build vessels for navigating Lake Ontario in the spring. Other troops were to collect warriors from "friendly Tribes" and, while marching to Niagara, "destroy the Seneka and other townships of Indians who are inimical." The largest body, of 5,000 troops, would penetrate Canada by way of the St. Francis River and "turn their attention immediately to the reduction of Montreal, St. Johns and the North end of the Lake Champlain." The ultimate end of the campaign was to be the "reduction" of the cities of Quebec and Halifax, disrupting the British fisheries and fur trade.

Washington opposed the Canada plan and was appalled that it had even been communicated officially.[71] One invasion had failed and plans for a second had already been scrapped. Congress, owing to Washington's apprehensions, countermanded the attack, but not before Franklin had gone beyond even these instructions in imprudently asking for French assistance in an attack on Rhode Island, a fact that he avoided mentioning in his report to Congress.

One of the felicities of studying the life of an historical personage two centuries after the event is that, with the opening of formerly secret archives, we can observe both sides of the shield, and thus understand the embroidery better, because we can see the unfaded colors on the other side. For example, Morris had reviewed the Canada plan, in rough draft, with Gérard. The latter's memoranda are now available; they allow us to see that the French minister had serious reservations about the scheme. We also know now that Vergennes had instructed Gérard to notify Congress that France would resist any move toward territorial aggrandizement in pursuit of final war aims. Vergennes naturally requested ("je demande") that the United States also explicitly abjure territorial conquest; in his opinion, the two nations could not soon be in a position to dictate terms that would expand the possessions of either.[72] For this reason, Gérard had argued against the plan's transmittal.

The instructions to Franklin had also proposed to beat the British vigorously out of American seaports, and simultaneously to establish a reputable American navy. Gérard stubbornly opposed this item; he believed it impractical to do both at once, besides which a British navy driven out of America might focus on European shores, to the detriment of French interests.[73]

In fact, Morris had deleted the navy article from his draft after conferring with Gérard in Philadelphia, and here is illuminated an important conflict between American revolutionary ambitions and French diplomacy. Vergennes and Gérard wanted the United States to agree, at an eventual peace settlement, to a territory coterminous with the British mainland colonies, as constituted at the outset of the American Revolution. Gérard presented this view to Morris in October 1778. Morris, perhaps imprudently, assured him that Congress would agree, and Gérard accepted this. But in February 1779, at the insistence of Vergennes, Gérard broached the matter with Congress directly, only to find that Morris had been wrong.[74]

One complication was that the western boundaries of some of the states were vague. By 1779, American settlers were moving across the Appalachians and toward the Mississippi. In doing so, they carried an at least wished-for American sovereignty with them. In addition, as a correlate of this settlement, the United States wanted the right to navigate freely on the Mississippi. Only, many Americans felt, if the river were recognized as part of the United States could a clear claim to the right of navigation be justified. Congress furthermore coveted the Floridas, and had approved plans to conquer Canada, which it soon hoped to bring under American control. (All this, at a time when Philadelphia was the only important seaboard city firmly under French-American control.)

What most alarmed the French was the push to the Mississippi, and the lust for the Floridas, both of which threatened to bring on nettlesome conflicts with Spain. That country still held title to the land west of the Mississippi, and laid claim to the territories between it and the Appalachians. Spain also zealously wished to retain the Floridas. France was thus in a complex position: her two closest allies had large and conflicting ambitions.[75]

Gérard shrewdly chose Gouverneur Morris as his audience for the Spanish point of view. Not only was Morris already, of course, a Francophile, but also he represented New York, a state without large interests in the western lands or the Floridas. Gérard urged on him the necessity of Congress's reassuring Spain by guaranteeing to it St. Augustine, Pensacola, and Mobile, as well as exclusive rights to Mississippi navigation. Morris promptly replied that he entirely appreciated the need to set limits to the Southern states, because the virtues necessary to the development of a republic were to be found and nurtured only in a hardy climate. Also, he said, Spain's control over the Mississippi from north of the Ohio to the Gulf would benefit the United States, by helping to keep the American population between the Ohio, the St. Lawrence, and the Mississippi dependent on the United States of the original colonies. But powerful American interests desired to make the Mississippi American. Armed with this friendly warning, Gérard began, in late December 1778, a diplomatic campaign in support of Spain's retention of the large waterway.[76] Meanwhile he and Morris continued to meet, for the last time on February 15, 1779.

In that month, thanks in no small part to the French, work on a Spanish-American treaty against Britain was completed. The result was not entirely what Vergennes and Gérard would have wished. The United States refused to limit itself to the territory it largely controlled at the outset of the war with Britain, and it insisted on the right to free navigation of the Mississippi. In other important respects, however, the treaty conformed to the general suggestions Gérard had made to Morris. Congress had agreed to Spanish control of the Floridas, but the United States had won freedom to navigate on the Mississippi.

According to Gérard's dispatches, his meetings with Morris were the most important congressional contacts he had on the key issues related to the enlistment of Spain in the alliance with France. Morris's work was both positive and significant, for the importance to America, especially with respect to sea power, of Spain's 1779 entry into the war against Britain should not be understated. In that year, the combined French and Spanish fleets comprised more than 120 vessels. The two navies dispatched squadrons to attack British forces in the Mediterranean; the threat of attack there and elsewhere put an end to Britain's ability to move troops at will. The British now had to guard their own shores (in July 1779 the French and Spanish planned to attack, but abandoned these plans in August) and step up patrols to protect their colonies in the Mediterranean, India, Africa, and Florida. France and Spain ultimately directed their main efforts at the British West Indies, thereby draining British resources from mainland America. With the Royal Navy stretched thin, British shipping was laid open to increased attacks by American privateers. As early as April 24, 1778, however, *The Ranger,* captained by John Paul Jones, entered Belfast Lough, flying the Independent Colonial American battle flag. There Jones and his crew engaged *The Drake,* a British warship. In the one-half hour engagement, Jones's eighteen 24-pound cannon inflicted heavy damage on *The Drake.* This early raid by Jones startled the British navy and signaled the first of many such surprise attacks.

Perhaps as important as the instructions to Franklin is the detailed "Observations on the Finances of North America." After drafting this document, Morris had shown it to Gérard, who passed on the information to Versailles, describing his meeting with "Moris" and offering a sometimes pungent commentary: "Congress's confession concerning its finances will probably be woeful" ("la confession du Congrès relativement à ses finances sera probablement douloureuse"). This document is almost exclusively, as we have seen, in Morris's hand, but is presented under the French representative's headings. Gérard's rhetorical methods and literary style resemble Morris's.[77]

Until the summer of 1778, Morris's work on behalf of the Revolution, from his brilliant late spring 1776 speech in New York advocating independence through his service in the Continental Congress, addressed mainly domestic matters—army provisioning and internal governmental functioning, for example. But he was almost equally vigilant in foreign policy matters, familiarizing himself with the issues and working hard whenever called upon. Perhaps it was in recognition of his diligence that he was appointed, in February 1779, to head the five-man committee established to consider important dispatches from the American commissioners abroad as well as communications from the French minister in the United States. The committee's report may have been the most important to issue from the American side during the war: it served as the basis of the peace, four years later, because it covered all the points deemed essential or useful in any eventual treaty with Britain. The report considered among other matters the new nation's boundaries, evacuation of British military posts within U.S. territories, fishing rights, and navigation on the Mississippi.

These subjects Morris's draft (or "draught" in eighteenth-century spelling) presents clearly under distinct headings, in a form suitable for examination and discussion in Congress's closed sessions in Philadelphia. Congress debated the report on and off for roughly six months. The delegates focused on the principles considered fundamental, leaving due latitude for the discretion of the negotiators. The papers, letters, and diaries of the participants reveal that Morris contributed to the debate in important ways. The resulting instructions to those future peace negotiators—who had not yet been chosen—were drafted by Morris. Congress adopted them unanimously, and on August 14, 1779, John Jay, who was now the president of Congress, sent them to Franklin.[78]

The "Instructions for a Treaty of Peace with Great Britain" announce that "the great object of the present defensive war on the part of the allies is to establish the independence of the United States." Accordingly, "a preliminary article to any negotiation [must be] that Great Britain shall agree to treat with the United States as sovereign and independent," governmentally and commercially. Six nonnegotiable stipulations follow: minimum geographical boundaries; evacuation by the British armed forces; fishing rights off New-foundland; rights to navigate the Mississippi to the U.S. southern boundary; free commerce with a port or ports below that boundary, and the cession of Nova Scotia, would the allies support this issue. The committee Gouverneur chaired also presented six conditional stipulations which might be used as bargaining points.[79]

In the six months of debate over the negotiating instructions, the fisheries off Canada had been an inexhaustible topic. On June 19, 1779, Congress-man John Fell wrote in his private diary that the Commercial Committee had discussed a memorandum from "Mr. Girrard"—Gérard, of course: "af-ter some debate ... the Eastern Members made a new motion about the Fishery, to which amendments were Propos'd and long and Idle debates en-sued according to custom, whenever the fishery is the subject." On July 22, Morris wrote to Robert R. Livingston, "The enclosed papers will shew you that the Fisheries are a daily subject of contemplation. . . ."[80]

If the question of the Canadian fisheries was inexhaustible, that had some-thing to do with its complexity. Sometime around March 22, Gouverneur Morris moved that Congress require Britain to pay "express regard" to the United States' "Exercise of the said Right" to "take Fish upon the ... Banks of North America." The motion essentially called on Great Britain to state an explicit policy of noninterference with American fishing vessels in Canadian waters. Henry Laurens offered a more logically presented and mildly worded amendment. But in the same July 22 letter to Robert Livingston quoted above, Morris wrote that the United States' insistence on a British "acknowl-edgment of [a] common right [with the United States] to fish" in North American waters indicates "much weakness" in American diplomatic think-ing and argumentation. In something like four months, then, Morris's posi-tion on the fisheries seemingly moved almost 180 degrees around.

Does this movement represent a nearly complete change of outlook? Prob-ably not. The Newfoundland fishing rights, so important to the United States and especially New England, came up over and over from 1779 to 1783 in de-bates, discussions, and memoranda about the terms of the future peace treaty.[81] Ideally, Morris (like, probably, nearly all his fellow citizens) would have wanted Americans to have unrestricted rights to fish in any waters. As the primary congressional liaison with Gérard and Vergennes, however, he was very well aware of how important the fisheries were to the French. The fish-eries off Canada were just as important to the British maritime trade and the dispute over fishing rights in a potential treaty was likely to prolong the war.

One of the primary French concerns, in addition to weakening the British hold on the New World, was to contain the territorial expansion of the

United States and limit their aim to achieving independence. Morris was amenable to keeping the United States compact, concerned as he was that expansion would jeopardize continued national unification.

On May 8, 1779, after a long, discursive preamble emphasizing the obligations of the United States to France, Morris moved to eliminate from the treaty terms all references to fishing rights as necessary either for a commercial treaty or a peace treaty with Britain. He must have known no such motion would pass; it may have been meant to placate Gérard. In a May 21 communiqué to Vergennes, the French minister wrote that he had persuaded Morris to present to Congress this resolution: should the war be sustained on the question of the fisheries alone, then if the overall issue be determined successfully, the fisheries would be divided equally among France, Spain, and the United States, and Britain entirely excluded from the relevant fisheries. (Gérard adverted to this question again in a memorandum to Vergennes of August 8, 1779.)

"La grande question relativement aux Pêcheries a été reprise," as Gérard put it in his May 16 letter to Vergennes. The great question never came to a vote, however, since Morris's motion was declared out of order. This was no doubt exactly what he had wanted. His twin concerns likely were these: first, the rapid French offer to back America up and sustain the war, if necessary, over the fisheries issue would set a malign precedent of undue American deference to France; second, if Congress formally insisted on U.S. fishing rights, as France wished, it would have to share those rights equally with France and Spain once a peace was signed. So Morris almost certainly believed that the French guarantee ought to be left out of the peace negotiations entirely. Following this path would enable America to avoid any explicit diplomatic commitment to sharing the Canadian fisheries with the French and Spanish and would signal that America was not to become a dependency of France.[82]

From October 1778 through August 1779, Morris served on *nineteen* congressional committees dealing directly with the details of the French alliance. Throughout, he was concerned to strike the right chord: to express proper respect for France while avoiding any hint of obsequiousness and preserving all the material gain diplomatically possible. This was wise statesmanship, and it probably encouraged France to provide more help to America. And—however selfish its motives—France provided ten million livres in gifts and loans to America from 1778 through the British capitulation. France also guaranteed a Dutch loan of the same amount, and permitted the American envoys in Paris to draw upon the money immediately. French aid increased every year of the war; in the crucial year 1781, the

French gave more than their previous gifts and loans combined. What was of equal importance, Vergennes assured American commanders that a fleet, led by Admiral François de Grasse, would sail for the West Indies that spring and be available for action on the American coast in early autumn: a strategically vital guarantee. The French also demonstrated remarkable fidelity. On several occasions during the war, emissaries from the British court made secret overtures for a separate treaty; Vergennes steadfastly insisted that American independence be recognized as a prerequisite. And, when Russia and Austria proposed to mediate between Britain and France, Vergennes accepted the offer but stipulated that American commissioners take part in the negotiations as the ministers of an independent power. He responded similarly to a negotiation proposal from Spain. And, in a secret convention with Spain, dated April 12, 1779—shortly before that country declared war on Britain—France insisted on a promise that Spain would not oppose American independence.[83]

In Europe, Benjamin Franklin worked to sustain the image of a strong nation that deserved to be met on terms of equality, and his ambassadorial presence elicited sympathy for the American cause. In America, at much the same time, Gouverneur Morris was doing much the same, primarily through his relationship with Gérard.[84]

In a somewhat less fruitful vein, Morris became involved in a political controversy involving Silas Deane, Arthur Lee, and Thomas Paine. Its outlines appear in contemporary essays; the parties' correspondence is less informative. As we know, in 1776 Congress sent Silas Deane to Paris to negotiate aid from France with the planted agent, Beaumarchais. Arthur Lee suspected the two of diverting to themselves funds meant for the American colonies, and his accusations induced Congress to recall Deane in July 1778, to have him give "a general account of his whole transactions" abroad. In a letter to the *Pennsylvania Packet,* December 5, 1778, Deane went public, castigating Lee for making accusations against him and accusing the Continental Congress of negligence in foreign affairs.

The subsequent turmoil led directly to Henry Laurens's resignation from Congress on December 9. Laurens, who had been inclined to believe Lee, was replaced the next morning by Gouverneur Morris's longtime friend John Jay. Along with Governor George Clinton of New York, Gouverneur Morris, and others, Jay tended to take Deane's side.

Deane's major antagonist in America was Thomas Paine. Using the title of his 1776 pamphlet "Common Sense" as a nom de plume, he wrote a passionate defense of Lee that was first published in the *Pennsylvania Packet* on December 15 and 29, 1778, and reprinted on December 2, 5, and 7, 1779.

Paine asserted that official papers in his possession made it clear that the money and supplies from Beaumarchais constituted a no-strings-attached gift from France to America. By making a public statement about governmental dealings meant to remain clandestine, Paine offended many congressmen who up to that point had been neutral.

The question of whether the money from Beaumarchais was a loan or a gift remains unclear, as does the question of their guilt. Beaumarchais and Deane were certainly taking commissions on the contributions, but such practice was then commonplace for the professional politician. The major issue for Congress ultimately became Paine's spilling of official secrets that he had access to as secretary to the Committee on Foreign Affairs. Not surprisingly, Gérard called for Congress to repudiate Paine's remarks. On January 7, 1779, when Congress considered the issue, Morris moved to have Paine dismissed from his position as secretary to the committee on the grounds that he had betrayed his trust by publishing information that ought to have remained secret.[85] Paine had reportedly gone so far as to invite any visitor to his office to look through the verifying documents of the king's gift. The affront to the French and dishonor to the king lay in this brazen disclosure of French secrets. At this time, both France and the thirteen colonies had agreed to try to conceal from the French people and the British enemy the extent of France's monetary assistance to the Americans. Domestically, the policy of secrecy made good sense for the French: as our story indicates in the chapter on Morris in Europe, France's generosity with America became a major factor in the economic downturn in France that led to revolution there. As regards foreign policy, often it is best conducted among allies when the rest of the world is kept in the dark as to how much funding is flowing from ally to ally, and for what purposes. In addition, how much financial help and logistical support France was then providing the American colonies was intelligence information the British spies would have paid a lot for, if they had been able to obtain it clandestinely.

Morris demanded Paine's dismissal without a formal hearing. In his view, the truth of the Beaumarchais-Deane agency was irrelevant; what mattered was that Paine had betrayed his public trust. Morris's speech begins with a word of disdain for the introduction, in the previous debates on the Paine-Deane question, of the factious "word *party*." He goes on to assert that "Gentlemen mean nothing but the public good, though sometimes they mistake their object." Morris proceeds to question the terms of Paine's tenure:

[H]e does not hold his office during good behavior; it is during pleasure. And what are we [meaning Congress]? The sovereign power, who appointed,

and who, when he no longer pleases us, may remove him. Nothing more is
desired. We do not wish to punish him.

What then do we ask? To turn a man out of office, who ought never to
have been in it.

Morris goes on to emphasize that Paine, as "Secretary to the Committee
of Foreign Affairs, styling himself *Secretary of Foreign Affairs,*" acknowledged having written a publication "highly dishonorable to his most Christian Majesty, and very injurious to him and to us." (In good lawyer-like
fashion Morris does not simply make this assertion and then move on, but
rather examines its consequences and "emanations" at length.)

Morris furthermore sensibly points out what surely was true: "Foreigners,
Sir, have not an adequate idea of the manner, in which business is conducted in this House." Not content with this angle of attack, Morris attacked Paine's social background:

[O]ur Secretary of Foreign Affairs . . . was a mere Adventurer *from England,* without fortune, without family or connexions, ignorant even of
grammar[.] Could he [a hypothetical "gentleman" in Europe] believe this?
And if assured of the fact, and if possessed of common sense, would he not
think that we were devoid of it? And yet, Sir, this is the man, who has been
just now puffed as of great importance.

Considering the case as it stands before us, there are three objects which
require our attention. The first is, to obviate the ill effects of his publication. The second, to remove him from office. And the third, to assign
proper reasons for that conduct, so as to connect the two first propositions
together, and give a greater weight to all our measures.

Morris goes on to argue that "in order to obviate the ill consequences of
[Paine's] mad assertions, we must pointedly contradict him." And, he asserts, "in the first place, [Paine] never was fit for [office]; and, in the second
place, he has abused it in the instance before us most flagrantly, and therefore is utterly undeserving of any farther confidence.

"Lastly, we must remove him, for without this, in contradicting him, we
shall not be believed." For if Paine kept his post, "the presumption is, that
he would not have written these things without our consent."[86]

It is not clear why Morris said Paine "styl[ed] himself *Secretary of Foreign
Affairs*"; Paine was secretary to the Congress's committee on foreign affairs,
and he signed his *Pennsylvania Packet* essays either "Common Sense" or
"Thomas Paine." However skillful Morris's arguments were technically, he

surely went too far in calling Paine unqualified for his post, and the ad hominem attack on Paine's social class and origins probably struck many of his fellow congressmen as a low blow. Perhaps partly for this reason, several motions for Paine's dismissal were defeated. He did resign on January 9, 1779, probably because he realized that his eventual dismissal was likely and his ability to fulfill the position compromised by the enemies he had made.

Nevertheless, Morris's speech had some of its intended effect: after it, seven states voted against giving Paine a hearing, four voted for; one delegation split, and one state was absent.

And what of the underlying charges against Deane? The evidence available at the time was inconclusive. Deane's instructions from Congress allowed him to take a commission on certain purchases from Beaumarchais; his claims for such commissions remained unpaid throughout his lifetime. Deane did not earn a salary, and the nature of the commissions is rather murky. Officials involved in procuring military supplies invariably extracted commissions, which were often indistinguishable from graft. Deane acted as both a buyer and a salesman; he was authorized to purchase and ship American goods and sell them upon return to the colonies.[87] In engaging French officers to fight on the American side, Deane was also charged with exceeding his mandate, and he probably did—but he secured the services of such officers as Lafayette and the Baron de Kalb. As one result of the controversy over Deane, on January 20, 1779, a committee of congressional representatives, one from each state, began a three-month investigation of the overseas agents' activities. The report on these inquiries solemnly announced "that the appointments of the said Commissioners be vacated, and that new appointments be made."

Deane, having thus lost his post, returned to France after the inquiry as a private citizen. Here he wrote a series of letters addressed to his brother, Simeon, but evidently intended to exculpate him before the public; in 1782, they were printed in *Rivington's New York Loyal Gazette*. In these letters Deane urged also that America surrender to Britain. He then shipped over to England, where he befriended the already notorious Benedict Arnold. He died there, impoverished, in 1789, almost as the U.S. Constitution was being ratified.

In the late nineteenth century, Congress paid Deane's heirs the then enormous sum of $35,000 to reimburse his wartime expenses. That Deane had almost certainly committed treason no one then could have known for sure. It is clear he did, however, as George III's correspondence with Lord North all but absolutely confirms.[88] While working for Congress, Deane apparently passed secrets to Edmund Bancroft, a double agent.

Governeur Morris's attitude toward the several pacifist religious sects in the Middle Atlantic region, in Pennsylvania especially, was characteristically complex. "The madheaded Governor of Pennsylvania" had been so harassing the Quakers "that they have serious thoughts of shifting their quarters," Morris wrote Robert Livingston in early January of 1778. The religious beliefs of the Quakers were of no moment to him or Livingston, since they conjointly "consider mankind from their relation to us by the same common Parent and not from the similitude of their ecclesiastical tenets." Even though "by an act of Parliament sometime in the year 1748 they are averse to taking arms . . . , they are Whigs in principle I believe. Could we [in New York] obtain these men [with all their human and material advantages] . . . at the trifling expense of an act of legislature I think we should make a good purchase." Yet he was impatient with pacifism. In February 1779, *The Pennsylvania Packet* published a letter he addressed "to the Quakers, Benthamites, Moderate Men, Refugees and other Tories whatsoever, and wheresoever, dispersed." The salutation read "Peace," but the thrust of the long essay that followed was to enjoin all those addressed to take up arms against Britain. "It is the will of Heaven," Morris argues, that "mankind should be free," but

> the idea that providence will establish such governments as he shall deem most fit for his creatures without their efforts is palpably absurd. Did he overturn the walls of Jerusalem by the mere breath of his mouth, or did he stir up the Romans to add Judea to their other provinces? In short, is not his moral government of the earth always performed by the intervention of second causes? How then can you expect that he should *miraculously* destroy our enemies, merely to convince you that he favors our cause? . . . Many of our measures which you perhaps justly considered as unwise, have by an amazing coincidence of circumstances become the corner-stones of independence.[89]

Of this letter, Morris observed to Joseph Reed that his intention "was to prevent our Friends from being alarmed and our Enemies encouraged by Appearances of Disunion."[90] In a letter dated April 26, 1779, Morris urged Washington to "accomplish New York"—that is, to attack and occupy the city—and he rejoiced that the British were campaigning in the south:

> When the Enemy went to the S[outhern] States I considered it as a Kind of Madness and I think they will feel the Consequences but certainly it cannot be worth while to loose a Moment unnecessarily in that Quarter for the

Climate will fight for us during the Summer and what shall remain may be compleated in the Autumn if the other Objects succeed.[91]

On May 8, Washington wrote Morris from army headquarters in Middle Brook, Virginia, explaining why "the relief of the S[outhern] S[tates] appears . . . an object of the greatest magnitude and . . . may lead to still more important advantages."[92] In the short run, the strategy did not work. In late May 1779, the British forces under Banastre Tarleton slaughtered numerous Continental soldiers in Waxhaws, North Carolina. On June 20, 1779, the British repulsed General Benjamin Lincoln's forces at Stono Ferry, South Carolina. And in the fall, the Americans tried and failed to retake Savannah, Georgia. In May 1780 General Lincoln's forces surrendered at Charleston, South Carolina, an abysmal defeat that cost the United States thousands of killed and captured Continental soldiers. And on August 16, 1780, at Camden, South Carolina, General Gates suffered a loss in the face of a superior division, commanded by Cornwallis. But these grave losses may have been counterbalanced by the brilliant successes of Generals Greene, Morgan, and Lee in North Carolina. And in each encounter, though the British had won they had also bled a bit more. Washington's army remained in the field, and Cornwallis's success in South Carolina may have made him overconfident, with costly results at Yorktown.

On the purely naval front, in 1779 the most spectacular victory was John Paul Jones's September 23 contest with the British frigate *Serapis,* then guarding a Baltic merchant fleet off Flamborough Head, Yorkshire. After Jones's creaking *Bonhomme Richard* defeated *Serapis,* the Americans sailed with their bounteous prizes to a Dutch port. When the Dutch refused to surrender the Americans to the pursuing British, the British government renounced all Anglo-Dutch treaties—an important additional step toward setting Britain in opposition to all too many continental European nations.

On June 5, 1780, General Clinton sailed for New York, leaving Cornwallis in command of southern operations. Whether or not Clinton, too, would have been defeated by the timely Franco-American combination in Virginia in October 1781, the result under Cornwallis is written in stone.

Some scholars have stated or implied that Gouverneur Morris's congressional involvement in the matter of Vermont was the main reason for his failure to be reelected in the fall of 1779.[93] I am not so sure, since the record indicates he developed a pro–New York stance.

The issue of Vermont's claim to territorial sovereignty occupied Morris over a long period. The dispute between New York and Vermont arose in the mid-eighteenth century because the British had never clearly defined New York's boundaries, so that both New York and New Hampshire claimed the region that is now Vermont. New York's governor, George Clinton, objected to land grants made in the late 1750s in the area by New Hampshire's royal governor, Benning Wentworth. In 1764, British authorities decided in favor of New York, and the New Hampshire land grants were rescinded, but the landholders resisted, often by force. At the outbreak of the Revolution the dispute faded into the background; in 1777, Vermont proclaimed its independence from both New York and New Hampshire.

After declaring itself an independent state in January 1777, Vermont applied to the Continental Congress for admission as the fourteenth colony and drew up a constitution in July, notable for allowing universal male suffrage. Given their state's interest in the territory, the New Yorkers in Congress, including Morris and John Jay, initially opposed acceptance of the application. Morris wrote to New York's Governor Clinton that he found "clearly from the best authority that without nice management we shall certainly loose [*sic*] the State of Vermont." He almost immediately continued, "What are their claims? Occupancy settlement cultivation and the Book of Genesis? What their plea? Their mountains their arms their courage their alliances. Against all these what can we [meaning, I believe, New York State specifically] produce?" In June 1778, Morris wrote to Clinton that he had been studying the congressional "Report on the Vermont business," and somewhat dubiously stated he "shall take the earliest opportunity to bring this business on and to procure such amendments as the nature of the Case requires." Congress, however, was understandably hesitant to force a settlement. On August 17, 1778, he wrote to Robert R. Livingston that "the Vermont Business doth indeed press and daily with additional Weight. Let our Situation be considered. The Attention of the Members of Congress to this Affair must be intreated not forced," for they had so much other more pressing business.

And yet at the end of May 1779, Morris was able to tell the governor that, as regards "our Vermont Business[,] . . . I hope we shall be able to render our State a good Account of that Business." Although nothing had yet been concluded, on Tuesday next "we are to take it up" again "in a Committee of the whole," and "I hope it will during the Course of the week be concluded to our Satisfaction." Thomas Burke of North Carolina, seconded by Morris, moved that Congress agree "that none of the said states ought to be, or shall be, divested of any lands or territories over which they respectively exercised jurisdiction . . . unless by judgment of Congress." Morris worked with Governor Clinton and other members of Congress to press New York's claims on Vermont, but Clinton believed rhetorical persuasion far superior to an armed conflict with the Vermonters. Once the Revolution was won, Vermont became in effect a sovereign nation, but the complicated question continued to boil until 1791, when Vermont finally became one of the United States.[94]

Writing to Governor Clinton on August 17, 1779, John Jay praised the conduct of the New York delegates, Gouverneur Morris, James Duane, and William Floyd; however, he hinted that there were attempts by other congressmen to damage their reputations. This was correct, especially as regards Morris. When the New York legislative body drew up its slate of delegates, elected October 1, 1779, Morris's name was not on it. In an October 5 letter to Jay, Clinton offered the opaque answer that "the Impudence of some of Morris' friends in voting, occasioned the loss of his Election."[95]

Yet in October, John Jay wrote Governor Clinton that "Morris is again with us, and I am glad of it. His Constituents must be either infatuated or wretchedly misinformed if they omit continuing him in the Delegation." Morris had in fact returned to Congress October 6, and was promptly appointed to a committee that was working on the issue of how much money each state should pay into the Continental Congress treasury.[96]

Morris's presence in Congress probably depended on the slowness of the mails, but the election of October 1 really was a complicated matter. The New York constitution of 1777 provided that delegates be elected yearly. The state House of Assembly had given Morris the same number of votes as Ezra L'Hommedieu, a rich farmer from Southold. Morris then lost by two votes in the run-off, which was decided by the assembly and the senate. Morris was again put in nomination to succeed Jay, but Schuyler was chosen instead.[97] Morris seems to have stopped attending sessions of Congress about November 19 (no votes are recorded for the sessions of November 20 through 22, 1779). Nevertheless, as late as November 17 he was appointed to a committee, and on November 27 two committee reports he had drafted were presented in Congress even though their author was gone.[98]

A graduate of Yale and also a lawyer, Ezra L'Hommedieu (1734–1811) was the brother-in-law of Morris's congressional colleague William Floyd. Like many of the distinguished American founders, he served nearly continually in public office from his first election to a New York office, in 1775, until his death, in Southold, thirty-six years later. When he died, he had held the post of Suffolk County clerk continuously for his last twenty-seven years. In

Congress he proved a solid but by no means spectacular replacement for Morris.

"Popularity is a crime from the moment it is sought," said the British statesman Lord Halifax. The extant correspondence—not to mention the results of the 1779 New York congressional election—indicates that, publicly at least, Morris never committed that crime. As early as January 29, 1778, Robert R. Livingston had written to Gouverneur from New York State to warn him, "[Y]our reputation suffers here most exceedingly." Subsequent cautionary letters came steadily from both Jay and Livingston. And yet, during the arduous years of his congressional service, Morris did about as little as anyone could to defend himself from the shallow attacks on him as a Tory.[99] Joseph Reed, the congressman from Pennsylvania, leveled a number of accusations against Morris. Among these, Reed claimed that Morris had infringed on Pennsylvania's rights by acting as an attorney in a disputed election, much to the dissatisfaction of the inhabitants "who suppose the delegates of the United States sent here to attend the affairs of the common Union, not to advocate the measures of any party." Morris insisted on his rights to continue legal practice and eventually made peace with Reed. The aspersion of his continuing associations with the Tories was more difficult to confront, as several of his close relatives and friends before the war were Loyalists, including his brother-in-law, Isaac Wilkins, and his mother, with whom he intermittently corresponded. Meanwhile, the family estate of Morrisania was overrun by the British, who were aware of Gouverneur Morris's patriot activities.

No doubt some of the sniping came from those who resented the fact that a congressman so young should also be so able. (Of the many dozens of delegates to the Congress during this period, only two—Frederick Frelinghuysen (1753–1804), of New Jersey, and Charles Pinckney (1757–1824), of South Carolina, neither of whom achieved much at York—were younger than Morris.)[100] Morris wrote to Jay on the subject in late July of 1778: "As to the Malevolence of Individuals It is what I have to expect. It is by no Means a Matter of Surprize that I should be hated by some Men but I will have my revenge. By laboring in the public Service so as to gain the Applause of those whose Applause is worth gaining I will punish them severely."[101] While combative at times, Morris was aware of his own failings and was committed to reconciliation. In some memorable lines to Livingston he remarked, "With all the faults both of you [Jay and Livingston] have, I have as many as you together. You both pardon me therefore you must pardon each other."[102]

The foregoing discussion of Morris's two years in Congress, as full as it is, has not delved into all of his important work. From May 1779 he served on the Committee of Provisions (writing long letters concerning, for instance, the purchase of flour); he also sat on the Commissary and the Medical Committees and on the Finance Committee, though not yet sworn in as representative of the Finance minister. Evidently his labors were much valued: General Nathanael Greene ordered that Morris be given fresh horses whenever he wanted them, a unique directive in the surviving records from the war.[103]

Much of Morris's work was less peripatetic, and some was indirect—recommending men such as Robert R. Livingston and John Jay to important positions, for example. And, of course, as he wrote Livingston on August 17, 1778: "I have drawn and expect to draw, almost [all] if not all the publications of Congress of any importance." This was not an idle boast. Edmund Cody Burnett, the first great scholarly authority on the Continental Congress, remarked that "With the simple quill of a goose, a little ink and the English language [Morris] could do ofttimes marvels in bringing the minds of men into unison."[104]

On October 19, 1779—no doubt in response to the news that he had not been reelected—Morris wrote Livingston, "That I have not untill [*sic*] this Moment written to you I beseech you to impute to my Situation which hath been and is much occupied. When I arrived the World (or at least such Part of it as I warmly love) was on the Wing. Old Systems are at once deranged and new ones to be adopted consistent with the old. . . . I should say . . . by what I learn from your Quarter I am no longer to be that wretched Creature a Statesman. The instant I came into the House [meaning Congress] I was placed upon an important committee . . . and that succeeded by a variety of others so that I am already again distracted with attention to different Things."[105] This letter, written with his uncommon stylistic flair, concluded: "We hope much, expect much and are Certain of this only That every Thing in this World is uncertain. There is from thence a strong Argument for acting inconclusively and so inconclusive an Animal is Man that it is kind to have found the Argumts. for him."

Some years later, a correspondent wrote to ask Gouverneur's permission to consult his papers from the Revolutionary era. Morris responded:

> I have no notes or memorandums of what passed during the war. I led then the most laborious life, which can be imagined. This you will readily suppose to have been the case, when I was engaged with my departed friend, Robert Morris, in the office of finance. But what you will not so readily suppose is, that I was still more harassed while a member of Congress. Not to

mention the attendance from eleven to four in the House, which was common to all, and the appointment to special committees, of which I had a full share, I was at the same time chairman, and of course did the business, of three standing committees, viz. on the commissary's, quartermaster's, and medical departments. You must not imagine, that the members of these committees took any charge or burden of the affairs. Necessity, preserving the democratical forms, assumed the monarchical substance of business. The chairman received and answered all letters and other applications, took every step which he deemed essential, prepared reports, gave orders, and the like, and merely took the members of a committee into a chamber, and for the form's sake made the needful communications, and received their approbation, which was given of course. I was moreover obliged to labor occasionally in my profession, as my wages were insufficient for my support. I would not trouble you with this abstract of my situation, if it did not appear necessary to show you why I kept no notes of my services, and why I am perhaps the most ignorant man alive of what concerns them.[106]

{4}

THE OFFICE OF FINANCE

MORRIS ACCEPTED HIS election defeat philosophically. He took up residence in Pennsylvania and became a citizen there. Pennsylvania was then one of four state governments to assume sovereign control over the naturalization of newcomers and establish procedures for admitting aliens to citizenship. A relative newcomer, such as Morris, who took an oath of allegiance could acquire real estate immediately but not vote. After one year, he was entitled to all the rights of a native-born subject of Pennsylvania, except that he could not be elected a representative. After two years, he was eligible for elected office. Soon after leaving Congress, Morris began to practice law in Philadelphia. He also wrote a series of essays on public finance, published pseudonymously in the *Pennsylvania Packet*. In February 1781, Robert Morris was appointed the first U.S. superintendent of finance, a post roughly equivalent to that of Treasury secretary. Having for some time been impressed by Gouverneur Morris's financial acumen, international political understanding, and facility with language, the new superintendent nominated him as assistant minister of finance. Congress approved the appointment, and Gouverneur Morris served from 1781 until November 1, 1784, when the office was eliminated. (In 1785, a Treasury Board was established; the U.S. Treasury Department came into existence after the ratification of the U.S. Constitution.)

In a July 4, 1781, memorandum Robert Morris enumerated the major problems facing his new department—which were also the reasons for its establishment: "The Derangement of our Money Affairs. The Enormity of our public Expenditures. The Confusion in all our Departments. The Languour of our general System. The complexity and consequent Inefficiency of our Operations."[1]

The colonies were in dire straits by the end of 1780. The Continental currency was nearly worthless; troops had begun steadily mutinying; General Arnold had gone over to the British; and General Horatio Gates's large-scale loss at Camden, coming along with other American setbacks in the region, led to the despondent feeling among many Americans and mainland Europeans that the British strategy in the South could win the war. Congress felt constrained to replace the potentially cumbersome congressional boards with executive boards, having one chief executive; hence the Office of Finance.

Gouverneur Morris's service in the Finance Office began in 1781; two years later, in a letter to John Jay, Robert Morris frankly acknowledged, "I could do nothing without him." Since Gouverneur Morris spoke and wrote French fairly well and Robert did neither, the former served as a reliable confidential interpreter and drafter of replies to the French. For the times, too, he had very advanced skills in cryptography, and he wisely persuaded Robert to abandon the codes then in use and replace them with others the younger Morris devised. In this period, too, Gouverneur drew up complicated proposals for a new American coinage system, which he employed in the winter of 1782–83, in preparing a set of annuity tables for Congress to use in considering pensions for Continental military officers. As our narrative has already noted, this was a favorite topic for Morris. He drafted or helped draft many of the superintendent's position papers, office reports, memoranda, and letters, and seems to have played a strong part in drawing up the plan for the Bank of North America, the nation's first commercial bank. He helped draft a vital report on credit, and presented Congress innovative essays on decimal coinage and on the utility of a federal mint. Last but perhaps not least, he worked to persuade the European powers to expand trade relations with America.

Many of these efforts of 1781–82 were effectively canceled in 1783, when congressmen exclusively concerned with states' issues failed to enact the import taxes that would have provided national revenues. But many of Gouverneur Morris's monetary proposals from this period found a place in the U.S. Constitution, and Alexander Hamilton's epochal series of Treasury Reports, disseminated in 1790–91, show that their author was much influenced by Gouverneur's fiscal writings. Hamilton's push for national centralization, especially his coinage plan and proposal that Congress assume states' debts, and his establishment of a central bank in 1791 were all policies earlier championed by Morris. Gouverneur may indeed lay claim in part to the economic stability that was Hamilton's legacy.

Setting out for Philadelphia from south of Wilmington, Delaware, in 1760, the British traveler Andrew Burnaby remarked of his movements through southeastern Pennsylvania, "upon the whole nothing could be more pleasing than the ride which I had this day. I ferried over the Schuylkill, about three miles below Philadelphia; from whence to the city the whole country is covered with villas, vistas, and luxuriant gardens." By 1778 Philadelphia seems to have had a population of at least 38,000, and by Morris's departure for Europe in 1789 more than 44,000; but the countryside had changed little.

During this period only about 6 percent of American citizens resided in the cities, and among those cities Philadelphia was in some ways unique. Like New York, it was a comparatively sophisticated American seaport and mercantile city, with a cadre of powerful elite families. For these reasons, and because he had attended school there, Morris obviously felt at home in the City of Brotherly Love.[2]

From 1778 through 1800, Philadelphia was the new nation's *de facto* capital. The Congress, of course, sat there. Thus, the military, financial, and legislative activities of the colonies and new nation had been largely administered here. Philadelphia, which also served as the state capital until 1799, was the seat of the national government from 1775 to 1789. In the latter year New York City succeeded Philadelphia for a brief period. But in 1790 Philadelphia again became the national capital and retained this distinction until the U.S. capital moved to Washington in 1800. Throughout these years, too, Philadelphia was the largest and fastest-growing American city: the main center for politics, journalism, law, theoretical science, and practical medicine. By 1770 the city was already very prosperous; it had a well-developed core of wealthy merchants, such as the furrier Samuel Neave (b.?–1774) and the merchant and importer Stephen Carmick (1719–1774), each of whom had a net worth of more than £6,000—a healthy fortune at that time. In part because of its vigorous economy, Philadelphia attracted such people as Robert Morris, who came from Liverpool to apprentice in a mercantile firm and became a partner in it after he cornered the city's lucrative export flour market. And Benjamin Franklin's abundant success as a Philadelphian needs no exposition.[3]

Ethnically and religiously, the region was then, as it is now, particularly diverse and comparatively tolerant, qualities Gouverneur Morris no doubt appreciated. By the time he embarked for Europe, southeastern Pennsylvania had become home to at least four religious sects and seven church denominations.[4]

Philadelphia's old town had already been planned and laid out with the gridiron system, including thoughtfully situated greens and squares; its buildings were mostly of brick, and in either the American Baroque or the American Roman style. During the founding period and even through the nineteenth century, the district below South Street remained mostly farmland and modest houses. (Still in the late twentieth century this part of the city had a flavor like none other.) But what we now think of as old central Philadelphia—north of South Street as far as Vine, and from roughly Thirteenth Street east to the Delaware—was steadily patrolled at night by hired constables. (Not until the early nineteenth century did the city's elite arrange a permanent and effective police force.) Philadelphia's streets were already paved, and kept quite clean; a trash removal firm, under contract with the municipality, cleared them daily. Schools, libraries, and newspapers flourished; there were two important hospitals and a number of clinics; and Benjamin Franklin had founded a fire brigade.

After arriving in Philadelphia Gouverneur Morris became a member of the Schuylkill Fishing Company, founded in 1732, and often considered the oldest angling club in America. Here—especially before his leg injury—Morris walked in the woods and swam in the river, as well as catching fish and playing quoits.[5]

As much as any American city in the pre-Federal era, Philadelphia was a center of artistic activity and of book publishing. Philadelphians enjoyed dancing and concert-going; Haydn was especially popular. After the British evacuated Philadelphia, its citizens "sharply increased the caliber and frequency of their cultural events, notably the dancing assemblies," says the historian Kellee Lynne Green. A concert series in 1783, for instance, featured dance divertissements between selections; generally, concerts also concluded with a ball managed by a dancing master.[6]

Unfortunately, Gouverneur Morris's social dancing days had ended on May 14, 1780. Planning a brief visit to the nearby countryside, he had had his phaeton brought from the stable south of Logan's Alley to his lodgement, on High (now Market) Street near Third. The horses—two powerful grays—were left untethered as Morris took his seat; he shouted to them before he had taken the reins, and they bolted. In the struggle—it lasted several hundred yards—to control the runaway horses, he fell, and his left leg was mangled in a wheel. His left ankle was dislocated and several bones in the same leg were broken.

Morris's personal physician, Dr. John Jones (1729–1791), who was also a friend and a native New Yorker, was out of town; several other well-respected doctors were summoned. They recommended amputation. In response Morris offered some hospital humor:

Gentlemen, I see around me the eminent men of your profession, all acknowledged competent to the performance of the operation. You have already secured renown, the capital by which you live. Now the removal of my leg cannot add to your celebrity; is there not one among you younger in your calling who might perform the act, and secure *éclat* for his benefit?

Dr. James Hutchinson (1752–1793), the same age as Gouverneur, performed a high below-the-knee amputation. Although some scholars have adjudged Hutchinson inexperienced because of his age, he had probably performed more surgeries than most North American physicians. He was a Continental Army surgeon; more than two years earlier, during the winter of 1778, he had written a memorandum complaining of the army's want of lancets. His skills were good enough to make him surgeon-general of Pennsylvania, a position he held until the peace. In fighting the severe outbreak of yellow fever in Philadelphia in 1793, Hutchinson succumbed to the disease himself.[7]

The record indicates that Morris's surgery was very well done. The stump never required "revision" (a euphemism for the surgical removal of more flesh and bone). And in an age when most major wounds became septic, Morris never developed a significant infection. Finally, the stump was sufficiently well-shaped that, after his rehabilitation, and before his last months, he often routinely walked nine miles a day. On his wooden leg he climbed to the top of the steeple at the Cathedral of Bruges. In France, at least, he had a stumble when he cursed the mud, but who has lived into his or her forties and has not?

After a brief experiment with a copper prosthesis, which proved too cumbersome, Morris settled on a thirty-six-inch-long oaken peg leg, having a leather-covered rest between a pair of securing arms. The length of the prosthesis, and its fittings, suggest that the leg was taken off as high as two inches below the knee.[8]

Was the amputation necessary? Pennsylvania—especially Philadelphia, of the late eighteenth century—was known for such outstanding surgeons as the Irish-born Edward Hand (1744–1802), the Scottish-born James Craik (1730–1814), and the German-born Bodo Otto (1711–1787). Morris's personal physician, John Jones, the founder of the New York Hospital, also organized the Continental Army medical corps and wrote the first American textbook on surgery, *Plain, Concise, Practical Remarks on Treatment of Wounds and Punctures* (1775). This slender volume served as the vade mecum of Continental Army surgeons. When Dr. Jones returned and heard the account of Gouverneur's injuries, he questioned the wisdom of amputating; Morris's case was often cited thereafter in medical training as an example of faulty surgical diagnosis. (Perhaps it was this professional opprobrium that prompted Dr. Hutchinson to refuse the appointment he was later offered as professor of surgery at the University of Pennsylvania.) But in an age before the advent of X-ray and MRI technology, a physician's judgment of injuries he had not seen deserves to be questioned stringently.

News of Morris's accident spread rapidly in Philadelphia. In his diary for that day, the Philadelphia silversmith Jacob Hiltzheimer, for instance, records that "Gouverneur Morris, member of Congress [*sic*], broke his leg by jumping out of his phaeton as the horses were running away."[9] Hiltzheimer ran the city's poshest stables, so he would have been among the first to hear of the case. Morris's friends wrote to one another reporting the accident and remarking on his condition. Robert R. Livingston wrote Clinton and John Jay, and Houston wrote Schuyler with the same essential message: that "he bears it [the amputation] with magnanimity and is in a fair way of recovery" (R.R.L.'s words to John Jay, July 6, 1780). Livingston added: "I feel for him and yet am led to hope that it may turn out to his advantage and tend to fix his desultory genius to a point in which case it can not fail to go far."[10]

After the amputation Gouverneur stayed with the Platers. George Plater (1735–1792), of Maryland, had served in Congress with Gouverneur throughout their tenure in York and Philadelphia; later he was governor of his home state. Mrs. Plater (née Elizabeth Rousby, 1749–1789) was a second wife, who married George, her cousin, in 1764 (such young brides were not unusual at the time). Several years older than Gouverneur, Eliza was evidently a very attractive woman, even though by this time she had borne at least five of her six children. Eliza's mother was so beautiful she was known as the White Rose of Maryland, and the discerning Marquis de Chastellux singled out Elizabeth's beauty for special mention in his diary.[11] From Madrid, John Jay before long wrote jocularly to Gouverneur Morris "that a certain married woman after much use of your legs had occasioned your losing one"— such was the toasty gossip surrounding Gouverneur by this time. The rumors concerning Mrs. Plater may have had much truth in them.

By his mid-twenties, Gouverneur already had become conspicuous for his resemblance to a hero in a William Congreve comedy. He remained a flirtatious man-about-town until his first and only marriage, well into his fifties. Gouverneur was the oldest of the major American founders to marry and also the oldest known to have fathered a child. From the King's College commencement oration he delivered at age sixteen, "On Wit and Beauty," Gouverneur's writings commented steadily on the charms of many of the ladies he met.[12]

The first reference I have found to Morris's amorousness appears in a letter from John Jay to Robert R. Livingston, of February 16, 1779: "Gouverneur is daily employed in making oblations to Venus." The normally straitlaced, future Supreme Court Chief Justice Jay also wrote to Robert Morris (September 19, 1780): "Gouverneur's Leg has been a Tax on my Heart. I am almost tempted to wish he had lost *something* else. I have been able to hear very little of him."[13]

When the Plater family returned to Sotterly Plantation, in what is now St. Mary's County, Maryland, Gouverneur corresponded secretly with Elizabeth Plater, through her cousin's wife, Mrs. William Bennett (Joanna) Lloyd of Annapolis. Gouverneur also sent roses to Eliza through Joanna Lloyd; and it was she who, at a dinner party in London in May 1790, brought him the news that Eliza had died, of tuberculosis, the previous November. In his private diary, Gouverneur poured out his emotions: "Poor Eliza! My lovely friend, thou are then at Peace and I shall behold thee no more. Never, never, never."[14] In his diaries, Morris rarely if ever expressed such strong emotion about anything or anyone.

Morris's sense of humor was famous. The day after the phaeton accident, a friend stopped by and proceeded to portray vividly the wonderful effect the injury would have on Morris's character and temperament; he enlarged on the temptations and pleasures into which young men are likely to be led, and on the diminished inducements Morris would now have to indulge in such dissipations. "My good sir," Morris replied, "you argue the matter so handsomely and point out so clearly the advantages of being without legs, that I am almost tempted to part with the other."[15]

Morris took pleasure in teasing his friends. By 1802, Robert Livingston had begun to lose his hearing; that same year, he was appointed U.S. minister to France. He knew enough French to get along, but James Bayard, his predecessor, had not. Morris told Livingston that "the French thought it very extraordinary that to succeed a minister who could not *speak* their language, we had sent one who could not *hear* it."[16]

Of the founders, Benjamin Franklin perhaps excepted, Gouverneur seems to have had the best sense of humor; but a reputation as a wit often proves dangerous in American public life. His election to the powerful Pennsylvania delegation to the Constitutional Convention was almost Morris's last; although Washington appointed him to the ministership to France, and the Federalist-dominated New York legislature elected him (against opponent Peter Gansevoort) 25 to 11 in the Senate and 54 to 48 in the Assembly to fill a three-year vacancy in the U.S. Senate, Morris was never popular with the mass of the people. In his intelligence and wit, Gouverneur Morris seems closest to Adlai Stevenson, who was also a brilliant writer and whose

humor was tongue-in-cheek, like Morris's. Stevenson had only limited electoral success, although a case could be made that he was intellectually superior to all of his political competitors. Superior intelligence and an
ineradicable sense of irony probably both distinguished and limited the
American congressman Thomas Braxton Reed. On the British side, Lord
Birkenhead's strong intellect, combined with his caustic wit, no doubt assured that this barrister would not attain the premiership.

Congress voted on May 20, 1781, to make Robert Morris the superintendent of the Department of Finance, which it had established in early February.[17] Robert Morris took the job, on two conditions. First, he required that
Congress sanction his continuance in private business while holding office.
This stipulation likely stemmed from criticism of his commercial activities
during his previous period of service with the federal government. He had
profited economically while serving in Congress. But it is only fair to mention that at one point he funded Washington's army from his own pocket.
From 1775 to 1784, Robert Morris was out of public office for just twelve
months, November 1779 to November 1780. Congress, well aware of the
sniping of contemporaries, accepted this proviso. Morris's second demand,
however, met with some resistance: he claimed the right not only to make all
the departmental appointments himself, but also to dismiss anyone, in any
branch of the government, who handled public property. Morris had seen all
too much incompetency and fraud; in his view, only such a sweeping power
would enable him to maintain government officials' financial integrity.[18]

Morris's terms implied that his authority would permeate every branch of
government. The objections to this were based on the fact that such power
could be readily abused, and some members disliked Morris personally. For
understandable reasons Congress, however, had come to believe extensive
powers should be granted its appointees; in 1781, after brief debate, it ac-
ceded to both of Morris's demands.

Robert Morris took office as Superintendent of Finance on May 24, 1781,
becoming the only person ever to hold the position. He was somewhat less
than fifty years of age, well-developed in physique and well-stocked with financial experience. His appointment was explicitly welcomed by George
Washington, Alexander Hamilton, Joseph Reed, and many others.[19]

The assistantship he offered Gouverneur Morris was officially created on
July 6, with a salary of $1,850 a year—about $5 a day, and, taking account of
inflation, a substantial cut in pay. (Gouverneur had earned $5 a day as New
York's representative in the Continental Congress.) The superintendent's

esteem may have been one of the job's attractions. In the letter formally offering Gouverneur the job, Robert wrote that "aided by . . . [Gouverneur's] Talents and abilities I feel better Courage, and dare indulge the fond hope that uniting our utmost exertions in the service of our Country we may be able to extricate it from the present embarassments." He further declared his "entire conviction" that Gouverneur's "genius, Talents and capacity" would enable him to serve his country well, and that Gouverneur's "aid, ease, and confidence" had made Robert choose him without hesitation. Gouverneur's letter of acceptance struck a similarly high note, referring to Robert's "Industry . . . , Abilities, and above all your Integrity," which "will extricate America from her Distresses." Yet he seems to have foreseen trouble, adding: "I will freely share in this bitter potion of Eminence."[20]

On August 8, 1781, Gouverneur was sworn in before Thomas McKean (1734–1817) of Pennsylvania, the president of Congress. He served three and a half years, the whole duration of his and Robert's unique offices, having begun work even before the swearing in. The collaboration was a happy one.

In his diary for August 4, 1781, when Gouverneur was still "unofficial," Robert wrote: "Having omitted in my Minutes to make mention of the Assistance I have received from Gouverneur Morris, Esqr., I think it proper to declare that he has chearfully afforded me every advice and Assistance which his Genius and Abilities enabled from my first Appointment to this time, and that I know him so Capable and Useful as to induce me to Solicit his Assistance in an Official Character."[21]

The affinities that lead to a good working rapport, not to mention a solid friendship, are often obscure, even where opportunities for observation are favorable. We do not have a complete picture of the relationship between the two Morrises. They were not, of course, a perfect match. One prospective source of discord proved important in Robert's subsequent life: Gouverneur, so long before government ethics laws, instinctively opposed the commingling of the public's commercial interests with his own. Moreover, although Gouverneur had something of the Midas touch in business, he also seems to have possessed a greater sense of measure than Robert did. This flaw in the older man eventually cost him and his family dearly.[22]

Both Morrises came from wealthy families, of course, Robert's father having become a well-to-do merchant before his death by accident at the age of forty. But Robert had been born in Liverpool, England, and apprenticed to a Philadelphia merchant. Like George Washington and Benjamin Franklin, for example, he lacked a college education.

Before and after their fruitful Finance Office tenure, the lives and careers of Robert and Gouverneur often converged. Both Morrises served in the

U.S. Senate, and they were two of only six men to sign both the Articles of Confederation and the U.S. Constitution. (Robert had also signed the Declaration of Independence.) In 1798, Robert began a roughly three-year sentence in Philadelphia's debtors' prison; he also had to declare bankruptcy. From his release, in 1801, until his death, in 1806, he and his family lived mostly on the charity of friends, among them Gouverneur.

Certainly Gouverneur Morris's praise of Robert in the letter by which he accepted the finance post was sincere. Well before then, in an August 1779 letter to Robert Livingston, Gouverneur expressed respect for Robert Morris: "indeed the thing could not be otherwise for an honester man is not on earth and the attacks on him [in connection with his business] have demonstrated it."[23]

As for Robert Morris's approval of Gouverneur, no doubt it had something to do with the latter's vigorous defense of him against attacks by Thomas Paine. Busy though he was with congressional service, Gouverneur made no small effort on Robert's behalf. Manuscripts exist of several replies by Gouverneur to Paine; each version bears substantial indication of alteration and revision, more than usual for the fluent Morris. In response to Robert's warning that Gouverneur Morris had become the subject of vile whispering attacks, Gouverneur wrote to Robert:

> I was infinitely obliged by your kind Letter. That Calumny directs her Shafts against me I believe. That Innocence alone is not a sufficient safe Guard I know. But I also know that Appeals to the Public on such Subjects by no Means remove the Ill Effects of the Attacks which are made. At the same time it is Inconsistent with the Office I hold to appear on the Public Stage agt. [against] Every one who shall amuse himself with Defamation. Be not however uneasy for your Friend. I venture to assure you that he will rise from the Stroke and pity the Envy of his Foes. The Tales circulated among the People I can trace back to Men who having inlisted themselves under the Banners of Faction & being disappointed in their Views burn with deadly Hate and seek Revenge in low Abuse and vilainous Insinuation. You will oblige if whenever any Member of Congress or other makes free with my Reputation you will question him as to Facts and Evidence. It would give me great Pleasure to fix upon some Scoundrel the deep Lie and open all his Infamy to his own View. . . . [24]

Robert Morris did not take the oath of office immediately after accepting the superintendency: he wanted to keep his seat in the Pennsylvania Assembly until certain laws that he considered "destructive of all credit" had been repealed. Meanwhile he also urged the Assembly to levy "effective Taxes in hard Money." This stance presages one of the pillars of his policy as finance chief. In a letter to Philip Schuyler, dated May 27, 1781, Robert wrote that "this poor distressed country is now threatened with ruin ... for want of system and economy and vigor in raising the public monies."[25] Robert Morris, assisted by Gouverneur, persuaded Congress to pass a law "for Regulating the Treasury, and adjusting the Public Accounts."

This law (September 11, 1781) allowed the restructuring of the former Board of Treasury as it passed into the Finance Office. The Board kept up its work during the transition to the superintendency, while Robert Morris wrapped up his congressional duties and private business. For several months, therefore, U.S. finances were administered according to a mixed system, rather like the current Italian practice.

The Treasury Board had never been notably efficient. To organize, from the very beginning, a government department is never easy, even in peacetime; to do so during a war with a powerful, rich enemy that enjoys a well-disciplined army and whose finances are constantly replenished by its vast colonial empire is nearly impossible. America was money poor because Britain had quickly drained away any specie that arrived on colonial shores. The colonial legislative assemblies were, by and large, the sole training grounds for the Continental Congress, so the congressmen had scant experience in the larger affairs of nation-states.

By whatever name—it was called, among other things, the Treasury Office of Accounts and the Board of Treasury—the Treasury was the first American governmental department. By law the Board grew from five members in 1776 to a virtually unmanageable ten men by 1778. Within the next several years, as the powers of the Board were more carefully delineated, the accounts and claims against the North American colonies for services or supplies had to be presented to a Committee of Claims. By the mid-war period, this committee and the Board of Treasury were dividing the examination of congressional accounts; and this system continued until a little less than six months before the Claims Committee folded, in 1777. The Board of Treasury alone then examined all unsettled claims and accounts. From 1778 until mid-1781, therefore, the Board had to develop public funds to sustain the government, as well as to examine and liquidate all public accounts.

On occasion, serving commissioners settled particular large accounts—those growing out of the Canadian expedition, for example, and the land disputes between the Confederation and New York and Virginia. But there was so much work as to make it impossible to handle Treasury business accurately, in particular because some Board of Treasury members were also members of Congress and had those duties to attend to as well. As Alexander

Hamilton perhaps first clearly recognized, the Board system was cumbersome and inefficient. This reality Robert Morris by 1781 clearly came to understand.[26] The Board later evolved to have an auditor, a comptroller, and a treasurer, but until Robert Morris's appointment as superintendent there was no one generally in charge. Considering this chaotic management, it is amazing that America had kept itself above water, if barely, until 1781— amazing, especially, because as is almost always the case, the fighting lasted far longer than almost anyone had foreseen.

Congress had passed the Articles of Confederation on November 15, 1777, providing an organizational framework for the revolutionary opposition to the authority of the British Parliament. The Articles reserved to the states most of the powers claimed by Parliament; Congress's powers were limited, so as to prevent their exploitation by powerful factions. Further complicating Congress's authority, the Articles did not take effect until March 1, 1781, when they were ratified by all the states. Meanwhile, Congress served as the de facto government, without the sanction of a written constitution. Thus, from June 1776 until March 1781, the Continental Congress essentially relied upon the steadily shifting framework of a draft of a plan of union. Even after the Articles became legally binding, the federal government had no sovereign power to raise money.[27] During 1780–1781 most governmental departments came under single heads. In previous years, however, the same congressmen had been chosen to serve repeatedly on committees in a particular line of governmental business; so a committee member in Congress, like Gouverneur Morris, probably exercised at least as much power as, for example, an assistant finance superintendent. Nor were Gouverneur Morris and Robert Morris the only members of Congress to wield enormous power. Thomas McKean, for instance, served altogether on fifty-two congressional committees, and chaired eleven, in addition to being Congress's president.[28]

Even apart from his affinity with the superintendent, Gouverneur Morris was in many ways the ideal candidate for the assistantship. He had always been interested in financial questions. In 1769, he was considering a bill by which the colony would meet its financial obligations by issuing loan certificates, rather than through taxation. Gouverneur, then just eighteen, wrote an anonymous essay against the bill; when the author's identity was discovered, his clear logic and elegant mathematics earned him some celebrity.[29]

Much as Benjamin Franklin's 1729 essay on paper money was the first major step in his political career, so Gouverneur Morris's May 30, 1775, "Report [from the New York Legislature] on the Expediency of a Continental Currency" did much to win him prominence. Herman E. Krooss, a scholar of money and banking, gave the report pride of place in the "Financing the

Revolution" segment of his comprehensive *Documentary History of Banking and Currency in the United States*.[30]

In 1777, John Jay, James Duane, and Gouverneur Morris were appointed to a special New York committee to devise ways and means to combat the decline in value of Continental paper currency. In this capacity, Morris (along with John S. Hobart) conferred with the political representatives of several New England states, in hopes that a cooperative effort might check depreciation and counterfeiting. The conferees' report recommended that state bills be removed from circulation as soon as possible, and that war expenses be met with increased taxation. Although New York did not receive these proposals enthusiastically, the legislature did take some steps toward reducing the flow of state currency.[31]

In his wartime correspondence, Gouverneur Morris frequently discussed American finances. In mid-1778 he succinctly observed that "if by Funding our Paper the immense circulating medium could be so reduced that the Bills were brought on a Par with Specie, the Debt tho nominally the same, would in Fact be much greater because the Produce of the Country being low, it would require so much more of it to pay the same Sum." Morris wanted to contract the colonial currency by selling foreign bills of exchange and locking up the currency received thereby. If it proved necessary later to expand the currency, this could be effected by releasing more of it into circulation, or, if need be, by coining more currency. He lamented the earlier failure to tax the citizenry.[32] In 1778–79 he drafted a "Proposal to Congress concerning Management of Government" which dwells primarily on finance. On July 30, 1779, he began service on a committee to prepare a plan to establish the Treasury Board.[33] And there was, of course, the series of essays by "An American," published first in the *Pennsylvania Packet* and then later in book form under his name.[34]

The manuscripts of these essays run eighteen, nine, eleven, and fourteen closely written foolscap pages. They begin with an overview of economic principles and of American currency and finances; he expresses opposition to inflation and espouses a laissez-faire economic policy similar to that advocated by Robert R. Livingston and articulated in 1776 by Adam Smith.[35]

Robert Morris's finance department worked to bring American public credit back to health, developing plans for the Bank of North America and for an American national mint. In addition Robert Morris issued monetary notes under the signature of the financier.

The two Morrises were not, of course, the Finance Office's only staff. The law establishing the department also provided for a comptroller, a treasurer, a register, auditors, and a sufficient number of clerks. By January 1, 1782, these posts had been filled.[36] Most of the newly appointed officers—Michael Hillegas (treasurer), James Milligan (auditor general), Joseph Nourse (assistant auditor general), and Robert Troup (secretary to the Board of Treasury)—had held important Board of Treasury positions before the new Finance Office's organization. Nevertheless, the rancor and friction that had pervaded the bureau all but disappeared from the new Finance Office, probably due to the leadership philosophy of Robert Morris, dictatorial to his critics and proficient to his adherents. Managerially, the new office was much improved: the duties of the offices were much more clearly defined than theretofore, and sub-officers were regularly consulted on matters relevant to their work. The former bureau's orders and practices were carefully studied; inefficiencies were weeded out and policies were clarified.[37]

Much as Gouverneur Morris assisted Robert, how much influence the younger Morris had on Finance Office policy is difficult to say. Probably he had a good deal to do with at least one of the three pillars of Robert Morris's superintendency, "the plan for establishing a national bank in the United States of North America." The editors of The Papers of Robert Morris judge that Gouverneur was "the one certain influence" on Robert's many-pointed plan. Robert Morris rarely, if ever, cited his authorities, unlike most of his effusively referential contemporaries, making conclusions about his literary and personal sources purely speculative. Gouverneur, however, was present for collaboration and, very late in life, wrote to Moss Kent that he had framed the concept of the bank.[38] And Robert Morris's letter to the French economist François, Marquis de Barbé-Marbois (1745–1837), containing questions on the national bank, is written in Gouverneur's hand, which may suggest that he had some part in framing those questions.

In Gouverneur's letter of June 4, 1781, to Robert Morris, we can see Gouverneur functioning as Robert's eyes and ears in Boonton (near Morristown), New Jersey. Gouverneur offered astute financial assessment and logistical detail, married with shrewd judgments on the New York–New Jersey political situation. Gouverneur was convinced that, owing to "infinite Abuses" of fraudulent sellers, "the whole Approvisionment of the Army should be thro one Channel and this cannot be too soon adjusted." He also opined that the "Distress of the army has been owing to a Want of Teams [transportation] more than of Flour and this Want can only be supplied by hard Money." Gouverneur advised Robert of the "Propriety of seeing the Jersey Legislature and conveying your Sentiments to that of New York" and delivered up-to-date information on the safety of the roads between Morristown and Philadelphia. He describes two routes and concludes that the "former of these roads is least liable to attempts from the enemy, but the latter is not dangerous."[39]

During the summer before his official appointment, Gouverneur also devised the Finance Office cipher ("number 4"), which assigns numbers to various combinations of words. It was both easy to use and very secure, quite sophisticated for its day.[40]

During this time, despite the fact that Gouverneur had not yet received his official appointment, he handled much of the Finance Office internal governmental correspondence (for example, with the Board of Treasury and the Board of War) and its outside correspondence as well. To the merchant Haym Salomon (1740–1785), for example, he wrote concerning the sale of bills of exchange. A bill of exchange is a written, signed instrument requiring the person to whom it is addressed to pay on demand (or on a future date) a fixed amount of money either to the person identified as payee or to anyone presenting the bill of exchange. Salomon, Philadelphia's leading dealer in this business, was employed by the French government to raise money for its army and navy by selling these bills in the colonies. With John Hazelwood (1726–1800), the former navy officer and military engineer and now state commissioner of purchases for the Continental Army, Gouverneur concluded a contract on July 19 for supplying rations to the post at Philadelphia, where the "People are in a Distressed Situation, and require Immediate Assistance."[41] On occasion Gouverneur kept the Finance Office diary; he drafted the office's correspondence in French to the Chevalier de La Luzerne, the French minister to America. In fact, he drafted all of Robert's letters in French on Finance Office business throughout the superintendency, and translated incoming French correspondence. He edited Robert's letters, sometimes helping to prepare them (some words and phrases in Robert's letters are in Gouverneur's hand).

In fall 1781, before Yorktown, Gouverneur also arranged for the sale of numerous bills of exchange. On Washington's suggestion, Morris urged General Greene to become secretary of war, and described for the benefit of Congress the qualities necessary in an American minister of navy and marines. Nathanael Greene was one of the three major candidates under final consideration for the secretaryship of war. Gouverneur Morris clearly believed that, as he wrote to Robert R. Livingston, "Green [*sic*] will be the man." The other two main candidates were Generals Henry Knox (1750–1806) and Benjamin Lincoln (1733–1810). As the former was Washington's extremely able chief of artillery, he was not a likely candidate for withdrawal from the field. Greene's presence in the field in the Southern campaign was also felt to be indispensable. And Washington refused to indicate which man he preferred in the position. Thus, Lincoln, arguably the least valuable military officer of the three major candidates, was offered and accepted the position. In any event, Greene's letter of November 21, 1781, clearly indicated that he had no serious interest in the newly created position. And Lincoln proved an honest, sensible, and patriotic first secretary of war.

Gouverneur made time to write warmly to Nathanael Greene, complimenting the general on his "extraordinary success" and asking him for an account of his army's exploits.[42] In truth, Greene's command was not the great success that Morris seems to have thought. The congratulations Gouverneur extended to Greene were on the general's efforts at Eutaw Springs, South Carolina. After an initial breakthrough of British General Stewart's front line, Greene's officers promptly lost control of their men, who commenced looting the British camp. While this mêlée occurred, Stewart's forces regrouped and counterattacked, inducing panic among Greene's men, who broke and ran. Although hundreds of Stewart's men were killed or wounded, since the British general remained on the field and forced Greene's men to flee, by eighteenth-century standards the British were, as so often during the Revolution, tactically victorious. Nonetheless, since Stewart then proceeded to Charleston, and had sustained so many casualties, Greene had rightly earned a strategic victory.

When Robert Morris was away on business, as he often was, Gouverneur in effect managed the office. At the end of September 1781, Gouverneur helped draft an important report on bills drawn by Benjamin Lincoln. This complicated matter involved the requested payment, with six percent interest, by Congress to General Lincoln, for his having paid out of his own pocket a large bill to a Continental Army supplier, John Owen. Although Pennsylvania Congressman George Clymer presented the report to Congress, no action on it was taken.[43]

Every Monday evening, beginning in the early fall of 1781, a conference assembled which included the secretary of war, the secretary of foreign affairs, the commander in chief, the secretary of Congress, Robert Morris, and Gouverneur Morris, the financier's assistant. This unofficial cabinet discussed a wide range of issues to all of which, of course, money was relevant. One of the primary goals of the cabinet, as evidenced by the departments represented, was unifying the government's executive power, and Gouverneur understood that financial reform would be necessary to the realization of this cohesion. A letter written to John Jay several months earlier expresses this awareness: "Finance, my Friend, the whole of what remains in the American Revolution grounds there."[44]

Earlier that year, the Revolution's outcome had seemed doubtful. The young but able General Lafayette loosely held ground not far from Williamsburg, Virginia, commanding not only his famous Light Division of French forces but also two brigades sent forward by Washington as reinforcements: one led by Colonel Alexander Hamilton and the other by Colonel John

Laurens. (Laurens's father, Henry, the former president of the Continental Congress, was still being held prisoner in the Tower of London.) Against them was ranged a more powerful and experienced army, fairly well entrenched, under General Cornwallis. General Rochambeau (1725–1807) occupied a portion of Rhode Island with the main French army on American soil, but had immediately accessible only six ships. These were under the command of Admiral de Barras (c. 1719–1793). General Washington's main army, a force roughly equal to Rochambeau's, was encamped outside New York, but Admiral de Grasse's substantial battle fleet, the only one the allies had, was in the Caribbean. On March 22, 1781, Louis XVI promoted Comte de Grasse (1720–1788) to rear admiral and ordered him back to the West Indies with twenty ships of the line, three frigates, and 156 transport ships. In the West Indies the French admiral's duties would again be to protect French commerce in the Caribbean, and to destroy as many British ships as possible.

On August 17, 1781, Washington announced his southern strategy, and that strategy culminated in the decisive victory at Yorktown. The first step had come on May 31, 1781, in a letter Washington wrote ostensibly for Major General Lafayette's eyes only: it included the false information that Washington and Rochambeau had decided to attack Clinton in New York. Washington arranged to have this deceptive missive intercepted by Clinton's troops, and as a result the British general stayed within his lines, awaiting an attack that never came. Washington and Rochambeau then swiftly marched around New York City and swooped down on Cornwallis in Virginia. Not until September 2 did Clinton realize that American troops were well on their way south.[45]

In April 1781, de Grasse apprised Rochambeau that he would be in St. Domingo by the end of June and could be in American waters by July 15, if necessary. Rochambeau promptly sent the fast cutter *Concorde* to St. Domingo to let de Grasse know of the plans Washington had communicated to the French general. He also notified the admiral of Cornwallis's arrival in Virginia and strongly hinted that he would prefer that de Grasse set sail right away for the Chesapeake. In this communiqué Rochambeau indicated that de Grasse should send a frigate to let de Barras and Washington know where he was.

About the same time, the Chevalier de La Luzerne, the French minister to America, emphasized to de Grasse that "it is you alone who can deliver the invaded states from that crisis which is so alarming that it appears to me there is no time to lose." Until September of 1781, Rochambeau seems to have kept Washington in the dark concerning the French naval plans for that year. But the French general disclosed to Washington de Grasse's plans for the late summer.[46]

For security reasons, Washington's forces traveled south independently of

Rochambeau's as far as Head of Elk, in Cecil County, Maryland, where the French and Americans united and sailed down the Chesapeake to join Lafayette.

At this point in our narrative the same Rivington whom Gouverneur Morris had tried to defend earlier in New York comes back onto the scene. In September of 1781 the printer turned over to Major Allan McLane, one of Washington's intelligence officers, the signal code for the Royal Navy. McLane as promptly as possible delivered the signals information to de Grasse. Given the time necessary to get the intelligence packet to the French admiral, and the casualties and ship damage sustained in the battle by the French, it is unlikely de Grasse received the signals intelligence in time to use it. Regardless, when the British fleet, under Admiral Thomas Graves (1725–1802), encountered de Grasse's ships in the battle known as the Chesapeake Capes, the French inflicted rapid and severe damage on the British fleet, which retired to New York, leaving de Grasse in command of Chesapeake Bay. Cornwallis's communications by sea were severed. An additional advantage afforded by this defeat is that it allowed Admiral de Barras to land reinforcements for the Continental Army.

The amphibious aspect completed, the French-American force commenced a classic siege operation. The Continentals Washington arranged in three divisions, commanded by Generals Lincoln, Von Steuben, and Lafayette. The militia, mostly from Virginia, came under the command of General Thomas Nelson, Jr., and Brigadier General George Weedon. Unaccountably, Cornwallis withdrew his men from the outermost defense works before the battle heated up, a grave tactical error.

After a heavy pounding of the defense works by Knox's artillery, on the evening of October 12, two storming parties of four hundred men each took the British redoubts. On October 19, Cornwallis surrendered. During this surprisingly brisk campaign, the British suffered 126 killed and 326 wounded; they surrendered some 6,630 men, of whom 2,500 were Hessian mercenaries and the remainder British soldiers. By this time, notably, at least 2,000 of Cornwallis's men were already in the field hospital, most of them from prior conflict. (Washington's forces, counting the men in Rochambeau's command, numbered about 16,000.) Although the official surrender occurred on October 19, Cornwallis had requested terms on October 17: the fourth anniversary of General Burgoyne's surrender near Saratoga.

The action was so fast mostly because of Admiral de Grasse's timely arrival in strength not far offshore on August 30; and the piecemeal tactical movement of the British fleet under Admiral Graves. Of course, Graves may conceivably have operated under nearly crippling conditions, since the French may have been able to read and interpret the British signals almost as fast as the British could send them, if McLane's signals intelligence reached the French fleet before September 5. Regardless, Graves's tardy maneuvers, combined with Admiral Sir George Brydges Rodney's (1718–1792) preliminary intelligence misassessments, led to the British navy's retreat. With their ships gone, the outnumbered British land forces at Yorktown could get no reinforcements; and thus Cornwallis's fate was all but sealed.[47]

When so important a battle is lost, blame and excuses fly as thickly as musket balls. In his October 20 letter to Clinton informing him of the surrender, Cornwallis claimed, "I never saw this post in a favorable light. But, when I found I was to be attacked in it in so unprepared a state by so powerful an army and artillery, nothing but the hopes of relief would have induced me to attempt its defense." Cornwallis claimed that his relief had been promised by Clinton's letters, and this claim had great influence in convincing the British public of Clinton's responsibility for the disaster. Clinton, who spent the remaining years of his life writing a lengthy narrative vindicating his role in the war, argued that he had never been deceived by Washington's plans for a siege of New York and that Cornwallis was guilty of "extraordinary neglect and misconception of my orders." Clinton informed his readers, "I am humbly of opinion that, had his plan of fortification been judicious and the works he had time to throw up been properly defended, such an army as His Lordship commanded ought not to have been reduced to extremity."[48]

Probably more print has been devoted to blaming the British in defeat than to praising the Americans in victory. Washington almost certainly deserves more credit than he has commonly received for concentrating his and Rochambeau's matériel and men at what proved the most opportune time and place. As Louis Pasteur has observed, "It is strange how the lucky accidents tend to take place in the same laboratories."[49]

Yet the British defeat at Yorktown need not have meant the end of the war. News of the debacle did not arrive in London until November 25, five weeks after the surrender. Germain at once made sensible-seeming (though necessarily belated) plans to keep fighting: the British would hold key positions that were already occupied, would build their British forces in North America to 28,000, would plan amphibious operations along the East Coast, including the retaking of Rhode Island, and would more thoroughly exploit Loyalist support in the lower mid-Atlantic region, an area where Clinton had through most of the war retained 25,000 troops. Germain also believed, correctly, that the Loyalist cause enjoyed strong support in Canada.[50]

Moreover, the British still held New York, Charleston, and Savannah, and their environs, so British shipping should be able to continue resupplying troops and providing logistical support. The defeat at Yorktown ended the war not because the British military in America had been crushed but because it enabled the British parliamentary opposition to overthrow Lord North's war government. On February 27, 1782, the House of Commons urged King George III to end the war; on March 20, the crisis forced Lord North to resign as prime minister, and the new government opened negotiations with the Americans.[51]

By the time the peace treaty was signed in September 1783, India had been retained, and Gibraltar had resisted attack by Spain. In the Battle of the Saintes (April 12, 1782), Admiral Rodney had gained a complete victory over the French fleet in the West Indies.[52] Britain thus emerged from the war relieved at having sustained little material loss beyond the American colonies. But the surrender had more far-reaching consequences. Indeed, as often happens, one war leads to another: Britain's war for America was arguably one cause of still more military conflicts with French successes in this, their second eighteenth-century war against the British in North America, helping to embolden France to continue waging war with Britain right up until Waterloo.

Of course, the war in North America did not officially end immediately after Yorktown. To begin with, it took news at least a month to cross the Atlantic. Not until November 30, 1782, did Britain sign (preliminary) peace treaties with the other European belligerents; not until February 1784 did the British Foreign Ministry officially end the hostilities with the United States, France, Spain, and the Netherlands. (The U.S. Congress had actually ratified this treaty on January 14, and Congress had demobilized the Continental Army almost entirely by November 3, 1783.)

The Yorktown victory had been a timely one. Before it came, Vergennes had been planning (despite his previous support for the Revolution) to accept from mediators then meeting in Vienna a peace founded on the status quo war map. Such a concession might have terminated the French-American alliance and gravely compromised the American drive for independence. The blow caused by Yorktown proved especially fortunate for the Americans, therefore, in that it short-circuited Vergennes's considerations of the developments in the Austrian capital.[53]

One highly regarded historian of the British army has remarked: "The fact is, as I must repeat, that the revolution was the work of a very small but busy and ambitious minority."[54] This is true. In the political sphere alone, we have seen how much energy was expended and power wielded by a comparatively few congressmen and congressionally approved appointees.

In the military sphere, in a war that lasted from 1775 to 1783, a surprisingly small percentage of the citizenry fought.

In 1775 and throughout the war, Britain seemingly enjoyed enormous advantages. It had much greater material resources than the thirteen colonies; the British military outnumbered the Americans at least four to one, nor does this take account of the large proportion of Loyalists—perhaps one in three people—on North American soil. Britain's warships outnumbered America's by about a hundred to one at the outset, and that ratio grew as the war progressed—besides which, the American "fleet" was only several dozen scantily outfitted boats. The British retained the naval advantage even after France, Spain, and the Netherlands joined the war. On both sides, musket balls inflicted most of the fatalities, although men were slain also by bayonet, sabre, and artillery (shrapnel was not employed in warfare until 1804, against the Dutch in the East Indies.)[55]

When still a young officer at headquarters who had already grown fond of the men he desired to command, and at whose head he was (very late in the war) slain, Colonel John Laurens remarked in a letter: "I would cherish those dear, ragged Continentals, whose patience will be the admiration of future ages, and [I would] glory in bleeding with them." Only two months before Yorktown the ranking French official in America, the Chevalier de La Luzerne, observed that the men of Washington's army had so little clothing that the French troops were joking about their near nudity. Gouverneur Morris wryly prophesied "that if the war is continued through the winter [of 1781–82] the British troops will be scared at the sight of our men, for as they never fought with naked men, the novelty of it will terrify them." And yet, when a pair of ships arrived from Spain with some red coats aboard, the Americans refused to wear them. Having described at length the Americans' material deprivations, the Hessian officer Johann von Ewald asked: "With what soldiers in the world could one do what was done by these men, who go about nearly naked and in the greatest privation? Deny the best-disciplined soldiers of Europe what is due them and they will run away in droves, and the general will soon be alone. But from this one can perceive what an enthusiasm—which these poor fellows call 'Liberty'—can do!" On this vital subject, let the last word belong to their commander in chief. In a February 6, 1783, letter to Major General Nathanael Greene, Washington expressed his wonderment at what the American forces were able to attain, though "composed of men often times half starved, always in rags without pay and experiencing, at times, every species of distress which human nature is capable of undergoing."[56]

As regards the fortunes of the subject of our story, his huge prewar income had, since he entered public service, shrunk to an average of just about $5 per day. In 1781 he learned not only that DeLancey's Brigade had been quartering troops in Morrisania and looting it, but also that Continental forces harassing British-held New York had captured the estate and nearly wrecked it.

At about the same time, he found out that his mother, whom he had not seen in five years, was in failing health. He applied for a pass to visit her. The Continental Army headquarters and Governor Clinton of New York approved; arrangements were made for Gouverneur to travel through New Jersey. But General Clinton refused to let him cross British lines: "The peculiar situation of the state exposed in almost every quarter renders it necessary to prevent as much as possible any intercourse with the enemy."[57]

In mid-March of 1782 George Washington sent Major General Henry Knox and Gouverneur Morris to meet with two commissioners appointed by General Henry Clinton: General William Dalrymple (1735–1807) and Mr. Andrew Elliott (1728–1797), the Loyalist lieutenant governor of New York. Their brief was to discuss an exchange of prisoners of war. Morris seems a logical choice to be the civilian half of the American delegation: On January 28, 1782, he had drafted a petition for a subscription in relief of American prisoners held in New York City; then he followed the issue in more than half a dozen meetings with the commissioners in the winter and spring of 1782 on the question of the treatment of patriot captives.

New York was the major British-held port in North America; moreover, most of the prisoners held by the British in North America had been captured on Long Island and at Fort Washington, on Manhattan. These captives, along with numerous civilians suspected of being a threat, constituted a prisoner population of many thousands. In addition, about 7,000 American privateersmen captured on the high seas were imprisoned in a dozen filthy hulks in the harbor. Letters of marque were issued to civilian ship masters to sail their ships armed, thereby becoming privateersmen, so that authoritative statistics on the deaths of privateersmen are hard to ascertain with precision. Altogether an estimated 11,644 American prisoners of war died on the prison ships alone. In some particularly poor quarters, approximately 75 percent of the American captives died of disease, malnutrition, and mistreatment. "Rebels, turn out your dead!" was the British jailers' first order of the day.[58]

Morris's concern for the treatment of all these prisoners was longstanding. On January 21, 1778, more than four years earlier, he and four other members of Congress were appointed to prepare "a manifesto on the injurious treatment the American prisoners . . . received from the enemy."[59]

The American and British prisoner exchange commission met on March 31, 1782, after a two-week delay requested by British general Sir Henry Clinton, probably to plan a negotiation strategy. On the agenda were three items: each side was to settle accounts for the maintenance of its prisoners on both sides, held by the other side; the prisoners' future support was to be provided for; and an exchange of prisoners was to be arranged. Two weeks of discussions produced no result: the American negotiators ostensibly objected to the limits set on the British delegates' powers to treat diplomatically, while the British commissioners balked at accepting the Americans as representatives of a sovereign nation.

I characterized the Americans' objections as ostensible. In fact, Morris and Major General Knox surely understood an ugly strategic truth, and probably understood it better than most U.S. leaders. The king's forces in the North American theater were overextended and constantly in need of more men. Since the American prisoners, almost to a man, refused to cross over in exchange for their freedom, the British POW camps proved unfertile recruitment soil. Moreover, the British treated captives far more harshly than the Americans did. Consequently, when American prisoners were exchanged, they had generally to be invalided out of the service, whereas British prisoners released in exchanges were almost always immediately fit to serve. And thus, as both Morris and Knox may have recognized, every American prisoner semistarving in appalling British jails was, in effect, serving the patriot cause. Evidently General Washington understood this brutal calculus as well. When he had read the dispatches of Knox and Morris, he told them he was confident that their progress was slow for good reasons.[60]

From mid-fall of 1781 through early winter of 1782, Robert Morris devoted three days a week exclusively to the discussion of financial measures. In addition, virtually every Monday and Friday evening George Washington, the secretary of foreign affairs, the secretary of Congress, Gouverneur Morris, and Robert Morris assembled in the Finance Office to discuss ways to fund the war's continuation. The Finance Office urged American ministers abroad to try to induce the governments to which they were accredited to grant the United States loans. During this period the office also made provisions for support of the government payroll; to evaluate numerous accounts and requisitions for money; to pay interest on Loan Office certificates; and to distribute funds obtained from Europe (this last had to be accomplished in accord with congressional resolutions). The office furthermore had to negotiate with private contractors for the supply of the army and recruits, as well as of the navy artificers—mainly carpenters, sail makers, and victualers—and to arrange to transport the supplies.

And there was more. The Finance Office duties included, on occasion, the import and export of goods, money, and other articles on account of the United States; preparing circular letters to the states, describing the conditions of the public finances; writing to the states to urge their compliance with Continental requisitions; the discharge of money to the French government for General Lafayette's financial engagements for his troops with merchants from Baltimore; and providing transportation for various French VIPs.[61] In addition, the finance chief and his assistant prepared, at congressional request, regular, extensive statements of America's overall commercial situation, including a listing of monies borrowed and paper money issued; and they wrote an essay on the state of the economy, including plans for protecting it.[62] They told Congress quite bluntly that the labors of the Finance Office could not include miracles, that the country's financial ills would require careful patience and economy. American economic self-sufficiency seems to have been Robert Morris's ideal, but it was never attained.[63]

The Bank of North America was among the creations of which the Finance Office was proudest; Robert Morris predicted it would "give a new spring to commerce in America." On May 17, 1781, he submitted to Congress the thirteen-point plan for the bank, which was adopted substantially unchanged. It envisioned that the Bank of North America should serve both public and private interests and attract private capitalists by making money for them. These attractants would serve as inducement to the private capitalists to provide effective aid to the American government. According to the Finance Office plan, the bank would have a capitalization of $400,000 in specie, secured through the sale of stock at $400 per share. This goal was not reached: the government appears to have invested roughly $250,000 in the enterprise, and individuals only about $70,000.[64] The bank actually opened for business with less than $40,000 worth of specie in the vault.

Chartered by Congress in 1781, the Bank of North America, as it came to be known, opened for business on January 7, 1782, in Tench Francis's store on Chestnut Street in Philadelphia. The BNA proved the first incorporated bank to be granted a charter by the Confederation Congress. And when the Congress approved the Bank of North America, this legislative body had forbidden the states from chartering any other bank for the duration of the war. The bank's affairs were managed by a board of twelve directors. The shares were freely transferable, and the directors could increase the capital from time to time. Every day except Sunday the board submitted a report of the bank's cash account and circulation to the Superintendent of Finance, Robert Morris. He retained full access to all of BNA's records. The bank's notes, payable on demand, were made receivable for duties and taxes in all the states, and were the equivalent of specie in adjustment of accounts between the several states and the United States. The bank was the first genuine commercial bank, as commonly understood today, in the United States. Moreover, in light of the BNA's national purpose, national charter, national subscription to its initial stock, services to the national treasury during 1782–1783, and temporary national monopoly, it is correctly called the first bank of the United States.

Robert Morris kept a tight grip on the accounting reins, cutting government outlays and personally overseeing military purchases. Not surprisingly, some contemporaries maintained that Robert's main interest with the Bank of North America was to enrich himself. Congress had given him permission to continue his own business ventures during his term, and like most public officials of the time, Morris found ways to line his pocket by conducting public and private enterprises in tandem. These contentions were sharpened by the fact that nearly half (about 40 percent) of the original stock actually bought was subscribed to by Robert Morris and four of his wealthy friends: John Swanwick (1740–1798), William Bingham (1752–1804), John Carter (1745–1814) and Jeremiah Wadsworth (1743–1804). In addition to mercantile pursuits, Swanwick published a volume of poetry and was later elected to Congress from Pennsylvania in 1795. Carter printed a pair of Providence newspapers, the *Gazette* and *Country Journal,* for almost fifty years after an apprenticeship with Benjamin Franklin in Philadelphia. Gouverneur Morris himself purchased one $400 share on January 1, 1782, a week before the public had access.

Undercapitalization hampered the bank in its operations, yet from the outset it was a success, profitable to Continental, state, and city governments as well as to commercial interests. As of 1806 its capital stood at nearly $900,000, and it easily surpassed $1 million in the following years. The bank remained viable until 1923, when it was folded into another organization. Finally, through the Bank of North America, Robert Morris was enabled to borrow for the American government more than three times the amount the government had invested in the institution, anticipating public revenue and doing valuable service for the United States. Alexander Hamilton's First Bank of the United States began operations in 1784 with much greater capital, but its predecessor had already demonstrated the procedures and policies necessary for commercial banking.

Despite the manifest overall success of the Bank of North America, before its inception naysayers were many. In 1785 and the following year, popular agitation over the question of a national bank reached its height with new opposition to the institution after four and a half years of operation. Established in Philadelphia, the Bank of North America provided financial services for city residents, but many citizens outside the city, particularly farmers, found themselves unable to obtain loans and began to lobby for assistance. Gouverneur Morris's essay in support of the bank deserves some exposition.[65] The bank, he argued, did not serve only the privileged class and monopolize purchasing power. He also pointed out that the Bank of North America had been granted a charter as a voluntary association, a basic right in any viable republic: "May not all charters be at once laid low, by a general law declaring the existence of corporations to be incompatible with the public welfare?" Morris worried that the courts would have to intervene if the charter were repealed and, though necessary to uphold a bill of rights, "such power in judges is dangerous."

Robert Morris and his assistant were close personally as well as professionally; Robert's letters and memos address the assistant Morris always as "My dear Gouverneur." In contrast, Robert began letters to Thomas Willig, his business partner of decades, with "My dear Sir." The closeness must have been nurtured by their long hours; during this period they often worked even on Sunday. For instance, on February 24, 1782, they went to work at the Philadelphia office through the lunch hour, then spent the afternoon "in pursuit of Health on Horseback." Gouverneur seemed to relish the long hours, writing to Robert, "If you see the Doctor tell him that Fatiguing from four in the Morning till eight in the Evening and sleeping only from eleven till three agrees with me much better than all the Prescriptions in all the phisical Works in all the Languages of all the World."[66]

Gouverneur also aided Robert vitally in deciphering encoded correspondence. In July 1781, Robert Morris had sent John Jay, the American minister in Madrid, a nomenclator that Gouverneur had prepared. This device consisted of two sheets with 660 word-and-letter combinations. One sheet, for encoding, was in alphabetical order; the other, for decoding, was in numerical order. These codes were used for correspondence with Jay. (Once Morris had to urge Jay to be more careful to encode his communications from abroad because letter "seals are, on this side of the water, rather matters of Decoration, than use.") Developed primarily by Gouverneur Morris, these codes superseded the scrambled book codes and ciphers used earlier, each of which had certain drawbacks. Although more complicated and somewhat slower both to encode and decode, they turned out to be much more flexible and secure than the previous systems; indeed, the code lists served as the basis for American secret communications until 1867. In roughly eighty-five years of heavy diplomatic usage, the system seems never to have been compromised.[67]

During the winter of 1781–82, a major concern of the Finance Office was the development of a uniform system of American coinage. Even after the colonies declared independence, they continued to use English pounds, shillings, and pence as the money of account, and relied even more on Spanish dollars and reals (one-eighth of a dollar). Naturally it was difficult to assess the value of any coin in such an environment. In spring 1781 the Finance Office was investigated by a congressional committee, one of whose purposes was to try to learn the precise amount of American public debt. The committee ascertained the approximate foreign debt but could not come up with even a near estimate of the domestic debt.

To bring order out of this chaos, Robert Morris proposed liquidating the public debt in specie, and borrowing the funds for it in the form of commercial loans. After the establishment of the Bank of North America, people began to prefer the notes as a medium of exchange. The dollar, divided into one hundred parts, became the unit of account and payment.

Gouverneur Morris suggested the decimal computation, and Jefferson the dollar as the unit of account and payment. Semi-annual statements of the public indebtedness began to be published by the Treasury Department in 1791.

On January 15, 1782, Robert Morris submitted to the President of Congress a report on the coinage of the United States; Gouverneur Morris actually wrote the report, although the two had worked on it very closely. As a result of a complex series of calculations, which took account of such factors as values per grain of fine silver, the report proposed that, at the mint price, the American dollar was to combine the British and Spanish systems. This plan was based on a monetary unit called a mill, defined as one quarter of a grain of silver. The proposal called for the minting of five denominations of coins, with values based on the decimal system. There would be two small copper coins: a five unit piece called a five and an eight unit piece called an eight. There would also be three silver coins: a 100 unit piece called a cent (sometimes referred to as a bit), a 500 piece called a quint and a 1,000 unit piece called a mark. There would not be a one unit piece.

To appreciate the Morris plan one must understand the complexity of the colonial monetary system. In many ways each state acted as an independent nation with its own laws, borders and customs inspectors, and currency rate. As each colony set its own value for its currency, the exchange rate among the various currencies was not always equal; a price in New York shillings was not the same as a price in Georgia shillings. These local currencies were both monies of account and paper currencies (but not coins) printed by the individual states. To complicate the colonial situation further, most interstate and many internal transactions took place using Spanish American silver dollar coins as the medium of exchange rather than paper currency shillings and pounds.

Thus prices and account books were kept in shillings and pounds, but payments were calculated and made with Spanish American dollars. For daily commerce one therefore needed to know the shilling exchange rate of a Spanish dollar for each of the states. Morris's system could be used to convert foreign coins, including the Spanish American silver dollar, into units that would be comparable in the different states. According to Morris's system, the Spanish American dollar was valued at 1440 federal units (or mills). This would be the value of the coin throughout the nation.

Congress took no immediate action on this proposal, but in 1783 referred it to a committee of which Thomas Jefferson was a member. Jefferson proposed the dollar as a unit of account and payment, with divisions and subdivisions in the decimal ratio. After he conferred briefly with Robert and Gouverneur Morris, the committee adopted Jefferson's views. The next year (1784) Congress adopted his system, although no coins were issued at that time.[68]

"Our civilization is inseparably linked with our methods of economic calculation," as Ludwig von Mises aptly observes in his classic *Human Action*. During the crucial late Revolutionary period the Finance Office was active in establishing those calculations for the new nation. It is true that, as some scholars have pointed out, some of the groundwork for Robert and Gouverneur had been laid by the sound money developments of 1780–81, during which time Congress had resolved to stop the paper money press (the usual solution to financial crisis), and the path had been opened by the amount of specie available in the country in 1781; still, we must not underestimate the size of the problem involved in providing a stable circulating currency at this time. Throughout the war years, the changing value of money in America warped all aspects of local trade. Two, sometimes three, currencies circulated simultaneously. Even within a region, the value of money could not be assumed, and this is not to mention that currency values fluctuated differently in different localities. Finally, all wartime bargaining was complicated by a preference for specie. The work of the Finance Office was enormously difficult and enormously important.

As Robert Morris had warned, the notes issued by the Bank of North America did not suffice to meet the need for a circulating medium by 1782, by which time the American Continental paper had become virtually worthless. Robert Morris still considered taxation impracticable even financially: the process would have drawn money (already scarce) out of circulation, thus exacerbating the problems posed by the most extreme devaluation of the Continental paper. He conceived of an additional, temporary, paper medium as a crossover currency: the "Morris notes" would circulate as cash, constitute a medium for establishing credit, and enable Congress to buy necessary supplies. Lack of security made people nervous over the Continental currency, but the "Morris notes" were backed by Robert Morris's personal fortune and ostensibly more reliable. When taxes could eventually be collected and steadily accumulated, Robert Morris hoped, then his Morris notes could be gradually eliminated.

To supplement this circulating medium and help revive the nation's public credit, Robert Morris inaugurated the first national mint, eventually established in Philadelphia. On January 15, 1782, Gouverneur and Robert submitted a proposal for the mint, which, in 1783, Congress approved. The first American coin was struck on April 2, 1783. Now Robert Morris's Finance Office had completed the three pillars of its economic platform: the foundational effort to regularize American currency, the creation of the Morris notes, and the founding of the mint.[69]

That same winter of early 1782, the Finance Office had the surprisingly difficult task of arranging to transport tobacco from Virginia to many other colonies and countries, especially in Europe and the West Indies. The office also quietly hired Thomas Paine, of all people, to write in support of "upright measures and a faithful administration," as the Finance Office saw them.[70] A written agreement on February 10, 1782, between Robert Morris and George Washington records that Paine was to be paid $800 a year and suggests the primary purpose of his employment: "the Propriety and even necessity of informing the People and rousing them into Action." In a memorandum later that month, Robert Morris wrote that Paine was "engaged to write in the public newspapers in support of the measures of Congress and their Ministers." For one thing, Paine was to encourage enlistment in the Continental Army: "We wish to draw the resources and powers of the country into action. We wish to bring into the field an army equal to the object for which we are at war." Morris was also interested in convincing people of the necessity of taxation; Paine's newspaper articles were to "prepare the minds of the people for such restraints and such taxes and imposts, as are absolutely necessary for their own welfare."

Over the course of the Revolution, paper money had been tried in all the colonies, but the experiment had worked satisfactorily only in Pennsylvania. Because of this—especially coupled with the conditions of war—accounting of the states' revenues was extremely difficult. Moreover, Congress could only recommend and request the states to pay money into the treasury; it had not a dollar's worth of enforcement power.

As Adam Smith remarked, the British had taxed their American colonies only moderately, in part because the colonies did not cost them much and in part because the local administrative apparatus was not well developed. And unlike France and Spain, for instance, the British conducted their imperial "government . . . upon a plan equally frugal" with the American administrative arrangements, thus sparing the colonists truly burdensome tithes.[71] Thus, the colonists had not become accustomed to paying heavy taxes.

Also, of course, the nascent nation needed to fund an expensive war. During the armed conflict Congress issued Continental bills amounting to roughly $191,552,000. From 1775 through 1779 there were huge increases in the face value of the bills issued, generally because the states failed to collect taxes which were to take the bills out of circulation. Virginia, for example, did not seriously attempt to obtain revenues from taxes until 1781, and the other states were, on balance, not substantially more ambitious. As mentioned above, Congress could only recommend taxes, not oblige their collection. The paper money scheme having failed, then, as late as the early 1780s the necessary supplies for the army had to be levied in kind, since they could not be paid for with tax revenues that did not exist.

One major problem was the inevitable result of a major administrative oversight: in order to have just requisitions, you must have accurate assessments; lacking these, Congress had no way to know how much each state should pay, nor was there adequate information concerning what each state had paid. The economic muddle that faced the new Finance Office in 1781 can only with difficulty be imagined.

The dilemma outlined above was exacerbated by electoral presumptions: the state governors felt they could not urge taxation upon the legislators without risking losing their election, while state legislators, who had the power to levy taxes, believed that in doing so they would also greatly injure their political opportunities. Moreover, popular catch-phrases concerning British taxation still rang in Americans' ears.[72]

Through 1782, paltry tax revenues made the prognosis poor for America's finances; it was more and more difficult to secure supplies for the army, and to obtain and pay for foreign loans was troublesome indeed. Robert Morris and Gouverneur Morris quickly understood that they must bring the old system to an end. As far as anyone in America then knew, the engines of war still had to be supplied. The Finance Office therefore primarily wanted taxes made payable in specie, which would provide the necessary revenue, and these taxes must be federal. Such revenue could pay most of the interest on the new nation's debt. The Finance Office also desired that the states make payments in advance for financing the war expenditure. In brief, they proposed to introduce retrenchment and economy into the American government.

Thomas Paine wrote an essay in favor of an import tax, but tiny Rhode Island (somewhat typically) obstructed its passage. In an unpublished essay, " 'Altogether in his Pay?' Robert Morris and the Nationalist Movement," the historian Elizabeth M. Nuxoll has pointed out that "states' rights partisans needed only to influence one or two state legislatures to defeat the mainstays of the nationalist program," and this they often did.[73]

The Finance Office had to accept that tax collection was politically impracticable; furthermore, borrowing, they came to accept, would have disastrous effects upon the country they served; and economic stabilization through legislation had already proven unsuccessful. The office therefore proposed to let depreciation work as a gradual and comparatively equitable tax, and to allow it to continue until the peace, when the remaining debt could be paid off at market value.

In the end most of Robert Morris's program broke down, mainly because of two eventualities: the narrow well of foreign loans dried up; and the still fragile Union lacked revenues from taxes to service its debts and support a robust currency in specie. The states failed to provide Congress with an income adequate to national needs. And Congress rejected Robert Morris's proposal for land, poll, and excise taxes.[74]

Historians often deprecate policies whose proponents have not succeeded in carrying them out. But the policies that Robert Morris and Gouverneur Morris's Finance Office managed to put into practice resulted in major and minor improvements on several fronts. As for what they wished to do but could not—collect taxes and obtain more foreign loans—the new country would have been wise to take their advice. To the critic who points out that America won the war regardless, and now is the world's financial leader, I would reply that American finances profited greatly by reason of the stewardship of Robert Morris and Gouverneur Morris and that, had the policies they advocated been adopted, America might well have prospered even more. Moreover, without the firm assistance of the French, in obtaining which Gouverneur and Robert played no small part—when might American strength alone have become sufficient to defeat their imperial enemy?

In late winter and early spring of 1782, Gouverneur Morris became much engaged in trying to obtain aid surreptitiously from Spain, via "Havanna," under the aegis of John Jay, then American Minister to Spain. "But if [aid] is obtained," Morris wrote, "give no notice to Congress, for we must plead Poverty to the States if we were rich as Croesus": clear indication of the friction between that august body and the Finance Office. This tension made somewhat more difficult the office's dealings with Congress concerning the domestic debt. On the other hand, Robert Morris informed Congress in 1782 that the best means of funding (repaying) the debt would be to pay the principal and interest by available revenues. Were this done, the market value of securities would rise to a level sufficient to flow "into those hands which would render it most productive." Robert Morris wished, in a word, to have those securities support an overall American system of credit and currency. He understood that such a plan would benefit the wealthiest Americans disproportionately.[75]

Despite many rumors of an imminent peace, the economic situation worsened in the spring of 1782. Although land battles were smaller and fewer, the British substantially strengthened their naval blockade. This fact, combined with a sharp increase in illicit trade (an ironic combination), placed great strain on the Finance Office's economic scheme outlined above. In this period, for the first time Congress appointed committees to oversee the executive departments, among them the Finance Office. After Robert seriously antagonized the states by publicizing in writing their failure to collect taxes and provide the national government with sufficient specie, the tension between Congress and the Finance Office grew stronger still.

In an attempt to save money, the Finance Office reduced the funds available for the care of British prisoners of war. (Even so, the British dealt far more harshly with the American prisoners than vice versa, and this although the British had far more money.) In the spring of 1782, Robert Morris conceived the idea of selling Hessian prisoners of war as indentured servants.

At this period an observant French visitor, Charles Louis Victor, Prince de Broglie (1756–1794), thus characterized Gouverneur:

> One of the men, who appeared to me to possess the most spirit and nerve amongst those whom I met at Philadelphia, was a Mr. Morris, generally called Governor [*sic*]. He is very well educated, speaks excellent French, is very sarcastic but generally liked. I fancy however that his superiority, which he has taken no pains to conceal, will prevent his ever occupying an important place.[76]

Morris enjoyed good company and had a penchant for the occasional battle of wits, and de Broglie's impression of his superciliousness accords with one's impression of Morris as both convivial and intensely competitive. That

Morris had any energy left over to socialize is remarkable, since his Finance Office activities became even more demanding that spring. Through May of 1782, the office operated out of William West's house on Front Street above Chestnut. Here, Gouverneur helped Robert Morris formulate a thoughtful essay for congressional perusal on American commerce and how to protect it. In April and May the office furthermore devised plans to try to break the enemy naval stranglehold on the Atlantic coast of America.[77] With several ships of the line, they thought the nascent country could successfully destroy the large British fleet patrolling America's coast.

While both Morrises (especially Gouverneur) were plainly overoptimistic concerning American military capabilities, with respect to finance both men had what Robert Lynd has termed "the genius of the long view . . . , another name for imagination in politics." Both also had an eye for short-term opportunity. For example, at this time in our story, when the illicit commercial trade and the British blockade had combined to shrink down imports of taxable goods almost to a nullity, Gouverneur sought relief for the American economy by recommending that the Bank of North America set exchange rates to give preference to Spanish silver dollars. This would encourage Americans to use silver coins domestically, reserving other coinage for illicit trade with the British. Thus, British money would be driven out of circulation in the United States. If the new nation adopted the silver standard, as Gouverneur Morris then hoped, and the national bank's notes were valued in Spanish silver dollars, then the bank would be able to back its notes with sufficient silver.[78]

In June 1782 the Finance Office shifted its headquarters from Front Street to a store rented from Jacob Barge (1721?–1808) on the southeast corner of High (Market) and Fifth Streets. Even in inclement weather both Robert and Gouverneur could easily walk to work: the new office was only one block east of Robert's large family house, where he lived with his wife and seven children, and two blocks west of Mrs. Dalley's boardinghouse at High and Third Streets. At Mrs. Dalley's, Gouverneur's fellow boarders included Alexander Hamilton and Elbridge Gerry (1744–1814). During the decade of his adult life that Gouverneur spent in Philadelphia, the street commissioners kept busy regulating paving, leveling the streets, and improving the sewers. These improvements must have been especially appreciated by the tall, peg-legged assistant to the financier.

On April 15, 1782, Benjamin Franklin received from Lord Shelburne the first communication relative to a treaty. During the summer of 1782, peace rumors began to circulate more widely, although a provisional treaty was not signed until November 30, 1782. A cessation of hostilities was declared on

January 20, 1783. Many more months passed, however, before John Adams, Franklin, and Jay signed the definitive articles known as the Treaty of Paris, on September 3, 1783, even though this treaty comprised the same terms as the provisional articles agreed to by both parties in November 1782. Still more time passed before Congress ratified the treaty on January 14, 1784.

Not everyone was eager to anticipate an end to the war, however. In an interesting letter to Matthew Ridley, dated August 6, 1782, Gouverneur Morris comments:

> I am well convinced of two things. One that a Peace will not easily be made, and another that it is not much for the Interest of America that it should be made at Present. Whoever will take a Retrospective View of our Affairs will find amid all their changes (and God knows they have been sufficiently variable) that we have made a silent but rapid and constant Progress towards Strength and Greatness. Our position, our Numbers, our Resources and our probable Increase are all important. Our Knowledge is not unimportant. Highly Commercial, being as it were the first born Children of extended Commerce in modern Times. We must be maritime. Freedom was secured by the several Constitutions, Freedom in the extreme. Nothing remained but Vigor, Organization and Promptitude to render this a considerable Empire. These can only be acquired by a continuation of the war, which will convince People of the necessity of Obedience to common Counsel for general Purposes. War is indeed a rude, rough Nurse to infant States, and the Consequence of being committed to her Care is that they either die Young, or grow up Vigorous. We have at least lived thro' the Cradle, and are familiarized to her Looks of Horror. . . .[79]

This is a capsule of one of the most extreme Federalist arguments. Both Robert Morris and Gouverneur, as well as such other luminaries as Alexander Hamilton, Rufus King (1755–1827), and possibly even Henry Knox, wished to extend the war because they believed it would perforce strengthen the ties between the states and the federal power, as well as greatly extend and deepen the powers of the federal government.

With his splendid contacts among those conducting America's foreign affairs—John Jay and Robert R. Livingston, especially—Gouverneur not surprisingly knew better than most American government officials the state of the negotiations under way in France; he was well aware that a formal peace was not immediately at hand. Still, his statements reveal that he was indifferent to the hardships long endured by the Continental Army and to the men's low morale. Food was abundant in Philadelphia to those of Morris's social class and financial means. The relative ease of life in the city was far different from the daily existence of the troops in the field. Since the Finance Office had been securing the army's and navy's supplies, Gouverneur Morris knew well the conditions under which most of the Continentals lived and fought, and that makes his desire for the war to continue even more unfeeling.

The peace arrangements concluded at Versailles in 1783 surprised contemporaries, and should surprise us even today. The main outlines can be presented with several strokes. Britain returned several territories to America's indispensable ally, France: St. Pierre and Miquelon; her West African settlements; the islands of Tobago and St. Lucia in the West Indies; and some trading posts and privileges in India. Florida was restored to Spain, which had lost it in 1763, and so was Minorca, lost in 1713. Spain, on the other hand, handed the Bahamas to Britain. And the thirteen colonies were recognized as the United States of America.

The new nation officially stretched westward to the Mississippi, and north roughly to the Great Lakes in the west and the St. Lawrence in the east; the nation's extent west of the Great Lakes remained to be settled later. The Americans also obtained fishing rights off Newfoundland. Debts owed to private contractors before the war were to be paid, no small problem for the American Treasury. The British and the Americans were, for the time being, to share the right to navigate the Mississippi. The United States promised that Congress would recommend to the states the restoration of property seized from Loyalists. And, of course, the military commanders of all the combatant nations received official orders to cease the fighting. (An unofficial cease-fire was already in place.) British withdrawal from the American ports took place with characteristic deliberateness during the ensuing months, after the signing of a separate treaty on the subject. The final withdrawals pursuant to the peace took place without further bloodshed or looting.[80]

Between midsummer and November of 1782, the Finance Office produced its report on public credit, on which Gouverneur had much influence. The Finance Office's assumption of the Revolutionary War debts of the states had formally created a national debt. So, not surprisingly, the report calls for federal land, poll, and excise taxes to fund all Continental obligations. The American dependence on foreign loans during this period proved immense.

Gouverneur also worked on the question of how America was to settle its financial accounts with Europe. In furtherance of the comprehensive strategy presented in the report on public credit, Gouverneur helped Robert develop a series of economic position papers, the chief aim of which was to try to convert the European powers to free trade, meaning trade absent tariff layers imposed by the European governments. In her essay "The Office of Finance and the Development of the Ideology of Free Trade," Mary Gallagher, the co-editor of *The Robert Morris Papers,* aptly characterizes Robert Morris and Gouverneur Morris as "impresarios" of free trade. Their views are set forth most clearly in Gouverneur Morris's essay addressed to the French minister, the Chevalier de La Luzerne, entitled "Ideas of an American on the Commerce between the United States and the French Islands." The inauguration of free trade alone, however, could not solve America's national debt problem. The Finance Office sought revenue-development powers for Congress; these, of course, would shift power dramatically away from the individual states.[81]

Throughout these months Gouverneur often wrote to his former King's College classmates John Jay and Robert Livingston, exchanging political insights and opinions.[82]

On August 18, 1782, George Washington wrote to the British general Guy Carleton to suggest restarting negotiations on a possible prisoner exchange. The British quickly agreed to go forward, and Washington again approached Gouverneur Morris and Henry Knox. Knox agreed, but Morris "signified [to G.W.] . . . it will be inconvenient . . . to attend as one of the Commissioners at the proposed meeting." Morris did not wish to become involved in what he anticipated would be an unsuccessful fishing expedition; and, perhaps more fundamentally, he believed, as indicated above, that America's best interests would not be served by most standard exchanges. Moreover, Gouverneur did have another more than full-time job.[83]

As summer turned to autumn, the Finance Office found that state-supplied revenues were extremely disappointing; Robert Morris ordered William Whipple (who had been instrumental in the overhaul of the Continental Army's commissary and quartermaster departments) to begin publicizing monthly the extent of each state's delinquent payments to the receivers of Continental taxes (a group of public officials then rapidly becoming as popular as the IRS).[84] That fall, the Finance Office negotiated a new contract with which the American army was temporarily satisfied. This arrangement also provided Robert and Gouverneur some much-needed flexibility in the sale of bills of exchange, a matter in which Gouverneur played an important behind-the-scenes part. The contract also relieved some of the pressure on the Morris notes.[85]

Gouverneur's character is revealed in a letter to Benjamin Franklin, dated September 28, 1782. After a brief remark on Finance Office–related resolutions before Congress, Gouverneur proceeds to "add a few hints as your friend"—specifically, that "your enemies industriously publish that your age and indolence have unfitted you for your Station, and your sense of obligation to France seals your lips when you ask their Aid, and that . . . both your

Connections and Influence at Court are extremely feeble." This was surprisingly frank—the more so because Franklin was twice Morris's age, already world-famous, and probably at the zenith of his career. Morris went on: "In addition to the general reflection how Envy has favored superior Merit in all ages, you will draw further consolation from this: that many who censure are well disposed to cast the censure on France, and would fain describe her as acting the part of self interest without a wish to render us effectual Aid."[86] Morris here hints what a number of congressmen had been thinking; namely, that France had been helping America for purely selfish national self-interest.

The letter to Franklin deserves to be read not only in light of Morris's knowledge of Franklin's relationship with the French, but also in the context of his pragmatism concerning the U.S. relationship with France. Gouverneur Morris and John Jay were among the most vociferous opponents of the congressional instructions presented on June 15, 1781. These instructions in effect placed the American peace commissioners entirely under the aegis of the French governmental representatives (it is noteworthy that these instructions were drawn up with the guidance of the French minister to the United States, the Chevalier de La Luzerne). However, the U.S. peace commissioners in France, led in this matter by Jay, took an independent path as regards the major points of disagreement—to the great and immediate benefit of America. Jay wrote to Gouverneur from Paris on October 13, 1782: "We may, and we may not have a peace this Winter. Act as if the War would certainly continue, keep proper Garrisons."[87]

At the outset of 1783, with the preliminary peace articles agreed on, and more favorable terms yet being negotiated by Jay, John Adams, and Franklin, the outlook for the fledgling United States seemed rosy. The peace led to a new nation, and this country looked something like this. As late as the 1790 census, it had just 4.5 persons per square mile, mostly in a half-dozen Atlantic coastal centers along with some isolated settlements. Free people, approximately 79 percent of the total population, lived primarily in widely spaced single-family wood-frame dwellings, and relied for heat and cooking on usually one open fireplace. This fixture consumed roughly six cords of wood per year, so Americans were probably often somewhat chillier than they would have liked, but also probably more inured to the cold. Almost no houses had stoves. In the early 1740s Franklin had invented his famous stove, but it did not become widely used until the 1790s, when it was redesigned in such a way as to remove the smoke from inside the houses. The Philadelphia inventor, David Rittenhouse (1732–1796), is generally accorded the honor of having made these design changes. Except in Philadelphia and Boston, moreover, houses nowhere had running water. People used outhouses to eliminate and washed using a pitcher and a basin. On frosty days, of course, the person who would wash or shave often had to break ice to do so. Candles were expensive, so most families seem to have used only one per night. Even prosperous Americans generally slept more than one to a bed; and bedsprings, by the way, were not invented until 1845.

Needless to say, canned food did not arrive until the late 1800s, and as there were no iceboxes for most people at the time, there was almost no such thing as storing frozen food. Some of the wealthiest citizens, such as Franklin, however, who had reasonable access to seasonally frozen bodies of water, had ice cellars, detached from the house, and filled with ice and sawdust. These storage pits sometimes furnished their owners with ice well into July. For most Americans, the dietary staples were salt pork, salt beef, lard, johnnycake—a bread made with cornmeal—oat bread, and molasses, as well as fruits and vegetables.

On March 24, 1782, Spain finally recognized U.S. independence; Sweden and Denmark had done the same more than a month before. On April 19, eight years after Lexington, Congress formally proclaimed the end of the war.

The previous day, Congress had urged the states to alter the Articles of Confederation to enable Congress to levy import duties for a period of twenty-five years. The duties were to be applied against the national debt. The request grew out of a meeting held on the evening of February 20. Present were Thomas Fitzsimmons (1741–1811), a Philadelphia merchant and future politician; Nathaniel Gorham (1738–1796), soon to be President of Congress and later active in the Constitutional Convention; Alexander Hamilton; Richard Peters (1744–1828), a congressman from Pennsylvania; Daniel Carroll (1730–1796), a Maryland congressman, and James Madison; they decided that time-limited import duties would be a good source of revenue. They also determined to obtain additional funds by asking the states to commit long-term taxes for federal use. Hamilton alone dissented from both ideas.

At the time, the request seemed reasonable to almost all Americans, and somewhat logically so: throughout the eighteenth century, the customs service had been one of Britain's most lucrative sources of revenue. With the state of New York alone opposed to it, however, the proposal was defeated, as changes to the Articles required the approval of all the states, a severe political problem.[88]

Despite the Finance Office's attempts to supply (and placate) the army, discontent in that institution steeply increased—not surprisingly, in light of the appalling lack of provisions, not to mention long droughts in pay and other fundamentals through most of the eight-year war. In early 1783, a pair of mutinies threatened the stability of the nation. In mid-March, in Newburgh, New York, a sizable group of veteran officers threatened serious internal violence; only their respect for George Washington, who made a personal appeal to them, held them back. As a result of the episode, Congress voted the officers five full years' pay. In late June a mutiny of unpaid Pennsylvania Line soldiers in Philadelphia forced Congress to leave the city and convene in Princeton, New Jersey. Thanks to the presence of mind of such veterans as Anthony Wayne, the mutineers were brought under control without much bloodshed less than two weeks later. On November 3, 1783, the Continental Army disbanded by order of Congress.[89]

As the reader already knows, Gouverneur had had some longstanding concerns about the hardships endured by our fighting forces. Indeed he had expended greater effort on trying to assure proper supplies, adequate pay and suitable pensions for the Continental forces than any other nonmilitary official. In the 1770s, for example, Morris worked intensively on a Revolutionary War pension plan that, in its clever use of equations, matches the elegant complexity of the coinage system proposals he presented to congressional leaders.[90]

In fall of 1782 the Finance Office had the first U.S. coins struck and submitted to Congress. But steady minting, which Robert Morris had hoped to inaugurate, was not instituted until 1789, when the Constitution was ratified.

As a reader of Bernard Mandeville's *The Fable of the Bees,* Gouverneur Morris may have believed that some vices "by the dextrous Management of a skillful Politician may be turned into Public Benefits."[91] He seems to have wished to use the army's capacity for violence, along with a disorganized citizenry's presumed incapacity to resist it, to force policy changes that he and Robert Morris desired. Before the Newburgh officers' revolt had reached its zenith, the less intransigent Federalists became convinced that they could not establish any federal taxes beyond the aforementioned import duties.

Congress had again asked for the power to levy customs duties, modifying the terms to eliminate some of the states' objections.[92] Robert Morris, who had already published his resignation, manifested scorn for the bill, and Gouverneur shared his sentiments. It seems likely that the latter, in particular, now conspired for a time with the military officers assembled at Newburgh to try to effect political reform. Both Robert and Gouverneur seem to have hoped that the threat of a military revolt would induce the states to increase congressional powers. If that failed, they hoped that Congress, supported by the army, would simply take those powers.

Gouverneur's correspondence suggests his connection to the conspiracy. When the mutiny was gaining force, he wrote Jay: "The army have swords in their hands. . . . Depend on it, good will arise from the situation, to which we are hastening. And this you may rely on, that my efforts will not be wanting. . . . I think it probable, that much of Convulsion will ensue, yet it must terminate in giving to Government that Power, without which Government is but a name." In February he wrote General Greene, then commander of the southern army, that "there is no probability the States will ever make such grants [to provide revenue to discharge all debts], *unless the army be united and determined in the pursuit of it; and unless they be firmly supported, and as firmly support the other public creditors.* That this may happen must be the entire wish of every intelligently just man, and of every real friend to our glorious revolution." He had written to Henry Knox in a similar vein, and with similar emphasis, roughly a week earlier.

To their credit, the two generals responded with better sense. Knox wrote that the army had always been Continental (meaning always a force loyal to the united thirteen colonies), that "A hoop to the barrel" and "Cement to the union" were favorite army toasts. He went on tactfully to tell the assistant U.S. financier that the army would gladly help strengthen the government in appropriate ways, but that such prospective efforts would have to be explained clearly "by proper Authority." Knox then asked: "As the present Constitution is so defective, why do not you great men call the people together, and tell them so? That is, to have a Convention of the States to form a better Constitution? This appears to us, who have a superficial view only, to be the most efficacious Remedy."

As for General Greene, he put to Gouverneur a pertinent question: "When soldiers advance without Authority, who can halt them?" The reply (May 18, 1783) was somewhat lame: "I entirely agree with you in sentiment as to the consequences, which must follow from any unconstitutional procedure of the military." Nevertheless, Morris continues revealingly, "*I did hope from their influence* . . . but neither time nor circumstances *will permit anything now.*"[93]

In an April 30, 1783, letter to William Hemsley, Gouverneur suggested a few ideas on the subject of a new coinage for America. Hemsley (1737–1812) was a Maryland congressman, appointed to the committee on April 23 to confer with Robert Morris on plans for coinage and a federal mint. Gouverneur's letter is one of several writings by him on the same subject. He discusses the denominations of such coins, the amount of silver to be in each, and how much it would cost to develop a system. Under the first of these rubrics he discusses the question of "Old Dollars," that is, where the official exchange rate changes domestically, for instance, where ten "old dollars" are exchanged for one new one. Morris also considers the comparative values of French crowns versus dollars; louis, which "pass for" dollars; and the "par of Exchange between London and Philadelphia." The louis d'or was the French 20-franc gold piece that was first struck in 1640 and continued to be issued up to the French Revolution. The par value here means the established value of the monetary unit of one country expressed in terms of the monetary unit of another country using the same metal as the standard of value. Next he demonstrates "the Arithmetical Operation" that allows discovery of "the Denomination of our Coin." Under this heading, he explores the dollar's "four . . . *nominal Values* in America," exclusive of the rate for sterling existent in South Carolina. Thirdly, Gouverneur considers the coins then circulating in the thirteen states, in order to determine "the Quantity of fine Silver" per coin. In a complicated and elegant series of calculations, he establishes the units of "Silver, Copper and if necessary Gold" that the mint must use for each. The exposition is intended to "render all [American] Accounts and Calculations extremely simple."[94]

Between early May 1783 and the New Year, the Finance Office worked mostly on developing American trade and lobbying against foreign trade barriers. In a September 24, 1783, letter to Gouverneur, John Jay observes some burgeoning opportunities for trade: "We have heard that the Ottoman and Russian Empires are on the Point of unsheathing the Sword . . . if Russia should extend her navigation to Constantinople, we *may* be the better for it. That Circumstance is an additional motive to our forming a Treaty of Commerce with her." Jay is also aware of the damaging potential of British restrictions toward American trade as he observes that "America is beheld with Jealousy, and Jealousy is seldom idle." Indeed, by July, a British Order of Council had already barred their West Indian colonies to American ships. Gouverneur responded to Jay in a letter dated January 10, 1784, in which he saw American unity as the benefit of British trade restrictions: "On this Occasion, as on others, Great Britain is our best Friend, and by seizing the critical Moment when we were about to divide, she has shewn clearly the dreadful Consequences of Division. You will find that the States are coming into Resolutions on the Subject of Commerce, which, if they had been proposed by Congress on the plain Reason of the Thing, would have been rejected with Resentment and perhaps Contempt." He concludes, "Do not ask the british [*sic*] to take off their foolish Restrictions. Let them alone and they will be obliged to do it themselves."[95] Around the same time, the Finance Office's applications (that is, U.S. applications) for French loans were turned down, although the Dutch seemed disposed to forgive the interest payments due on their sizable loan, which encouraged Robert and Gouverneur to hope that that obligation could be retired.[96] Despite the concerted efforts of both Morrises, "the obstacles to reduction of defense expenses" remained great "even after the cessation of hostilities." Their frustration is palpable in a typical Finance Office diary entry (July 30, 1783): "Being in great distress for want of Money Mr. [Gouverneur] Morris and myself spent much time in considering ways and means but as yet unsuccessfully."[97]

A military sketch of 1783: On May 13, the Society of the Cincinnati was formed—a group mainly of distinguished commissioned officers from the Continental Army who agreed to gather regularly after disbanding, to reminisce and discuss matters of common contemporary interest. They took their name from the Roman general Lucius Quinctius Cincinnatus, who was much admired for his republican virtue. The society's founding president was Henry Knox, who was to succeed Washington as the head of America's army. On November 25, the last of the British army finally left New York. On the following day Congress met at Annapolis, rather than Philadelphia. On December 4, George Washington took leave of many of his most cherished fellow officers at Fraunces Tavern in New York City. And on December 23 he formally resigned as military commander in chief.

On January 3, 1784, General Knox reported to Congress that the army had been reduced to fewer than seven hundred men. An obvious duty for them would have been the protection of the new western and southwestern frontiers, except that strong opposition to a standing army dictated more reductions: on June 2, Congress voted the discharge of all but eighty privates and several junior officers to guard the federal storehouses. The navy, consisting for the most part of several thousand privateers, was steeply reduced (and the War of 1812, preceded by many years of galling naval impressments by the British Royal Navy, was the inevitable result).[98]

From the New Year, 1784, through October of the same year, the Finance Office overdrew on the Dutch loan. Robert specifically postponed his retirement until he could meet his financial commitments. Somewhat in a similar vein, from his office Robert made statements opposing the creation of a rival bank in Philadelphia. In Europe, John Adams negotiated to have Robert's bills of exchange covered by a new Dutch loan. During this period, too, Robert, with Gouverneur's assistance, established a fund for the retirement of the Morris notes. This effected, on November 1 Robert, followed by Gouverneur, resigned from office. The Congress, then convening at Trenton, abolished the Finance Office and reinaugurated the Board of Treasury. The new Board began on an unpropitious note, since the first appointees refused to serve; not until nearly eight months later (January 25, 1785) were men finally found to serve.

This Board administered the U.S. finances until the last day of September 1788—that is, for three years and five months, almost the same amount of time as the Finance Office. Over that time, the receivers of taxes paid into the Treasury less than $997,000, and the funds received by Congress came almost entirely from three sources: interest on certificates, or indents, accounted for just over $1,881,000, and shockingly small sums came from the sale of substantial war materials and huge acreages of public lands. The taxes collected by the new Board had not been deposited into the Treasury, and large sums allotted for secret service, such as spying and privateers' services, proved unaccounted for. The Treasury Board was suspended when a congressional committee, assembled to examine its affairs, reported its pitiful mismanagement. This with no war to excuse it.

The Robert Morris Finance Office had effected many reforms that led to large reductions in expenses, preventing large-scale corruption and lessening governmental liabilities. Robert Morris's notes were in due time redeemed. Every financial obligation he had officially assumed while superintendent of finances was eventually fulfilled. Small wonder Congress had proved extremely reluctant to accept his resignation.[99]

When Gouverneur Morris retired from the office of assistant financier, he resumed his private legal practice; various business ties kept him in Philadelphia, where he remained until he left for Europe in 1788. Their years of intimate acquaintance had made Gouverneur perfectly comfortable with Robert; in the years after the dissolution of the Finance Office, the two worked together in business speculations, Gouverneur on occasion serving either as Robert's agent or his legal counsel. At other times he devised plans for mercantile voyages over land and sea, or purchased stocks and lands.

The ethical character of these speculations seems to have been mixed; so also the character of the speculators. And, as J. H. Robinson and H. W. Rolfe write in their *Petrarch,* "The public man, whatever his character and aims, is pretty sure, if he rises above mediocrity, to be accused of unscrupulousness."[100] Gouverneur himself was only so accused twice: both times when in the Finance Office, and both times by Pennsylvania officials. The matters were trivial (the first concerned a supposedly missing bag of flour), and were easily dismissed.

Robert Morris, however, had been frequently investigated when in public service. On one occasion he was charged with shifting ownership of a cargo from private to public account, after the vessel which carried it had been captured by the enemy, in order to throw the loss from himself onto Congress. Although vehemently pursued, the charge proved false. At another time, he was accused of violating Pennsylvania's antimonopoly laws, but cleared himself by demonstrating that his actions had been within the laws against forestalling. In disproof of another charge, he demonstrated he had been acting as agent for John Holker (1745–1822), a supplier to the French navy.[101] Moreover, George Washington thought well enough of the former superintendent of finances to offer him the position of treasury secretary, but Robert Morris declined the president's offer and recommended Alexander Hamilton.[102]

As for Robert and Gouverneur together, they had begun to seek the main chance economically well before the abolition of their office. Along with John Vaughan (ca. 1738–1795), as early as March 20, 1783, Gouverneur and Robert agreed to borrow funds in Europe to pay for the purchase of American lands which the three hoped to resell for substantial profits. Land is, as Ludwig von Mises has cogently articulated in his treatise *Human Action,* a factor of production like machinery, tools, or technology; Gouverneur and Robert perceived this reality clearly. "Let us for Heaven's sake get rid of undue restrictions on the Rights of Property unless we mean entirely to quench the Spirit of Industry that Parent of private Virtue and punish [word unclear] Felicity," exclaimed Gouverneur in a March 9, 1781, letter to his friend Governor George Clinton. From 1784 until 1789, especially, Gouverneur accumulated much property, but often undercover. In 1787, for example, a group including Gouverneur and Robert Morris purchased the substantial piece of land known as St. Lawrence Ten Towns, but they kept their names secret by operating behind their front man, Alexander Macomb. Gouverneur's land speculation included not only the St. Lawrence region, where the towns of Gouverneur and Morristown, New York, form a pair of his monuments, but also in the western wilderness. Countinghouse speculations were not enough for Morris, who went on several expeditions in the late 1790s and in the first decade of the new century. To survey the lands he thought to purchase, he made his way along shadowed trail and through gladed forest by foot and oaken peg, by birch canoe along the Mohawk Valley, and steadily westward to Niagara. From there he traveled into Canada.[103] Most new settlers were beginning to deal with private land dealers like Morris rather than the state because of the unstable land policies effected by the transition between prewar and postwar governments. According to Gouverneur, it was "absurd to suppose a person with scarce a second shirt to his back can go two or three hundred miles to look [scope] out a farm, have it surveyed, travel back again to the office for a patent, etc., clear the land, cut a road, make a settlement, and build a house and barn and then an owner under a prior grant may come forward and take possession."[104] Gouverneur's picturesque description and comprehension of the situation was made possible by traveling the trails himself.

Had Robert shown similar care before his land purchases, during the nineties particularly, he might not have strained his substantial credit to bursting. For his activities after the Revolution were at least as ambitious as Gouverneur's. By 1787, thanks in no small part to Robert's efforts, the economic climate of Philadelphia was profiting greatly from a vast trade in tobacco with the British. In a March 16, 1785, letter, for example, he told Tench Tilghman (1744–1786), a Maryland businessman, former business partner with Morris, and aide-de-camp on George Washington's staff during the war, that he had recently urged a successful campaign to drive down the crop's domestic price. In keeping with these efforts, Robert secured monopoly contracts in 1785, 1786, and 1787 to supply the French 20,000 hogsheads of Virginia and Maryland tobacco a year, for which the French government agreed to pay him a million livres. Gouverneur helped lay the foundation for Robert's tobacco fortune by arranging the shipments to Europe in 1786 and 1787.[105] He also engaged in the "tedious disagreeable business" of sorting out Robert's attendant legal problems, particularly extracting money owed Robert by Congressman Carter Braxton. The two profited immensely from buying shares in mercantile partnerships; Robert Morris bought both Gouverneur and himself shares with a New York City firm operated by William Constable.

At this period, many American farmers were struggling to make ends meet. What shall we make of Robert's and Gouverneur's apparent rapacity? The latter had no dependents until well into his fifties; although Robert already had a large family by the mid-1780s, he also had a large appetite for luxuries, as evidenced by his purchases of large homes in Philadelphia as well as vacation estates above the Schuylkill and in New York. The dubious nature of his dealings reveals a man overextended by business ventures and attempting to cover his interests, which far from justifies his behavior. Like many Americans, Robert and Gouverneur saw the establishment of the new nation as both political and economic opportunity.

Robert Morris's avarice may be difficult for many of us to understand. Unlike Benjamin Franklin, for example, he did no publicly known charitable work, and made no known charitable contributions. He undertook his financially ruinous enterprises ten years after he had left public office, when he had had a large salary and numerous investments. At last his mammoth land speculations vastly overextended even his Croesus-like fortune; by 1796, his credit had entirely collapsed, and in 1797 he went bankrupt, with $3 million in unpayable debts. In 1798 he entered Philadelphia's debtors' prison, the Walnut

Street Gaol, near Sixth Street, where he remained incarcerated until 1801. When he died, in 1806, he still owed the United States nearly $100,000 in unpaid fines and unrepaid court costs. From the time of his imprisonment until his death, his entire large family subsisted on the charity of his friends— especially of Gouverneur Morris, who established a fund to help keep his friend's family afloat. (He was to do the same later for the family of Alexander Hamilton.)[106]

Sarah Morris died on January 15, 1786, when she was seventy-one years old after several lonely years as an invalid. From the written record there is no indication that Gouverneur had visited or written to her during the two-year period after Britain's armed forces departed from New York. In the absence of any revealing statements to or about his mother during this period, or even shortly after her death, we have no way of knowing how he felt about Sarah. He was certainly very busy with commercial dealings. He and Robert Morris, for instance, found time to make several lengthy trips to "tobacco country" in hopes of sealing the deal on their then elusive tobacco contract. Moreover, in pursuit of his extensive land purchases, Gouverneur ventured far and wide in upstate New York. But he does not seem to have made any time to write or to visit his mother. And his diary records no statement of grief such as he makes when he learned, belatedly, that Elizabeth Plater had perished.[47]

By his father's will, Morrisania now devolved upon the second son, Staats Long Morris. As already indicated, in England he had married the widowed Duchess of Gordon, and he was still an active-duty general in the British Army. (The eldest son, Lewis, had received his portion of the estate before his father perished.) The father's will also provided that Staats Long Morris distribute the sum of £7,000 to the other surviving children; of this sum, £2,000 was apparently intended for Gouverneur. Since Staats Long Morris did not plan to return to America to live, he negotiated the purchase of Morrisania with Gouverneur, who much desired its return. The transaction, involving both loans and concessions, was absurdly complicated; its upshot was that Gouverneur wound up with both Morrisania and a large portion of Staats Long's lands in New Jersey.[107] Through commercial and real estate ventures, Gouverneur Morris had, by 1787, laid the foundation of a fortune. During the next quarter-century he raised an impressive superstructure on this substantial base.

In 1787, as a delegate from Pennsylvania, of which state he was now a citizen, Gouverneur Morris took his seat in the convention that assembled to frame a U.S. constitution. To that convention we now turn.

{5}

THE CONSTITUTIONAL CONVENTION

THE VIRGINIA LEGISLATURE believed the Articles of Confederation an inadequate foundation for a permanent governmental structure; early in 1786, it proposed that all the state legislatures meet at Annapolis and adopt a resolution calling for a convention to amend the Articles. In early August of the same year, Charles Pinckney, of South Carolina, moved in Congress to amend the Articles, but the motion was defeated. The convention proposed by Virginia took place from September 11 to September 14, attended by representatives of just five states: New York, New Jersey, Pennsylvania, Delaware, and Virginia. The convention they called for would amend only the Articles enacted into law in 1781. In late February 1787, the Congress endorsed that resolution, and the Constitutional Convention was set to meet in Philadelphia in late May for several months' deliberations.

The delegates first considered the radical Virginia Plan put forth by Edmund Randolph on May 29, and then the New Jersey Plan, proposed on June 17, which was in some ways more moderate. On June 19, however, the delegates decided that, rather than merely try to amend the flawed Articles of Confederation, the Convention would establish an entirely new framework for the national government.[1]

From 1774 on, administrative departments with individual directors had evolved out of the revolutionists' original committees and boards; after 1781, when Congress was becoming steadily weaker, these departments were unable to demonstrate their advantages over the pre-Confederation system. The department heads had insufficient freedom; Gouverneur Morris wrote that they shouldered "the arduous task before them to govern without power, nay, more, [without the ability] to obtain the power necessary to govern. They must persuade where others command, and the strong phalanx of private interest, with the impetuous sallies of private politics and party, encounters them at every step."[2] In writing from Philadelphia to the businessman Matthew Ridley, on July 25, 1783, he lamented "the scattered fragments of Chaos" and "the Intricacies and Contradictions of our loose and jarring System." In the winter of 1783, he met in Philadelphia with Robert Morris, Robert R. Livingston, and Thomas Paine to propose the development of "a Continental Legislature to Congress, to be elected by the several States."[3]

The first to push for reconstructing the Confederation government were those who had served it during the Revolution: high-ranking military officers, such as Washington, Greene, Lincoln, and Knox; diplomats such as Livingston, Adams, and Franklin; and congressional representatives and federal financiers, such as Robert Morris, Gouverneur Morris, James Madison, and Alexander Hamilton. As for the resistance to a unified government, it must be understood in what we might call its geographical context.

A Yankee seaman who sailed into Wilmington or Savannah must have felt very far from home, and the Carolinians and Georgians he met would probably know little of New York or Massachusetts. Life on a South Carolina plantation was far different from life in a New England village. Then, too, the colonies had come into existence at different times, and for different reasons.

The roads were mostly terrible. The pike from New York to Boston was not too bad, but even in the best weather making the journey between the two cities took four days in a clumsy coach. Pennsylvania's highways were often nearly impassable; travel on them was little less than miserable. South of the Potomac matters were worse; a bridge crossing was a rare luxury.

As for the mails: they passed between Portland, in southern Maine, and Suffolk, Virginia, three times a week during the summer, but from Suffolk they went south only twice a week in summer, and in winter only once a week. Just a few courageous souls had ventured to settle in the wild and almost trackless forest west of the Appalachians.[4]

No surprise, then, that real political union seemed a near impossibility. But it was a prerequisite for the economic, political, and military power America has enjoyed.

Despite the conditions just cited, by 1787 the states were not so dissimilar in political structure; in fact, even five years after the Declaration of Independence, the process of making the state constitutions had been pretty well completed. To form a viable *national* system, however, was less simple. For some years after 1776, congressional delegates conducted the new nation's business without constitutional restraints; Congress did what needed doing, and, on occasion, showed energy and intelligence. But it often sank into sloth and incompetence.

Under no conditions would the American states surrender all political authority to any national central government; but by the Articles of Confederation they granted Congress almost every power of a general or national character. Three powers that the central authority much needed, though, the Articles withheld: the power to raise money, the power to regulate commerce, and what might broadly be termed the executive authority. Consequently, Congress could not enforce the laws it passed. It could request money but not compel its payment. It could enter into treaties but not enforce their stipulations. It could request the raising of an army but could not fill the ranks. It could borrow new money but could take no adequate measure for repayment. It could advise and recommend but not command.

Furthermore, although the Articles did specify the appointment of a member of Congress to preside over its sessions, no one could serve in this post more than one year in any three. The Articles also allowed for the appointment of civil officers to manage the general affairs of the United States under congressional direction. Neither provision made for anything like an executive branch.[5] Thus, under the Articles, no steady, effective driver held the reins. The delegates at the convention were concerned to provide for an executive branch to make the unwieldy political machine more immediate and responsive. The president would have the power to appoint the managers of government departments and unify them in the pursuit of various presidential objectives. The president would also have the prerogative to issue an Executive Order in urgent circumstances. Hamilton in particular urged the need for the executive power to issue pardons, arguing that mercy would be dispensed more equitably by an individual than by a body.

The gathering that has become known as the Constitutional Convention had been scheduled to begin May 14, 1787. Of the out-of-town delegates, Washington seems to have arrived first, on May 13; the trip had taken him four days over difficult roads from Mount Vernon. (It is remarkable that he came so promptly, since he had at first balked at attending. His aide wrote him that "Gouverneur Morris and some others have wished me to use whatever influence I might have to induce you to come.")

As this may suggest, so few delegates arrived on time that the body did not attain a quorum until May 25, when the South Carolina delegation and two New Jersey delegates finally arrived. Even after the convention at last met officially (it chose George Washington to preside), Rufus King of Massachusetts had not yet arrived; when he did, he found himself the lone representative from any of the New England states. He quickly wrote to his good friend Jeremiah Wadsworth of Connecticut, indicating that the situation was embarrassing, and urging other New England delegates to hurry to Philadelphia. But not until July 23, when the two New Hampshire delegates arrived, were all attending states present. Rhode Island, known as "Rogue Island" to some cynics, was to boycott the entire convention. The state was suspected of harboring some Shays's Rebellion insurgents, and the state administration's cupidity supported its fraudulent paper money system. According to one apologetic Rhode Islander, James M. Varnum, "the measures of our present legislature do not exhibit the real character of the state. . . . The majority of the administration is composed of a licentious number of men, destitute of education, and many of them void of principle. From anarchy and confusion they derive their temporary consequence, and this they endeavor to prolong."[6]

Those who come to prominence in a crisis—such as the American Revolution—are probably considered great more often than they deserve to be. But exigencies do often call forth great individuals, and dozens of such Americans stepped forward during the Revolution. In that seagoing age, people remained aware that the word "founder" is not a noun only, but also a verb meaning "to sink." The majority of those at the Constitutional Convention took their duties seriously.

Of the fifty-five men who served as delegates, roughly half had fought in the Continental Army or a state militia. And of the forty who signed the Constitution, twenty-three were combat veterans of the Revolutionary War. Forty-four of the fifty-five had already served as members of the Continental Congress. Gouverneur Morris of course had served in the Congress from New York, and he was one of only six individuals to sign both the Articles of Confederation and the U.S. Constitution (only two, Robert Morris and Roger Sherman, had underwritten all three major documents from the period, the Declaration of Independence, the Articles of Confederation, and the Constitution). Governmentally, too, the delegates were much experienced: the Framers had amassed altogether roughly a thousand years of elected and appointed public service.

Fewer than thirty men attended all or nearly all of the convention's sessions over its roughly four-month span. Ten others, including Gouverneur Morris, missed a few weeks. Four members attended for only short periods. And twelve, notably including Alexander Hamilton, John Lansing Jr., and Robert Yates, of New York, were absent much of the time. Hamilton left after his five-hour presentation of the Hamilton Plan at the beginning of the convention, but returned in August and September and urged the delegates to sign the completed document. Lansing and Yates departed from the convention together after six weeks, explaining in a letter to New York governor George Clinton that they had not been aware the convention was considering the consolidation of the colonies into one federal government.[7] Yates had apparently been under the impression that the delegates were merely going to revise the Articles of Confederation. At the ratifying convention in 1788, both again voiced opposition to the centralized system. Yates, who failed in an election bid for the governorship of New York, died almost penniless in 1801, while Lansing, after a long career as New York's chief justice, was mysteriously murdered in New York City in 1829.

Twenty-six delegates had served as state legislators, Morris of course among them. Thirty-two had been state judges or attorneys, or at least had legal training. Thirteen delegates, again including Morris, had had experience in state constitutional conventions, and seven had already served as governors. Roughly fifteen held slaves (Morris had long before manumitted the slave he had inherited from his father). Eleven had represented either shippers or manufacturers as legal or business agents. Nine were planters. Six, again including Morris, had been financiers, and four were practicing physicians. The subsequent careers of the delegates were also distinguished. Two (Washington and Madison) became U.S. presidents, and one (Elbridge Gerry) became vice president. Two delegates became chief justices of the U.S. Supreme Court: John Rutledge (1739–1800), who served briefly as acting chief justice, although the Senate refused to confirm his nomination because of his mental illness, and Oliver Ellsworth (1745–1807). Alexander Hamilton served as Washington's secretary of the treasury; Edmund Randolph (1753–1813) became attorney general (1789–1794) and then secretary of state (1794–1795). Fourteen delegates, including Gouverneur Morris, became U.S. senators. Eight were elected to the House of Representatives in the first Congress alone. And four delegates, again including Gouverneur Morris, went on to represent the United States abroad.

Not surprisingly, the delegates were generally rich (ironically, Robert Morris seems to have been the richest) and well educated. Two dozen of them were among their home states' chief creditors (although Gouverneur Morris remained a debtor due to his extensive land speculation). Of the thirty-two delegates with some professional connection with the law, half had graduated from American universities—Harvard, Yale, King's College (Columbia), the College of New Jersey (Princeton), or the College of William and Mary, of which only King's and William and Mary had substantial Loyalist elements. Twenty-eight of the fifty-five delegates had attended college; the comparable figure among free Americans generally was about one in two thousand.

The average age of the delegates was forty-three. Gouverneur Morris was in his mid-thirties and thus, as usual, on the young side in the circle in which he moved. But not the youngest—fourteen delegates were younger than Gouverneur Morris: Jonathan Dayton (1760–1824), John Francis Mercer (1759–1821), Richard Dobbs Spaight, Sr. (1758–1802), Charles Pinckney (1757–1824), Nicholas Gilman (1755–1814), Rufus King (1755–1804), Alexander Hamilton (1755–1804), John Lansing, Jr. (1754–1829), Jacob Broom (1752–1810), James McHenry (1753–1816), Edmund Randolph (1753–1813), William Richard Davie (1756–1820), Abraham Baldwin (1757–1807), and William Houstoun (1755–1813). Benjamin Franklin, eighty-one, was the eldest.

Eight of the delegates had been born outside North America. One of them, William R. Davie (1756–1820), had to leave the convention in mid-August and did not sign the Constitution, though he argued strongly for its ratification. William Jackson (1759–1828), the secretary of the Constitutional Convention, had been born in England. He signed the document to authenticate it; not an elected delegate, he had had no voice in the deliberations. Jackson's work, therefore, had to be especially accurate and reliable because the public and the press were barred from the deliberations, which were held behind closed windows and doors. The delegates had agreed before the convention that utter secrecy would prevent outside interference by state legislatures. Delegates were to be free to speak their minds. George Washington, after receiving a convention document that had been dropped in the State House, addressed the group later that day: "I must entreat the gentlemen to be more careful, [lest] our transactions get into the newspapers and disturb the public repose by premature speculations. I know not whose paper it is, but there it is. Let him who owns it take it." The paper was never claimed but the message had been received.[8] All of the delegates were Christians, and all but two were from Protestant denominations. Pennsylvania's Thomas Fitzsimmons (1741–1811), born in Ireland, and Daniel Carroll (1730–1796), of Maryland, were the Convention's only Roman Catholics.

The Convention adjourned only twice: on July 3 and 4 and from July 26 to August 6. Otherwise sessions ran steadily through the hot, humid summer, six days a week, from ten or eleven A.M. through three or four P.M.

The State House was not only stiflingly hot, it was noisy. In the 1780s the Philadelphia street commissioners had spent money mostly on leveling the city's streets and paving them with cobblestones. The clatter of carriage wheels on stone was so loud that at last loads of gravel were deposited on the stretch of Chestnut Street in front of the State House to muffle the sounds.[9]

As an elected delegate from Pennsylvania, Gouverneur Morris became one of the first seven elected individuals to represent Pennsylvania in the Convention; the others were Robert Morris, George Clymer, Thomas Fitzsimmons, Jared Ingersoll, Thomas Mifflin, and James Wilson. On Benjamin Franklin's return from France, Pennsylvania added his outstanding, although ailing, personage to its delegation. Born in Philadelphia, Clymer (1739–1813) recommended independence after British economic restrictions impinged on his mercantile firm. His financial expertise had made him invaluable to commerce committees in the Continental Congress, but he rarely spoke and had only a small role in the formation of the Constitution during the Convention. The Irish-born Fitzsimmons was also commercially oriented and had helped found the Bank of North America in 1781; despite his regular attendance, his impact on the Convention was slight. Born in Connecticut to a British official, Ingersoll (1749–1822) studied law in London, returned to Philadelphia, caught Revolutionary fervor, and won election to Congress in 1780. Like several of the Pennsylvania delegates, he remained largely reticent at the Convention, as did the fourth-generation Pennsylvanian Mifflin, who had served as Congress president for six months in 1784. Wilson (1741–1797), on the other hand, exerted an influence second only, perhaps, to that of Madison. He emigrated from Scotland in 1765 and soon after involved himself in Revolutionary politics. His shift to conservatism and defense of Loyalists after independence made him some radical enemies, and in 1779 a mob forced him to barricade himself in his home, thereafter dubbed "Fort Wilson." Wilson's expertise—an understanding of the importance of form and structure in formulating theories of governance, married with political foresight—and numerous speeches on political theory made him invaluable to the Convention.

Of the middle colonies, in 1787 Pennsylvania proved the most populous and probably also the most cosmopolitan state. The observant eighteenth-century British traveler, Andrew Burnaby, refers to Pennsylvania as "this wonderful province."[10]

Early in the convention, Gouverneur Morris argued that the large states should, at the outset, unite to oppose the equality of the states in voting in the Convention. According to James Madison's account, the members from Virginia believed that such a move could prove fatal to the union; rather, they thought, during the deliberations the small states could be persuaded to trade equality in voting power for an efficient government. This view prevailed for the House of Representatives while a compromise gave the small states equal representation in the Senate.

On May 29, Edmund Randolph proposed fifteen resolutions—the so-called Randolph Plan, or Virginia Plan, whose outline was to become the basis of the finished Constitution. (Madison and Randolph, at least, had been working on it for months; but there is no clear reason to suppose that either deserves more credit for the plan than any other member of the Virginia delegation.) Madison proposed that Randolph should present the plan because of his oratory skills and because he was known as a moderate, not a radical nationalist. The main points of the Virginia Plan were the establishment of a bicameral national legislature with seats allocated by state size, a national executive who would be chosen by the legislature and possess "general authority to execute the national laws," and a national judiciary with a "supreme" and several "inferior" tribunals. Finally, the state governments would be compelled by oath to support this constitution. In short, the Virginia Plan did not correct the Articles of Confederation; it proposed an entirely new form of government.

A committee of the whole proceeded to consider the plan, at which crucial time Gouverneur Morris took an important step; he suggested that Edmund Randolph move to postpone consideration of the first point of the plan and instead present an innovative resolution. Inspired by Morris's challenge, Randolph drew up the resolution in three points. This resolution's importance can hardly be overstated. It declared that no "Union of the States merely federal" nor any "treaty or treaties among the whole or part of the States" would be acceptable, and: "That a *national* government ought to be established consisting of a *supreme* Legislative, Executive and Judiciary." In other words, the convention would not simply produce a federation with a weak central government. In the debate that followed, Morris argued "that in all Communities there must be one supreme power, and one only"; this sovereign power, he proposed, should be able to compel obedience and should be constituted formally as a national government. A "federal" government, as Morris used the term, meant "a mere compact resting on the good faith of the parties." The resolution was adopted—only Connecticut dissented—although a number of delegates objected to it as obliterating the sovereignty of the states. The convention's commission had been to *amend* the Articles of Confederation; now it had moved, instead, toward development of a centralized national government, a far more radical project.[11]

On May 30, Charles Pinckney presented a detailed draft of a federal constitution, but the convention took no official action on it.

The Committee of the Whole then proceeded to consider the Virginia Plan clause by clause. On June 13 it reported out the result, in nineteen resolutions substantially based on those offered by Randolph. They directed themselves to the formation of a new government, radically different from the one provided for by the Articles of Confederation and meant to provide the framework for a national government.

But support for a mere reform of the Articles of Confederation was not dead. On June 15 William Paterson, of New Jersey, proposed a plan in that vein; after a day of debate, and following the eloquent urging of Alexander Hamilton, the Committee of the Whole voted for the amended Virginia Plan. And now the delegates took up the framing of the Constitution. The delegation subsequently adopted twenty-three resolutions which declared the sense of the Convention as regards the matters the Constitution should contain. On July 26 these resolutions were turned over to a Committee of Detail so that it could prepare and report a draft of the Constitution. This committee reported out a draft Constitution on August 6. The delegates spent a little more than a month debating and revising the draft; the revisions were incorporated into a new draft, and, after a few more changes, the U.S. Constitution was adopted on September 17, 1789.

Morris had left the Convention on May 31, primarily to make the final financial arrangements to take title of the Morrisania estate. Morris needed to train the new overseer and lay out his building and crop plans for his laborers. Morris was certainly cognizant of how momentous the proceedings were, later writing that the "fate of America was suspended by a hair." [12] Morris's choice to prioritize personal business over the nation's formative process suggests that, though a passionate nationalist, he had prominent individual interests. William Pierce (1740–1789) of Georgia decried Morris's negligence, but Pierce himself left in June to deal with pressing financial issues, as did several other delegates. Morris proved able to sustain substantial indebtedness for his purchase of Morrisania for several reasons; his brothers had agreed to several mortgages; he could sign off more than £2,000 indebtedness from the estate to himself; and his four sisters were all willing to defer their share of the payment of their inheritances. In April, Gouverneur had made plans to buy from Staats Long Morris valuable tracts of land in New Jersey: along the Raritan at Morristown, and also in Sussex and in Somerset Counties. These purchases were essentially speculative—Morris planned to resell the properties in future. [13]

Once Morris returned from New York on July 2, he contributed to the debates steadily and substantially. No previous scholarship has presented clearly the extent of Morris's contributions to the development of the Constitution; the exposition that follows endeavors to do so. On September 8, when the delegates had almost finished reviewing the draft presented by the Committee of Detail, they voted into being a five-man style committee comprising Morris, William Samuel Johnson, Hamilton, Madison, and King. On September 12—roughly ninety-six hours later—they reported a revised draft. This was a prodigious feat. Although the document they started with was in the form of a rough constitution, it was convoluted, with many clauses haphazardly piled together and many sections out of place; there were few signs of the orderly arrangement a legal instrument ought to have. The style committee not only brought admirable logical order to this chaos but brought to the document's prose its familiar elegance and lucidity.

Gouverneur Morris did this work. His skill as a draftsman was widely recognized, and the other members of the committee were doubtless glad to leave the work to such an able hand. Many years later, in a letter to Thomas Pickering, Morris referred thus to his part in the final document: "That instrument was written by the fingers which write this letter. Having rejected redundant and equivocal terms, I believed it to be as clear as our language would permit." More than forty years after ratification, Madison commented in a letter to historian Jared Sparks that "The finish given to the style and arrangement of the Constitution fairly belongs to the pen of Mr. Morris; the task having, probably, been handed over to him by the chairman. . . . A better choice could not have been made, as the performance of the task proved."[14]

On September 13 the convention delegates perused the instrument, making a number of minor amendments and two amendments of substance: U.S. representatives were allotted to the states at a rate of one for every thirty thousand people, rather than one for every forty thousand; and Article V, the amendment clause, was made to provide that "no State [should], without its Consent, . . . be deprived of its equal Suffrage in the Senate." In the latter change, Gouverneur Morris played an important part. Connecticut's Roger Sherman had argued to the convention on June 11 that a proportional vote in the lower house would express the will of the people and an equal vote for states in the upper house would reflect the states' majority opinion. Sherman's motion was defeated by a single vote, the large states finding no reason to compromise their position, but it was revived after two compromises: Franklin suggested that the lower house should have exclusive power over the drafting of "money bills" or taxing power, and the Southern states successfully pushed the three-fifths formula for representation, in which each slave counted as three-fifths of one free resident in determining representation. Sherman then moved, unsuccessfully, to strike the entire Amendment Clause. Dismay among the delegates from the smaller states was so great that Morris renewed Sherman's first motion. This time it passed, without a single dissent.

Even matters of punctuation came under review. The Committee of Style deviously inserted a semicolon in the phrase that described the power of Congress "to lay and collect Taxes, Duties, Imposts and Excises, to pay the Debts and provide for the common Defence and general Welfare, of the United States." This semicolon, inserted between "Excises" and "to pay," would have made the phrase "to pay the Debts and provide for the common Defence and general Welfare of the United States" an additional power of the Congress. The change of punctuation here would seem, at first glance, to be a devious move by penman Morris, a nationalist who had demonstrated some interest in a government bank. But the debates indicate that, in contrast to other members of the Committee of Style, Morris tended to be against the expansion of congressional money-raising powers and responsibilities. Thus it seems likely that, in this instance, Morris was prevailed upon by the other members of the committee to change the punctuation, and therefore, to an extent, the sense, of Article I, Section 8.[15]

Lastly, when the entire instrument had been gone over and agreed to by all the states present, and orders for the document to be engrossed had been promulgated, Gouverneur devised the attestation clause of Article VII, this with a view to avoiding the scruples of those delegates who would be unwilling to sign the Constitution because they did not wish to seem to approve it. Morris therefore proposed that they should sign after the words "Done in Convention by the Unanimous Consent of the States present [on September 17, 1787]"; the idea was that this formula would signify that the instrument had received the approval of each *state* but not of each *delegate*. Morris had the enormously popular Franklin introduce the suggestion, to increase its chance of passage, and the move succeeded. (Virginia's Randolph and Mason, and the New Englander Gerry still refused to sign.) The delegates who signed represented twelve states.

Morris's contributions to the development of the Constitution can probably best be understood if we consider the document article by article, section by section, and clause by clause, from draft through ratification.

The Preamble originated in the Committee of Detail, although earlier discussions in the convention as a whole of course bore upon the purposes and nature of the intended government and seem to have influenced the Preamble's development.[16] Unfortunately, the steps by which it grew from the suggestions in the debates of May 30, June 13, and June 20 remain opaque. On August 6, the Committee of Detail reported a draft of the Constitution which begins

We, the people of the states of New Hampshire, Massachusetts, Rhode Island and Providence Plantations, Connecticut, New York, New Jersey, Pennsylvania, Delaware, Maryland, Virginia, North Carolina, South Carolina, and Georgia, do ordain, declare, and establish, the following Constitution for the government of ourselves and our posterity:—

Article I. The style of this government shall be "The United States of America."

Article II. The government shall consist of supreme legislative, executive, and judicial powers.

This text was approved in August and sent to the style committee. Morris drafted a new version of the Preamble, which does not mention the individual states but substitutes the phrase "We, the people of the United States." This alteration was necessary because the draft's Article VII provided that the Constitution should go into effect when ratified by nine states, not all thirteen. Morris's version omitted Articles I and II and included the inspiring, lucid, and forceful statement of purpose with which we are familiar today:

We, the People of the United States, in Order to form a more perfect Union, to establish Justice, insure domestic Tranquility, provide for the common defence, promote the general Welfare, and secure the Blessings of Liberty to ourselves and our Posterity, do ordain and establish this Constitution for the United States of America.

On September 13, the convention approved these lines with a single change: they struck the word "to" before "establish justice."

The passage dealing with Congress's legislative powers began as Article III, as reported by the Committee of Detail in its draft of August 6. After some changes by the convention on the floor on August 7, this article eventually moved to the Committee of Style. The committee (which is to say Morris) clarified the diction and syntax to produce what we know as Article I, Section 1, and Article I, Section 4.

The next section of the first draft to be incorporated into the finished Constitution started life as Article IV, Sections 1 and 2: who was eligible for membership in the House of Representatives, and how they were to be elected. When these matters came before the Convention on August 7, Gouverneur Morris sought to limit the federal suffrage to property owners—a restriction he had urged successfully in the development of the first New York State constitution, where it had sharply diminished the number of eligible voters.

In Philadelphia, Morris lost. He and John Dickinson (of Delaware)

advanced the argument that a limited franchise would keep out the dangerous influence of the multitudes. In opposition, a formidable and geographi-
cally diverse phalanx formed, including James Wilson and Benjamin
Franklin, of Pennsylvania; Hugh Williamson, of North Carolina; Oliver
Ellsworth, of Connecticut; George Mason, of Virginia; and Pierce Butler,
of South Carolina. Their principal argument was, strikingly, that it would
be unwise to excite the jealousies of the people by denying them the right
to vote in federal elections when the same citizens could vote in state con-
tests. Franklin alone urged the argument that is probably most obvious to
twenty-first-century readers: namely, that a property restriction would
damage the public spirit of the common people.

In further discussion on voter eligibility, George Mason moved to change
the residency requirement for citizens from three years to seven. On August
13, when the section again came up for discussion, Gouverneur Morris
moved to add a proviso that the seven-year requirement would not affect
the rights of anyone who was already a citizen. Unfortunately, this proposal
lost a vote of six to five.

On August 9, the delegates debated the period of citizenship required for
eligibility to sit in the Senate. Opinions ranged widely, from four years (John
Rutledge) to fourteen (Gouverneur Morris). In the end, the convention set
the citizenship requirement at nine years.

Gouverneur Morris's position deserves brief examination; it reveals a cor-
nerstone of his political philosophy, as does his support for setting twenty-
five as the age below which one was ineligible for election to the House.
(The House age minimum was also unpopular at first.) Here is Morris's rejoinder to Rutledge (who urged a minimum four years' citizenship for senators) and to Pinckney (who suggested ten years):

> The citizenship requirement should be fourteen years. The lesson we are
> taught is that we should be governed as much by our reason and as little by
> our feelings as possible. The language of reason on this subject is that we
> should not be polite at the expense of prudence. The privileges which im-
> migrants will enjoy among us, though they shall be deprived of that of be-
> ing eligible to the great offices of government, exceed the privileges allowed
> to foreigners in any other part of the world.
>
> As every society, from a great nation down to a club, has the right of de-
> claring the conditions on which new members shall be admitted, there can be
> no room for complaint. As to those philosophical gentlemen, those citizens of
> the world, as they call themselves, I do not wish to see any of them in our
> public councils. I would not trust them. The men who can shake off their

attachments to their own country can never love any other. These attachments are the wholesome prejudices which uphold all governments. Admit a Frenchman into your Senate, and he will study to increase the commerce of France; an Englishman, and he will feel an equal bias in favor of that of England.

Foreigners cannot learn our laws nor understand our Constitution under fourteen years. Seven years are requisite to learn to be a shoemaker, and double this term will be necessary to learn to be an American legislator. It would be preferable to confine the senators to natives, except for the appearance of such a requirement and the effect it might have against the system.

Even on the page this shows a pleasing balance and pace; its hearers evidently found it compelling, for Pinckney, Butler, and Mason, who were often at variance with Morris's opinions, fell into line behind him.

Morris's power to move an audience—legislative, judicial, or personal—must have been considerable. Although it is not possible to hear him, and there is no known description of his voice, we know he was physically impressive—over six feet tall, in an age when the average American male seems to have been about five feet seven. (Among his nicknames were Tall Boy and Big Fellow.) The amount of work he performed from age nineteen and for decades beyond indicates robust health. Contemporary descriptions and portraits show that he had lively, large blue eyes, a large head beneath an ample brow, and an expressive mouth. We may imagine him using his oaken peg leg to good effect, tapping the floor for emphasis as he paced and spoke. The Georgia delegate William Pierce (1740–1789) provides this description of Morris at the Convention:

Mr. Governeur Morris is one of those Genius's in whom every species of talents combine to render him conspicuous and flourishing in public debate:—He winds through all the mazes of rhetoric, and throws around him such a glare that he charms, captivates, and leads away the senses of all who hear him. With an infinite stretch of fancy he brings to view things when he is engaged in deep argumentation, that render all the labor of reasoning easy and pleasing. But with all these powers he is fickle and inconstant, never pursuing one train of thinking, nor ever regular. He has gone through a very extensive course of reading, and is acquainted with all the sciences. No Man has more wit,—nor can any one engage the attention more than Mr. Morris. . . . This Gentleman is about 38 years old, he has been unfortunate in losing one of his Legs, and getting all the flesh taken off his right arm by a scald, when a youth.[17]

William Pierce probably called Morris "fickle and inconstant" because of Morris's seemingly unwarranted absence from the convention over the month of June.

In the debates concerning the apportionment of members of the House and of federal taxes, Morris again exerted considerable influence. Following a motion on the subject made by Franklin in early July, the Committee of Detail offered a lengthy draft text. The country, he said, would certainly be united one way or another; if persuasion failed, the sword would succeed. South Carolina's Rutledge followed by proposing to allot representatives in proportion to how much federal revenue each state supplied; the apportionment would be fixed at the convention, then recalculated every few years. This motion lost; the next day, Morris moved to refer back to the committee the part of the draft that fixed one member for every forty thousand inhabitants. The idea was that the committee could set the numbers of representatives each state would initially send to the House, and that subsequent legislatures might be authorized to make changes. After brief debate, this motion carried. Gouverneur Morris, Gorham, Randolph, Rutledge, and King were immediately appointed by ballot to a special committee, chaired by Morris, which was to absolutely fix the number of representatives.

He thus played a leading role in the committee's report of July 9, which apportioned fifty-six members per state for the first anticipated meeting of the U.S. House. Sherman immediately questioned the number, observing that it did not appear to follow any numerical rule, and Morris conceded that the "Report is little more than a guess. Wealth was not altogether disregarded by the Committee . . . [which] meant little more than to bring the matter to a point for the consideration of the House."[18] Gouverneur's motion to authorize the legislature to alter the number of representatives from time to time was easily agreed upon, but the question of how many to apportion for the first meeting required further consideration by another committee. Of the eleven members appointed to this committee, only Morris and Rufus King had been on the previous. Owing to his presence on both predecessor committees, it seems likely that Morris exerted disproportionate influence on the eleven-man committee as well.

This body estimated that sixty-five members would be needed for the first U.S. House of Representatives; also, it reapportioned them. Its report stimulated much dissent, and many motions were made to alter the size of the delegations. All such motions, however, were defeated, and the motion apportioning sixty-five representatives was approved. In the course of the discussion on this report, Rufus King remarked that the true line of separation between the states was not between large and small but between South and North, a reality Gouverneur Morris also acknowledged.[19]

On July 11 and 12 the Philadelphia delegates presented numerous and often conflicting motions concerning the methodology for a federal census, since the numbers of citizens by state would affect the apportionment of legislatures. Some wanted wealth considered in the apportionment equation. Gouverneur seems to have favored this approach to an extent. Several delegates furthermore argued that the anticipated western states should be represented only to the extent the original states allowed. Morris advocated this position, opposed eloquently by Mason and Madison. (Madison once referred to Morris's "disrelished ideas"; this was almost certainly one of them.)[20]

On July 12, Morris addressed himself to the legislature's power to change the apportionment of representatives; he proposed a "proviso that taxation shall be in proportion to Representation." George Mason objected that Morris's plan might drive the legislature to make requisitions. Other delegates apparently protested that Morris's proviso would be unfair if applied to taxes and duties on imports, exports, and consumption, so Morris amended his motion to provide "that *direct* taxation . . . be proportioned to representation [emphasis added]." In this form, the motion passed unanimously. In the final Constitution, the idea put forth by Mason and Madison prevailed, namely that direct taxation and representation were not to be proportioned in relation to each other but according to the respective populations of the states.

In the entire U.S. Constitution the word "slavery" appears only once; namely, in the Thirteenth Amendment, which formally abolished the brutal institution. Slavery had already dissolved, however, in the crucible of the Civil War; that only a war would settle the issue, Morris had suggested on the Convention floor in Philadelphia.[21]

Morris had long been opposed to slavery. The reader will recall that in 1777 he had attempted to persuade his colleagues in the New York legislature to instruct the framers of the state constitution to insert into that document a pledge of future liberation. His fellow legislators, finding the proposal "inexpedient," gave it no further consideration. At the Philadelphia Convention, Morris was representing the state with the best antislavery record. Thanks largely to the conscientious efforts of the Society of Friends, Pennsylvania was the first state to abolish slavery. In November 1778 the Council asked the lower chamber to prepare a bill to manumit infant "Negroes" born of slaves. A matter of protocol between the two legislating Houses, though, prevented the passing of the relevant act until March 1, 1780. The result freed no one immediately and outright: it automatically freed the children of slaves at the age of twenty-eight. During the Revolutionary War, many slaves in Pennsylvania and other colonies were freed in exchange for military service.[22]

In assailing slavery, Gouverneur Morris was attacking a well-entrenched American institution. Of the roughly 600,000 African-American slaves in the fledgling country, the South held the majority: more than 222,000 in Virginia, nearly 100,000 in South Carolina, nearly 95,000 in North Carolina (and the Carolinas then were very thinly populated overall), roughly 83,000 in Maryland, and nearly 23,000 in Georgia. Nearly 23,000 slaves, however, also lived and labored in New York, well over 21 percent of the state's population. More than 11,000 slaves were still held in New Jersey, which, of the northern states, was the last to abolish slavery. Pennsylvania still had more than 8,000 slaves, Connecticut more than 6,000, and Massachusetts more than 5,000. Moreover, apologists for slavery, with the eloquence of Augustine and the seeming rationality of Thomas Aquinas, steadily turned out books defending slavery. Probably the summa of such treatises is Thomas R. R. Cobb's *An Inquiry into the Law of Negro Slavery,* which argues that the paternal relationship between the master and the slave ensured basic necessities and protection for the slave. "Southern slavery," wrote Cobb, "is a patriarchal, social system. The master is the head of his family. Next to his wife and children, he cares for his slaves." Cobb called for some reforms in the institution, such as laws restricting abuse and rape, reasoning that the role of a master called for kindly responsibility to his group of slaves interested only in "the gratification of a few animal passions."[23] Anthony Trollope sagely refers to "that subtle, selfish, ambiguous sophistry to which the minds of all men are so subject."

This is the context in which we must see Morris's July 12 proposal that "taxation should be in proportion to representation." The chief slaveholding states sought to be represented in Congress in proportion to their whole population—including the slaves, who of course could not vote. The voters of the slaveholding states would, under such a system, be overrepresented in comparison with the voters in states whose populations were not inflated by the politically silent human chattel; to link taxation with representation would add a cost to that disproportion. Although the motion was supported mostly by southern states, slavery profited some very influential people in every colony, so that Morris's speeches against slavery would earn him some enmity from every corner. Because few but the wealthiest elites could afford slaves anywhere in the colonies at the time, Gouverneur's public stand, like many of his actions, required a store of civil courage.[24]

The July 12 debate did not, however, address slavery directly. The issue did surface explicitly in Philadelphia on numerous occasions, from the fourth day of the convention through the final day's debate, on September 15. Gouverneur Morris contended with George Mason, a Virginia delegate, in denouncing slavery: "a nefarious institution," as Morris called it. And elsewhere: "The curse of heaven on the States where it prevails." Like some others, Morris believed that to count slaves in apportioning federal representation would spur the importation of yet more captives from Africa. But Roger Sherman and Oliver Ellsworth favored leaving importation to the states. The former did not consider the admission of African American slaves as open to "such insuperable objections." Ellsworth felt certain that abolitionists' headway and "the good sense of the several States would probably complete it" (emancipation) . . . eventually. Gerry of Massachusetts concurred.

It is noteworthy that the strongest opposition to slavery was expressed by the delegates from Maryland and Virginia—states that were among the leaders in slave breeding. And although Georgia and the Carolinas—at the time, the three southernmost states—were slavery's strongest defenders, it is also true that several New England states were quite willing to see the states prohibit or allow the Atlantic trade, as they liked. Also worth remarking on is that Pinckney and Baldwin, of the two states then most attached to the importation of black slaves, believed that local public sentiment might soon force slavery's end. Meanwhile, as readers are no doubt aware, the convention reached its notorious compromise on the matter of counting the population of slaves: each was treated as three-fifths of a man. As for the importation of slaves from Africa, it was not to be forbidden prior to 1808, although a small tax was levied on it in the meantime.[25]

On the slavery issue, Gouverneur Morris may have played the strongest role of any delegate at the convention. Pennsylvania's was the largest, and probably the most influential, delegation in Philadelphia. As Paul Finkelman has thoughtfully underlined, and as noted above, since Pennsylvania was the first state to emancipate its slaves (albeit gradually), it also figured to be "the northern state most familiar with the problems that could emerge in the transition from slavery to freedom."[26]

With respect to explicit antislavery arguments introduced at the Constitutional Convention, Morris emerged as the most vociferous opponent of slavery; but his position was subtle and complex. On July 11, he argued that the counting of slaves for representation would offend "the people of Pennsylvania," who would thereby be "put on a footing with slaves."[27] James Wilson, also of Pennsylvania, followed, expounding at length on the practical dilemmas and plumping for "the necessity of compromise."

In rebuttal Morris rose to say he felt "reduced to the dilemma of doing justice to the Southern States or to human nature," and he "must therefore do it to the former." He "could never agree to give such encouragement to the slave trade as would be given by allowing a representation" that reflected the numbers of slaves. Morris thought the South, with its slave-heavy economy, would never accept a constitution that prohibited the slave trade, but he opposed counting slaves for representation. After this speech, which evidently deeply moved many delegates, the convention voted 6 states to 4 against the three-fifths clause; the Pennsylvania delegation voted with the majority. New Hampshire, Rhode Island, and New York were absent.

Morris's July 12 motion, that taxation should "be in proportion to Representation," seems to have shown the way to a compromise. He apparently hoped to discourage southern support for counting slaves by linking the number of representatives a state had in Congress with the taxes it was expected to contribute; but, as indicated above, this scheme failed. On the same day, James Wilson suggested, cleverly, that there would be "less umbrage" against counting slaves for representation, were the clause so drafted as "to make them indirectly only an ingredient in the rules." This motion the convention accepted. Thus, by a vote of 6 to 2, with two states' delegations dividing, the convention adopted the three-fifths clause.

On July 13, the day after the three-fifths clause was formally adopted, Morris began a last, desperate stand on the subject of the relationship between slavery and legislative representation. Here he uttered his Cassandra-like words: if "this distinction" between the North and the South "be real, instead of attempting to blend incompatible things, let us at once take friendly leave of each other."[28] With his usual tenacity, Morris kept pressing. On July 24, Morris suggested that the plan for direct taxation that would incorporate the three-fifths rule, with representation based on the taxation formula, had only been presented to the Convention "as a bridge to assist us over a certain gulph" but "having passed the gulph the bridge may be removed." However, the plan was on the Convention floor and ready to go to committee, and the three-fifths clause remained.

Still Morris persisted in challenging the link between slaveholding and representation. On August 8 he moved to amend the representation formula so as to insert the word "free" before "inhabitants": "the Legislature shall regulate the number of representatives by the number of *free* inhabitants, according to the provisions herein after made, at the rate of one for every forty thousand." He went on to remark, with what we can now see as understatement, that "much . . . would depend on this point," and to give a speech that must have mesmerized his listeners.

"I never will concur in upholding domestic slavery," he began. "It is a nefarious institution . . . the curse of heaven on the States where it prevails." He compared the general impoverishment of the slave-heavy southern states—the Carolinas and Georgia—with "the free regions of the middle States, where a rich and noble cultivation marks the prosperity" of the environs. "Proceed southward, [however], and every step you take [through slave state territory] presents a desert increasing with the increasing proportion of these wretched beings."[29]

Morris posed four confounding rhetorical questions:

Upon what principle shall slaves be computed in the representation? Are they men? Then make them citizens, and let them vote. Are they property? Why, then, is no other property included?

He mocked the logical implications of counting slaves:

The admission of slaves into the representation, when fairly explained, comes to this: that the inhabitant of Georgia and South Carolina who goes to the coast of Africa, and in defiance of the most sacred laws of humanity tears away his fellow-creatures from their dearest connections and damns them to the most cruel bondage, shall have more votes in a government instituted for protection of the rights of mankind than the citizen of Pennsylvania or New Jersey, who views with a laudable horror so nefarious a practice. I will add, that domestic slavery is the most prominent feature in the aristocratic countenance of the proposed constitution. The vassalage of the poor has ever been the favorite offspring of aristocracy.

The slave states would be a burden on the free:

They [the northern states] are to bind themselves to march their militia for the defence of the southern states against those very slaves of whom they complain. They must supply vessels and seamen, in case of foreign attack. The legislature will have indefinite power to tax them by excises and duties on imports, both of which will fall heavier on them than on the southern inhabitants.

On the other side, the southern states are not to be restrained from importing fresh supplies of wretched Africans, at once to increase the danger of attack and the difficulty of defence; nay, they are to be encouraged to it by an assurance of having their votes in the national government increased in proportion; and are, at the same time, to have their exports and their slaves exempt from all contributions for the public service. I will sooner submit myself to a tax for paying for all the negroes in the United States than saddle posterity with such a constitution.

Gouverneur's dramatic skills, as already indicated, were impressive: he had been versed in Shakespearean acting from adolescence on. Launched without much in the way of preliminaries, the peroration soars without pause to its conclusion. The sense of measure in the body, the rapid, clear style, and the climactic power reflect Gouverneur's study (in college and afterward) of Demosthenes' Crown speech; the oration's cadences echo Cicero.

Morris may also have had in mind Sallust's *Histories,* which take up what the former senator believed to be the causes of Roman decline. Sallust saw as especially corrupting the sloth and weakness bred by the extreme wealth—much of which depended on slave labor—of pre-Jugurthan Africa, and he decried slavery as an institution inflicted on the European continent.[30]

Not only had Morris read widely and deeply in classical literature, philosophy, and history, so that he well understood the effects of slavery on the ancient world; not only had he observed slavery in his nation; he had also seen it intimately, in his father's household.

New Jersey's Jonathan Dayton (1760–1824) promptly seconded Morris's motion. South Carolina's Charles Pinckney drolly declared "the fisheries and the western frontier as more burdensome to the United States than the slaves," and went on to say that under other circumstances, he would have responded in a "proper" fashion. This terse statement reflected Pinckney's belief that Morris's speech would prove fruitless at this Convention. The South Carolinian was certainly right. James Wilson spoke earnestly against Morris's motion, which went down by a vote of 10 to 1. Only New Jersey voted to have slaves removed from the population counts used to allot U.S. representatives. New Hampshire, Rhode Island, and New York were again absent.

That matter was not discussed again at the Convention, but warm skirmishes over the slave trade continued, in particular between August 21 and August 28. Two matters were up for debate: the importation of slaves; and what proportion of vote in Congress would be needed to pass a so-called navigation act—a law requiring that goods be shipped only on U.S.

vessels. The South wanted to stipulate a two-thirds supermajority because its exporters feared that a navigation act would free Northern shipping companies, with a monopoly in the market, to set extortionate rates.[31] Morris proposed to "form a bargain among the Northern and Southern States," and this was what took place; Congress could not bar slave imports before 1808, but no supermajority would be needed for a navigation act to pass.

And so, although Morris remained in principle an implacable opponent of slavery, he showed the way to two key compromises on the subject. He did endeavor to allow only the Carolinas and Georgia to keep importing slaves; he suggested that only those states desired the trade, so that the restriction "would be most fair" and would obviate "ambiguity." George Mason argued that such a measure would "give offence to the people of those states"—which, as Paul Finkelman correctly infers, "was precisely Morris's intention." He withdrew his motion: he had made his point, and he must have known that not enough votes were available to stop the slave trade.[32]

As already noted, throughout the Revolutionary and Confederation periods Gouverneur Morris had been a staunch advocate of a strong central government, a position doubtless made even firmer by his extensive experience in the Continental Congress and the Finance Office. In Philadelphia, he said that he had come to the Convention "in some degree as a representative of the whole human race"—in whose perfectibility he, like Diderot, disbelieved. He generally seems to have been quick to understand which goals were attainable, which not, and to have accepted these positions realistically. But in his public statements, he did not usually relinquish his principles. He cherished a lifelong hatred of chattel slavery, and although he showed the ways to some of the compromises that allowed the formation of the central government embodied in the U.S. Constitution, virtually every one of his arguments foreshadowed the lines of attack that the abolitionists thickened in their writings of the 1830s and later.

Morris's influence on presidential impeachment procedures proved substantial. At his insistence, on August 27 a motion to assign jurisdiction over such trials to the Supreme Court had been postponed, not to be taken up. Morris also argued that the U.S. Senate would constitute the only trustworthy impeachment tribunal. If the President were impeached, he pointed out, and the chief justice sat on the Privy Council (the Cabinet), the situation would be particularly undesirable. For one thing, the Supreme Court was to try the president after the impeachment trial; also, the Supreme Court would comprise too few and presumably too narrow a band of citizens.

Roger Sherman agreed on the latter point; and, he urged, the Court's consisting of some members appointed by the President (Sherman actually misspoke somewhat on this matter) would make it an unfair tribunal. The Committee of Style incorporated a provision that the Chief Justice, not the vice president, preside in the Senate when a presidential impeachment proceeding is on the floor. Rutledge and Morris suggested adding "that persons impeached be suspended from their offices until tried and acquitted"; but Madison and King argued successfully that this would leave the President far too dependent on the legislature.

The reader may remember that before 1913, U.S. senators were chosen by their state legislatures, not directly elected. Morris's belief in the wisdom of having a strong and stable Senate no doubt became ingrained during his studies at King's.[33]

Article I, Section 4, Clause 1 assigns to the states responsibility for setting "the times, places and manner" of elections for the federal legislature. Morris sided with Nathaniel Gorham, Madison, and King in arguing for what might be broadly termed a federalist position. They held that allowing the state legislatures to elect members of the Senate would ensure a means of defense against the national government's encroachments. Rakove attests to the power of this argument in the delegates' minds by submitting that "it was probably this consideration that led all ten states present to approve the amendment." Congress was finally barred from changing the state regulations concerning the election of senators in a move to ensure state sovereignty over an area of power with which the federal government could not interfere.[34]

During the debates concerning Article I, Section 5, Clause 2, Morris held that to expel a member of either house of Congress ought to require a simple majority vote; Madison argued for a two-thirds vote. Madison's motion, of course, won. On Article I, Section 6, Clause 1, Gouverneur led a cohort that included Langdon, Madison, Mason, Carroll, and Dickinson in arguing successfully to have the legislators paid from the Treasury of the United States. On July 16 the Convention had resolved that with regard to the salaries of government officials, "no money shall be drawn from the Public Treasury." This position implied that the states were responsible for paying their own representatives, but such dependence soon became problematic to some of the delegates, and on August 14 the resolution was reversed. Carroll summarized the majority's opinion that the "Senate was to represent and manage the affairs of the whole, and not to be the advocates of State interests. They ought then not to be dependent on nor paid by the States." This position does not resolve the question of the Senate's ultimate obligation. As Rakove argues, "The Senate itself would embody the mixed character of the Constitution: It would be 'federal' in origin but 'national' in orientation, somehow protecting state sovereignty and the national interest simultaneously."[35]

As regards Article I, Section 6, Clause 1, Morris urged going forward in accord with the issue of the privileges of each House as produced by the Committee of Detail. In doing so Morris helped carry the vote over Randolph and Madison. The draft he produced clarifies the detail committee's version substantially and elevates its style. With respect to Article I, Section 6, Clause 2, Morris felt that serving military officers should be eligible for election to Congress; otherwise they would despise "those talking lords who dare not face the foe." Morris also warned of the army's inclination, if excluded, to "cut their way" into Congress before laying down their arms at the end of a war. He argued that there was little danger of corruption because these men would be elected based on their merits and justification of public confidence. "Why should we not avail ourselves of their services if the people chuse [*sic*] to give them their confidence," he inquired. In his final point on the issue, he argued the benefits of having, in the case of war, a member of Congress "most capable of conducting it." His motion failed. Randolph cited the merits of Morris's last point but urged closing any opening for "influence and corruption" which might arise from military presence in the Congress. As Sherman argued, "The Constitution should lay as few temptations as possible in the way of those in power."[36] In the subsequent debates on September 3, Morris fell in with King, Gorham, Baldwin, and Charles Pinckney in seeking a refinement and clarification of the ineligibility matter.

Article I, Section 7, Clause 1, reserves to the House of Representatives the power to originate revenue bills. In character, Morris joined Rutledge, Carroll, and McHenry in opposing the limit on the Senate's power. Although his side lost, the more elegantly expressed version put forth by the Committee of Style is in Morris's hand. In discussion of Article I, Section 7, Clauses 2 and 3, Morris expressed the wish that some plan for a more effective check on hastily proposed legislation could be devised, or "bad laws will be pushed." Morris professed to believe "the public liberty in greater danger from Legislative usurpations than from any other source"; but who was to hold this power, the Executive or the Judiciary? Put on the spot, he suggested without elaboration that perhaps the President should hold the power to block legislation; this, with the addition of a congressional override, became the veto power.

To Article I, Section 8, enumerating Congress's powers, Morris's motion resulted in the addition of the phrase that makes "all Duties, Imposts" and Excises . . . uniform throughout the United States." (This concept is also reflected in Section 9, which specifies that each state's ports must be treated equally and that duties may not be charged on interstate commerce.)[37]

Article I, Section 8, Clause 2, passed to the style committee as granting Congress the power "to borrow money and emit bills on the credit of the United States." On August 16, when the clause came before the convention, Morris moved to strike everything but "to borrow money." He reasoned that if the United States had credit, a Treasury bill clause would be unnecessary; if it had not, they would be unjust and useless. A Treasury bill is a short-term security that matures in one year or less from its issue date. You buy a Treasury bill for a price less than its face value. When it matures, you receive payment at par value. The interest constitutes the difference between the purchase price of the security and what is paid at maturity, or what is paid if the bill is sold before it matures. The phrase "On the credit of the United States" is still there, but Morris's wording may have been an improvement.

The next section of the Constitution to which Morris contributed substantively is Article I, Section 8, Clause 10, which empowers Congress "to define and punish Piracies and Felonies committed on the high Seas, and Offenses against the Law of Nations." On August 14, Morris moved to eliminate the word "punish" before "Offenses against the Law of Nations," so as to enable Congress to define them as well as to punish them. His Pennsylvania colleague Wilson maintained that to pretend to define the law of nations, which depends on the civilized nations' authority, would seem arrogant and thus make the United States look ridiculous. Morris replied that it was correct to speak of defining the law of nations, because it was too vague to be authoritative otherwise.

We have already seen what his role was in the matters of importing slaves, representation, and taxation of exports (Article I, Section 9, Clauses 1, 4, and 5). Neither he nor any other delegate seems, however, to have understood that the prohibition of *ex post facto* laws in the U.S. Constitution would apply to the powers of Congress only, and not to the states.

In the brief discussion of what became Article I, Section 10, Clause 2, Morris supported an amendment by King, who moved to insert the "or Exports" in the line which stated that "No State shall . . . lay any Imposts or Duties on Imports or Exports" to prohibit the states from levying either tax. Morris believed this amendment would prevent the Atlantic states from endeavoring to tax the western states. Friction produced by such sectional taxations, Morris argued, could in turn lead to struggles over Mississippi navigation rights; a further consequence, Morris feared, might be to "drive the Western people into the arms of Great Britain." But Morris did not consider the danger of the western states' return to Great Britain as real enough to give them equal rank with the other states, desiring to encourage growth without casting power into unready hands.

As a welcome break from the (as usual) hot, muggy late-July weather, the convention went into recess from July 26 to August 6. The date the recess began proved not arbitrary: by the twenty-sixth, the Convention had reconsidered and discussed all the resolutions of the Virginia Plan that Randolph had formally introduced.

Throughout the convention the delegates had socialized often at the Man Full of Trouble Tavern, built in 1760, when Gouverneur was only eight, and which early in the twenty-first century still stood and served at 127 Spruce Street. Also the delegates frequently dined at the Indian Queen Tavern, on the southwest side of Fourth and Chestnut streets. This large establishment had stables which held eighty-three horses; its rooms could accommodate as many as a hundred people. City Tavern flourished, then as now, at Second and Walnut streets, not far from the juncture of Dock Street and Goforth Alley, where, in 1780, Morris had the accident that cost him his leg.

In an age when one place was not interchangeable with another, Philadelphia had numerous substantial charms, especially for someone with interests similar to Gouverneur's. The city's libraries had no equal in North America.[38] A "Society for Political Inquiries" met at the one established by Franklin; among its forty-two members were Washington, Wilson, Robert Morris, Clymer, Rush, Bingham, Paine, and Gouverneur Morris. They gave new meaning to the term "festive." The tab for an evening's socializing for a dozen of these American Founders that summer included sixty bottles of madeira. They ate well, too, and one midsummer Wednesday, August 22, 1787, the majority of the delegates and some family members and friends gathered at the river to observe John Fitch's self-propelled steamboat and to picnic by the water.

Morris and his friends also sometimes patronized the Opera House, where musical entertainments were frequent that summer. The works of the Philadelphia composer Alexander Reinagle (1750–1809) were well-liked, even more so were Joseph Haydn's. The American colonists, as is well known, were great dancers, and the most popular music was that composed for dancing. European visitors remarked on the beauty of Philadelphia women; Morris did not fail to take notice of it, too, in his scant leisure time.

Theatrical performance was banned in Philadelphia, and had been since the outset of the Revolution, but in June a New York acting company came down to give dramatic performances. These had to be cautiously advertised as concerts or operas. (Entertainment in Philadelphia was surprisingly inexpensive. At the time the Convention assembled, prices in the city had begun to drop, and they continued to do so until roughly 1789, by which time Morris had already sailed for Europe.)[39]

The city also had a pious side (although, what was unusual for the time, Pennsylvania had no established church). Probably the leading clergyman was Bishop William White, leader of the Episcopal Church and Robert Morris's brother-in-law. Bishop White's impressive house, at 309 Walnut Street, was completed in 1787. The Bishop was rector of both Christ Church and St. Peter's, so that through his churchly duties alone he exerted considerable influence on the city's cultural milieu. Many of the visiting luminaries enjoyed his supper table.

After Washington arrived in the city on May 13, he stayed first at the boardinghouse kept by Mrs. Mary House, at Fifth and High (Market) Streets. Robert and Mary Morris called on him almost right away, and insisted that he stay at their home on the north side of High and Sixth. There Gouverneur Morris passed much time in Washington's company. Along with Robert and Mary Morris, they occasionally went on weekend carriage rides into the nearby countryside, and sometimes farther. Once they ventured to Trenton, where Washington fished "not very successfully" one afternoon, and the next morning "with more success" (he landed perch). During the ten-day recess, Washington went with Gouverneur Morris "in his phaeton with my horses" to the vicinity of Valley Forge "to get trout." While Morris fished, Washington "rid [*sic*] over the old cantonment of the Continental American Army of the winter of 1777 and 1778, visited all the works which were," he added, with mixed emotions, "in ruins."[40] They stayed at Robert Morris's country house, now squarely in the middle of Philadelphia's Fairmount Park. This house, with its cozy oval parlor and plummy feel, must have been a companionable place to spend the convention break.

The story of how Gouverneur offended the dignified Washington concerns this period. Supposedly Morris accepted a wager with Alexander Hamilton "for supper and wine for himself and a dozen friends," if Morris "would take a liberty with Washington at a forthcoming dinner" by clapping the general on the back and exclaiming, "You look fine tonight, old boy!" Washington's glare was so deadly, the story goes, that Morris told Hamilton: "I have won the bet although paid dearly for it, and nothing could induce me to repeat it."

This anecdote is recounted in virtually every biographical narrative on Gouverneur Morris, but its provenance is elusive. The story appears unfootnoted in the 1874 *Life of Jefferson* by James Parton; John Fine regaled Martin Van Buren with it in the spring of 1857, eighty years after the supposed incident. Van Buren relates that Fine (1794–1867), a retired lawyer and New York senator, said he first heard the story in 1852 from Jacob Burnet (1770–1853), a retired judge and legislator who had served briefly in the U.S. Senate. Burnet in turn claimed to have heard it from Alexander Hamilton. In 1852, Hamilton had been dead for forty-eight years. William R. Read's *Life and Correspondence of George Read* (1870) recounts a slightly different version. Among those supposedly present were Hamilton, Dr. John Morgan, and Generals Lafayette, Knox, Greene, Von Steuben, and Wayne, not to mention Gouverneur Morris and George Washington himself, yet none of these recorded the incident. And most of them were prolific writers; Hamilton may have written more letters than Gouverneur Morris, while Washington kept voluminous diaries. In none of these materials have I found anything resembling the story of the backslap.

Besides, although Gouverneur was not given to fawning, every letter he wrote to or about Washington shows his earnest and deep admiration of the general; and Washington's letters to Gouverneur, too, evince a respect. On May 18, 1778, for instance, Washington commented disparagingly to Gouverneur on General Mifflin's return to active service. It was rare indeed for General Washington to criticize a colleague to a (much younger) civilian. Given the utter absence of contemporary verification of the back-slapping episode, and the tone of respect and confidence that consistently marks the two men's communications, the most famous Gouverneur Morris story seems almost certainly apocryphal.[41]

On August 6, the delegates reconvened. The weather continued warm, but seems not to have troubled the fundamentally robust Morris; he never complained, either, of the discomforts that must have been associated with his heavy oaken peg leg. Over the next five weeks, he spoke—and spoke constructively—more than any other delegate, making the majority of his 173 speeches during the convention. Probably only a select few, such as Madison and King, had as much influence as he on the portions of the Constitution debated during this time. His imprint is strong on Article II, which treats the executive branch. Indeed, the extent of his contributions may not have been recognized as fully as it deserves before now.[42]

The seventh of the Randolph resolutions, as originally presented to the Committee of the Whole, declared that a national executive should be instituted, to be chosen by the national legislature for a term left blank; to receive a fixed compensation; to be ineligible for a second term; and (besides having general authority to execute the national laws) to enjoy the executive powers vested in Congress by the Confederation. The committee of the whole began to consider the resolution as early as June 1. The question first raised was whether the executive ought to be a single person.

When Wilson moved that it should, James Madison records, there was a pregnant pause. Benjamin Franklin somberly stated that this was "a point of great importance." After some warm debate, the Committee of the Whole agreed that there should be a national executive, but found itself not prepared to settle the question of how many persons "the executive" should comprise. As for the length of the executive's term, opinion varied between three and seven years; by a mere majority, the latter prevailed.

Throughout the convention, as one member observed, Gouverneur Morris was the floor leader of the drive for a strong and independent chief executive. He and Wilson argued strongly for election by the people themselves. As Morris put it, he did not wish the chief executive to be "the flunkey of the Congress"; and, he reasoned, an executive both appointed by the legislature and impeachable by it would be its mere creature. The executive should be elected by the people at large: "The magistrate [that is, the president] is not the king, but the prime minister. In the U.S. the people are the king." If the people elected the chief magistrate, they would not fail to select a person of distinction in character and services; if the legislature elected him, Morris said, the choice would arise out of intrigue, cabal, and faction. Accordingly, Morris moved to strike the words "national legislature" and replace them with "citizens of the United States." On this point he sharply debated Charles Pinckney over several days. But the convention agreed on election by the national legislature.[43]

With his usual tenacity, however, Morris persevered. His arguments were compelling: (1) When the interests of members were opposed to the general interest, the legislature, otherwise trustworthy, could not be too much distrusted. (2) In all public bodies there are two parties; the executive would necessarily be more connected to one than the other. And not enough had been said concerning the possibility of intrigues to get the chief executive out of office.

As for the danger of monarchy, Morris asserted, the result of election by legislature could prove even worse, if the executive were not properly chosen. So that the executive would not be too dependent on the legislature, the expedient of having him be ineligible for a second term had been devised. In other words, America should deprive itself of the benefit of experience. At the end of a long term, too, the chief magistrate would wish to continue in office. By the Constitution this road would be severed; so he would make a road with the sword. Make the executive too weak, Morris argued, and the legislature would usurp his authority; make him too strong, and he would usurp legislative powers. Morris urged a short term, with the possibility of reelection; and it should not be the legislature doing the electing.

Charles Pinckney, seconded by Mason and Gerry, still supported election by the national legislature but now proposed a rotation system, by which the chief magistrate could serve no more than six years in any twelve. No, Morris replied; rotation was a school in which the scholars, not the masters, governed. He enumerated the evils to be guarded against in establishing the executive: first, the undue influence of the legislature were it to elect the executive; second, the instability of counsel since the president's council would not be elected; third, misconduct in office. In attempting to prevent the first, rotation would produce the second, instability; and change of men would lead to unsalutary change of measure. Nor would rotation prevent intrigue and unhealthy dependence on the legislature. The executive would look forward to the time, however distant, when he would again be eligible to hold office. Finally, to avoid the third evil, that of misconduct in office, impeachments would be necessary—another reason against election by the legislature. Once again, Morris said, he favored election by the people, or, as a second choice, that the electors should choose the executive by lot from among the legislators.[44]

On the last day of August the delegates elected a committee (one member from each of the states) to complete the unfinished or postponed portions of the Constitution. On this committee, James Madison represented Virginia and Gouverneur Morris represented Pennsylvania. The committee delivered its vital report on September 4. Given the style of the section of the report that treated of the presidency, and given Morris's intense and vocal interest in the matter, it seems certain that he wrote those passages. The language of the vesting clause of Article II also surely is Morris's. The report furthermore stipulates a presidential term of four years, with the possibility of reelection. The latter provision, particularly, is in keeping with Morris's ideas—he envisioned a second term as a reward for good behavior in the first. This idea he helped persuade his fellow committee members to go along with.

Although the first draft had provided for election by Congress for a single seven-year term and, provided for the chief magistrate's election by Congress, the report of the Committee of Eleven set up a different system. Each state was to elect a group of electors equal in number to its total of senators and representatives. This quasi electoral college was to vote for two candidates in each state; the one getting the most votes would, ideally, become a candidate for president, while the runner-up stood for vice president.[45]

On August 27, the succession to the presidency was debated. Morris objected to making the president of the Senate the provisional successor to the president. The issue was referred to the committee of eleven dealing with unfinished portions of the Constitution; it reported back naming the vice president the successor first in line. This became the substance of Article II, Section 1, Clause 6. As recounted in chapter 3, Gouverneur Morris had been one of the three primary developers and drafters of the 1777 New York Constitution. That document's provisions for the governorship and lieutenant governorship greatly influenced the U.S. constitutional provisions for the presidency and vice presidency. Like the New York State lieutenant governor, the U.S. vice president would take over in the event that the chief executive died or resigned. Even the wording of the two constitutions' clauses is similar.[46]

In 1802, the speaker of the New York State Assembly wrote to then–U.S. Senator Gouverneur Morris, inquiring about how the Constitutional Convention had settled on a mode of electing the vice president. On Christmas Day, Morris replied:

> The Convention was aware that every Species of Risk and Contrivance would be practiced by the ambitious and unprincipled. It was therefore conceived that if in Elections the President and Vice President were distinctly designated there would generally be a Vote given for two rival Presidents, while there would be numerous Candidates for the other office; because he who wished to become President would naturally connect himself with some popular Man of each particular District for the sake of his local Influence so that the Vice Presidency would be but as a bait. . . . The Person [as Vice Presidential running mate] would have only a partial Vote [of confidence], be perhaps unknown to the greater Part of the Community and probably unfit for the duties which the Death of a President might call on him to perform.[47]

The Constitution makes no reference to a presidential cabinet. On August 20, Gouverneur Morris proposed a council of state, to comprise the Chief

Justice and the secretaries of domestic affairs, of commerce and finance, of foreign affairs, of war, of the marine, and of state. Morris furthermore moved that the president be able to submit any matter to this council for their discussion and opinions, but should retain a free hand to do as he thought proper. But in the debate on September 4, the idea of such a council encountered opposition; Gouverneur Morris, too, opposed it. He had changed his mind, he said, primarily because he now believed that a council would simply shield the president from responsibility for his wrong-headed measures. He also believed that the U.S. Constitution should not properly go into "such minutious" matters.

In the debate over what became Article III, Section 2, Gouverneur and his Pennsylvania colleague Wilson successfully resisted the proposal that so large a body as the Senate have the power to appoint ambassadors and Supreme Court justices.

Scholars sometimes too quick to jump to conclusions have often labeled Gouverneur Morris a monarchist; they do not mean the label as a compliment. He did indeed make statements such as "There never was, and never will be a civilized Society without an Aristocracy"; but surely he meant a Jeffersonian "natural aristocracy," not a hereditary class of nobles.[48] The evidence can be found in the records of the Constitutional Convention, if one has the perseverance to study them.

Just as he had at the New York State constitutional convention in 1777, Morris in 1787 was a staunch defender of civil liberties. At Poughkeepsie in 1777, he had fought a losing battle to eliminate quitrents; at Philadelphia in 1787, he opposed George Mason's motion to empower Congress to enact sumptuary laws. Morris believed that such laws had historically favored already wealthy families, since the main purpose and effect of sumptuary laws had been to mark class distinctions clearly, and thus prevent any person from assuming the appearance of a superior class. In Philadelphia, too, Morris opposed the establishment of an official religion in America. He implicitly urged strongly the official separation of religious institutions from government.

Morris also played, in 1787, what John Dickinson described as a peacemaking role at crucial times (James Madison also seems to have seen Morris in this light). One such occasion was a vituperative battle between representatives of the small states and those of the large on the matter of the election of the president; popular election would favor the large states, and election by the national legislature would favor the small states. Dickinson had temporarily defused one potentially explosive issue—the best means to commit massive executive power to one "Man of the People," as Dickinson phrased it—and Morris, sensing the time right for compromise, immediately said—"Come, gentlemen, let us sit down again and convene further on this subject." The resulting discussion enabled Madison to sketch "a mode for electing the President agreeable to the present issue as drafted before us."[49]

The chief architects of Article III, whose subject is the federal judiciary, were Charles Pinckney, Ellsworth, Wilson, Randolph, and Rutledge. But James Madison and Gouverneur Morris were responsible for several crucial points. For example, in late August, the convention was examining the article's opening sentence, by which the federal judiciary is established. The version read: "The jurisdiction of the Supreme Court shall be exercised in such manner as the Legislature shall direct." Madison and Morris urged that the phrase "jurisdiction of the Supreme Court," provided by the Committee of Detail, be replaced by "judicial Power." The change was agreed to; its result is to emphasize that this third branch had power that extended nationally; the Court's power was up for debate, but its jurisdiction was limited only by national borders.

Madison and Morris also succeeded in persuading their fellow delegates to excise clauses that would have sanctioned legislative direction of the federal judiciary, thus guaranteeing that the courts would remain free of congressional meddling.[50]

Some of Morris's drafting for the style committee was also significant. The Constitution gives Congress the power "to constitute Tribunals inferior to the supreme Court" (Article I, Section 8). The circumstances under which this power is to be exercised appear in Article III, and the relevant passage left the detail committee as follows:

> The Judicial Power of the United States both in law and equity shall be vested in one Supreme Court, and in such Inferior Courts as shall, when necessary, from time to time, be constituted by the Legislature of the United States.

Morris's style committee produced this: "The judicial Power of the United States, both in law and equity, shall be vested in one supreme Court, and in such inferior Courts as the Congress may from time to time ordain and establish."[51]

By eliminating the phrase "as shall, when necessary," the style committee's version deprives Congress of the power to determine the need for inferior federal courts and thus serves to assure that such courts *must* be created. That the committee meant to convey the sense of an imperative power in the federal judicial branch can be inferred from the affirmative diction—"to ordain and establish"—to show what Congress was to do. The choice of these words to substitute for the less forceful "constitute" seems unlikely to have been happenstance.

Congress of course retained authority to organize the lower-level courts and to determine the manner in which jurisdiction is to be settled upon in cases of treason (Article III, Section 3). That the lower courts might be assigned some appellate as well as original jurisdiction could be inferred: Section 2 empowered Congress to make exceptions to the appellate jurisdiction of the Supreme Court. The permissive language "may from time to time" secured the right of Congress to reorganize the federal judiciary. Thus, the intent expressed by the style committee's language is that public convenience, not necessity, is to govern congressional decisions on these structural matters. Morris's Committee of Style furthermore rectified an important oversight: the convention had neglected to give the Supreme Court jurisdiction over disputes between states. Section 3 of Article III concerns treason. In the floor debate, Morris moved unsuccessfully to use the wording of the 1696 British statute, which had permitted those accused of treason to be defended by counsel and allowed the defense to examine and cross-examine witnesses and address the jury. The delegates did adopt the statute's requirement of two witnesses or confession for conviction. Morris, in an effort to give the federal government the power to define treason, wished to substitute more words, so that the article would declare it treason "if a man do levy war against the United States within their territories." Several delegates objected that treason against the one state was not necessarily against all and that the power to define treacherous behavior belonged to the states.[52]

Morris's prose skills are reflected in the full faith and credit clause of Article IV. What came out of the detail committee was drawn from Article XVI in the Virginia Plan, and it read as follows: "Full faith shall be given in each state to the acts of the legislatures, and to the records and judicial proceedings of the courts and magistrates of every other state."

When this provision came before the Convention on August 29, Hugh Williamson, of North Carolina, moved to substitute the wording from the Articles of Confederation: "Full faith shall be given, in each of these states, to the records, acts and judicial proceedings of the courts and magistrates of every other state." Williamson may have misunderstood the meaning of this text; James Wilson and William Samuel Johnson thought it to mean that legal judgments in one state could be the ground of legal action in another. Madison wanted to make it possible to execute one state court's judgments in other states in situations that might be suitable. But Randolph countered that there was no instance of one nation executing the judgments of another nation; he proposed the following substitute:

> Full Faith ought to be given, in each State, to the public Acts, Records and judicial Proceedings of every other State, and the Legislature shall by general Laws, determine the State and Effect of such Acts, Records and Proceedings.

This still being somewhat fuzzy, Morris proposed a clearer phrasing substituting "the legislature may . . . prescribe the manner in which such acts . . . shall be proven" for "the legislature shall determine the state . . . of such acts. . . ." The draft article and the proposed revisions were then turned over to a five-man committee (Rutledge, Randolph, Gorham, Wilson, and Johnson), and the article emerged thus:

> Full faith and credit shall be given in each State to the public acts, records and judicial proceedings, in every other State; and the legislature may, by general laws, prescribe the manner in which such acts, records, and proceedings shall be proved, and the effect thereof.

Having considered this, the convention sent it to Morris's style committee, whose internal debates produced the following:

> Full faith and credit shall be given, in each state, to the public acts, records and judicial proceedings, of every other state. And the Congress may, by general laws, prescribe the manner in which such acts, records and proceedings, shall be proved and the effect thereof.

In drafting the section for final consideration by the full convention, Morris made only three changes, but their effect was significant in clarifying the section's import and shifting its focus. First, Morris changed uppercase "State" to lowercase "state," thus deemphasizing the states' importance relative to the federal power. (Except that "State" is capitalized in the final version of the Constitution, as are most nouns.) Second, he divided the clause into two sentences by changing the semicolon after "every other state" to a period. The effect is to stress the special power that this clause assigns to Congress. Third, he changed "the legislature" to "the Congress," thereby obviating potential serious problems of interpretation.

Regarding Congress's power to admit new states (Article IV, Section 3, Clause 1), the detail committee's version dictated that new states be admitted to the Union on the same terms as the original states, except that "the Legislature may make conditions with the new States, concerning the public debt." Morris moved to strike that part of the clause, saying he did not want to bind the federal legislature to admit the western states on altogether equal terms. Madison and Mason objected that new states ought not to be degraded and "the best policy is to treat them with that equality which will make them friends not enemies." According to Madison's convention journal, "Morris did not mean to discourage the growth of the Western Country. He knew that to be impossible. He did not wish however to throw the power into their hands." Despite opposition from Mason, Madison, Sherman, and Williamson, Morris's motion carried; only Maryland and Virginia voted no.

Morris also proposed wording that would make passage into the Union more difficult for the western states than the detail committee's language had made it. He proposed that "New States may be admitted by the Legislature into this Union: but no new State shall be erected within the limits of any of the present States, without the consent of the Legislature of such State, as well as of the General Legislature." In the warm debate that followed, Luther Martin (1748–1826), a delegate from Maryland, pointed out that if Morris's wording were adopted, difficulties would arise for a territory like Vermont, which had obtained its independence from New York. Vermont, Luther argued, would be in danger of being "reduced by force in favor of the States claiming it" and compelled to join the Union. The motion passed after much more flexible changes in the wording so that it read "no new State shall be formed or erected within the Jurisdiction of any other State."[53]

The last part of Article IV deals with, among other things, protecting the states from domestic insurrection. Morris again proves helpful here. The Committee of Detail report specified congressional power "to subdue a rebellion in any state, on the application of its legislature." During discussion of this clause (August 17), Morris pointed out both that the executive might be at the head of the rebellion, and that "we are acting a very strange part. We first form a strong man to protect us, and at the same time wish to tie his hands behind him" (by requiring the application of the legislature).

Article V provides for the Constitution's amendment. The version being debated on September 15 included only a *congressional* procedure for changing the Constitution; George Mason expressed the concern that the effect might be to foreclose all amendment entirely.

Morris and Elbridge Gerry then moved to provide that a constitutional convention be called if two-thirds of the states desired it. Connecticut's

Roger Sherman feared lest the Constitution be amended to encroach on states' rights and urged a proviso "that no State shall without its consent be affected in its internal police, or deprived of its equal suffrage in the Senate." But Madison did not want to multiply inessential provisions—they might effectively gut the amendment clause altogether. It was Morris who came up with the solution: "that no State, without its consent, shall be deprived of its equal suffrage in the Senate." This assuaged everyone's concerns and was agreed on without debate. Article V was soon approved in its final form. By the design of the Framers, to amend the Constitution is an extremely arduous process. More than seven thousand amendments have been introduced in Congress but only twenty-seven have become part of the Constitution.[54]

In his 1971 discussion of the U.S. Constitution and the judiciary branch, Julius Goebel remarks on the crucial importance of the second paragraph of Article VI. Morris's Committee of Style, he points out, "wrought a fine bit of rhetorical magic": where the Constitution, federal law, and federal treaties had been "the supreme law of the several states," the committee made them "the supreme Law of the Land."[55] The change clearly signified the subordination of the states to the federal power—a matter of no small philosophical and legal import. By the first paragraph of Article VI, the United States assumed all the obligations the nation had incurred before the Constitution was ratified. The move was essential to the new nation's international credibility. On August 22, the issue of the U.S. legislature's stance with respect to dealing with the federal debt came to the floor. Morris suggested that the clause specify that "The Legislature *shall* discharge the debts and fulfill the engagements of the United States," a wording clarifying and strengthening the previous clause's declaration that "the U.S. *shall have power* to fulfill the engagements." He recognized that possessing the power and following through on obligations were two different things. The convention determined on August 24 that the new government would honor the old Confederation's debts, although the final wording does not specify that just the Congress's debts are still valid; Madison observed that "attempts made by the Debtors to British subjects to shew that contracts under the old Government were dissolved by the Revolution . . . destroyed the political identity of the Society."[56]

Under what became Article VI, Clause 2, in the debates on the floor on August 25, Morris seconded Madison's motion to insert after "all Treaties made" the words "or which shall be made." The astute Virginian and the delegate from Pennsylvania clearly wished to obviate all doubt about preexisting international compacts by making the language explicitly cover both past and future ones. Without change, this clause later passed to the Committee of Style. This committee reported the clause back, under Morris's hand, with this major change incorporated.

Morris had substantial influence on the final enactment of Article VI, Clause 3. This text, dealing in large part with the oaths binding federal officials and judges to uphold the Constitution, originated in the fourteenth resolution of the Randolph Plan. On June 11 Sherman spoke against it as intruding needlessly into the states' jurisdictions. When the clause came up again on August 30, Charles Pinckney wished to insert a provision that "No religious test, or qualification shall ever be annexed to any oath of office under the authority of the United States," and although Sherman opposed it— this time he argued that the prevailing liberality was a sufficient protection against such tests—the motion passed, with Morris in support.

The relation of church to state in the colonial era was, let us say, enmeshed. In New Hampshire, Massachusetts, and Connecticut, for instance, taxpayers were obliged to support the Congregational or town church whether they were members or not. Virginia, the Carolinas, and Georgia all recognized the Church of England as the state church, as did Maryland, which had formerly been under Catholic and Puritan jurisdiction. Of the aforementioned colonies, however, in truth the Anglican establishment took substantial hold only in Virginia. Pennsylvania, New Jersey, Delaware, and Rhode Island established absolute freedom of religion. In New York the situation until 1777 proved muddled owing to the region's extraordinarily polyglot population, which included, among other groups, English, Irish, Scots, Poles, Dutch, French, Portuguese, Danes, Norwegians, Swedes, Germans, and Italians. Nevertheless, the Anglican Church was established in New York in 1693. Morris felt so concerned about religious intrusions into New York state politics that, in helping to develop the first state constitution, in 1777, he labored to bring about the passage of a clause that declared "the free exercise and enjoyment of religious profession and worship, without discrimination or preference, shall forever hereafter be allowed, within this State, to all mankind."[57]

Article VII—concise in the version drafted by Morris, which is the one that appears in the ratified Constitution—arose out of the verbose fifteenth resolution of the Virginia Plan. It specifies that the Constitution will go into effect among the states ratifying it, as long as at least nine do so. On this matter Gouverneur joined with Mason, Randolph, Gorham, and Madison in support of the reference to conventions. Morris's arguments for this approach proved cogent and forceful. As the debates wound down, on August

30 and 31, Morris suggested that the conventions ought to proceed in a two-fold way, so as to provide for the situations of the ratifying states either being contiguous, which would render a small number sufficient, or being dispersed, which would require a greater number. Madison argued that the article should specify the number of states necessary for ratification, whether seven, eight, or nine, lest it be "put in force over the whole body of people, though less than a majority of them should ratify it."[58] When this article came up in the Philadelphia convention on August 31, it was decided that nine states would be necessary to ratify the Constitution.

Morris moved to strike the requirement of conventions and leave the states to pursue their own modes, but after some debate, the motion lost. Morris's chief contribution to this article was therefore his draft of it, approved without alteration in mid-September.

Morris's significant contributions to the debates and the drafting were now completed, but work remained to be done. For the Committee of Style, he drafted the document governing the transition of Congress from the Articles of Confederation to the Constitution. In doing so, he made a number of alterations to the document as it came from the floor of the Convention on September 10. The style committee also incorporated part of the twenty-third resolution from the Virginia Plan ("Introduction of Government") into the transitional document, which appears to have been approved without debate immediately after the Constitution was signed.

On the matter of the formal Introduction of Government following ratification, Morris again contributed substantively. The provision originated wholly in the Committee of Detail and appeared first as Article XXIII of the Draught of the Committee of Detail, which read:

> To introduce this government, it is the opinion of this Convention, that each assenting Convention should notify its assent and ratification to the United States in Congress assembled . . . should elect Members of the Senate, and direct the election of Members of the House of Representatives . . . and should, as soon as may be, after their meeting, choose the President of the United States, and proceed to execute this Constitution.[59]

At this time Morris moved successfully to strike the words "choose the President of the United States" from the article's list of imperatives for the ratifying conventions, arguing that the mode of choosing the president had not yet been decided. Although the mode of choosing had been addressed in Article II, Morris correctly anticipated further debate on the subject, which took place four days later. Afterward the style committee made changes bringing the document into line with some later decisions of the convention. For instance, with regard to choosing the President, the final document specified the procedure much more closely: "Electors should be appointed by the States which shall have ratified the [Constitution], and . . . the Electors should assemble to vote for the President."[60] The result seems to have been approved without debate directly after the signing of the Constitution on September 17.[61]

So far I have emphasized Morris's positive contributions to the framing of the U.S. Constitution, but he was instrumental, too, in keeping certain provisions *out* of the document. For instance, over a nearly two-month period, the Convention repeatedly debated the general subject of controlling the states' presumed tendency to encroach on the federal government. On July 17, there was a brief debate on whether the federal government should have the power to negate state laws; Morris argued that such a power would disgust the states. This view eventually prevailed over Madison's contention— made that day and repeated afterward, until September 12—that the power was essential.

Once all of the delegates had commented on the draft Constitution that emerged from the Committee of Detail, the conclusion came quickly. On September 8, the Committee of Style was elected by ballot, with representation from New York (Alexander Hamilton), Connecticut (William Johnson), Massachusetts (Rufus King still resident there), Virginia (James Madison), and Gouverneur Morris (Pennsylvania). "The finish given to the style and arrangement of the Constitution fairly belongs to Gouverneur Morris," Madison wrote to Jared Sparks in 1832. Indeed, the other four members of the committee could not have had much input, because the draft was completed just four days later. Discussion of the draft began as soon as it was reported out on September 12, and concluded on the fifteenth. On that day, with a few changes incorporated, the Constitution was approved and a fair copy was made. With restraint, Madison records in his notes for the day: "On the question to agree to the Constitution all the states Ay."

On September 17 the delegates gathered for their last session, to sign the fair copy. On that morning Franklin rose with a speech, which his Pennsylvania colleague Wilson read for him: the famous plea for all present to put aside their hesitations and support this Constitution. Franklin moved that the members sign the document, "Done in Convention by the unanimous consent of the States present . . ." In this way all members could signify that their state delegations had approved the Constitution, even if some of the individuals in those delegations had not. This lawyerly motion had been drawn up for Franklin by Gouverneur Morris.[62]

Forty-two delegates were present on this last day, and all but Gerry, Mason, and (ironically) Randolph stood ready to sign. At the last minute, Gorham indicated a desire to change the number of representatives per state to "one for every thirty thousand people. "For the first and only time, Washington intervened, and asked that the change be made. The alteration was done by Morris on the spot. That night Gouverneur Morris drafted the letter by which Washington would formally submit the Constitution to Congress, convening in New York. That last Constitutional chore elegantly completed, he joined the rest of the delegates, who by this time were already celebrating at the City Tavern, along with the Pennsylvania Assembly. (This body had been meeting concurrently with the Convention, across the hall in the State House.) In the engrossed Constitution, which is the official version, the Pennsylvania delegation signed last. After all of the other Pennsylvania delegates had affixed their signatures to the charter, there is a period; and after this full stop appears only the signature *Gouvre Morris,* the characteristic way that Morris signed his name. There is a poetic rightness about the way this signing has been executed.

The next day, having dined at one P.M. at Robert Morris's house one last time, Gouverneur Morris, George Washington, and Robert Morris rode together the several miles west to Gray's Ferry, on the Schuylkill River. Here the three parted. Washington headed south to Mount Vernon; Robert Morris returned to his High Street house; and Gouverneur Morris turned his horse north, to his newly acquired Morrisania.[63]

On June 21, 1788, New Hampshire cast the ninth and deciding vote to ratify the United States Constitution. Now began the first transition of a modern national government by democratic vote, rather than by the sword or by heredity. Roughly two thousand men served as delegates to the state U.S. Constitutional adoption conventions; many thousands more state citizens had voted to elect those delegates. Benjamin Rush wrote rhapsodically about "the hand God . . . employed in this work," Thomas Jefferson of the demigod delegates who created it. Morris's assessment, made in July 1788, was less exalted. The U.S. Constitution, he said, was just "the work of plain honest men."[64]

A great deal has been written about the essays pseudonymously published by "Publius," which have come to be known as *The Federalist Papers.* Two large states, Virginia and New York, had, somewhat predictably, wavered at first on the matter of ratification. Alexander Hamilton accordingly enlisted several deft hands to draft essays advocating the Constitution's acceptance. Although ailing, John Jay was a partner from the outset; he produced essays number 2 through 5. In November, James Madison took a turn as "Publius." Hamilton expected William Duer to share the burden of the writing, but Duer wrote only two pieces, and his essays were not printed in the collection. Late in life, Gouverneur Morris said, "I was warmly pressed by Hamilton to assist in writing *The Federalist,* which I declined." Although Morris supplied no reasons, this biographer surmises that Gouverneur did not wish to become involved as an advocate for a charter he had had such a great share in bringing to fruition.[65] Morris may well have felt that in both style and content the Constitution's merit was self-evident and would be recognized.

In the event, the efforts of "Publius" probably did not exert a significant influence on ratification. Virginia and New York had approved the Constitution by the end of July 1788. North Carolina ratified it in November 1789, and Rhode Island in May 1790. By this time, the United States of America had already begun to function under the Constitution.

At the time the U.S. Constitution was drafted, English was far from being the world's most prestigious language. Ahead of it were French, German, Spanish, and perhaps Russian. In the years since, the English language has spread steadily and become more and more important in international relations. Before the end of the nineteenth century, this change likely had something to do with Britain's imperial preeminence. But even as England's empire shrank, the predominance of the English language has increased, and now English is more nearly the world's language than any tongue has ever been. Surely, this has to do with the development of the United States as a global power. That at its foundation the subject of our biography had some small, valuable part, the careful reader may now aver.

$\{6\}$

IN EUROPE

AFTER PARTING FROM George Washington and Robert Morris at Gray's Ferry, Morris rode to his estate, where he stayed for several weeks, assessing the extensive war damage and making plans to restore the mansion and repair the grounds. By the end of October, he was back in Philadelphia on business, and here he had some interesting conversations with influential American political figures. Their assessments alarmed him enough to prompt a letter to George Washington: "Living out of the busy World [while at Morrisania], I had nothing to say worth your Attention, or I would earlier have given you the Trouble you now [are about to] experience [from this importuning letter]." Morris reports he believes the Constitution will be ratified, but only with the popular understanding that Washington will allow himself to be nominated for the presidency. "Should the idea prevail that you would not accept of the Presidency, it would prove fatal [to ratification] in many Parts. Truth is that your great and decided Superiority leads Men willingly to put you in a Place which will not add to your personal Dignity, nor raise you higher than you already stand: but they would not willingly put any other Person in the same Situation. . . . Men must be treated as Men and not as Machines, much less as Philosophers, and least of all Things as reasonable Creatures; seeing that in Effect they reason not to direct but to excuse their conduct." As he then observes, "public Opinion on these Subjects must not be neglected in a Country where Opinion is every Thing," in addition to which it is the "Conviction that of all Men you are best fitted to fill" the office of President. "Your cool steady Temper," he continues, "is *indisputedly necessary* to give a firm and manly Tone to the new Government."

Morris compares the political leadership of a large country to the operation of a complex piece of machinery: "the Task of no common Workman," who must, especially at the outset, establish properly "the mighty Power of Habit, and the Custom, the law both of Wise Men and Fools." For "no Constitution is the same on Paper and in Life." Powerful office is dangerous to those un-equal to it: "The Exercise of Authority depends on personal Character . . . the Whip and Reins by which an able Charioteer governs unruly Steeds will only hurl the unskillful Presumer with more speedy and headlong Violence to the Earth. . . . And . . . among these thirteen horses now about to be coupled to-gether there are some of every Race and Character. They will listen to your Voice, and submit to your Control: you therefore must I say *must* mount the Seat." Morris hints strongly that the duty would likely not prove "pleasing" to Washington. "You will however on this, as on other occasions, feel that inte-rior Satisfaction and self Approbation which the world cannot give; and you will have in every possible Event the Applause of those who know you enough to respect you properly."[1]

This earnest letter made a notable imprint on the general, who was just be-ginning again to enjoy the farming life he had cherished steadily throughout his adulthood. Within three weeks Gouverneur and Robert had additional opportunities to plead their case to Washington: they stayed with him at Mount Vernon from November 19 through November 21. After that, they rode to Richmond, primarily for the sake of the tobacco trade, on which both Morrises soon hoped to become enormously wealthy. They remained in Rich-mond for the better part of seven months, much of their visit coinciding with the state's constitutional ratification convention. Gouverneur attended as many of these sessions as his business appointments would allow. Here, as in Philadelphia, it seemed that the document he had drafted would be ratified. From the New York state capital, Morris wrote to Washington: "It is the gen-eral Opinion of those with whom I converse that the federal Ticket will pre-vail thro this State with a very great Majority."[2]

By the time the Constitution had been ratified and the consequent cele-brations begun, Gouverneur had returned, briefly, to New York. Here he observed the low-key parade down the Broadway to honor the official event. That Richard Morris had been chosen to serve as one of the thirteen deputy marshals in the procession must have pleased him, too.[3]

On November 12, 1788, Gouverneur wrote from Morrisania to "Gen-eral Washington" to say that he expected to make his departure "soon from Philadelphia for the kingdom of France." He also planned to visit Holland and England. Washington asked him to purchase a gold watch for personal use: "Not a small, trifling nor a finical, ornamental one, but a watch executed in point of workmanship, large, flat and with a plain, hand-some key." (Morris dealt with this matter quickly once he reached Paris.

On April 29, 1789, he wrote, "Six Days ago I got from the Maker your Watch, with two Copper Keys and one golden one, and a Box containing a spare Spring and Glasses, all of which I have delivered to Mr. Jefferson who takes charge of them for you.")[4] Washington also sent him letters of introduction to Lord Shelburne, the Marquis of Lansdowne, Rochambeau, Lafayette, now a French hero for his military victory in America, and Chastellux, among others—opening to Morris many offices and salons. Morris's ship, *Henrietta,* passed Cape Henlopen, Delaware, on December 18, 1788, and arrived at Le Havre on January 27, 1789—forty days of rough wintertime passage. On this trip Morris, who probably regretted not waiting for a gentler springtime passage, made well-phrased observations about the weather and the waves. Of his first trip to Europe and first ocean voyage, he wrote that "the greatest Part of the twenty four Hours was cloathed in Darkness." While on board, he penned letters to friends and produced a fascinating essay on the finances of the United States, a piece he subsequently discussed with Jefferson. Morris pondered the means by which the United States could obtain the import duties the states received without creating "disgust among the many friends of the new Constitution and [providing] weapons to its enemies."[5]

Gouverneur's main purpose in going abroad was to represent Robert Morris in business. As so often, however, life presented him with a few unexpected turns. What began as a business trip expected to last, at most, several months developed into a decade of adventurous sojourn on the Continent and in the British Isles. Over that decade, Morris was variously a commercial agent, a private agent for the American government, an "in the clear" American public official, and, in inimitable, and, for the biographer, somewhat confounding fashion, an informal public agent, first for Washington and then for the British Foreign Office.

Morris went straight from Le Havre to Paris, where he checked into the historic Hôtel Richelieu. It happens that he stepped out of his carriage onto the streets of the City of Lights at a time when a great conflagration had just begun to spark, and he lived more or less in the midst of the greatest turmoil for a total of roughly five years. Of the hundred or so Americans who are known to have visited France between 1789 and 1799, Gouverneur stayed the longest.

Thanks largely to Washington's letters of introduction and to his own aristocratic charm, Morris moved in interesting circles when abroad. He wrote steadily and informatively to Washington and sent him packets of newspapers. From March 1789 to January 1792 he kept a fascinating and voluminous journal, which is now one of the primary sources of information on the French Revolution. (He stopped keeping it out of concern for his French friends' safety as well as his own.)

On October 17, 1789, Washington—he was now President Washington—wrote to Gouverneur asking him to go to England and approach the British government informally, with a view to easing the serious differences between it and the United States. Morris thus became the fledgling nation's first known private agent abroad, but not its first successful one, as we will see. Thanks to modern scholarship, we have learned in large part why: a clever British spy had preempted Morris even before he received his commission.

Last and not least, Morris served in a fully official capacity as the new nation's first minister plenipotentiary to France from January 12, 1792, to August 9, 1794. He was the only chief emissary from a foreign country to remain on post throughout this violent period. Well before his appointment, though, Morris had become deeply involved in French governmental affairs, so much so that he became one of the only non-French personages to exert a considerable impact on the period.[6]

Morris's financial business in Europe enjoyed some noteworthy successes. By the time he had returned to America, in 1800, for example, as a result of various trades and sales he owned more than forty-five acres of choice land in Cambray, France, and nearly thirty-nine acres of The Hague.

But that came later. The first thing Morris did in Paris in 1789, even before his bags were unpacked, was to make the rounds of the city to present his letters of introduction. Nature and nurture had given Morris a subtle touch of drama in the way he did business. His French was adequate for commercial dealings, but he found, not surprisingly, that it was insufficient at first to enable him to understand much social conversation. Although Gouverneur went out to France primarily as agent and partner of Robert Morris, he got along financially quite well apart from the latter. For one thing, he already had independent partnerships before he sailed (and good for him he did). At this period especially, however, all these firms were greatly handicapped in trying to profit from the rise in security values overseas by lack of sufficient capital at home. And like most American merchants at that time, Gouverneur was financially overextended, in a variety of enterprises, especially real estate. Robert Morris was stretched even thinner. American merchants had often depended on Europe for credit. Now, with the market spiraling upward, they wished to involve more European capital in their speculations. These would succeed as long as whatever they produced or bought could be sold in Europe at prices higher than those current in the United States. In theory, European capital would enable speculators to buy any commodity without limit, making money at every step while debt was transferred to Europe.[7]

Having gone abroad in large part to try to restore Robert's fortunes and advance his own fortunes, Gouverneur soon found that his friend's "various debts and engagements," combined with his inability to deliver the ordered tobacco shipments on time, made it impossible to help Robert substantially. "Here I have to perform the task of the Israelites in Egypt," he wrote to the older Morris, "make bricks without straw."[8]

Largely out of frustration over the "stock not ready for delivery" messages he steadily received from America, Gouverneur Morris soon became deeply involved in securities speculation and in major efforts to restructure the American debt to France. Morris met with the French statesman Maréchal de Castries on April 1 (April Fools' Day!), 1789, and proposed to provide France with large, steady shipments of tobacco, flour, rice, and other provisions. These items, Morris stipulated, would be purchased in part with money and in part with U.S. debt to France. Some months later Gouverneur arranged to contract to import thirty thousand barrels of flour from America. He also attempted to negotiate with France's finance minister, Jacques Necker (1732–1804), on the American debt. In these efforts he anticipated having the assistance and cooperation of Robert, whose influence still seemed considerable.

Necker desired ten million livres a year for three years. With characteristic complexity, Morris offered three hundred thousand a month, to proceed until twenty-four million was paid, at which point the U.S. obligation would be deemed fulfilled. Necker desired to have part of this arrangement secured in hard currency, so no bargain was struck. Morris's efforts to speculate on the debt collapsed in 1790, since the United States seemed prepared to pay its debts outright, which was of course preferable to Necker. France, bankrupted after supporting the American Revolution, desperately needed the cash, and efforts at financial reform had failed.

If such direct private dealings with U.S. governmental financial matters by a private businessman with no official portfolio seem breathtakingly brassy, that is because they are. But in attempting to purchase the American debt to France, Gouverneur Morris was far from alone. American credit was rising at the same time that the French government needed money; many speculators had had the notion of purchasing the American debt to France, selling it on the securities market in Holland, and taking a rich profit.[9] Morris's strictly commercial schemes, developed at roughly the same time and in collaboration with the American merchant Daniel Parker, who was also in Europe, were even grander in scale.

In 1789 Gouverneur and Parker planned the organization of an international syndicate of European investors to purchase the entire U.S. domestic debt. They aspired to organize a cadre of European merchants at Antwerp, and soon thereafter forge an alliance with the Amsterdam Society. This society of Dutch trading houses had already been doing business with Parker. In this helium-filled scheme, Morris and associates were to obtain two-thirds of the shares.

This plan soon fell apart, but in the process of floating it, Gouverneur shipped over to London. Here he made the acquaintance of several British investors: the poet Samuel Rogers (who also kept what became a famous journal); the hugely wealthy banker Sir Francis Baring; Edmund Boehm, a director of the East India Company; and Thomas Hinchman. With these investors Morris was able to raise the funds necessary to purchase the U.S. debt and sell it at a profit. These transactions netted Morris more money than most people earned in a lifetime.

Morris not only profited handsomely in the deals he actually executed but also made surprising headway in elite circles. There are a number of reasons for this. Bad as his French at first was, it was nevertheless almost certainly superior to that of most foreign visitors. He was well educated in the European classics. And he had a well-deserved reputation for brilliance of achievement in governmental matters. During the American revolutionary period, he had already had numerous contacts with such French officials as Rochambeau, Gérard, Vergennes, Luzerne, and Lafayette. So, ironically, the French political elite of 1789 almost certainly appreciated Morris's value as a constitution builder better than almost any Americans have.

French women, married and otherwise, also seem to have found Gouverneur Morris particularly attractive. The average European man of the era, at just a bit over five feet tall, was smaller and less robust than his American counterpart, and Morris towered over most of his countrymen.[10] The vitality and vigor, charm and intelligence apparent in Morris's writings must have carried twice the force when embodied in the man himself.

The France of 1789 was the country that Georg Christoph Lichtenberg (1742–1799), perhaps history's only physicist/satirist, had referred to as "free France, where people are now free to string up anyone they want to." Yet in a certain respect, it resembled the America of the time. Both nations were largely agricultural. In 1789, only about 3 percent of Americans lived in what were then termed cities, and only five cities had more than 8,000 people. France at the time likewise had only five or six cities of more than 8,000 people. Most citizens of this most populous Western European nation lived either in the countryside or in isolated small towns in the midst of the country. Perhaps because France was a much older country than the United States, its social divisions were much more complex and varied. As the journalist Jacques Mallet du Pan wrote to a fellow writer on political matters, P. E. Dumont, at about the time of Morris's arrival, divergent branches of French society had sprung out in all directions in a pattern difficult even for a native to discern.[11]

Morris moved easily amid these complexities. As Theodore Roosevelt, his second biographer, put it, "Before a month [in Paris] had expired, Mr. Morris had become a social success, thanks to his wit, ability and engaging manners."[12]

It is difficult to abridge Morris's diaries or to provide a context for brief quotations; on the other hand, how can passages be quoted out of context? The diaries seem not to have been meant for public viewing, but rather as a source for Morris himself to refer to privately in later years, as a register of first impressions. He evidently let himself be influenced by feelings of sympathy or antipathy, and (consciously or not) he sometimes presented the facts in the light most flattering to himself. But the biographer who would rely strictly on those diaries, journals, or memoirs that are completely objective and truthful would have little to work with.

The revolution that Morris's European diaries partially chronicle could well be the most written about subject in history. To this period belong the first political apologias by women (that of Madame Roland [1754–1793], especially, trembles with life). And yet none of the central protagonists left an autobiography. Of course, many were guillotined before they had a chance; during 1793 and 1794, more than 2,500 died this way. Thousands of others were hanged, stabbed, or beaten or kicked to death. And most of those thus slain were among the most highly educated elite. Small wonder that, in *Democracy in America,* Alexis de Tocqueville remarks that "the great advantage of Americans is that they have [attained] a democracy without having to undergo a democratic revolution."

Despite the volatile political circumstances in which he found himself, Morris's first impressions were delight at the pursuits Paris could afford. Morris's diary commences on March 1, 1789, when he was "employed in writing all morning," after "a business breakfast," on how best to move forward "with respect to the tobacco." That night he watched Molière's *The Misanthrope* acted "inimitably well" and dined with a small party, reflecting that his "Manner of thinking and speaking however is too masculine for the Climate I am now in." Morris was soon to find that "I have not a Moment's Time": "The Amusements I cannot partake of because my Business in the Morning and my Engagements till Midnight keep me in perpetual Hurry."

Although the political division between them was great, Jefferson was characteristically courteous to Morris in Paris. Despite their philosophical differences, the two had much in common. Both must have felt some unease in embarking from Philadelphia, a city of roughly forty thousand in a country with roughly three million citizens, and arriving a few weeks later in Paris, where seven hundred thousand of France's twenty-four million people resided. Both men were bibliophiles of the best kind: they not only bought thousands of books but also read many of them. (Morris's diary and letters are replete with quotations from Shakespeare, Swift, the *philosophes,* Sterne, and Chesterfield.)

Jefferson was a widower, Morris a bachelor, and both enjoyed amours in France. Morris's draft for a French constitution, written for Lafayette and Talleyrand (1754–1838), in many ways resembles the one Jefferson drew up for Lafayette on June 3, 1789. Jefferson and Morris also would share some family connections. On the commercial trip he made in the American South before leaving for Europe, Gouverneur had stayed at Tuckahoe, the plantation on the James River that belonged to his friend Colonel Thomas Mann Randolph. Jefferson's father had served as this Randolph's guardian, and Thomas Jefferson had lived seven years at Tuckahoe. Colonel Thomas Randolph had fathered thirteen children. The fourth child, also Thomas, married Jefferson's daughter, and then became governor of Virginia. The eighth child, Anne Cary, whom Morris first saw when she was fourteen and he thirty-six, was born in July 1774. After tumultuous decades, and an evidently mostly in-house courtship, Anne—called Nancy—became Mrs. Gouverneur Morris.

Mostly from Madison's letters, Jefferson learned a great deal of what took place at the Constitutional Convention, and what found its way into the seven articles of the ratified document. Both Morris and Jefferson believed in the positive value of federal taxation, and both would have wished for a more powerful president. Jefferson, however, believed ardently in the cause of the French revolutionists, whereas Morris was a monarchist with respect to France, and naturally he found government-by-mob abhorrent. But Louis XVI (1754–1793) impressed him as "a small beer character."[13]

On March 5 Jefferson took Morris to the governmental seat, then at Versailles, where he met Armand-Marc, Comte de Montmorin–Saint Hérem (1745–1792), the minister of foreign affairs, and was treated gruffly by him. Montmorin's attitude would change as his situation became more perilous; of his end, the reader shall learn below. The same day Morris met the Duchess of Orléans, to whom he later gave much assistance, and encountered an old acquaintance, Admiral Charles d'Estaing (1729–1794), who had commanded the French fleet in the American Revolution. Within a few years D'Estaing made the one-way trip to the guillotine. Jefferson also introduced Morris to the Comte d'Angiviller, administrator of the king's buildings—in effect, the keeper of a gigantic ring of desirable keys. D'Angiviller was also the older brother of the Comte de Flahaut. Thanks to this connection, the family (D'Angiviller, Flahaut, his wife, Adélaïde, and her son) had an apartment in the Louvre.

Jefferson soon invited Morris to dinner at the Champs-Elysées legation, where on March 8 he met Jefferson's and Crèvecoeur's daughters and General Greene's sons. When the royalist reformer Chrétien Guillaume de Lamoignon de Malesherbes (1721–1794), former French minister of Marine, heard that Morris was in the city, he recalled Morris's paper on West Indian commerce and expressed a desire to see him on behalf of a friend whose extensive holdings in Saint-Domingue would be augmented by American maritime trade with these islands. But Morris declined to negotiate on these financial matters: "I had rather leave our affairs in the hands of our minister" (Jefferson, of course). Morris, however, was captivated by the benign, serene Malesherbes, writing of him to the London ambassador Luzerne that "I am in love with one of your family, and this is not singular, for everyone else has the same passion." In 1793 Malesherbes conducted a compelling defense of Louis XVI before the Convention. This good man, too, soon died on the scaffold.

Morris was again at Versailles on March 21, when Madame de Flahaut appeared. At the time she was twenty-eight, her husband sixty-three; and although the count spoke no English, Adélaïde did. In his diary that evening, Morris called her "a pleasing woman" and "not a sworn enemy to intrigue."

A week later Morris was walking to Madame Corny's—she was one of Jefferson's friends—when he happened upon Madame de Flahaut. While he believed the encounter accidental, she knew of the handsome American's presence in Paris because of their meeting at Versailles and had likely sent out a servant to scout his whereabouts. She invited him to the Louvre to view the artwork. At the very end of March, he took her up on the invitation, and for months afterwards they entertained each other in an *amitié amoureuse,* a romantic friendship, with the major emphasis on the *amitié* (friendship). Madame de Flahaut had been married seven years and had a four-year-old son, Charles, who bore no strong resemblance to her husband the count. She seems to have had a captivating personal presence; it comes across even in portraits, where she appears as a full-figured brunette with large, heavy-lidded eyes and graceful-looking hands. Acquaintances remarked on her mesmerizing demeanor.

On April 20, 1790, Gouverneur went to the Louvre to see Adélaïde and found Talleyrand there. Charles Maurice de Talleyrand–Périgord (1754–1838), born of a noble family, became an abbot even before he was ordained a priest. In 1789, he had been made bishop of Autun. Much as some wealthy members of the House of Commons were unfamiliar with their constituencies, so the bishop seldom visited his diocese. Indeed, he spent more time at the apartments of the Comte de Flahaut. Irrespective of his religious calling (an accident in youth had rendered him unfit for commissioned military service, the natural career path for someone of his background), Talleyrand had exceptional political interests, ambitions, and talents. In the First Estate he had become a forceful advocate of what was then termed a liberal political philosophy, and he subsequently served in the French National Assembly. Two years Morris's junior, Talleyrand was of medium height and wore his clerical vestments. Morris found his tone of voice annoying and noted with disapproval his large snuffbox.

Talleyrand was a notable political survivor. During most of the Terror, he lived in England and America. But he re-entered French political life powerfully in 1796 under the Directory, and in 1797 he became foreign minister, a post he held for a full decade. During this period, of course, he served under Napoleon. Even after his official dismissal, Talleyrand continued to provide important services for Napoleon. Along with the former security chief Joseph Fouché (1759–1820), however, he spearheaded Napoleon's deposition by the Imperial Senate. Talleyrand's skilled diplomatic maneuvers at the Congress of Vienna (1814–1815) were crucial to restoring France's station in world affairs. Years after Morris's death, Talleyrand was still serving the Bourbons (he was foreign minister under Louis XVIII) and, latterly, the July Monarchy, almost until he died at eighty-four.[14]

On April 22, Lafayette went to Jefferson's to ask his and Morris's advice on security for the king. Gouverneur made the commonsense suggestion that Louis XVI's Swiss bodyguard be replaced by French soldiers. He noted in his diary that "Mr. Jefferson does not think this important," but Jefferson was wrong. The Swiss Guard was a substantial provocation and was soon slaughtered by the French "populace." On May 5 Morris attended the king's address to the Estates-General, at which the queen, too, was present. It was an extraordinary spectacle: imagine the State of the Union address to Congress, but with exponentially more color, pageantry, and historical resonance. Morris was moved, calling it "a spectacle more solemn to the mind, than gaudy to the eye":

> there was displayed everything of noble and of royal in this titled country. A
> great number of fine women, and a very great number of fine dresses,
> ranged round the Hall. On a kind of stage the throne; on the left of the King

and a little below him the Queen. . . . When the King entered, he was saluted with a shout of applause. He read his speech well, and was interrupted at a part, which affected his audience, by a loud shout of Vive le Roi! After this had subsided, he finished his speech, and received again an animated acclamation of applause. . . . Here drops the curtain on the first great act of this great drama in which Bourbon gives freedom. His courtiers seem to feel, what he seems to be insensible of, the pang of greatness going off.[15]

On May 13, he met with Jefferson and they talked at length about French politics. Afterward, Morris wrote that the American minister "does not form very just estimates of character, but assigns too many to the humble rank of fools, whereas in life the gradations are infinite and each individual has his peculiarities of fort and feeble." This may be a case of the pot calling the kettle black; after dealing with Jacques Necker for a time, Morris dismissively described him as "one of those People who has obtained a much greater Reputation than he had any Right to." Necker, he continued, though a "Man of Genius," was utterly devoid of talent, ignorant of politics, and "a very poor financier."[16]

On June 4, Jean-Antoine Houdon (1741–1828) asked Morris to stand in for the figure of George Washington, whose bust the sculptor had cast on a visit to America. Houdon's reputation had been made in the early 1770s, with his bust of Denis Diderot. Morris was much flattered by the invitation and, as he told Adélaïde, he readily consented to "the humble employment of a manakin." Like many great works of art, the sculpture of Washington was long in the making. The trip to America on which the bust was cast had taken place in 1785. The body now took several "standings." The result is generally considered, along with his seated *Voltaire,* the artist's finest work. It stands in the Virginia State Capitol.[17]

Throughout the late spring and early summer, Morris continued to visit Adélaïde at the Louvre. To his surprise and chagrin, although the count was always absent, Talleyrand was often there.

In June, Thomas Jefferson had written a ten-point charter of rights for Lafayette to deliver in the governmental assembly. It stipulated that the Estates-General alone should levy taxes and formulate laws (with the consent of the crown), and should have the power to command that a person be detained and brought before the court; it clearly subordinated the military to the civil power; and it provided for the abolition of all pecuniary entitlements and special privileges. Morris predicted that the document would too swiftly "annihilate distinctions of order"—that it would change too much and too soon (diary entry for June 12, 1789). On the nineteenth of June, by a small majority, the clergy agreed to side with the Third Estate; Morris quickly foresaw that the nobility would soon be in grave trouble.

Morris, however, was soon chided for expressing his opinion to various people, including Madame de Tessé, on the dire position of the nobility. At supper on June 23, Lafayette commented that Morris had already caused damage to the cause of *Liberté,* telling him he injured the cause, for his "sentiments are continually quoted against the good party." Morris rejoined that he "opposed . . . the [French kind of] democracy, from regard to liberty." The last day of June a mob broke into a Parisian prison, this time to free some of the incarcerated—soldiers being held temporarily for inebriation. From then on, mob violence escalated. Adélaïde expressed alarm at finding her husband's name on a printed list of "furious aristocrats," a kind of popular most-wanted list. On the evening of July 12, 1789, a Sunday, Morris courageously drove the Abbé Bertrand and another timorous aristocrat home from a salon. On the way to Jefferson's afterward, he saw a troop of French cavalry stoned in the Place Royale. Jefferson informed him that Montmorin had resigned, and that Necker had already been banished (actually, he had just been ordered to leave but had not yet done so).

On Monday, Morris affixed to his hat a green bow, symbol of the Third Estate, and walked to the Louvre to try to calm Adélaïde. The next day the lightly manned Bastille fell after a bloody battle. With the city rife with rumors, alarms, and random searches, Morris managed to visit Adélaïde several more times the following week. On Sunday, again, Talleyrand was present when Morris arrived. On July 25, Morris sketched out "some thoughts respecting the Constitution of this country." The object of this inveterate federalist was to, as he put it, "urge strongly the danger of a Constitution too democratical." In the meantime, before the constitution would be completed, Morris proposed an additional safeguard for the monarch: "an Association to protect the Prince and to declare those who may insult him Enemies both public and personal." The next day, Adélaïde asked him to ride with her to Versailles "to confer with the committee" charged with reporting out a constitution. On the way, Morris went over with her what he had written, explained the document a bit, and then they had "a little wild chit chat." On Monday, Morris went to Jefferson's for dinner, obtained the passport he needed to do some imminent commercial business in England, and then went on to the Louvre. The count was present, but soon left on "a long visit," and after a brief interval of working together on a literary translation, Gouverneur and Adélaïde moved on to other matters.

On the last day of July, Morris embarked from Dieppe for Dover. He spent a month in London, and for the time being put the frantically accelerating French violence behind him.

The revolution now beginning to flare throughout the country of course sprang from a variety of sources. Given the complexities of the economic facts, political situation, cultural nuances, social customs, religious beliefs, and internecine conflicts, few visitors could have grasped even the largest cords of the broad historical movement. And Morris had never even been to France before 1789.

Of course, he had studied French history, and he had had extensive dealings with French government officials, although mostly by letter and otherwise entirely in America. He was a quick and often keen observer of human affairs—although it is true that quickness is not the same as accuracy. He had important roles in developing two governmental founding charters. Finally, he was knowledgeable about both private and public finance.

Yet the ease with which he was able to insert himself into French elite circles may have proven a hindrance, giving him the illusion that he understood what was happening around him. He advised the leading figures in Louis XVI's cabinet during his first year in France—but how relevant this advice proved to be is open to question. The humdrum—in this case, the world of Paris's elite salons—continued to hum along for quite some time despite the surrounding chaos. This too can mislead the naïve observer.[18]

In broad terms there seem to have been five causes of the French Revolution, each of which, not surprisingly, overlapped with and colored the others. These causes were economic, social, political, cultural, and religious.

As soon as we begin to consider economic issues, demographics also enters the picture. On the eve of the Revolution, France had roughly 20 percent of Europe's people, although the proportion had begun to shrink in the later eighteenth century, as J. F. Bosher emphasizes. Moreover, as Jacques Necker noted, the percentage of young men in positions of governmental authority was, in the late 1780s, at a recent high. According to Bosher, Necker "believed that the outbreak of revolution owed something to young men with general ideas, little experience, and less judgment who had become 'dominant.'"[19] Furthermore, by 1789, France had endured an extraordinary number of years of poor harvests. Food supplies had been running low, and this reality had prompted a number of food riots.

In the Peace of Paris (1763), which concluded the Seven Years' War, the French gave up Canada to Great Britain, and abandoned all claims to India. These material losses were somewhat offset by the positive charge to French morale provided by the American Revolution, but, owing partly to the costs incurred in that extended foreign expedition, France's service on its national debt consumed more than half of all government expenditures by 1789. By this time the government was relying, probably too heavily, on indirect taxation—that is, taxes not on revenue but on articles of commonly consumed articles like wine, playing cards, soap, salt, and tobacco.[20] As R. R. Palmer makes clear, the burden of this taxation was "borne mainly . . . by the least wealthy" of the people. Few serfs remained, but peasant life had changed little for a very long time. French peasants were vexed in many ways. If they owed no labor, then they paid a quitrent. If they sold their farms, then they had to pay part of the proceeds to the local lord. At market they often had to pay dues or fees. Their grain had to be ground, their olives or grapes pressed, and their bread baked at the lord's mill, press, or oven, and a fee was exacted for these services. Generally, only the lord could hunt, and he often ran his horses and dogs gallingly over the peasants' fields. The Catholic Church extracted a tithe, often a twelfth of a poor farmer's crop.

There was more: royal taxes, of which the *taille* was one of the most onerous. Sometimes the *taille* was a land tax, and sometimes a tax on the peasants' total resources. Villagers were obliged to choose tax collectors, who were sent to jail if sufficient sums were not forthcoming. Indeed, Bosher, probably the leading expert on the economy of the period, characterizes the French financial system in the 1780s as a "venal" one, managed by independent financiers who collected and spent all government funds, "partly on commission, partly for fees, and partly in the hope of social advancement." These financiers were "accountable only to the magistrates in the Chamber of Accounts,"[21] which means they were independent to a dangerous degree, being neither elected officials nor subject to any controls by the office of the minister of finance. Abuses were multitudinous. Rather than reform the system by discovering and disciplining the rampant dishonesty of these financiers, who were by now embedded in the ruling class, the government of Louis XVI chose to assume the burden of the state debt and attempt to pay it off by raising taxes still more widely and deeply, reducing expenses, and streamlining administratively.[22]

Although unemployment had become a serious problem, the French peasantry—still most of the nation's population—probably fared better than any other in Europe except perhaps the Low Countries. On the other hand, from about 1735 onward, wages had not kept pace with the rising prices of goods. In the period from 1785 to 1789, a French worker paid roughly 25 percent more for the same basic goods than he or she would have between 1726 and 1742. Land rents, too, had risen fairly steeply. This trend benefitted the landowners, of course: they not only did not pay their fair share of taxes, but also received proportionally and steadily more for their products while paying relatively less in wages. The 1788 harvest was another exceptionally poor one, so grain prices rose precipitously. And even before that, the poorer half of the French had been spending roughly two-thirds of their total income for food.

The church in France could not be said to have aided the economic situation. It contributed nothing to the support of the state except an annual gift. During the reign of Louis XVI, this gift averaged less than four and a half million francs; at the same time, the annual subsidy the church received from the king was two and a half million francs. In 1789, when Louis XVI's governmental ministers favored the granting of religious freedom for Protestants, the church withheld its gift altogether. With its untaxed capital of four hundred million francs and a yearly income of fifteen million francs from tithes, the church naturally wielded tremendous political power. Parish priests struggled to do the best they could on a scant income. But the leading figures in the church's hierarchy—the cardinals and the bishops, especially—lived like princes.

Apart from what went to keep the royal family and the elite clergy, a very high percentage of the kingdom's revenues were expended on the nobility and on the financiers who administered the nation's funds. All of these individuals received large annual salaries, huge pensions, and numerous expensive gifts and perquisites (at the time, the king's chief dispenser of patronage was the Comte d'Angiviller, whose connection to the Comte de Flahaut has already been noted). The comte, incidentally, was also a close friend of Turgot (1727–1781), who had been a relatively activist finance minister: he had floated an ambitious program of reforms. Louis's minions easily defeated them and drove their proponent out of office.

The newly arrived Gouverneur Morris could hardly have perceived and understood all these realities.[23]

Although the foregoing presents the major economic facts that led to the French Revolution, "facts," as Coleridge purportedly said, "are not truths." In a general sense, most of the aristocrats of pre-1789 France must have concurred with the unnamed French nobleman who, after the Revolution, remarked of the conflagration period: "Never was there a more terrible awakening preceded by a sweeter slumber and more seductive dreams. We [the aristocrats] believed it [the high life they had been living] to be indestructible." This was plainly true of the king and queen as well.

Near the beginning of the Terror, Louis XVI was charged with counterrevolution, tried and convicted, and guillotined, as was his queen, Marie Antoinette, the Austrian archduchess he had been married to in 1770. He had ascended the throne upon his grandfather's death in 1774.

Despite his excellent memory and special abilities in languages, history, and
geography, Louis was unfit to rule. He had traveled little, his thought was insular, and he had a broad and deep insolent streak. In addition, Louis had a
weak grasp of politics, and small understanding of public finance.

In a parliamentary system, such as Britain's, such a king as Louis XVI might
have done far less damage to the nation. An able prime minister and cabinet
could have made up for his deficiencies. But as the French monarchy had
evolved, too much depended on the abilities of the king. By 1789, the royals'
waste and extravagance had become notorious; one brief glimpse is emblem-
atic. Louis XVI gave Benjamin Franklin "the King of France's picture set with
four hundred and eight diamonds," and that was only one of a number of similarly extravagant gifts. Louis also made a huge donation to the University of
Pennsylvania in 1786. Such largesse was delivered without oversight or ac-
countability, and without the consent of those who bore a disproportionate
share of the cost: the poorest of the French. Again, Morris, so newly arrived
from America, could hardly have grasped the extent of the royal profligacy.[24]

Social causes too operated in stimulating the uprising, but French social
categories and subcategories were more numerous and complicated than
many historians and social commentators have understood. The prideful Morris could not have comprehended them quickly and competently. Consider,
for example, the nobility, which could be divided into two classes, the non-
feudal and the enfeoffed. However, there were subdivisions of these. French
jurists of the 1780s, for instance, employed three subdivisions in their legal
reasonings and judicial decisions. First, hereditary nobility, *noblesse de race,*
was transmitted through the bloodlines (most often the father's). *Noblesse de
lettres* was awarded by the state upon official registration at the Chambres
des Comptes and the payment of a stiff set fee. *Noblesse de dignité* could be
first attained by the holding of official office and was conferred by the king.
It in turn was legally recognized as having two distinct branches, *noblesse de
robe* and *noblesse de cloche.* Furthermore, there existed a *demi-noblesse,*
whose members held offices that entailed noble privileges but not full noble
status. Army officers, for example, after twenty years' service were exempted
from the *taille.* And lawyers were exempt from forced service in the militia.
There were still more distinctions, having to do with, for example, place of
residency. *Noblesse* of whatever branch or subbranch held different kinds of
perquisites in the countryside, the village, and the cities.

Politically, separate castes existed. The First Estate comprised the privileged nobles with their membership in the *parlements,* while the Third Estate
consisted of rich commoners at the top and of the peasants and urban poor at
the bottom, who, combined, constituted most of the population. Indeed, as

the historian John McManners puts it, one could "no longer describe France in the simple terms of the three orders of clergy, nobility and third estate, for this horizontal stratification of society was . . . in dissolution" by 1789.[25]

As to what might be called the cultural reasons for the Revolution, many French citizens felt a not unreasonable sense of deprivation, especially with respect to freedom of expression, women's rights, and university education. Recent scholarship has clarified the extent to which writers of both sexes, and women of every class, benefited from the changes the Revolution wrought. And Lawrence Brockliss's *French Higher Education in the Seventeenth and Eighteenth Centuries* describes some of the major deficiencies in French education at the outset of the Revolution. Even the French language changed between the years 1789 and 1793.[26]

The political situation in 1789 may have been even more baffling. When the Estates-General met at Versailles in May 1789, Louis more or less rolled out the red carpet, but neither he nor his ministers had a coherent, unified strategy for dealing with the Third Estate. Some of his councilors urged a resolute, conservative stance, while others were inclined to compromise. The king expected the Estates-General to devote its attention solely to the country's financial problems, which even this dim bulb of a monarch had noticed. Louis had ordered that the nobility, the clergy, and the Third Estate vote separately, in the hope that the first two would outweigh the latter. The nobility organized itself into a separate chamber (by a vote of 141 to 47), as did the clergy (133 to 114), but the Third Estate refused. If the Estates all voted together, and if the delegates from the Third Estate (the largest one) voted as a bloc, then the Third Estate could always prevail. But if the Estates voted separately, the clergy and the nobles could combine against the interests of the Third Estate.

The Estates remained deadlocked for nearly three weeks. On June 17, the Third Estate declared itself a "National Assembly" and invited the other orders to convene to work together, so as to bring about the legislative reform of the nation. On the twentieth, the Third Estate found that Louis had barred them from the Estates' assembly hall; they proceeded to another building, one that had often been used either as a riding hall or a tennis court. Here the Third Estate took the so-called Tennis Court Oath, swearing that they would not adjourn until they had drafted a constitution for France. The Tennis Court Oath is generally thought of as the beginning of the Revolution, in that the Third Estate then acted not only against the desires of Louis XVI, but also went far beyond the vague agenda he had outlined for the assemblage. The king, perhaps secretly doubting his own wisdom and leadership, vacillated and temporized. Soon some members of the lower ranks of the clergy and a few of the more liberal nobles joined the Third Estate. With a huge army still loyal to him, Louis could have disbanded the assembly by force. Instead, he yielded.

Politically the way was now paved for the new National Assembly to draw up a constitution. But there was no time for deliberation such as the delegates in Philadelphia had enjoyed. The rioting that led up to the storming of the Bastille had spread rapidly across France. In many regions peasants attacked the opulent châteaux and burned the records of the dues and fees they owed. Some monasteries were looted, and scores of landowners murdered. Needless to say, the courts almost all ceased to function.

Many nobles, not surprisingly, soon fled the country. In early October a mob of both men and women, many of whose members carried clubs, marched from Paris to Versailles, where they menaced the royal family. The royals, surrounded by the National Guard with Lafayette commanding, promptly left Versailles for Paris. (The guard was in turn hemmed in the whole way by the mob.) The National Assembly soon followed the king; Paris became the de facto French capital.[27]

In Paris, the Assembly kept the national financial crisis in view. One of the major ways they hoped to address it was, for the first time, to sell church property, which comprised roughly 8 percent of French lands (some estimates go as high as 10 percent). The Assembly simply appropriated much of this property. In December 1789 the government ordered notes (*assignats*), primarily to underwrite the assessed value of this land. The intent was to sell the newly appropriated land to public bidders, who would pay for it with *assignats,* which would then be retired. In this way, the sale would pay off the national debt, forestall the need to obtain still more loans, and perhaps allow a steep cut in internal taxes. Before long the abundant lands abandoned by those fleeing the Revolution also entered the governmental marketplace. Both these properties and those confiscated earlier went overwhelmingly to the richest and best connected.

To get ahead of our story a bit, the plan failed. The notes were issued in April 1790, paying 3 percent interest. Far more *assignats* were produced than were needed; accordingly, prices began to rise steeply. The notes immediately lost 8 to 10 percent of their value, and specie rapidly disappeared. By February 1792, *assignats* had fallen in value by 30 percent, and the situation continued to worsen. By 1796 a new kind of paper, the *mandats territoriaux,* had to be issued, but the *mandats* precipitously fell to 5 percent of face value. By 1797, the 2.5 billion *mandats* and the thirty-six billion *assignats* had to be repudiated and became worthless. So much for the revolutionary government's experiments in public finance.[28]

The Assembly also instituted the large-scale reorganization of the church's diocesan territories—a move much of the church hierarchy found especially galling. In November 1790, the Assembly also pressed all of the sitting French bishops and priests to take an oath of submission to the new revolutionary government. Only two of the country's 160 bishops professed loyalty to the crown (at least for the moment). One of these was Talleyrand.

It is generally accepted that the eventual Bishop of Autun fathered at least one son, Charles (1785–1870), the offspring of his liaison with Adélaïde de Flahaut. By 1790 the fact of Talleyrand's relationship with Adélaïde had dawned on Morris; the diary suggests that, on some level, he sensed the truth almost immediately. Morris estimated him on June 6, 1789, a "sly, cool, cunning and ambitious Man" and confessed "I know not why Conclusions so disadvantageous of him are formed in my Mind, but so it is and I cannot help it." Adélaïde's husband, it seems, was to be kept entirely in the dark during their affair; in late September, when he was gone to Madrid, Adélaïde felt unusually *"triste"* and feared "Consequences." Gouverneur sat with her for a long time and wrote in his diary: "If, however, nothing happens, we are to take Care for the future until the Husband returns, and then exert ourselves to add one to the Number of human Existences" (*Diary,* October 1, 1789). When Talleyrand and Morris became aware of their involvement with the same woman is uncertain; the three dined together on October 4, with Morris informing Talleyrand that the defect in the bishop's ideas on finance was that "he must get Men about him who understand Work and who love Work." The tension between the two men is palpable on the diary's page as it records how the bishop avowed his own proclivity for labor. Talleyrand took leave, but with the promise, Morris observes, "to return and bid her Good Night." The next day, Adélaïde informed Morris of his subsequent "Importunities" and her fear that without Talleyrand she would be lost. "She wishes me to make some Sacrifices," he wrote, "but this is I know a Business to which there is no End and therefore I refuse." Adélaïde approached him later and promised to leave town without seeing Talleyrand, and Morris seems reassured: "She insists that she will be only mine." A week later she wrote a letter, which Morris looked over, to the Bishop, apparently ending their understanding. But three days later, the three again dined together and Morris confides in his diary that "I leave her to go Home with him and thus risque heroically the Chance of Cuckoldom." However, Gouverneur and Adélaïde continued their passionate affair uninhibited. On January 6, 1792, Morris records one of their typical interludes: "Monsieur (her husband) leaves the room. We seize the Occasion and taste the genial Joy." Talleyrand chose to disregard the affair until February, when he "reproached her with Infidelity in the most injurious Terms."[29]

Undeterred by his newness to France, Morris showered various French officials with notes, letters, draft speeches, and memoranda during his first twenty or so months in Europe. He sent a note to the queen concerning the attitude the royals should now adopt (January 26, 1790). On May 25, 1791, he wrote to Montmorin, thus demonstrating that he knew at least something about who was well connected. Armand Marc Montmorin-Saint Hérem was by 1789 a veteran official, and since February 14, 1787, he had been the very powerful foreign minister. Morris's letter suggested some improvements in government administration. The author followed up with two more letters, one evidently written later the same day, the other drafted and sent on July 30, advising Montmorin on the state of public affairs in France. On August 27, 1791, Morris drafted a speech for the king to deliver and with it offered some observations on the country's constitution. Later he wrote Louis a long memo on the same subject. On September 21, 1791, Montmorin was again the happy recipient of a letter, this one outlining ways to facilitate the movement of supplies to Paris.

Montmorin does not seem to have resented the newcomer's stream of advice. Perhaps the letters of introduction from Washington helped; and, of course, there was the force of Morris's personality. Perhaps his ideas even struck their recipients as useful in such frightening times.

Montmorin had served the government a long time: he became ambassador to Madrid in 1777; served as Brittany's commander-in-chief from 1783 to 1786; and then became the secretary of state for foreign affairs. He was, moreover, a close associate of Necker, and, like Necker, had moved in and out of office. But whereas Necker was merely banished from France, Montmorin was killed. He had remained with the king as long as he could, and it was he who issued the fake passport the royal family was supposed to use in its 1791 attempt to flee. In November of that same year, Montmorin was again dismissed, for allegedly planning counterrevolution. After the extreme mob violence of August 10, 1792, he went into hiding, but on the twenty-first, he was discovered in the dwelling of a laundress. A crowd seized him, beat him severely, and sent him to the notorious Abbaye prison. Here he was slain by a mob on August 31.

It was thanks to Montmorin, mainly, that Morris spoke often to Necker in 1790. He gave much advice to Talleyrand, as well; most of it, in fact, was solicited. For example, the bishop asked Morris's opinions of his speeches to be given at the Assembly. (Morris attended as many legislative sessions as he could, and he paid close attention to the proceedings.)

Morris's diary and letters from his time in France are superb sources of information of all kinds, but they are often charming as well, as when after dinner at Lafayette's, Morris was regaled by one of the general's musically gifted little daughters, who sang him a song that turned out to be "one of my own composition."

That same evening, after the children were put to bed, Lafayette and the American reviewed together a draft of the Declaration of the Rights of Man. Morris suggested several amendments meant "to soften the high colored expressions of freedom," which the French language has in abundance, because, as Morris notes, "not by sounding words" are "revolutions . . . produced."[30]

Morris's letters to William Short (1759–1849) are especially appealing; here, for instance, are a pair of comments in a letter from London, dated March 18, 1790:

> My fair friends you say complain of my Silence. They will at least own that it is only in my Absence that such Complaints can have any Foundation. . . . I would deputize you to the Handling of Madame de C[hastellux]'s Teapot, but since every Thing now goes by Election I cannot hazard such Encroachment upon the Droits d'homme.[31]

On March 3, 1789, he spent a couple of hours at the home of the Comte de Ninni, then went to dine at the Comtesse de B's (her name is not given, and I have no good guesses). The house was a mess, with the maid scurrying to clean up, and the valet struggling to start a good fire: "Three small sticks in a deep bed of ashes gave no great expectation of heat. By the smoke, however, all doubts are removed respecting the existence of fire." The comtesse was a poetess, and the other guests were of "that exalted part of the Species who devote themselves to the Muses." The meal was meager and ill-prepared; Morris consoled himself

> in the persuasion that, for this day, at least, I shall escape an Indigestion. A very narrow Escape, too, for some rancid Butter, of which the Cook had been liberal, puts me in bodily fear. If the repast is not abundant, we have at least the consolation that there is no lack of conversation. . . . As for the rest of the Company, each being employed either in saying a good thing or in studying one to say, it is no wonder if he cannot find time to applaud that of his Neighbor.

Morris's presentation of the king and queen's appearances at Versailles before the legislature on May 5, 1789, ranks among his most memorable creations, particularly his account of the hat-doffing ceremony:

> After the King has spoken he takes off his Hat and when he puts it on again his Nobles imitate the Example. Some of the Tiers do the same, but by Degrees they one after the other take them off again. The King then takes off his Hat. The Queen seems to think it wrong and a Conversation seems to pass in which the King tells her he chuses [*sic*] to do it, whether consistent or not consistent with the Ceremonial.

Jacques Necker's speech follows the king's:

> He tries to play the orator but he plays it very ill . . . he falls into Action and Emphasis, but a bad Accent and an ungraceful Manner destroy much of the Effect which ought to follow from a Composition written by Mr. Necker and spoken by Mr. Necker. He presently asks the King's Leave to employ a Clerk, which being granted the Clerk proceeds in the Lecture . . . The clerk delivered it much better than the Minister, and that is no great praise. It was three hours long, and contained many excellent things, but too much of compliment, too much of repetition, and indeed too much of everything, for it was long by two hours.[32]

Morris's offhand remarks are often striking or instructive. In a December 21, 1792, letter to Jefferson: "There are Cases in which Events must decide on the quality of Actions, which are bold or rash according to the Success." In the diary entry for June 24, 1795: "There is nothing perfect in this World, and we must therefore take Things as we find Them."

Like Jefferson, Morris was of no special religious opinion, and strongly opposed the union of church and state. On February 28, 1790, he described a dinner party conversation: "A Gentleman present observes that in all Countries there is an established Religion. I assure him that there is none in America." Some discussion followed, in the course of which Morris told his interlocutor "that God is sufficiently powerful to do his own business without human Aid, and that Man should confine his care to the Actions only of his fellow Creatures, leaving to the supreme Being to influence the Thoughts as he may think proper."

In *Memoirs from Beyond the Grave* (1849–1850), Chateaubriand (1768–1848) observes that "the Revolution made me understand the possibility of living in . . . conditions . . . [where] moments of crisis produce a reduplication [meaning redoubled vigor] of life in men." The atmosphere in France at the time evidently produced this effect on many of those living through the troubled era. No signs of depression or ennui can be found in any of Morris's large circle of extremely active friends. The revolutionists, too, were vigorous, if not always for the better.[33]

From mid-1789 to mid-1791 Morris drafted several essays which proved philosophically interesting and revelatory of his political vision, while his epistles (for such they often are) to William Short continue, as always, to provide lively reading. In one letter on April 7, 1790, he expressed his frustration with the bureaucracies he had to deal with in negotiating a low percentage loan:

> Among those who are now at the Helm there is neither the Mind to conceive, the Heart to dare nor the Hand to execute such Things. They will therefore continue to pile up System upon System without advancing one Inch. The dreadful primeval Curse is repeated upon them all. Paper thou art and unto Paper thou shalt return.[34]

The thirty-year-old Short, Jefferson's secretary, had frequent correspondence with Morris on both matters of state and matters of the heart. He had fallen in love with a woman a year younger than he was and twenty years younger than the uncle to whom she was married; the two conducted only a brief affair but continued to exchange letters for fifty years. On one occasion, Morris reassured an insecure Short that "Jefferson considers him as one of the ablest Men in America" (May 14, 1791).

In the essay "On Government" (July 4, 1789—the "birthday of our Republic"), with particular applicability to France, Morris ruminates on freedom and despotism, and on social and economic rank. He opines that the notion of "freedom" can be taken too far:

> I have steadily combated the Violence and Excess of those Persons who, either inspired with an enthusiastic Love of Freedom or prompted by sinister Designs, are disposed to drive every Thing to Extremity. Our American Example has done them good; but like all Novelties, Liberty runs away with their Discretion, if they have any. They want a King instead of a President, without reflecting that they have not American Citizens to support that Constitution.

Morris characterizes the king as "an honest Man" who "wishes really to do Good" and the nobility as "hugging the dear Privileges of Centuries long elapsed." He is not kinder to their adversaries, however, remarking on the opposition leadership's lack of talents and virtue: "The Chief has not even

Courage, without which you know that in Revolutions there is nothing." Nonetheless, for many months he worked, vainly of course, for a powerful French monarchy. How he expected this to develop remains mysterious. In keeping with this scheme, he tried to cultivate Lafayette as a military leader, but he thought not much more of the general than of the king. Lafayette, he wrote, was "very much below the business he has undertaken [in France], and if the sea runs high he will be unable to hold the helm."[35] Still, in June 1790 Morris drafted an elaborate "Plan of a Campaign for France," which he had presented to Lafayette (Morris was abroad), imagining, one supposes, that the general would somehow summon the power needed to execute it.

The plan was strategically grandiose—even delusionary—like most of Morris's military schemes. Its purpose, so Morris told the queen, was to start an armed conflict so that war "shall come to rescue the state, and reestablish its affairs." He proposed, in brief, to provide "freedom to Flanders, and perhaps to Holland"; to "mend," unqualifiedly, Poland's political situation; possibly to free the Greeks from Turkish domination; and to deliver India from the British yoke. Besides which it would open for France the free navigation of the Black Sea, make Egypt independent, and restrain the pirates from Barbary. The idea was that French warships would make a feint in the Caribbean while French infantry menaced "the Island of Britain . . . [got] possession of Plymouth, and extend[ed] from the city of Exeter across the Irish Channel." In the course of this expedition, the French forces should impress into service numerous Britons.[36] The scheme was short-lived. William Carmichael, the American chargé d'affaires, who had also received a version by letter, disregarded it entirely; the French National Assembly was far too occupied with the revolution; and Lafayette did not respond.

Once he began keeping a diary, Morris continued it almost without interruption until his death. But from August 1792 until October 1794, he sought to protect both himself and his numerous royalist acquaintances by steeply cutting back detail. Up to that point, the diary provides an especially valuable record, presented, as the best such literary productions often are, with the sense of life as lived: Henri Bergson's *durée*. The obvious comparison is with Samuel Pepys. Pepys's canvas, of course, is much bigger, and Pepys did not anticipate the guillotine. But both he and Morris were primarily businessmen, public officials, and statesmen. Both, too, were cultural virtuosos. Morris records nothing like Pepys's extended seduction and then abandonment of Deb Willet, nor, in Morris's dealings as a government official, is there anything like Pepys's financial irregularities.

Morris's diary is not panoptic; largely absent are descriptions of or reflections on the material culture of his France—its furniture, its impressively decorated dining tables, its palaces (Compiègne, Fontainebleau, Versailles). He had nothing to say about fashions in clothing. Salvatore Vigano (1769–1821), the outstanding name in dance history from 1789 to 1810, appeared, along with his wife, in Paris and in Vienna often from 1790 through 1795, but these performances Morris entirely missed. His strength lies almost entirely in his unique observations of the human scene.

In 1790, President Washington appointed Thomas Jefferson secretary of state, making him one of the four members of the first U.S. cabinet. Earlier, however, the president had made Gouverneur Morris the new nation's first official private agent, on a mission to Britain in the fall of 1789. His Majesty's Government had still not appointed a minister to the United States, and there had been no American minister to the Court of St. James since John Adams's departure from London in February 1788. This was just over two years before Morris arrived in the British capital. In the meantime, King George had begun to show symptoms of serious illness, and the British government was in some consequent disarray. Morris's broad official charge, which he received on January 21, 1790, was to resolve a number of differences between England and the United States.

Among other matters, Morris was to negotiate with the Duke of Leeds, the Foreign Secretary from 1783 to 1791, concerning still-unexecuted clauses of the 1783 peace treaty. Chief of these was the British military's continued occupation of seven military posts in what was then termed the Northwest, including what is now Michigan, Ohio and western New York. Morris was also to enter into discussions for a commerce treaty. Washington did place significant limits on Morris's negotiations. Regarding the treaty, Morris had to "be careful not to countenance any idea of our dispensing with [the northwest territories] in a treaty" while at the same time ascertaining, "if possible, their views on this point." Morris, it seems, was to determine the British hand without laying any cards of his own.

Morris set off for London on February 15, traveling via Holland and visiting Brussels, Antwerp, and Amsterdam on the way. He crossed the Channel from Hellevoetsluis to Harwich. At the time, the fastest possible trip from Paris to London seems to have taken four full days; even urgent messages generally took five. Morris checked into his London hotel, the Froome, about five weeks after departing Paris.[37] The British capital was then, as now, the nation's center of politics, fashion, the arts, sciences, and commercial business.

Morris was in some ways ideal for the job Washington had given him: those who have to play a weak hand need, at the least, a reasonably aggressive spirit and sound nerves. These Morris had, despite his flaws. He engaged with Leeds and the Prime Minister, William Pitt the Younger, on many topics, among them the impressment of American seamen; reimbursement for slaves taken off by the British upon evacuation; the treaty of commerce; the British government's failure to make reparations payments to American landowners; and the occupation, already mentioned, of the frontier posts. Throughout this and his second trip, Morris was irked by what he saw as British rigidity and indifference to American interests.

In the first months of his 1790 sojourn, Morris found the Duke of Leeds, the foreign secretary, and Pitt to be full of amiable professions of friendship, but otherwise unforthcoming. Morris felt the British statesmen desirous of a "real and *bona fide* system of commercial intercourse," but not disposed to take a step toward negotiating a treaty on the subject, despite his assurances that the new federal government was prepared to make and to execute such agreements. As for the frontier posts, Pitt hinted that, as a precondition, Britain would require security for the payment, according to the guaranty of the peace treaty of 1783, of prerevolutionary debts owed to British creditors by American individuals.

After months of such fruitless conversation ("negotiation" would be too strong a word), Morris was frustrated and angry. He had little choice but to inform Washington that England showed no sign of wanting to change the existing state of relations.

Jefferson was soon convinced that nothing would come of negotiations with Britain as long as England remained at peace with mainland Europe. In December 1790, he submitted to Washington a report on the entire matter, to which he attached Morris's dispatches through September 18 of that year. Jefferson concluded that on the matter of the forts—by far the most important source of contention—Britain had no plans to compromise, no matter what security the United States offered for its prewar debts.

The Nootka Sound crisis brought Spain and Britain close to war; the fledgling United States might have been caught between Scylla and Charybdis. The crisis arose when Spain seized some British trading vessels in the sound, on the coast of Vancouver Island. British outrage seemed likely to lead to war, in which Britain would surely attack Spain's North American possessions—the Floridas and Louisiana—taking the route overland from Canada through the United States. If the United States did not permit the British to cross its territory, the result might be war with Britain; if the United States did permit the British to cross, the result might be war with Spain. Jefferson instructed Morris to tell the British that the United States would remain neutral, if Great Britain executed the 1783 treaty fairly, and did not take over any Spanish territory adjoining the United States. He sent more or less comparable instructions to the U.S. minister in Madrid. Before Jefferson's messages arrived, however, Spain accepted Britain's ultimatum, and war was avoided, to the relief of all concerned. But the important issue of the seven British forts, with their concomitant threat to U.S. commerce and sovereignty, was not resolved until the execution of the Jay Treaty, in 1794.[38] The treaty provided for the British to evacuate all their military posts in the Northwest by June 1, 1796. The property of British settlers would be protected, and they would be given the option to retain their British allegiance or become American citizens.

As for Morris's inquiries concerning an exchange of ministers, the British response seemed to him murky; yet he may have helped push the decision forward. As early as May 17, 1791, William Grenville, the foreign secretary who had replaced Leeds, received official approval to appoint the first British minister to the United States. This was less than a year after his meetings with Morris. The appointee was George Hammond (1763–1853). Grenville told him to proceed "to America without delay."

Morris reported that at first Pitt insisted that America should give Great Britain "particular privileges, in return for those . . . [Americans] enjoy" in England. Tartly, Morris "assured [Pitt] . . . that I know of none, except that of being [militarily] impressed . . . a Privilege which of all others we least wished to partake of." Pitt, clearly amused, observed that Americans "were at least treated in that respect as the most favored nation, seeing that we [Americans] were treated like themselves." (To obviate the professed confusion between British seamen and American, Morris suggested that the Americans be issued IDs, an experiment to which Secretary of State Jefferson strongly objected. Jefferson observed that paper evidence of citizenship would not survive the "casualties of their calling," the rigors of sea travel, and "thus the British government would be armed with legal authority to impress the whole of our seamen." Jefferson insisted that the "simplest rule will be that the vessel being American, shall be evidence that the seamen on board her are such."[39] Morris also strenuously protested British press gangs' "enter[ing] American Vessels with as little ceremony as those belonging to Britain." In this he actually exceeded his mandate, threatening that the American ships' captains, upon returning home, would "excite much heat in America." He speculated that this would "perhaps occasion very disagreeable Events."[40]

On the slave compensation the British did not budge. The peace treaty ratified in 1784 provided that the British army was to withdraw from U.S. territory "with all convenient speed, and without . . . carrying away any

Negroes or other Property of the American inhabitants." A number of slaves, however, had fled to British lines during the war. The British considered some of these slaves manumitted and took them back to England with the rest of the army. Many thousands of other slaves were removed by the British forces throughout the early 1780s, however, and were sent by the king's government to British holdings in the West Indies, where conditions proved generally even harsher than they had been in the thirteen mainland colonies. The U.S. contention that these men, women, and children were U.S. property fell on deaf ears.[41]

Morris reportedly expressed no happiness that the British refused to return these escapees from slavery to America. This may seem an odd silence from the statesman who had spoken so eloquently and vehemently against the detestable institution during the Constitutional Convention. At the same time, Morris was well aware that the President and his Secretary of State at this time were large-scale slaveholders.

Only a miracle worker could have made headway on this issue. Washington's willingness to discuss a trade agreement and his decision to send a diplomatic agent to London had been leaked by Hamilton to the British agent George Beckwith, who promptly informed the Foreign Office. Hamilton's intention remains a mystery, but his disclosure emptied Morris's negotiating toolkit. The British, convinced that Hamilton provided a closer approximation of the American government's desire for British alliance, did not feel compelled to accept Morris's tougher demands.

In pressing for a commercial treaty, Morris argued that the House of Representatives had already exhibited restraint in not imposing heavy restrictions on British vessels entering American ports. As Washington had written to Morris in his instructions, "in the late session of Congress a very respectable number of both houses were inclined to a discrimination of duties unfavorable to Britain, and that it would have taken place but for conciliatory considerations."[42] Curiously, although Morris's efforts were not obviously fruitful, impressment did abate as soon as the Nootka Sound crisis ended, and it did not become a major problem again until some years later. Furthermore, Britain soon resumed its role as America's chief trading partner.

As has been mentioned, the most serious diplomatic problem between the two nations was the seven forts on the U.S. frontier. It is possible that Morris's negotiations were helpful. As late as May 21, 1790, Pitt and Leeds were still saying that England would not give up the forts. But on May 29 Morris wrote, with confidence in his source's reliability, that on that day Grenville had consulted British fur merchants and had consequently decided to let the forts go. Grenville desired informed opinion about how much the surrender of the forts would impact the vital fur trade, which would lose the protection and navigation rights ensured by a British military presence. One firm, Phyn, Ellice, and Inglis, estimated that its gains would be cut by over fifty percent, but other advisers argued that more Americans in the region would open the market even further. In discussions with Captain Schank, the navy commander of the Great Lakes, Grenville decided that establishing new garrisons on the Canadian side of the line could as readily regulate the area. Although Grenville made these extensive inquiries, there is no hard evidence that his meetings with Morris were the reason for the change in Britain's position. As the historian Alfred L. Burt puts it, "The sudden disposition to yield the posts is a little mysterious." But that Morris may have had something to do with it does seem likely, since he was the only American agent in England at the time.[43] As for Morris's remarkable connection to Grenville, it shall be discussed a bit more below.

One other important question was that of British payments—or the lack of such payments—to American landowners for depredations by British troops. Here Morris made no visible headway.

Overall, however, commercial relations vastly improved once Morris began meeting with British officials. The timing is suggestive, although earlier biographers of Morris have generally believed otherwise.[44] Before February 14, 1791, when Washington provided the U.S. Senate a belated and somewhat understated report on the then terminated mission, Morris had already received from Jefferson a note (December 17, 1790) in "testimony of approbation from the President of the United States." Jefferson often took a stuffily Olympian tone in communications with people of whom he fundamentally disapproved, and that tone appears in the note. He broached the subject of compensation for Morris ("a draught on our bankers in Holland for a thousand dollars, as an indemnification for those sacrifices"). Characteristically, Morris had never asked for payment. Jefferson also remarked that Gouverneur "will of course have the goodness to inform us of whatever may have passed further since the date of your last [communication]."[45] Morris, however, had been faithful in posting lengthy reports on his activity, most recently on September 21 and 24 and November 22.

A review of Morris's work in England would not be complete without mention of the British spy George Beckwith (1753–1823). Thanks to Beckwith, the British authorities knew, even before Morris did, the entire scope of his mission and the narrow range of options George Washington had afforded him. Beckwith, the central figure of British intelligence in America during the war, returned to New York several times after 1788 in the guise of a British army officer on a personal tour, all the while establishing his intelligence network from Florida to Vermont. Lacking any sort of effective counterintelligence operation, the American government granted him diplomatic access. Alexander Hamilton, for mysterious reasons, let him in on the treaty proposal. Beckwith also obtained information in a secret meeting with Creek chief Alexander McGillivray, one of the Indian leaders Washington had invited to New York in 1790 in his attempt to stabilize the Southwest. Remarkably, McGillivray was living in the house of Secretary of War Henry Knox at the time, where the government expected to keep him under close watch. Beckwith's able work apprised Pitt's government that there was no hurry to appoint a minister to the United States, although Grenville did name Hammond promptly. What negotiator can be effective in such circumstances?[46]

In returning to France, Morris detoured through the Netherlands and Germany, visiting Dunkirk, Ghent, Antwerp, Aix-la-Chapelle, Cologne, Coblenz, Frankfurt, Darmstadt, Mannheim, and Strasbourg. His diary for this period dwells mainly on bad roadways, transportation, and drinking water, and on the uncomfortable inns. On one good day with fine weather and a well-paved toll road, Morris reported that they traveled thirty-three miles in just under seven hours, with an hour of that time taken changing horses. Some days the carriage could cover up to forty miles, while on others they had to be content with less than half that if the roads were too pitted or gravelly for the horses to gain good footing. The company in the coaches varied; on October 14, Morris, sympathy likely roused by his own unfortunate experience with a carriage, reported a delay when "the poor Dog in following the Carriage gets his Foot much hurt by the Wheel, and we are obliged to take him in." The accommodations and fare along the way received varied marks from the discriminating diplomat. One morning he took a breakfast which "from the Badness of the Butter is reduced to a Dish of Tea" and the "Indifferent Repast" of a subsequent meal requires him to give most of it to the dog. In one inn on October 21, he refused, in order, the soup of "greasy Crusts," half-eaten veal, a "sodden Partridge," and a shoulder of a "starved" calf, finally settling for "salt Cheese made of Hog's Head." Such complaints are leavened by his persistent good humor. That very night he remarked on his short bed "out of the foot of which however I can poke only one Leg, having left the other in America."

When Morris was in England, as he notes, he received "no letters from Paris"—he seems to mean "no letters from Adélaïde"—"which amazes me." On the evening of his return to Paris, he sent a note to inquire about Madame de Flahaut, but she was away. Some eight days later he received a welcome note from her. She had just learned that he was back, and had come ninety miles in fifteen hours by a rickety carriage to see him. He dressed and hurried to the Louvre to possess her at once. The next day she took him to the convent of Chaillot, to meet the elderly English nun to whom she owed her education and her fluency in English. While they waited, they enjoyed a hurried intimacy in the convent's reception room for guests (facilitated by the fact that in the eighteenth century, women did not wear underpants).

By this time Morris seems to have overshadowed both Talleyrand and the elderly count, her husband. She literally saw her home and finances disappearing in the increasing flames of the revolution. From the time of Gouverneur's return from Britain until the last day of August 1792, when the Tuileries was stormed, Adélaïde's appetite for him was insatiable. Although Gouverneur proposes indifference "to keep her passion alive," they spent a great deal of time together, shopping, attending the opera and theater, visiting art galleries, and eating both at home and at cafés. Morris seems to have been monogamous. His most explicit description of their relations had come the year before, on Sunday, October 11, 1789: "After dinner we join in fervent adoration to the Cyprian Queen, which . . . conveys to my kind votary all mortal bliss which can be enjoyed. I leave her reclined in the sweet tranquility of nature well satisfied." Usually, he was more discreet.[47]

Adélaïde grew more and more desperate as the revolution wore on, suggesting to Morris more than once that her husband be sent as minister to America, instead of the Comte de Moustier. Adélaïde hoped to marry Morris in America after her older husband died, but Morris, despite his connections, was in no position to affect the French choice of an ambassador. By this time she understandably feared for her entire family's lives. She knew Morris to be both wealthy and well connected but she seems also to have been at least deeply infatuated with him. At the end of October 1790 she offered to end her relationship with Talleyrand. Morris recorded this in his diary, notably without comment.

Back in France after his failed diplomatic mission to Britain, Morris remained engaged in public affairs, though some of his activities might better be called clandestine, such as the plan for the king's escape from the city in July 1792. Three years later, his royalist activities continued as he planned with Grenville how to reinstate the Bourbons in the person of the king's brother, the Comte de Provence. His diplomatic immunity enabled him to shelter several refugees in his house, including the Comte d'Estaing and Adélaïde herself before she fled to England in 1793. Morris was the only envoy representing any foreign country to remain during the Terror, though his relations with the new government grew increasingly worse. He wrote out comments to various American officials concerning trade with France, the U.S. debt to Spain, U.S. assistance to Saint-Domingue (the eighteenth-century French designation for the island that now comprises Haiti and the Dominican Republic), the ministerial changes occurring rapidly in France, U.S. policy toward émigrés from Europe, and other governmental business.

Morris's labors, along with his knowledge of French, fairly strong grasp of history, vigor, wit, intelligence, and substantial store of relevant experience seem to have made him an obvious selection for U.S. minister to France. It may be recalled that in October 1778 he had been chosen by the Continental Congress to draw up the first instructions ever sent to an American minister abroad. It was Morris who planned for the reception of the first minister to America, Conrad-Alexandre Gérard. The instructions for Franklin, like many written by Morris, emerged from the meetings of a committee, this one including such eminent personages as Richard Henry Lee and Samuel Adams. Congress discussed the draft report for five days; Morris wrote the final version.[48] Thus, Morris's familiarity with the intricacies and expectations surrounding the position of an American minister abroad naturally made him the leading candidate when he was nominated by Washington on December 21, 1791.

Yet, so far from sailing through, Morris's nomination drew heavy fire. The Senate confirmed Morris's nomination on January 12, 1792, but not without acrimonious debate and vituperative correspondence. Among his leading opponents were Roger Sherman, of Connecticut, Aaron Burr, of New York, and James Monroe, of Virginia. That Rufus King, Robert Morris, and John Carroll supported him is to be expected, but that Connecticut's Oliver Ellsworth, New Jersey's Dickinson, and South Carolina's Butler should have argued on his behalf is worthy of remark. Ellsworth's closest friend was Roger Sherman; Dickinson's political philosophy seems to have been at least somewhat at variance with Gouverneur Morris's; and Butler had skirmished with Morris for months over the slavery question.

Senators opposed Morris's nomination for various reasons. Monroe found Morris's "manners not conciliatory—his character well known and considered as indiscreet. . . . Besides he is a monarchy man & not suitable to be employed by this country nor in France." Burr said, "Morris conducted himself so offensively in his intercourse with the English Ministers that they were offended" and broke off negotiations. Roger Sherman seems actually to have liked Morris:

> I have never been borne down by his superior talents, nor have I experienced any mortifications from the manner in which he has treated me in debate. . . . I allow that he possesses a sprightly mind, a ready appreciation,

and that he is capable of writing a good letter and forming a good draft. I have never heard that he has betrayed a Trust, or that he lacks integrity.

With regard to his moral character [however], I consider him an irreligious and profane man. [And] it is a bad example to promote such characters.

Sherman proceeded, remarkably, to remind his auditors of Benedict Arnold, and to say that he and Morris were two of a kind.[49]

French protests, official and otherwise, against Morris's nomination arrived on George Washington's desk as well. These mostly expressed concerns over Morris's monarchist views; indeed, when Morris was finally confirmed, in January 1792 (the vote was 15 to 11; two senators abstained), both Washington and Jefferson warned him to conceal his opposition to the revolution. Washington candidly observed:

Whilst your abilities, knowledge in the affairs of this country and disposition to serve it were adduced and asserted on one hand, the levity and imprudence of your conversation, and in many instances of your conduct were as severely arraigned on the other.... Tho' your imagination is brilliant the promptitude with which it is displayed allows too little time for deliberation or correction, and is the primary cause of those sallies which too often offend ... and which might be avoided ... [with] more caution and prudence.[50]

Morris responded with suitable earnestness on April 6: "I *now promise you* that Circumspection of Conduct which has hitherto I acknowledge formed no part of my character. And I make the *Promise* that my Sense of Integrity may enforce what my Sense of Propriety dictates."[51]

Despite this undertaking, Morris's royalist inclinations for the king and queen drew him into at least one perilous plan to save their lives. The king confided in Terrier de Monciel, one of his ministers, who engaged Morris to form a typically complicated—but seemingly practicable—escape plan. A short time later, Louis XVI sent Morris the immense sum of 547,000 livres to help effect the plan. Louis also expressed the wish that Morris take custody of all of the royals' papers. (Morris accepted the first offer but declined the second.) Louis's offer of such a large sum suggests that he favored Morris's plan. There were probably half a dozen others. One scheme had been put forward by De Molleville. Count Axel Fersen, a Swedish friend of Marie Antoinette, and evidently another lover of Adélaïde de Flahaut, planned the escape in disguise, which failed when the king and queen, having missed a crucial rendezvous, were apprehended in Varennes. It was time to attempt the plan made by Monciel and Morris, but the king temporized. While he did so, the all-important date, August 10, arrived: the Tuileries was that day taken by attack, and the Swiss Guard massacred. The king and queen were now very near their ends.

On March 10, 1792, Jefferson sent Morris secret instructions to provide "assurances of [America's] friendship" toward France, and on all occasions to impress "the national assembly with this truth." Jefferson commented on trade relations with France and stressed the importance of sustaining *"our agricultural interests."* A study of the correspondence between the Secretary of State and the U.S. minister to France makes clear that, apart from the colossal misjudgment he displayed in the plot he cooked up with Monciel, Morris did a good job in a constantly fluctuating situation. It should be remembered, for example, that the sovereign to whom he presented his credentials was Louis XVI. Morris seems seldom to have exceeded his instructions, and he diligently kept Washington's four-member Cabinet informed of developments in Europe.[52] (As he put it in an April 6, 1792, letter thanking Rufus King for the latter's support of his nomination: "If I have not *good* information and *early* Information, I can do little or nothing. . . . It happens also, not infrequently, that by knowing good or bad Tidings before anyone else, we can make the most of one, and obviate the worst of the other.")[53]

While, as I have said, Morris seldom exceeded his instructions, when he did so, he did it spectacularly. In 1796 he acknowledged that in 1792 Louis XVI had passed him an immense sum—nearly a million livres—to pay for "a sort of royal army" to try to crush the revolution. Morris consented to hold the king's money, though he warned him that "his house did not strike him as any safer than the palace of the Tuileries, since he had long been an object of hatred to the conspirators." Most of the money was distributed later that summer "to individuals who, with other trustworthy people, were to repair to certain places and there to fight under their chiefs." Some of the money was used to help friends of the king hide and escape, although Davenport records that Morris returned a substantial portion to the king's daughter, Madame Royale, in Vienna in 1796.[54] Washington and Jefferson would have needed ice packs and strong brandy had they heard of Morris's meddling.

After the bloodshed on the tenth of August, the monarchy effectively ended. More than two dozen of those loyal to the king sought sanctuary at Morris's house, 488 Rue de La Planche, Faubourg St.-Germain. (Among the refugees were Adélaïde and her son, and D'Estaing, the former French naval commander.) They presented Morris with a serious problem: he could not extend to this crowd diplomatic immunity, but neither could he bring himself to turn them out. Not surprisingly, their presence soon became known, antagonizing the revolutionists further.

Adélaïde fled with young Charles to England in September 1792, and stayed there for three years. Her husband, although sixty-six years old, had fought for Louis at the Tuileries on August 10; he had been captured and then imprisoned. He bribed his turnkey and escaped, but his attorney was arrested for complicity in the escape. Upon learning this, the count turned himself in so as to free his lawyer; he remained incarcerated until he was guillotined, several months later. D'Estaing, after speaking in favor of the queen, was guillotined as well.

After Adélaïde returned to France, Morris saw little of her. The flame had all but gone out by then; during her exile, she had become involved with a Portuguese ambassador, whom she later married. Meanwhile, too, she was disporting herself with a young Englishman, Lord Wycombe. Morris had been suspicious of Wycombe, having found him alone with Adélaïde often after the mission to England. It was Wycombe who paid for Adélaïde's modest residence in London, on Half Moon Street.[55]

After the slaughter at the Tuileries, Talleyrand urged Morris to flee France, as Talleyrand himself did. Every other member of the diplomatic corps in France—except Morris—exited, just as quickly as they could obtain their passports from the new republican government. Morris explained in a letter to Jefferson that although his position was not without danger, he presumed that when the President appointed him it was not for his own pleasure and safety, but to serve the interests of his country. This he could best do by staying put. Whether because of this letter is not known, but Jefferson never ordered Morris to withdraw. In any case, Morris could certainly have justified a flight. His decision to remain pleased the new goverment, since it suggested that America was thus proving itself the nation's only steadfast ally.

Unsurprisingly, Morris's (carefully concealed) diaries express his distaste for the Revolutionary Tribunal. He also commented trenchantly on the Jacobins, making cynical note of their "*parole* energy," and he accurately predicts that these loquacious and violent men will not hold power long. Morris's handling of financial exchanges with the rapidly shifting French government of course required astuteness. See, for instance, the complexities with which Morris became involved in making allowances for the American debt payment to France. France, dealing with an insurrection of slaves and free blacks in Saint-Domingue in late 1791, required supplies for the colony. The American government wished to open trade with the French and British West Indies, and so Morris agreed that commodities for

Saint-Domingue would pay down their debt. To avoid the chicanery of the Parisian money exchangers, Morris arranged for the payment to be made in the United States, where the supplies would be purchased.[56]

Within two weeks of the king's execution, France declared war on England and Holland. The revolutionaries, able to swiftly raise "volunteers" by terrorizing the public, hoped to expand their frontiers and were confident that their conquest would be abetted by foreign revolutions. Spain soon joined the British and Dutch coalition. The declaration of war had more or less the same effect on the morale of the new republican government that Morris's similar plan had intended for the royals.

Lafayette, fearing for his life, took flight to Luxembourg; he ended up imprisoned by the Austrians, in Olmütz, on the grounds that "the existence of Lafayette is incompatible with the security of the governments of Europe." His claim of American citizenship made no difference, of course. Morris advanced him ten thousand florins and also loaned a hundred thousand livres of his own money to Mme. de Lafayette, and used his influence to save her from the guillotine. She remained grateful to him for the rest of her life. Thomas Paine, too, wrote to Morris from prison. Paine had become a French citizen and, although he knew very little French, had already served in the National Assembly. Morris did not care for Paine, and as the historian William Howard Adams notes in his biography *Gouverneur Morris: An Independent Life,* "given that Paine had claimed French citizenship and in light of the fragile diplomatic relations between France and America, there was little the envoy could do beyond writing a diplomatic letter to the minister of foreign affairs."[57] Morris's successor, James Monroe, eventually obtained Paine's release in 1794.

Surely it is always challenging to serve as ambassador to a sovereign power that changes constantly; Morris's position was complicated even further by the revolutionary government's strong suspicions that he had harbored a sizable crowd at his Paris home, not to mention the incriminating documents, the "Notes on the Form of a Constitution for France" that he had presented to the king, and the scheme for Louis's flight.[58] Besides the complicated questions related to the American debt, to English-French trade, and to American-French trade, Morris was also obliged to protest French privateering against American shipping and to reclaim the vessels thus unlawfully seized; to aid American captains whose vessels had been detained illegally; to help American citizens improperly seized and imprisoned; and to express U.S. objections to certain decrees of the French Convention. To the U.S. Secretaries of State (Jefferson and then Edmund Randolph) and to the President, Morris sent numerous long memoranda and reports, attempting to predict where the revolutionary turmoil was leading. He tried, too, to gauge the temperature of relations between France and her neighbors Spain, Britain, and the Netherlands. In October 1792 he wrote to Jefferson that "I am clearly of Opinion that the great decided effective Majority is now for the Republic. What may be the Temper and Opinion six Months hence, no prudent sensible Man would I think take upon him to declare." Morris seemed sure of one thing, however, writing to Washington that same month that "the King is accus'd of high Crimes and Misdemeanors. . . . What may be his Fate God only knows, but History informs us that the Passage of dethron'd Monarchs is short from the Prison to the Grave." Morris also accurately anticipated the imminent war with England, informing Washington that the British required that France "deliver the royal Family to such reigning Branch of the Bourbons as the King may chuse, and . . . recall her Troops from the Countries they now occupy." French compliance, Morris knew, was improbable. Immediately following the king's execution, Morris wrote to Jefferson, "I consider a war between Britain and France as inevitable [but] Britain will, I think, suspend her blow until she can strike very hard." Although he saw the war coming, it was France that struck first.

Morris's efforts, and those of others, were unavailing; Lafayette was finally freed thanks to a victorious Napoleon, on September 19, 1797. Mme. de Lafayette had voluntarily come to Olmütz with her two daughters, then aged eighteen and thirteen, more than two years earlier, so that the family might at least be imprisoned together. In October 1797, Morris arranged to be in Hamburg where, on October 4, at the house of the former U.S. consul John Parish, the freed prisoners were formally received. Morris called the ceremony "very worthy" and said it was carried off with "much dignity." Bear in mind that George Washington esteemed Lafayette above all the other foreign officers serving with the Americans, Baron von Steuben included.[59] Although Morris did not believe Lafayette equal to the task of leading the revolution in France, his appreciation of the general's service to America was undiminished. So was his affection for Lafayette, his wife, and the children.

Morris's generosity toward desperate French aristocrats extended beyond government business. According to the Duc d'Orléans, in the fall of 1797 Morris made a "generous loan" of $4,000 to the duke's mother, who was at the time in deep financial distress. He also advanced the duke money to go to the United States and provided him with unlimited credit at two banking houses in New York.[60]

Remarkably, Lafayette too was shabby in his treatment of Morris—who, years later, had to dun the general for payment. The debt was finally settled in 1804, when Lafayette paid Morris 53,500 livres. How this sum was decided upon is difficult to determine; it seems to have involved complicated and not very accurate calculations involving depreciated currency values. Morris was chagrined, but he should have recognized certain clues in the character of Lafayette, evident nearly three decades earlier. In 1777–1778, after the American retreat at Brandywine and the loss of Philadelphia, there occurred the episode known as the Conway cabal. The Irish-born American officer Thomas Conway, who had fought heroically at Brandywine and had a low opinion of George Washington's generalship, asked Congress to promote him to a major generalship and also criticized the commander in chief in his correspondence. Word of this backbiting reached Washington; then Congress promoted Conway to the new post of inspector general, where the two men worked closely together and with considerable hostility. At last, Conway and Horatio Gates, who shared his views, asked Congress to remove Washington. Lafayette protested, saying that France might withdraw its support from the revolutionists if Washington went. The result was that Gates returned to his troops, Conway was demoted, and the inspector generalship went to Baron von Steuben. But although Lafayette professed himself George Washington's "first admirer" and "warmest friend," yet he wrote both Henry Laurens and Richard Henry Lee in support of the anti-Washington cabal, claiming that Conway was "much known by a friend of mine" and desiring "to be some what useful to him."[61] Lafayette's public defense of Washington seems to have been sincere, but his letters to Lee and Laurens indicate that he prioritized the maintenance of his reputation on both sides of the struggle over Washington. Ingratitude commonly accompanies this sort of duplicity.

Morris's prompt generosity toward the Duc d'Orléans and the Lafayettes in a way reinforces the impression of meanspiritedness made by his indifference to Thomas Paine's plight. Although Paine had been serving the French government, he probably still had some claim to U.S. citizenship, and the American minister could have pressed forcefully for his release. At the least, he should have been able to arrange superior legal representation for so powerful and eloquent an American revolutionist—and one whom Morris himself had worked with. Yet he now added injury to the insult he had flung at Paine some fifteen years earlier, when he had scorned Paine for his humble ancestry during the quarrel over Paine's indiscreet exposure of diplomatic correspondence in the winter of 1778–1779.

Morris treated John Paul Jones carelessly as well. He had served in 1788–1789 as a rear admiral in the Russian navy, then had come to Paris, where he fell seriously ill. Jones's mistress summoned Morris to their humble apartment, where Jones asked him, with a stammer, to draft his will. Morris agreed, but then left for supper; by the time he returned, a few hours later, Jones was dead. He had been virtually without a sou; Morris seems to have thought Jones should have an elaborate funeral, but did little to help pay for it. Nor did he attend. (He did help the admiral's family sell Jones's possessions.) This failure, besides being disrespectful of Jones's memory, could be seen as a dereliction of duty. His calendar for the day was crowded with social visits.[62]

Despite his neglect of Jones, Morris was one of the earliest and most persistent advocates of a powerful U.S. Navy. However, he overestimated—as he almost always did—how much a force of a given size could accomplish. For instance, in a May 31, 1794, letter from his country house in Seine-Port, he remarked to Secretary of State Edmund Randolph "that while the United States of America pursues a just and liberal conduct [of foreign policy], *with twenty Sail of the line at sea,* no Nation on Earth will dare to insult them."[63]

Those who expect far more of a person or an institution than that person or institution can possibly deliver often find themselves disappointed. But if Morris looked down on Jones for his naval freelancing, he should have remembered that the United States at the time had no navy at all. Jones's correspondence makes it clear that, had there been one, the admiral would have served with it. And surely, at a time when Morris was lavishly forking out loans to various imperiled French, he might have spared a few louis for Jones's funeral. The ceremony was arranged by a generous French citizen.

Did Morris do a good job in France and England? The U.S. government seems to have thought so: in September 1779, John Jay and others expressed the wish that Gouverneur might be spared from Congress to serve in Europe, where his abilities would do "Honor as well as Service to his Country." In forming our own judgments, we should remember that he was handicapped by important breaches of security that it was not within his power to prevent. What meager resources he had for negotiating with the British had been revealed in advance, thanks to Alexander Hamilton's incautious dealings with the British spy Beckwith. But Morris's voluminous letters home make plain that he provided his government with a tremendous amount of potentially valuable information on European (especially, of course, French and English) political factions; on the state of many of the European economies; on the temperaments of several European leaders; on the Western European harvests.

Morris was careful about the security of his official correspondence; a very high percentage got through unintercepted, and in good time. His government seems to have been more lax. Intercepted letters came late (one from Jefferson, dated June 13, 1793, did not reach Morris for over a year) or not at all. Throughout the first half of 1794, in particular, Gouverneur complained steadily about the casual attitude to security. On June 15, Washington attempted to explain the "disappearance" of numerous important letters en route abroad; but he was clearly flummoxed by the situation. On August 31, 1794, Morris remarked to Randolph that the Secretary's letter of April 19 had just arrived; furthermore, "it came through the hands of the *Comité de Salut Public,* and was, of course, read by them." "Which is just as well," Morris added, but it was not always to the U.S.'s benefit to have the Secretary of State's official correspondence read in advance by whatever overheated cabal happened to be in charge at the time.[64]

"I could be popular [here]," Morris wrote President Washington on February 14, 1793, "but that would be wrong. The different French political parties pass away like shadows of a magic lantern, and to be well with any of them would, in a short period, become the cause of unquenchable hatred with the other." This was surely correct. James Monroe, a very different man, came to the same conclusion soon after he succeeded Morris in France. On June 25 of the same year, Morris promised Washington that he would "be cautious to commit the United States as little as possible to future contingencies." But his ministerial behavior in some ways remained unusual. Even after he left Paris (Talleyrand had advised him to leave the country entirely), trouble followed him: his royalist friends soon found him and again his house became a refuge. The revolutionists were particularly vexed by Morris's sheltering of the Comtesse de Damas, for whom the Paris Committee of Safety had issued an arrest warrant. Morris's refusal to recognize French law and surrender the countess supplied the pretext for his recall.[65]

What happened was this. Edmond Genêt replaced Jean Baptiste Ternant (1750–1816) as the French minister to America. Morris dined with Genêt before he left and described him to Washington as an "upstart." Washington's impression did not much improve after meeting the man, whose primary mission was to draw America into France's impending war with Britain. Genêt received a warm reception, but his act wore thin as he persisted in reaching over the administration to raise popular support for the war.[66] Washington's cabinet determined to request his recall. Genêt, who detested Morris, had heard from Paine that "Gouverneur Morris who is here now is badly disposed towards you." He responded by accusing Morris of favoring counterrevolutionary projects. France responded to Genêt's withdrawal by throwing Paine in prison and calling for Morris's recall.[67]

Morris's view of French affairs was straightforward: he approved of the French Revolution as long as he thought it would end in a constitutional monarchy. Constitutional democracy, he believed, would prove disastrous, since the multitudes without money and property would sell their votes, making despotism even likelier than before. We cannot know whether he was right, but it is worth reminding the reader that, less than two decades after 1789, the French nation had adopted a constitutional monarchy, which lasted for more than three decades after the Restoration in 1814 until Napoleon's nephew came to power in 1848.[68]

In late summer 1792 Morris lamented to Washington and others "the distressful State of . . . [this] Country for which we have both a sincere Regard." On January 3, 1793, Jefferson wrote to William Short, then U.S. minister at The Hague, that President Washington wanted Short instructed that "France . . . [is] the sheet anchor of this country and its friendship . . . a just object." The leaders of the new nation felt deeply indebted to France for what they believed, in their naiveté, to be its largely selfless support of the Revolution in America. They freshly recollected the Continental Congress's receipt of millions of livres from their French allies. They remembered that French influence had enabled them to obtain valuable loans from Dutch bankers, without which the American Revolution would almost certainly have collapsed. As regards the governmental leadership supplied by Louis XVI, in particular, Morris seems to have been especially cognizant and grateful. The reader may recall Morris's dismissive initial assessment of the king as "small beer" upon his arrival in 1789; the American envoy had recognized the need for reform and encouraged the reformers' desire to base a new government on the American model. Three years later, he feared the revolution's turn toward despotism and had changed his estimation of the king. The king had lost his power and the respect of his people, but now Morris began to informally advise him, perhaps determining, as Richard Brookhiser speculates, "to prop up the weakest, lest its equally unworthy enemies prevail."[69]

What the American leadership, Morris included, failed to understand was that France had virtually "no genuine interest in the American cause as such. . . . What Vergennes had in mind was really the balance in powers in Europe and the colonial world, and not the support to any . . . [foreign] cause."[70] Vergennes's *Mémoire* of March 29, 1784, makes this starkly clear, and a *Mémoire* by Rayneval written in 1781 indicates how soon this attitude had solidified.

Besides having an interest in the European balance of power, France confidently expected to become America's leading trade partner as soon as independence was won. But, despite the postwar chill between them, by the mid-1790s Britain had easily resumed its prewar eminence as America's foremost trading partner. Such a surprise development for France seems to have arisen from several causes. The British had goods—particularly sturdy hardware and fabrics—that Americans desired. They delivered those goods promptly to U.S. ports, whereas deliveries from French merchants were routinely late. In addition, the Americans correctly believed that French merchants were taking advantage of the early commerce treaty to ship goods of less than the highest quality, and they resented it. Last but not least, the huge American debt to France led the balance of trade to work against a strong Franco-American trade relationship.[71]

After revolutionary France went to war, Morris's sympathies turned sharply toward the British. From mid-August on he had written to such confidants as Robert Morris of how glad he felt to be obtaining relief from his ministerial duties. As he wrote to Robert Morris on August 14, "I shall be relieved from a burden which has pressed on my shoulders, and which I am happier to be rid of than you can easily conceive. . . . I desired much to be recalled, but I would not ask it because I conceived my honor concerned in seeing the thing through." On June 19, 1794, after he had decided to change ambassadors, President Washington wrote Morris an eloquent letter, marked "Private." After a brief and stoutly courteous opening, Washington assured Morris that "my confidence in, and friendship and regard for you remain undiminished." Washington's tone seems sincere, not just a measure to assuage his envoy's feelings; he remained loyal to Morris and genuinely approved of his accomplishments.[72]

Once Monroe took over, Morris at first intended to return to America and had found a ship, *Superba*. He packed up his goods, including his books, liquors, linens, furniture, plate, and carriages, and had them shipped to New York. The liquor included a huge quantity of Marie-Antoinette's Imperial Tokay, which Morris had bought for twenty-five cents a bottle during the Terror.

Monroe initially had trouble obtaining Morris's passport. Morris, relishing an open schedule, wished to go see where philosopher Jean-Jacques Rousseau (1712–1778) had lived in Switzerland. As Monroe reported to Washington, "the French Government said [Morris] might choose his route to leave France but they did not like to permit him to go into Switzerland where the emigrants were and return back into the Republic."[73] Morris finally obtained the passport when he agreed not to return to France. Morris remained so interested in European affairs that four years passed before he followed his household goods home. In addition to Switzerland, he traveled to Hamburg, and thence to England. Sir James Bland Burges, the head of England's American department, had formally introduced him to Lord Grenville, who was now the Foreign Secretary. (Grenville was also an intimate and cousin of Pitt the Younger, still the Prime Minister.) William Wyndham Grenville (1759–1834) was British foreign secretary from 1791 to 1801. Heretofore he had not been notably pro-American; indeed, in 1794 he had negotiated an Anglo-American treaty so stringent that the U.S. Senate had rejected it.

Morris traveled widely throughout England and Scotland, especially in late 1795 and early 1796. In June 1796 he returned to the Continent, traveling mostly in Switzerland, in parts of Europe which are now simply Germany, in Holland, and in Austria.

All the mainland European courts received him; whenever he required an introduction, the British ambassador supplied it. Throughout these years, he steadily sent George Washington his impressions—for the most part, astute ones—of the European political scene. More remarkably, he did the same for Lord Grenville. His advice was generally wise, and his reports contain material of substantial interest. To be sure, he did a great deal of sightseeing, but his primary focus seems to have been supplying the British Foreign Office with intelligence.[74] The work was unpaid.

The reader may be startled to learn that the man who (signing himself "An American") wrote potent anti-British essays for the *Pennsylvania Packet* would then spend four years working for the British Foreign Office. While this generation of intelligence for Britain might seem active disloyalty, Morris did so with the best interest of his country in mind. To Morris, the nascent republic in France had become the real threat, and he hoped to restore the Bourbon dynasty with British assistance. He also wished to demonstrate the British interest in discontinuing interference with American vessels on the Mississippi and elsewhere.

Grenville had begun to learn about Morris's political opinions, personality, and abilities some time before Burges introduced him to the man. In early 1794, Francis Drake had mailed him three bulletins from Paris that concern Morris; no doubt reports had also come from the active British secret agents who worked the streets of Paris and the nearby countryside.[75] That the British spy network abroad should have been so good seems a bit ironic, because "all important decisions had to be made by the secretaries of state who belonged to the small governing elite," and "many members of this elite had little personal knowledge of foreign countries and languages."[76] Precisely for that reason, Grenville often attended closely to

Morris's advice; he would probably have done well to follow it even more than he did. Needless to say, information provided by even the most astute spy will generally fall far short of reports by a well-connected observer acting for the most part openly. Morris's assiduity certainly warmed His Majesty's Government toward America; against this must be weighed the fact that it was the younger Pitt's party that had instituted impressment of Americans at sea.[77] At the same time, Britain was at war with France, which seized three hundred American vessels in 1797 alone. Furthermore, Alexander Hamilton had advocated siding with the British in that war, and Washington had adopted his views as policy.

In an audience with George III, Morris cleverly reminded the monarch that his eldest brother, Lieutenant General Staats Long Morris, was at that very moment serving the king by commanding the fortress of Plymouth, England. Staats had married the dowager Duchess of Gordon, whose eccentric son Lord George Gordon had, in 1780, led the disturbances known as the Gordon Riots. Having thus endeared himself to the king (and therefore to Grenville), Morris omitted to mention something that is clear from his letters and diary. To wit, he had neither written to Staats nor talked to him until Washington's policy had clearly shifted toward England and away from France. Only then did Gouverneur approach his eldest brother.[78]

Superficially, it may seem surprising that Grenville and Morris should have gotten along. Acquaintances described the British statesman as unassuming to the point of shyness, frank and simple, although hardly affable.[79] Morris, of course, was generally flamboyant and gregarious. But such disparate natures sometimes complement each other nicely, like an acid and a base. Grenville entered the usual dynastic marriage of nobility. (In the Britain of the time the elite families tended to augment their fortunes through marriages which would enlarge their estates, so that these families' large properties often extended over several counties.) When Morris finally wed, at age fifty-seven, it was for love.

The shared traits of Grenville and Morris outnumbered the dissimilarities. In the political world, both men got off to very fast starts, and began hitting marks consistently by their mid-twenties. These speedy takeoffs were enabled by both substantial abilities and outstanding formal educations. Both men, incidentally, seem to have raised some hell at school. Grenville once wrecked an Eton schoolmate's room in two short minutes; Mintz records an occasion on which Morris and his classmates pelted one unfortunate Latin instructor with their no doubt weighty volumes of Ovid and Virgil, though such behavior was arguably not out of the ordinary for eighteenth-century schoolboys.[80]

Like Pitt and Charles James Fox, Grenville was among the foremost British politicians of his generation. Perhaps a key to his success was another trait he and Morris shared. Grenville was a sound scholar (indeed, he seems to have been much more learned than either Pitt or the drunken Fox). He spoke French fluently enough to be taken for a native, had nearly the same command of Italian, and could get along in Spanish. Like Morris, he had carefully studied geography—a tremendous asset for a statesman, but rare in British cabinet ministers of the day. That both men were highly intelligent goes without saying, though Morris's mathematical abilities were superior. Both men, too, were very conscientious and resolute, qualities for which Morris has not been fairly credited until now. Unlike Morris, however, Grenville freely enjoyed the many perquisites of office. Morris made his money on his own.

Interestingly, neither man held very high office for very long. Grenville served as prime minister less than fourteen months; he was far more important in his decade as foreign secretary. Both Morris and Grenville were youngest sons who had lost their fathers in childhood. Both opposed slavery; as Speaker of the House of Commons, Grenville made an excellent speech in support of Wilberforce's abolitionist program. Indeed, the most important achievement of his brief prime ministry was the abolition of the slave trade, which took effect on the very day in March 1807 when his government left office.[81]

On December 22, 1795, George Washington described to Morris the "indifference, nay more than indifference, with which the government of Great Britain received the advances of this country towards a friendly intercourse with it." Britain continued to impress seamen, stir up the Indians against American settlers, and send "ungracious and obnoxious" representatives. "If you should again converse with Lord Grenville on the subject," Washington instructed Morris, "you are at liberty, unofficially, to mention [these details] according to circumstances." Whilst steadily following George Washington's hints as to how to make the most, for American purposes, of his relationship with Grenville, Morris also provided important advice to Grenville from 1795 through 1798. At the earlier date, the British economy temporarily faltered and the country saw serious hunger riots. In 1797, the government prohibited the Bank of England from paying notes in gold, because of the strain the war with France had put on the gold reserves, and the restriction remained until 1821.[82] Against this bleak economic backdrop, Morris provided sound reasoning on foreign policy.

The British foreign policy of the day blended overseas conquests with continental expeditions and allied subsidies. In this context, Gouverneur believed that Grenville relied too exclusively on England's ties to Austria. Both Grenville and Pitt immensely underestimated the strength and staying power of the French armed forces, the army in particular. Napoleon's easy conquest of Italy took Whitehall completely by surprise. And neither the Prime Minister nor the Foreign Secretary seemed able to imagine that this same French army would prove sufficiently well organized and well disciplined to maintain effective military pressure on Austria and distant Prussia as well.

Gouverneur Morris had, as early as July 1795, warned Grenville of the vulnerability of Italy to French conquest. He had also predicted that Sardinia (Piedmont) would remain allied to France, "and the enemy of Austria." Corsica, too, being Napoleon's homeland, would fly the tricolor. On this basis, Morris forcefully pointed out to Grenville British overreliance on Austria. Pitt had formed a Treaty of Alliance with Austria on August 3, 1793, but the alliance failed because Austria had more interest in territorial conquest in Italy and Germany than a joint military campaign against France. Austria was also vulnerable, and after Napoleon defeated the Austrians in 1797, they signed the Peace of Campo Formio with France, only to join the Second Coalition and again declare war on France in 1799. Morris urged the Foreign Office to press for a strong Prussian alliance, a nation whose military had achieved a fearsome reputation after Prussia doubled its size in the Seven Years' War, but the British government stubbornly resisted. This resistance permeated the government; Morris's tenaciously promulgated aide-mémoire would have had to persuade the king (George III remained stubbornly opposed), Pitt (slightly less strongly opposed), and Grenville (who remained, to the last hour, hostile to the notion).

Anti-British feeling was growing in Austria, and a note of internal discouragement was heard throughout Britain. In a letter of October 5, 1796, from Vienna, Morris told Grenville that some in Austria were accusing Britain of protracting the miseries of Europe in a war, so as to complete the conquests of the East and West Indies. Granted, he went on, that Grenville had to appease the home audience by expatiating on the value of Britain's colonial acquisitions; but these very statements, when reported by the European press, embarrassed Austria's rulers. Morris therefore suggested that Grenville issue a public, reasoned defense of his foreign policy. The Foreign Secretary should explain that although the security of other British possessions required the seizure of the French and Dutch colonies, that seizure was not the ultimate objective of the war. That strategic aim, too, should be explicitly stated: namely, that England fought to protect Germany and the Netherlands. (Morris was, in effect, advising the Foreign Office to proclaim a spurious motivation to do what, nakedly stated, he felt, even the British public would not easily accept.)

Whether Morris's advice would have helped, we cannot know, for Grenville disregarded it. He seems to have felt that such public statements would have constituted an unheard-of (and therefore unwelcome) departure from the reserve traditional in the British Foreign Office. However, we may judge the actual British policy by its results. While the nation's military was overextending itself in the Indies, its leadership hesitated to move aggressively toward an alliance with Prussia, instead maintaining only the existing alliance with Austria. Meanwhile, the French approached the Prussians and made a secret treaty, committing their nations to neutrality. At the same time, France began massing its forces confidently on its Austrian border, whence they thrust northeast through the Austrian towns. The French inflicted defeat after bloody defeat on the hapless, now isolated, Austrian army. Owing to this development alone, Britain was to remain at war with France for another decade and a half. (The war with France, which had begun in 1793, continued until the Treaty of Amiens, in 1802, but resumed in 1803 and continued until Napoleon was crushed at Waterloo in 1814.)[83]

Sometimes Morris's advice to Grenville did bear fruit. A case might be made that his urgings to the Foreign Office tipped the decision-making balance in favor of the 1798 treaty between Great Britain and Russia, forming the Second Coalition against Napoleon.[84] In the treaty, Britain agreed to provide substantial loans and subsidies to its allies.

Throughout his years overseas, Morris continued his commercial ventures, in matters as disparate as trading in West Indian markets and bidding on the Penn family's land. A typical business letter from this period is the one to Tench Coxe, of April 13, 1796, from London, asking Coxe for prices and other particulars of the Pennsylvania land.

On October 2, 1798, Alexander Hamilton wrote to Rufus King to ask: "Why does not Gouverneur Morris come home? His talents are wanted. Men like him do not superabound." Hamilton did not have long to wait: Morris was booking his passage that very day. He sailed from Hamburg, aboard *Ocean,* on October 7. After a rough voyage, he landed at New York in late December 1798. He had been in Europe for ten years. Now that he had returned, he would not go overseas again.

{7}

SENATOR FROM NEW YORK

Rough seas had slowed Morris's passage; *Ocean* did not enter the eastern end of Long Island Sound for fifty-four days. Even there, the winds, seas, sleet, rain, and snow were so heavy that, from Point Judith Light, at Narragansett, *Ocean* had to run back up to Newport, Rhode Island. Not until December 23 did she enter New York Harbor—seventy-seven days to make landfall. Morris was met by his nephew David Odgen, Alexander Hamilton, newly promoted to general, and John B. Church, an Englishman who had been commissary-general under Lafayette during the Revolution. (Church returned to England after the war and, despite Tory resistance, claimed a seat in Parliament from Wendover, where Morris had visited him.) Morris did not proceed immediately to Morrisania, but stayed in the city through the holidays. On New Year's Eve, at Trinity Church, he sat in the pew of Isaac Low, a friend since the provincial congress in 1775. Subsequently he paid "calls on the [local] clergy and the Mayor." Finally, on January 5, 1799, after dusk, he returned to Morrisania, where he dined and went to bed.

At Morrisania he had hoped to settle for life, entirely free of any more governmental duties, official, public, semiofficial, or private. The nation, he felt, could get along without him: "There is . . . a fund of good sense and a calmness of character here, which will, I think, avoid all dangerous excesses. We are free; we know it; and we know how to continue free.

"Some of my friends have . . . [been] talking to me of [returning to] public life, but I turn a deaf ear to all that[.] I have got safe into the Port of private life, unless something should happen . . . to make it my Duty." He had already attained a substantial fortune, and grew even wealthier during the next seventeen years. Lewis Morris (1726–1798), the de facto lord of the manor during Gouverneur's absence from Morrisania, had died some months before. Morris's other half-brother, Richard, had retired from public life nine years earlier, and now lived on a large property in Scarsdale, New York. Not surprisingly, Morrisania was in a "leaky and ruinous" condition. The estate house, servants' quarters, and grounds, as earlier noted, had been used by the British as a horse park through most of the Revolution. An attack by the Continentals late in the war had caused further extensive damage. And Lewis had been too ill in the last several years of his life to manage and restore the place. This was what Morris now meant to do. He hoped, also, to invest further in stocks, bonds, and land, and to litigate a bit, in select cases or on behalf of close friends.

Not only was his property in a parlous state but also his books from overseas (roughly one hundred volumes) "had been so packed up at Paris, that an edition of half a dozen volumes was sometimes scattered through as many crates." It took him until January 27 to arrange his paperwork and library, while carpenters and stonemasons worked loudly all around him. Morris was then just days away from his forty-seventh birthday, and his friends had begun to wonder whether the wealthy, handsome, and accomplished bachelor might not desire a helpmate.[1]

To one of these friends, John Parish, he also wrote on a loftier plane. From a letter of April 6, 1799: "You wish rather the relation of our Realities. And yet, my excellent Friend, what are the Realities of the earth but a less vapory Dream? What are our best conclusions from most solid Facts, but light Conjecture, built on airy Vision?" This in the middle of several paragraphs on international affairs.[2]

Among his European correspondents was Jacques Necker, about whom Morris had dramatically changed his opinion. He had enjoyed visiting the Neckers in their Swiss exile, and they wrote to each other warmly. On May 13, 1799, Necker remarked, "I regret that I can no longer derive advantage from the sagacious speculations of your mind, and from your prognostications, so frequently verified." He went on to ask, "Will Europe never see you again?"[3]

In April of that year Gouverneur traveled to Philadelphia, primarily to visit Robert Morris in debtors' prison. Among his creditors was Gouverneur, to whom he owed a small fortune. Gouverneur was making no attempt to collect and had no part in Robert's imprisonment. In late May Washington invited him to Mount Vernon: "If either business or inclination should induce you to look towards the South, I shall be very happy to see you in this seat of my Retirement." But business took Morris to Albany that summer, to defend two prominent New York merchants, Isaac Gouverneur, a kinsman, and Peter Kemble in a suit brought against them by the French trader Louis Le Guen for business fraud involving shipments of cotton and indigo. The case had been dragging on since July 1796 when Morris stepped forward to present his arguments. The plaintiff was represented by Aaron Burr and Alexander Hamilton. Morris proved so combative before the jury that the judge had to admonish him for his "indiscreet" and "injurious" comments to Hamilton. Morris evidently apologized to the judge's satisfaction, but Le Guen won his case.

Courtroom opponents or otherwise, Hamilton, Burr, and Morris remained political allies in opposition to President Adams, even though Morris was a Federalist. Morris, who judged Adams an inept chief executive, on December 9 wrote George Washington urging him to come out of retirement and run for the presidency again. Probably Washington never read the letter: he became suddenly ill on the evening of the thirteenth and died the next day, at age sixty-seven.

Washington's funeral was on the nineteenth. The city fathers of New York asked Gouverneur Morris to give the funeral oration at St. Paul's Chapel; he replied, "The request is distressing and I pray time till tomorrow to consider." Morris loved and respected Washington most of all men; the blow was a heavy one.

Gouverneur chose to speak, but the result was a dry and lackluster narration of Washington's achievements. Perhaps he knew that Washington's will, dated just that July, asked "that my corpse be Interred in a proper manner, without parade, or funeral Oration." Too, the weather was ugly, exceptionally cold and damp, on the day of the funeral, and owing to the slowness of the procession Morris waited some hours in the cold before he spoke. Last but not least, of course, there was his grief. In his diary, Morris tersely notes: "Pronounced my oration badly."[4]

Morris had written to John Parish that he was spending "much more money than necessary to put ourselves in a respectable position of Defense" against the temptation to return to public life. These efforts notwithstanding, he was soon back in government. U.S. Senator James Watson, of New York, resigned from his office in March 1800 with three years left before his term expired. Morris successfully contended with Albany native Peter Gansevoort for the post, and the Federalists had him elected just before the party dramatically lost power. He joined the Senate on April 3—less than two weeks before it adjourned—and served out the term to 1803.[5]

The Senate that Morris joined was even more exclusive a body than it is today. One reason is probably that in the early nineteenth century, senators were elected by their state legislatures, not directly by the people. Candidates therefore did not need to appeal to all the voters. (This, by the way, no doubt had at least something to do with Morris's election.) Also, it was almost a necessity to be independently wealthy, because a U.S. senator's annual salary was only six dollars per diem.[6]

The Senate was in summer recess before its move to Washington, D.C., from the former national capital, Philadelphia. During the interval, Morris spent most of the summer traveling through upper New York and lower Canada, an opportunity he continued to take whenever the Senate was in recess. On this journey, he explored the large tract of land he owned on the southern borders of the St. Lawrence River and on Lake Ontario. He described his travels vividly to John Parish, the former U.S. consul in Hamburg, who, like William Short, brought out some of his most trenchant observations. The New York landscape had changed much since his European service: "They begin, I am told, on some farms to feel the loss of wood. It is now very thickly settled, and the banks of the river are covered for miles with timber and boards." Since settlements had commenced in 1785, "a whole region is converted from a wilderness into a settled country." Traveling up the St. Lawrence and Genesee Rivers, Morris proclaimed the country "the finest I ever saw" and described a "river whose banks are composed of the richest land, a sky bright, an atmosphere brilliant, fish and game in abundance." At Niagara Falls, a "stupendous object," he remarked that the falls had worn the rock back about twenty yards in almost three decades. Reflecting on these scenes, Morris prognosticated, "The proudest empire in Europe is but a bubble compared to what America will be, must be, in the course of two centuries—perhaps of one." Writing to Henry (Light Horse Harry) Lee, the former Revolutionary War commander who was serving in Congress, on January 22, 1801, he took up the topic of developing a canal in New York State. He returned to that project during his "retirement," but he had been turning over the idea in his mind since before Ticonderoga.[7] In November, Morris traveled to the District of Columbia for the opening of the Senate.

Morris's first official act as a senator—this was still in Philadelphia, before the recess—was a motion to increase diplomatic pay. It carried. That night he dined in prison with his old friend Robert Morris. On May 14, he voted against permission "in certain cases [of] the bringing of slaves into the Mississippi Territory." The negatives carried the vote, 14–5. He also voted with the 13–5 majority in favor of prosecuting a fellow New Yorker, William Duane, for the slander of Federalists in the *Aurora Gazette*. For Morris, as for the others, the main issue was the importance of confidential senatorial proceedings. The anti-Federalist Duane's Philadelphia publication had printed a proposed Federalist bill, leaked by the Senate's Democratic-Republicans, concerning how disputed presidential elections would be determined. Duane asked to speak to his lawyer and never returned for the trial, although the Senate did not prosecute further.[8]

In the Sixth Congress, the first one to meet in Washington, the most pressing matter was the vote for president: Burr and Jefferson had tied at 73 votes from the electors. (John Adams had 65 and Charles Cotesworth Pinckney 64.) Materially important, too, was how to handle the new treaty with Napoleon, recently made First Consul, whose star was steeply rising. America wished to obtain compensation for the ships and cargoes that the French republic had destroyed and, until these claims were met, offered to suspend the old treaty, which guaranteed French possessions. Napoleon, eager to ensure that America would not join forces with Britain, promised full compensation if America would continue the alliance. Meanwhile, however, France commenced negotiations with Spain for Louisiana.

After thirty-six rounds of voting, Jefferson at last prevailed over Burr and became the third U.S. president. He thus also left the presidency of the Senate, which promptly elected a committee of three, including Morris, to produce an address to be delivered to him. Not surprisingly, the committee chose Morris as its spokesman; in this capacity, he read the brief, eloquent farewell address on the Senate floor.[9]

Morris had opposed Jefferson at first, but changed his mind after concluding that the majority of the electorate supported him. This did not affect his friendship with Burr, and they dined together several times after Morris returned to New York in May 1801.

The primary diplomatic matter of concern before the Senate was ratification of the Convention of 1800, the treaty ending the undeclared war with France, which had begun in 1798. Morris accepted the treaty solely as a legal manifestation of the termination of U.S. hostilities with France. But he voted with the majority to eliminate Article II of the Convention. This article suspended the 1778 treaties until American claims on the French for $20,000,000 were settled. Although the full reasons for this senatorial vote for expungment remain somewhat opaque, Morris seems to have been in part concerned that the French would bribe the American elites to lobby against French repayment. Morris evidently reasoned that this maneuver, if successful, could greatly extend the conflict, one that the lightly armed new nation had already proved militarily unable to sustain with success.

Life in Washington did not impress Morris favorably. On December 14, 1800, he wrote to the Princesse de la Tour in Ratisbone:

We want nothing here but Houses, Cellars, Kitchens, well informed Men, amiable Women, and other little Trifles of this kind, to make our City perfect; for we can walk here, as if in the Fields and Woods, and, considering the hard frost, the air of the City is very pure. I enjoy more of it than any one else, for my Room is filled with Smoke whenever the door is shut. . . . It is the very best City in the World for a *future* Residence.[10]

At the end of April 1802, Congress approved the Enabling Act, which allowed the territories that were organized under the Northwest Ordinance to become states. (On March 1, 1803, Ohio would become the seventeenth state to join the Union.) It was in this context that Congress debated whether to repeal a new federal judiciary law. In midwinter 1801, the Federalist-led Congress had passed a judiciary bill creating seven new district judgeships and sixteen circuit judgeships. The outgoing President Adams signed the legislation; all the seats went to Federalists. Arguing that the judgeships entailed "unnecessary additional expenses," Jefferson's Democratic-Republican administration sought the judiciary law's repeal.

Morris led the Federalist counterattack. On January 8 and 14, 1802, he delivered a pair of powerful speeches opposing the repeal. A shorthand recorder on the floor of the Senate reported that these two speeches alone numbered roughly seventeen thousand words. The thrust of Morris's arguments was that inferior courts, once established by law, ought to retain the power vested in them and their judges: "If as a precedent, Congress would *ex post facto* destroy such courts, [then] the people of America have vested all power incontinent to the national legislature." He continued: "They [the American people] have not done so. They have provided a check of the first Necessity to prevent an invasion of the Constitution by unconstitutional Laws."

On the more pragmatic side, Morris pointed out that the expansion of population and admission of new states, and the predictable increase in litigation, would lead the half-dozen aging justices of the Supreme Court to exhaust themselves in riding circuit "from one end of the continent to the other." He argued that the "ostentatious economies" supposedly to be wrung from repeal were so negligible as to be absurd. Despite the good sense of both the constitutional and the practical arguments, the repeal passed on February 3.[11] Jefferson's attack on the judiciary only reinforced the pragmatic Morris's opinion of the president's unfitness as an administrator. After dining with the third president in April, Morris commented only, "He is Utopia, quite." A month later he was less reticent, calling Jefferson "cold as a frog."

In summer 1802, the penniless Robert Morris received his discharge from jail after a new law permitted him to declare bankruptcy. After Robert had visited his family, Gouverneur Morris took him to Morrisania for a rest. The state of Pennsylvania had imprisoned the sixty-eight-year-old for the last three and a half years, and he was a broken man. Gouverneur wrote to Parish that "he came to me lean, low-spirited, and as poor as a commission of bankrupt can make a man whose effects will, it is said, not pay a shilling in the pound. . . . I sent him home fat, sleek, in good spirits and possessed of the means of living comfortably the rest of his days. So much for the air of Morrisania." After the summer with Gouverneur, Robert rejoined his family in a small house in Philadelphia, where he remained until his death five years later. Among Gouverneur's gifts to his old friend was a $15,000 annuity.

Toward the end of Morris's Senate term, rumors were circulating that the Spanish had been forced to cede the vast Louisiana territory to France. The rumors raised concerns that Americans might no longer be able to navigate the Mississippi River freely, blocking the transport of their goods to market. Morris, along with several western Federalists, advocated the use of force to keep the Mississippi open for American navigation. He supported the resolutions of Pennsylvania senator James Ross to authorize Jefferson's seizure of New Orleans, forestalling a French invasion. In rallying support, he made an unfortunate concession to slavery, arguing to Southern delegates that control of New Orleans would also enable the suppression of Caribbean slave insurrections: "That event will give to your slaves the conviction that it is impossible for them to become free. Men in their unhappy condition must be impelled by fear, and discouraged by despair. Yes—The impulsion of fear must be strengthened by the hand of despair!" How could such an ugly argument come from a man who had vilified the slave trade and the three-fifths rule? The conclusion of one biographer is difficult to deny. "Whatever his reasons," writes Brookhiser, "it was a wicked argument, and if he had come to the point of saying such a thing, it was just as well that he was leaving public life."[12] The other side held that navigation rights might be acquired by means other than a war with France, a move that Morris admitted would devastate the western states, and Ross's resolutions were defeated 15–11 (with six senators abstaining).

In the winter of 1803, following instructions from Jefferson, James Monroe and the American envoy in Paris, Robert R. Livingston, opened negotiations with the French to buy the city of New Orleans and some nearby land on the east bank of the Mississippi. The French, however, offered to sell all of the Louisiana territory to the United States for $15 million (this was accomplished by way of a roughly $12 million U.S. direct payment combined with a nearly $3 million loan forgiveness). The astonished Americans signed the Louisiana purchase treaty on April 30, 1803, just a few days before Morris's term in the Senate ended on March 3.

The Louisiana Purchase was controversial at the time. Opponents contested Jefferson's constitutional right to purchase land without the states' consent and questioned the incorporation into the union of unknown people and uncultivated territory. Many of the senators who were large landowners worried that their own eastern holdings would depreciate in monetary value if the nation were to double its size. Amazingly, the cost was also an issue. According to Delaware senator James White, "even supposing that this extent of territory was a desirable acquisition, fifteen million dollars was an enormous sum to give." The Federalists feared that the political center of gravity would shift south or west. Morris attributed his party's concerns to this one reason: "it cost money the greater part of which we to the northward must pay, and it gains territory which will, in their apprehension, by giving strength to the Southern representation, diminish the Eastern influence in our councils." Finally, there were concerns that Spain's agreement with France had included stipulations that disallowed its sale to another country, thus rendering any agreement null and void. That neither Morris nor his major Federalist colleagues kept pace with the president on this issue should come as no great surprise. But Hamilton and Morris, who feared the acquisition would destabilize the union, soon changed their minds, realizing that the purchase could also secure insularity. As Morris wrote to Senator Jonathan Dayton of New Jersey, "I am prepared to pay my share of fifteen million to deprive foreigners of all pretext of entering our country." Morris may have overpraised Robert Livingston's negotiating savvy, and he gave scant direct credit to Jefferson at the time.[13]

The U.S. Senate ratified the purchase treaty on October 20, 1803, doubling the size of the new nation. In time, all or parts of thirteen new states would be carved from the vast Louisiana territory.

During his senatorial period, Morris sustained a very active private correspondence which, in itself, is remarkable for the variety of the subjects discussed and the superlativeness of the literary style. In a letter from Morrisania, dated June 20, 1802, to the Princesse de La Tour, Morris comments:

> He, therefore, who wishes to glide through Life on a smooth surface, should
> seek the Capital of some large Monarchy, where an individual is of too little

importance to occupy the attention of that Government, by whose Power he is protected, and by whose Laws he is secured. The Result of this mild state of being is mildness of Manners, but it occasions also a want of Energy.

This letter concludes with a gentle rumination on "the changes and chances of human life": "There is compensation everywhere and in everything. To be happy we must learn to be content with our lot where it is cast, and our condition, whatever it may be. In studying this lesson I shall never forget that I once enjoyed the charms of your conversation, lovely Princess, and while I remember the sweets of your society I will endeavor not to regret."

To Robert Livingston, August 21, 1802, Morris expressed dismay at a consequence he expected from universal suffrage, which "takes from men of moderate fortune their proper weight, and will, in process of time, give undue influence to those of great wealth . . . a different state of things seems to be approaching, and slight circumstances will perhaps decide whether we are to pass through a course of revolutions to military despotism, or whether our government is to be wound up, by constitutional means." "Much will depend," Morris concludes, "on the union of talents and property." Yet the qualities which Morris continued to esteem were universal. On October 10 of the same year, again writing to Livingston, Morris asked: "What renders a nation respectable?" His answer was "Power, courage, wisdom."[14]

With the end of Morris's Senate term in May, he was free to spend much of the rest of 1803 traveling through New England, New York State, and southern Canada. Since the March before last he had been writing to old friends, such as Robert R. Livingston, that he wished "to get out of this galley [the U.S. Senate, of course], and live for myself." Not surprisingly, he did not seek reelection.

During these travels, a ship Morris was on encountered rough autumn weather while sailing on Lake Ontario. "The sea [was] running very high," he noted in his diary, "with the surf of the whole lake tumbling on them unsheltered." The ship's captain became so ill he could not retain the helm; he asked Morris to pilot the vessel. "With no other resource than my recollection of a former Voyage," Morris steered safely through the high surf and rocky waters to a safe harbor. This was his second such adventure, though he had no nautical training whatever. Having enjoyed his adventures, Morris at last returned to settle into Morrisania.[15]

That autumn, he responded to a letter from Henry W. Livingston asking about the intent of the Constitution's framers on a particular point: "It is not possible for me to recollect with precision all that passed in the Convention while we were framing the Constitution; and, if I could, it is most probable that meaning may have been conceived from incidental expressions different from that which they were intended to convey, and very different from the fixed opinions of the speaker." Constitutional scholars, take heed.

Not that Morris was always so circumspect concerning the framers' intent. The reader will recall here Morris's Christmas Day 1802 reply to the Speaker of the New York State Assembly, wherein he reviewed the framers' concerns with respect to the choice of a vice-presidential running mate in the national elections. "The Convention was aware that every Species of Risk and Contrivance would be practiced by the ambitious and unprincipled. . . ."[16]

As Morris entered his fifties, he was still much interested in the ladies. On January 9, 1802, he enountered Dolley Madison at a tea at Thomas Jefferson's, where she arrived with Mrs. Robert Morris. She was wearing a low-cut dress. Might she be amenable to seduction? he wondered in his diary. She had, he believed, "good dispositions," by which he meant he was optimistic. On another day, he remarked that a Mrs. Morton was receptive but temporarily "indisposed," and also that she had a jealous husband (no doubt Perez Morton). Writing to Jonathan Dayton on November 9, 1803, Morris discussed real estate for three and a half pages, but then closed thus: "Present me respectfully and affectionately to my friends male and female of all Parties. You are not to be told that the Heart knows nothing of Politics especially when it approaches a Petticoat."[17]

{8}

IN RETIREMENT

ONCE HE WAS back at Morrisania, Gouverneur's political activities fell steeply and deliberately into abeyance, but his pen became even more active. He enjoyably occupied many of his remaining hours writing numerous essays and hundreds of letters. As William Blake remarks, "The cistern contains: the fountain overflows." Most of the essays deal with political subjects, some with more general cultural topics. They appeared primarily in the *Evening Post,* the *Examiner,* and the *United States Gazette.* In the *Post* he sometimes used his old nom de plume, "An American."

Of his voluminous correspondence from this period, some of the most interesting exchanges are with Lewis B. Sturges, Rufus King, Robert R. Livingston, Jonathan Dayton, Jonathan Mason, the Ogdens, John Penn, the Merediths, Timothy Pickering, and W. B. Randolph.[1]

In May 1804, the same month that Napoleon became emperor of the French, his youngest brother, Jérôme Bonaparte, and his new bride, the former Elizabeth Patterson, of Baltimore, dined at Morrisania. The bride's imperial brother-in-law had banned the couple from France, and perhaps it was for this reason that the bride continued to dress in the largely see-through, scanty style of the Directory. "An almost naked woman," observed Margaret Bayard Smith. The Bonapartes brought along with them a still unknown poet, the twenty-five-year-old Thomas Moore, a friend of Lord Byron.

On the first day of July 1804, Morris went to Alexander Hamilton's office "to settle the affairs of William Constable and Company," of which Hamilton was the legal representative. In 1789, Morris had entered a partnership with Constable in order to speculate on the wheat trade. Hamilton did not mention his impending duel with Aaron Burr, and the next time Morris saw his friend, Hamilton was unconscious and on his deathbed. His family asked

Morris to deliver the oration at Hamilton's funeral. He agreed, although he was deeply affected by grief. (He had grieved more only for Washington and for Elizabeth Plater, with whom he had fallen in love while recovering from his amputation in 1780. She had died in 1790 while Morris was in Europe.)

Morris's diary records that he thought the result a failure and its delivery no better. We cannot judge the latter, though the hearers were impressed, but about the former Morris was surely wrong. The sentences are clear and generally brief, intensified by occasional antitheses and verbal emphases, and with some longer periods that have climactic power. The effect is poignant and restrained: "Far from exciting your emotions, I must try to repress my own, and yet, I fear, that instead of the language of a public speaker, you will hear only the lamentations of a wailing friend. But I will struggle with my bursting heart to portray that heroic spirit which has flown to the mansions of bliss."

The grief-stricken Mrs. Hamilton asked Morris to look into the family's financial condition; he discovered, to his dismay, that they had nothing. Having discussed the matter with a number of his friends, Morris decided to establish a Hamilton family trust; the capital was supplied by Hamilton's friends and administered by the reliable Rufus King. As Chamfort put it: "In great matters, men appear as they wish to appear; in small matters, they appear as they are."

Another sequel of Hamilton's untimely death was that Morris took his place on the Columbia College board of trustees, working conscientiously to strengthen the teaching and make the school more rigorous.[2]

Morris joined several other influential New Yorkers to found the New-York Historical Society in the autumn of 1804. And soon thereafter he became the society's president. Eight years later, on one gouty leg, he delivered a formal address to the society's membership. Surprisingly, he struck a pious note:

> There must be something more to hope than pleasure, wealth, and power. Something more to fear than poverty and pain. Something after death more terrible than death. There must be religion. When that ligament is torn, society is disjointed and its members perish.[3]

Despite his intellectual and personal history, his conviction rings true; national independence, he believed, required a grounding principle that religion might very well provide.

His long-held interest in building a canal system for New York State now was coming to fruition. Along with Robert Fulton and George Clinton, he was instrumental in the development of the Erie Canal; on May 4, 1811, he was elected president of the nine-member Canal Commission. Unfortunately,

although he retained his deep interest all his adult life, he died before ground
was broken on the project (1817); the Erie Canal finally opened in 1825.[4]

Morris's influence on the development of the Erie Canal, however, like almost everything else in his life, was complicated. He seems to have been the
first person to conceive the idea of a canal between Lake Erie and the Hudson River. After the evacuation of Ticonderoga in 1777, Morris arrived at
General Schuyler's headquarters, on a mission from the Committee of General Safety of New York. Here he met with Schuyler, to inquire into and report on the state of the military force in that region of the state. According
to Morgan Lewis (1754–1844), who served in the New York Senate and
later became governor, Morris then stayed several days in the same house as
the general and Lewis. Morris, "never doubting the ultimate triumph of our
arms, and the consequent attainment of our independence," announced one
evening "in language highly poetic . . . that at no very distant day, the waters
of the great western inland seas would, by the aid of man, break through
their barriers and mingle with those of the Hudson."

In response to a direct question by Lewis as to how these barriers could be
surmounted, Morris replied "that numerous streams passed through natural
channels, and that artificial ones might be conducted by the same routes."

Lewis goes on to state that "this object" was one of which he never lost
sight. In 1810, Morris went to Albany for the express purpose of engaging,
if possible, the state legislature in his plans for the canal's construction. In
Albany, Lewis, then a senator himself, accompanied Morris to the lodgings
of New York State Senators Clinton, Platt, and Hall with the purpose of inducing in them the zeal needed to excite the rest of the legislature with the
canal project.

On August 26, 1811, Morris drafted a report to the New York State surveyor general, from the Committee on the Erie Canal, arguing the case for the
canal. Simeon De Witt, the surveyor general for many years, states that "the
merit of first starting the idea of a direct communication by water between
Lake Erie and the Hudson River . . . unquestionably belongs to Gouverneur
Morris." In the first volume of *New York Canals,* De Witt traces in detail Morris's efforts beginning in 1803. Indeed, as early as 1800 Morris had written
that, for "one-tenth the expense borne by Britain in the last campaign," ships
could in future "sail from London through the Hudson River into Lake Erie."

According to Judge Benjamin Wright (1770–1842) of Utica, however,
"Morris looked only to canalling along the valleys of the natural water-
courses to Lake Ontario, and then connecting Lake Ontario and Lake Erie
by improvements around Niagara Falls." Fellow Canal Commissioner
Thomas Eddy remarks that "no one of the [Erie Canal] commissioners were

more ardent [than Morris] in promoting the object of connecting the waters of Lake Erie and the Hudson." Eddy, nonetheless, goes on to adjudge "that Mr. M. in some respects infused the undertaking—or, in other words, was the means of preventing the legislature engaging in the project so soon as they otherwise would have done." Eddy's reason for saying this is that Morris drafted the first report and had an undue influence on the promulgation of its concept. As Eddy phrases the matter, "Mr. M. gave scope to his fancy, and proposed the project of a canal on an *inclined plane* from Erie to the Hudson." For reasons that Eddy's undated communication never makes clear, Morris "certainly . . . (as has been shown) prevented the legislature adopting the plan prior to 1816."

Nonetheless, Morris had proven the first individual to conceive the idea for the canal. He also spearheaded the campaign to drum up interest in it in the state legislature. Furthermore, Morris also drafted the second report of the commissioners. As a result of this report, the legislators passed an act, giving the commissioners authority to borrow from Europe, on the state's credit, five million dollars toward the initial engineering plan and construction. This scheme, however, did not move to fruition, much to Morris's chagrin. After all has been written, said, and done, however, Evan Cornog's statement seems best to encapsulate Morris's influence on the Erie Canal, namely, that "his prominence helped carry the plans forward."[5]

Morris did live, however, to travel up the Hudson River on a steamship. Years earlier, on a Sunday afternoon during the historically eventful summer of 1787, he had seen an ancestor of it demonstrated in Philadelphia.

During this period Morris took sardonic pleasure in the exile of Napoleon Bonaparte. While still in Europe, Morris had opposed the French Directory and had even more strongly opposed Bonaparte. He saw Bonaparte's ascension to First Consul and then to Emperor as the embodiment of his early 1790s prophecy that the French Revolution would produce a dictator.

Although Morris had steadily opposed British impressment of American seamen, he opposed the War of 1812. He had objected to the embargo as a foredoomed American attempt to induce Great Britain to cease boarding U.S. ships at will. He saw that the embargo would lead to war, and he felt it was promulgated mainly to protect "foreign Sailors in our Merchant ships against the Power of their Sovereign." He also believed that the real reason for the embargo was the unstated U.S. goal of conquering Canada. When the fighting seemed imminent, Morris proposed a convention of the two political parties north of the Potomac to overcome what he saw as the South's domination of the government by eliminating representation based on the three-fifths clause.

In Morris's opposition to James Madison's lead-up to the congressional declaration of war, and his underlying concern that the South had undue influence in national affairs, Morris went so far as to advocate secession. For this purpose he wrote to Harrison Gray Otis, of Massachusetts, to propose what was to become the Hartford Convention. This meeting was to convene the states that were "friends of peace and commerce" to discuss ways to circumvent the embargo. The reasons why Morris did not attend the convention are not clear. It may be that the increasingly painful physical condition, which eventually led to his death, prevented him from making the trip. After the convention met, in December 1814, Morris felt it did not go far enough in the direction of a peace formulation.

Productive though he had always been, Morris also knew how to be idle. In clear weather he always enjoyed the view from Morrisania of the Bronx Kills and Randalls Island and the numerous sailing craft of all kinds and sizes, along with innumerable porpoises, which played back and forth in clean waters. His guests, who often arrived by boat, found a mansion with large rooms and lofty ceilings. There was a dark parquet floor, imported from France, that showed the marks made by Morris's peg leg. The guests could also expect a fine repast. By contemporary accounts, during his retirement, Morris became one of the best chefs in North America. Usually starting at four P.M., the meal was followed by interesting conversation over good wine, and oysters brought in from the fertile collection beds in New Jersey's Raritan and Sandy Hook bays. In Paris he had kept "a tun of sauternes and a tun of claret," not to mention ample supplies of Madeira and Port, and Morrisania was soon even better stocked.[6] With Voltaire's comment "the superfluous, a very necessary thing," Morris would have heartily agreed.

The best letters, like the best conversations, color theories with personality, and enrich autobiography with ideas. Thus Morris's correspondence, and thus, judging by the comments of his guests, Morris's talk. His sense of humor, too, remained as strong as ever. Less than eight months before his death, Gouverneur wrote a jocular letter to Moss Kent about lawyers, the national bank, and a certain General Brown: "I think the Want of Sincerity indecorous in Men of a certain Size. A Giant should not encroach on a Pigmy's Patrimony."[7]

Morris's friends had all come to believe he would remain a bachelor for life. Well into his fifties, he continued to have "a roving eye." At the end of a letter of April 1808, for example, in which he gave David Parish, a young lawyer, advice on a legal complaint in Pennsylvania, Morris added a postscript: "Remember me properly to all Friends Male and *Female*." On Christmas Day,

1809, however, in a surprise ceremony at Morrisania, the fifty-seven-year-old Morris married his housekeeper, thirty-five-year-old Anne Cary Randolph (1774–1834).

Although the bride came from one of the great Virginia planter families, the scandal that attached to Anne's name had long since made her unwelcome in the clan. Anne's history was as follows. Her mother had died in 1789, and her father, Thomas Mann Randolph of Tuckahoe, Virginia, then remarried. His new wife disliked Anne, so when Thomas died, the girl (then sixteen years old) went to live with her older sister, Judith, in early 1791. The evidence strongly suggests that Judith's husband (and cousin), Richard Randolph, conceived a child with Anne. The infant seems to have been stillborn; its corpse was discovered in a trash dump by a slave.

Criminal indictments of Richard and Nancy (as Anne was known) followed. The charges were incest and infanticide. The Randolphs hired Patrick Henry and John Marshall, probably the two strongest criminal attorneys in the state; the family was prominent and powerful; the slave's testimony was not admissible; and Judith testified that Nancy's pregnancy had never shown, indeed that it could not have occurred. According to Marshall's closing argument, the "publick fondness" between Richard and Nancy indicated that they had nothing to hide. The justices acquitted the defendants after little deliberation. Though the court had dismissed the charges, the verdict of public opinion was much less decisive, and the story of this "Jezebel of the Old Dominion" circulated in tavern and marketplace.

Not too many months afterward, the still young and evidently hale Richard (1770–1796) died under mysterious circumstances. A sudden fever turned to delirium, which the doctor could not diagnose, and Richard died within two days. An admirer of the American and French revolutions, Randolph subscribed to their principles of human rights and in his will freed all of his ninety slaves.

The presence of both Judith and Nancy in the house at the time he became ill leaves ample room for suspicion of poisoning, and some saw Nancy as the prime suspect. Judith, frantic during his illness, wore only black for months afterward and seems not to have been suspected. The sisters' relationship, which had deteriorated during the trial, continued to sour. As Judith's resentment grew, Nancy felt her sister treated her like a servant. Her options were limited, however, as the scandal had made the possibility of a good marriage unlikely.

Morris was not put off by this history, of which he was sufficiently aware, whatever the whole truth may have been. He visited her in October 1808 and after corresponding for five months, Morris invited her to join him at

Morrisania as a housekeeper. He told her that his servants required supervision, as the previous housekeeper had caused considerable dissension. Morris assured her that his intentions were honorable and that his conduct would be proper, but he did leave open the possibility that the relationship might advance beyond that of master and servant. Her salary would be the same as the other housekeepers in order to keep up appearances, but, Morris wrote to her, "I can only say that our real relations shall be that of friends." Anne moved to Morrisania from Manhattan in April 1809. The facts of their relationship at this time are unknown, though, naturally, there were rumors of an illicit connection.

Christmas Day, 1809, dawned and remained beautiful. Nine guests, including the Wilkinses and the Ogdens, arrived for what they thought would be simply a fine, early Christmas dinner. After the meal, however, Morris rose to say a word: "I marry this day Anne Cary Randolph." The bride, who until then had remained upstairs, out of sight, now descended the front stairway. Rather than a bridal gown, she wore the plain brown housedress in which she worked. It was patched on both elbows. Her wedding dress was a statement that they both very much enjoyed, Nancy because it showed her gratitude for his past kindness and Morris likely because of the element of surprise for their guests.[8] Isaac Wilkins, the husband of Gouverneur's oldest sister, Isabella, and rector of St. Peter's Church of Westchester County, was among the family present and performed the ceremony.

"Of all actions of a man's life," John Selden supposedly remarked in his seventeenth-century *Table Talk,* "his marriage does least concern other people; yet of all actions, 'tis the most meddled with by other people." With varying degrees of venom the families of Samuel and Euphemia Ogden, Isaac and Isabella Wilkins, Gouverneur's niece Gertrude Meredith of Philadelphia, and other relatives—almost all of whom as a result of his marriage faced the prospects of lost inheritances—expressed shock and outrage at Morris's marriage. Several small-souled others also had opinions to impart. With characteristic equanimity, Morris wrote to Gertrude Meredith:

> If I had married a rich Woman of seventy, the World might think it wiser than to take one of half that Age without a Farthing, and if the World were to live with my Wife I should certainly have consulted its Taste—but as that happens not to be the Case, I thought I might without offending others endeavor to suit myself, and look rather into the Head and Heart than into the Pocket.[9]

On Tuesday, February 9, 1813, a little more than three years after their wedding, the couple's only child, Gouverneur Junior, was born. Morris was then sixty-one, and the oldest of the Founding Fathers to father a child. In October 1813, from Stillwater, where much of the battle of Saratoga had taken place, Gouverneur sent Nancy a letter in verse. Their son was then eight months old, and the poem captures the tender feelings of the husband and father:

> Kiss for me, my love, our charming boy
> I long to taste again the joy
> Of pressing to his father's breast
> The son and mother. Be they blest
> With all which bounteous Heaven can grant
> And if among us one must want
> Of bliss, be mine the scanty lot.
> Your happiness, may no dark spot
> Of gloomy woe or piercing pain
> Or melancholy ever stain. . . .

Two years after Gouverneur's death and probably with the desire to reveal a side of her husband seen only by his close friends, his widow mailed this tender poem to *The Columbian,* the college's magazine, where it was published. On it she wrote, "After this was written Mr. Morris and myself were never absent from each other except one night."

Morris died on November 6, 1816, at Morrisania. The death throes were acutely painful, being brought on by a slowly progressing blockage of the urinary canal, the first symptoms of which he had noticed nearly two decades before, when he was traveling in what is now Belgium. On November 5, Rufus King had reported to a friend in greater detail on Morris's condition: "He has been long subject to a stricture in the urinary Passage; and have unskillfully forced a piece of whale bone thro' the Canal so lacerated the parts, as to create a very high degree of inflammation, which has been followed by a mortification that I am told will prove fatal. Some years ago, and in the interior of our State, he performed the same operation with a flexible piece of hickory; the success on this occasion probably emboldened him to repeat the experiment, that is now to prove fatal."

Gouverneur Morris expired with his closest family members by his side, in the same large second-floor room, at the front of the house, where, in 1752, he first saw light. He is interred next to Nancy in the graveyard of St. Ann's Episcopal Church, 295 St. Ann's Avenue, in the lower Bronx.[10]

{ *9* }

CONCLUSION

T HE GENERAL TENOR of a man's life is the rule by which to judge his Character"—so said Robert R. Livingston in an unpublished letter of 1778. On the personal side of Morris's life, both his genetic inheritance and his childhood environment evidently afforded him significant advantages. From his mother's side, he received his aptitude for French and a well-developed sense of social grace and cultural style. One of his paternal great-grandfathers had served as an officer in Cromwell's army; his paternal grandfather, as Eugene Sheridan has ably revealed, was a man of considerable abilities in public affairs. Morris also no doubt profited from observing his father's insouciant but capable management of Morrisania, and from the huge library the elder Morris kept.

Perhaps, too, it was an advantage to be the only son of a second marriage—and a late birth, at that. The youngest boy from the first marriage, Richard, was already twenty-two when Gouverneur arrived in this world. Before the younger brother had left the schoolroom, the older had already succeeded their father as a judge of the vice admiralty. Though the closest in age, Richard is not known to have helped his fatherless little brother much, but Gouverneur also does not seem to have faced any of the family opposition that often saps the energies of the talented and unarmored young. Moreover, not only was he his mother's favorite, but also his several sisters dearly loved him. Such benign factors can only help in the development of people who achieve much. Certainly Morris was a man of substantial vitality. He also had strong nerves, no small store of courage, a massive intellect, and a healthy sensitiveness. All these traits, his home environment helped to flourish.

Some people seem formed by nature to delight in opposition, and pass their most agreeable hours in storms mostly of their own creating; not so

Gouverneur Morris. Unlike many of those who make history, he needed no sense of struggle and conquest to enjoy life. It was not that he had no quarrels, but in a letter to Nathanael Greene he described his usual response to personal and professional attacks: "There is nothing which speaks so intelligibly as expressive Silence." Like many exceptional people, Morris had a polar quality, attracting love and hatred with a force from which meaner natures seem exempt. Enemies seem to be a concomitant of any robust life; sometimes the number of one's enemies is an accurate indicator of strength.

Gouverneur was never cowed by any person, mob, or civic assembly, either in the New World or the Old. (He did admit having been "hellishly scared" after Ticonderoga.) Civilly, as he himself put it, he was "not a cautious man." This incaution seemed to liberate him. In philosophical spirit he suggests the Voltaire who, in a 1765 letter, remarked: "The great consolation in life is to say what one thinks."[1]

His schooling seems to have been perfectly suited to a future statesman. As Robson ably highlights in *Educating Republicans,* Morris's King's College was "uniquely inhospitable to American patriotism in the years before the [revolutionary] war." Despite the Loyalist cast of the board of trustees and the faculty, King's produced a number of important revolutionary figures, among them John Jay, Robert Livingston, Egbert Benson, and Alexander Hamilton.[2]

As our narrative has made clear, after his large-scale failed land speculation of 1773, Morris eventually became very adept at honest moneymaking. Like every very successful person in any realm, however, he enjoyed a share of lucky breaks and timely rescues. Few could have afforded a formal education as expensive as his—but many others have had equally expensive schooling, and have done much less good with it. When he first became a lawyer, too, his family connections brought him many important clients; but it was his able handling of their cases that moved him a giant step in the direction of a lucrative, lifelong practice and the amassing of a small fortune from the law. Among the public issues with which he became involved, his defense in writing to various well-connected colonists of the newspaperman Rivington strengthened the freedom of the press; we still feel its positive effects today.

Gouverneur made his mark, too, as a legislator. He served for two crucial terms each in the New York legislature and the Continental Congress, then went on to perform distinguished work at the Constitutional Convention and later, for nearly three years, in the U.S. Senate. Many of his speeches before these bodies are models of both style and substance. One fine example is his speech to the New York Provincial Congress on May 30, 1775, on the currency issue in the colonies. Less than a year later came an even more masterful oration, concerning the necessity of forming a new government, which he delivered before the Fourth Provincial Congress on May 24, 1776.

He served faithfully as assistant superintendent of finance for four key years—labors that still may not have received their proper due—was briefly a private agent to Britain, and spent several eventful years as minister plenipotentiary to France.

He was an early, hardworking, and foundation-laying member of the New York Committee of Safety; on the Secret Committee of the New York Provincial Congress, as a member of the New York Provincial Congress, he first met George Washington, with whom he later developed a long-standing close relationship and friendship. With Jay and Livingston, his talented classmates at King's College, he played an important role in drafting the final version of the state's first constitution (1777). Not only did this document serve as the state's official charter for decades, but also it influenced deeply the Constitution of the United States. Morris strove to expunge religiously prejudicial language from the state charter, and in the debates in Philadelphia he advocated freedom of worship. He labored, unsuccessfully, to introduce into the New York State charter an article prohibiting domestic slavery, and we have seen his complex efforts on this matter at the debates in Philadelphia years later.

In the Continental Congress, Gouverneur served on fourteen committees, many of them vital. He performed critical work on the Committee of Conference and as chair of the committee elected to respond to Lord North. It was he who drafted the instructions to the American peace commissioners in Paris.

From its fifty-two-word Preamble through its seventh and final article, the Constitution of the United States bears the marks of Morris's vigorous, crisp prose style. He had much to do with the content, too, of Articles I through IV. And he was graceful in debate: as Madison observes, he added to "the brilliancy of his Genius . . . what is too rare, a candid surrender of his opinions, when the lights of discussion satisfied him."

Scholars have neglected Morris's achievements at Philadelphia in 1787. To offer two recent examples: In *A Machine That Would Go of Itself: The Constitution in American Culture,* the historian Michael Kammen cites Morris just once, with a trenchant quotation from his correspondence that, however, has little to do with Morris's work on the convention floor and at his writing desk. And in a lengthy lecture, mainly on the U.S. Constitution, Supreme Court Associate Justice Antonin Scalia mentioned a number of lesser lights from the convention while citing Morris not at all.[3]

Morris's adventures in Europe would supply more than one entertaining novel, except that the details would be called incredible. On balance, he gave outstanding service to the United States, as Washington clearly recognized. When minister plenipotentiary to France, Morris occasionally went over the edge, as in his plans to liberate the king and queen; in hiding dozens of royalists; and in a 1794 episode I have omitted, the vetting of James Donatien Leray de Chaumont as U.S. emissary to Morocco and Algiers, which was unauthorized and clearly exceeded his instructions. Even then, his letters and memoranda reveal, he almost always had in mind his nation's best interest. This remained true even when he was volunteering his services to the British Foreign Office. Indeed, this office would have done well to take more of his advice, notably on the matter of Britain's European allies.

In stating, in the late 1880s, that Morris's diary and letters outdo those of any other American public official for their "amusing, light, and humorous touch," Theodore Roosevelt does not exaggerate.[4] But Roosevelt fails to give Gouverneur credit for his numerous accurate political predictions. In general, European scholarship has done better on this point than has American. Indeed, Morris came up often in the European table talk of his day, when the strength and accuracy of his prognostications was admired.

One of the statesman's first duties is to see situations clearly and make the proper deductions from them. Some people are able to see clearly and distinctly what is on the horizon, but do not foresee that the horizon will change. On many issues Morris was able to do both. In the short run, for example, he recognized the wisdom of having George Washington be the first U.S. head of state, and wrote Washington an eloquent, vigorous letter urging him to seek office, demonstrating his awareness of Washington's ability to mold the united colonies in what he knew would be times of tremendous and unforeseeable change.

Great writers often perceive clearly and express aptly what is only dimly perceived and ill expressed by their lesser contemporaries. Thanks to Morris's robust ability to enjoy life as the gift it generally is, his keen mind, and his understanding—worthy of Racine—of the complications in human character, his letters, and even some of his official documents and public speeches, rise to the level of literature. Especially to be prized are his letters to Carmichael, Greene, Grenville, Hamilton, Jefferson, King, the Merediths, Robert Morris, Necker, Parish, the Penns, Short, and, especially, Washington.

The family of Hamilton had explicitly asked Morris to deliver the eulogy for Alexander. And with the assent of Martha Washington, the city fathers of New York chose Morris to deliver the eulogy for the president and commander in chief. Only the one for Hamilton is up to Morris's standard, but it may be one of the finest such performances. Its phrasing is lovely in cadence, its sentiments are expressed with dignity and restraint, and its structure is harmonious; it ranks with the best public speeches of Burke, Disraeli,

Gladstone, and Lincoln. Several of those who heard it recorded their deep admiration of its delivery, as well.

Not that Morris led a blameless life. As U.S. minister to France, he treated Thomas Paine and John Paul Jones shamefully. Nor was he infallible; his military schemes, such as the early 1780s "New York strategy," were grandiose to the point of harebrainedness.

By the early 1780s, he had a reputation as something of a rake. It seems to have been well deserved. Until his marriage, at age fifty-seven, he apparently did not discriminate much between married and unmarried women. Indeed, of his known lovers, married women outnumber single women by two to one.

Wit seems to be the quality that suffers most from the passage of time, nor is it necessarily widely appreciated when it is offered. The acerbic wit of such public figures as U.S. Congressman Thomas Brackett Reed (1839–1902), British statesman Lord Birkenhead (1872–1930), and American statesman Adlai Stevenson (1900–1965) evidently worked strongly against their advancement to the highest positions in public life, and the same might be said about Morris.

Palmerston and Stevenson may be the historical figures best compared with Gouverneur Morris. Palmerston's rise was even faster: at age twenty-two he was a cabinet minister; and at twenty-five he was offered the Chancellorship of the Exchequer, which he declined. Both men served their countries for decades—though Morris's service was not continuous, nor was it always official.

Neither Morris nor Palmerston ever held the highest elected office in his country, although both were politically prescient. Both men were patient, physically and emotionally robust, and generally brilliant and hardworking public servants. Palmerston, however, lasted longer in politics. In 1864, he became Britain's Foreign Secretary a third time, and by this period he seems to have been nearly as popular as the Prime Minister, Lord John Russell. Palmerston seems to have been well liked in all layers of British society, whereas Morris seldom had any appeal for the "masses."

Both men were fascinating to women. Both were tall and strongly built, with a somewhat jaunty air, a large face, a broad brow, and blue eyes (Morris's were described by contemporaries as "China blue"). Palmerston, who did not marry until he was fifty-five years old, had so many mistresses that he was nicknamed Lord Cupid. Unlike Morris, however, Palmerston married a woman who greatly strengthened his social position: Lady Cowper, the famous Whig hostess and sister of Lord Melbourne.

On the American side of the Atlantic the public figure most like Morris might be Adlai Stevenson. Both men came from patrician families; Stevenson, like Morris, enjoyed the superlatively enriching friendships (at least) of intelligent and interesting women from his Ivy League days onward. (Stevenson married, however, much earlier than Morris, and not successfully; the marriage ended in angry divorce.) Like Morris, Stevenson was also a lawyer by schooling, and a brilliant speechmaker, letter writer, and wit.

After World War II, Adlai helped launch the United Nations and served twice as a delegate to this body (once under John F. Kennedy). He won a single term as governor of Illinois, then ran for president twice, in 1952 and 1956, against Dwight D. Eisenhower. One of his biographers remarks that Stevenson "was great more for what he was and stood for than what he directly accomplished."[5] From that sketch, it will be clear that Morris and Stevenson were alike in that neither appealed to a broad political constituency. Given the restricted state of the franchise at the time, Morris easily won election to the New York Provincial Congress and to two terms in the Continental Congress (his first appointment expired, but he was reappointed and relieved James Duane on October 22, 1799). Interestingly, some of his ablest colleagues in both chambers strongly supported his retention. In the voting for the Pennsylvania delegation to the Constitutional Convention, however, Gouverneur received just 33 votes of a possible 63, the fewest of any candidate elected. (It would be instructive to compare each delegate's rank in that vote with his record of achievement at the convention.) Morris's fourth major *elected* position, that of U.S. Senator, was not the outcome of a direct popular vote, but rather that of a ballot by the state legislature.

Human nature being what it is, we may not be surprised that a rich, witty man with literary, rhetorical, oratorical, and legislative skills such as Morris's should not be widely popular. Harder to understand is New York's failure to recognize his achievements. He represented his state with great credit in three important legislative bodies. He was a driving force behind the construction of the Erie Canal. He was a founder and an early president of the New-York Historical Society. He settled and raised a small family at the same place in the lower Bronx to which he had felt strongly attached his entire life. He served assiduously on the board of trustees of Columbia, the school from which, when it was King's College, he had received his two degrees. And yet, more than two and a half centuries after he was graduated, Columbia has yet to dedicate a building to his name, though it has honored, among others, his friends Hamilton and Jay. Surely Columbia ought to recognize and take pride in this alumnus.

Every man and woman is unique, and the most exceptional, such as Gouverneur Morris, defy comparison and calculation. At the outset of our story we took notice of our subject's name: "Gouverneur," which means, literally, "governor" in French, and which also carries echoes of the nautical terms which mean "to steer" and "to take the helm"; and "Morris," which is also the name for a lively British dance. Our subject distinguished himself by the manner of his pilotage, and he understood well how, and when, with a flourish and snap, to *Morris*. Let the final words, then, belong to our subject. He wrote of his last years thus:

I lead a quiet, and more than most of my fellow mortals, a happy Life. The Woman, to whom I am married, has much Genius, has been well educated, and possesses, with an affectionate Temper, Industry and love of Order. Our little Boy grows finely, and is generally admired. You may, then, opening your mind's Eye, behold your Friend, as he descends with tottering steps the bottom of Life's hill, supported by a kind Companion, a tender female Friend, and cheered by a little Prattler, who bids fair, if God shall spare his Life, to fill in due time the space his Father leaves.[6]

ACKNOWLEDGMENTS

NEEDLESS TO SAY, this biography of Gouverneur Morris's life and career, imperfect as it is, could never have been written without the courteous assistance and warm encouragement of many helpers. Juanita, Joseph, and Linda Kirschke have served as a steady source of joy and inspiration. Joe, a fine journalist, typed and edited an important portion of the manuscript.

Over the years of work on this biography, I have profited steadily from thoughtful conversations and correspondence with many distinguished colleagues whose minds are engrossed by similar Colonial, Revolutionary, and early Federal American problems and who gave me their kind counsel. Professors Clarence L. Ver Steeg, Mary A. Y. Gallagher, and Elizabeth M. Nuxoll, all at one time of the Robert Morris Papers; Eugene Sheridan, formerly senior associate editor of the Jefferson Papers; William R. Casto; Wythe H. Holt, Jr.; Frank Shuffleton; Roger J. Fechner; Dorothy Twohig, formerly of the Alexander Hamilton Papers and then of the George Washington Papers; Wendy Hilton; and David Moltke-Hansen have all contributed to the research on this biography. Professor Hans S. Haupt has examined this biography in manuscript with great and characteristic care.

Thanks largely to our Graduate English Committee, chaired successively by Professors Robert P. Wilkinson, Robert A. Kantra, Vincent B. Sherry, and Heather Hicks, I have benefited by having a succession of reliable, intelligent, and likable graduate assistants, especially Vicky Perdios, Jennifer Farthing, Ed Doran, Stanley Moyer, Jr., Jennifer Sherman, David Walls, Sean Flanagan, Patty Crouch, and Vic Sensenig. Vic's help has been beyond praise. My university students have, by their interest and suggestions, proven helpful and stimulating. Our department chairmen, especially Professors Sterling F. Delano, Robert P. Wilkinson, Charles Cherry, and Evan Radcliffe, have so arranged my heavy teaching schedule as to abet the completion of this book. Our departmental secretaries, Susan Burns, Madeline Di Pietro, and Cindy Farrell, have provided indispensable support. Last but not least, Kail Ellis, O.S.A., dean of arts and sciences at Villanova University, has helped with crucial scheduling adjustments and quiet confidence.

Over the past several years I have presented papers on aspects of Morris's life and career, and on these occasions I have received tactful and beneficial advice from the collegial audiences. These forums were as follows: "Gouverneur Morris (1752–1816): An Overview" (fall 1990), chaired by Professor Deborah A. Thomas, Villanova University; "Gouverneur Morris in Europe After the Revolution," East Central Conference/American Society for Eighteenth-Century Studies (EC/ASECS) (fall 1991), chaired by Professor Beverly Schneller, Millersville University; "Gouverneur Morris: An American Cassandra," ASECS (spring 1992), chaired by Professor Daniel E. Williams, University of Washington; "Gouverneur Morris as Literary Stylist," EC/ASECS (fall 1992), Philadelphia, chaired by the author; "Gouverneur Morris at the Constitutional Convention" (spring 1993), chaired by Professor John Engell, Providence College; "On Writing a Biography of Gouverneur Morris" (spring 1994), chaired by Professor Kenneth Silverman, the Biography Seminar, New York University; and "Gouverneur Morris and George Washington" (1999), Washington Bicentennial, Mount Vernon, Virginia.

Without the assistance of numerous librarians, the writing of this biography would have proven impossible. As always, the staffs of the Villanova University and Bryn Mawr College libraries have been meticulous, big-spirited, and efficient. The support provided by Villanova's Falvey Memorial Library reference staff is nearly beyond praise. I am also greatly indebted to the staffs of the three major Gouverneur Morris collections: the Morris Collection, bequeathed in the mid-1990s by the Smith family to the American Philosophical Society Library (4.5 cubic feet; about 2,000 items); the Morris Papers at the Butler Library, Columbia University (1,374 Morris items); and the Library of Congress (more than 700 items). At the production phase of my book, Princeton University's library generously loaned me the Papers of Gouverneur Morris (53 volumes) on microfilm. At the APS Library, Scott DeHaven and Robert Cox proved extremely helpful. At the Butler, I received assistance from the following: Kenneth Lohf, Rare Books; Rudolph Ellenbogen; Bernard R. Crystal, assistant librarian for manuscripts; and Patricia Cahill, reference librarian in the Rare Books and Manuscripts Library. Also at Columbia University the librarian of the Columbiana Collection, Holly Haswell, proved unstintingly helpful. At the

Library of Congress's Madison Library, the large staff could not have been any more efficient or helpful. The staff at the New York State Library at Albany provided useful information. At the New-York Historical Society (for whose foundation Morris was largely responsible), the papers of Robert R. Livingston and William Duer proved especially valuable, and I received generous assistance there from Margaret Heilbrun, as well as from Daphne Arnaiz and Elliot Meadows. The staffs of the Historical Society of Pennsylvania and its neighbor, the Library Company of Philadelphia, were, as always, uniformly helpful. Also in Philadelphia, Dr. Thomas A. Horrocks made available the collections of the College of Physicians and put me in touch with some otherwise unobtainable medical information. The librarians of the Van Pelt–Dietrich Library of the University of Pennsylvania, the British Library (London), and the British Public Record Office extended me every possible scholarly courtesy.

Wendy Schmalz, Laura Bucko, and Emma Sweeney, of Harold Ober Associates, have provided "Oberesque" help with this project; to them I offer my sincerest thanks. My publisher, Thomas Dunne, has waited for this manuscript with a patience for which I am very grateful. Also at Thomas Dunne Books, Peter Wolverton has proven understanding and helpful. I would also like to thank Carolyn Chu, the tactful, intelligent, and efficient former associate editor at Thomas Dunne Books; and Peter Joseph, the biography's thoughtful point editor. Associate editor Katherine A. Carlson has been additionally helpful. Jolanta Benal has proven a fantastic copy editor. Darren Poley and Paul and Kathy Barents have generously and thoughtfully perused the first pass manuscript; and Darren closely reviewed the second pass as well. Cynthia J. McGroarty has helped in important ways with the Morris Chronology and the Historical Time Line and has provided much additional assistance and support. I alone, however, am responsible for any of my book's defects.

Lastly, I would like to thank the lady to whom this book is dedicated. For a boy without siblings and then a young man who grew up without a father, and whose mother was perforce seldom around, she proved the ideal understanding, supportive, and confidence-emanating aunt.

NOTES

PREFACE

1. *Observations on the American Revolution* was published in the *Pennsylvania Gazette,* 1780. (For a full discussion, see Chapter 3.)
2. Gouverneur Morris, *A Diary of the French Revolution,* ed. Beatrix Cary Davenport (Boston: Houghton Mifflin, 1939), vol. 1, p. xiii.
3. *The Proceedings of the Provincial Congress,* New York, February 28, 1776. See also *New York in the Revolution,* comp. Berthold Fernow (Albany: New York State Archives Series, 1887), vol. 1, pp. 75–76.
4. Alan C. Aimone and Eric I. Manders, "A Note on New York City's Independent Companies, 1775–1776," *New York* (January 1982), pp. 59–73.
5. Jacob Hiltzheimer, *Extracts from the Diary, 1765–1798,* ed. Jacob Cox Parsons (Philadelphia: W. F. Fell and Company, 1893), p. 43.
6. Letter from George Washington to Gouverneur Morris, New York, October 13, 1789. Add. MSS. Folio 233.28065. British Museum MSS. British Library, London, England. For Morris's service as a private agent, I am indebted to the generosity of Professor Kenneth R. Bowling.
7. See Hippolyte Taine, *Derniers essais de critique et d'histoire* [1894]. 6th ed. (Paris: Hachette, 1923), p. 307.
8. Jared Sparks, *The Life of Gouverneur Morris* (Boston: Gray and Bowen, 1832).
9. See, for example, Sparks's journal and correspondence for February 11, 1831, in Herbert B. Adams's *Life and Writings of Jared Sparks* (Boston: Houghton Mifflin, 1893), vol. 2, pp. 164–65.
10. Theodore Roosevelt, *Gouverneur Morris* [1889] (reprinted, New Rochelle, N.Y.: Arlington House, 1970).
11. Howard Swiggett, *The Extraordinary Mr. Morris* (Garden City, N.Y.: Doubleday, 1952).
12. Mary-Jo Kline, *Gouverneur Morris and the New Nation, 1775–1788* (New York: Arno Press, 1978).
13. Max M. Mintz, "Gouverneur Morris, 1752–1779" (Ph.D. dissertation, New York University, 1957); and Max M. Mintz, *Gouverneur Morris and the American Revolution* (Norman: University of Oklahoma Press, 1970).
14. Richard Brookhiser, *Gentleman Revolutionary: Gouverneur Morris—The Rake Who Wrote the Constitution* (New York: Free Press, 2003).
15. William Howard Adams, *Gouverneur Morris: An Independent Life* (New Haven: Yale University Press, 2003).

1. FAMILY ROOTS AND EDUCATION

1. In 1759, at the Verrazano Narrows, Andrew Burnaby reports "innumerable porpoises playing upon the surface of the water." *Travels Through North America . . . 1759–60.* 3rd ed. (London: H. Wessels, 1904), p. 111.

    Max M. Mintz's *Gouverneur Morris and the American Revolution* (Norman: University of Oklahoma Press, 1970) and "Gouverneur Morris, 1752–1779: The Emergence of a Nationalist" (Ph.D. dissertation, New York University, 1957), as well as Mary-Jo Kline's *Gouverneur Morris* (New York: Arno Press, 1978), have been largely used for this chapter. For Morris's ancestry, childhood, and early education, use has also been made of these sources and repositories: Stephen Jenkins, *The Story of the Bronx: 1639–1912* (New York: Putnam, 1912); *Biographical Directory of the American Congress, 1774–1971* (Washington, D.C.: Government Printing Office, 1974); *Dictionary of American Biography,* vol. 13 (New York: Scribners, 1934); *Encyclopedia Americana,* vol. 19 (New York: Grolier, 1990); W. W. Spooner, "The Morris Family of Morrisania," *American Historical Magazine,* vol. 1, no. 1 (winter 1906), pp. 25–44; the Genealogy Room of the New York Public Library; the Morris collection at Columbia University; and Monroe Johnson, "The Gouverneur Genealogy," *New York Genealogical and Biographical Record,* vol. LXX (January 1939), pp. 134–136.

2. On Sarah's Huguenot roots, see Mintz (1957), pp. 11–12, in particular. Concerning the commercial success and political acumen of Sarah's uncle (Gouverneur Morris's maternal great uncle), Abraham (or "Brom" as he was known within the family), see Mintz, *Gouverneur Morris,* pp. 12–13.

    Not irrelevant to Sarah's family in the New World is the early segment of W. F. Eccles's *France in America* (New York: Harper and Row, 1972). On the Huguenots' difficulties in North America after the revocation of the Edict of Nantes, see, in particular, pp. 9–10 and 26–27. On the same general subject, see Henry P. Beers, *The French in North America: A Bibliographical Guide* (Baton Rouge: Louisiana State University Press, 1957).

3. Eugene R. Sheridan, *Lewis Morris* (Syracuse, N.Y.: Syracuse University Press, 1981), pp. 19–24 and 46–48; and Charles M. Andrews, *The Colonial Period of American History* (New Haven: Yale University Press, 1937), vol. 3, pp. 138–39.

4. Sheridan, p. 114.

5. Dixon Ryan Fox, *Caleb Heathcote: Gentleman Colonist* [1926] (reprinted, New York: Cooper Square, 1971).

6. See Eugene R. Sheridan, *Lewis Morris,* especially pp. x–xi; 2–5; and Chapter 2, "Morris's Inconsistencies," *passim,* but, in particular, pp. 19–25. See also Stanley Katz, *Newcastle's New York: Anglo-American Politics, 1732–1753* (Cambridge: Harvard University Press, 1968), especially pp. 70–73. Sheridan points out that age-induced infirmity made Lewis Senior unable to carry out his duties as governor of New Jersey. That at this age he was made governor, however, seems remarkable.

7. Bernard Bailyn, *The Origins of American Politics* (New York: Knopf, 1970), p. 111. See also Eugene Sheridan, ed., *The Papers of Lewis Morris* (Newark: New Jersey Historical Society, 1993) 3 vol., *passim.*

8. Eustace Percy, *Some Memories* (London: Eyre and Spottiswoode, 1958), p. 12. After growing up at Etchingham, Sussex, Percy (later first Baron Percy of Newcastle, 1887–1958) served in the British diplomatic corps and wrote eight books. My generalization in the next paragraph of the text concerning the development of talent in public affairs potentially induced by the "large private responsibility" (Percy, p. 15) of running an estate, is based on the perusal of books by authors such as Percy who had managed Morrisania-style estates, from conversations with acquaintances among the few remaining members of Philadelphia Main Line society with large land holdings, and from a dollop of imagination.

9. Jared Sparks, *The Life of Gouverneur Morris,* vol. 1, p. 4.

10. See *Staats Long Morris, Mary Lawrence and Richard Morris v. Sarah Morris,* Packet 68, Exhibit D, Testimony (New York State Court of Appeals, 1785), for a detailed inventory of the personal property of Lewis Morris.

11. Jon Butler, *The Huguenots in America: A Refugee People in New World Society* (Harvard Historical Monographs LXXII, Harvard University Press, 1983). See especially pp. 140–141 and 243, n. 83; see also pp. 194–97 and 248–49. And see the chapter on the Huguenots in Amsterdam in Lucian Fosdick, *The French Blood in America* (New York: Gotham Press, 1906), as well as James P. Wickersham, *A History of Education in Pennsylvania* (Lancaster: Inquirer Publishing, 1886), chapter 4, in particular.

12. Information about the Academy's curriculum and students is culled from a wealth of detail in the archives of the University of Pennsylvania, Rare Books and Manuscripts Collection, Van Pelt Library. See also Thomas H. Montgomery, *A History of the University of Pennsylvania from its Foundation to A.D. 1770* (Philadelphia: G. W. Jacobs, 1900), especially pp. 52–60; 531, 543; and 549.

13. New York Wills, Liber 23: 426–30 (Nov. 19, 1760). Surrogate's Office, Hall of Records, New York City, as well as New York Surrogate's Court, *Abstracts of Wills on File in the Surrogate's Office, City of New York,* vols. VI and VII.

   Nevertheless, Richard received a Yale degree in 1752, Lewis in 1746. See Franklin B. Dexter, *Biographical Sketches of the Graduates of Yale College, with Annals of the College History, May 1745–May 1763* (New York: Holt, 1896), vol. 2, pp. 82–83.

14. At that time roughly 14,000 people lived on Manhattan Island, mostly near the docks in the area now known as the Battery, and the city had roughly 3,000 dwellings. The College was bounded by what now are Murray, Barclay, Church, and Greenwich Streets. At the time Gouverneur applied for admission to King's only three of the American colleges—Harvard (1636), William and Mary (1693), and Yale (1701)—were more than fifty years old.

15. Martin, *Men in Rebellion* (New Brunswick, N.J.: Rutgers University Press, 1973), p. 128. In his masterful study *The Colonial Colleges in the War for American Independence* (Millwood, N.Y.: Associated Faculty Presses, 1986), John F. Roche estimates the number of American colonists then living who had graduated or even attended college as very small. The 1776 figure has been estimated at between 2,500 and 3,000, about one of every one thousand males.

   Among those who did not attend college were Ben Franklin, Washington, Robert Morris, and Patrick Henry. But they understood the value of University study. "Education generally," Washington, for example, writes, is "one of the surest means of enlightening and giving just ways of thinking to our Citizens" (George Washington to Alexander Hamilton, September 1, 1796). In *The Papers of Alexander Hamilton,* vol. 20, Harold C. Syrett ed. (New York: Columbia University Press, 1974), p. 311. In this letter, Washington essentially expresses his regrets for not having incorporated into his farewell address a proposal for a national university.

   To compare in detail the curriculum of King's with that of contemporary colleges— Thomas Jefferson's William and Mary; James Madison's College of New Jersey (now Princeton); and Nathan Hale's Yale—would require a separate monograph. The groundwork for it has been prepared; see in particular James J. Walsh, *Education of the Founding Fathers of the Republic* (New York: Fordham University Press, 1935); Roche, op. cit.; and David W. Robson, *Educating Republicans: The College in the Era of the American Revolution, 1750–1800* (Westport, Conn.: Greenwood, 1985).

   As regards Yale College, excellent exposition has been provided by Louis Leonard Tucker. See, for example, *Connecticut's Seminary of Sedition: Yale College* (Chester, Conn.: The American Revolution Bicentennial Commission of Connecticut, 1974); *Puritan Protagonist: President Thomas Clap of Yale College* (Chapel Hill: University of North Carolina Press, 1962); and "President Thomas Clap and the Rise of Yale College, 1740–1766," *The Historian* (November 1956), 66–81. On Hale's education, see also John W. Maguire, "Nathan Hale: Connecticut Teacher and Patriot," *Journal of Rural and Small Schools* 8 (spring 1989), 48–50.

   On Jefferson's William and Mary, see Dumas Malone, *Jefferson and His Time* (Boston: Little, Brown, 1961), 43–61. For James Madison's education, his papers provide an abundance of valuable documents, as well as helpful commentary. See, for the period

1751–1779, *The Papers of James Madison,* William T. Hutchinson and William M. E. Rachal, eds. (Chicago: University of Chicago Press, 1961), vol. 1, pp. XLI–61 and 78–79 especially. For analysis of Madison's education, see Irving Brant, *James Madison: The Virginia Revolutionary, 1751–1780* (Indianapolis: Bobbs-Merrill, 1941), pp. 56–103. Also valuable on Madison's College of New Jersey are Sheldon S. Cohen and Larry R. Gerlach, "Princeton in the Coming of the American Revolution," *New Jersey History* XCII (winter 1974), 62–92, as well as Francis L. Broderick, "Pulpit, Physics and Politics: The Curriculum of the College of New Jersey, 1746–1794," *William and Mary Quarterly.* 3rd ser. VI (Jan. 1949), 42–57; see especially pp. 46ff.

During the late Colonial period, many sons of well-to-do parents still traveled abroad for their university educations. An excellent essay on the Oxford and Cambridge schooling available during this period can be found in "The Training of a Statesman," *The Edinburgh Review* CCXII (July 1910), 54–84.

As concerns French university education during the period, L.W.B. Brockliss's masterful *French Higher Education in the Seventeenth and Eighteenth Centuries: A Cultural History* (Oxford: Clarendon Press, 1989) can be recommended. In *The Papers of Robert Morris* (Pittsburgh: University of Pittsburgh Press, 1977) can be found extensive discussion of R.M.'s reasoning concerning a European university education for his sons. In the *Papers* (vol. 3, n. 2, pp. 58–59) the editors neatly survey the documents available on this question. In brief, the problems R.M. encountered in trying to provide his two eldest with a first-quality education abroad led him to have them educated at home.

Also recommended for the subject of late Colonial American college education are Howard Miller, *The Revolutionary College: American Presbyterian Higher Education, 1707–1837* (New York: New York University Press, 1976); and a more specialized monograph, Jurgen Herbst's *And Sadly Teach* (Madison, Wisc.: University of Wisconsin Press, 1989). On the subject of how much King's College students favored the Revolution, see also Howard H. Peckham, "College Ante Bellum Attitudes of College Professors and Students Toward the American Revolution," *Pennsylvania Magazine of History and Biography* XCV (January 1971), 50–72. College of New Jersey, Harvard, and Yale students also had their oars in.

16. For the early years of King's College, see *A History of Columbia University, 1754–1904* (New York: Columbia University Press, 1904), especially books 2 and 3; and Herbert Schneider and Carol Schneider, eds., *Samuel Johnson, President of King's College,* vol. 4 of 4 (New York: Columbia University Press, 1929). *From King's College to Columbia 1746–1800* (New York: Columbia University Press, 1976) is the most valuable source for the King's College years.

Of daily work in the King's College classroom of Morris's time, little is known; there are few such primary sources as lesson plans, student diaries, tutorial outlines and student papers, quizzes and examinations. All these were no doubt dispersed to wind and fire by the British, who also systematically destroyed the college library.

The major British campaign in 1776 centered on New York City. Although the King's building was spared the torch when New York was overrun, in mid-1776 the British turned it into a British army hospital, and so it remained until November 25, 1783. Between its first graduating class, in 1758, and 1776, when it was closed "for the duration" by the British army, it graduated only 108 students, 56 percent of those matriculated. See the *New York Public Library, Research Libraries Dictionary Catalog of the Manuscript Division* (Boston: G.K. Hall, 1967), *passim.* The statutes of King's College from our period are printed in Richard B. Morris, ed., *John Jay, The Making of a Revolutionary: Unpublished Papers, 1745–1780* (New York: Harper & Row, 1975), pp. 55–64.

17. See *Robert Morris Papers,* vol. V, pp. 435–446; letter, GM to Samuel Osgood, October 30, 1785 (Osgood Papers, BV sec "O," New-York Historical Society); and GM to John Rutledge, February 3, 1783 (*Robert Morris Papers,* vol. VII, pp. 393–99).

18. On Gouverneur's fondness for Shakespeare, see Sparks, vol. 1, pp. 5–6.

By the advent of the American Revolution, most schools for girls remained sex segregated, and had shorter class attendance periods. These schools offered another means of gaining literary and mathematical competence which was already quite high for both sexes. Despite formal proposals by such individuals as Benjamin Rush to create regular school systems for girls and young women, most females of the period were educated at home, if at all. On the subject, of more than passing interest is Fred G. Robbins, "Salaries of School Teachers in Colonial America," *Monthly Labor Review* 28 (winter 1929), 27–31.

19. Ancillary information concerning Morris's King's years can be found in the four volumes edited by Herbert and Carol Schneider, *Samuel Johnson, President of King's College* (New York: Columbia University Press, 1929), as well as in Max M. Mintz's *Gouverneur Morris and the American Revolution* (Norman, Okla: University of Oklahoma Press, 1970). The Iselin Collection (formerly at Katonah House, Bedford, New York; now at the New-York Historical Society) contains virtually all the textbooks used during Gouverneur Morris's period at King's.

20. On the challenges presented Morris's American college class cohort, surprisingly scant relevant periodical literature currently exists. The reader can, however, refer to Robert Middlekauff, " 'The Persistent Tradition': The Classical Curriculum in 18th Century New England," *William and Mary Quarterly* 18 (January 1961), 54–67. Middlekauff's article considers the curricula of Brown, Harvard, and Yale. The King's College requirements seem, on paper at least, more demanding than those.

In the "Bibliographic Essay" of his *Education in the Forming of American Society* (Chapel Hill, N.C.: University of North Carolina Press), pp. 86–103, especially, Bernard Bailyn provides numerous suggestions for scholarly research; thus far, most of his suggested research topics remain "uncovered."

21. Morris seems to have absorbed most from Demosthenes, on whom the most cogent commentator is Lionel Pearson. See especially *The Art of Demosthenes* (New York: Scholar's Press, 1981). Pearson also demonstrates the ways Demosthenes influenced Cicero: See, for instance, his "Cicero's Debt to Demosthenes in the Verrines," *Pacific Coast Philology* 3, no. 3 (1968), 49–54, and "The Development of Demosthenes as a Political Orator," *Phoenix* 18 no. 2 (1964), 95–109. In the latter article Pearson remarks that "Cicero . . . would have been quite ready to admit that he had learnt more about narrative from Demosthenes than from rhetorical textbooks or teachers of rhetoric" (p. 109).

Demosthenes provided Morris a salutary public example: he too began his speech-giving career early—as soon as he came of age, at eighteen.

22. Austin B. Keep, *The Library in Colonial New York* (1909; reprint, New York: B. Franklin, 1970) p. 200. On the "book world" of eighteenth-century America, a useful compendium of source materials has concisely been assembled by Cathy N. Davidson: *Revolution and the Word* (New York: Oxford University Press, 1968), pp. 266–74, notes 24 and 29 to chapter 1 and notes 6, 9, and 39 to chapter 2. Throughout Morris's adolescence and the remaining years before the Revolution, three newspapers were regularly published in New York.

23. As a final demonstration the British officers had their men grease the flagpole in New York Harbor.

24. Further evidence of the available library resources in New York at the time emerges from several scholarly surveys and assessments. See: Keep, op. cit., especially pp. 16–17, 58–59, 62–63, 80–85, 94–97, 118–127, 130–135, 150–151, and 198–99; Esther Singleton, *Social New York under the Georges, 1714–1776* (1902; reprint, New York: Blom, 1969), especially pp. 337–39; and Henry F. May and David Lundberg, "The Enlightened Reader in America," *American Quarterly* 28 (May 1976), 262–95. Letters and diaries by foreign observers of America during Morris's period often corroborate these scholars' work. For example, in 1771 the reliable British observer William Eddis remarks that "in short, very little difference is, in reality, observable" between the cultural background "of the wealthy colonist and the wealthy Briton." *Letters from America,* ed. Audrey C. Land (Cambridge, Mass.: Harvard University Press, 1969), pp. 57–58.

Additional material on the library of King's College, 1757–1776, and other colonial libraries in New York can be found in miscellaneous manuscripts, Austin Baxter Keep (1875–1932) Collection, Boxes I and V, New-York Historical Society. For the book-reading tastes of Morris's American contemporaries, see James D. Hart, *The Popular Book* (New York: Oxford University Press, 1959), 24–25; and Frank L. Mott, *Golden Multitudes* (New York: Macmillan, 1947), pp. 303–305 and 315–317 in particular. In "Importation of French Literature in New York City, 1750–1800," *Studies in Philology* 27 (October 1931), 235–51, Howard M. Jones helpfully summarizes Americans' taste in French books.

According to Eugene Sheridan, Gouverneur's grandfather Lewis Morris had accumulated a personal library of roughly "3,000 historical, legal, literary, philosophical, political, scientific, and theological works." This number compares "favorably in terms of size to the 3,500 volumes in Harvard College's 1723 library." Sheridan also highlights the evidence that Lewis Morris, Sr., had actually read many of his books. See Eugene R. Sheridan, ed., *The Papers of Lewis Morris, vol. 1: 1698–1730* (Newark: New Jersey Historical Society, 1991). p. xv and p. xxxi, notes 6 to 8.

25. In 1987, the Library Company of Philadelphia presented a six-month exhibit of copies of these books, called "The Delegates' Library." There was no catalogue. Circulation records for the delegates do not exist.

26. David W. Robson, *Educating Republicans: The College in the Era of the American Revolution, 1750–1800* (Westport, Conn.: Greenwood Press, 1985), p. 78. My analysis draws substantially on the researches of Robson, pp. 76–87 in particular; and on James Walsh, *Education of the Founding Fathers of the Republic* (New York: Fordham University Press, 1935), pp. 187–205.

Isocrates seems to have been the first author who wrote to be read rather than recited. There is no trace of a reading public in the ancient world until about the end of the fifth century. At Rome, apart from archives of official documents, there is no trace of libraries before the first century B.C. Most scholars probably underestimate how well the educated elite of Morris's day knew the Greek writers. For lack of typographic fonts for classical Greek, colonial Americans very seldom quoted Greek in print, and no Greek books were printed in America until after the Revolution. (The late Edwin L. Wolf, of the Free Library of Philadelphia, provided this information in private conversation.)

In America, Franklin's fustigations on the "unaccountable prejudice in favor of ancient customs and beliefs" (1789) are better known, but in 1787 William Vans Murray, in his *Political Sketches,* argues that analogies from antiquity were not valid, were indeed dangerous. He maintained that the new nation was a unique society, and that history had no lessons to teach America. In such beliefs Franklin and Vans Murray followed the often short-sighted Machiavelli. Regardless, the founders had frequent recourse to ancient Greek and Roman examples (not to mention Old and New Testament ones). On this topic generally, see Meyer Reinhold's scholarship. And see, for example, J. W. Eadie's *Classical Traditions in Early America* (Ann Arbor: University of Michigan Press, 1976).

27. In a struggle for control over the North African country of Numidia (approximately present-day Algeria), Jugurtha's attack on his cousin Adherbal provoked a war with Rome, which ended in Jugurtha's capture and execution.

28. See, for instance, C. Nicolet, *The World of the Citizen in Republican Rome,* P. S. Falls, trans. (Los Angeles: University of California Press, 1980). On pp. 383–84 Nicolet ably summarizes his narrative and presents the lengthy list of scholars who have made substantial contributions in the same vein. In *The Nobility of the Roman Republic,* Robin Seager, trans. (New York: Barnes & Noble, 1969), Matthias Gelzer indicates further the way "the nobility ruled the Roman republic" (p. 53). See also pp. 18–27, 52, and 139, especially.

29. Minutes of the Governors of King's College. Meetings of May 13, 1766, and February 6, 1767. This prank was the merest peccadillo beside the student disorders at Harvard and Yale. See, for instance, Theodore Crane, "Harvard Student Disorders in 1770," *New England Quarterly* 61 (March 1988), 25–54. This essay relates substantially more than its title indicates. In the Harvard disorder of 1770, perhaps significantly, one of the worst transgressors was Winthrop Sargent, who became one of his college's most distinguished graduates. Sargent deserves a worthy biography. This author's sketch of him in *American*

National Biography, volume 19 (New York: Oxford University Press, 1999), might be a good starting point for prospective biographers.

30. Myles Cooper to Samuel Johnson, August 27, 1766. Samuel Johnson correspondence, III (Columbia University Libraries Special Collections).

31. For Morris's fortitude, see Julia L. Delafield, *The Biographies of Francis Lewis and Morgan Lewis,* volume 1 (New York: A.D.F. Randolph, 1877), p. 75. For the extent of his injuries, see, for example, William Pierce's sketch of Morris at the Constitutional Convention of 1787, first published in Max Farrand, ed., *The Records of the Federal Convention of 1787* (New Haven: Yale University Press, 1937).

32. The newspaper accounts were: *New York Gazette, Weekly Mercury* (both May 23, 1768), and *New York Journal* (May 26, 1768). See Milton H. Thomas, "King's College Commencement in the Newspapers," *Columbia University Quarterly* XXII (1919–1920), 226–47. On the Literary Society, see also Beverly McAnear, "American Imprints Concerning King's College," *Papers of the Bibliographical Society of America* XLIV (4th quarter, 1950), 336.

   Benjamin Moore later became the second Episcopalian bishop of New York. In this position, in 1806, after some hesitation, he administered the church's last blessings to the dying Alexander Hamilton.

33. The "Oration on Wit and Beauty" is in the Gouverneur Morris Collection, Columbia University Library Special Collections.

   For a pioneering analysis of the topical breakdown of commencement speeches of the day, see Howard H. Peckham, "Collegia Ante Bellum," *New England Quarterly* 54 (January 1971), p. 55 in particular.

34. "Oration on Love," 1771. Gouverneur Morris Collection, Columbia University Library, special collections.

35. The rules, regulations, and minutes of the debates, and the drafts of the arguments, are all but one in the handwriting of Peter Van Schaack. The introductory remarks on the Society are by Henry C. Van Schaack. Altogether, eighteen items are included in the New-York Historical Society Collections, 512 (Debating Society, N.Y.C.). Admittedly, there is no direct evidence that Morris was a member, but the membership records are incomplete, and there are a few insignificant references to him in the extant documents.

36. The first law school in America—the Litchfield Law School, now defunct—opened in 1784, followed by Harvard in 1817 and Yale in 1826. The first university law lectures did not begin until 1779, at William and Mary. Thus, there is some justification to Roscoe Pound's assertion that the profession did not begin in America until the nineteenth century. See "Legal Education in the United States," *Encyclopaedia Britannica* (1948). In a market economy, it seems likely that the number of lawyers would reflect the size and diversity of the population. At the time of Morris's birth, the population of the colonies was approximately 1½ million; by 1774, this figure had grown to roughly 2½ million. These population estimates come from Richard Morris, ed., *Encyclopedia of American History* (New York: Harper & Row, 1953), p. 442, 486.

37. See Alfred Z. Reed, *Training for the Public Profession of the Law* (Boston: The Merrymount Press, 1921), especially chapter IV, "Authorities Admitting into the Practice of the Law." Reed points out that "the law and the legal education of England, of England's self-governing colonies and of the United States resembled the branches of a great tree, which reveal at all times their common origin, and yet have each developed along independent lines of their own" (p. 5). As a result, even as early as the mid-eighteenth century, New York's official means of appointing members of the bar was an anachronism.

38. "My" curriculum draws on the following accounts: Herbert A. Johnson, "John Jay: Lawyer in a Time of Transition, 1764–1775," in *Essays on New York Colonial Legal History,* Herbert A. Johnson, ed. (Westport, Conn.; Greenwood Press, 1981), pp. 125–57; the same author's *John Jay: Colonial Lawyer* (Ph.D. diss., Columbia University, 1965); Frank Monaghan, *John Jay* (New York: Bobbs-Merrill, 1935), pp. 39–42 in particular; Max Mintz, *Gouverneur Morris,* especially pp. 23–27; but see also pp. 28–29 for additional commentary

on the import of Morris's legal clerkship readings; Julius Goebel, "The Courts and the Law in Colonial New York," in Alexander C. Flick, ed. *History of the State of New York*, volume 3. (New York: Columbia University Press, 1933), pp. 36–43 in particular; and on some valuable grazing in the manuscript records of the New York colonial courts.

That case law was not part of legal studies then may seem odd. In the colonial period, however, only Pennsylvania, Maryland, and Virginia reported cases and opinions. Throughout the colonies, the acts of the Assemblies were regularly printed and periodically revised to eliminate repealed statutes. But in pre-Revolutionary New York, no attempt was made to reduce case law to a written or printed form. Although the colonial New York laws were compiled and published twice during Morris's lifetime—in 1752 and 1773—and the sessions laws regularly reported, regular reporting of New York cases did not begin until 1794.

On this question, as on several others, Charles Warren's highly acclaimed *A History of the American Bar* (1911; rpt. New York: Howard Fertig, 1966) is slightly off, and therefore misleading. See, for example, p. 4.

On the importance eventually assumed by Blackstone's *Commentaries* (first published in 1765–1769) in America, see William S. Holdsworth, *The Historians of Anglo-American Law* (New York: Columbia University Press, 1928), pp. 54–59.

39. In *Legal Evolution* (Cambridge, Eng.: Cambridge University Press, 1980).

40. The "Treatise" is in New-York Historical Society B. V. Sec. TREATISE.

Not surprisingly, other colonies also had professionally useful and handy legal documents—in Pennsylvania, for example, James Logan's "The Charge to the Grand Jury" (Philadelphia, 1723) and "A Dialogue Shewing What's Therein to Be Found" (Philadelphia, 1725). These documents are now in the Historical Society of Pennsylvania Rare Manuscripts Collection.

41. Information concerning the Moot Club is primarily from New-York Historical Society, B. V. Sec. M, Breton #555. This archive includes the minutes, the questions debated, and the rules and regulations of the Club on various debate topics. In the same volume are abstracts relating to the rules of the New York Provincial Supreme Court, 1699–1788.

Of the twenty-two meetings for which notes survive, Gouverneur Morris attended ten. Reliable commentary on the activities of the Moot can be found in Herbert A. Johnson, *John Jay: Colonial Lawyer*, pp. 177–81.

42. Edmund Morgan and F. X. Dwyer, *Introduction to the Study of Law*, 2nd ed. (Chicago: Callaghan, 1948), pp. 40–41.

43. Minute Book of the Supreme Court of Judicature, April 18, 1769–May 2, 1772, 448–49. Office of the County Clerk, Hall of Records, New York City.

44. Felix Frankfurter, *Of Law and Life and Other Things That Matter: Papers and Addresses of Felix Frankfurter, 1956–1963,* Philip B. Kurland, ed. (Cambridge, Mass.: Harvard University Press, 1965), p. 7.

45. On this subject see especially Paul M. Hamlin, *Legal Education in Colonial New York* (1939; rpt. New York: Da Capo Press, 1979), p. 6 and p. 11, n. 22. See also the comment on "the prestige question" in Charles Warren, *A History of the American Bar* (1966; rpt. New York: H. Fertig, 1991).

Since the ancient Greeks, at least, most sensible people have recognized the importance of having good lawyers. On this subject, see especially Werner Jaeger, *Paideia,* tr. Gilbert Highet (New York: Oxford University Press, 1939), vol. 1, p. 107 especially and n. 2 in particular.

2. EARLY LEGAL PRACTICE AND NEW YORK POLITICS

1. Morris to William Smith, Jr., February 20, 1772. This letter appears first in Sparks, vol. 1, but I quote from Max Mintz, *Gouverneur Morris and the American Revolution* (Norman, Okla.: University of Oklahoma Press, 1970), p. 31. Gouverneur's physical description is

drawn in part from Howard Swiggett, *The Extraordinary Mr. Morris* (New York: Double-day, 1952), p. 4.

This letter alone tends to give the lie to the sense many of Morris's contemporaries had and many scholars still have that, from puberty onward, Gouverneur always possessed an unfailing self-confidence. See, for example, the sketches of Gouverneur Morris in both versions of the original Dictionary of American Biography.

During Gouverneur Morris's lifetime, to be over six feet tall was remarkable. The average American male was roughly five feet, six inches tall, and the average European male likely even smaller.

For the elite Americans of the pre-Revolutionary era, a post-graduation trip to Britain often served some of the functions of the Grand Tour for post-Oxbridge students. See Christopher Hibbert, *The Grand Tour* (London: Thames Methuen, 1987), pp. 20, 50, 52, 56.

2. See Joyce Goodfriends's *Before the Melting Pot: Society and Culture in Colonial New York City* (Princeton, N.J.: Princeton University Press, 1992).

3. In these statistics I extrapolate from the data provided by J. Potter in D. V. Glass and D.E.C. Eversley, *Population in History* (London: Edward Arnold, 1965), pp. 653–54; and Alice Jones Hanson, *American Colonial Wealth: Documents and Methods,* vol. 3, 2nd ed., rev. (New York: Arno Press, 1978), p. 1790. Relevant information concerning colonial travel can be found in the ultimate chapter of Charles M. Andrews, *Colonial Folkways* (New Haven: Yale University Press, 1919).

4. New York City census, which shows 18,726 whites and 3,137 African Americans. See Evarts B. Greene and Virginia D. Harrington, *American Population Before the Federal Census of 1790* (New York: Columbia University Press, 1932), p. 102. My interpolation profits from the statistical data provided by J. Potter, "The Growth of Population in America, 1700–1860," in D. V. Glass and D.E.C. Eversley, *Population in History,* p. 639.

5. Karin Calvert, "The Function of Fashion in 18th Century America," in *Of Consuming Interests: The Style of Life in the 18th Century,* Cary Corson and Ronald Hoffman, eds. (Charlottesville, Va.: University Press of Virginia, 1994), p. 272. Concerning the musical interests and performances of the time, see especially Esther Singleton, *Social New York Under the Georges, 1714–1776* (1902; rpt. New York: Blom, 1969), pp. 286–91 and 296–99; and Wye J. Allanbrook and Wendy Hilton, "Dance Rhythms in Mozart's Arias," *Early Music* (February 1992), pp. 142–49. The first American book on dancing appears appropriately early: John Griffith, *A Collection of the Newest and Most Fashionable Country Dances and Cotillions* (Providence, R.I.: Carter, 1788).

As regards eighteenth-century dance, I am particularly indebted to the advice of the following: Professor Wendy Hilton, the Juilliard School and Stanford University; Ms. Paige Whitley-Baugess, New Bern, N.C.; Ms. Diane Feingold and Ms. Suzanne Day-one of the Library of the Performing Arts, Lincoln Center, New York; and Ms. Jane Peck of Minneapolis. All five have helped with information in conversations, and Professor Hilton and Ms. Whitley-Baugess have made interesting and educational tapes of dance performances in eighteenth-century style available to me for viewing.

Valuable secondary sources on eighteenth-century American music are Ronald L. Davis, *A History of Music in American Life,* volume 1, *The Formative Years* (Malabar, Fl.: Kreiger, 1982), and H. Wiley Hitchcock, *Music in the United States: An Historical Introduction,* 2nd ed. (Englewood Cliffs, N.J.: Prentice-Hall, 1974), pp. 32–49 especially.

For the cultural background generally, Kenneth Silverman's *A Cultural History of the American Revolution* (New York: Crowell, 1976) is a cogent overview. Professor Silverman points out that the first known public performance of Haydn in America was in New York, and not until April 27, 1782. By this time, however, as the newspaper records reveal, Haydn had already been performed very often in salons and in private dwellings. Further valuable details on the New York social milieu of the time can be found in Bayard Tuckerman, *Life of General Philip Schuyler, 1733–1804* (1903; rpt. New York: Books for Libraries Press, 1969), pp. 2–3 and 96–97 in particular.

6. The Charles Hamm quotation is from his *Music in the New World* (New York: Norton, 1983), p. 90. See also pp. 92–93 for the quotations on the atmosphere of the theaters in New York, Philadelphia, and Boston at the time. On this matter, see also John T. Howard, *Our American Music,* 3rd ed. (New York: Thomas Y. Crowell, 1954), pp. 32–33 especially. Both Hamm and Howard have valuable bibliographies.

   Ancillary information can be found as well in Susan L. Porter, *With an Air Debonair: Musical Theatre in America, 1785–1815* (Washington, D.C.: Smithsonian Institution Press, 1991). Chapter one, "The Establishment of Musical Theatre in America," is especially helpful, as are the last 200-odd pages. These in part list musical entertainments and performances in selected cities during the period. Porter does well to emphasize the legally enforced blackout on the American stage, 1774–1783.

   The drama of the pre-Revolutionary period is well discussed in Walter J. Meserve, *An Emerging Entertainment: The Drama of the American People to 1828* (New York: Norton, 1977), and in Thomas J. Wertenbaker, *The Golden Age of Colonial Culture* (New York: New York University Press, 1942), pp. 54–55, a terse summation. On American colonial cultural conditions generally, see James T. Adams, *Provincial Society, 1690–1763* (New York: Macmillan, 1927), chapter three in particular.

7. *Journals of the General Assembly of New York, 1691–1743* (Early American Imprints. First series; Evans no. 9756 and no. 10418), vol. I, p. 712. On the early history of the Jews in colonial New York, see especially Nathan Glazer, *American Judaism,* 2d ed. (Chicago: University of Chicago Press, 1972), pp. 14, 19, and 191, as well as Jacob R. Marcus, *The Colonial American Jew, 1492–1776* (Detroit: Wayne State University Press, 1970), pp. 305–12, 398–412, 862–74, and 890–94, and Leo Hershkowitz and Isadore S. Meyer, eds., *Letters of the Franks Family* (Waltham, Mass.: Brandeis University Press, 1968), passim.

8. An American who could not afford a lamp would have had difficulty reading by candlelight. In 1762 it cost one and three-quarter pence an hour to burn a common candle. See wages discussion later in this chapter.

   On the contemporary architecture of New York, see Fiske Kimball, *The Domestic Architecture of the Colonies and the Early Republic* (New Haven: Yale University Press, 1923), as well as Russell V. Whitehead, ed., *Monograph Series Recording the Architecture of the American Colonies and Early Republic,* vols. 15–18 (New York: Dial, 1929–1932). See also Mintz, *Gouverneur Morris,* pp. 32–35, and Bayard Tuckerman, *Life of General Philip Schuyler* (1903; reprinted, Freeport, N.Y.: Books for Libraries Press, 1969), an early and admirable "life and times"; see especially chapter 1.

9. Gouverneur Morris to Robert Morris, October 20, 1778. Robert Morris Papers, Box 3, New-York Historical Society.

10. Thomas Jones, *History of New York during the Revolutionary War.* vol. 1 (New York: New-York Historical Society, 1879), 140n. See, for instance, S. Alexander DeAlva, *A Political History of the State of New York,* volume 1 (New York: Henry Holt, 1909), p. 73, where the historian refers to G.M.'s "self-confident and conceited demeanor."

11. Morris's law register, held in the Madison Library of the Library of Congress, records some of his cases; Jared Sparks, who had access to records and materials no longer extant, said that Gouverneur's practice proved quite successful. Morris's law register is also accessible in microfilm format at the New York Public Library. Many of the records, which Sparks saw, of GM's legal cases were destroyed in the fire in the New York State archives at Albany in 1911. On Sparks's conclusions concerning the success of Morris's legal practice, see *Gouverneur Morris,* volume 1, p. 20. Also valuable has proven a survey of period documents from *New York Legal Mss,* New-York Historical Society.

12. A brief excursus on American wealth and income of the time may illuminate the sums of money in this section. To give contemporary real-worth equivalents of eighteenth-century monetary units would be impossible. But the reader should know that, for the entire colonial population (1774) of roughly 2,355,000 people, private, nonhuman tangible wealth averaged about £37.5 sterling. Slaves and servants by law had no claim on this wealth, and the free blacks affected the average only slightly; so free whites' average wealth in 1774 was

£47.5. If we include "human capital" (free—mostly indentured servants—and slave), then the figure reaches roughly £73.4 sterling. (At the time roughly 23 percent of the American population was enslaved.)

In 1774 nearly half the total population was in the South, and the balance divided between the Middle Atlantic and New England regions. The latter regions between them had almost two-thirds of the free population, and only 15 percent of the slave. The slaves, of course, were concentrated in the South, but there were significant numbers in Delaware and New York (as we shall soon note, the number of slaves in New York in the eighteenth century was surprisingly high). In aggregate wealth, when the value of the slaves is included, the South at the time was outstandingly the richest of the three regions; significantly, however, free wealthholders in the North, especially in the Middle Atlantic colonies, held comparatively more wealth in the form of liquid, nonhuman assets.

Wealth was most equally distributed in the Middle Atlantic colonies. In the thirteen colonies, overall the top 1 percent of the population held approximately 13 percent of the material wealth, while the bottom half had less than 7 percent. (Britain's economic breakout at the same time proves similar.)

For the foregoing estimates, see Edwin J. Perkins, *The Economy of Colonial America,* 2nd ed. (New York: Columbia University Press, 1988); John McCusker and Russell Menard, *The Economy of British America, 1607–1789* (Chapel Hill, N.C.: Institute of Early American History and Culture/University of North Carolina Press, 1985); Alice Hanson Jones, *American Colonial Wealth: Documents and Methods,* 2nd ed., vol. 3 (New York: Arno Press, 1978) and *Wealth of a Nation to Be* (New York: Columbia University Press, 1980); and Joseph A. Ernst, *Money and Politics in America, 1755–1775* (Chapel Hill, N.C.: IEAHC by the University of North Carolina Press, 1973).

Estimates for the eighteenth century mainland British economy draw on the sources provided in a pair of exceptionally fine social histories: Roy Porter, *English Society in the 18th Century* (New York: Penguin, 1982), and Louis Kronenberger, *Kings and Desperate Men* (New York: Vintage Books, 1959).

13. Law Register, 2. Papers of Gouverneur Morris, New-York Historical Society.
14. H. R. Pleadings Pl. 1076. The attorneys' arguments and the testimony of the witnesses can be found in *J. T. Kempe Lawsuits C-F Sub nom.* Benjamin Ferris. On the judgment, see *Minute Books of the Supreme Court of Judicature, 1750–1781,* Microfilm Copy, Queens College Historical Documents Collection (Rolls SC1–SC8). See also the Miscellaneous Morris file at the New-York Historical Society. Douglas Greenberg, *Crime and Law Enforcement in Colonial New York, 1661–1776* (Ithaca: Cornell University Press, 1976), is a fundamental scholarly resource. Greenberg employs court records to examine the social history of the law and to shed revealing light on the New York society of the period.
    A useful guide to the legal terminology of the period is Edmund M. Morgan and F. X. Dwyer, *Introduction to the Study of Law,* 2nd ed. (New York: Callaghan, 1948). See especially pp. 37–41 and 76–77.
15. Morris's Law Register 2. Papers of Gouverneur Morris, New-York Historical Society.
16. Sarah Morris. Waste Book. Entry October 20, 1772, in *Morris et al. v. Morris* (1785). Exhibit F testimony. Packet 68. New York State Court of Appeals, Albany. See also Archives of the State of New Jersey, vol. 19 of "Extracts from American Newspapers Relating to New Jersey, 1773–74." 1st series. XXIX, 398–99.
17. On the subject, see William H. Ludlow's sworn testimony in *Morris et al. v. Morris,* 1785, Packet 68, New York State Court of Appeals, Albany, as well as Mintz, *Gouverneur Morris,* pp. 38–39, n. 26.
18. For more details of this extended flirtation with Kitty Livingston, see Howard Swiggett, *The Extraordinary Mr. Morris,* pp. 15–19. The note appears in Mintz, *Gouverneur Morris,* p. 41.
19. During the war, the Club's monthly meetings and meals were at Kip's Bay, on the East River.
20. Morris to the Penns, January 7, 1774. In Sparks, vol. 1, pp. 20–21. The last sentence, of course, is ironic. John Penn (1729–1795), a grandson of William Penn, inherited (1771) life use of a quarter of the proprietary rights in Philadelphia. From 1752 to the end of

proprietary rule on September 26, 1776, he served virtually continually in important political positions in Pennsylvania.

Elias Boudinot (1740–1821) is a historically neglected but important statesman of the Revolutionary period, and also a close associate of George Washington.

Many of Gouverneur's close associates—John Penn, Boudinot, Robert Morris (1734–1806), James Duane (1733–1797), and even George Washington (1732–1799)—were a generation older than Morris.

Since early July 1769 the New York Sons of Liberty had exerted pressure on the merchants to respond to the various British duties on British goods sold in America.

21. Morris's letter to John Penn (May 20, 1774) is worth studying in its entirety not only for what it reveals of his social attitudes, which have been much criticized, but also for its astute political analyses and accurate predictions. It has been reprinted several times; I rely on Sparks, vol. 1, pp. 23–26.

The "riotous mob" observation proved to have some accuracy, as the scholarship of Henry B. Dawson revealed. See *The Sons of Liberty in New York* (1859; reprinted, New York: Arno Press, 1969). Significantly, this volume is part of Arno's "Mass Violence in America" series.

22. See Jonathan Powis, *Aristocracy* (Oxford, U.K.: Blackwell, 1994), p. 22. See also p. 77 and throughout, especially Powis's observation that "success in government also carried aristocratic associations of its own" in the eighteenth century. Then as now, in America as in England, money, access, and prestige reinforced one another.

In his *Preface to Eighteenth-Century Poetry* (Oxford, U.K.: Clarendon Press, 1948), James Sutherland aligns these attitudes with Matthew Arnold's generalization concerning the state of affairs in nonrevolutionary periods, which Arnold calls "epochs of concentration" (pp. 38–39, especially). Also relevant is Lawrence Stone, *The Crisis of the Aristocracy* (Oxford, U.K.: Oxford University Press, 1967).

23. From his December 20, 1787, Letter from Paris to James Madison. In Merrill D. Peterson, ed., *The Portable Jefferson* (New York: Penguin Books, 1977), p. 432.

24. Thomas Jefferson's culminating statement on this subject appears in a letter to John Adams, from Monticello, dated October 28, 1813. In this letter Jefferson also states that "the artificial aristocracy is a mischievous ingredient in government and provision should be made to prevent its ascendance." Valuable general insight into the Jefferson-Adams debate can be found in Arthur Ponsonby, *The Decline of Aristocracy* (1912; reprinted Millwood, N.Y.: Kraus, 1973), pp. 26–29.

25. See Anton-Hermann Chroust, *The Rise of the Legal Professions in America* (2 vols.; Norman, Okla.: University of Oklahoma Press, 1965), vol. 1, pp. 146–47 especially. And see Eugene Sheridan's percipient book-length scholarly works—a biography and volumes of papers—on Lewis Morris. Ancillary insights are provided by Paul Hamlin, *Legal Education* (New York: Da Capo Press, 1979), pp. 116–17.

26. Nicholas Canny's remark appears in his article "England Over the Water," *Times Literary Supplement,* August 12–18, 1988, p. 878. Information on access to libraries, such as it was at the time, is handily available in James D. Hart, *The Popular Book: A History of America's Literary Tastes* (New York: Oxford University Press, 1950)—see especially pp. 24–25—and in Frank L. Mott, *Golden Multitudes* (New York: Macmillan, 1947), pp. 303–305, in particular. In 1774 the bestselling book in the colonies was the modern-seeming *The Life and Opinions of Tristram Shandy,* published in Philadelphia by James Humphreys. In the next year, when the armed hostilities officially began, the also durable and fascinating *Robinson Crusoe,* published by Hugh Gaine in New York City, sold best.

Despite the Americans' somewhat strained condition, an Englishman named William Addis judged that "the common [American] people are on a footing, in point of literature, with the middle ranks of Europe. It is scarce possible to conceive that number of readers with which even every little town abounds." This casts an admirable light on the "Poor Reptiles." By Morris's birth in 1752, the thirteen colonies on the mainland already had more than twenty-five printing presses, a number that had roughly doubled by the time the Revolution began.

In some fundamental ways, such as fine and accessible libraries, Britain has historically lagged far behind America. England, for instance, did not have a public library until Warmington's opened in 1848; and even by 1860 only nine public libraries were in existence in the entire United Kingdom. At the same time in the United States there were 188 public lending libraries. See U.S. Bureau of Education, *Public Libraries in the United States of America: Their History, Condition, and Management* (Washington, D.C.: Government Printing Office, 1876), pp. 452–56.

27. Carl L. Becker, *History of Political Parties in the Province of New York, 1760–1776* (Madison: University of Wisconsin Press, 1909), p. 16.

28. On this subject the best secondary accounts are again, Carl L. Becker, chapter 7 and pp. 266–69, as well as Montgomery Schuyler, *The Patroons and Lords of Manors of the Hudson* (New York: Order of Colonial Lords of Manors in America, 1932), pp. 12–21 and 24–32 especially; and Alexander Flick, *Loyalism in New York* (New York: Columbia University Press, 1901), passim.

Relevant to the prerevolutionary power concentration is that (as David E. Narrett has cogently pointed out in his *Inheritance and Family Life in Colonial New York City* [Ithaca, N.Y.: Cornell University Press, 1992]) the first American colonial group to arrange that their children's inheritances be used to generate interest income were the wealthy New Yorkers of this period. Also relevant to the concentration of power are Cadwallader Colden, *The Colden Letter Books* (New York: New-York Historical Society Collections, 2 vols., 1877–88), pp. 61–62, 71, and 92 in particular; and Virginia D. Harrington, *The New York Merchant on the Eve of the Revolution* (New York: Columbia University Press, 1935), pp. 11–15. As Sung Bok Kim has ably shown, the New York Livingstons, at least, experienced more than a few headaches resulting from their method of managing their estate. See *Landlord and Tenant in Colonial New York: Manorial Society, 1660–1775* (Chapel Hill, N.C.: Institute for Early American History and Culture/University of North Carolina Press, 1978). See especially chapter 3.

29. The roots of the British colonial system, as it relates to the American revolutionary era, are revealingly analyzed by Herbert L. Osgood, *The American Colonies in the Seventeenth Century*, 3 vols. (1904; reprint, New York: Peter Smith, 1957). Osgood accomplishes substantially more than his title indicates. Valuable and penetrating governmental systems analysis is also provided by Esmond Wright, *Fabric of Freedom: 1763–1800*, rev. ed. (New York: Hill and Wang, 1978). See pp. 6–9 in particular.

30. See Oscar Theodore Barck, *New York City During the War for Independence* (1931; reprinted, Port Washington, N.Y.: Ira J. Friedman, 1959), pp. 36–43; and Carl J. Becker, *The History of Political Parties in the Province of New York, 1760–1776* (1909; reprinted, Madison: University of Wisconsin Press, 1960), pp. 112–23.

31. Becker, *The History of Political Parties in the Province of New York*, pp. 210–11, 223–27, and 262–67.

32. Force, *American Archives*, 4th Series (Washington, D.C.: M. St. Clair Clarke and Peter Force, 1837–46), II, 529, 832. Henry B. Dawson, "Westchester County, New York, During the American Revolution," in J. Thomas Scharf, *History of Westchester County, New York, Including Morrisania, Kings Bridge, and West Farms, Which Have Been Annexed to New York City*, vol. 1 (Philadelphia: L. E. Preston, 1886), pp. 242–60.

33. Quoted by Theodore Roosevelt, *Gouverneur Morris* (Boston and New York: Houghton Mifflin, 1888), pp. 35–36.

34. Morris's work on the currency report is treated cursorily by Jared Sparks in his first volume, pp. 36–40, and analyzed in Mintz, *Gouverneur Morris and the American Revolution*, pp. 48–51. See also his June 30, 1775, letter to John Jay. Upon receipt of the report, the New York delegation in the Continental Congress—which included, in addition to John Jay, two close Morris friends, Philip Livingston and James Duane (1716–1778)—eliminated the anti-Catholic statement and the equally foolish proviso about trade and fisheries. Gouverneur had objected to both proposals with admirable strength, as the initial draft of the first New York State Constitution (of 1777) indicates.

35. On this question, see Richard Henry Lee to Morris, May 28, 1775, in Paul H. Smith, ed., *Letters of Delegates to Congress, 1774–1789* (Washington, D.C.: Library of Congress, 1976), vol. 1, pp. 415–16. And on the entire Rivington matter, see the documentation in *American Archives,* 4th series, II, 726, 836–37, 899–900. See also Morris to Richard Henry Lee, May 1775, "The Lee Papers," *Collections I* (New-York Historical Society), pp. 178–79.

36. On this incident, see especially Henry B. Dawson, ed., *New York City During the American Revolution* (New York: Mercantile Library Association of the City of New York, 1861), pp. 61–65.

37. Gouverneur Morris, June 5, 1776, *Journal of the Provincial Congress,* vol. 2, p. 204; Force, ed., *American Archives* (4th ser.) VI, 1385. See also Wilbur C. Abbott, *New York in the American Revolution* (New York: Scribners, 1929), chapters 6 and 7, in particular.

38. Of the persistence of the Loyalist problem, voluminous evidence is supplied in the following: *Proceedings of the Albany Committee of Correspondence,* January 24, 1775, to June 10, 1778, and Victor H. Palstits, ed., *Minutes of the Commissioners for Detecting and Defeating Conspiracies in the State of New York, Albany County Sessions, 1778–81,* 3 vols. (Albany: State of New York, 1909).

    On the patriots' lamentable combination of will, system, and method see Alexander C. Flick, *Loyalism in New York, passim,* but chapters 3 and 4 in particular, and Robert M. Calhoon, *Loyalists in Revolutionary America, 1760–1781* (New York: Harcourt, Brace, Jovanovich, 1973), *passim.* In his bibliographical essay, Calhoon provides a helpful annotated survey of the pre-1971 scholarship on the subject (pp. 359–63). Throughout the Revolutionary period, New York was one of the smaller colonies, ranking only seventh in point of population, but it was strategically the most important: the large territory separated New England from New Jersey, Pennsylvania, Maryland, Virginia, and the Carolinas. Control of New York furthermore put British military forces in good strategic position to descend on Pennsylvania, which in resources was the richest of the middle colonies.

    George Washington was one of the first to see clearly the comparatively ineffectual institution of the states before they officially became united in 1789. See his December 1778 letter from camp to Benjamin Harrison (1726[?]–1791), the president of the Virginia House of Burgesses: "The states separately . . ."

    The reader should know that on July 10, 1776, the Fourth Provincial Congress of the Colony of New York renamed itself the Convention of the Representatives of the State of New York; see *American Archives,* 5th series (Washington, D.C.: M. St. Clair and Peter Force, 1848–53), I, 1393. This surely was wishful thinking: from August 1776 to 1783, British troops occupied five New York counties and parts of two others. And New York City remained occupied from November 1776 until the evacuation in 1783. As two members of the Committee of Safety drolly observed, it might have been more sensible "first to endeavor to secure a State to govern, before we established a form to govern it by." The Provincial Congress continued to press its claim to represent even the occupied areas. See Christopher Tappen and Gilbert Livingston to the convention, August 14, 1776, *American Archives,* 5th ser., I, 1542; and Alexander C. Flick, ed., *History of New York* (New York: Columbia University Press, 1933), vol. 3, p. 269, and vol. 4, p. 43.

39. Morris's contemporaries publicly said as much, and often. See, for example, Force, ed., *American Archives,* 4th ser., VI, 825–26, 1351. See also *American Archives,* 5th ser., I, 403; and Frank Moore, ed., *Diaries of the American Revolution* (New York: Evans Jones, 1860), pp. 253–54. Dixon Fox, "New York Becomes a Democracy," *History of the State of New York,* vol. 6, Alexander C. Flick, ed. (New York: Columbia University Press, 1934), *passim.* Also relevant is Arthur J. Alexander. "Exemption from Militia Service in New York State During the Revolutionary War," *New York History* XXVII (spring 1946), 204–212, especially pp. 205–207; and Flick, ed., *History of the State of New York,* vol. 4 (New York: Columbia University Press, 1933), pp. 9–25.

40. Force, ed., *American Archives,* 4th ser., V, 1054, 1101, 1117–19, and 1148. See also Moore. *Diary of the American Revolution,* vol. 1, p. 256; and Oscar T. Barck, *New York City During the War for Independence* (1931; rpt. New York: Ira J. Friedman, 1968), chapter 2.

41. These figures draw on the following: Evarts B. Greene and Virginia D. Harrington, *American Population Before the Federal Census of 1790* (New York: Columbia University Press, 1932), pp. 6–7; J. Potter, "The Growth of Population in America, 1700–1860," in D. V. Glass and D.E.C. Eversley, *Population in History* (London: Arnold, 1965), pp. 632–39; and Alice H. Jones, *American Colonial Wealth: Documents and Methods,* vol. 3 (2nd ed., New York: Arno, 1978), pp. 178–91.

  The number of free, white, sufficiently wealth-holding males with no felony conviction record in the New York of the time—in other words, the only individuals eligible to vote and to hold public office—seems to have numbered roughly 45,000 or approximately 22 percent of the total population.

  Directly relevant to the slavery issue are several trenchant scholarly analyses: James G. Lydon, "New York and the Slave Trade 1700–1774," *William and Mary Quarterly* 35 (April 1978), 375–94; Thomas J. Davis, *Slavery in Colonial New York City* (Ph.D. diss., Columbia University, 1974); and Shane White, *Somewhat More Independent: The End of Slavery in New York City, 1770–1810* (Athens, Ga.: University of Georgia Press, 1991).

42. Montgomery's second in command was Benedict Arnold, not yet the traitor he was to become. Morris's opinion of the expedition appears in a note of October 13, 1775, to Robert R. Livingston, in the Robert R. Livingston Papers at the Library of Congress.

43. On this subject, see *American Archives,* 4th series, VI, 793, 1332.

44. For this, ironically, she paid dearly: the British forces occupying New York used the Morris property as a park for their horses. The troops who lived in her house treated it and her grounds with the shameful disrespect that one would expect given the redcoats' burning and sacking of many American towns.

45. Gouverneur Morris to Lewis Morris, February 26, 1776, Emmet Collection, New York Public Library. This letter is misdated 1775 (an error caught by Max Mintz).

  Most of Gouverneur's biographers, and a high percentage of historians, including even his grand-niece, seem to find Gouverneur's declaration to Lewis puzzling. On this matter, see also the exposition by Sparks, *Gouverneur Morris,* vol. 1, p. 89 fn.

46. Georgia, a strongly royal colony, was generally considered to have the smallest population of the thirteen and was farthest south. She therefore at first broke with her northern neighbors, but soon came to see the folly of such separation. The historical literature on late colonial Georgia is especially rich. On the issues discussed above, a good reliable secondary source is Kenneth Coleman, *Colonial Georgia* (New York: Charles Scribner, 1976), pp. 266–71 and 273–75.

47. See the discussion in David W. Robson, *Educating Republicans: The College in the Era of the American Revolution, 1750–1800* (Westport, Conn.: Greenwood Press, 1985), pp. 84–85. On Morris's separation speech, see Mintz, *Gouverneur Morris,* pp. 16–22.

48. The Athenian symmories were groups of taxpayers responsible for certain public services—the upkeep of ships, for example.

49. *American Archives,* 4th series, VI, 1332.

50. For Morris to Washington on November 12, see W.W. Abbot and Dorothy Twohig, eds., *Papers of George Washington, Presidential Series,* vol. 1, p. 103, and Washington to Chastellux in the same volume, p. 131.

51. See especially Washington's letter to Morris from New York on October 13, 1789, and Morris's letters of report in Sparks, *Morris,* pp. 340–45.

52. As late as July 1, 1776, John Dickinson argued for postponing outright revolution. See *Pennsylvania Magazine of History and Biography,* vol. 65 (1941), 468–81. Nevertheless, the Middle Temple–educated Dickinson became an ardent leader in the independence movement.

  With respect to the leadership question, a historically typical revolutionary situation is the advent of the early Roman Republic. In the overthrow of the monarchy, the initiators were the Roman aristocracy, with the concurrence, at least, of the mass of the Roman people. On this subject see especially Ulrich von Lübtow, *Das Römische Volk sein Staat und sein Recht* (Frankfurt, Germany: Klostermann, 1955), pp. 87ff.

53. C. G. Jung, "The Language of Dreams," in *The Symbolic Life: Miscellaneous Writings,* Trans. R.F.C. Hull (Princeton: Princeton University Press, 1976), p. 208.

54. *The Journal of Nicholas Cresswell* (New York: Dial, 1924), p. 127 (Monday, October 30, 1775). On Monday, November 6, however, news arrives of the burning of the town of Falmouth (now Portland, Maine) by "the King's Ships." The picture thereafter appears substantially bleaker, even to Cresswell.

   Cresswell's journal covers almost exclusively his American residency from 1774 to 1777, when he was between twenty-four and twenty-seven years old. He lived from 1750 to 1784.

   For the wish of Maryland and Pennsylvania, for example, to avoid revolution, see the following: for Maryland, Force, ed., *American Archives,* 4th ser., IV, 653–54, and 4th ser., V, 1588–90; and for Pennsylvania, 4th ser., III, 1793.

55. George L. Beer, *British Colonial Policy* (New York: Macmillan, 1907), p. 314. The literature on the causes of the Revolution is unusually rich, and the sources cited in the footnotes below represent a rigorously selected few.

56. C. H. McIlwain, *The American Revolution: A Constitutional Interpretation* (New York: Macmillan, 1923). A selection of readings that well illustrate the arguments put forward by the leading Colonial and British thinkers is that edited by Max Beloff, *The Debate on the American Revolution, 1761–1783.* 3rd ed. (London: Sheridan House, 1989). This text includes essays and speeches by James Otis, John Dickinson, Samuel Adams, and Jefferson, as well as equally interesting material by William Pitt and George Grenville.

57. Franklin to Reverend Samuel Cooper (of Boston), June 8, 1770, in William B. Willcox, ed., *The Papers of Benjamin Franklin,* vol. 17 (New Haven, Conn.: Yale University Press, 1973), p. 163.

58. David Ramsay, *The History of the American Revolution* (Philadelphia: R. Aitken and Son, 1789; reprinted, Indianapolis: Liberty Classics, 1990), vol. 1, p. 28.

59. On these complicated issues, see Romney G. Sedgwick, ed., *Letters from George III to Lord Bute, 1756–1766* (London: Macmillan, 1939), pp. 201–202 (letters 282 and 283).

   Able discussions of the topics sketched out in the foregoing paragraphs can be found in the following: Lewis Namier, *Crossroads of Power* (London: Macmillan, 1962), in particular pp. 132–39; Herbert L. Osgood, *The American Colonies in the Eighteenth Century,* vols. 3 and 4 (New York: Columbia University Press, 1924); W. H. Nelson, "The Revolutionary Character of the American Revolution," *American Historical Review* 70 (1964–1965), 998–1014; H. E. Egerton, *The Causes and Character of the American Revolution* (Oxford, U.K.: Clarendon Press, 1923), pp. 135–47, 158–83, 200–201.

60. See James Henretta, *The Evolution of American Society* (Boston: Heath, 1973), in particular pp. 9–11.

61. See, for instance, the typical entries on the commercial matters for 1752, the year of Gouverneur's birth. In particular, consult the entries for January 15, on Georgia, in the House of Commons, on "the better preservation of his Majesty's woods in America." Leo F. Stock, ed., *Proceedings and Debates of the British Parliaments of Great Britain Respecting North America,* vol. 5 (1730–54) (Washington, D.C.: Carnegie Institute, 1941), pp. 518, 521, 524.

62. On these subjects, see *British Public Record Office, Colonial Office, Class 5 Files: The Board of Trade Entry Books on Proprietary Colonies, 1761–1773.* Reel VI. Vol. 1296. 0739 (1769) and 0742 (1770); Henretta, *Evolution,* pp. 48–49, especially the chart on p. 48; and Charles M. Andrews, "The Acts of Trade," in J. Holland Rose, et al., *Cambridge History of the British Empire* (London: Cambridge University Press, 1929), pp. 280–99 especially. In late 1989, Professor Daniel A. Baugh kindly mailed me a copy of his then unpublished paper "The Navy and the Atlantic Empire: The Limits of Power," which he had presented at the David Center Colloquium on October 27, 1989, in Washington Crossing, Pennsylvania. The paper brilliantly elucidates how the British used maritime and commercial trade to develop the empire's prosperity and security.

63. For discussion of the various British trade laws and acts imposed on the American colonies, see Derek Jarrett, *Britain, 1688–1815* (New York: St. Martin's Press, 1965), in particular

chapter 2, "The Collapse of Management: 1770–1782," especially the section entitled "The Problem of the American Colonies," pp. 297–315.

Samuel Adams is quoted in an enclosure in a letter from Sir Francis Bernard (1711?–1779) to the First Earl of Hillsborough (1718–1793), February 25, 1769 (British) Colonial Office Records, 5, 758, Folio 147. By 1775, with nearly one-third the number of inhabitants of Britain, the thirteen American colonies had a proportionate gross domestic economic output.

On the ways the comparatively moderate response to the enactment of the Stamp Act induced the British to favor the Caribbean colonies over those on the mainland, see Arthur J. O'Shaughnessy, "The Stamp Act Crisis in the British Caribbean," *William and Mary Quarterly,* 3rd ser., vol. LI, no. 2 (April 1994), 203–226. See also Thomas Barrow, *Trade and Empire* (Cambridge, Mass.: Harvard University Press, 1967), passim.

With the Navigation Laws, the overall aim of Great Britain was to export manufactured goods to America, to import raw materials, and at the same time to retain the balance of trade firmly in her favor. This she usually succeeded in doing. As part of British mercantilist policies, certain colonial products were only allowed to be exported from the place of origin in America to England. From 1660 through 1767 various items emanating from the colonies were thus "enumerated" by laws. Over the years these products variously included sugar, tobacco, indigo, cotton, ginger, certain dyewoods, rice, molasses, naval stores, furs, copper, hides and skins, iron, lumber, and so forth and so on—a very extensive list!

The Stamp Act was a law passed by the British Parliament in 1765 to raise revenue by requiring that taxes be placed on various types of printed matter, such as newspapers, broadsides, and pamphlets, practically all kinds of legal documents, and even dice and playing cards. Taxes were to be paid in specie. Transactions in violation of the act were to be invalid. Penalties for infringements could be imposed by British-dominated Vice Admiralty Courts as well as by colonial common law courts.

The colonial governors prorogued their assemblies when they learned that they were about to condemn the Stamp Act. The assemblies therefore met mainly in inns and taverns, in hopes that their informal protests would lead the British government to retract the act.

64. On the general question there now exist in print two exceptionally informative monographs: A. Roger Ekirch, *Bound for America: The Transportation of British Convicts to the Colonies, 1718–1775* (Oxford, Eng.: Clarendon Press, 1987), and Wilfred Oldham, *Britain's Convicts to the Colonies,* W. Hugh Oldham, ed. (Sydney, Australia: University of London dissertation, 1939). These two studies complement each other well.

J. M. Beattie's *Crime and the Courts of England, 1600–1800* (Princeton, N.J.: Princeton University Press, 1986) examines the policy primarily from the British point of view. From this angle the historical records reveal some surprises. For example, Grenville, Pitt's foreign minister, wrote a letter in late November 1789, stating: "the landing convicts in the territories of the United States, even if the masters of the ships perform their contracts for so doing, is an act highly offensive to a country now foreign and independent." Needless to say, the events that prompted this memorandum followed the sailing of the First Fleet bound for Australia. That had sailed at dawn on Sunday, May 13, 1787, from Portsmouth, England, and had arrived in Sydney Cove on January 26, 1788.

The course of the British governmental discussion on the subject of Australian transportation can be followed in the correspondence between William Pitt and William W. Grenville. See, in particular, Pitt to Grenville, October 2, 1785, and Grenville to the Marquis of Stafford, September 29, 1789 (Whitehall), in *The Dropmore Papers,* Historical Manuscripts Commission, vol. 1 (London: Eyre and Spottiswoode, 1892), pp. 257 and 524.

The British "reach" as regards transportation to America is revealed as well in the *Records of the Parliaments of Ireland.* On January 20, 1752, the year of Gouverneur's birth, Sir Archibald Acheson presented to the House heads a bill "for the more effectual transportation of felons and vagabonds, and for preventing the pernicious practice of kidnapping children, and seducing people on board ships, and transporting them to America."

65. *The Provincial Governor in the English Colonies of North America* (1898; reprint, New York: Russell and Russell, 1966), p. 205. On this matter see also pp. 103 and 109.

On this head see further the imperial tone in very many of the memoranda in Leonard Woods Labaree, ed., *Royal Instructions to the British Colonial Governors, 1670–1776.* 2 vols. (reprint: New York: Kraus, 1967). These British pronouncements often show complete ignorance of colonial business methods and of colonial conditions generally. Attempts to enforce these rulings, particularly after 1763, disclosed as never before the difficulties of applying the British system to the colonies. Indeed, the colonists sometimes thought, as was said in a controversy over a governor's instruction in New York, that the King would never have so instructed his governor had he known the effect of such an instruction on the welfare of the province.

As John L. Bullion has remarked: not surprisingly, "well before 1783, the king had realized that if Britain lost its North American possessions, it would be in a very different relationship with other European powers." See "George III on Empire, 1783," *William and Mary Quarterly,* 3rd ser., vol. LI, no. 2 (April 1994), p. 309. On this topic the entire essay, pp. 305–310, merits study.

66. On these judicial questions, see Instructions, 1761, *New York Colonial Documents,* VII, 479; and Leonard Woods Labaree, *Royal Government in America: A Study of the British Colonial System Before 1783* (New Haven: Yale University Press, 1930), pp. 384–89. On some of the economic leveraging employed by New York and three other provinces see also pp. 340–41. More generally see Charles M. Andrews, "The Government of the Empire," *Cambridge History of the British Empire* (London: Cambridge University Press, 1929), vol. 1, pp. 418, 420, 432–34, and 436. The complications of the Crown's struggle with the colonies are concisely presented by John Brewer, *The Sinews of Power: War, Money, and the English State, 1688–1783* (New York: Knopf, 1989), p. 176.

67. Mellen Chamberlain, *John Adams, the Statesman of the American Revolution* (New York: Houghton Mifflin, 1898), p. 248. Piers Mackesy's book is *The War for America, 1778–1783* (1964; rpt.: Lincoln: University of Nebraska Press, 1993).

68. See "An Uneasy Connection" in Stephen G. Kuntz and James H. Hutson, eds., *Essays on the American Revolution* (Chapel Hill, N.C.: University of North Carolina Press, 1973), pp. 3–51, in particular pp. 35–43; Jack P. Greene comments, with trenchant examples, on the cited advantages. From 1700 to the 1761 presentation by James Otis of his powerful argument on behalf of the sixty-one colonists in the Writs of Assistance case, the population of the American colonies had increased more than six and a half–fold, from 257,060 to roughly 1.6 million. This population increase was a significant factor in the development of the revolutionary movement.

69. New York's delegation to the Continental Congress had not been empowered to act independently of the New York legislative body.

70. Howard H. Peckham, ed., *The Toll of Independence: Engagements and Battle Casualties of the American Revolution* (Chicago: University of Chicago Press, 1974). In his introduction, Peckham lucidly discusses his subject's methodological difficulties and approaches (pp. vii–xv). Peckham's list of "Military Engagements and Casualties" begins with Lexington, April 19, 1775 (p. 3), and ends with the skirmish at Fort Carlos III in what is now Arkansas (p. 99). His "Summations and Implications" (pp. 131–34) also provides valuable exposition.

The engagements and military casualties Peckham cites represent "the ascertainable minimum number" (p. 105), so any errors are likely to add to the toll. Moreover, Peckham does not include the numerous American civilian casualties of the war.

New Jersey had the most military engagements of all the colonies (238). With 228 battles and skirmishes, New York came in second.

71. In *The Winter Soldiers* (New York: Doubleday, 1973), Richard M. Ketchum interestingly narrates the New York Campaign of 1776–77. The American troops' confusion was not surprising for men not yet tested in battle: at Brooklyn Heights, for example, the American line units sustained fifteen hundred casualties in the same engagement. Few, if any, untried outfits in history could have sustained such heavy casualties in a first engagement without experiencing at least some panic.

72. John Jay is quoted in Jay Monaghan, *John Jay* (New York: Bobbs-Merrill, 1935), p. 83.

73. *American Archives,* 4th series, vol. VI, 1465–66; 5th series, vol. III, 202, 307, 331, 371.

Although records of the New York Convention were apparently kept for the period December 14, 1776, to March 5, 1777, to my knowledge they have not been preserved. See also *American Archives,* 5th series, vol. I, 374, 1391, 1394, 1410.

74. Morris to New York Convention, in *American Archives,* 5th series, II, 323. See also 1023; and Robert R. Livingston to Morris, October 8, 1776, Robert R. Livingston Papers, New-York Historical Society.

In a rare volume in the Department of Special Collections of the Van Pelt–Dietrich Library at the University of Pennsylvania is an entry which contains, under the signature of "Schuyler," what purports to be six pages of published notes, drawn from the original papers, then held by John McKesson, Esq. He was an heir of the John McKesson who was one of the two secretaries of the New York Convention at the time (the other was Robert Benson).

These notes also record that "on August 1, 1776, on motion of G. Morris, seconded by Mr. Duer, a Committee [was] appointed to prepare and report a constitution as form of government" (p. 692), the committee of thirteen elsewhere alluded to. Here we read that the committee was supposed to report on August 16. "But owing to the state, and the distracted state of affairs in various parts of the country, little or nothing appears to have been done . . . on this subject." On December 5, 1776 "the committee [was] appointed to prepare a form of government, and other members, having withdrawn, the remainder acted as a committee of safety" (p. 692). "From the early part of August 1776 to February or March 1777, the Convention had been obliged frequently to change its place of meeting—its members sometimes serving with the troops in the field, sometimes returning home, and others being elected, some dispatched on other trusts, and sometimes not enough left to transact business" (p. 692). The notes, however, revealingly emphasize that "the most considerable part of the constitution now stands as it came from the hands of Mr. Jay" (p. 692).

The notes moreover indicate that the copies of the New York constitution were printed at the courthouse in Kingston on the Tuesday morning following, by the other secretary, Robert Benson, "from a platform erected on the end of a hogshead, Vice-President Cortlandt presiding" (p. 696). The information and quotations under the hand of "Schuyler," cited above, are from *Reports of the Proceedings and Debates of the Convention of 1821, Assembled for the Purpose of Amending the Constitution . . .* [of New York], reported by Nathaniel H. Carter and William L. Stone (Albany, N.Y.: E. and E. Hosford, 1821), pp. 690–99.

75. Morris to Mrs. Morris, Dec. 19, 1776. Martin Wilkins was Morris's nephew. Emmet Collection, New York Public Library.

76. See *Journal of the Provincial Congress,* I, 827 and 920–21. See also Robert A. East, preface to *A Bibliography of Loyalist Source Material in the United States, Canada, and Great Britain*, Gregory Palmer, ed. Westport, Conn.: Meckler, 1982, p. vii. In the New York legislature, Morris served on four separate committees dealing with the Loyalists; the first commenced duties May 25, 1776.

77. The Massachusetts Constitution of 1780 was the first to be produced by a convention elected for that sole purpose, and the first to be submitted to the voters of the state. On this general subject, see W. F. Dodd, "The First State Constitutional Conventions, 1776–1783," *American Political Science Review* 2 (Summer 1908), 545–61.

The voters' relationship to the development of the first Maryland state constitution is unique in a different way. When the Maryland constitution had been formulated by the Revolutionary Assembly, it was submitted to the voters for approval and suggestions, but not for decisive action. The Assembly then reconsidered the constitution in light of the popular suggestions, and then voted the revised document into law.

78. See, for example, Richard B. Morris, *John Jay, the Nation and the Court* (New York: Scribners, 1976), p. 10; Charles Z. Lincoln, *The Constitutional History of New York* (Rochester, N.Y.: Lawyer's Co-op., 1906), vol. 1, pp. 471, 630. Lincoln calls John Jay "the chief author" and "the principal author" of the first state constitution. Max M. Mintz, "Gouverneur Morris, 1752–1779" (Ph.D. dissertation, New York University, 1957), p. 72, quotes John Jay's son, William, who claims his father repaired to "someplace in the country" in late February

1777 to prepare the first draft of the document. In *John Jay: The Making of a Revolutionary* (New York: Scribners, 1980), pp. 389–94, Richard Morris qualifies his judgment somewhat, insofar as he suggests reasons why Jay's contributions could not be said to be definitive. My own study of the correspondence among John Jay, Gouverneur Morris, and Robert R. Livingston in April 1777, the most relevant month, validates this assessment.

79. On this last matter, the only scholar to come to similar conclusions, to my knowledge, is Merrill D. Peterson. See *Democracy and Liberty* (New York: Bobbs-Merrill, 1966), pp. 126–27. Interestingly, Thomas Jefferson preferred the New York State version of the veto to the federal one, since in the former the judiciary is involved. See Jefferson's letter to Francis Hopkinson from Paris, May 13, 1789, in *The Portable Jefferson,* Merrill D. Peterson, ed. (New York: Penguin Books, 1977), p. 436 in particular.

During the colonial period, the power of the executive reached a maximum in New York and Maryland. For an analysis of this question with regard to New York especially, see Herbert L. Osgood *The American Colonies in the 17th Century* (1940; reprint, New York: Peter Smith, 1957), vol. 1, pp. 94–95 and 438–39.

80. The New Jersey constitution of 1776 did indeed extend the franchise to women who met the property requirement. The constitution's unusually permissive suffrage provision was intended to ensure that New Jersey residents who had previously been denied eligibility would respond by providing money and manpower for the war effort. Joseph Cooper, a Quaker lawmaker who believed in equality between men and women, is often credited with incorporating "he or she" in the Election Law of 1790. Irwin N. Gertzog suggests, on the other hand, that women retained suffrage because conservative legislators were convinced that the female votes would swing elections in the Federalists' favor. Women did turn out at the polls in subsequent post-Revolutionary elections but were ultimately deprived of the vote in 1807. Unable to hold political office, women could not prevent the reform of the election process by both Federalist and Republican legislators who supported for political advantage the disenfranchisement of all but "free, white, male citizens." See Irwin N. Gertzog, "Female Suffrage in New Jersey, 1790–1807," *Women, Politics, and the Constitution,* vol. 10, no. 2 (1990): 47–58.

81. At that time the New York Supreme Court was the state's highest court, whereas today the highest court is the Court of Appeals.

82. Charles Z. Lincoln, *The Constitutional History of New York . . .* (Rochester, N.Y.: Lawyers Co-operative, 1906), vol. 1, p. 13.

83. *Journals of the Provincial Congress,* vol. 1, p. 845.

84. For a discussion of the debates over fundamental liberties during the composition of the Constitution, see Max M. Mintz, *Gouverneur Morris and the American Revolution* (Norman: University of Oklahoma Press, 1970), pp. 72–76.

The permutations of these amendments can be followed in Lincoln, vol. 1, pp. 543–45. See also Alfred F. Young, *The Democratic Republicans of New York: The Origins, 1763–1797* (Chapel Hill, N.C.: University of North Carolina Press for the Institute for Early American History and Culture, 1967), pp. 17–22.

The original states' constitutions can be most readily studied in Francis N. Thorpe, comp. *The Federal and State Constitutions, Colonial Charters, and Other Organic Laws of the States, Territories, and Colonies now or Heretofore Forming the United States of America.* 7 vols. (Washington, D.C.: U.S. Government Printing Office, 1909). Of the first New York State constitution, three thousand copies were distributed. Lincoln includes the first New York constitution in vol. 1, pp. 162–88.

The first draft was gone over in a close chamber above a prison; the air soon became so fetid from the human emanations that, after a few days, Gouverneur jocosely moved that "the members be permitted to smoke in the convention Chamber to prevent bad effects from the disagreeable effluvia arising from the jail below." *Journals of the Provincial Congress, Provincial Convention, Committee of Safety and Council of Safety of the State of New-York, 1775–1776–1777* (Albany: T. Weed, 1842), vol. 1, p. 242.

85. See *Journals of the Provincial Congress,* vol. 1, pp. 834, 836, 860, as well as Lincoln, vol. 1, p. 533.

86. See *Journals of the Provincial Congress,* vol. 1, pp. 860–61. From 1789 on, of course, naturalization became a federal matter.
87. See Lincoln, vol. 1, pp. 553–56. For Morris's proposal and the Convention's response, see *Historical Magazine* 10 (1866), p. 238; and Sparks, vol. 1, pp. 125–27. On pp. 126–27 John Jay provides a clear statement of his position, which accords very much with Gouverneur's.

That Gouverneur gave way on the slavery issue is to be regretted, but even large historical actors must shape their actions within their contexts.

At his death, Lewis Morris, Jr., owned forty-six slaves. (His property, except the reportedly well-stocked library, is listed in detail in *Staats Long Morris, Mary Lawrence and Richard Morris v Sarah Morris,* 1765, Packet 33, Exhibit D. Testimony, New York State Court of Appeals, Albany.)

To my knowledge, Gouverneur's first public rejection of slavery, made in Kingston in March 1777, was only the second such public utterance in a similar forum in the colonies. In August 1775, the Quaker merchant Moses Brown had led a movement to goad the Rhode Island legislature into acting on an emancipation measure, but his attempt did not bear full fruit until 1784. Pennsylvania, which adopted the most democratic of state constitutions, was also the first state to take positive steps toward abolition. In November 1778, the Pennsylvania Council requested the legislature's lower chamber to prepare a bill for manumitting the newborn children of slaves, but even this measure did not take effect until March 1, 1780. Children born from slaves following the effective passage of this law could be held in bondage until age twenty-eight. Thus it would have been possible for a slave boy born in Pennsylvania in late February 1780 to have lived his life in slavery. And his children, born as late as 1820, to remain enslaved until 1848. Such a scenario actually played out thus in this "progressive" state. See Gary B. Nash and Jean R. Soderlund, *Freedom by Degrees: Emancipation in Pennsylvania and Its Aftermath* (New York: Oxford University Press, 1991).

New Jersey formally outlawed slavery in 1846, when it passed its second emancipation law. But this law did not entirely liberate all of the Garden State's slaves; children of slaves born after the passage of the act were no longer slaves but were to be "apprentices" for life. This law was only superseded by the passage of the 13th Amendment to the U.S. Constitution in 1865.

In New York, needless to say, slave owners were much wealthier and more aggressive than their counterparts in Pennsylvania and New Jersey. On this subject generally, see Edgar McManus, *A History of Negro Slavery in New York* (Syracuse, N.Y.: Syracuse University Press, 1966); Thomas J. Davis, "Slavery in Colonial New York City" (New York: Ph.D. dissertation, Columbia University, 1974); and James G. Lydon, "New York and the Slave Trade, 1700 to 1774," *William and Mary Quarterly,* 3rd ser., 35 (April 1978), 375–94.

As Lydon indicates, between 1748 and 1774 "at least 103 vessels" took part in slave trading in Africa, and these ships made "a minimum of 130 separate voyages" (p. 378). Moreover, he points out, since smuggling was evidently common in the eighteenth century and traders would have attempted "to avoid the heavy provincial duties on slaves" (p. 385) in New York, the total slave trade—official and unofficial—was almost certainly substantially bigger.

In the context of world history, the colonial efforts to abolish slavery may even have been relatively progressive. As late as 1797, the proportion of slave to free in Africa seems to have been roughly three to one. See, for instance, Mungo Park, *Travels in the Interior Districts of Africa, 1795 to 1797* (London: George Newness, 1799), p. 296. The Jamaican Consolidated Slave Law was not passed until 1784. The significance of this statute is explained concisely by James Pope-Hennessy in *Sins of the Fathers* (New York: Knopf, 1968), p. 111. Also revealing in this regard is Philip D. Morgan's depressing "Slaves and Livestock in Eighteenth-Century Jamaica: Vineyard Pen, 1750–51," *William and Mary Quarterly,* 3rd series (January 1995), vol. LII, pp. 47–76.

Under the *asiento,* British slave traders carried more than a million and a half Africans during the eighteenth century. At this time, of course, most of the world accepted slavery.

The last British slave did not perish (in Scotland) until 1819, and Britain did not banish slavery in its Caribbean colonies until passage of the Emancipation Bill in August 1833, a month after the death of William Wilberforce (1759–1833).

This wealthy, evangelical, and well-connected M.P. for Hull began an emancipation campaign in the British House of Commons in 1789. Thanks largely to his efforts, along with those of his valuable foot soldiers Thomas Fowell Buxton (1786–1845) and Thomas Clarkson (1760–1846), the slave trade was abolished in Britain in 1807.

The legislation was spearheaded by George Canning, who wrote to William Windham (1750–1850), on February 26, 1802, asking "to have some talk with you about my Slave Trade Motion." Even this initial communication, however, approached the matter in terms of the best interests of the planters, not the slaves. Canning's letter appears in Windham's published *Diary* (1784–1810), ed. Earl of Rosebery (London: Herbert Jenkins, 1915), pp. 183–84.

The playing of the fountain of honor is sometimes erratic. Although Wilberforce generally receives the lion's share of credit for the abolition of the slave trade in Britain, Canning's 1802 introduction of a slave trade cessation motion in the Commons first had positive effect. And Wilberforce's actions of 1807 and 1830 were a positive follow-on effort, but Clarkson and Buxton's Herculean daily labors have gone without sufficient praise.

88. See, for instance, his eloquent letter on this subject to Alexander Hamilton, dated May 16, 1777 (Alexander Hamilton Papers, Library of Congress).

89. Mintz (p. 111) furthermore remarks that Morris's forward-looking effort to remove what should have been seen as outmoded feudal imposts was far ahead of its time. "It did not succeed until 1845, and then only after a bitter political battle." See in addition Edward P. Cheney, "The Anti-rent Movement and the Constitution of 1845," in Alexander C. Flick, ed., *History of the State of New York* (New York: Columbia University Press, 1934), vol. 6, pp. 317–18.

On the quitrent issue, see also *Journals of the Provincial Congress,* vol. 1, pp. 913, 914, and Flick, *History of the State of New York,* vol. 2, pp. 81–82.

90. See *Journals of the Provincial Congress,* vol. 1, p. 931. The administrative fluidity may have been necessary. The same New York legislature had to flee Kingston in October 1777, ahead of a rapid British advance, and the Council of Safety had to hold the reins of government entirely for more than three months. The legislature, along with the other two incipient branches, did not convene again until January 1778, which explains in large part the gap in the paper record for the early governance of the state. See *Journals of the Provincial Congress,* vol. 1, p. 1111.

91. Morris to the President of the Council of Safety, July 16, 1777, *Journals of the Provincial Congress,* vol. 1, p. 511. An undated, formal report was submitted "to the Hon'able the Representatives of the United States of America" by John Jay and Gouverneur Morris. This report, however, is presented in Gouverneur Morris's obfuscatingly best style, and in a manner even Henry James might have learned from. It is printed in full in *Public Papers of George Clinton* (Albany, N.Y.: Wynkoop, Hallenbeck, Crawford, 1900), vol. 2, pp. 233–36.

Morris's July 16, 1777, letter is more critical but must be read attentively for this to be clear. It ends: "I have this morning been with the General [Schuyler] to the place he intends to occupy. One fortnight will, I hope, put it in a proper posture of defense, which I am extremely happy to inform the council is nothing more than a few open redoubts, with an abbatis; these commanding the roads over a morass on each side of the river . . . will give General Burgoyne some trouble should he attack them, which I am in great hopes he will not be in the capacity of doing," in *Public Papers of George Clinton.* vol. II, p. 117. Indirect as this is, it was as close as Morris, a loyal friend, could come to frank condemnation of Schuyler's poor tactical judgment.

92. Morris to the President of the Council of Safety, July 16, 1777, *Journals of the Provincial Congress . . .* (Albany, N.Y.: T. Weed, 1842), vol. 1, p. 511.

93. Colonial Office Papers, Public Record Office, London, 42/36, folio 7. See "Remarks" at the end of the volume for 1778.

94. Gouverneur Morris Collection, Columbia University Libraries.
95. Piers Mackesy, *The War for America: 1775–1783* (1964; reprinted, Lincoln, Neb.: Bison Books, 1993), p. 134. Better in my view than any American scholar, the British Mackesy reveals the extent to which military victory for the Americans was by no means assured.
96. The important terrain aspect of the New York campaign is well analyzed by Hoffman Nickerson, *The Turning Point of the Revolution* (1928; reprinted, Fort Washington, N.Y.: Kennikat Press, 1967).

3. MORRIS AND THE CONTINENTAL CONGRESS

1. During this arduous winter, Morris and Washington cemented the lifelong friendship that had first taken root in the spring of 1775, when Morris served as one of Washington's two official escorts through New York. At that time, Washington was riding north to assume command of the Continental Army, then fighting around Boston.
2. For the presentation of the New York delegates' credentials, see *Journals of the Continental Congress,* vol. 9, p. 906. Incidentally, the credentials demonstrate the inefficiency of the Congress's administration and structure. They were so ambiguously drafted that Henry Laurens, the president of the Congress, had his clerk note: "[I]t appears that the honorable Philip Livingston, James Duane, Francis Lewis, William Duer, and Gouverneur Morris, or any two of them, are empowered to represent [New York] in Congress" (*Journals,* vol. 9, p. 906). The following year, the number who could represent New York was changed. See also *Journals,* vol. 8, pp. 396–97.

The delegates' credentials do not specify the date by which they were to report to Congress, and since more were elected than were eligible to vote, it is possible that Gouverneur's late arrival was less delinquent than it seems. The credentials also fail to specify a term of service.

The three fundamental sources for the Continental Congress are these.

(1) *Journals of the Continental Congress 1774–1789* (Worthington C. Ford and Gaillard Hunt, eds., 34 vols. [Washington, D.C.: U.S. Government Printing Office, 1904–1937]; the *Journals* are indexed by Kenneth E. Harris and Steven D. Tilley [Washington, D.C.: NARS/GSA, 1976]). The journal entries are brief, not addressing many of the difficulties faced by the Congress or providing adequate information about how the delegates addressed many vexing issues.

(2) *The Papers of the Continental Congress 1774–1789* (available on 204 rolls of microfilm and published by the National Archives and Records Administration, Record Group 360, item M247).

(3) *Letters of Delegates to Congress 1774–1789* (Paul Smith, et al., eds. [Washington, D.C.: U.S. Government Printing Office, 1976]). Twenty-two volumes of the letters have been completed as of this writing; another three are expected. For GM, the most helpful volumes are 10 and 11. Except for the period not yet covered by Smith et al., this work mostly supersedes the eight-volume edition by Edmund C. Burnett, published from 1921 to 1936.

See also *Index of the Papers of the Continental Congress, 1774–1789,* 5 vols. (Washington, D.C.: U.S. Government Printing Office, 1978). Most of the Morris-related entries are indexed in volume 3, pp. 3357–59.

With institutions as with people, we can often best understand them by watching them grow from their inception. The Continental Congress represented the colonies' attempt to present a unified response to the Coercive Acts—that is, it first met as an ad hoc measure, and hence, perhaps, its administrative disarray. The problem was no doubt compounded by the Congress's moves from place to place as the war progressed. It met in eight different cities: Philadelphia, Baltimore, Lancaster, York, Princeton, Annapolis,

Trenton, and New York City. (On November 13, 1777, Henry Laurens wrote to George Washington: "[As it] is a rule in Congress to commit letters to the consideration of particular Boards these being dispersed in different parts of the town and governed by Rules of their own for meeting, it is not always, or I should rather say, it is seldom in the power of the President [that is, Laurens] to answer with that dispatch that may seem necessary" [*Journals of the Continental Congress,* vol. 9, p. 90]).

Yet another problem was that the Congress had some authority and dignity but, having come into being extralegally, no sovereignty. The Articles of Confederation, intended to further the colonies' unification, were drawn up in 1777 but were not ratified (and thus were not effective) until 1781. Consequently, up to that time Congress was acting as a de facto government but without the benefit of a written constitution. The drawbacks of this condition have been ably discussed; see Mitchell Broadus, "Disabilities of Congress," in *The Price of Independence* (New York: Oxford University Press, 1974), and Jennings P. Sanders, *Evolution of Executive Departments of the Continental Congress, 1774–1789* (Chapel Hill, N.C.: University of North Carolina Press, 1935), pp. 4–5 in particular. Sanders quotes GM as having remarked, essentially, that as a committee chair and sole member of a committee he was often compelled to do all the work, and so, while democratic in form, the committee's operation was in fact monarchical. See also *The Diary and Letters of Gouverneur Morris* (New York: Charles Scribner's Sons, 1888), vol. 1, p. 12.

For a valuable general discussion of the Continental Congress, see Jack B. Rakove, *The Beginnings of National Politics: An Interpretive History of the Continental Congress* (New York: Knopf, 1979), and Edmund C. Burnett, *The Continental Congress* (New York: Macmillan, 1941).

In 1759 the often astute British observer Andrew Burnaby wrote: "The colonies, therefore, separately considered, are internally weak; but it may be supposed, that, by a union or coalition, they would become strong and formidable; but a union seems almost impossible . . . [due to] the difficulties of communications, of intercourse, of correspondence, and all other circumstances considered" (Andrew Burnaby, *Travels Through North America,* 3rd ed. [London: A. Wessels, 1904], p. 152. See also pp. 153–54).

3. "Broad-brush" discussion of the Valley Forge encampment can be found in several secondary accounts, foremost of which are Donald B. Chidsey, *Valley Forge* (New York: Crown, 1960) and Frank H. Taylor, *Valley Forge* (Philadelphia: James W. Nagle, 1905).

4. For an account of the Americans' hardships, see James K. Martin, ed., *Ordinary Courage: The Revolutionary War Adventures of Joseph Plumb Martin* (St. James, N.Y.: Brandywine Press, 1993), chapter 4 in particular. See also George Washington's long letter to John Banister, a Virginia delegate to the Continental Congress: "To see men without clothes . . ." (April 21, 1778; in W. B. Allen, ed., *George Washington: Selections* [Indianapolis: Liberty Press, 1985]; and also Washington to George Clinton, February 16, 1778, and Colonel Philip van Cortlandt to George Clinton, February 13, 1778, in *Public Papers of George Clinton,* Hugh Hastings, ed. (Albany: Published by the State of New York/Wynkoop, Hallenbeck, Crawford, 1899–1914), vol. 2, pp. 843–44.

For details of the British commissary, see CO 5/254-ff. 58–83 and 88–89. British Secretary of State to Admiralty. British Public Records Office, London.

5. Francis Dana (1743–1811) was elected to the Congress in 1776 and remained active there until 1779. Dana subsequently served with Morris on the committee appointed by Congress to consider the conciliatory propositions of the British commissioners, Johnson and Eden (see below). After his service in Congress, Dana served as secretary of legation to France. In 1780 he was appointed minister to Prussia, although not publicly received as such. In 1784 he again received election to Congress. In 1792 he became chief justice of Massachusetts.

Joseph Reed (1741–1785) had served as deputy to the Provincial Convention of Pennsylvania in 1774. The next year he was elected as a delegate to the Provincial Convention of Pennsylvania. From July 4, 1775, to mid-May 1776, Reed served as lieutenant colonel and military secretary to General Washington. In early June 1776 he became adjutant general of the Continental Army. This position he resigned in late January 1777, when he became a member of the Continental Congress from Pennsylvania, 1777–1778. Subsequently Reed served as attorney general of Pennsylvania, and then as president of the Supreme Executive Council of Pennsylvania.

Nathaniel Folsom (1726–1790) was elected as a delegate from New Hampshire to the Continental Congress in 1774 and 1777–80. Prior to the Congress, however, he had fairly extensive military experience, having served as a captain in Colonel Blanchard's regiment during the French and Indian War, and then as a field grade officer in the Fourth Regiment of New Hampshire Militia, which he commanded when the Revolutionary War began. As brigadier general, he commanded the New Hampshire troops sent to Massachusetts in 1775. In this leadership position he participated in the siege of Boston. And as major general he planned the details of the movement of the New Hampshire troops to Ticonderoga.

John Harvie (1742–1807) served as a delegate to the Continental Congress from Virginia in 1777. Afterward, he became secretary of state for Virginia.

Charles Carroll (1737–1832) was a propertied Marylander with huge wealth. Prior to his service on the Committee of Correspondence, he had been an unsuccessful commissioner to Canada in the attempt to bring about a union between Canada and the colonies. He was the sole Roman Catholic signatory of the Declaration of Independence.

See also Kate Mason Rowland, *The Life of Charles Carroll of Carrollton,* 2 vols. (New York: G. P. Putnam, 1898), in which she asserts that Carroll, one of the richest men in America at the time, served on the Committee of Conference for three months. But records of the Congress do not support his having done any service at the camp. Not surprisingly, subsequent scholars have often followed Rowland's error.

See *American National Biography,* John A. Garraty and Mark C. Carnes, eds. (New York: Oxford University Press, 1999).

6. The Council of Pennsylvania was then sitting in Lancaster, the scene of all the excitement, so a personal call would have been possible.

7. The essential primary sources for this teapot tempest are Morris to Joseph Reed, April 9, 1779 (Reed Manuscripts, vol. VI, 1779, at the New-York Historical Society); Edmund C. Burnett, ed., *Letters of Members of the Continental Congress,* vol. III, pp. 49, 62–63; *Pennsylvania Archives* (Philadelphia: Joseph Severns, 1853), 1st series, vol. VI, pp. 201–202; George Washington to Board of War, January 26, 1778; to Lt. Col. William S. Smith, January 27, 1778; and to Horatio Gates, January 27, 1778 (*The Papers of George Washington, Revolutionary War Series,* Philander D. Chase and Edward G. Lengel, eds. (Charlottesville: University Press of Virginia, 2002), vol. 13; copies of the letters were graciously supplied to me by Dorothy H. Twohig, Philander Chase, and Frank Grizzard. See also deposition of James Christy, February 3, 1778, *Pennsylvania Archives,* 1st series, vol. VI, pp. 233, 263; and Robert L. Brunhouse, *The Counter-Revolution in Pennsylvania, 1776–1790* (1942; reprint, New York: Octagon, 1971), p. 47. In my view, Edmund C. Burnett's account in *The Continental Congress* (New York; Macmillan, 1941) is unhelpful.

8. Nor was Laurens alone in getting a bad first impression of GM. Robert Morris, a delegate to the Continental Congress from Philadelphia, observed that Gouverneur had "first-rate abilities" but added, "I think he will be immensely useful if he pursues his objects steadily (for I have been told his only blemish is being a little too whimsical)." The two men later became close associates and friends.

Henry Laurens's letter to the Marquis de Lafayette (from York), January 28, 1778, *The Papers of Henry Laurens,* David R. Chesnutt, et al., eds. (Columbia, S.C.: University of South Carolina Press, 1990), vol. 12, p. 366.

Robert Morris's assessment of GM is in a letter to Richard Peters, also of Pennsylvania, dated January 25, 1778, in the General Wayne Papers at the Historical Society of Pennsylvania, in Philadelphia.

9. Morris's letters are in the John Jay Papers, microfilm edition, Columbia University Libraries. It seems that at least one Pennsylvania regiment did not lack food and other comforts. Lieutenant James McMichael recorded the abundant feasting at the mess of Colonel Stewart's 13th Pennsylvania Regiment. See "The Diary of Lieutenant James

McMichael of the Pennsylvania Line, 1776–78," *The Pennsylvania Magazine of History and Biography,* vol. 16, no. 2 (1892).

10. See *American National Biography.*

    The Committee of Conference Minutes, Jan. 28, 1778, *Papers of the Continental and Confederation Congresses* (Washington, D.C.: NARS Microfilm edition). See also therein the letters from Dana to the president of Congress, January 28 and 29, 1778. Also cf. Document number 33, n. 71.

11. The "Establishment of the American Army," as reported out of Congress on May 27, 1778, can be examined in clear and convenient schematic form in *Public Papers of George Clinton, First Governor of New York* (Albany: Published by the State of New York/ Wynkoop, Hallenbeck, Crawford, 1900), vol. 3, pp. 434–39. This report also includes addenda resolutions of May 29 and June 2, 1778.

    As an example of how Washington, who was then forty-six, worked with the twenty-six-year-old Morris, the general wrote the congressman in April 1778 to point out that "the commanding officer of Artillery" had been "negatively excluded" from the Council of War as set up by the Congress: the council had been stipulated to include the infantry's "major generals and the chief engineer." Morris conceded the point at once, writing that the artillery commander, General Knox, "is to attend the council."

    Some of Morris's other proposals for army reorganization that the Congress did not accept may also have been sensible. For instance, on May 28, 1778, he submitted to Congress a plan calling for "some mode" to be "adopted to keep the Regiments full as to Officers, and some Line of Promotion chalked out for their Satisfaction." He suggests "that generally seniority shall be regarded but that a Power be given in extraordinary Cases of merit or Demerit to vary from that Principle" (GM no. 1440, *Public Papers of George Clinton,* vol. 3 [1900], pp. 371–72).

    Even before the completion of the committee's report, Washington was steadily using his leadership to improve the morale of the Continental soldiery; in a sense, the general essentially told his men at Valley Forge how strong they were, in order to bolster their courage. See, for example, Washington's speech at Valley Forge of March 2, 1778. In his morale-boosting Washington had a job of work, not least because of a clever British disinformation campaign. See, for instance, General George Weedon's *Valley Forge Orderly Book, 1777–78* (New York: Dodd, Mead, 1902), pp. 244–47, and the message of April 23, 1778 (pp. 296–97, for example). See also *Journals of the Continental Congress,* vol. 11, pp. 533–43.

12. See George Washington to the President of Congress, December 23, 1777, and to Wharton, March 7, 1778, Worthing Chauncey Ford, ed., *Writings of George Washington* (New York: G. P. Putnam's, 1889–92), vol. 6, pp. 258 and 394–96. Although Washington's army no doubt suffered more, food shortages were felt throughout the eight-year war by many American civilians: during this period, at least thirty-seven civilian food riots occurred.

    As Barbara Clark Smith remarks, "Most of these riotous crowds objected to 'exorbitant' prices that shopkeepers demanded for their goods or to merchants' practice of withholding commodities from the market altogether." "Food Rioters and the American Revolution," *The William and Mary Quarterly,* 3rd ser., vol. LI, no. 1 (January 1994), 3–38. In an appendix, Smith lists "American Food Riots, 1775–1779."

13. See, for example, Board of War to the Continental Congress, June 11, 1979. *Board of War Papers.* III, pp. 418–33.

    On October 4, 1778, Washington wrote to GM from Fishkill, New York: "A Rat, in the shape of a Horse, is not to be bought at this time for less than £200." At the time a good horse usually sold for about £15, although prices often varied wildly.

    Adrienne D. Hood suggests some of the domestic reasons for the persistent clothing shortages: "The Material Worlds of Cloth: Production and Use in Eighteenth Century Rural Pennsylvania," *William and Mary Quarterly,* 3rd ser., vol. 53, no. 1 (January 1996), 43–66. See especially pages 58–59 and footnotes 45 and 46. Hood's work suggests that a combination of selfishness, rapacity, and indolence largely accounted for the deprivation of the troops. See also E. Wayne Carp, *To Starve the Army at Pleasure: Continental Army Administration and American Political Culture, 1775–1783* (Chapel Hill, N.C.: University of North Carolina Press, 1984), and Don Higginbotham, *The War of American Independence: Military Attitudes, Policies, and Practices, 1763–1789* (New York: Macmillan, 1971), pp. 398–99. (The evaporation of officers resigning their commissions is discussed on pp. 400–401.)

The British were well aware of American clothing shortages: they obtained detailed lists of materials ordered from Europe for the American forces by studying the manifests of America-bound ships taken into Guernsey by the Royal Navy. See, for example, State Papers Domestic, S.P. 47, Channel Islands (to 1782), Public Records Office, London.

14. See John C. Fitzpatrick, ed., *Writings of George Washington from the Original Manuscript Sources, 1745–1799* (Washington, D.C.: U.S. Government Printing Office, 1931), vol. XI, p. 237; and Charles H. Lesser, *The Sinews of Independence: Monthly Strength Reports of the Continental Army* (Chicago: University of Chicago Press, 1976). Lesser clearly indicates that enlistments dropped every year from 1776 through 1781. The colonies had to quickly initiate the draft. Even so, by 1779 no more than one in sixteen male Americans of military age was in uniform, less than half the number in 1776. See Franklin Jameson, *The American Revolution Considered as a Social Movement* (Princeton: Princeton University Press, 1926), p. 48.

In *The Morale of the American Revolutionary Army* (1943; rpt., New York: Kennikat, 1964), Allen Bowman indicates that roughly 30 percent of American courts-martial dealt with line officers and noncommissioned officers. This percentage is high for any army at any time.

15. See Jared Sparks, ed., *Correspondence of the American Revolution* (Boston: Little, Brown, 1853), vol. 2, p. 67; Worthington Chauncey Ford, ed. *Writings of George Washington* (New York: G. P. Putnam's, 1889–93), vol. 6, pp. 301–304, 445, 466, 477–79; vol. 7, pp. 16, 20, 348–55, 449–52, 454–68.

16. Morris to Washington, October 25, 1778, in Smith, ed., *Letters of Delegates,* vol. 10, p. 78. The history of the half-pay/pension bill can be traced in William H. Glasson, *Federal Military Pensions in the United States,* David Kinley, ed. (New York: Oxford University Press, 1918), pp. 26–47. Glasson also explains the major plausible objections to the various versions of the legislation.

17. The land and river obstacles produced by Washington's engineers and infantry officers have thus far been afforded insufficient credit. Effective water obstacles, for instance, were chevaux-de-frise. These were sharp spikes, strung together with wire, placed into large boxes, and weighed down with stones. These devices were positioned in the approach rivers and streams, just under the surface of the water. Thus canoes and boatmen acting as British reconnaissance units unwittingly moved their hulls over these obstacles and punctured the bottoms of their crafts.

The British political leadership harshly criticized Howe's inaction during this period. See, for example, William Bodham Donne, ed., *The Correspondence of King George the Third with Lord North from 1768 to 1783* (London: J. Murray, 1867), vol. 4, pp. 345–52.

18. See, for instance, George Ewing's diary, excerpted in George F. Scheer and Hugh F. Rankin, eds., *Rebels and Redcoats* (New York: Da Capo, 1977), pp. 308–309; and Albert Manucy, *Artillery Through the Ages* (Washington, D.C.: Government Printing Office, 1949), pp. 55, 73–85.

Reliable British officers, such as Frederick Mackenzie (*Diary,* 2 vols. [Cambridge, Mass.: Harvard University Press, 1930]), admitted that the colonists were much the superior marksmen in this war. Some obvious reasons for the American superiority are not difficult to find: the British were almost completely innocent of aimed musket fire. Contemporary drillbooks reveal that the position of the soldier at "Present" and "Fire" has him aiming with the butt of his firelock pressed against his shoulder and his head erect, rather than aiming even down the barrel of the piece. The British longarm of the eighteenth century lacked rear sights; with the bayonet affixed, even the bayonet lug, which could have served as some rough guide, was invisible.

Moreover, in the kneeling position the front-rank men failed to support the weight of the rifle by placing the rifle on the knee. In addition, slings were evidently never adjusted to appropriate tightness. Some of these commonsense soldierly deficiencies are pointed out by J. A. Houlding. *Fit for Service* (Oxford: Clarendon Press, 1981). See especially pp. 279–81.

Serious marksmanship training flaws, combined with the fact that, in the British army of the time, "free commissions" (meaning merit based) were scarce, leads the sober reader to marvel at what a tough fight the Revolution proved to be. Marksmen the British were not; but they were disciplined, proud, and brave.

The American drills with the bayonet counted for a great deal in such tactical victories as the attack at Stony Point in 1779, led by General Anthony Wayne. This battle, in which the Pennsylvania line proved so effective, constituted payback for the British success at Paoli, Pennsylvania, not far from Wayne's house.

Needless to say, the author has checked out these generalizations in relevant British historical repositories such as the Marines' Museum, Naval Station, Portsmouth, England; the Imperial War Museum; and the Victoria and Albert, London, England.

19. This committee's work alone would have exhausted most. Morris somehow managed to juggle it with the work of his other eight committees *and*, in the same period, to publish "An Address of the Congress to the Inhabitants of the United States." (This was a trenchant essay on the significance of the recently cemented alliance with France.) With Richard Henry Lee and Roger Sherman, he also drafted the initial instructions to the American peace commissioners in Europe. And in mid-September the same year, he chaired a committee to prepare draft instructions to Benjamin Franklin, the American minister plenipotentiary to France.

20. As prime minister from 1770 through 1782, North occupied a position of crucial importance throughout the Revolutionary period. His policies, however, had the support of George III and, until the end of 1779, the majority of his subjects. For an eagle's eye view of the subject, see Richard Pares, *Limited Monarchy in Great Britain in the 18th Century* (London: Historical Association, 1957), pp. 12–15, 20–27. That George III spurred North's policies is clear from the monarch's correspondence. See, for example, numbers 2170, 2179, 2180, 2161, and 2162 in volume 4 of *George III: Correspondence, 1760–83,* J. W. Fortescue, ed. (London: Macmillan, 1927–1928). In my view, much of the blame that North has been assigned for the American debacle belongs rightly to George III, who not only appointed North but also refused his repeated requests to be relieved of the premiership.

Nevertheless, historians generally have agreed with Henry Gratton's son, who calls North "the best of private men and the worst of public ministers": "from 1769 to 1782 he ruled with fatal sway, and urged headlong, in his impetuous career, the fates, the fortunes and the reputation of Great Britain." Henry Gratton, *Memoirs of the Life and Times of Rt. Hon. Henry Gratton* (London: Henry Colburn, 1849), vol. 1, p. 211.

On North's February 1778 proposals, see William Cobbett, *Cobbett's Parliamentary History of England from the Norman Conquest in 1066 to the year 1803* (London: R. Bagshaw, 1806), vol. 19, pp. 867–70; *Journals of the Continental Congress,* vol. 10, pp. 374–80; *Pennsylvania Gazette* (June 20, 1780, *passim;* and Robert Leckie, *George Washington's War* (New York: HarperCollins, 1992), pp. 452–57.

21. Headlam's assessment appears in his chapter "International Relations, 1763–1783," in *The Cambridge History of the British Empire,* J. Holland Rose et al., eds. (Cambridge, U.K.: Cambridge University Press, 1929), vol. 1, pp. 701–15 in particular.

22. Piers Mackesy is quoted from his "British Strategy in the War of American Independence," *Yale Review* 52 (Fall 1963), pp. 539–57; the quotation is from p. 550. I disagree with some aspects of William B. Willcox's "British Strategy in America, 1778," *Journal of Modern History* 19 (June 1947), 97–121, but he usefully supplements Mackesy's analysis of Germain's political reasoning and strategy. So does Gerald S. Brown, *The American Secretary: The Colonial Policy of Lord Germain, 1775–1778* (Ann Arbor: University of Michigan Press, 1963); see in particular chapter 6, "The Plans for the Campaign of 1777." Max M. Mintz's *The Generals of Saratoga: John Burgoyne and Horatio Gates* (New Haven: Yale University Press, 1990) is well worth attention. And for a view of the battle within the larger tapestry of the war, I recommend chapter 9 of David H. Zook, Jr., and Robin Higham, *A Short History of Warfare,* 2nd ed. (New York: Simon & Schuster, 1966).

Lord Germain, who presided over the American Department during this strategically disastrous period for Britain, is George Sackville Germain (1716–1785). He was known as Lord George Sackville until he assumed the name of Germain in 1770. He was created Viscount Sackville in 1782.

In his *Historical Memoirs of My Own Time* (London: A. C. Black, 1815), vol. 2, pp. 305–311, Nathaniel W. Wraxall endeavors to characterize Lord Germain, whom he knew well, liked, and admired. Wraxall says he rarely "opened an Author," even in retirement, and Germain's ignorance of history was surely a serious deficiency in a statesman. His policies during the revolutionary era were failures. For more on Germain's weaknesses as a statesman, see *The Papers of Lord Germain*, Randolph G. Adams, ed. (Ann Arbor: The William L. Clements Library, 1928).

23. Jan Willem Schulte Nordholt and Wim Klooster, "The Influence of the American Revolution in the Netherlands," in *A Companion to the American Revolution*, ed. Jack P. Greene and J. R. Pole (Oxford: Blackwell, 2000), pp. 545–49.

On this subject, see also Friedrich Edler's still valuable *The Dutch Republic and the American Revolution* (Baltimore: Johns Hopkins University Studies in Historical and Political Science. 29th series, 1911); and Jan W. Schulte Nordholdt, *The Dutch Republic and American Independence*, Herbert H. Rowen, trans. (Chapel Hill, N.C.: University of North Carolina Press, 1982), especially chapters 13 and 17.

On January 23, 1783, a treaty of amity and commerce and a convention concerning recaptures of commercial items were ratified by Congress, having been signed by the Dutch and American plenipotentiaries at the Hague on October 8, 1782. The agreements went into effect in early summer 1783. In the event, America proved a rival rather than a customer of the Dutch republic. By 1786 American merchants had taken over from the Dutch a great amount of the China trade and had established a flourishing illicit commerce with the Dutch West Indian colonies, Surinam, and the Cape of Good Hope, all to the commercial disadvantage of the United Provinces. See Edler's chapter 8 in particular; for Britain's maneuverings against the Dutch, see his chapter 9.

24. Vergennes had become minister of foreign affairs at the accession of Louis XVI in 1774 and held the position until 1787, the year he died. The fullest biography is Orville T. Murphy, *Charles Gravier, Comte de Vergennes* (Albany: State University of New York Press, 1982), which is old-fashioned in the best sense of the term: Murphy presents Vergennes's robust career in a well-balanced manner and gives a clear and economical explanation of his subject's vision (p. x).

In Murphy's words, "Vergennes believed with almost a mathematical certainty that war [with Britain] was inevitable" (p. 526, n. 8). Regarding the treaty of alliance, the most important articles are 2, 5, 6, and 8. In *Leading American Treaties* (New York: Macmillan, 1992), C. E. Hill presents a readable and cogent summary. Both treaties appear in D. Hunter Miller, *Treaties and Other International Acts of the United States of America* (Washington, D.C.: The Carnegie Institution, 1931), vol. 2.

On the presentation of the relevant Franco-American treaties to the British government, see (British) State Papers, Public Record Office, London, 78/306, folios 345–46 and 365–66. For the start of hostilities and the declaration of war, see G. S. Brown's lucid "The Anglo-French Naval Crisis, 1778: A Study of Conflict in the North Cabinet," *William and Mary Quarterly*, 3rd ser., 13 (January 1956), 3–25. Especially pertinent is n. 4 on p. 4.

On the shipping losses inflicted by American privateers on the British, see John Fortescue, ed., *Correspondence of George III*, vol. 2, p. 275, as well as House of Lords (British) Sessional Papers, February 1778.

Valuable primary source material for the Franco-American alliance may be found in the following: the Auckland Papers, British Museum Additional Mss. 29475, 34412–34417; and Henri Doniol, *Histoire de la participation de la France à l'établissement des États-Unis d'Amérique: Correspondance diplomatique et documents,* 5 vols., and a supplementary volume (Paris: Imprimerie Nationale, 1886–1892). The Auckland Papers comprise the official papers, correspondence, and dispatches to and from William Eden, who became first Lord Auckland, under secretary of state, and, one of the three members of the Carlisle Commission. They are especially revelatory on the British reaction to Burgoyne's surrender and on the Carlisle Commission. Doniol's collection is particularly valuable, since it includes documents from the archives of the French Foreign Office concerning the eventual alliance with America.

The secondary literature on the Franco-American pact is unusually rich and voluminous; the bibliography that follows is therefore rigorously selective. Laura C. Sheldon, *France and the American Revolution, 1763–1778* (Ph.D. diss., Cornell University, 1895) is an admirable, compact, pioneering monograph. Edward S. Corwin, *French Policy and the American Alliance of 1778* (Princeton: Princeton University Press, 1916) is a well-balanced exposition of the subject. Alexander DeConde, *Entangling Alliances* (Palo Alto: Stanford University Press, 1958) contains controversial revisionist views. Samuel Flagg Bemis, *The Diplomacy of the American Revolution* (1935; rpt., Bloomington: Indiana University Press, 1957) is now somewhat superannuated. William Stinchcombe's *The American Revolution and the French Alliance* (Syracuse, N.Y.: Syracuse University Press, 1969) is a lucid study, particularly valuable for its emphasis on the subject from the institutional perspective of the Continental Congress. Ronald Hoffman and Peter J. Albert, eds., *The Franco-American Alliance of 1778* (Charlottesville, Va.: University Press of Virginia, 1981) present five thought-provoking essays on aspects of the subject and its primary actors. Jonathan Dull, *The Diplomatic History of the American Revolution* (New Haven: Yale University Press, 1985) provides a detailed exposition, which seeks to clarify many aspects of the alliance. Dull somewhat overemphasizes Benjamin Franklin's ambassadorial accomplishments and underestimates the extent of French diplomatic casuistry. In H. M. Scott's *British Foreign Policy in the Age of the American Revolution* (Oxford, Eng.: Clarendon Press, 1990), chapters 1, 10, 11, and 12 and the conclusion are especially relevant. Scott examines the subject from a British standpoint, and with a much broader international perspective than any diplomatic historian before him. He correctly emphasizes the extent to which the eighteenth-century British "formulation and execution of official policy" relied on "the central importance of personalities," a generalization he ably clarifies and qualifies (see pp. 27–28). In this regard, that the British Foreign Office was not established until 1782—a full year after the ultimately decisive Battle of Yorktown—appears relevant. Stanley J. Idzerda, ed., *France and the American War for Independence* (New York: Scott Ltd. Eds., n.d.) is in some ways cogent, but utterly lacks scholarly documentation. Needless to say, the journal literature on the subjects surveyed in the foregoing paragraphs is vast.

25. For more detail, see George L. Clark, *Silas Deane* (New York: Putnams, 1913) and C. H. Van Tyne, "French Aid Before the Alliance of 1778," *American Historical Review* 31 (October 1925), 20–40. Clark concentrates chiefly on Deane's less than seemly and successful French episodes.

In *British Foreign Policy in the Age of the American Revolution,* cited earlier, H. M. Scott says "the recruitment of British diplomats" during this period "could be, and often was, remarkably haphazard" (p. 25). This may be true, but the training, placement, and handling of Britain's spies was superb. Several chapters hence, our narrative will indicate how one British spy crippled Gouverneur Morris's first official overseas assignment.

The subject of British spying during the American Revolutionary era is fascinating, but the story has not yet been adequately told. Several authors, however, have made attempts. Carl Van Doren's *Secret History of the American Revolution* (New York: Viking, 1941) in fact concerns the Arnold-André affair almost exclusively. Helen Augur's *The Secret War of Independence* (New York: Duell, Sloan & Pearce, 1955) is an insufficiently detailed treatment and of course suffers from lack of access to many sources now available. John E. Bakeless's *Turncoats, Traitors and Heroes* (Philadelphia: Lippincott, 1960) suffers from much the same lacunae and emphasizes American-based military-related espionage activities to the substantial neglect of the numerous clever British and continental European clandestine movements.

26. Albert Sorel, *L'Europe et la révolution française,* 8 vols. (Paris: E. Plon, Nourrit, 1889–1904). See the labyrinthine nature of continental diplomacy at the time as portrayed

by Sorel in vol. 1, *Les moeurs politiques et les traditions,* passim. Some notion of the lack of diplomatic security, the bad judgments, and the oversights is conveyed by Samuel Flagg Bemis, "British Secret Service and the French-American Alliance," *American Historical Review* 29 (April 1924), 474–95. The account in Elias Boudinot's *Journal . . . During the Revolutionary War* (Philadelphia: F. Bourquin, 1894), pp. 26–29, of Silas Deane's "profoundly secret" dealings with the French induces a sardonic smile.

27. Doniol, vol. 3, p. 281; translation mine. Also relevant here is C. H. Van Tyne's "Influences Which Determined the French Treaty with America in 1778," *American Historical Review* 21 (December 1915), 528–41.

28. Bonvouloir's 1775–1776 mission was unofficial but bore much fruit. See Joseph Hamon, *Le chevalier de Bonvouloir, premier émissaire sécret de la France auprès du Congrès de Philadelphia avant l'indépendance américaine* (Paris: Jouve, 1953), a rare monograph on the secret emissaryship to Congress in Philadelphia, which also provides some post-1778 information, including memoranda from the Archives Nationales, for the years 1778–1781. Regarding the '75–'76 mission, see also James B. Perkins, *France in the American Revolution* (Boston: Houghton Mifflin, 1911), who concludes that "though he [Bonvouloir] had no official position, his expedition must be regarded as the first formal step towards action in behalf of America taken by France" (p. 46). Relevant biographical material on Bonvouloir can be found in Mark M. Boatner III, *Encyclopedia of the American Revolution* (New York: David McKay, 1966), pp. 2–4. Also somewhat helpful is "Bonvouloir" in John Durand, *New Materials for the History of the American Revolution* (New York: Henry Holt, 1889), pp. 1–16.

29. Georges Edouard Lemaître, *Beaumarchais* (New York: Knopf, 1949), pp. 180–86.

Beaumarchais's life and career have occupied many biographers. Of the numerous lives, probably the best are Béatrice Didier, *Beaumarchais* (Paris: Presses Universitaires de France, 1994), and Lemaître, *Beaumarchais*. Didier's study focuses on Beaumarchais as an artist, whereas Lemaître emphasizes his achievements as a man of the world; the two biographies complement each other well.

The strongest of these statements was drafted April 1776, the same month as Lexington (!): "Reflections on the Present Situation of the English Colonies, and on the Conduct Which France Ought to Hold in Regard to Them," in Doniol I, 243–49. All of Beaumarchais's *aides-mémoires* on America are in Doniol. On this subject see also John J. Meng, ed., *Despatches and Instructions of Conrad Alexandre Gérard, 1778–1780* (Baltimore: Johns Hopkins Press, 1939), p. 57, n. 2. On the memorandum matter, see also Meng, "A Footnote to Secret Aid in the American Revolution," *American Historical Review* 43 (Fall 1953), 791–95.

30. Without the French and Spanish munitions, Saratoga would likely not have been the breakthrough victory that led the French to make formal treaties with the Americans. On the Spanish commitments to the American cause, the indispensable source is Valentin Urtasun, *Historia diplomatica de America*. Vol. 1: *La alianza francesca* (Pamplona, Spain: H. Coronas, 1920).

Considering the early French interest (would "eagerness" be too strong a word?) in the American cause, the fact that Beaumarchais was one of the early French envoys seems almost too perfect: the earliest American overtures in France were treated with seeming coolness that Deane, for one, read as rebuff. Beaumarchais is remembered today as a master of French drama, but the comic intrigue he created for *The Barber of Seville* and *The Marriage of Figaro* could not improve on the drawing-room comedies enacted during these years by Silas Deane, Arthur Lee, and Benjamin Franklin as they were manipulated by French officials. Nonetheless, the Americans owed the successful outcome of the war, in large part, to French aid. In *France in the American Revolution* (Boston: Houghton Mifflin, 1911), James Breck Perkins readably pursues this thesis, although too single-mindedly.

31. North's motions, along with the relevant ancillary materials, can be found in *The Parliamentary History of England from the Earliest Period to the Year 1803,* vol. 19 (London: T. C. Hammond, 1809), pp. 762–870. The Papers of Lord North, Prime Minister,

1770–1782 (British Library Additional Manuscripts, 61860–61876) are now available in microform from Harvester Press Microform Publications, Ltd., in the "Prime Ministers of Great Britain Series." The understanding of North's premiership necessitates the study of the papers of a great many of his leading contemporaries. Some insights from the French standpoint into the committee responding to the Carlisle Commission can be found in John J. Meng, ed., *Despatches and Instructions of Conrad Alexandre Gérard, 1778–1780* (Baltimore: Johns Hopkins Press, 1939).

32. Benjamin F. Stevens, *Stevens's Facsimiles of Manuscripts in European Archives Relating to America, 1773–1783,* vol. V, no. 500, and vol. XI, nos. 1099 and 1100. On the members of the Commission, see *Carlisle Manuscripts,* p. 377. An adequate number of the Carlisle papers germane to our story can be read in Great Britain, Royal Commission on Historical Manuscripts, *Fifteenth Report,* Appendix, Part VI, *The Manuscripts of the Earl of Carlisle Presented at Castle Howard* (London: for H.M.S.O. by Eyre and Spottiswoode, 1897). The lengthy memoranda and letters reveal, in particular, the frustrations and difficulties experienced by Carlisle and his commission, even before disembarkation. In early July 1778, aboard *Trident,* on the Delaware, Carlisle complained of gnats "as large as sparrows" off what is now South Philadelphia (p. 345).

33. Lord North's ministerial difficulties at this period are cogently analyzed by Alan Valentine in *Lord North* (Norman: University of Oklahoma Press, 1967), vol. 2, chapters 29–32.

   On the British elite of the day, Alan Valentine's two-volume *The British Establishment, 1760–1784: An Eighteenth Century Biographical Dictionary* (Norman: University of Oklahoma Press, 1986) is clearer, more accurate, and more up-to-date than the *Dictionary of National Biography.* Unfortunately, it does not include a bibliography, which greatly diminishes its usefulness to scholars.

34. *Carlisle Manuscripts,* p. 377.

35. In a March 30, 1778, letter to Lord North, Eden hints strongly that this was so, complaining of "the coolness with which this business has been from the first treated by the cabinet." The letter is in B. F. Stevens. *Facsimiles of Manuscripts . . . 1773–1783,* vol. IV, no. 411. Secondary scholarship on the commission sheds additional light on these issues. See especially Weldon A. Brown. *Empire or Independence: A Study in the Failure of Reconciliation, 1774–1783* (Baton Rouge: Louisiana State University Press, 1941), chapters 9 and 10 in particular. Also valuable, for Germain's viewpoint, is Gerald S. Brown, *The American Secretary* (Ann Arbor: University of Michigan Press, 1963), especially chapter 8. See also William B. Willcox, "British Strategy in America, 1778," *Journal of Modern History,* vol. 19 (June 1947), pp. 97–121 and 249–260, a brace of essays that are notably illuminative.

   Britain's numerous spies provided ample and reliable early warning of French intentions, so it is telling that Germain put off until March 18, 1778, a first meeting to consider defense plans for the Leeward Islands against the French fleet. It suggests that the ministership was behindhand; the courageous British military deserved better. On this and other matters related to Germain's handling of the American war, see William Oxenham Hewlett, ed., *Report on the Manuscripts of Mrs. Stopford Sackville, of Drayton House, Northamptonshire* (London: H. M. Stationery Office, 1904–10). The report is in two volumes, the first mostly concerned with the British Isles, Europe, and India, the second bearing mostly on America, Canada, and the West Indies. For the March 18 meeting, see, in particular, vol. 2, p. 272.

   In *The British Navy in Adversity* (London: Longmans, Green, 1926), W. M. James describes the Admiralty's war plan at this period of the Revolution in four appropriately brief paragraphs (chapter seven). "There was no plan," he says, "nor, indeed, was there very much to plan with." James's account of naval tactics is brisk and clear; his maps are uncluttered, straightforward, and useful.

   Needless to say, Americans at this period were not prepared for a war in which they were part of an alliance against England. In a June 13, 1778, letter to GM, for example, Robert Livingston speculates that America may make peace with England and then let England and France fight it out (Gouverneur Morris Collection, no. 783, New-York Historical

Society). See also Alan S. Brown, "The British Peace Offer of 1778: A Study in Ministerial Confusion," *Papers of the Michigan Academy of Science, Arts and Letters* 40 (1955), 249–60.

36. See Morris to Jay, Aug. 18, 1778, in Richard B. Morris, ed., *John Jay: The Making of a Revolutionary* (New York: Harper & Row, 1975), p. 88. See also *Journals of the Continental Congress,* XI, pp. 507, 733–34; XII, pp. 1213–14, 1222–23; and *Papers of the Continental Congress* (microfilm edition), item 23 (p. 351). And on Morris as one of three members of Gérard's reception committee, see *Journals of the Continental Congress,* XI, p. 733.

37. That the British loss at Saratoga provided much of the impetus for the dispatch of the Carlisle Commission is strongly indicated by the following incident: in his November 18, 1777, "Address to the throne concerning Affairs in America," Lord Chatham (1708–1778) seized the occasion of a traditionally bland annual address to the throne to move an amendment to protest again very boldly against what he believed to be the injustice and folly of the war: "My Lords, *you cannot conquer America. . . .*"

    Unbeknownst to Chatham, the British force under Burgoyne had surrendered at Saratoga on October 13, although America's alliance with France had not as yet become solidified. Despite Chatham's *gravitas* in the British political world at the time, not to mention the lustrous eloquence of his speech, his proposed amendment was soundly rejected, 97 to 24. See Cornelius B. Bradley, ed., *Orations and Arguments by English and American Statesmen* (Boston: Allyn and Bacon, 1895). Needless to say, evidence of the pro-war feeling at the time abounds in the official records. After the news of Saratoga arrived, the British government decided to give conciliation a try.

38. Johnstone to Robert Morris, Feb. 5, 1778. In Burnett, *The Continental Congress,* p. 330, and *Journals of the Continental Congress* X, p. 398n.

39. Morris to Jay. April 28, 1778. *Letters of the Continental Congress,* Burnett, ed., vol. III, pp. 199–200. Like about half of Morris's letters to Jay in this period of several months, it never reached its destination. These letters may indeed have been intercepted by British spies.

    The attentive reader will see the dramatic irony in Morris's reference to "as well as him from England." The "three months" to victory pronouncement is typical of Morris's oversanguine vision of American military prowess.

40. As regards the official notification of Congress, see also Robert Morris to Henry Laurens, April 26, 1778, *The Papers of Henry Laurens* (Columbia: University of South Carolina Press, 1992), vol. 13, p. 195. Morris's April 27 note to Jay reveals that he assumed Britain's *known* presence at the negotiations in Paris.

41. *Journal of the Continental Congress,* vol. XI, 605–606, 608–611, 614–15, and 776. For a British assessment, see *Carlisle Manuscripts,* p. 341.

42. On these exchanges, see Cobbett, *Parliamentary History,* vol. 19, pp. 867–70; Chestnutt, et al., *The Papers of Henry Laurens,* vol. 13, pp. 420–21; *Journals of the Continental Congress,* vol. X, pp. 374–80; and *The Pennsylvania Gazette,* June 20, 1778.

    The drafts of Lee and Witherspoon may be found in *Letters of Members of the Continental Congress,* ed. Peter Smith, vol. 3, pp. 296–297.

43. The text of this response, signed "AN AMERICAN," can be found, along with helpful annotations, in Smith, ed., *Letters of Delegates,* vol. 10, pp. 154–162. On Morris's central role in the four responses to the Carlisle Commission, see, for example, notes 1 and 2 in Smith, p. 162. See p. 105, note 1 in Smith, however, to explain how Morris adapted Richard Henry Lee's draft to produce the finally promulgated version.

44. The undated, fourteen-page manuscript is in the Gouverneur Morris Collection at Columbia University. Its many emendations and insertions offer much insight into Morris's thought processes. His friends immediately recognized the responses as his. See, for example, Richard B. Morris, ed., *John Jay: The Making of a Revolutionary: Unpublished Papers, 1745–1780* (New York: Harper & Row, 1975), p. 482, for Jay's letter to Morris, dated May 20, 1778: "The report of Congress on the subject of Lord North's Bills was too strikingly marked with Morris not to be known by his friends to have been produced by his pen."

45. The letter appears in vol. 12, pp. 146–52, of *Letters of Delegates to Congress* 12 (Washington, D.C.: Library of Congress, 1987). The series is superbly edited by Paul H. Smith.

46. On the special nature of Morris's public audiences, see *Journals of the Continental Congress,* vol. XI, p. 688; vol. XII, p. 1063; vol XIII, p. 421. *Observations* was published in 1779 both in Philadelphia and, by the *Remembrancer,* in London; it has been less noticed that an entire volume of the *Remembrancer* in 1780 was devoted to a complete republication of *Observations.* See also Carlisle's minutes dated August 29, 1778, in *Carlisle Manuscripts,* p. 362.

The low morale among both civilians and soldiers in America in 1778 is suggested by the status of paper money. Henry M. Muhlenberg, for example, reports how "Congress" money went only a third as far as gold or silver coin. Financial fears, he writes, were stimulated by fears that the Revolution might fail, for "if the British side should win, the paper money will lose its value." See *The Notebook of a Colonial Clergyman,* translated and edited by Theodore G. Tappert and John W. Doberstein (Philadelphia: Muhlenberg Press, 1959), p. 187.

Unlike, I believe, many American public officials, Morris was always aware of the importance of the pen, especially in a struggle involving a fundamentally democratic political entity. For example, in a letter dated January 6, 1777, and addressed to "Dear General" (presumably Washington), he wrote: "We intend publishing an accurate Account of the various Successes since crossing the Delaware [after the attack on Trenton] in our Retreat and therefore wish you would send us all the Intelligence in your Power for that Purpose. But let us be sure to say nothing by Authority but that which is strictly true. I wish to God that [this] war [were] over. A great Stroke might be struck in Conjunction with Maxwell and yourself. I am a friend most respectfully yours, Gouv. Morris" (Historical Society of Pennsylvania, Case 1, Box 9/Old Congress Collection).

Brigadier General William Maxwell of the New Jersey brigade was Washington's first commander of the light infantry troops. As such, Maxwell's brigade often served as a probing arm for Washington's army. Maxwell had crucial roles in the battles of Cooch's Bridge (Iron Hill), Brandywine, Germantown, and Monmouth.

I surmise that Morris had been directed by Congress to send this letter, although I have found no documentation to that effect. (That Morris was entrusted with the responsibility of publicizing Washington's successes seems significant.) In several ways the letter is pure Morris: the insistence on strict truth; the desire to serve the patriot cause; the hatred of the war; the warm respect for Washington.

47. While the manuscript is undated, the evidence for assigning it to this period is fairly strong. I rely on the document's content and presentation and on remarks Morris made in letters he wrote around this time. For instance, Morris wrote to John Jay from Philadelphia on August 16: "We are at Length fairly setting about our Finances and foreign Affairs." Drafting the essay would have taken a couple of weeks, so that pushes the writing back to late July. The proposal itself refers to medical department equipment and financial reports that did not reach Congress before May 21. Finally, in late July, Morris was appointed to a committee on the treasury, which later submitted a report (written by Morris) that draws on ideas in the proposal. Morris's memorandum appears in Paul H. Smith, *Letters of Delegates,* vol. 10, pp. 202–13.

48. Morris was not alone in predicting a prompt victory. For instance, Congressman Oliver Wolcott (1726–1797), in a June 5, 1778, letter from York to his wife, Laura, in Connecticut, writes rosily: "Oliver will attend to the objects of Peace. The War will have but a Very Short Duration in my Opinion." See Smith, ed., *Letters of Delegates,* vol. 11, p. 34.

49. See, for example, Elaine Forman Crane, ed., *The Diary of Elizabeth Drinker,* vol. 1, 1758–1795 (Boston: Northeastern University Press, 1991), entries for 1777–78; Henry M. Muhlenberg, *Notebooks,* entry of May 20, 1778; Robert F. Seyboldt, ed., "A Contemporary British Account of General Sir William Howe's Military Operations in 1777," *American Antiquarian Society Proceedings* 39 (April 1930), 69–92. This document, evidently by one of Howe's general staff, indicates that Howe's failure to mount an effective offensive against Washington at Valley Forge may have been due to Washington's defensive tactics and clever use of deception as much as to the British general's timidity. See, for example, pages 83–84 on the American engineers' water obstacles. For more about British depredations, see

Harry M. Tinkcom, "The Revolutionary City, 1765–1778," in *Philadelphia: A 300-Year History,* Russell F. Weigley, ed. (New York: W. W. Norton, 1982), pp. 109–154.

50. On these matters, see *The Papers of Henry Laurens,* June 1778 volume, p. 467, pp. 470–471, p. 487; *Journals of the Continental Congress,* vol. XI, pp. 608–628; and Paul H. Smith, *Letters of Delegates,* vol. 10, pp. 194–95.

51. In Paul H. Smith, *Letters of Delegates,* vol. 11, p. 145.

52. See, for example, Nathanael Greene to Morris, June 1, 1778. In Sparks, vol. 1, pp. 180–83. Greene, almost certainly one of Washington's three best generals, was a Quaker who had been read out of his congregation for having taken up arms. Henry M. Muhlenberg records in his diary a caustic assessment of the Revolutionary War pacifism of the Pennsylvania Quakers. *Notebooks,* translated and edited by Tappert and Doberstein, pp. 178–79. Many shared that disgruntlement, but the Quakers' charitable work was impressive by any standards.

53. Morris to George Washington, Aug. 2, 1778. In Paul H. Smith, ed., *Letters of Delegates,* vol. 11, p. 383. On related congressional matters, see George Washington, *Writings,* edited by John C. Fitzpatrick (Washington, D.C.: Government Printing Office, 1931), vol. 12, pp. 226–28, and *Journals of the Continental Congress,* vol. 11, p. 728, and vol. 12, p. 1010.

54. William Gilmore Simms is quoted from his memoir, in *The Army Correspondence of Colonel John Laurens in the Years 1777–78* (New York: Bradford Club, 1867; reprinted, New York: Arno Press, 1969), p. 24. John Laurens is quoted on p. 196 of the same book. Besides Laurens, a major reliable source on the battle is Henry Dearborn. *Revolutionary War Journals of Henry Dearborn, 1775–1783,* edited by Lloyd A. Brown and Howard H. Peckham (New York: Caxton Club, 1939), pp. 127–29.

For the British side, see especially Howard H. Peckham, ed., "Sir Henry Clinton's Review of Simcoe's Journal," *William and Mary Quarterly* 21 (2nd ser., 1941), p. 364, and the *Clinton Papers* (Ann Arbor: University of Michigan), letter to Eden, July 3, 1778. Clinton here blames the result of the battle on the heat, but in his *Historical Detail,* vol. 1, he blames the terrain instead. See Sir Henry Clinton, "An Historical Detail of Seven Years Campaigns in North America from 1775–1782"; printed as *The American Rebellion: Sir Henry Clinton's Narrative of His Campaigns, 1775–1782,* William B. Willcox, ed. (New Haven: Yale University Press, 1954). Carlisle wrote, on the basis of what witnesses told him, that "we had undoubtedly the advantage in the action, though the enemy sung also *Te Deum*; and had not the heat been beyond all belief severe, several of our men running mad and instantly dropping down dead from its intenseness, the thermometer in the shade at 96, we are taught to believe that it [the outcome] would have been very decisive in our favor."

55. The July 23, 1778, letter from Morris to Jay is in Richard Morris, ed., *John Jay: The Making of a Revolutionary,* p. 486. Jay to Morris, Oct. 21, 1778, appears on p. 501; Morris to Jay, Aug. 16, 1778, is on p. 487.

There is no evidence that Morris ever took a bribe, although he must have had ample opportunity. At about this time, he was serving on the Committee of Treasury and Finance, on the Commissary Committee, and on the Quarter-master Committee. He was also providing New York's governor, George Clinton, with unsolicited advice on how to handle the state's accounts with Congress (see, for instance, Morris to the New York Assembly, July 23, 1778, in Paul H. Smith, *Letters of Delegates,* vol. 11, pp. 342–43).

56. G.M. to Robert Livingston, August 28, 1778. Robert R. Livingston Papers, 1777–1799. Special Collections. New York Public Library. *277 Bancroft* (143).

57. See Morris to George Washington, Aug. 31, 1778, Smith, *Letters of Delegates,* vol. 10, p. 542.

58. "Observations on the American Revolution Published According to a Resolution of Congress by Their Committee for the Consideration of Those Who Are Desirous of Composing the Conduct of the Opposed Parties and the Several Consequences Which Have Flowed from It" (Philadelphia: Styner and Cist, 1779), p. 4.

59. *Observations,* p. 75 ff. Morris always did write vigorously. In an October 8, 1777, letter from Kingston, N.Y., to Robert R. Livingston, he remarked of his New York State congressional colleagues: "*We are hellishly frightened but don't say a word of that* for we shall

get our spirits back again and then perhaps be so full of valor as to smite the air for blowing in our faces. . . . We shall beat them [the British]." Robert R. Livingston Papers, 1777–1799. Special Collections, New York Public Library. *227 Bancroft*. 58–59. On January 2, 1781, the same correspondent received from Morris a characteristically invigorating letter, which concludes: "Tell the Antiverrontians that America is now busied in teaching the great Lesson, that men cannot be governed against their wills. Adieu." Robert R. Livingston Papers, 1777–1799. Special Collections, New York Public Library. *277 Bancrofts*, 225.

60. Longinus, *On the Sublime in Classical Literary Criticism,* trans. T. S. Dorsch (New York: Penguin, 1965), p. 72.

Morris's "Observations" occupied an entire issue of Almon's *Remembrancer* in 1780. Helpful information concerning prior publication appears in the footnote on page 3 of that issue.

I consulted the original editions of "Observations" and of *The Remembrancer* in the Rare Books and Manuscripts Collection at the Dietrich Van Pelt Library, University of Pennsylvania.

61. *Observations* as printed in the *Remembrancer,* p. 72. Morris's use of the term "the United States of North America" reflects contemporary practice. The name "United States of America" first appears, to my knowledge, in the Declaration of Independence, but the French-American treaties of 1778 use "United States of North America," and so do some other official documents. On July 11, 1778, Congress resolved to use "United States of America" on all U.S. money. But the usage remained inconsistent for several years, even in official documents.

The curious reader can see bills of exchange from the period in the Thomas Addis Emmet Collection, in the Special Collections Department at the New York Public Library, Emmet Reserve.

62. For Almon's life and career, see primarily the sketch in *Dictionary of National Biography,* Leslie Stephen and Sidney Lee, eds. (London: Oxford University Press, 1917) and the sources provided in the bibliography (vol. 1, pp. 340–42). See also J. N. Larned, ed., *The Literature of American History* (Boston: Houghton Mifflin, 1902), p. 1219.

63. On these appointments, see *Journals of the Continental Congress,* vol. 12, pp. 892, 908, 921, and 961.

64. The Clinton and Livingston letters are in Paul H. Smith, *Letters of Delegates,* vol. 10, pp. 549–51, 590–92; and the Potts letter (September 17, 1780) is in the Jonathan Potts Papers, Historical Society of Pennsylvania, vol. 4, p. 83.

65. Gouverneur Morris Collection, Columbia University, no. 517.

66. Morris to Van Schaack on September 8, 1778, in Smith, *Letters of Delegates,* vol. 10, pp. 605–06; Morris to George Clinton on September 6, 1778, in Smith, *Letters of Delegates,* vol. 10, pp. 590–91.

67. The letter of credence, the "Instructions," and the "Plan of Attack" are all printed in Claudia Lopez, ed., *The Papers of Benjamin Franklin* (New Haven: Yale University Press, 1988), vol. 27, pp. 596–97, 633–42. On Franklin's mission in Europe, see especially Claude Anne [Claudia] Lopez, *Mon Cher Papa* (New Haven: Yale University Press, 1990), the most authoritative discussion of this phase of Franklin's career. It supersedes Carl Van Doren's *Benjamin Franklin* (1938; reprint, New York: Penguin, 1991). See also Edward E. Hale, *Franklin in France,* 2 vols. (Boston: Roberts Brothers, 1887–88). Hale's second volume, which concentrates on the peace treaty, is especially valuable. In preparing his first volume, Hale did not have access to the fullest possible range of French communiqués on American developments.

With respect to those, see especially the collections edited by Henri Doniol, *Histoire de la participation de la France à l'établissement des États-Unis d'Amérique: Correspondance diplomatique et documents* (Paris: Imprimerie Nationale, 1886–92), and Benjamin Franklin Stevens, *Facsimiles of Manuscripts in European Archives Relating to America, 1773–1783,* 25 vols. (London, 1889–98). For the French point of view, see John J. Meng, ed., *Despatches and Instructions of Conrad Alexandre Gérard, 1778–1780* (Baltimore: Johns

Hopkins Press, 1939). These documents, carefully annotated by the editor, provide an interesting view of the American revolutionary movement as seen by the key interpreter of it for Versailles. Gérard actually translated the writings Morris did for Congress in this period.

68. James's definition of artistic "insistence" appears in *William Wetmore Story and His Friends* (Boston: Houghton Mifflin, 1903), vol. 2, p. 217.

69. See Vergennes's letter of October 31. Gérard's wrote to Vergennes a memo suggesting that the French temporize on this matter, in order to teach the Americans a lesson in "inequality." See Meng, *Despatches of Gérard,* p. 346.

70. On Gérard's meeting with Morris concerning what became of this Article 5, see Meng, *Despatches of Gérard,* pp. 341–42.

71. As noted earlier, the "Plan of Attack" is in Lopez's edition of the Franklin Papers, vol. 27. Lafayette's plan for North America appears in Stanley J. Idjerda, Robert E. Smith, et al., eds., *Marquis de Lafayette in the Age of the American Revolution: Selected Letters and Papers* (Ithaca: Cornell University Press, 1978), vol. 2, pp. 145–46. On November 11, Washington wrote Congress to argue that the plan to seize Canada was unworkable. The letter was referred to a committee which, significantly, was headed by Morris, who responded, "You know more of the Subject than all of us together." After accepting the general's objections, Morris nevertheless recommended that preparations for the expedition continue in the expectation that the British would begin a strategic withdrawal. Washington thereupon asked for a consultation on the matter in Philadelphia. Here, in early winter, he met with a five-person committee, again including Morris. On New Year's Day, 1779, the Congress permanently terminated the scheme for the invasion of Canada. *Journals of the Continental Congress,* vol. 12, pp. 1227, 1230. See also the exposition first presented in Max M. Mintz, *Gouverneur Morris and the American Revolution* (Norman: University of Oklahoma Press, 1970), p. 117.

72. See Meng, *Despatches of Gérard, 1778–80,* no. 50 in particular.

73. By the end of 1778, the United States had lost some nine hundred vessels, but not one of these was a genuine battle frigate; they were privateer gunboats, or merchant ships converted to military duty with the addition of a few guns. A genuine American navy would have had to be built from scratch. See Cecil Headlam, "International Relations, 1763–1783," in *Cambridge History of the British Empire,* vol. 1, p. 713, esp. n. 4.

74. By the terms of the 1763 Treaty of Paris, France transferred to Britain Canada and, with a few small exceptions, all French territories east of the Mississippi. At no time from 1778 through the 1783 treaty negotiations did France say a word officially about renewed claims on Canada.

75. On June 21, 1779, Spain, backed by a new French alliance, ratified the Convention of Aranjuez (April 12, 1779). Politically cautious, Spain had been negotiating the Convention for months. However, Spain refused to recognize American independence and of course never directly allied with the United States. In signing the Convention, it officially declared war on Britain.

76. The story of the westward movement of the late 1770s (and its dangers) is told well by, among others, James A. James, *The Life of George Rogers Clark* (Chicago: University of Chicago Press, 1928). See especially pp. 181–93. For a fuller description of the French-American alliance, and of the hoped-for Spanish-French-American alliance, see James's chapters 5–9.

On all the diplomatic issues discussed here, see also Gérard's memorandum no. 47 in Meng, *Despatches*; Gérard to Vergennes, Oct. 10, 1778, in Doniol, *Histoire de la participation de la France,* vol. 2, pp. 72–73; and Francis Wharton, *The Revolutionary Diplomatic Correspondence of the United States,* vol. 2 (Washington, D.C.: U.S. Government Printing Office, 1889), pp. 807–08. Morris's correspondence corroborates the French accounts. See also Meng's commentary, pp. 114–15.

77. See, for example, Gérard to Vergennes, in Meng, *Despatches,* pp. 339–47. Morris began meeting with Gérard in Philadelphia in midsummer of 1778. The French representative was skeptical of the plan to seize Canada but did not demand that it not be

sent to Franklin. On this matter, see his memorandum to Vergennes of July 19, 1778, especially the second paragraph (Meng, *Despatches,* p. 311) beginning "On m'a fait depuis . . ."

French is especially well suited to the synthesis and analysis of documents. See in particular J. P. Vinay and J. Darbelnet, *Stylistique Comparée du Français et de l'Anglais* (Paris: Didier, 1958), chapter 4.

78. On these documents, see Francis Wharton, *Revolutionary Diplomatic Correspondence,* vol. 3, pp. 300–305, and *Secret Journals of the Acts and Proceedings of Congress, from the first meeting thereof to the dissolution of the Confederation by the adoption of the Constitution* (Boston: T. Wait, 1821), 4 vols. Sparks, *Morris,* vol. 1, chapter 12, passim.

79. See "Instructions . . ." in Wharton, *Revolutionary Diplomatic Correspondence,* vol. 3, pp. 300–303, and compare the transmitted "Instructions" with the three-page "Resolution" (drafted by Morris) "concerning [a] treaty with Great Britain." Morris outlines a series of precautions to be considered before the composition of "Instructions" to be sent in the post. (Gouverneur Morris Collection, Columbia University Libraries Manuscript Collections.) The memorandum is undated, and the records of the Continental Congress do not make it absolutely clear when this resolution was presented. See also Edmund C. Burnett, *The Continental Congress* (New York, Macmillan, 1941), pp. 429–33.

80. Fell is quoted in Edmund Cody Burnett, *Letters of the Members of the Continental Congress* (Washington, D.C.: Carnegie, 1921), p. 279. Morris to Robert R. Livingston, Robert R. Livingston Papers, 1777–1779, New York Public Library.

81. That is, it came up chiefly among the French, Americans, and British. The Canadian fisheries were of less concern to Spain.

82. As the exposition by Burnett, *Continental Congress,* vol. 4, (pp. 112–14, footnotes 1–5), makes clear, there is some question as to the date of the motion Morris proposed, which is speculatively dated as March 22. There is also doubt as to the actual date of Henry Laurens's proposed amendment, presumed to be of the same date. The relevant Gérard memoranda to Vergennes are nos. 118, 120, and 117 in Meng, *Despatches* (pp. 654–59, 650–51). Gérard's remark beginning "La grande question" is on p. 651. Meng's footnote commentary supplements that in Edmund C. Burnett, *Letters of Members of the Continental Congress,* vol. IV (New York: Smith, 1963), pp. xxii–xxv. The interested reader should also study the instructions from the Continental Congress, August 14–October 16, 1779, along with the helpful annotations, in Barbara B. Oberg, ed., *Papers of Benjamin Franklin,* vol. 30 (New Haven: Yale University Press, 1993), pp. 226–98. Oberg's work permits an accurate tracking of the few but significant changes Congress made to Morris's draft. See also *Journals of the Continental Congress,* vol. XIV, p. 744, and the reliable summary and commentary by Jonathan R. Dull in his *A Diplomatic History of the American Revolution* (New Haven: Yale University Press, 1985), pp. 59–61.

Although Max Mintz and I have studied many of the same primary sources, our assessments of Morris's behavior vary. For Mintz's view, see *Gouverneur Morris and the American Revolution* (Norman: University of Oklahoma Press, 1970).

83. See also Doniol, *Histoire de la participation de la France,* vol. III, "Spain" entry in index. When General Pershing arrived in France during World War I, he almost immediately took an armful of roses to Lafayette's tomb, saying, "Lafayette, we have arrived." He might as justly have performed the same gesture at the tomb of Vergennes.

84. On this general subject, the reader may consult Ralph L. Ketcham, "France and American Politics, 1763–1793," *Political Science Quarterly* 78 (Fall 1963), 198–223.

85. On these developments, see *Journals of the Continental Congress,* vol. XI, p. 801, and vol. XII, pp. 1202–1206; and *The Deane Papers,* ed. Charles Isham five volumes (New York: New-York Historical Society, 1887–1890), vol. 11, pp. 66–76. On January 26, realizing that he had gone too far, Paine published a letter in which he said that his earlier publication had not mentioned "the King of France by any title nor yet the nation of France." This was, of course, unlikely to be persuasive. British leadership at all times was aware of the truth concerning French aid to the American revolutionists.

See also George Clinton to GM, February 2, 1779, in *Public Papers of George Clinton,* vol. 4, p. 536. Hugh Hastings and J. A. Holder, eds., 10 vols. (Albany: James B. Lyon 1909–14).

86. Morris's "Speech made in Congress ab: Mr. Payne—[on back of sheet] taken down afterwd from Memory to obviate Misrepresentation." Gouverneur Morris Collection, Columbia University Libraries. See also the exceptionally helpful scholarly commentary on the Deane-Lee controversy, as well as Morris's part in it, in Paul H. Smith, ed., *Letters of Delegates,* vol. 13, pp. 367–368.

87. For a more comprehensive analysis of Deane's transactions, see Coy Hilton James, *Silas Deane—Patriot or Traitor?* (East Lansing: Michigan State University Press, 1975).

88. See William Bodham Donne, ed., *The Correspondence of King George III with Lord North from 1768–1783* (London: J. Murray, 1867), pp. 145, 363, 380, 381, and 384. See also *Pennsylvania Packet* (Philadelphia: J. Dunlop, D.C. and S. Claypoole, Z. Poulson, 1771–1850).

89. Morris's February 1779 address is from Paul H. Smith, ed., *Letters of Delegates,* vol. 12 pp. 114–15. The letter to Livingston, dated January 8, 1778, is in the Gouverneur Morris Papers, Columbia University Libraries Special Collections.

90. Morris to Reed, quoted in Paul H. Smith, *Letters of Delegates,* vol. 12, p. 120, n. 1.

91. Morris to Washington, April 26, 1779, in ibid., p. 391.

92. Washington to Morris, *Writings of George Washington,* John C. Fitzpatrick, ed., vol. 15, pp. 23–26.

93. See, for example, David Sloan, "Gouverneur Morris," in *American Writers Before 1800: A Biographical and Critical Dictionary,* edited by James A. Levernier and Douglas R. Wilmes (Westport, Conn.: Greenwood Press, 1983), p. 1033; Beatrix Cary Davenport, "Introduction," *A Diary of the French Revolution by Gouverneur* Morris (Boston: Houghton Mifflin, 1939), vol. 1, p. xiv; Theodore Roosevelt, *Gouverneur Morris,* p. 80.

94. See Morris to Livingston, August 17, 1778, in Paul H. Smith, *Letters of Delegates,* vol. 11, p. 468; Morris to George Clinton, May 30, 1779, Paul H. Smith, *Letters of Delegates,* p. 55; Morris to George Clinton, June 16, 1778, no. 1511, in *Public Papers of George Clinton,* vol. 3, pp. 460–61; Morris to George Clinton, March 4, 1778, Robert R. Livingston Papers, 1777–1799, New York Public Library Special Collections 277, Bancroft 101. Incidentally, Morris's statement about Vermont is followed by a detailed plan for the recapture of what is now Manhattan, the Bronx, and Long Island.

The congressional resolves of the end of May 1779 can be found in *Journals of the Continental Congress,* vol. XI, pp. 630–33. All four members of the New York delegation— Jay, Duane, Morris, and Floyd—voted yes on Burke's motion, as well as on the question of moving the issues to committee.

For more on the Vermont question, I recommend several works. In "Ethan Allen: An Interpretation" (New England Quarterly 2 [Fall 1929], 561–84), C. W. Rife reveals Allen to have been a leader of a Vermont whose citizens preferred the rule of the British to that of New York. See also Ethan and Ira Allen: Collected Works, J. Kevin Graffagnino, ed. (Benson, VT: Chalidze Publications, 1992). Helpful commentary can also be found in John P. Kaminski, George Clinton: Yeoman Politician of the New Republic (Madison, Wisc.: Madison House, 1993), pp. 64–65; Mintz, Gouverneur Morris and the American Revolution; and Sparks, vol. 1, pp. 208–209. Vermont scholars sometimes oversimplify the case; for instance, in "Vermont as a Sovereign and Independent State, 1783–1791," in Collections of the Vermont Historical Society, vol. 2 (Montpelier, Vt.: 1871), pp. 394–498, the author reports that Gouverneur Morris was "favorable to Vermont" as early as 1778 (p. 436, n. 2), a statement not supported by the evidence.

95. The letter from John Jay to George Clinton, August 27, 1779, appears in *The Papers of John Jay,* James Johnstone, ed. (New York: Putnam, 1890–1893), vol. 1, 214–18. Clinton's letter of October 5 appears in Clinton's *Public, Papers,* vol. 5, p. 309.

96. Jay's letter of October 7 to Clinton in vol. 14, p. 39. See also Paul H. Smith, *Letters of the Delegates,* vol. 15, pp. 1148–49.

97. See *Votes in the Proceedings of the Assembly of the State of New York* (Fishkill, N.Y.: Samuel London, 1779), August 18, 1779, to March 14, 1780 no. 565, note 2 (microform in Falvey Memorial Library, Villanova University).

98. The *Journals of the Continental Congress* report that the delegation's credentials were presented at nine A.M. on October 15, vol. 12, p. 1144, but the credentialing papers themselves have the term of service begin on October 29.

    The delegates' salary was five dollars a day, even then no king's ransom.

99. The Livingston letter to Morris, dated January 29, 1778, is in the Robert R. Livingston Papers, New-York Historical Society. Halifax's remark concludes, popularity "is only a virtue when men have it whether they will or no."

100. At York and at Valley Forge, Morris suffered in a number of ways, the least of which was being resented. He worked extremely hard at both places; moreover, as he wrote to Robert Livingston, who was then at Clermont, New York, "there are no fine women in York Town. . . . Worse still I am now in camp [at Valley Forge] and Lady Kitty [Alexander] and Miss Brown within three miles of me [but] I can't go to see them" (Morris to Livingston, March 21, 1778, Morris Papers, Columbia University Libraries Special Collections).

    In *The Life of Henri Brulard,* Stendhal observes, "The great DRAWBACK of being witty is that you have to keep your eyes fixed on the semi-fools around you, *and steep yourself in their commonplace way of feeling*" (translated by Jean Stewart and B.C.J.G. Knight [New York: Funk & Wagnalls, 1968], p. 11). This may have had something to do with Morris's propensity to have detractors. On this point, see his replies to overheated letters from Joseph Reed and John Dunlap.

101. Paul H. Smith, *Letters of Delegates,* vol. 10, p. 341. Morris's letter to Jay is evidently a response to a July 4 letter from Jay that I have not been able to locate.

    Morris may have drawn inspiration from some of Caesar's letters—for instance, that concerning those who had surrendered and been spared at Confinium.

    Morris served New York well in Congress. See, for instance, *Journal of the Continental Congress,* vol. 11, pp. 627, 630, where it is recorded that he and Duer secured for the state "an Advance of 100,000 Dollars." Additional evidence of Morris's concern for the welfare of New York abounds in the *Journal* and in the papers of the Continental Congress, as well as in his correspondence with Governor George Clinton and others. See his letters to Clinton of September 1, 1778, September 27, 1778, March 2, 1779, and October 7, 1779 *Public Papers of George Clinton,* vol. 3, pp. 100, 740; vol. 4, p. 606; Smith, *Letters,* vol. 14, pp. 44–45. Also see Morris to Clinton, *Public Papers of George Clinton,* vol. 4, pp. 325–26, 403.

    As early as January 1778, Robert R. Livingston urged Morris to absent himself from the Continental Congress in order to attend the state legislature: "You know too much of Some People in power here to think the State safe in their hands" (Robert R. Livingston Papers, New-York Historical Society).

102. This letter from Morris to Robert L. Livingston, dated September 22, 1778, is available in Paul H. Smith, *Letters of Delegates,* vol. 12, pp. 684–85, where it is most helpfully annotated. The letter is extraordinarily revealing to the biographer. Morris wrote that "it is possible my good star may prevail to take me from this Scene and place me in a better. I mean among my friends. For certainly I was formed for the sweets of Private Life." Morris then makes an effort to make peace between Livingston and John Jay.

103. See Nathanael Greene's order from headquarters dated August 8, 1781, in the Gouverneur Morris Collection, Manuscript Collection, Columbia University Libraries. On these matters, see for instance Morris to Caesar Rodney, April 12, 1779, in the Old Congress Papers, Gratz Collection; Morris to William Whipple and John Armstrong, May 18, 1779, in William Whipple Folder, and Morris to Jermiah Wadsworth in "Government Officials in the Revolution," in William Whipple File, all at the Historical Society of Pennsylvania. See also on this matter the May 18, 1779, entry in John C. Fitzpatrick, ed., *The Writings of George Washington.*

104. Morris to Robert R. Livingston, August 17, 1778, in Burnett, *Letters of Members of the Continental Congress* (Washington, D.C.: Carnegie Institution, 1921–36), vol. III,

p. 377. For Burnett's assessment of Morris's skills, with which I concur, see, for example, vol. III, p. 377n. Max Mintz was the first to draw similar conclusions: see his *Gouverneur Morris and the American Revolution*, pp. 88–97.

105. Morris to Robert R. Livingston, October 19, 1779, Paul H. Smith, *Letters of Delegates,* vol. 14, pp. 78–79. In the eleven days following October 6, when Morris returned to Congress from New York, he was appointed to several more committees.

106. Paul H. Smith, *Letters of Delegates,* vol. 10, p. 469, n. 3. This letter first appears in Sparks. Although Morris is describing his own work, he was not prone to exaggeration, and in years of studying him I have learned nothing to cast doubt on his assertions here.

Regrettably, Morris seems to have kept no record of his reading after King's. The following chapter, for instance, would have benefited from information concerning whether, or how closely, Morris had read Adam Smith and Jeremy Bentham, or the French philosophes.

4. THE OFFICE OF FINANCE

1. Robert Morris is quoted in Nelson S. Dearmont's sketch "Gouverneur Morris (1752–1816)," in Richard L. Blanco, ed., *The American Revolution, 1775–1783: An Encyclopedia* (New York and London: Garland, 1993), vol. 2, p. 1114.

2. My description of Philadelphia and its environs draws on Andrew Burnaby, *Travels Through the Middle Settlements in North America in the Years 1759 and 1760* (London: A. Wessels, 1904), pp. 88–89; Merrill Jensen, *The Founding of a Nation: A History of the American Revolution* (New York: Oxford University Press, 1968), p. 9 and notes 1 and 2; Henry F. May, *The Enlightenment in America* (New York: Oxford University Press, 1976), p. 197; Max M. Mintz, *Gouverneur Morris and the American Revolution* (Norman: University of Oklahoma Press, 1970); J. Potter, "The Growth of Population in America, 1700–1800," in D. V. Glass and D.E.C. Eversley, eds., *Population in History: Essays in Historical Demography* (Chicago: Arnold, 1965), pp. 631–85. Potter's figures for the Philadelphia population for the period of 1778 to 1789 are several thousand people higher than the other estimates. On this topic, see also Susan E. Klepp, *The Swift Progress of Population: A Documentary and Bibliographic Study of Philadelphia's Growth, 1642–1859* (Philadelphia: American Philosophical Society, 1991), especially the items annotated on pp. 16–18 and 26; and John K. Alexander, "The Philadelphia Numbers Game: An Analysis of Philadelphia's 18th Century Population," *Pennsylvania Magazine of History and Biography* 98 (Fall 1974), 314–24. The first U.S. federal census did not occur until 1790.

That Burnaby's description of the lusciousness of the southeastern Pennsylvania landscape is accurate can be inferred from the fact that the growing season lasts between 165 and 200 days. On this general theme, see James T. Lemon, *The Best Poor Man's Country: A Geographical Study of Early Southeastern Pennsylvania* (Baltimore: Johns Hopkins University Press, 1972).

3. See, for instance, Alice H. Jones, *Wealth of a Nation to Be* (New York: Columbia University Press, 1980), pp. 297–341.

4. See especially Lemon, *Best Poor Man's Country,* pp. 18–19, 14–15, and 46–47.

5. See, for example, John F. Watson, *Annals of Philadelphia and Pennsylvania,* vol. 3 (Philadelphia: E. S. Stuart, n.d. [ca. 1891]), p. 296. This work contains much valuable material on the social activities and customs of that time and place.

In Riches, Class, and Power Before the Civil War (Lexington, Mass.: D. C. Heath, 1973), Edward Pessen concludes that in the Boston, Manhattan, Brooklyn, and Philadelphia of the day, the richest people were insular in every way—no surprises there—and that the rich of Philadelphia were the most insular of all. Given Morris's social tastes, he would have found the city particularly enjoyable for just that reason.

6. On these cultural matters, see Edwin Wolf II, *The Book Culture of a Colonial American City: Philadelphia Books, Bookmen, and Booksellers* (Oxford, Eng.: Clarendon Press,

1988), pp. 78–130; Robert B. Winans, "The Growth of a Novel-Reading Public in Eighteenth-Century America," *Early American Literature* 9 (Winter 1975), 267–75; H. Wiley Hitchcock, *Music in the United States: An Historical Introduction,* 2d ed. (Englewood, N.J.: Prentice-Hall, 1974), pp. 32–49; and Kellee Lynne Green, "The Politics of Dancing: Social Dance in Philadelphia, 1750–1800" (M.A. thesis, Villanova University, 1989), pp. 82–83 and 105.

> After the 1780s, Alexander Reinagle was Philadelphia's favorite composer.

7. Hutchinson's memo is quoted by Francis R. Packard in *The History of Medicine in the United States, 1660–1800* (Philadelphia: Lippincott, n.d. [1910]), p. 299. Hutchinson was professor of chemistry at the University of Pennsylvania, having turned down an offer to make him professor of surgery.

> Packard's work includes a previously published monograph, "The Medical Profession in the War for Independence" (pp. 233–320), which has not been entirely superseded.

8. Morris's late 1780 below-the-knee prosthesis is still on view in the Luce Collection, New-York Historical Society. Anesthesia was, of course, unknown in his time. See Packard, *History,* pp. 468–69. Eighteenth-century surgery of all kinds frequently resulted in sepsis; see Richard H. Shryock, *Medicine and Society in America* (New York: New York University Press, 1960), p. 59. For contemporary surgical procedures, see Larry Burkhart, *The Good Fight: Medicine in Colonial Pennsylvania* (New York: Garland, 1989). For thumbnail sketches of the major physicians and surgeons of the day, see Howard A. Kelly and Walter L. Burrage, *American Medical Biographies* (Baltimore: Norman Remington, 1920), which remains unsurpassed in its coverage of the revolutionary era.

> In none of Morris's letters or diaries does he complain of the stomach disorders and toothaches that were distressingly prevalent in a time of poor sanitation and primitive dentistry. Perhaps he had a higher than average pain threshold, or perhaps he was lucky; Philadelphians enjoyed an abundance of fresh fruit, vegetables, fish, and meat. He did, however, complain occasionally of migraines.

9. Jacob C. Parsons, ed., *Extracts from the Diary of Jacob Hiltzheimer* (Philadelphia: W. F. Fell & Co., 1893), p. 43. Hiltzheimer's stables were used by the city's upper crust, so he would have learned of the accident almost at once. For more on the accident, see also the sources cited by Max Mintz, *Gouverneur Morris and the American Revolution* (New Haven: Yale University Press, 1970), pp. 139–40, footnotes 3 and 4.

10. Robert R. Livingston to John Jay, in Richard B. Morris, ed., *John Jay: The Making of a Revolutionary* (New York: Harper and Row, 1975), p. 78. Mrs. Jay reported similarly to Mrs. Robert Morris.

11. The adventure of finding biographical information about the Rousbys and Platers was made much easier thanks to the kind assistance of the reference staff at the Sotterly Plantation (formerly the property of George Plater III) and at the Calvert County (Maryland) Historical Association. I am especially indebted to Ms. Caroline Leray, at Sotterly Plantation, and to Mrs. Carla Rose, of the Calvert County Historical Association. Eliza's father, John Rousby III, seems to have died at the age of twenty-five, leaving behind his widow, the former Anne Frisby ("the White Rose of Maryland"), and their infant daughter, Elizabeth; this is made clear in his will. John Rousby III left an immense fortune and a vast estate, including Rousby Hall. The estate was not far from today's Washington, D.C., city limits, between the Chesapeake and the Patuxent. William Fitzhugh, the Maryland attorney who drew up the will, was determined to marry Anne Rousby, and he wished to force her hand. Just after the estate was settled, or possibly even before, he seized baby Elizabeth, rowed out onto the Patuxent, held the infant over the water, and threatened to drop her in unless Anne agreed to marry him. The wedding took place in January 1752.

> Elizabeth's birthdate is not recorded; the date of 1749 has been inferred from other historical details.

> The reader may also consult the articles entitled "Plater Family" and "Morgan Family" in *Maryland Historical Magazine* 2 (December 1907), pp. 370–77.

12. See, for example, Gouverneur Morris to Robert R. Livingston, October 13, 1777, on the beauties of Isaac Low's eldest daughter, "at all times sufficiently affecting to the sight but

now ... [a] second Medusa" (George Dangerfield, *Chancellor Robert L. Livingston of New York* [New York: Harcourt, Brace, 1960], p. 103). To Mrs. Penn, GM described with zest the wife and daughters of Governor Dunmore of Virginia (Jared Sparks, *The Life of Gouverneur Morris* (Boston: Gray and Bowen, 1832), vol. 1, p. 21.

13. Jay's letters of February 16, 1779, and September 16, 1780, appear in Richard B. Morris, ed., *John Jay*, p. 556. But Jay's latter remark did not appear in print until Frank Monaghan's *John Jay: Defender of Liberty Against Kings and Peoples* (New York: Bobbs-Merrill, 1935) was published; before that, the family had suppressed the letter (even though two of them wrote biographies of Jay). On Jay's reputation for stodginess, see, for example, Robert R. Livingston to GM, September 16, 1778. Livingston Papers, New-York Historical Society Special Collections.

14. Mintz provides this entry of May 5, 1790, pp. 143–45, where there is also a sketch of Mrs. William Bingham's fling with Gouverneur.

15. Sparks, vol. 1, p. 113. Morris's spirits were raised by his friends on the day before the surgery, which was to proceed without anesthesia. The Marquis de Chastellux observed drily that Morris's friends had "congratulated him on this event [the amputation] saying that he would now devote himself wholly to public business." *Travels in North America in the Years 1780, 1781, and 1782,* revised translation by Howard C. Rice (Chapel Hill: University of North Carolina Press, 1963), p. 131.

16. Morris to Robert R. Livingston, in Anne Carey Morris, ed., *Diary and Letters of Gouverneur Morris,* vol. 2 (New York: Scribners, 1888), p. 422.

17. Burnett, *Letters,* vol. 5, p. 464n; *Journals of the Continental Congress,* vol. XIX, p. 180. Robert Morris was nominated by New York's William Floyd (1734–1821). His election was nearly unanimous; there were two abstentions, by Samuel Adams and Artemus Ward (1727–1800), both of Massachusetts. For this period, volume 16 of Smith, *Letters,* is especially valuable for its thoroughness. It ends with Maryland's delayed, decisive ratification of the Articles of Confederation.

18. The primary records of these matters are Francis Wharton, ed. *The Revolutionary Diplomatic Correspondence of the United States,* vol. IV (Washington, D.C.: Government Printing Office, 1889), pp. 297–99, 330–33, 412–14; *Journals of the Continental Congress,* vol. XIX, pp. 180, 255, 263, 287–89, 290–91. 326–27, 337–38, 429, 432–33, and vol. XX, pp. 455–56, 499. Volume 16 of Smith, *Letters,* provides valuable ancillary material.

19. On Morris's acceptance, see *Journals of the Continental Congress,* vol. XX, p. 499.

20. Both letters are in Mintz, pp. 144–45.

21. Robert Morris's diary, August 4, 1781. In James Ferguson, John Catanzariti, Mary A. Gallagher, and Clarence VerSteeg, eds., *The Papers of Robert Morris, 1781–1784.* Vol. 2 (August–September 1781) (Pittsburgh: University of Pittsburgh Press, 1975), p. 14. The reader may recall a letter from Robert Morris to John Jay, January 3, 1783, that was cited earlier: "I could do nothing without him [GM]." Still later, Robert Morris wrote to Jay that GM "has more virtue than he shows, and more consistency than anybody believes." This letter to Jay is from *The Papers of Robert Morris,* vol. 8, 4 November 1783, pp. 708–09.

22. Although he was generous with those he saw as his peers, GM could be a skinflint in doing business with the less advantaged. For instance, in 1779 he wrote to George Washington that he was reluctant, even under the necessity of stimulating recruitment, to offer a ten-dollar bonus, lest it stimulate the "rapacity" of the soldiery. Ten dollars was two days' pay for GM.

Robert Morris came to dominate the huge American export market for flour; if some rapacity were not revealed in this, it would be surprising, especially given his later record in land speculations. But the man who was probably the wealthiest American of the day did not seem to think GM was particularly suited for business: "I have learned it said that G. Morris is [now] in trade. I hope the report is groundless. I have a high opinion of that gentleman's Abilities, and Integrity; the latter may be warped by the prospect of amassing great wealth—*ceci entre nous*" (Charles Carroll of Carrolton to William Carmichael, May 31, 1779; in Burnett, *Letters,* vol. 4, pp. 238–39).

23. GM to Robert R. Livingston, August 8, 1779. Robert R. Livingston Papers, 1777–1799, New York Public Library.

24. GM to Robert Morris, in Smith, *Letters,* vol. 13, p. 81.

25. Robert Morris to Philip Schuyler, in Francis Wharton, ed., *Revolutionary Diplomatic Correspondence,* vol. IV, pp. 458–59, "Taxes in hard Money" is from Robert Morris's letter to George Washington of June 15, 1781, *New-York Historical Society Collections,* vol. XI (1878), pp. 461, 62. See also Jared Sparks, ed., *Correspondence of the American Revolution* (Boston: Little Brown, 1853), vol. III, pp. 339–41, Wharton, *Revolutionary Diplomatic Correspondence,* vol. IV, pp. 505–06, and, last but not least, *The Papers of Robert Morris,* edited and with scholarly commentary by E. James Ferguson, John Cantanzariti, Elizabeth M. Nuxoll, and Mary A. Gallagher, in nine volumes (Pittsburgh: University of Pittsburgh Press, 1973–1996). Elizabeth Nuxoll's forthcoming biography of Robert Morris will certainly be the best.

26. See Robert Morris's early objections, in Peter Force, ed. *American Archives,* 5th series, vol. III (Washington D.C, 1837–1853), p. 1241.

27. See the exposition by E. S. Corwin, "The Progress of Constitutional Theory Between the Declaration of Independence and the meeting of the Philadelphia Convention," *American Historical Review* 30 (April 1925), pp. 511–36.

28. Thomas McKean, too, deserves an up-to-date biography. For additional specifics on the managerial deficiencies of the Board of Treasury before mid-1781, see Jennings B. Sanders, *Evolution of Executive Departments of the Continental Congress, 1774–1789* (Chapel Hill: University of North Carolina Press, 1935), pp. 64–74.

29. See Sparks, *Morris,* vol. 1, pp. 13–15, and Howard Swiggett, *The Extraordinary Mr. Morris* (Garden City: Doubleday, 1952), p. 16. But Swiggett is not quite correct on the facts.

30. Herman E. Krooss, *Documentary History of Banking and Currency in the United States,* vol. 1, part II (New York: Chelsea House, 1969), pp. 95–98. The reader will recall that Morris's essays were analyzed in chapter 2. The latter speech, as recorded, sketched out a system for financing the Revolution; it was not wholly satisfactory in practice, but that does not necessarily signify that Morris's logic was faulty. See the commentary by William Graham Sumner, *The Financier and the Finances of the American Revolution,* vol. 1 (New York: Dodd, Mead, 1891), pp. 39–42. See also his astute analysis of the Morrises' financial endeavors while Robert Morris was superintendent of finance.

31. See Andrew C. Flick, *History of the State of New York,* vol. 4 (New York: Columbia University Press, 1933), pp. 116–19 especially. Also of interest in this context is some of GM's correspondence from his New York friends—for example, Robert R. Livingston to GM, April 6, 1778, New-York Historical Society. And see *Journals of the Provincial Congress,* vol. I, p. 1009.

32. GM to George Clinton, *Public Papers of George Clinton,* vol. 3 (1900), no. 1722, p. 725. See also GM to George Clinton, February 20, 1779, and GM for the Committee of Congress to Jeremiah Wadsworth, February 17, 1779, in Smith, *Letters,* vol. 12 (1987), pp. 100, 86.

33. *Journals of the Continental Congress,* vol. XI, p. 731. An elegantly prepared three-page draft is in the Gouverneur Morris Papers at Columbia University.

     The finance report, drafted by GM on September 19, 1779, for the committee of Morris, R. H. Lee, Elbridge Gerry, and Robert Morris, was presented for the delegates' consideration. Many of the points in the draft received scant official notice, but the memorandum offers acute insights into congressional thinking on financial matters. Gouverneur Morris Collection, Columbia University.

34. Morris's "Letters of Appreciation," originally published in 1780 in Philadelphia by Thomas Bradford, are available in Clifford Kenyon Shipton, ed., *Early American Imprints, First Series,* Evans no. 16820 (Worcester, Mass.: American Antiquarian Society, 1967–71), which reproduces Charles Evans's *American Bibliography* (Chicago: C. Evans, 1903–59); Shipton's edition was also issued as a microfiche (New York: Readex Microprint, 1985).

35. Since GM kept no record of his reading, I cannot be sure that he read *The Wealth of Nations,* but Robert Morris had read and admired it, and lent it to friends. It is suggestive that some of the economic arguments he and Robert Morris made resemble Adam

Smith's. It may simply be that they arrived at the same ideas at more or less the same time, although the fact that Robert Morris had a copy and had read it strongly suggests that he borrowed the ideas rather than arriving at them independently.

36. See *Journals of the Continental Congress,* vol. XXI, pp. 976, 995, vol. XXII, p. 60, and vol. XXI, p. 1283; and *Papers of the Continental Congress.* On the various offices and appointments, see Jennings B. Sanders, *Evolution of Executive Departments in the Continental Congress, 1771–1781* (Chapel Hill: University of North Carolina Press, 1935), pp. 132-33; and Clarence VerSteeg's relatively brief and very valuable, *Robert Morris: Revolutionary Financier* (Philadelphia: University of Pennsylvania Press, 1954), chapter 5.

37. See especially *Journals of the Continental Congress,* vol. XV, pp. 1241–42, 1251–52, vol. XVI, pp. 225, 750, 1054–55, and vol. XVII, 779–80.

38. See GM to Moss Kent, March 15, 1816 (Gratz Collection, Historical Society of Pennsylvania).

39. On the "Plan for Establishing a National Bank in the United States of North America," see especially Ferguson, et al., *Papers of Robert Morris,* vol. 1, pp. 68–73; GM's June 1, 1781, letter to Robert Morris appears on pp. 106–109. The footnotes on pp. 109–110 are illuminating.

40. Almost any code or cipher is superior to text sent in the clear. Codes and ciphers allow for an increased number of mathematical combinations, thereby decreasing the probabilities of cracking the encoded system by chance. The German Enigma code, for example, was not cracked until the British obtained the German machine.

   Morris's interest in codes likely began with his classics studies at King's. The Roman ruler Julius Caesar (100–44 B.C.), whose work Morris knew, employed a simple cipher for secret communication. He substituted each letter of the alphabet with a three-letter combination further along. Afterwards, any cipher that used this kind of displacement system to create a cipher alphabet became referred to as a "Caesar cipher." Morris's system expanded on Caesar's concept.

   See also Ferguson, et al., *Papers of Robert Morris,* vol. 1, pp. 232–36.

41. See Ferguson, et al., *Papers of Robert Morris,* vol. 1, pp. 122–23 for Salomon and pp. 280, 341, and 352 for Hazelwood.

42. On GM's Finance Office work in this period, see Ferguson, et al., *Papers of Robert Morris,* vol. 2, pp. 230–35. The editorial commentary on 230–33 is especially excellent even by the standards of this superb work. I relied on the same source for the preceding paragraph; see vol. 2, Haym Salomon: pp. 50, 60, 92–93, 107, 32, 37, 39, 43, 47, and 109; Bills of Exchange: pp. 27, 38, 43, and 47; John Hazlewood: pp. 110, 175, 244–245, and 343–344; GM and the Finance Office Diary: pp. 28, 32–33, 38–39, 43–47, 50, 58–60, 66–67, 69, 73 and 285–286; GM as translator of French letters in the Finance Office: pp. 173; GM's prepping of RM's letters: pp. 13, 26, 92, 103, 200–201, 219, 274, 336, and 356. The Finance Office diary reveals that Morris rarely missed a day at work because of illness.

43. See ibid., vol. 3, pp. 36–37, and n. 1 in particular.

44. This letter of March 31, 1781, is in the Gouverneur Morris Collection, Columbia University.

45. On the misleading letter, see Randolph G. Adams, ed., *The Headquarters Papers of the British Army in North America During the War of the American Revolution* (Ann Arbor: William L. Clements Library, 1926). See also *New York City During the American Revolution* (New York: Mercantile Library Association, 1861), pp. 177–84, a collection of original papers.

   Washington's Southern strategy, as presented to de Grasse on August 17, 1781, is in Jared Sparks, ed., *The Writings of George Washington,* vol. 9 (Boston: American Stationers' Company, John B. Russell, 1835), pp. 130–33. Washington's strategic skills are still underappreciated.

   On Washington's effective use of intelligence, see, for instance, Edmund R. Thompson, "George Washington, Master Intelligence Officer," *American Military Intelligence Journal* 6, no. 2 (1984), 3–9; and Philander D. Chase, ed., *The Papers of George Washington, Revolutionary War Series* 13 volumes (Charlottesville: University Press of Virginia, 1985). There does not appear to be a full-scale study of Washington's use of military intelligence, but two helpful works are Edmund R. Thompson, "Intelligence in

Yorktown," *Defense* 81 (October 1981), pp. 25–28; and (in some key ways, not yet superseded) Henry P. Johnston, *The Yorktown Campaign and the Surrender of Cornwallis, 1781* (New York: Harper & Brothers, 1881).

46. See Robert A. Selig, "DeGrasse and Yorktown (François Joseph Paul Compte de Grasse, the Battle Off the Virginia Capes, and the American Victory at Yorktown)" on the Web site www.americanrevolution.org.

47. The best French treatment of the subject remains Georges La Cour Cayet, *La Marine militaire de la France sous le règne de Louis XVI*, vol. 2 (Paris: H. Champollion, 1905), chapters 7 and 8, especially pp. 130–179, and chapter 21, pp. 399–418.

It should be explicitly stated that the obvious hopelessness of the naval situation almost certainly precipitated Cornwallis's early surrender.

Throughout the Revolution, and for decades afterward, the U.S. Navy remained understrength. Not surprisingly, then, Alfred Thayer Mahan depicted naval operations during the Revolution as comparatively minor in importance; see *Major Operations of the Navies in the War of Independence* (Boston: Houghton Mifflin, 1913). The most spectacular American naval engagement of the war was John Paul Jones's defeat of the British frigate *Serapis* off Flamborough Head, on the Yorkshire Coast, September 23, 1779.

48. Sir Henry Clinton's narrative and an appendix of useful letters may be found in William B. Wilcox, ed., *The American Revolution: Sir Henry Clinton's Narrative of His Campaigns, 1775–1782* (New Haven: Yale University Press, 1954). See pages 332–350 for the siege and fall of Yorktown.

49. Especially valuable in this regard is *The American Campaigns of Rochambeau's Army, 1780, 1781, 1782, 1783;* 2 vols., edited and translated by Howard C. Rice, Jr., and Anne S. K. Brown (Princeton: Princeton University Press, 1972).

50. A work critical of Germain (as most histories are) is John W. Fortescue, *A History of the British Army*, vol. 3 (London: Macmillan, 1902), pp. 397–98. In my view, Fortescue does not give Washington's generalship its due.

That Loyalism was strong in the mid-Atlantic region is demonstrated in, for example, Victor H. Paltsits, ed., *New York Commissions for Detecting and Defeating Conspiracies, 1778–1781,* 3 vols. (New York: J. B. Lyon, 1909–1910). These records follow the Committee on Safety, which occupied many of Morris's working hours. Hugh E. Egerton, ed., *The Royal Commission on the Losses and Services of American Loyalists, 1783–1785* (Oxford: H. Hart at the Oxford University Press, 1915; reprinted New York: Burt Franklin, 1971) also does much to fill in the picture. See, finally, Gregory Palmer, ed., *A Bibliography of Loyalist Source Material in the United States, Canada, and Great Britain* (Westport, Conn.: Meckler, 1982), p. viii.

51. Rockingham, the new prime minister, soon died, and Lord Shelburne then became prime minister and assumed control of the peace negotiations. Through an envoy, Richard Oswald, he started diplomatic conversations with the Americans, following a hint from Benjamin Franklin. Charles James Fox, the former opposition leader, began discussions at Paris with the European belligerents through the accredited Foreign Office envoy, Thomas Grenville. Shelburne aimed to defer the recognition of the United States until the completion of a treaty, so as to hold formal diplomatic recognition as a trading point for various British objects.

52. The commercial value of the West Indies to Britain, both before and after the American Revolution, is deftly related by Herbert C. Bell in *Studies in the Trade Relations of the British West Indies and North America, 1763–1773* (Philadelphia: University of Pennsylvania Press, 1917). See especially pp. 281–87.

53. On the aftermath of Yorktown, see a pair of fascinating narratives: Esmé Wingfield-Stratford, *The History of British Civilization* (New York: Harcourt Brace, 1938), especially the chapter entitled "The Loss of an Empire"; Jeremy Black, *The War for American Independence* (New York: St. Martin's Press, 1991). Neither author, however, elucidates the connections between the American Revolution and the onset of the long period of warfare on the European mainland in which Britain became engaged.

As regards the peace negotiations, foundational documentation can be found in the following: *British Diplomatic Instructions, 1689–1789* (London: Royal Historical Society, 1934). Documents relating to the interactions with France are in Part IV, 1745–1789, in selected form. This portion provides adequate illumination of Vergennes's acute inclination to follow the Vienna negotiations, which tempted him to sue for a separate peace with Britain, had the Yorktown victory not occurred. The Doniol supplement to Volume V, published in 1899, proves directly relevant here also, as does B. F. Stevens's *Transcripts Relating to the Peace Negotiations, 1782–1783.* The Jared Sparks collection at the Harvard College Library contains transcripts of Oswald's official correspondence as on-the-spot negotiator. And the Rockingham and Shelburne correspondence and memoranda are now available on microfilm.

54. J. W. Fortescue, *A History of the British Army* (London and New York: Macmillan, 1899–1930), vol. 3, p. 32.

55. As marksmen, the Continentals were vastly superior to the British; they probably had more practice, and this was the golden age of the Pennsylvania long rifle, which was far more accurate than any contemporary European weapon.

Congress, however, deserves some censure. Even when it was plain that war with Britain was imminent, Congress made no attempt to establish a national army until the act passed by the Second Congress on June 14, 1775. Subsequent to this, each of the states raised their initial quotas of men to fill the ranks of the Continental Army. The colonies had enough gunmakers, as Sawyer notes, "to make 100,000 stand of muskets per year at 28 shillings each." Moreover, powder stores were ample. See Charles W. Sawyer, *Firearms in American History, 1600–1800* (Boston: privately printed, 1910), p. 71.

On British manning levels and casualties, see C. T. Atkinson, "British Forces in North America, 1774–1781: Their Distribution and Strength," *Journal of the Society of Army Historical Research* 16 (Winter 1937), 3–23. On the high proportion of casualties among the Americans, see Howard H. Peckham, ed., *The Toll of Independence: Engagements and Battle Casualties of the American Revolution* (Chicago: University of Chicago Press, 1974), in particular pp. vii–xiv, and the tables on pp. 3–128, as well as Peckham's conclusions. And see Henry B. Carrington, *Battles of the American Revolution: Battle Maps and Charts of the American Revolution* (1876; reprint, New York: Arno Press, 1968), especially p. 653, where he explains clearly how he arrived at these figures. By Carrington's measure, Massachusetts provided the most service, with Connecticut, Virginia, and Pennsylvania next, providing about half as much service as Massachusetts. (But Massachusetts then included almost all of what is now Maine.) Georgia and then Delaware bring up the rear.

In terms of the percentage of the entire population, only the American Civil War cost more military lives than the American Revolution.

56. John Laurens is quoted in Charles Knowles Bolton, *The Private Soldier Under Washington* (New York: Scribner's Sons, 1902; reprint, Port Washington, N.Y.: Kennikat, 1964), p. 126; Luzerne's comments are quoted in John Durand, ed. and trans., *New Materials for the History of the American Revolution* (New York: H. Holt, 1889), p. 250. Morris's prediction appeared in his private journal and is quoted in Bolton, p. 104. George Washington's letter to Nathanael Greene appears in the forthcoming *The Washington Papers, Revolutionary War Series,* and is quoted here by courtesy of the editors. Finally, see Johann von Ewald, *Diary of the American War: A Hessian Journal,* translated and edited by Joseph P. Tustin (New Haven: Yale University Press, 1979), pp. 340–41.

On the pathetically ill-supplied men of Washington's army, see Arnold Whitridge, *Rochambeau* (New York: Macmillan, 1965), p. 102, and Don Higginbotham, *War and Society in Revolutionary America: The Wider Dimensions of Conflict* (Columbia: University of South Carolina Press, 1988), pp. 398–99. To study the war from the British point of view makes clear how uncertain the American victory was. See the British War Office files on the war, which are now available on microfilm (Amherst Papers, Stanford University).

Other valuable works on the Revolution include Edward Countryman, *The American Revolution* (New York: Hill & Wang, 1985); Ronald Hoffman and Peter J. Albert, eds., *Arms and Independence: The Military Character of the American Revolution* (Washington, D.C.: Published for the Capitol Historical Society by the University Press of Virginia,

1984); John Shy, *"A People Numerous and Armed": Reflections on the Military Struggle for American Independence* (New York: Oxford University Press, 1976); and especially Harry M. Ward, *The War for Independence and the Transformation of the American Society* (London: UCL Press, 1999).

57. On this doleful subject, see also Royal Commission on Historical Manuscripts, *Report on Manuscripts in the Royal Institution of Great Britain* (the Carleton/Dorchester Papers), prepared by B. F. Stevens and edited by H. J. Brown, vol. 1 (London: published for His Majesty's Stationery Office by Mackie and Co., 1904), pp. 391, 432–35.

58. For more information, see *US Army Center of Military History: The War of American Independence*. <http://www.army.mil/cmh-pg/reference/ revbib/pows.htm> (accessed 10 December 1996 and 10 June 2003).

59. Published in the *Journals of the Continental Congress,* vol. XII, pp. 1080–82 (October 30, 1778). On Morris's January 21, 1778, committee appointment, see idem., vol. X, pp. 81–82.

On the issue of prisoners, see Olive G. Anderson, "Establishment of the British Supremacy at Sea and the Exchange of Prisoners of War, 1689–1783," *English Historical Review* 75 (Spring 1960), 77–89. With admirable understatement, Anderson makes clear how desperate for men the British forces were by the midpoint of the war. See also John K. Alexander, "The Treatment of Prisoners of War in Britain During the American War of Independence," *Bulletin of Historical Research* 18 (Spring 1955), as well as John K. Alexander, "American Privateersmen in the Mill Prison: An Evaluation," *Essex Institute Historical Collections* 102 (1966), 318–40; John K. Alexander, "Forton Prison During the American Revolution: A Case Study of British Prisoner of War Policy and the American Prisoner Response to that Policy," *Essex Institute Historical Collections* 103 (1967), 365–89; and Sheldon S. Cohen, *Yankee Soldiers in British Gaols* (Newark: University of Delaware Press, 1995). The articles by Anderson, Alexander, and Cohen on the subjects they treat are extremely relevant.

60. Insight into the prisoner exchange issue from the other side is provided by William B. Willcox, ed., *The American Rebellion: Sir Henry Clinton's Narrative* (New Haven: Yale University Press, 1954), p. 358. Also relevant here are Clinton's appointment instructions to the two-member commission, March 25, 1782, which may be found in the Manuscript Division, Special Collections, Columbia University Library.

Washington's instructions on the same head, dated March 11, appear in John C. Fitzpatrick, ed., *The Writings of George Washington,* vol. 23, 1745–1799 (Washington, D.C.: Government Printing Office, 1931), pp. 456–59. See also *Papers of Robert Morris,* vol. 4, pp. 438–41, 490–91. And see Elias Boudinot to Morris and Knox, March 14, 1782, Gouverneur Morris Collection, Columbia University. Historians have sometimes been confused about Morris's participation on this commission, probably because Sir Henry Clinton referred to him as "Mr. Morrison" in that British officer's narrative.

Some illuminating commentary may be found in North Callahan, *Henry Knox* (New York: Rinehart, 1958), chapter 11, and in Betsy Knight, "Prisoner Exchange and Parole in the American Revolution," *William and Mary Quarterly* 48 (3rd series) (April 1991), 214–222.

61. See, for example, *Journals of the Continental Congress* XXI, p. 1039; XX, pp. 597–98, 721, 734; XXII 813–14, 908, 954–55, 1024–25, 1027, 1062, 1068, 1070, 1135, 1149–50.

62. On these matters, the reader can consult not only the rich, abundant materials in *Papers of Robert Morris,* but also *Journals of the Continental Congress,* vol. XXII, pp. 9, 74, 173, 201–202, 209, 219, 238, 244, 263–74, 321, 324, 343, 363–65.

63. *Papers of the Continental Congress,* John P. Butler, ed. (Washington, D.C.: National Archives, 1978), no. 137, vol. I, p. 9; Ellis P. Oberholtzer, *Robert Morris: Patriot and Financier* (New York: Macmillan, 1903), p. 306.

64. See Robert Morris to Thomas Jefferson, June 11, 1781, *Papers of Robert Morris,* vol. 1, pp. 142–43. For the official naming of the president, directors, and company of the Bank of North America, see *Journals of the Continental Congress,* vol. VII, p. 257 (entry dated December 31, 1781). The plan for the bank, as submitted to Congress on May 17, 1781, can be found with the usual helpful annotations in *Papers of Robert Morris,* vol. 3, pp. 68–74.

The extent of Gouverneur Morris's input is suggested in footnote 10. I have never found an instance in which GM exaggerated his professional achievements—rather, the contrary.

Also helpful in understanding the bank's development are Robert Morris to John Hancock, July 2, 1781 (*Papers of Robert Morris,* vol. 1, pp. 211–12), and John H. Michener, *The Bank of North America* (New York: Putnam, 1906). Especially reliable is Clarence Ver Steeg, *Robert Morris: Revolutionary Financier* (Philadelphia: University of Pennsylvania Press, 1954); see, in particular, chapter 5.

For a broader view, see Paul A. Gilje, "The Rise of Capitalism in the Early Republic," *Journal of the Early Republic* 16 (Summer 1996), 159–81.

65. Trenchant commentaries on the roles of both Morrises in the history of the Bank of North America can be found in the relevant volumes of *Papers of Robert Morris;* William G. Sumner, *The Financier and the Finances of the American Revolution,* vol. 2 (New York: Dodd, Mead, 1891), especially pp. 17–46; Albert S. Bolles, *The Financial History of the United States from 1774 to 1789,* 2nd ed. (New York: Appleton, 1884), pp. 272–79; and the commentary in Herman Krooss ed., *Documentary History of Banking and Currency in the United States* (New York: Chelsea House, 1977), especially pp. 86–92. Krooss wisely points to the long-range currency and banking legacies of Robert Morris, Gouverneur Morris, Alexander Hamilton, and Thomas Jefferson (p. 89). Also valuable is the chapter entitled "Banking Companies" in Joseph S. Davis's *Essays in American Corporations,* vol. 1 (Cambridge: Harvard University Press, 1917) and Edwin J. Perkins's *American Public Finance and Financial Services, 1700–1815* (Athens: Ohio University Press, 1994), especially pp. 130–35. Gouverneur's "Address on the Bank of North America" appears in Jared Sparks, *Life of Gouverneur Morris* (Boston: Gray & Bowen, 1832), vol. 3, pp. 438–40.

The Bank of North America was viable until 1923. At this time it was folded into the Commercial Trust Company, and became known as the Bank of North America and Trust Company. This institution prospered for six more years. In June of 1929, it merged into The Pennsylvania Company for Insurances on Lives Granting Annuities.

66. On the February 24, 1782, Sunday workday, followed by a horseback ride, see *Papers of Robert Morris,* "Diary," vol. 4, p. 299. Gouverneur remarks on his hours in his June 4, 1781, letter to Robert Morris in *Papers of Robert Morris,* vol. 1 (Pittsburgh: University of Pittsburgh Press, 1973), pp. 106–09.

67. In GM's nomenclator, printed numbers appear on the decoding sheet, along with words, letters, and syllables, carefully written. The encoding sheet has code elements, in alphabetical order, with the number listed after each element. This durable cipher was adapted for use by the U.S. diplomatic corps and remained in use until the installation of the transatlantic cable. See Ralph E. Weber, *United States Diplomatic Codes and Ciphers, 1775–1938* (New York: Precedent, 1979), in particular pp. 68–71, 80–81, 110–111, and Appendix WE006.

Thomas Jefferson's wheel cipher was probably more sophisticated. See David Kahn, *The Codebreakers: The Story of Secret Writing* (New York: Macmillan, 1967), p. 195.

For an example of an encoding error by Morris in the Finance Office, see the letter from Matthew Ridley to Robert Morris, February 16, 1782, written from Rouen (*Papers of Robert Morris,* vol. 4, pp. 242–47).

GM's letter to Jay is in *Papers of Robert Morris,* vol. 6, p. 146.

68. The twin proposals are capably explained by Sumner, *The Financier,* vol. 2, pp. 40–45. A lucid examination and criticism of the systems can also be found in Sparks, *Morris,* vol. 1, pp. 273–81. The editors' introduction to these questions, and their annotations, in *Papers of Robert Morris,* vol. 4, pp. 25–29 and 39 n. 10 are especially valuable, clear, and insightful.

For information on the conversion of coin value, see Louis Jordan, "Colonial Currency," *The Coins of Colonial and Early America* (10 Dec. 1997) University of Notre Dame, Department of Special Collections. June 2003. <http://www.coins.nd.edu/Col Currency/CurrencyText/Contents.html>.

69. Ludwig von Mises, *Human Action* (New Haven: Yale University Press, 1949), p. 231. On the currency, see John J. McCusker, *How Much Is That in Real Money?* (Worcester, Mass.: American Antiquarian Society, 1992), pp. 351–52, and especially also footnotes

46, 49, and 50; and John J. Knox, *United States Notes: A History of the Various Issues of Paper by the United States,* 3rd ed. (New York: Scribners, 1899).

Both Robert A. East, *Business Enterprise in the American Revolutionary Era* (New York: Columbia University Press, 1938), p. 210, and, surprisingly, Clarence Ver Steeg, *Robert Morris,* pp. 192–93. For a lucid discussion of American prices and monetary values at the time of the Finance Office, see the conclusions of Anne Bezanson, *Prices and Inflation During the American Revolution: Pennsylvania, 1770–1790* (Philadelphia: University of Pennsylvania Press, 1951). For Robert Morris's comprehension of the short-term power of the Morris notes, see Robert Morris to GM, April 3, 1782, *Papers of Robert Morris,* vol. 4, pp. 510–511.

During the Finance Office period, clipped and debased gold coins were circulating, largely from British-held New York. Morris solved the problem by having the bank value silver coins by the weight of the coins rather than the number of coins. This became the Bank of North America's normal policy, and it was adopted by the banks developed in the Confederation period. It was of some help to the dire American economic situation; in a slowly sinking bark, steady bailing always helps.

70. On the tobacco matter, see, for example, Robert Morris's diary entry of February 12, 1782, in *Papers of Robert Morris,* vol. 4, pp. 216–17. Regarding Thomas Paine, the agreement with George Washington on February 10, 1782, appears in vol. 4, p. 201, and the "Memorandum on Thomas Paine" in vol. 4, pp. 327–28.

71. On these points, see Adam Smith, *The Wealth of Nations* (Glasgow: Glasgow University Press, 1979), vol. 2, p. 574. Smith's work, which Robert Morris read well before he assumed the superintendency of the Finance Office, also directly influenced Lord North's thinking. In 1777, in order to find fresh revenue of nearly £250,000, North imposed a tax on manservants, an idea borrowed from *The Wealth of Nations* (Smith in turn had borrowed it from Holland). In 1785, Pitt extended the tax to maidservants.

72. Such attitudes partly account for GM's dislike of the American "love of popularity . . . our endemial disease," as he put it in a 1782 letter to Benjamin Franklin (cited in Sparks, *Morris,* vol. 1, p. 274). For detailed information on Congress's insurance of Continental bills, see Ralph V. Harlow, "Aspects of Revolutionary Finance, 1775–1783," *American Historical Review* 35 (October 1929), pp. 46–68; chart, pp. 49–50. For ancillary background information, see John A. Stevens, *Albert Gallatin* (Boston: Houghton Mifflin, 1896), especially chapter 6.

73. For a glimpse of the antinationalist sentiment on the economic side, see Clarence Ver Steeg, *Robert Morris: Revolutionary Financier,* p. 197, and Glenn W. Fisher, *The Worst Tax? A History of the Property Tax in America: Studies in Government and Public Policy* (Lawrence: University Press of Kansas, 1996), pp. 28–29.

74. On all the measures discussed above, Robert and GM worked together so closely it is fair to speak of them in tandem. See *Papers of Robert Morris,* vol. 4, pp. 218–20, 572–74, 577–78. On the paper-money taxation question, see Kroos, *Documentary History of Banking,* p.88, and Burnett, *Letters of Members of the Continental Congress,* vol. 4, pp. xvi–xvii.

When Washington's troops were still at Valley Forge, GM had proposed mandating "contributions" from the residents of Philadelphia, an idea Washington tactfully discouraged (see George Washington to Morris, May 29, 1778, in *The Writings of George Washington,* ed. John C. Fitzpatrick (Washington, D.C.: Government Printing Office, 1931), vol. 11, pp. 482–86. For relevant commentary, see E. James Ferguson, *The Power of the Purse: A History of American Public Finance, 1776–1790* (Chapel Hill: University of North Carolina Press, 1961), pp. 30–31, 67–71, 149–53.

75. On Gouverneur Morris's and Jay's dealings concerning Spain, see, for instance, *Papers of Robert Morris,* vol. 4, p. 82. For Robert Morris's presentations to Congress on the least painful ways to handle the domestic debt, see Ferguson, *Power of the Purse,* pp. 122–25, and William G. Anderson, *The Price of Liberty: The Public Debt of the American Revolution* (Charlottesville: University Press of Virginia, 1983), pp. 14–15, 37–45. Anderson's monograph deserves wider scholarly notice. Consolidation raised the federal domestic debt from $11 million (the specie value of loan certificates) to over $27 million; Anderson points out that Robert Morris saw this as a good sign, reasoning that a large debt would require large amounts of revenue and therefore a federal taxing power.

Both Anderson and Ferguson explain how Robert Morris's policies boomeranged; see Anderson's p. 18 and Ferguson's p. 222. Also relevant here is Sumner, *Finances,* vol. 1, p. 41, on the Morrises' attempts to regularize the coinage.

76. Prince de Broglie, "Narrative of the Prince de Broglie [1782], Translated [by E. W. Balch] from an Unpublished MS," *Magazine of American History, with Notes and Queries* 1 (March 1871), p. 234.

77. On these schemes, worked out in writing between about April 10 and May 10, 1782, see *Papers of Robert Morris,* vol. 5, pp. 145–59. The May 10 report emphasizes the potential windfalls available from the American tobacco trade; see especially "Estimate No. 1" and "Observation on the Estimates." These passages consistently overestimate how much could be attained by a small American naval force against the powerful and experienced Royal Navy, a quality that suggests the authorship of Gouverneur Morris. His military notions were usually overoptimistic.

78. Robert Lynd, *Books and Authors* (New York: G. P. Putnam's Sons, 1923), p. 37. For Gouverneur Morris's sound reasoning on the silver question, see *Papers of Robert Morris,* vol. 5, pp. 444–46 (June 18 essay), where he compares the values of various national currencies with the value of silver and gold. (As usual, the editors provide exceptionally helpful annotations [see vol. 5, pp. 442–44].) Concerning "Money [being] carried away [from America] and the Influence which it has on the Welfare of the Country," see Gouverneur Morris's astute letter (June 18, 1782) to Robert Morris's business partner Thomas Willig in *Papers of Robert Morris,* vol. 5, pp. 435–44.

With characteristic thoroughness, GM began his ventures into currency policy by carefully examining all the categories of coins then circulating in America. He consulted James Steuart's *An Inquiry into the Principles of Political Oeconomy* (1767), which he had read during the summer of 1781. See GM to President of the Bank of North America, June 18, 1781, draft version, Gouverneur Morris Collection, Columbia University Library. Steuart's work concerns such matters as money of account, material money, metals analysis, and how the value of a money unit affects a nation's domestic interest, banks, the valuation of coinage, public debt, and taxation. Steuart's book is hard to find, even in the helpfully annotated reprint edition (2 vols., Andrew S. Skinner, ed. [Chicago: University of Chicago Press, 1966]).

See also *Papers of Robert Morris,* vol. 5, pp. 435–40, and Fritz Redlich, *The Molding of American Banking: Men and Ideas, 1780–1784,* vol. 1 (New York: Hafner, 1951), pp. 3–7.

79. This revelatory letter is in the Ridley Collection, Boston Public Library.

80. The treaty's language was not unambiguous. See, for example, David Demeritt, "Representing the 'True' St. Croix: Knowledge and Power in the Partition of the Northeast," *William and Mary Quarterly,* 3rd series, vol. 54 (July 1997), 515–48.

The most reliable source for an American perspective on the negotiations is John Jay; see Frank Monaghan, ed., *The Diary of John Jay During the Peace Negotiations of 1782* (New York: Bibliographical Press, 1934). This diary covers the crucial period, June–December 1782. For the treaty's text, see D. Hunter Miller, *Treaties and Other International Acts of the United States of America,* vol. 2 (Washington, D.C.: Carnegie Institution, 1931). It is helpful to consult John Mitchell's map, which the negotiators used; it has been reproduced often. John Mitchell's map may be found in John R. Sellers and Patricia Molen Van Ee. *Maps and Charts of North America and the West Indies, 1750–1789: A Guide to the Collections of the Library of Congress* (Washington, D.C.: Library of Congress, 1981), pp. 11–14. B. F. Stevens's *Transcripts Relating to the Peace Negotiations of 1782–1783* (Washington, D.C.: Library of Congress, 1885) includes many valuable primary documents.

The most reliable discussion of the treaty is Samuel F. Bemis, *The Diplomacy of the American Revolution* (New York: Appleton-Century, 1935); chapters 14 through 19 are especially valuable, and the author includes "the Preliminary and Conditional Articles of the Peace," as well as providing an extended bibliographical note. On the diplomatic prelude and the making of the treaty, still worth consulting is Andrew C. McLaughlin, *Confederation and Constitution* (New York: Harper & Bros., 1905), pp. 10–17, 18–21, 29–30.

81. Mary Gallagher, "The Office of Finance and the Development of the Ideology of Free Trade," unpublished. Robert Morris viewed the national debt as an immense impediment to the prompt establishment of national credit. He felt so strongly on the matter that he threatened to resign if steps could not soon be taken to reduce it; he did not wish, he said, to be "the Minister of Injustice." See *Papers of Robert Morris,* vol. 7, pp. 368–71 (January 24, 1783). In 1783, the congressional committee on the debt converted the total into dollars at five livres and eight sous to the dollar. *Journals of the Continental Congress,* vol. VIII, p. 151; also somewhat germane is vol. VII, p. 386. As of the end of 1783, the United States owed France $6.35 million; Holland, $1.304 million; and Spain, just over $174,000.

The situation with regard to Spain's contributions to American independence is exceptionally complicated. The munitions supplied through the French representative Beaumarchais seem to have been sent by way of a loan approved by the Spanish king. The negotiations of the relevant American representatives—Deane, Lee, Franklin, and Jay—with the Spanish representatives—Floridablanca and Aranda, especially—were indeed byzantine. In the end, the Americans had proposed paying back this loan with large shipments of tobacco, potash, and rice. But these repayments had been thwarted mainly by the strong British blockade. Also, early in the war, gunpowder from the same king's stores was paid for by a draft, drawn in Spanish milled dollars, on the "Grand Council of Viriginia." In an odd development, some of the struggling missions and forts in the west, in what is now California, Texas, New Mexico, and Arizona, collected funds in support of the war. These funds were evidently sent as gifts. But the $174,000 figure as the loan amount owed to Spain in the early 1780s is the same amount listed several times by the extremely knowledgeable editors of the *Papers of Robert Morris.* See also Thomas E. Chávez. *Spain and the Independence of the United States: An Intrinsic Gift* (Albuquerque: University of New Mexico Press, 2002), pp. 31, 68, and 215.

82. On these issues, see *Papers of Robert Morris,* vol. 6, pp. 579–80. On the major goals of the Robert Morris Finance Office, see idem, vol. 6, pp. xxv–xxxvii, a compact, thoughtful, and clear presentation. For GM's involvement with the report on public credit and the sale of bills of exchange, see especially idem, vol. 6, pp. 26–51; on settlement of American financial accounts with Europe, see vol. 6, pp. 227–29, 257–59.

83. On the prisoner-exchange issue, see, especially, *Papers of Robert Morris,* vol. 6, pp. 299 and n. 2 there.

84. See Robert Morris to William Whipple, June 4, 1782, in *Papers of Robert Morris,* vol. 5, pp. 336–37.

85. These three economic matters are both complex and interconnected. The editorial annotations in *Papers of Robert Morris,* vol. 6, pp. 565–68, clearly sketch the outlines. In the same volume (p. 47), the editors assess the extent of Gouverneur Morris's involvement with Robert Morris's plan of public credit; I believe they underestimate that involvement, as do Clarence Ver Steeg, *Robert Morris: Revolutionary Financier,* pp. 78–84, and Mary-Jo Kline, *Gouverneur Morris and the New Nation, 1775–1778* (New York: Arno Press, 1978).

Who influenced the economic thinking at the Finance Office, besides Adam Smith and James Steuart? *Papers of Robert Morris* mention Hume, Richard Price, Sully, Necker, and Chastellux (see vol. 6, pp. 43–44). Gouverneur Morris, too, seems to have been influenced by all of these.

86. This document first appeared in print, though with typographical errors, in Francis Wharton, *The Revolutionary Diplomatic Correspondence of the United States,* vol. 5 (Washington, D.C.: U. S. Government Printing Office, 1889), p. 779. It is unsigned but there is no mistaking the prose style.

87. On January 1, 1783, GM wrote approvingly to John Jay of Jay's diplomatic initiatives overseas. He objected to what he called the "Servility" that Congress's instructions of spring 1781 would require of the American commissioners; see his letter to John Jay, June 17, 1781, in Richard B. Morris, ed., *John Jay: The Winning of the Peace, 1780–1784* (New York: Harper & Row, 1980), pp. 86–87. Jay paid heed to his younger friend, so GM's influence on the peace negotiations was substantial and positive from their outset.

88. The event sharply highlights one of the major deficiencies of the Articles of Confederation as a national governing instrument. The efficiency of the English customs office is ably demonstrated by Elizabeth E. Hoon, *The Organization of the English Customs System, 1696–1786* (1938; reprint, New York: Greenwood Press, 1968). Hoon's monograph is essential reading on the subject.

89. On the mostly nonviolent Pennsylvania mutiny, see the following: Samuel Hazard, ed., *The Register of Pennsylvania* (Philadelphia: W. F. Geddes, 1828–1831), vol. II, pp. 275–78 and pp. 328–33; Henry Cabot Lodge, ed., *The Works of Alexander Hamilton* (New York: G. P. Putnam's Sons, 1885–86), vol. VIII, pp. 124–44; and *The Papers of Robert Morris,* vol. 7, p. 341, n. 54, n. 58 (the two footnotes are especially valuable for their brief presentation of the essential facts and for drawing attention to Kenneth Bowling's essay, "New Light on the Philadelphia Mutiny of 1783: Federal-State Confrontation at the Close of the War for Independence," *Pennsylvania Magazine of History and Biography* 51 [1977]). Mary Gallagher's "Soldiers, Citizens, and Rationalists: The Philadelphia Mutiny of 1783," a typescript of which she generously provided me before its publication, neatly discusses the revolt. Her conclusion is well worth quoting: "We should not fail to see the mutiny as one more demand for governmental response to the needs and sufferings of Pennsylvania soldiers and recognition of their role in bringing about the triumph of revolutionary objectives." Gallagher demonstrates that although GM's tone may have offended some of the soldiers, he attempted to ease tensions to mollify the soldiers and to limit the damage they did. For more on his participation in quelling the mutiny, see *The Papers of Robert Morris,* vol. 8, pp. xxxiv–xxxv, 196, 220, 222–26, 228, 236, and 483.

90. On the pension scheme, see, for instance, *Papers of Robert Morris,* vol. 7, pp. 393–99. On GM and the coinage system, see his letter to Samuel Osgood, October 30, 1785, in Osgood Papers, BV section "O" in the Field-Osgood Papers at the Library of Congress. The computations here follow the proposal GM outlines in his June 18, 1782 letter to Thomas Willig (*Papers of Robert Morris,* vol. 5, pp. 435–46, with the usual excellent annotations).

91. Bernard Mandeville, *The Fable of the Bees,* ed. Philip Harth (New York: Penguin, 1971), vol. 1, p. 369. By 1760, Mandeville's book had appeared in nearly a dozen editions in Gouverneur Morris's two main languages, English and French. During his lifetime, it was published rather like a prose *Leaves of Grass,* with each new edition adding some material and leaving other passages out. The quoted passage appears in every edition published before 1783.

92. On these matters, see especially *Journals of the Continental Congress* XXIV, pp. 144n, 170–74, 188–92, 195–261, and XXV, pp. 920–62; and Joseph Jones to George Washington, February 27, 1783 (Burnett, *Letters,* vol. VII, pp. 60–61).

93. The letters to John Jay, Henry Knox, and Nathanael Greene were first published in Sparks, *Morris,* vol. 1, pp. 248–51, 255–56, but with altered spelling and punctuation, and with some passages deleted. The originals are in the Columbia University Library, Gouverneur Morris Papers.

   That Washington's army passed the winter of 1782–1783 better fed, clothed, and sheltered than, probably, at any other time in the past eight years, should not surprise us; memories of oppression tend to be cumulative.

   On the conspiracy question, as usual the editors of *The Papers of Robert Morris* provide insightful commentary. See, for instance, vol. 7, pp. xxvi–xxix, 307. On the nationalist policies of the Morrises, see also Kline, *Morris,* pp. 210–14. For commentary on the relationship between GM and Knox, see *The Papers of Robert Morris,* vol. 7, pp. 412–17, 419–20; on the correspondence between GM and Greene, see vol. 7, pp. 426–27.

94. *Papers of Robert Morris,* vol. 7, pp. 761–65. Robert Morris passed this letter to Jefferson on May 1, 1784.

95. These two letters are in *Papers of Robert Morris, 1781–1784,* Jay to Morris on September 24, 1783, in vol. 8, pp. 540–41 and Morris to Jay on January 10, 1784, in vol. 9, pp. 17–18.

96. The writings in which GM attempts to develop postwar commercial activity can be seen to clear effect in *Papers of Robert Morris,* vol. 8, pp. 593–95 and 687–98, including

annotations. Both GM and Robert Morris advocated free trade but argued that British attempts to thwart free trade with America would nevertheless provide a further incentive for American unity, since any such attempts by Britain at monopolizing American trade would drive the former colonies even close together. On these points, see *Papers of Robert Morris,* vol. 8, pp. 552–53 notes 14 and 15, p. 550, n. 17, p. 565; GM to Jeremiah Wadsworth, as well as the two letters from GM to John Jay of September 24, 1783, and January 10, 1784, Gouverneur Morris Collection, Columbia University Library. And see *Papers of Robert Morris,* vol. 8, p. 511, n. 5, last paragraph.

97. For commentary on the still steep American military expenses after the war, see *Papers of Robert Morris,* vol. 8, p. xxxiii; see also p. xxxii. The diary entry for July 30, 1783, appears in vol. 8, p. 358.

98. On the breathtakingly ill-considered troop reductions, see the *Journals of the Continental Congress,* vol. IX, pp. 290–91 (June 2, 1784).

99. On these subjects, see Eric P. Newman, *The Early Paper Money of America* (Racine, Wisc.: Whitman, 1967), pp. 43, 359–60, and Albert Sidney Bolles, *The Financial History of the United States, 1789–1860* (New York: D. Appleton, 1885).

Surely a thorough biography of Robert Morris is due. Thus far the most satisfactory is still that by Ellis P. Oberholtzer, *Robert Morris: Patriot and Financier* (New York: Macmillan, 1903). But most writers have taken a too simplistic view of his achievements. Either he "financed the Revolution" and "ruined his own fortune for the state, and a grateful country allowed him in later years to gain experience in a debtors' prison" (F. S. Oliver, *Alexander Hamilton* [New York: Putnam, 1921], pp. 84–85) or, perhaps because he wound up in debtors' prison, his worth is undervalued. As an example of the latter, see Howard Swiggett, "The Patriot Financier: Robert Morris," in *The Forgotten Leaders of the American Revolution* (New York: Doubleday, 1955), chapter 6.

In *American Public Finance and Financial Services, 1700–1815* (Columbus, Oh.: Ohio State University Press, 1994), Edwin J. Perkins judges Robert Morris "among the most important and powerful financial leaders in American history" (p. 106, and see pp. 107–13). He also provides a good overview of Morris's accomplishments; but he provides relatively little scholarly documentation, and this detracts from the usefulness of his work.

100. J. H. Robinson and H. W. Rolfe, eds., *Petrarch, the First Modern Man of Letters* (New York: G. P. Putnam's Sons, 1898; 2nd ed., revised and enlarged, 1914), p. 124.

101. The ninth and last volume of *Papers of Robert Morris* lists the numerous fruitless investigations of the Finance Office head's financial dealings and details the primary sources for each.

102. Interestingly, Hamilton was instrumental in developing the first conflict-of-interest law. By such legislation the intercourse between business and government has not been entirely terminated, but at least legal standards have been put in place.

103. The memorandum of agreement involving GM, Robert Morris, and John Vaughan appears in *Papers of Robert Morris,* vol. 8, pp. 616–17. The footnotes are illuminating. On the importance of real estate, see Ludwig von Mises, *Human Action* (New Haven: Yale University Press, 1949), passim. GM's letter to George Clinton is quoted from the photocopy in the Historical Society of Pennsylvania collection.

On GM's New York State and lower Canadian land ventures, see J. C. Churchill, *Landmarks of Oswego County* (Syracuse, N.Y.: University of Syracuse Press, 1895), p. 13. On his western land speculations, see also the correspondence docketed as "Gouverneur Morris–Kingsbury" in the Tioga Point Museum, Athens, Pennsylvania; Anne Cary Morris, ed., *Diary and Letters of Gouverneur Morris* (New York: C. Scribner's Sons, 1888), vol. 2, p. 459; C. R. King, ed., *Rufus King, Life and Correspondence* (New York: Appleton, 1894–1900), vol. 4, p. 404.

For other New York State speculators of the time, see D. R. Fox, *The Decline of Aristocracy in the Politics of New York* (New York: Columbia University, 1919), chapter 4. From 1784 through 1789, Robert Morris also executed some of his most ambitious private business deals. From the Genesee region, he sold 120,000 acres to an Englishman, Sir William Pulteney. This transaction alone netted Robert $100,000, or about 80 percent of the sum that Spain loaned to America for the Revolutionary War. Robert's

"Holland Purchase" comprised three and a half million acres. On this topic, see, for example, William G. Sumner, *The Financier and the Finances of the American Revolution,* vol. 2 (New York: B. Franklin, 1891), chapter 33.

It may be useful to remind readers that corruption among American officials—corruption that pre-dated conflict-of-interest laws—was petty compared with what went on in contemporary Europe. Many British offices, for example, allowed the incumbents to take commissions for contractors, to accept sweeteners, and to use as their private kitties huge sums of public money, with which they manipulated the Exchange. Marlborough, Cadogan, Amherst, Robert Walpole, Bubb Dodington, Henry Fox, James Brydges, and others made their fortunes on the Paymaster Generalship. Lord Chancellor Macclesfield was caught stealing from the Exchequer outright; he had embezzled at least £100,000, and it took him less than six weeks to pay his £30,000 fine.

104. Information on the land dealing and this excerpt from Gouverneur's letter of May 3, 1816, may be found in Alfred F. Young, *The Democratic Republicans of New York: The Origins, 1763–1797* (Chapel Hill: University of North Carolina Press, 1967), pp. 65 and 261–62.

105. See Anne Cary Morris, ed., *The Diary and Letters of Gouverneur Morris,* vol. 1, p. 17; GM to Constable, Rucker & Co., October 31, 1787, in Gouverneur Morris Collection, Library of Congress; Le Contelux to Rucker, April 23, 1787, Pennsylvania Mss—Additional Miscellany, Historical Society of Pennsylvania. For GM on the tobacco trade, see Manuscript Collection No. 76, folders 1 through 6, American Philosophical Society.

106. John Stuart Mill's remarks, in *Principles of Political Economy* (1871), on "the utility of [having] money" may provide some insight into the avarice of Robert and Gouverneur Morris.

Hamilton died of a gunshot wound to the thigh in 1804, less than two years before Robert Morris died in a modest house in Philadelphia. On Robert Morris's houses and estates from the 1780s to the late 1790s, see, for instance, Oberholtzer, *Robert Morris,* passim, and H. D. Eberlein, *Portrait of a Colonial City: Philadelphia, 1670–1838* (Philadelphia: J. B. Lippincott, 1939), pp. 383–97. The debtors' prison was not more than three hundred yards from the large city square that Robert had once owned.

On the debts under which many American farmers labored in the period 1784–1789, see Curtis P. Nettels, *The Emergence of a National Economy, 1775–1815* (Armonk, N.Y.: M. E. Sharpe, 1962), pp. 79–81. The farmers' debts and tax obligations caused them to oppose the merchants' banks, which offered only short-term loans. Farmers needed cash loans that could extend through growing and harvest seasons, and the state governments' "land banks" fit that bill. "Land banks" lent bills on land security, and not only charged less interest, but also allowed farmers time to hold surplus produce for good prices and still pay their taxes. Useful as a supplement is Christopher Clark, "Rural America and the Transition to Capitalism," *Journal of the Early Republic* 16 (Summer 1996), 223–36.

Many of Gouverneur Morris's famous American contemporaries found themselves impoverished in middle age or old age. That Alexander Hamilton left his family virtually penniless may be accounted for in part by the suddenness of his death, and in part by his honesty in public service. But dishonesty was no guarantee of wealth. William Duer (1747–1799) died during his seventh year in debtors' prison. As assistant treasury secretary under Hamilton, Duer seems to have operated on the principle "One for the people and one for me," and his land speculations with the Scioto Company suggest how little effect conflict-of-interest laws may have. (See Robert F. Jones's biography of Duer, *King of the Alley* [Philadelphia: American Philosophical Society, 1992].) John Cleves Symmes, the pioneer settler of the Ohio Valley, died penniless, as did Elias Boudinot, who was once a magnate in New Jersey. Of the handful of the best American general officers who survived through the Confederation period virtually all died poor: Knox, Lincoln, Moultrie, Parsons, and Sullivan, among others. Furthermore, as a biographer of Edmund Pendleton has observed, "imprisonment for debt hung like a nightmare over some of the first families of Virginia." Light Horse Harry Lee and Thomas Jefferson ended more or less in penury.

107. The financial maneuverings by which Gouverneur Morris obtained Morrisania can be traced in manuscript collections. In a letter dated March 21, 1787, from Philadelphia, GM advised his business agent, Richard Harison (1748–1829), concerning strategy for

the purchase. At Morrisania, GM received some sound advice from Walter Rutherford on developing the farm at his estate. The letter to Harison is in the Papers of Richard Harison, 1860 Box 1, Cage GG7B, New-York Historical Society. The most relevant Walter Rutherford letter, of August 31, 1787, is in the Stuyvesant-Rutherford Collection, New-York Historical Society.

5. THE CONSTITUTIONAL CONVENTION

1. For the entire Confederation period, the work of three scholars stands out: Merrill M. Jensen, *The New Nation: A History of the United States During the Confederacy, 1781–1789* (New York: Knopf, 1950); Gordon S. Wood, *The Confederation and the Constitution: The Critical Issues* (Lanham, Md.: University Press of America, 1979) and *The Creation of the American Republic, 1776–1787* (Chapel Hill: University of North Carolina Press, 1969); and Jack N. Rakove, *Original Meanings: Politics and Ideas in the Making of the Constitution* (New York: Knopf, 1996). Wood's *The Radicalism of the American Revolution* (New York: Knopf, 1992) dovetails interestingly with his treatises on the Confederation era. On the Annapolis Convention, especially valuable is Arthur T. Prescott, *Drafting the Federal Constitution* (1941; reprinted, New York: Greenwood Press, 1968).

2. To General Greene, December 24, 1787, in Jared Sparks, *The Life of Gouverneur Morris,* 3 vols. (Boston: Gray and Bowen, 1832), vol. I, p. 239. See also Anne Cary Morris ed., *The Diary and Letters of Gouverneur Morris* (New York: Charles Scribner, 1888), vol. 1, p. 15.

3. GM to Matthew Ridley, in *The Papers of Robert Morris,* Elizabeth M. Nuxoll and Mary A. Gallagher eds. (Pittsburgh: University of Pittsburgh Press, 1995), vol. 8, p. 340. George Washington seems to have been the first to realize, and to say clearly, that there must be a strong and efficient central government. See his letter to Benjamin Harrison, who was then president of the Virginia House of Burgesses, on December 18, 1778, in Jared Sparks, ed., *The Writings of George Washington,* vol. 6 (Boston: Russell, 1834), pp. 142–44. Washington writes that "the States, separately, are too much engaged in their local concerns, and have too many of their ablest men withdrawn from the general council, for the good of the common weal." From 1781 to 1786, New Hampshire, North Carolina, South Carolina, and Georgia paid none of the money requisitioned by Congress, and they went unpunished. See Joseph Story, *Commentaries on the Constitution of the United States,* 2nd ed. (Boston: C. C. Little and J. Brown, 1851), vol. 1, p. 177. Between 1784 and 1789, nearly 60 percent of the states' payments to the Confederation consisted of state-printed "indents." Needless to say, the Confederation government was impoverished.

    For a good discussion of the states' domestic affairs during this period, see Allan Nevins, *The American States During and After the Revolution, 1775–1789* (1924; reprint, New York: A. M. Kelley, 1969). For the difficulties in foreign relations, see Mary A. Giunta, ed., *Foreign Relations of the United States Under the Articles of Confederation,* 3 vols. (Washington, D.C.: National Historical Publications and Records Commission, 1984–1995). Some valuable commentary on the systemic weaknesses of the Confederation can also be found in Edward A. Channing, *A History of the United States,* vol. 3 (New York: Macmillan, 1912), chapter 15. On the weakness of Congress during this period, see the foreword by Eugene R. Sheridan and John M. Murrin, eds., *Congress at Princeton* (Princeton: Princeton University Press, 1985), especially pp. xxi, xxvii, xxxi, xxxiii, and xxxv. Foreign observers commented on the weaknesses of Congress, too; see, for example, the reports drafted for the British Foreign Office (Foreign Office Papers, America, Folio 5. Sir John Temple, Mr. Bond, 1787).

4. As often during the late eighteenth and early nineteenth centuries, European visitors' observations are more revealing than accounts by natives. On the above subjects, see especially Brissot de Warville, *New Travels in America,* vol. 1 (London: J. S. Jordan, 1792), passim but especially pp. 49–99. See, too, Edmund Quincy, *Life of Josiah Quincy*

(Boston: Little, Brown, 1874), pp. 35–40; "Letters of Phineas Bond," American Historical Association *Report* 1896, pp. 520–24; *Pennsylvania Archives,* 1st series, vol. 10, pp. 128–31; and New-York Historical Society Collections 1878, pp. 23–33.

5. Merrill Jensen's *The Articles of Confederation: An Interpretation of the Social-Constitutional History of the American Revolution, 1774–1781* (Madison: University of Wisconsin Press, 1948) and "Democracy and the American Revolution," *Huntington Library Quarterly* 20 (1956–1957), pp. 321–41, offer especially sophisticated analyses of these subjects. See also Richard C. Haskett, "Prosecuting the Revolution," *American Historical Review* 59 (Winter 1954), pp. 578–87, which examines the structural difficulties of the governmental systems provided by the Continental Congress and the Articles of Confederation.

6. This letter by Varnum to George Washington on July 18, 1787, may be found in Max Farrand, ed., *The Records of the Federal Convention of 1787* (New Haven: Yale University Press, 1966), vol. 3, pp. 47–48.

7. This letter of July 1787 is located in Jonathan Elliot, ed., *Debates on the Constitution* (Philadelphia: Lippincott, 1941), vol. 1, pp. 480–82.

8. See Fred Barbash, *The Founding: A Dramatic Account of the Writing of the Constitution* (New York: Linden Press, 1987), pp. 53–54.

9. The information presented above, concerning the Constitutional Convention and the Framers, draws on numerous sources. Chief among them are John P. Butler, ed., *Papers of the Continental Congress, 1774–1789* (Washington, D.C.: National Archives and Records Association, 1978), and *The Miscellaneous Papers of the Continental Congress* (Washington, D.C.: National Archives and Records Association, 1962). Also from NARA, microfilmed records relating to Revolutionary War accounts and pensions.

　　Valuable secondary sources include Dorothy H. McGee, *Framers of the Constitution* (New York: Dodd, Mead, 1968); Clinton Rossiter, *1787: The Grand Convention* (New York: Macmillan, 1966); Fred Rodell, *Fifty-five Men* (Harrisburg, Pa.: Telegraph Press, 1936). The latter, however, lacks scholarly documentation. Of value as a survey of the early-twentieth-century scholarship on the subject is Stanley Elkins and Eric McKitrick, "The Founding Fathers: Young Men of the Revolution," *Political Science Quarterly* 76 (Winter 1961), 181–216.

　　See also the generalizations concerning the delegates made by James Kirby Martin in *Men in Rebellion: Higher Governmental Leaders and the Coming of the American Revolution* (New Brunswick: Rutgers University Press, 1986), on pp. 66–67. See also Bertrand de Jouvenel, *The Politics of Redistribution* (Cambridge: Cambridge University Press, 1952), p. 38, and James Sutherland, *Preface to the Eighteenth Century* (Oxford: Clarendon Press, 1948), p. 38.

　　From its inception, the United States was far larger, at nearly 900,000 square miles, than any European state; the population on which Congress was based was 2.568 million, but that figure treats the slaves at three-fifths of a person each. The real total was probably about 2.776 million. On the important demographic matters, see especially Evarts B. Greene and Virginia D. Harrington, *American Population Before the Federal Census of 1790* (New York: Columbia University Press, 1932), tables pp. 7, 8, and footnotes 12, 13.

　　In "The Rocky Road," *The Philadelphia Inquirer,* April 28, 1987, Susan Caba provides a vivid description of transportation in and around Philadelphia at the time.

10. That Pennsylvania was the most populous state is from Evarts B. Greene and Virginia D. Harrington. *American Population Before the Federal Census of 1790,* p. 8. Germane demographic information on the middle colonies can be found in Potter's essay in D.V. Glass and D.E.C. Eversley, eds., *Population in History* (London: E. Arnold, 1965). pp. 652–54, especially. Relevant here, too, is Mary Schweitzer, "Revolutionary Pennsylvania: 1760–1790," in *A Guide to the Study of History,* eds., Dennis B. Downey and Francis J. Bremer (New York: Greenwood Press, 1993). Additionally helpful information on Pennsylvania demographics can be found in Donna Bingham Munger, *Pennsylvania Land Records: A History and Guide for Research* (Wilmington, Del.: Scholarly Resources, 1991).

　　Benjamin Franklin's estimate that one-third of the population was foreign-born, although untrue of the colonies at large, may well have proven true of the Pennsylvania of 1787. Penn's colony had by this time an already established tradition of separation of church and state, pluralism, toleration and, compared to most other state governments, equal justice. America's moral campaigns for equal rights for women, African Americans, and Native Americans all originated in the churches of Pennsylvania.

The Commonwealth incorporated the first independent black churches and played a crucial part in the history of Episcopalianism, Methodism, Lutheranism, and the German Reformed Church. Not surprisingly the Moravians, Rappites, and the German Swiss and Dutch Anabaptists also settled near to Philadelphia, mainly in Lancaster and Lehigh Counties. Last but not least, although anti-Catholic prejudice manifestly existed thickly among the elites in the Philadelphia region until the early 1960s, still, at the early date of the Convention in Philadelphia, Roman Catholics already enjoyed in the Keystone State a freedom to worship without parallel in the former North American colonies.

In many ways, then, Pennsylvania's history through the early Republic era proves illustrative of the attitude toward American religion. In that Gouverneur Morris was, along with Franklin and Jefferson, among the most religiously tolerant of the Founders alone makes his selection for the strong, seven-member Pennsylvania delegation seem appropriate. The reader may also need reminding that Gouverneur had already proven one of the three key drafters and signers of the first New York State constitution. And certainly the comparatively high degree of cultural sophistication in the Pennsylvania of the era made it appealing to GM. Although scholars have sometimes indicated that GM as Pennsylvanian was merely a transient there, the reader deserves to be reminded that, by the time Gouverneur had sailed for Europe in 1788, he had lived in Philadelphia for more than sixteen of his thirty-five years.

The Burnaby quotation is from *Travels Through North America,* 3rd ed. (London: A. Wessels, 1904). p. 91.

11. The resolution offered by GM and Edmund Randolph, and the debates over it on May 30, can be followed in Max Farrand, ed., *Records of the Federal Convention of 1787* (New Haven: Yale University Press, 1937), vol. 1, pp. 38–39. On the same day there was a debate between GM and James Madison over which legislators would be allowed to vote; Madison prevailed. See also the debates of June 13 (vol. 1, pp. 232–39), July 13 (vol. 1, pp. 600–06), and July 14 (vol. 2, pp. 2–11), and Rufus King, "First Report of the Committee of the Whole Convention." Formerly in the Manuscripts Collection at the New-York Historical Society, this manuscript was destroyed in a fire at the Society.

The most valuable primary source that has been published is Max Farrand, ed., *The Records of the Federal Convention of 1787.* (There is also a 1987 reprint from the same publisher.) This is a day-by-day account of the Convention, including the secretary's journal entries and the notes kept or made later by James Madison, Robert Yates, James McHenry, William Pierce, Alexander Hamilton, and Rufus King. Farrand also includes relevant letters and papers and the major plans (such as Randolph's and Paterson's). James Hutson has edited a *Supplement to Max Farrand's "The Records of the Federal Convention of 1787"* (New Haven: Yale University Press, 1987), with a useful general index (Farrand's index runs clause by clause.) A helpful addendum to all this is John Lansing, Jr., *The Delegate from New York,* Joseph Reese Strayer, ed. (1939; reprint, New York: Kennikat, 1967).

A useful one-volume edition of many Convention documents is Charles C. Tansill, *Documents Illustrative of the Formation of the Union of the American States,* House Document 398, 69th Congress, 1st Session (Washington, D.C.: U.S. Government Printing Office, 1927). And see Philip B. Kurland and Ralph Lerner, eds., *The Founders Constitution,* 5 vols. (Chicago: University of Chicago Press, 1987).

There are many useful reference works on the Constitution's gestation. Among the best are Carol Berkin, *A Brilliant Solution: Inventing the American Constitution* (New York: Harcourt, 2002); Leonard W. Levy, ed., *Encyclopedia of the American Constitution,* 4 vols. (New York: Macmillan, 1986); Alfred H. Kelly, et al., *The American Constitution: Its Origins and Development* (New York: Norton, 1983); Arthur T. Prescott, *Drafting the Federal Constitution* (Baton Rouge: Louisiana State University Press, 1941); Max Farrand, *The Framers of the Constitution* (New Haven: Yale University Press, 1913); Charles Warren, *The Making of the Constitution* (1928; reprint, Boston: Little, Brown, 1937);

David G. Smith, *The Convention and the Constitution* (New York: St. Martin's Press, 1965); Merrill Jensen, *The Making of the American Constitution* (New York: Macmillan, 1969); Michael Kammen, *A Machine That Would Go of Itself: The Constitution in American Culture* (New York: Knopf, 1986); Thornton Anderson, *Creating the Constitution* (University Park: Pennsylvania State University Press, 1993); John P. Roche, "Founding Fathers: A Reform Caucus in Action," *Political Science Review* 55, no. 4 (December 1961), 799–816. Still valuable is Henry Cabot Lodge, "The Constitution and Its Makers," in Lodge's *The Democracy of the Constitution and Other Essays* (New York: Scribners, 1915), pp. 32–87; Jack N. Rakove, *Original Meanings: Politics and Ideas in the Making of the Constitution* (New York: Knopf, 1996).

In *Gouverneur Morris and the New Nation, 1775–1788* (New York: Arno, 1978), Mary-Jo Kline gives a strong analysis of this phase of Morris's career. Robert J. Janosik, *The American Constitution* (Metuchen, N.J.: Scarecrow Press, 1991), provides a book-length bibliography with valuable annotations.

For readers who wish to compare the unwritten British constitution and the U.S. Constitution, I recommend F. W. Maitland, *Constitutional History of England* (London: Cambridge University Press, 1926), and Maurice Amos, *The English Constitution* (London: Longmans, Green, 1930). Amos emphasizes the importance of the Cabinet in Britain; the U.S. Constitution makes no provision for such a body, although the President has had a Cabinet since 1797. Amos also points out that in the early eighteenth century the British government had three parts, each of which enjoyed considerable independence: "the King in his executive capacity, the King-in-Parliament, and the judges." See Amos, pp. 55–64.

12. Richard Brookhiser, *Gentleman Revolutionary: Gouverneur Morris, The Rake Who Wrote the Constitution* (New York: Free Press, 2003), p. 81.

13. The reader can follow these deals in Max M. Mintz, *Gouverneur Morris and the American Revolution* (Norman: University of Oklahoma Press, 1970), in the chapter "Unofficial and Private." See especially the sources cited in footnotes 28–40, pp. 172–75.

14. Morris's letter to Thomas Pickering, December 22, 1814, was first published in Sparks, *Morris,* vol. 3, p. 323, and in Jonathan Elliot, *The Debates in the Several State Conventions on the Adoption of the Federal Constitution . . . ,* 2nd ed. (1836–1845; reprint, Lippincott, Philadelphia, 1941), vol. 1, pp. 506–507; James Madison's letter to Jared Sparks, April 8, 1831, was first published in Elliot, vol. 1, pp. 507–508.

15. Barbash, *The Founding,* p. 199.

16. Like all the debates, these are best followed in Farrand, *Records of the Federal Convention of 1787.* Randolph's motion of May 30 (pp. 33–38) was made on GM's suggestion. See also the debates on June 13 (pp. 232–39) and June 20 (pp. 335–44).

17. Pierce is quoted in Jane Butzner, *Constitutional Chaff* (1941; reprint, Port Washington, N.Y.: Kennikat, 1967), p. 166.

18. See Madison's entry for July 9, 1787, in Farrand's *Records,* vol. 1, pp. 559–562.

19. See, for example, Elliot, *Debates on the Constitution,* vol. 5, p. 308 (Madison's rejoinder is on pp. 314–15), and the debates for July 7–10 in Farrand, *Records,* vol. 1, pp. 503–47.

20. For Morris's views on the potential western states, see Elliot, *Debates on the Constitution,* vol. 5, pp. 279, 294, 298, 491–93, and the debates for July 11 in Farrand, *Records,* vol. 1, pp. 548–74.

21. On American slavery, especially its economic aspects, see Elizabeth Donnan, ed., *Documents Illustrative of the History of the Slave Trade to America,* 4 vols. (1930–35; reprint, New York: Octagon Books, 1965). Volumes 2 through 4 are especially relevant. A moving book on the trade is James Pope-Hennessy, *Sins of the Fathers: A Study of the Atlantic Slave Traders, 1441–1807* (New York: Knopf, 1968). W. E. B. Du Bois, *The Suppression of the African Slave-Trade to the United States of America, 1638–1870* (1896; reprint, New York: Russell and Russell, 1965), is an admirable history of this festering subject.

See also Philip D. Curtin, *The Atlantic Slave Trade: A Census* (Madison: University of Wisconsin Press, 1969); Sylvia R. Frey, *Water from the Rock* (Princeton: Princeton University Press, 1991); David B. Davis, *The Problem of Slavery in the Age of Revolu-*

tion, 1770–1823 (Ithaca, N.Y.: Cornell University Press, 1975); Benjamin Quarles, *The Negro in the American Revolution* (Chapel Hill: University of North Carolina Press, 1961).

For the issue in the context of the Constitutional Convention, see David Brion Davis's "Constructing Race: A Reflection," *William and Mary Quarterly,* 3rd series, vol. 54, no. 1 (January 1997), pp. 7–18. I disagree, however, with his endorsement (p. 7) of the thesis that "slavery was not born of racism; rather, racism was the consequence of slavery," which Eric Williams had put forth in *Capitalism and Slavery* (Chapel Hill: University of North Carolina Press, 1944).

22. For GM and his antislavery proposal for the New York constitution, see my chapter 2, and also "Historical Notes on Slavery in the Northern Colonies and States," *Historical Magazine* 10 (1866), p. 238 especially; Sparks, *Morris,* vol. 1, p. 125; and A. H. Payne, "The Negro in New York, Prior to 1860," *Howard Review* 1 (1923), pp. 1–29.

On the earliest efforts in Pennsylvania to manumit the slaves, see *Pennsylvania Packet,* November 28, 1778 (Penn State University, Microfilm E1); James T. Mitchell and Henry Flanders, eds., *The Statutes at Large of Pennsylvania* (Harrisburg: State Printer, 1915), vol. X, pp. 67–70; Edward R. Turner, *The Negro in Pennsylvania: Slavery-Servitude-Freedom* (1911; reprint, New York: Arno Press, 1969); and Darold D. Wax, "The Negro Slave Trade in Colonial Pennsylvania" (Ph.D. diss., University of Washington, 1962). See also Quarles, *The Negro in the American Revolution,* especially pp. 43–52.

23. See Thomas R. R. Cobb, *An Inquiry into the Law of Negro Slavery in the United States of America* (Philadelphia: T. & J. W. Johnson; Savannah: W. T. Williams, 1858; reprint, with an introduction by Paul Finkelman, Athens: University of Georgia Press, 1999), pp. ccxvii–ccxviii.

24. The periodical literature on this subject is abundant. I found the following especially valuable: Earl M. Maltz, "The Idea of the Proslavery Constitution," *Journal of the Early Republic* 17 (Spring 1997), pp. 37–59; Howard A. Ohline, "Republicanism and Slavery: Origins of the Three-Fifths Clause in the United States Constitution," *William and Mary Quarterly,* 3rd series, vol. 28 (October 1971), pp. 563–84; Paul Finkelman, "The Pennsylvania Delegation and the Peculiar Institution: The Two Faces of the Keystone State," *Pennsylvania Magazine of History and Biography* 112 (January 1988), pp. 49–71.

25. As so often in the American treatment of race, the question of voting rights for black freemen was handled irrationally. Several states that began by allowing them to vote later withdrew the right, for example. Knots the law cannot untie sometimes have to be cut by the sword; so it happened in the United States, as GM predicted in 1787.

26. Finkelman, "Pennsylvania Delegation," p. 50.

27. All quotations on this subject are drawn from Farrand, *Records,* vol. 1, pp. 583–97.

28. Ibid., pp. 603–605.

29. Frederick Law Olmsted, *The Cotton Kingdom,* ed. Arthur M. Schlesinger (New York: Knopf, 1953), which was based on Olmsted's writings about the South where he traveled in the 1850s, presented similar arguments, but more expansively.

30. Jugurtha was king of Numidia—roughly, Algeria—in the second half of the second century B.C. Before 206 B.C., when Numidia's ruler allied himself with Rome, the kingdom had been part of the wealthy and oligarchic Carthaginian empire.

31. See the discussions in Jack N. Rakove, *Original Meanings,* pp. 85–89, and Fred Barbash, *The Founding* (New York: Simon and Schuster, 1987), pp. 156–59; also see Farrand, *Records,* vol. 2, pp. 373–75, 400–416, 449–51.

32. Finkelman, "Pennsylvania Delegation," p. 68. Finkelman points out that, at every turn, Benjamin Franklin supported James Wilson's positions rather than the more radical ones staked out by GM. See also Farrand, *Records,* vol. 2, p. 375, 400–416.

33. During the mature republican era, the Roman Senate was the state's leading body. An interesting scholarly excursus would examine the extent to which ancient Greek notions of governance, too, influenced the formulation of the U.S. Constitution.

34. See Jack N. Rakove, *Original Meanings,* pp. 62, 67, and 170–71.

35. For the July 16 resolution, see Farrand, *Records of the Federal Convention of 1787,* vol. 2, pp. 13–15. The August 14 proceedings are found in the same volume, pp. 282–93. Rakove's insightful analysis is on pp. 170–71 of *Original Meanings.*

36. See the August 14 deliberations in Farrand, *Records,* vol. 2, pp. 282–93.

37. See Farrand, *Records,* vol. 2, p. 594.

38. See, for example, Robert A. Rutland's delightful *"Well Acquainted with Books": The Founding Framers of 1787* (Washington, D.C.: Library of Congress, 1987), p. 13; Edwin Wolf II, *The Book Culture of a Colonial American City: Philadelphia Books, Bookmen and Booksellers* (Oxford, Eng.: Clarendon Press, 1988).

39. On musical tastes in Philadelphia, see H. Wiley Hitchcock, *Music in the United States: An Historical Introduction,* 2nd ed. (Englewood Cliffs, N.J.: Prentice-Hall, 1974), pp. 32, 36–37, 40–45; on the women of Philadelphia, see, for instance, Andrew Burnaby. *Travels through the Middle Settlements in North America in the years 1759 and 1760* (New York: A. Wessels, 1904), p. 97; on prices, see Anne Bezanson, *Wholesale Prices in Philadelphia, 1784–1789* (Philadelphia: University of Philadelphia Press, 1936), especially p. 5. Thomas Jefferson shared Burnaby's enthusiasm for the state; see his letter to Chastellux, dated September 2, 1785, The Avalon Project at Yale Law School, <http://www.yale.edu/lawweb/avalon/jefflett/let34.htm>.

40. George Washington, *Diary,* Fitzpatrick, ed., July 30.

41. Martin Van Buren told the story in his *Inquiry into the Origin and Course of Political Parties in the United States* (1867; reprinted, New York: Augustus M. Kelley, 1967), pp. 105–106. James Parton's biography of Thomas Jefferson was published in Boston by J. R. Osgood in 1874; see page 369.

    See the interesting testimony of Washington's stepson, George Washington Parke Custis, in his *Recollections and Private Memoirs of Washington* (New York: Putnam's, 1860), p. 236.

    Nothing about the "Washington glare" at GM appears anywhere in Robert Morris's writings, although GM and Washington were often his houseguests, and often simultaneously.

42. Nonetheless, see the admirable and judicious scholarship of Donald L. Robinson, "Gouverneur Morris and the Design of the American Presidency," *Presidential Studies Quarterly* 17 (Spring 1987), 319–28; and Robert N. C. Nix and Mary M. Schweitzer, "Pennsylvania's Contributions to the Writing and the Ratification of the Constitution," *Pennsylvania Magazine of History and Biography* 113, no. 1 (January 1988), 3–24.

43. Relevant to these considerations is Simon P. Newman, "Principles or Men? George Washington and the Political Culture of National Leadership, 1776–1801," *Journal of the Early Republic* 12 (Winter 1992), pp. 477–507. For GM's remarks, see "The people are the King," in Farrand, *Records,* vol. 2, p. 69 (July 20).

44. Tansill, *Documents,* p. 136; see also Mintz, *Governeur Morris,* pp. 189–94.

45. In the 1800 elections, the two Republican party candidates, Thomas Jefferson and Aaron Burr, received equal numbers of votes in the electoral college, so the final choice had to be made by the House of Representatives. The resulting bitterness led directly to the passage of the Twelfth Amendment, requiring, among other things, separate electoral college votes for president and vice president.

46. An exception was that under the New York State constitution, the lieutenant governor took over in the event of the governor's absence from the state. The U.S. Constitution included no such provision, but did speak of the president's "inability" to function in office.

47. GM to Speaker of the Assembly of the State of New York, December 25, 1802. Gratz Collection, Federal Convention Papers, M-2/Case 1, Box 26. Historical Society of Pennsylvania. The letter is five pages long.

48. GM quoted in Farrand, *Records,* vol. 1, p. 545. It is worth mentioning that the British Cabinet was, and remains, outside the formal governmental structure. Blackstone's *Commentaries on the Laws of England* (1765) includes not a single reference to the Cabinet.

49. John Dickinson to James Logan, November 1802. Folder 18, Box 17-33 LD/LCP. Logan Collection of Dickinson's Papers, Library Company of Philadelphia. For intelligent

commentary on this episode, see the chapter "Rewriting Constitutions" in Milton E. Flower, *John Dickinson: Conservative Revolutionary* (Charlottesville, Va.: University Press of Virginia, 1983), pp. 235–262.

On the presidency's development at the Convention, see Forrest McDonald, *The American Presidency: An Intellectual History* (Lawrence: University Press of Kansas, 1985), and Donald L. Robinson, *"To the Best of My Ability": The President and the Constitution* (New York: Norton, 1987).

50. See, for instance, James Madison's *Journal of the Federal Convention* (Chicago: Albert, Scott, 1893), E. H. Scott, ed., pp. 401, 423–24, 430–31. W. B. Gwyn's interesting commentary on the subject appears in *The Meaning of the Separation of Powers: An Analysis of the Doctrine from Its Origin to the Adoption of the United States Constitution,* Tulane Studies in Political Science 9 (New Orleans: Tulane University Press, 1965); see especially chapters 3 and 7. On August 27, GM moved successfully to delete the proviso making federal judges removable "by the executive on the application by the Senate and House of Representatives." Morris was ably supported by Rutledge, Wilson, and Randolph. See Farrand, *Records,* vol. 2, pp. 422–33.

51. Farrand, *Records,* vol. 2, p. 600; see also pp. 603–604.

52. This debate can be found in Farrand, *Records,* vol. 2, pp. 345–50. The final wording appears as Article III, Section 3, Clauses 1 and 2. An excellent discussion of Article III is Julius Goebel's *Antecedents and Beginnings to 1801,* vol. 1 of *History of the Supreme Court of the United States,* Paul A. Freund, ed. (New York: Macmillan, 1971); especially useful are pp. 222–26 and 233–51. With respect to most of the Article III matter I discuss above, King and Madison, GM's colleagues on the style committee, were his close allies during the debate on the floor.

The British Settlement Act of 1696 had introduced important procedural modifications in cases of treason, some of which GM wanted to include in the U.S. Constitution. Hostility to the British would almost certainly have prevented the incorporation of any provision traceable directly to British legal procedure; GM's proposal sank without a trace. On the Settlement Act, see F. W. Maitland, *The Constitutional History of England* (Cambridge, England: University Press, 1920), pp. 316–19.

53. For the debates over state admission, see Farrand, *Records,* vol. 2, pp. 454–56.

54. See CongressLink (23 October 2003) http://www.congresslink.org/lessonlans/amending.htm)

55. See Julius Goebel, Jr., *Antecedents and Beginnings to 1801,* pp. 247–78.

56. For the debates of August 22 and 25, see Farrand, *Records,* vol. 2, pp. 376–77, pp. 412–14.

57. On the larger issue of religious influences on American revolutionary leaders and on the Framers, see, especially, Ellis Sandoz, *A Government of Laws: Political Theory, Religion, and the American Founding* (Baton Rouge: Louisiana State University Press, 1990).

58. Farrand, *Records,* vol. 2, p. 469.

59. See Charles C. Nott, *The Mystery of the Pinckney Draught* (New York: The Century Co., 1908), p. 332.

60. Farrand, *Records,* vol. 2, pp. 665–67.

61. For some of the complications surrounding the endorsements, see Elliot, *Debates on the Constitution,* vol. 5, p. 602, n. 266.

62. See Tansill, *Documents,* p. 740, as well as *They Knew the Washingtons: Letters from a French Soldier with Lafayette and from His Family in Virginia.* Trans. by Princess Catherine Radziwill (Indianapolis: Bobbs-Merrill, 1926).

63. For Washington's account of September 18, 1787, see Donald Jackson and Dorothy Twohig, eds., *The Diaries of George Washington* (Charlottesville: University Press of Virginia, 1976–79), vol. 5, p. 113.

64. GM quoted from Carl Van Doren, *The Great Rehearsal* (New York: Viking, 1948), p. 189. The original of the letter (July 21, 1788) is in the Morris-Croxhall Papers, Library of Congress.

65. A great deal has been written about the process of ratification. See Merrill Jansen, John P. Kaminski, Gaspare J. Saladino et al., eds., *The Documentary History of the Ratification of the Constitution,* 9 vols. (Madison: State Historical Society of Wisconsin, 1976–2003).

    John P. Kaminski and Richard Leffler are the editors of *Federalists and Antifederalists* (Madison, Wisc.: Madison House, 1998). Also see Robert J. Storing, ed., *The Complete Anti-Federalist,* 7 vols. (Chicago: University of Chicago Press, 1981); Bernard Bailyn, ed., *The Debate on the Constitution* (New York: Library of America, 1993). Despite its title, Bailyn's book does not duplicate either Farrand or Adrienne Koch's *Madison's "Advice to my Country"* (Princeton: Princeton University Press, 1966). Finally, Colleen A. Sheehan and Gary L. McDowell have edited the quite useful *Friends of the Constitution: Writings of the "Other" Federalist, 1787–1788* (Indianapolis: Liberty Fund, 1998).

    GM to W. H. Wells, February 24, 1815, in Sparks, *Morris,* vol. 3, p. 339. See also P. L. Ford, "The Authorship of the Federalist," *American Historical Review* 2 (1896–1897), pp. 677–78.

    The U.S. Constitution is the world's oldest continuously functioning government charter. See Henry Maine's assessment of its importance: "The Constitution of the United States is much the most important political instrument of modern times," in his *Popular Government* (London: John Murray, 1886), p. 196. William Gladstone agreed with Maine ("Kin Beyond the Sea," *North American Review,* September–October 1878), as did James Bryce, *The American Commonwealth* (New York: Macmillan, 1897). Thomas Macaulay called the Constitution "all sail and no anchor," but fortunately he was wrong.

    "On all great subjects," observed John Stuart Mill, "much remains to be said." Nevertheless, much of value has been said on the subject of the Constitution; see, for instance, Wilbourn E. Benton, ed., *1787: Drafting the U.S. Constitution,* 2 vols. (College Station: Texas A & M University Press, 1986); John A. Jameson, *The Constitutional Convention: Its History, Powers, and Modes of Proceeding* (New York: Scribner's, 1867); Calvin C. Jillson, "Constitution-Making: Alignment and Realignment in the Federal Convention of 1787," *American Political Science Review* 75 (September 1981), 598–612; Philip B. Kurland and Ralph Lerner, *The Founders' Constitution,* 5 vols. (Chicago: University of Chicago Press, 1987); Jack N. Rakove, *Original Meanings* (cited in full earlier); Gordon Wood, *The Radicalism of the American Revolution* (New York: Knopf, 1992).

6. IN EUROPE

1. Washington's copy of the letter, dated October 30, 1787, appears in W. W. Abbot and Dorothy Twohig, eds., *The Papers of George Washington: Confederation Series* (Charlottesville: University Press of Virginia, 1997), vol. 5, pp. 398–401.
2. This letter of November 28, 1788, may be found in Dorothy Twohig, ed., *The Papers of General Washington: Presidential Series* (Charlottesville: University Press of Virginia, 1987), vol. 1, pp. 137–38.
3. See Sarah H. J. Simpson, "The Federal Procession in the City of New York," *New-York Historical Society Quarterly Bulletin* 9 (July 1925), 39–56.
4. GM to George Washington, in Dorothy Twohig, ed., *The Papers of George Washington Presidential Series,* vol. 2, p. 148.
5. See Howard Swiggett, *The Extraordinary Mr. Morris* (New York: Doubleday, 1952), p. 139.
6. A typical packet of information from GM to Washington can be found in the Gratz Collection of Manuscripts, Case 1, Box 21 (July 2, 1787), Historical Society of Pennsylvania. On the subject of GM's important vantage point during the Terror, see, for example, William Matthews, ed., *American Diaries* (Boston: J. S. Conner, 1959), p. 175, and Hippolyte Taine, *Les origines de la France contemporaine* (New York: American Book Company, n.d. [ca. 1911]), pp. 13, 61. GM's diaries also feature in, for example, François Furet, *Revolutionary France, 1770–1880,* Antonia Nevill, trans. (London: Blackwell, 1992), and J. F. Bosher, *The French Revolution* (New York: Norton, 1988).

    These works, however, do not detail the extent of GM's extraordinary activities in

France, some of which were rather unusual: helping (or trying to help) extricate members of the royal family from the country; drafting a constitution to present to the king; advising French officials on the national finances; and in general making suggestions to the French government concerning its foreign policy. These activities could supply material for a sensational and not very believable novel; the facts are presented eloquently in Adhemar Esmain, *Gouverneur Morris: un témoin américain de la révolution française* (Paris: Hachette, 1906), and also Daniel Walther, *Gouverneur Morris: Witness of Two Revolutions,* Rae Foley, trans. (New York: Funk & Wagnalls, 1934).

On the Americans in France around the time of the Revolution, particularly impressive is Yvon Bizardel, *The First Expatriates: Americans in Paris During the French Revolution,* Jane P. Wilson and Cornelius Higginson, trans. (New York: Holt, Rinehart, & Winston, 1975).

7. On GM's landholdings in Europe, see the Matthew Ridley Collection, Manuscripts Division, Boston Public Library. Some valuable information on his land speculations is in the Richard Harison Papers at the New-York Historical Society (see Boxes 1 and 2).

8. Quoted in William Sumner, *The Financier and the Finances of the Revolution* (New York: B. Franklin, 1970), vol. 2, p. 277.

9. The story of GM's financial maneuverings in this period is ably told in E. James Ferguson, *The Power of the Purse: A History of American Public Finance, 1776–1790* (Chapel Hill: University of North Carolina Press, 1961), vol. 1, pp. 264–73; see the documentation in footnotes 27–36 and 38–47. Ferguson rightly points out that "in the eighteenth century, the distinction between public and private businesses was vague" (p. 345). There still is no book-length treatment of GM as a financier, however.

10. See Romain Rolland, André Maurois, and Édouard Herriot, *French Thought in the Eighteenth Century* (London: Cassell, 1953), p. 195.

11. On this subject, the following are especially valuable: Gordon Wright, *France in Modern Times, 1769 to the Present* (Chicago: Rand McNally, 1960), pp. 8–106, and J. McManners, "France," in A. Goodwin, ed., *The European Nobility in the Eighteenth Century* (London: A. C. Black, 1953), pp. 22–25. McManners's bibliographical citations on p. 191 are especially useful.

12. For this period of GM's life, the Gouverneur Morris Papers at the Library of Congress are most valuable. They exist both in manuscript and on microfilm; Container 1, Microfilm Reel 1, volumes 2 and 3, includes GM's diary for September 13, 1789, through April 30, 1791. Here GM has recorded much useful information on British-related financial affairs. For his travels in Europe, see Containers 8, 9, and 10, Microfilm Reel 3, volumes 21–23, which include substantial portions of GM's commercial correspondence for 1789–1795. Even a cursory inspection of his dealings reveals that he was making an enormous amount of money.

Until 1938, Morris's descendants restricted access to or publication of the diaries, and his literary heirs withheld many of the letters from scholarly examination until relatively recently. The fullest publication is Beatrix Cary Davenport, ed., *A Diary of the French Revolution,* 2 vols. (Boston: Houghton Mifflin, 1939).

13. Morris's belief that a more powerful executive was to be desired emerges in his remarks throughout the Convention; many are mentioned in the preceding chapter. He had been consistent in this view since the days when the New York constitution was being framed. And see his letter to Alexander Hamilton, May 16, 1777 (Alexander Hamilton Papers, Library of Congress).

Jefferson, too, saw a "want of power in the federal head" as constructed in the Constitution, a phrase from his letter to Richard Price, February 1, 1785, in Merrill Peterson, ed., *The Portable Thomas Jefferson* (New York: Penguin, 1977), p. 372. (For the word "endanger" in this copy, read "engender.") For Jefferson's views on the French Revolution, see Eugene R. Sheridan, "Thomas Jefferson and the Giles Resolutions," *William and Mary Quarterly,* 3rd series, vol. 49 (October 1992), 589–608, especially p. 592 and footnote 8. Sheridan was also the senior associate editor of *The Papers of Thomas Jefferson* (Princeton: Princeton University Press, 1950–). Jefferson also wrote to Madison from Paris, March 15, 1789, that "we were educated in royalism; no wonder some of us retain idolatry still." Quoted in Peterson, *Portable Thomas Jefferson,* p. 440.

On Jefferson in Paris, see William H. Adams, *The Paris Years of Thomas Jefferson* (New Haven: Yale University Press, 1997), and Howard C. Rice, *Thomas Jefferson's Paris* (Princeton: Princeton University Press, 1976). On his francophile reading, see Douglas L. Wilson, "Thomas Jefferson's Library and the French Connection," *Eighteenth Century Studies* 26 (Summer 1993), pp. 669–85. For Jefferson on the Continent generally, see George Green Shackleford's *Thomas Jefferson's Travels in Europe, 1784–1789* (Baltimore: Johns Hopkins University Press, 1995).

14. See Jean Orieux, *Talleyrand; ou, le Sphinx incompris* (Paris: Flammarion, 1970). The original is preferable to the translation, *Talleyrand: The Art of Survival,* Patricia Wolf, trans. (New York: Knopf, 1974).

15. This account of the beginning of the end of Louis XVI's reign can be found in the May 5 entry in Davenport, ed., *A Diary of the French Revolution.* vol. 1, pp. 67–70.

16. See Morris to Washington on January 24, 1790, in *A Diary of the French Revolution,* vol. 1, pp. 384–85. Necker's only child, the brilliant intellectual and novelist Madame de Staël (1766–1817), was certainly a woman of genius.

17. A generally informative article on the subject is Ronald E. Heaton, "The Image of Washington: The History of the Houdon Statue," *The Picket Post,* Pamphlet Winter 1971, pp. 24–32, to which I would like to offer one correction: the cast for the body was done after Houdon returned to France on Christmas Day, 1785.

Three years after the statue's delivery, Houdon was paid in full—in assignats, which by then had depreciated substantially. On July 29, 1796, he made a claim to the governor of Virginia for the original value, which he subsequently received.

18. I cannot claim to have mastered the vast array of primary materials and secondary scholarship on the French Revolution. What follows is simply a sketch of what I have found most helpful.

Martin Wolfe, ed., *The Maclure Collection of French Revolutionary Materials* (Philadelphia: University of Pennsylvania Press, 1966) is an annotated guide to the more than 25,000 pamphlets and other printed items that, bound into 1,460 volumes, constitute the Maclure Collection. Also see L. G. Wickham Legg, ed., *Select Documents Illustrative of the History of the French Revolution,* 2 vols. (Oxford, Eng.: Oxford University Press, 1905), and John Hall Stewart, ed., *A Documentary Survey of the French Revolution* (New York: Macmillan, 1951). Newly available on microfiche from Inter Documentation Company (IDC), Leiden, The Netherlands (postal address: POB 11205, 2301 EE LEIDEN; email address: info@idc.nl; and website: http://www.idc.nl/index.html) is an extensive collection of documents directly related to the revolution's economic roots: Collection de Documents inédits sur l'Histoire économique de la Révolution française, Paris 1906–1952. Also newly available from IDC is a collection of documents concerning Paris during the revolution: Collection de Documents relatifs à l'Histoire de Paris pendant la Révolution française, Paris 1883–1923.

Alexis de Tocqueville's *The Old Regime and the French Revolution* is, of course, a classic. I used the Stuart Gilbert translation, published by Peter Smith in Gloucester, Massachusetts, in 1978. Indispensable in researching this chapter was William Doyle, *Origins of the French Revolution* (New York: Oxford University Press, 1980). See also Georges Lefebvre, *The Coming of the French Revolution,* R. R. Palmer, trans. (Princeton: Princeton University Press, 1947). Louis R. Gottschalk, *The Era of the French Revolution* (Boston: Houghton Mifflin, 1929) is somewhat outdated but still useful. François Furet's work is outstanding; see, for instance, Furet and Denis Richet, *The French Revolution,* Stephen Hardman, trans. (New York: Macmillan, 1970). See also Furet and Mona Ozouf, eds., *A Critical Dictionary of the French Revolution,* trans. Arthur Goldhammer (Cambridge: Harvard University Press, Belknap Press, 1989). Another helpful reference is Samuel Scott and Barry Rothaus, *Historical Dictionary of the French Revolution, 1789–1799,* 2 vols. (New York: Greenwood Press, 1985).

For the period through 1793, an early but well-balanced work is H. Morse Stephens, *The French Revolution,* 2 vols. (New York: Scribners, 1900). Valuable for the light shed on the interplay among social, economic, and political spheres are several of the essays in Keith M. Baker, *Inventing the French Revolution* (Cambridge, Eng.: Cambridge University Press, 1990).

19. J. F. Bosher, *The Revolution* (New York: Norton, 1988), p. 4.

The *Encyclopaedia Britannica* is a helpful guide to many aspects of the revolutionary period.

As complicated as my account is of the revolution's causes, the reality was even more confusing, since it included numerous shifting coalitions, cadres, cabals, and clubs—the Girondins, the Conventionalists, the Jacobins, the sans culottes, the Montagnards, and the Feuillants.

20. See Palmer's footnote on pp. 8–10 in his translation of Lefebvre's *The Coming of the French Revolution* (Princeton: Princeton University Press, 1947).

21. Bosher, *The Revolution*, p. 75.

22. Ibid., p. 76.

23. On Turgot's reforms, see Thomas E. Watson, *The Story of France*, vol. 2 (New York: Macmillan, 1899), pp. 56–57. On the national debt of prerevolutionary France, see Lefebvre, *The Coming of the French Revolution*, p. 22; on the government's decision to rely heavily on indirect taxation, see the translator's footnote on pp. 8–10. On the corruption endemic in the collection of taxes in France, see J. F. Bosher, *The Revolution*, pp. 75, 308, notes 26, 28.

Turgot was finance minister from 1774 to 1776; Necker held the same job in the late 1780s but had been appointed director of the treasury in 1776 and comptroller general shortly thereafter. He resigned that position in 1781. Necker also spent many years as a banker.

Jacques Necker was a financier and statesman of impressive talents. Born in Geneva, he was ordered to leave France in July 1789 and did so in 1790. He died in 1804, in Switzerland. Between 1781 and 1802, he wrote half a dozen intelligent books—two valuable accounts of French finances under the king; a narrative of the revolution; a collection of his observations on politics and finance; and a book on the importance of religious opinions.

On the onerousness of the taille, see Friedrich A. Hayek, *The Constitution of Liberty* (Chicago: Gateway reprint, 1972), p. 43.

24. For the long view of this subject, see A. J. Grant, *French Monarchy 1483–1789*, vol. 2 (Cambridge, Eng.: Cambridge University Press, 1925). In Book 10 of his *Histoire de la révolution française* (Charles Cocks, trans. [Chicago: University of Chicago Press, 1967]), Jules Michelet explores the confrontation between the monarchy and the Convention. Another interesting—and roughly contemporary—assessment of Louis is in Nathaniel W. Wraxall, *Historical Memoirs* (1815; reprint, London: Kegan, Paul, Trench Tubner, 1904). See especially pp. 66–69, 70–71, 204–205, and the footnotes on p. 703.

The king, having renounced his governmental powers too late, was executed on being convicted of counterrevolution. The extent to which he was foredoomed is made clear by David Jordan, *The King's Trial: Louis XVI and the French Revolution* (Berkeley: University of California Press, 1979). Michael Walzer has a somewhat different view of the subject, expressed in his introduction to *Regicide and Revolution: Speeches at the Trial of Louis XVI*, Marian Rothstein, trans. (New York: Columbia University Press, 1992). See also John Hardman, *Louis XVI* (New Haven: Yale University Press, 1993); Simon Schama, *Citizens* (New York: Vintage Books, 1989), and M. D. Charlesworth, "The Virtues of a Roman Emperor: Propaganda and the Creation of Belief," *Proceedings of the British Academy* 13 (1937), pp. 105–33.

See also Millie Considine and Ruth Pool, *Wills: A Dead Giveaway* (New York: Doubleday, 1974), p. 98. My discussion of the economic background of the period draws largely on B. R. Mitchell, *European Statistics, 1750–1970* (New York: Columbia University Press, 1975); Shepherd B. Clough, *France: A History of National Economics* (New York: Scribners, 1939); and Ralph W. Greenlaw, ed., *The Economic Origins of the French Revolution* (Boston: Heath, 1958). In Greenlaw's book, see especially the essay by J. F. Bosher.

25. J. McManners, "France," in *The European Nobility in the Eighteenth Century: Studies of the Nobilities of the Major European States in the pre-Reform Era,* edited by Albert Goodwin (New York: Harper & Row, 1967), pp. 22–27. The material quoted is on p. 22. On the social causes of the revolution, see Norman Hampson, *A Social History of the French Revolution* (London: Routledge & Kegan Paul, 1963); Alfred Cobban, *Social Interpretations of the French Revolution* (Cambridge, Eng.: Cambridge University Press, 1964); and Orville T. Murphy, *The Diplomatic Retreat of France and Public Opinion on the Eve of the French Revolution, 1783–1789* (Washington, D.C.: Catholic University Press, 1998). Hampson and Cobban provide broad views of their topic, while Murphy focuses on the extent to which the perception of Louis XVI's inabilities permeated French society and helped stimulate the violence that erupted.

On the nobility, see the magisterial study by Henri P.M.F. Carré, *La noblesse de France et l'opinion publique au XVIIIième siècle* (Paris: Plon, 1920). Of the many histories of French society at the time, I have found most useful Philippe Sagnac, *La formation de la société française moderne,* 2 vols. (Paris: Presses Universitaires, 1945–1946). Volume 2 is the more relevant.

Many of the nobles filled the highest ranks of the French army: see particularly Emile-G. Leonard, "La question sociale dans l'armée française au XVIIIième siècle," *Annales, economies, sociétés, civilizations* 3 (1948), 135–49.

On the economic activities of the nobility around the time of the revolution, see Henri Lévy-Bruhl's "La noblesse de France et la commerce à la fin de l'ancien régime," *Revue d'histoire moderne* 8 (new series, vol. II, 1933), pp. 209–235.

26. On authorship generally, see, especially, Carla Hesse, "Enlightenment Epistemology in the Laws of Authorship in Revolutionary France, 1777–1793," *Representations* 30 (Spring 1990), 109–137; Jeffrey S. Ravel, "La Reine Boit! Print, Performance, and Theater Publics in France, 1724–1725," *Eighteenth Century Studies* 29/4 (1996), pp. 391–411; and Henri-Jean Martin, *Le livre français sous l'ancien régime* (Paris: Promodis, 1987).

On women and the revolution, see Jules Michelet, *The Women of the Revolution* (Philadelphia: Baird, 1955). Linda Kelly, *Women of the French Revolution* (London: Hamilton, 1987); Joan B. Landes, *Women and the Public Sphere in the Age of the French Revolution* (Ithaca, N.Y.: Cornell University Press, 1988); and Amelia Ruth Gere Mason, *The Women of the French Salons* (New York: Century, 1891) are informative and insightful. Lawrence Brockliss's magnum opus is *French Higher Education in the Seventeenth and Eighteenth Centuries: A Cultural History* (Oxford, Eng.: Clarendon Press, 1989).

27. On the constitutional history of the revolution, see Léon and Henri Monnier, *Les constitutions et les principales lois politiques de la France depuis 1789: collationées,* 4th ed. (Paris: Librairie générale de droit et de jurisprudence, 1925). Jacques Godechot presents an intriguing survey of the revolution's institutions: *Les institutions de France sous la révolution et l'empire* (Paris: Presses Universitaires de France, 1951). Valuable for an understanding of the weakness of parliamentary institutions in France is D.W.S. Lidderdale, *The Parliament of France* (New York: Praeger, 1952).

28. The facts of this mismanagement are set forth in Andrew Dickson White, *Fiat Money Inflation in France* (New York: Foundation for Economic Education, 1959).

29. On Charles de Flahaut, see Françoise de Bernardy, *Son of Talleyrand: The Life of Comte Charles de Flahaut* (London: Collins, 1956), and Duff Cooper, *Talleyrand* (London: Murray, 1938), pp. 32–37, 69, 357. See also J. Christopher Herold, *Mistress to an Age: A Life of Madame de Staël* (New York: Bobbs-Merrill, 1958). De Staël's mother, incidentally, had first been engaged to marry Edward Gibbon, but when her mother disapproved, she married Necker.

30. Theodore Roosevelt, *Gouverneur Morris* (Boston: Houghton Mifflin, 1888; reprinted, New York: Haskell House, 1968).

31. See George Green Shackelford, *Jefferson's Adoptive Son: The Life of William Short, 1759–1849* (Lexington: University Press of Kentucky, 1993).

32. *The Diary and Letters of Gouverneur Morris,* edited by Anne Cary Morris (New York: Charles Scribner's Sons, 1888), vol. 1, 67–70.

33. François René de Chateaubriand, *Memoirs,* selected and translated by Robert Baldick (London: Hamish Hamilton, 1961), p. 109. This is a modern translation of Chateaubriand's classic *Mémoires d'outre-tombe* (1849–1850).

34. *Diary and Letters of Gouverneur Morris,* vol. 1, p. 470.

35. *Diary and Letters of Gouverneur Morris,* vol. 1, p. 158.

36. A long draft of the plan is in the Gouverneur Morris Collection at the Columbia University Library. Its purpose is stated in the third paragraph. Concerning the plan, J. R. Jones, *Britain and the World, 1649–1815* (London: Harvester Books, 1980), pp. 248–53, is somewhat germane.

37. Washington's letters appointing GM and instructing him are conveniently available in Dorothy Twohig, ed., *The Papers of George Washington, Presidential Series* (Charlottesville: University Press of Virginia, 1995), vol. 4, pp. 176–83. Volume 3 (1989). The same series contains valuable detailed reports from Washington's Board of Treasury, dated June 15, July 23, and August 14, 1789. These reports, which detail the U.S. financial condition, the history of its foreign debt, and the status of payments on the debt, make clear why the new nation's armed forces were so anemic; otherwise, the U.S. negotiating position would have been very different.

Somewhat belatedly, on February 14, 1791, Washington wrote the Senate to inform them of his instructions to GM; see Linda Grant De Pauw, ed., *Documentary History of the First Federal Congress* (Baltimore: Johns Hopkins University Press, 1974), vol. 2, p. 116. Other valuable primary documents on GM's mission can be found in *American State Papers: Foreign Relations* (Buffalo, NY: W.S. Hein, 1998); vol. 1 William R. Manning, ed., *Diplomatic Correspondence of the United States: Canadian Relations 1784–1860,* vol. 1 (Washington, D.C.: Carnegie Endowment for International Peace, 1940); and Sparks, *Morris,* vol. 2, pp. 1–56.

For the British perspective, see *The Manuscripts of J. B. Fortescue . . . preserved at Dropmore* (also known as the *Dropmore Papers,* being the correspondence and papers of Lord Grenville), vol. 2 (London: Printed for H. M. Stationery Office by Eyre and Spottiswoode, 1894), part V.

Especially valuable histories include Ephraim D. Adams, *The Influence of Grenville on Pitt's Foreign Policy, 1787–1798* (Washington, D.C.: Carnegie Institution of Washington, 1904); Alfred L. Burt, *The United States, Great Britain, and British North America from the Revolution to the Establishment of Peace After the War of 1812* (New Haven: Yale University Press, 1940), pp. 16–17, 26–29, 36–39, 106–113; H. C. Allen, *Great Britain and the United States: A History of Anglo-American Relations, 1783–1952* (New York: St. Martin's Press, 1954), pp. 268–85; and Alexandre de Conde, *Entangling Alliances* (Durham: Duke University Press, 1958). Max Mintz's discussion of this phase of GM's life and career in *Gouverneur Morris and the American Revolution* (Norman: University of Oklahoma Press, 1970), pp. 205–240.

38. On this treaty there are two indispensable scholarly studies: Samuel Flagg Bemis, *Jay's Treaty: A Study in Commerce and Diplomacy,* rev. ed. (New Haven: Yale University Press, 1962), and Jerald A. Combs, *The Jay Treaty,* 2 vols. (Berkeley: University of California Press, 1970). For the Nootka Sound controversy as seen by Washington's Cabinet, see Dorothy Twohig et al. eds., *The Papers of George Washington, Presidential Series,* vol. VI, pp. 474, 493, 503–05, 596–09. On the matters concerning which the United States and Britain were negotiating, see Samuel Flagg Bemis, *A Diplomatic History of the United States* (New York: Holt, Rinehart & Winston, 1965), pp. 70–73, 86–91.

Grenville had intended to retain the frontier forts, as can be seen from his correspondence with Lord Dorchester. See, for instance, his letter of October 29, 1789, in *The Manuscripts of J. B. Fortescue (Dropmore Papers),* vol. 2. GM simply did the best he could; see, for instance, *Diary and Letters,* vol. 1, p. 330.

On the commercial issues between the two nations, see De Pauw, *Documentary History,* vol. 2, pp. 451–67. Also valuable is Samuel Flagg Bemis, *The American Secretaries of*

State (New York: Knopf, 1927), vol. 2, pp. 21–24, 40–43, 106–109. Morris's handling of the five major issues addressed in Washington's appointment letter of October 13, 1789, is highlighted in Donald Jackson and Dorothy Twohig, eds., *The Diaries of George Washington* (Charlottesville: University Press of Virginia, 1976).

39. This letter to Thomas Pinckney of July 11, 1792, appears in John Catanzariti, ed., *The Papers of Thomas Jefferson,* vol. 24 (Princeton: Princeton University Press, 1990), pp. 59–63.

40. See GM's *Diary and Letters,* vol. 1, p. 310; Sparks, *Morris,* vol. 2, pp. 344–45; and Burt, *The United States, Great Britain, and British North America,* pp. 106–113 especially.

On Grenville's selection of Hammond, see the *Dropmore Papers,* vol. 2, p. 80. The relevant volume of *Diaries of George Washington* is the sixth, pp. 81–82.

41. See David Hunter Miller, *Treaties and Other International Acts of the United States* (Washington, D.C.: Government Printing Office, 1931–1948), vol. 2, p. 99. On this subject, see my "Steps Toward Nationhood: Henry Laurens and the American Revolution in the South," *Historical Research* 78 (May 2005), pp. 3–4 and p. 9, n. 16.

42. Morris, *Diary of the French Revolution,* vol. 1, pp. 462–64.

43. Burt, *The United States, Great Britain, and British North America,* p. 112. For the issues just discussed, see also pp. 110–13. See also Allen, *Great Britain,* p. 282; and *Papers of George Washington,* vol. 4, 182–83. Evidence of Grenville's continued concern about the ongoing British possession of these forts, as late as August 6, 1794, can be found in the memos he exchanged with the Marquis of Buckingham: see *Dropmore Papers,* vol. 2, pp. 610–11.

44. See, for instance, Theodore Roosevelt, *Gouverneur Morris* (New York and Boston: Houghton Mifflin, 1916), pp. 266–67.

45. Thomas Jefferson's letter of December 17, 1790, appears in William R. Manning, ed., *Diplomatic Correspondence of the United States: Canadian Relations,* vol. 1 (Washington, D.C.: Carnegie Endowment for International Pence, 1940), p. 45. For the British change of mind concerning commercial relations with America, see W. C. Ford, ed., "Report of a Committee of the Lords of the Privy Council of the Trade of Great Britain with the United States" (January 1791) (Washington, D.C.: U.S. Department of State, 1888). Also pertinent is De Pauw, *Documentary History,* vol. 2, pp. 451–67.

46. On the Beckwith spy mission see, first, Harold Syrett, ed., *The Papers of Alexander Hamilton,* vol. 26 (New York: Columbia University Press, 1979), pp. 526–35; Frank T. Reuter, " 'Petty Spy' or Effective Diplomat: The Role of George Beckwith," *Journal of the Early Republic* 10 (Winter 1990), 471–92; and George J. A. O'Toole, *Honorable Treachery: A History of U.S. Intelligence, Espionage, and Covert Action from the American Revolution to the CIA* (New York: Atlantic Monthly Press, 1991), pp. 71–75 and 502.

I was startled to find, in the British Museum Manuscripts (item 28065, f. 233), a copy of Washington's October 13, 1789, appointment letter to GM. Beckwith secured and copied the original and sent it to the Foreign Office. Pitt, Leeds, and Grenville all had their own copies before the original reached Morris.

47. Concerning his mistress after Adélaïde, Elise de Chaumont, Morris wrote nothing at all. But her letters to him (in the Gouverneur Morris Collection at the Columbia University Library) are rather too heated for quotation in polite biography.

48. See *Secret Journals of the Acts and Proceedings of Congress* . . . (Boston: Thomas B. Wait, 1820–21), vol. 2, pp. 94–96.

49. My summary of the Senate debate on GM's confirmation draws mostly on Rufus King's notes, whose accuracy is corroborated by other sources. See Charles R. King, *The Life and Correspondence of Rufus King,* vol. 1 (New York: Putnam's, 1894), pp. 419–21. Sherman's speech concerning GM's appointment as minister to France is in the Rufus King Papers, at the New-York Historical Society.

Senator William Maclay, of Pennsylvania, called GM "half pimp, half envoy [for Robert Morris] . . . or more properly . . . a political eavesdropper about the British Court." See Edgar S. Maclay, ed., *Journal of William Maclay, U.S. Senator from Pennsylvania, 1789–1791* (New York: Appleton, 1890), p. 389.

50. Washington's letter of January 28, 1792, is enclosed with Thomas Jefferson's cautionary letter of January 23, informing GM that the president had appointed him U.S. minister to

France. These letters, along with helpful scholarly commentary, appear in Charles T. Cullen, ed., *The Papers of Thomas Jefferson,* vol. 23 (Princeton: Princeton University Press, 1990), pp. 55–57 and 85–86. Jefferson's letter to GM January 23, 1792, is in the Gouverneur Morris Collection, Columbia University Library.

51. GM to George Washington, *Papers of Thomas Jefferson,* vol. 23, p. 86n.
52. See Thomas Jefferson to GM, March 10, 1792, in *Papers of Thomas Jefferson,* vol. 23, pp. 248–49. Also relevant are GM's letter of April 6, and Jefferson's to GM, April 28, in the same volume, pp. 381–83, 467–68. With his usual considerateness, GM promptly wrote to thank Washington, Ellsworth, and King for their support: see letters of April 6, 1792, to Oliver Ellsworth, in 17 Gouverneur Morris Papers (Letterbook) 101–102, Library of Congress. To Ellsworth, GM wrote: "The favorable Sentiment of virtuous and judicious Men has ever appeared to me (next to an approving Conscience) the highest earthly Reward for our Exertions."
53. Printed in Jared Sparks, *Life of Gouverneur Morris* (Boston: Gray and Bowen, 1832), p. 59.
54. Beatrix Cary Davenport, ed., *A Diary of the French Revolution,* vol. 2 (Boston: Houghton Mifflin, 1939), pp. 473–79.
55. On Adélaïde's dispositions, see André de Maricourt, *Madame de Souza et sa famille,* 4th ed. (Paris: Emile-Paul Frères, 1913), pp. 142–44, 452–55.
56. See GM, *Diary and Letters,* vol. 2, p. 54, where Morris expresses his essential opinion on the new Tribunal. For his view of the Jacobins, see Sparks, *Morris,* vol. 2, p. 336. For his thinking and action on the trade issues with France, see Mintz, *Morris,* pp. 224–25. Also extremely valuable is Catanzariti, *Papers of Thomas Jefferson,* vol. 26, pp. 347–52.
57. Quoted in Simon Schama, *Citizens: A Chronicle of the French Revolution* (New York: Knopf, 1989), p. 870. See also William Howard Adams, *Gouverneur Morris: An Independent Life* (New Haven: Yale University Press, 2003), p. 247.
58. The constitutional plan GM offered Louis XVI was long and elaborate, with a verbose section on principles, and articles entitled "Executive Power," "Police and Administration," and "Education and Worship," as well as sections on a possible cabinet, on finances, foreign relations, legislation, and on the judiciary. The plan is in the Gouverneur Morris Collection at the Columbia University Library.
59. See George Washington's letter to GM of July 24, 1778. It is best studied in the Columbia University Library's Collection, because the version published by Sparks contains significant errors and omissions.
60. Louis-Philippe, *Memoirs: 1773–1793,* trans. John Hardman (New York: Harcourt, Brace, Jovanovich, 1977), p. 422. Louis-Philippe began writing his memoirs for this period only in 1802. See also John J. Conway, *Footprints of Famous Americans in Paris* (London: Lane, 1912), pp. 32–33.
61. See Stanley J. Idzerda, Roger E. Smith, Linda J. Pike, Mary Anne Quinn, eds., *Lafayette in the Age of the American Revolution: Selected Letters and Papers, 1776–1790,* vol. 2 (Ithaca: Cornell University Press, 1977), p. 72. It should be noted that the letter to Laurens mentioned was sent on June 8, 1778, the day before Lafayette took the oath of allegiance to the United States. Also relevant is W. E. Woodward, *Lafayette* (New York: Farrar and Rinehart, 1938), pp. 356–57, 370–73. Woodward is generally sharply critical of GM.
62. See Phillips Russell, *John Paul Jones: Man of Action* (New York: Brentano's, 1927), pp. 275–79, and Samuel Eliot Morison, *John Paul Jones: A Sailor's Biography* (1959; reprint, New York: Time-Life Books, 1964), chapter 21.
63. The entire letter, in the Gouverneur Morris Collection of the Columbia University Library, is revealing.
64. Morris took care to keep his communications secure. In a letter to Randolph, July 22, 1794, he says he has been waiting three weeks till he had the "opportunity" for a secure "transmission." Gouverneur Morris Collection, Columbia University Library.
65. GM to George Washington, February 14 and June 25, 1793, in Gouverneur Morris Collection, Columbia University Library. On the sanctuary issues involving the Comtesse de

Damas, see the summary treatment in Daniel Walther, *Gouverneur Morris: Witness of Two Revolutions,* trans. Elinore Denniston (New York: Funk and Wagnalls, 1934), pp. 240–43.

66. On Genêt's mission, see, above all, Catanzariti, ed., *Papers of Thomas Jefferson,* vol. 26. In a letter to James Madison, Jefferson expressed his angry exasperation with Genêt's conduct (p. 652).

67. When the Washington administration demanded Genêt's recall, Morris was soon ousted by the French. See also Noble E. Cunningham, ed., *Circular Letters of Congressmen to Their Constituents, 1789–1829,* vol. 1 (Chapel Hill: University of North Carolina Press, 1978), pp. 18–19, and Howard Swiggett, *The Extraordinary Mr. Morris* (Garden City, N.Y.: Doubleday, 1952), pp. 263–69.

On the "intemperate conduct of the French minister," see the capsule treatment by John W. Foster, *A Century of American Diplomacy* (Boston: Houghton Mifflin, 1900), pp. 153–56; the quotation is from p. 156. Foster justly remarks that GM "had become a persona non grata to the French government" (p. 172). For more on Genêt, see Edward A. Channing, *A History of the United States,* vol. 4 (New York: Macmillan, 1917), pp. 129–33, and Alexander de Conde, "A Time for Candour and a Time for Tact," *William and Mary Quarterly,* 3rd series, vol. 17 (Fall 1960), 341–445. De Conde's assessment of GM's performance as American minister in Paris is harsher than mine.

68. Especially useful are Jacques Léon Godechat, *Les institutions de la France sous la révolution et l'empire* (Paris: Presses Universitaires de France, 1951), and Philippe Sagnac, *La legislation civile de la révolution française, 1789–1804* (Paris: Librairie Hachette, 1898).

69. GM's letter to George Washington, September 13, 1792, is in the Gouverneur Morris Collection, Columbia University Library. On GM's awareness of the value to America of France's seemingly unselfish largesse, see his letter to Robert R. Livingston, May 5, 1778, in Robert R. Livingston Papers, 1777–1799, New York Public Library Special Collections. See also Richard Brookhiser, *Gentleman Revolutionary: Gouverneur Morris—The Rake Who Wrote the Constitution* (New York: Free Press, 2003).

70. The assessment of French interest in the American cause was made by Claude B. Fohlen in "The Peace 1783: A French View," paper delivered at the Two Hundredth Anniversary of the Ratification of the Treaty of Paris, a conference that took place at the Woodrow Wilson Center, Washington, D.C., May 15, 1984.

For the rest of this paragraph, see Archives du Ministre des Affaires Etrangères, Paris, Mémoires et Documents, and Mémoire de Rayneval à Louis XVI, 1781, in the Library of Congress. In chapter 4, we noted how close France came to making what we might call independent arrangements, just before Yorktown.

71. Claude Fohlen's scholarship (see preceding note) nicely highlights these realities. On the renewal of America's trade relations with Britain after the Revolution, see also William Whitlock, *The Life and Times of John Jay* (New York: Dodd, Mead, 1887), chapter 5.

72. See Anne Cary Morris, *Diary and Letters of Gouverneur Morris,* vol. 2, p. 66. George Washington to GM, Woodhouse Collection, F. 132 #5, Historical Society of Pennsylvania. On the change of French ministers, see also Stanislaus Murray Hamilton, ed., *The Writings of James Monroe* (New York: Putnam's, 1898–1899), vols. 1 and 2.

73. Swiggett, *The Extraordinary Mr. Morris,* p. 290.

74. The end of the grand tour was generally Italy, and the first known use of the term in print is by Richard Lassels, *The Voyage of Italy,* published by Vincent du Moutier in Paris and London, 1670. Morris's grand tour, of course, had a political and economic character rather than an artistic and philosophical one. Fichte, Novalis, Schelling, Goethe, Kant, Schiller, and Herder were all alive, but he met none of them.

It should be noted that, for security reasons, GM never sent some of the long dispatches he meant for Grenville. Even in communicating with foreign leaders he was more cautious than some early American statesmen were in dealing with their own country's secrets.

75. Drake's bulletins from Paris on GM are dated February 10, February 27, and March 11, 1794. They appear in the *Dropmore Papers,* vol. 3, pp. 68–70. See also the *Dropmore*

Papers, no. 607, which deals with Pitt's meeting with a group of American merchants to discuss the American governmental debts.

76. J. R. Jones, *Britain and the World, 1649–1815* (London: Harvester Press, 1980), p. 12.

77. Pitt the Younger was prime minister from 1783 to 1801. When he reached the top of that greasy pole, he was the fifth prime minister in a year; he became the longest-serving prime minister of the eighteenth century.

78. On GM's audience with King George, see *Dropmore Papers,* vol. 3, pp. 87, 226, 563. On Staats Long Morris, the only reference in George III's correspondence is a letter by the Duke of York, December 14, 1797. See A. Aspinall, ed., *The Later Correspondence of George III,* vol. 2 (Cambridge, Eng.: Cambridge University Press, 1963), p. 646.

79. For Grenville's personality and character, see William J. Copleston, *Memoir of Edward Copleston, D.D.* (London: Meuvay, 1851), p. 48, and John W. Fortescue, *British Statesmen of the Great War, 1793–1814* (Oxford, Eng.: Clarendon Press, 1911), pp. 75–78. A portrait of Grenville at about age forty-nine shows a receding hairline, thick eyebrows, a prominent nose, a broad forehead, and a dimpled chin, at the Historical Society of Pennsylvania, Ferdinand J. Dreer Autograph Collection.

80. Mintz, *Gouverneur Morris and the American Revolution,* pp. 11–12.

81. Grenville's father was the first British prime minister whose son eventually held the same office.

Despite their great intelligence, interesting personalities, and historical importance, neither Grenville nor GM has received his historical due. The only really substantial biography of Grenville is Peter Jupp, *Lord Grenville, 1759–1834* (Oxford, Eng.: Clarendon Press, 1985). A good starting point for research would be A. D. Harvey, *Lord Grenville (1759–1834): A Bibliography* (Westport, Conn.: Meckler, 1989). Informative sketches of Grenville's life and career also appear in William Gould, ed., *Lives of the Georgian Age: 1714–1837* (New York: Barnes & Noble, 1978), pp. 200–201, and Alan Valentine, *The British Establishment,* vol. 1 (Norman: University of Oklahoma Press, 1980), pp. 390–91.

82. Washington's letter may be found in John C. Fitzpatrick, ed., *The Writings of George Washington,* vol. 34 (Washington, D.C.: Government Printing Office, 1940), pp. 398–403. For more information on the history of the Bank of England, see its Web site at <www.bankofengland.co.uk/history.htm>.

83. For an understanding of the relationship between GM and Grenville, I consulted the following: *Dropmore Papers,* vol. 3, pp. 222, 224, 230, 258; Sparks, *Morris,* vol. 3, p. 93; Ephraim D. Adams, *The Influence of Grenville on Pitt's Foreign Policy, 1787–1798* (Washington, D.C.: Carnegie Institution, 1904), pp. 40–44, 51–52, 58–59, 66–67, and 70–74; A. W. Ward and G. P. Gooch, eds., *Cambridge History of British Foreign Policy,* vol. 1 (Cambridge, Eng.: Cambridge University Press, 1922), pp. 266–67; and Jupp, *Lord Grenville,* pp. 163–64, 175, and 180–95.

While the new U.S. government was still closely allied with France, GM wrote Luzerne helpful memoranda like those he wrote Grenville. See, for instance, GM to Luzerne, October 12, 1790, from Antwerp: "I promised you, my dear Sir, to communicate some information respecting this country . . ." in the Gouverneur Morris Collection at the Columbia University Library.

A historical atlas can be revealing. See, for instance, Map 86 in Oddvar Bjørklund, *Historical Atlas of the World* (New York: Barnes and Noble, 1986). France's border snakes around Lombardy, so that at that time France shared a border with Austria.

84. See Nikolai N. Bolkhovitinov, *The Beginnings of Russian-American Relations, 1775–1815,* Elena Levin, trans. (Cambridge: Harvard University Press, 1975), pp. 103–105. For more on the Second Coalition, see J. R. Jones, *Britain and the World, 1649–1815,* pp. 269–83.

7. SENATOR FROM NEW YORK

1. Alexander Hamilton had been made a general during the undeclared war with France (1798–1800), although the combat was exclusively naval and he never saw a battle.

The quotations in this paragraph, as well as the description of Morrisania's condition as "leaky and ruinous," are from GM's letter to John Parish, January 27, 1799 (Letterbooks, Gouverneur Morris Collection, Library of Congress, microfilm edition).

Among the inquirers on the matrimonial question were Parish, John Dickinson, John Rutherford, and the Schuylers. To one friend, GM replied, "I should not hesitate if I could light upon such a person as Mrs. R. [probably Mrs. Rufus King, who is recorded as having been beautiful and charming], and light up in her Bosom such Flame, as would on such an occasion warm my own" (Gouverneur Morris Collection, Columbia University Library).

Accounts for the extensive repairs to Morrisania can be found in Box 1 onward, MS Collection, No. 76, Smith Family Papers, Series 41—Gouverneur Morris at the American Philosophical Society, Philadelphia.

2. GM to John Parish, Letterbooks, Gouverneur Morris Collection, Library of Congress.

3. Necker wrote on May 13, 1799, from Copet, Switzerland. The letter is in the Gouverneur Morris Collection at the Library of Congress.

4. On this subject generally, see *Eulogies and Orations on the Life and Death of General George Washington* (Boston: Manning and Lorring, for W. P. and L. Blake, 1800). This now rare item can be consulted in Joseph Sabin, *Dictionary of Books Relating to America* (New York: Readex Microprint, 1963).

5. Life being often odder than fiction, Morris was the fifth senator from New York in three years. In 1797, Philip Schuyler had succeeded Aaron Burr, but Schuyler became gravely ill; John Sloss Hobart held the office for only three months; after he resigned, William North was senator for just ten months before resigning as well; James Watson, elected after him, held the office until March 1800.

6. On the composition of the Senate, see, especially, Elaine K. Swift, *The Making of an American Senate: Reconstitutive Change in Congress, 1787–1841* (Ann Arbor: University of Michigan Press, 1996); particularly relevant are Swift's remarks on p. 121.

7. These observations from his expedition can be found in Anne Cary Morris, ed., *The Diary and Letters of Gouverneur Morris,* vol. 2 (New York: Scribner's, 1888), pp. 385–91.

8. In a letter dated June 4, 1800, after this vote, GM told Rufus King that "the thing, which, in my opinion, has done most mischief to the Federal party, is the ground given by some of them to [have others] believe, that they wish to establish a monarchy" (Sparks, *Morris,* vol. 3, p. 128).

9. See Thomas Jefferson, *Jefferson's Parliamentary Writings,* Wilbur S. Howell, ed., *Papers of Thomas Jefferson,* 2nd series (Princeton: Princeton University Press, 1988), pp. 25–26.

10. Sparks, *Morris,* vol. 3, p. 130.

11. The Federal Judiciary bill became law on March 31, 1802. On this subject, see Thomas Hart Benton, ed., *The Abridgement of the Debates of Congress, from 1789 to 1856,* vol. 2 (New York: Appleton, 1856), pp. 480–81, 488–97; 540–65. Sparks reproduces GM's entire speech in *Morris,* vol. 3, pp. 378–402. The circuit-riding system entailed wear and tear on the judges; the first nine Supreme Court Justices served an average 8.6 years, whereas in the late twentieth century the average has been well over sixteen years, some of which may be attributable to longer life expectancy. See Kathryn Turner, "Federalist Policy and the Judicial Act of 1801," *William and Mary Quarterly,* 3rd series, vol. 3 (1965), pp. 3–32.

A similar reading of the Judiciary Act appears in Jerry W. Knudson, "The Jeffersonian Assault on the Federalist Judiciary, 1802–1805: Political Forces and Press Reaction," *American Journal of Legal History* 14/1 (1970), 55–75. For a still broader view of the subject, see Richard E. Ellis, *The Jeffersonian Crisis: Courts and Politics in the Young Republic* (New York: Oxford University Press, 1971), especially chapters 2–4, 15.

Valuable background is offered by John P. Frank, "Historical Bases of the Federal Judiciary System," *Indiana Law Journal* 23 (April 1948), 236–70, and Edmund M. Morgan and F. X. Dwyer, *Introduction to the Study of Law,* 2nd ed. (New York: Callaghan, 1948), pp. 19–21. Still earlier, but with sound general insights, is Robert L. Schuyler, "Working Toward a Federal Domain," *Political Science Quarterly* 28 (Fall 1913), 496–511.

Further valuable commentary and analysis are offered by Wythe H. Holt, Jr., in "The First Federal Question Case," *Law and History Review* 3 (Spring 1985), pp. 169–89, especially pp. 169, 172–73, 182–89; and in the same author's "If the Courts Have Firmness Enough to Render the Decision: Egbert Benson and the Protest of the 'Midnight Judges,'" in William Nourse and Wythe L. Holt, Jr., *Egbert Benson: First Chief Judge of the Second Circuit* (New York: Second Circuit Committee of the Bicentennial, 1976), pp. 9–23, especially p. 16.

The Republicans' arguments for repeal of the "midnight judges" act signed by John Adams are cogently explored by James M. O'Fallon in "Marbury," *Stanford Law Review* 44 (January 1992), 219–60. I would like to thank Wythe Holt for bringing this article to my attention before it was published, and Professor O'Fallon for graciously sending me an early reprint.

Morris saw the federal judiciary as "a system of salutary checks," "that fortress of the constitution" which could counterbalance excess powers aggrandized by either of the other two branches. As he wrote, too, to Robert R. Livingston, "in some parts of this union, justice cannot be readily obtained in the State courts" (February 20, 1801, in Sparks, *Morris,* vol. 3, p. 153).

Writing to Alexander Hamilton on January 5, 1801, GM intimated his resolve to make the best of Jefferson's victory over Burr (Gouverneur Morris Papers, Library of Congress).

12. See Richard Brookhiser, *Gentleman Revolutionary: Gouverneur Morris—The Rake Who Wrote the Constitution* (New York: Free Press, 2003), pp. 169–70.

Abridgement of the Debates, vol. 2, pp. 668–92, covers all the relevant congressional speeches in 1803. Sparks (*Morris,* vol. 3, pp. 403–34) reproduces GM's speech in its entirety. It runs thirty-one pages and must have lasted several hours; it is a masterpiece of rhetoric. See also American Philosophical Society, Manuscript Collection, No. 76, Box 6, p. 46.

Some other useful works are C. W. Alvord, *The Mississippi Valley in British Politics,* 2 vols. (Cleveland, Oh.: World Books, 1917); A. C. McLaughlin, *The Western Posts and the British Debts* (Washington, D.C.: American Historical Association [Annual Report], 1894); and Arthur P. Whittaker, *The Mississippi Question, 1795–1803* (1934; New York: Peter Smith, 1962).

13. See Morris's November 28, 1803, letter to Livingston in Anne Cary Morris, ed., *Diary,* vol. 2, p. 444. The Louisiana Department of State offers a useful resource in "The Louisiana Purchase Exhibit" at <http://www.sec.state.la.us/purchase/purchase-index.htm>.

Debate in each house of Congress was limited to one day. See *Annals of Congress,* 8th Congress, 1st Session, 1803, pp. 35–73, 432–515; and, on the ratification, *Annals of Congress,* 8th Congress, 2nd Session, 1803–1804, pp. 1054–1079. Only the House debate on the Louisiana Territory is reported.

See also Thomas Jefferson to Robert R. Livingston, April 18, 1802, and to John Breckinridge, August 12, 1803. These letters may be found in "The Letters of Thomas Jefferson: 1743–1826" at *From Revolution to Reconstruction,* a hypertext on American history from the colonial period to modern times, University of Groningen, The Netherlands, http://odur.let.rug.nl/~usa/. At the time of these letters, Livingston was minister to France, Breckinridge U.S. senator from Kentucky. See also John Mayfield, *The New Nation, 1800–1845* (New York: Hill & Wang, 1982); still valuable historically is Binger Hermann, *The Louisiana Purchase* (Washington, D.C.: U.S. Government Printing Office, 1898).

14. The letters to Livingston appear in Sparks, *Morris,* vol. 3, pp. 170–73, 179–80. The letter to the Princesse de la Tour is in the Gouverneur Morris Collection at the Library of Congress.

15. See GM to Robert R. Livingston, March 20, 1802, in Sparks, *Morris,* vol. 3, pp. 164–66. Anne Cary Morris, ed., *Diary,* pp. 276 and 440.

16. GM to the Speaker of the Assembly in the State of New York, December 25, 1802, Gratz Collection, Historical Society of Pennsylvania, Federal Convention, M-2, Case 1, Box 26.

17. GM to Dayton, November 9, 1803, Gratz Collection, Historical Society of Pennsylvania, Federal Convention, M-2, Case 1, Box 26.

8. IN RETIREMENT

1. See John W. Francis, "Gouverneur Morris," *The Historical Magazine,* 2nd series, vol. 3 (April 1868), 193–98. And the Houston Smith Collection of the American Philosophical Society, as well as the New York State Library, are rich in unpublished materials.

2. For the background and consequences of the duel, along with Morris's oration, see Harold C. Syrett, ed., *The Papers of Alexander Hamilton,* vol. 26 (New York: Columbia University Press, 1979), pp. 322–29; Mary-Jo Kline, ed., *Political Correspondence and Public Papers of Aaron Burr,* vol. 2 (Princeton: Princeton University Press, 1983), pp. 876–92, especially.

Scholarly commentary on the duel often induces puzzlement in the present-day reader. Burr challenged Hamilton to the illegal duel. Hamilton agreed as a point of honor, but fired into the air, while Burr shot to kill. Hamilton left eight children, an unemployed wife, and a mountain of debt. Yet the scholarly consensus seems to be that Hamilton deserved what he got. Typical is Milton Lomask, who writes of Hamilton's being "hoist on his own petard." See his *Aaron Burr: The Years from Princeton to Vice President, 1756–1805,* vol. 1 (New York: Farrar, Straus & Giroux, 1979), pp. 350–56.

Two recent articles provide interesting commentary on the "field of honor" and give fine complementary surveys of scholarship on the subject: William J. Rorabaugh, "The Political Duel in the Early Republic: Burr v. Hamilton," *Journal of the Early Republic* 15 (Spring 1995), 1–23; and Joanne B. Freeman, "Dueling as Politics: Reinterpreting the Burr-Hamilton Duel," *William and Mary Quarterly,* 3rd series, vol. 53, no. 2 (April 1996), 289–318.

On the Hamilton family trust, see Morris's diary, July 14, 1804, especially pp. 457–59, and Charles R. King, ed., *The Life and Correspondence of Rufus King,* vol. 4 (1801–1806) (New York: Putnam's, 1897), pp. 403–405.

Chamfort is my translation, from N. Chamfort, *Oeuvres Choisis,* ed. M. de Lescunre (Paris: Librairie des Bibliophiles, 1892), vol. 1, pp. 4–5.

For GM's work for Columbia, see his letter to his niece Gertrude Meredith, of Philadelphia, May 21, 1810, in the Gouverneur Morris Collection at Columbia University Library.

3. Speech given on December 6, 1812; printed in *Collections of the New-York Historical Society,* vol. 2 (New York: AMS Press, 1974), pp. 117–148.

4. Minutes of the Canal Commissioners of New York meetings, May 1811–March 1812. Bound in volume no. 1847, New-York Historical Society.

On the Erie Canal, see Noble A. Whitford, *History of the Canal System of the State of New York,* vol. 1 (Albany, N.Y.: New York State, 1905), especially chapter 2. See also Dorothie Bobbe, *DeWitt Clinton* (New York: Putnam's, 1968), pp. 83–84, 88–89, 96, 98–99; Carol Sheriff, *The Artificial River: The Erie Canal and the Paradox of Progress, 1817–1862* (New York: Hill & Wang, 1996); Evan Cornog, *The Birth of Empire: DeWitt Clinton and the American Experience, 1769–1828* (New York: Oxford University Press, 1998), and my review of this work in *William and Mary Quarterly,* 3rd series (April 2000), pp. 457–459.

5. The quotation from Cornog, *The Birth of Empire,* is from page 159.

6. On the oyster beds, I am indebted to Jack Putnam of the Education Department at New York City's South Street Seaport Museum, who spoke with me on the subject in the early 1990s. The details of Morrisania come mainly from Stephen Jenkins, *The Story of the Bronx* (New York: Putnam's, 1912), pp. 2–5, 358–61. Jenkins also includes maps and photographs.

While GM was in Europe, Lewis Morris had tried to have the nation's capital situated at Morrisania, according to Jenkins (p. 3). Some poorly coordinated civic attempts to preserve the house as a museum and the grounds as a park proved unsuccessful. In 1905 the New York and Harlem Railroad secured the property; soon after the mansion was demolished. See also *New York Tribune,* May 7, 1922.

7. GM to Moss Kent, March 15, 1816. Articles of Confederation file, Gratz Collection, Historical Society of Pennsylvania, and Mintz, *Gouverneur Morris,* pp. 213–217 and 237–239. Case 1, Box 21.

8. GM to David Parish, April 28, 1808, Historical Society of Pennsylvania. For Anne Cary Randolph, see first and foremost the splendid biography by Alan Pell Crawford, *Unwise Passions: A True Story of a Remarkable Woman—and the First Great Scandal of Eighteenth-Century America* (New York: Simon and Schuster, 2000). For Richard Randolph and the emancipation of his slaves, see Melvin Patrick Ely, *Israel on the Appomattox* (New York: Knopf, 2004). See also Charles C. Tansill, *The Secret Loves of the Founding Fathers* (New York: Devin-Adair, 1964), pp. 156–63; Mintz, *Morris,* pp. 134–45; Howard Swiggett, *The Extraordinary Mr. Morris* (New York: Doubleday, 1952), pp. 379–82, 391–402; and William C. Bruce, *John Randolph of Roanoke, 1773–1833,* vol. 2 (New York: Putnam's, 1922), pp. 274–95, 300–302.

9. Quoted from Mintz, *Morris,* p. 235. The letters GM and Anne wrote each other (June 5–15, 1812; October 13, 15, 25, 1813) can be found at the American Philosophical Society.

10. On the cause of GM's death, see *Papers of Rufus King,* vol. 6, p. 34. The tombstone reads "Ann," rather than "Anne." The church was consecrated in June 1841; Gouverneur Junior donated the land in memory of his mother.

CONCLUSION

1. Robert Livingston to the historian William Gordon from Clermont, New York, November 27, 1778, in the Bancroft Papers, Special Collections, The New York Public Library. GM to Nathanael Greene, in John Catanzariti, Elizabeth M. Nuxoll, and Mary A. Gallagher, eds., *The Papers of Robert Morris,* vol. 7 (Pittsburgh: University of Pittsburgh Press, 1988), p. 348. See also "The Statesman," in Edward Dowden, ed., *The Works of Sir Henry Taylor,* vol. 4 (London: Kegan, Paul, Trench, 1883), p. 291.

2. David W. Robson, *Educating Republicans: The College in the Era of the American Revolution* (Westport, Conn.: Greenwood Press, 1995); see especially p. 77 and p. 138, n. 56.

3. For Madison's encomium, see James Madison to Jared Sparks on April 8, 1831, in Max Farrand, ed., *The Records of the Federal Convention,* vol. 3 (New Haven: Yale University Press, 1937), p. 500. Michael Kammen, *A Machine That Would Go of Itself: The Constitution in American Culture* (New York: Knopf, 1986). Scalia's lecture, cosponsored by the Intercollegiate Studies Institute and Villanova University, was given at the Villanova University School of Law, November 20, 1987.

4. Roosevelt, *Gouverneur Morris,* p. 189.

5. Palmerston, like Grenville, has still probably not had the biography he deserves, but the following are to be recommended: Jasper Ridley, *Lord Palmerston* (New York: Dutton, 1970), and D. G. Southgate, *The Most English Minister* (New York: St. Martin's Press, 1966).

   Of the published scholarship on Adlai Stevenson, what follows is only a sample: Herbert J. Muller, *Adlai Stevenson: A Study in Values* (New York: Harper & Row, 1967); the quotation in the text above appears on p. xi; Bert Cochran, *Adlai Stevenson: Patrician Among the Politicians* (New York: Funk & Wagnalls, 1969); and John Martin's two-volume biography *Adlai Stevenson of Illinois* (New York: Doubleday, 1976) and *Adlai Stevenson and the World* (New York: Doubleday, 1977).

6. Sparks, *Gouverneur Morris,* vol. 1, p. 495.

INDEX

GM stands for **Gouverneur Morris.** The **War** stands for **American Revolutionary War**.